M000198767

ORACLE®

Oracle Press™

Portable DBA: Oracle

Oracle Press™

Portable DBA: Oracle

Robert G. Freeman

McGraw-Hill/Osborne

New York   Chicago   San Francisco
Lisbon   London   Madrid   Mexico City   Milan
New Delhi   San Juan   Seoul   Singapore   Sydney   Toronto

The **McGraw·Hill** Companies

McGraw-Hill/Osborne
2100 Powell Street, 10th Floor
Emeryville, California 94608
U.S.A.

To arrange bulk purchase discounts for sales promotions, premiums, or fund-raisers, please contact
McGraw-Hill/Osborne at the above address. For information on translations or book distributors outside the
U.S.A., please see the International Contact Information page immediately following the index of this book.

Portable DBA: Oracle

1234567890 DOC DOC 01987654

ISBN 0-07-222980-2

Vice President & Group Publisher Mike Hays	**Proofreader** Claire Splan
Vice President & Publisher Scott Grillo	**Indexer** Claire Splan
Editorial Director Wendy Rinaldi	**Composition** Lucie Ericksen, John Patrus
Project Editor Janet Walden	**Illustrators** Kathleen Edwards, Melinda Lytle
Acquisitions Coordinator Athena Honore	**Series Design** Jani Beckwith, Peter F. Hancik
Technical Editor Pete Sharman	**Cover Designer** Damore Johann Design, Inc.
Copy Editor William McManus	

This book was composed with Corel VENTURA™ Publisher.

This book is dedicated to Lisa, my personal iron rod.

About the Author

Robert Freeman has been an Oracle DBA for almost 15 years. He currently lives in Chicago, where he works for TUSC as a management consultant. Robert presents at Oracle-related user groups such as IOUG-A and the UKOUG on a regular basis. He is the author of three other best-selling Oracle Press titles, *Oracle Database 10g New Features*, *Oracle9i RMAN Backup & Recovery*, and *Oracle9i New Features*. Robert is the father of five teenagers, husband of a wife who is incredible, and the owner of a moody cat. In his spare time he works on getting his third-degree black belt in tae kwon do and sits at the edge of local runways with a sign that says "Will DBA for blocks of flight time."

Contents at a Glance

Contents

Acknowledgments

This book has been a long project. First I need to acknowledge my wife, Lisa, who makes my world a very nice place to live in. Imagine being newly married, and you are already a book widow, well that's Lisa. She is a trooper, though, supporting me through it all (well, after I bribed her with a cruise once this was all done...). So, I acknowledge the support and love of Lisa, and without it this book would be still somewhere in a stage of completeness. I truly am a lucky man, and often find myself saying, "Wow! I'm with her?"

Thanks also to my kids, who put up with my writing habit and have for a number of years. At first, they thought it would be cool for dad to be a writer. They figured I'd be famous and get rich. Now that they know that neither is going to happen, they look at me and just sigh and mention something about interventions. They love me, and that makes all this work somehow easier to do.

Thanks to Clifford, he keeps my feet warm.

Thanks to my dad. It is what I learned from him that allows me to even think I might be able to write a book.

To all my Karate friends, thanks!

Thanks to the great folks at TUSC who provide lots of support and who are some pretty smart Oracle people.

Thanks to the folks at Oracle Press who really made it possible to write this book. I am constantly amazed at how much work goes into one of these books, not just from my side, but from the production side, and the Oracle Press folks don't miss a beat. From Wendy Rinaldi, to Janet Walden and Bill McManus, to all the production folks and management at Oracle Press, thanks. A big thank you to Athena Honore, we miss you. Pete Sharman was the technical editor of this book. He is tops and a great Oracle employee. Pete technical edited this book while moving from the sunny coast of California to the outback and did a great job. Thanks for all the hard work Pete!

I'd also like to offer a special word of thanks to Kevin Loney who allowed us to "cut and paste" some of his material from *Oracle Database 10g: The Complete Reference* (Oracle Press, McGraw-Hill/Osborne, 2004) for Appendix C. We were on a tight schedule and needed an easy way to get you this information. Kevin came to the rescue! He truly is an Oracle legend.

I need to make special mention also of some folks who contributed to the writing of this book. Brian Peasland contributed to chapters in this book in a big way. Without Brian this book would have never made it to press when it did. Brian's writing is excellent, and he really added some great content. Mike Killough helped out with a couple of chapters as well. Thanks guys for the help, it was much needed! Of course, if you like this book, remember that I wrote it. If you don't like it, then you just read a chapter that Mike or Brian wrote.

Also, thank you, the reader. Without you, who would I write for? So, thanks a bunch and enjoy *Portable DBA: Oracle.*

Introduction

elcome to *Portable DBA: Oracle*! This book sprung from a seed of an idea that was planted almost two years ago. One day I was pondering what kind of book a DBA really needs, what is it that we were missing? It seemed to me that in my early DBA days, what I needed was sort of quick reference cheat sheet. I needed something to jog my memory, and to help remind me how to do certain operations. I knew what a table was, but I could not quite remember the structure of the command to create it. What I needed was the syntax diagram, and perhaps a handy example…. Voilá! I was off to the races.

As my Oracle experience grew (and my memory diminished) I needed my cheat sheet more and more. I didn't need examples as frequently, unless I was doing something rare, but I did need the syntax diagrams now and again to make sure I was constructing my SQL statement correctly.

As I pondered this need, I also pondered the fact that I hate online documentation, and the fact that few Oracle DBAs actually have a published, bound copy of the Oracle documentation available to them. So, we have to surf the Web, cruise over to Tahiti.oracle.com, and find what we want in the docs. Then we need to print it so we can take it over to our colleagues for discussion. All very time consuming.

Then there is the moment of the dreaded database crash, when you find yourself asking questions about the specifics of a point-in-time recovery command. You bring up your web browser, and promptly find that you get a 404 error when you try to access the Oracle documentation web site. Perhaps your Internet connection is down and you can't get to metalink either. Now what do you do? Where do you go? Your boss is sweating, your coworkers who thought you were Mr. Oracle are now laughing at your inability to perform a database recovery, and you are at a loss.

Enter *Portable DBA: Oracle*. In the pages of this book, you will find the answer to many a question. New DBAs, if you want examples of how to create tables, or indexes, or foreign key relationships, they're in this book. More experienced DBAs, perhaps you want examples or just a quick "carry it with you" reference; well, *Portable DBA: Oracle* is just for you.

In the pages of this book, I have tried to give you somewhat condensed coverage of all the major Oracle commands. In the very first chapter, I have provided a cheat sheet of sorts, with many examples of how to issue specific commands, to perform specific database actions. In the following chapters, I delve into most of the SQL commands with more detail, but in a condensed format. This is not a book for learning, but for doing. So, if you want to learn about the benefits and costs of using table compression, you will want to look at the Oracle documentation or *Oracle Database 10g: The Complete Reference*. If you want to actually know how to enable compression on a table, this is the place to go. If you want to know the benefits of index-organized tables over other types of tables, you should find your way to one of the other great Oracle Press books. If you want a book that you can carry with you to your buddy's cube so you can help him create that table, this book is the one.

Check out the appendixes too! Lots of meat there, such as a SQL quick reference guide that you can take with you wherever you go!

It is my hope that this book will not become a doorstop of good intention but low practicality, but will become a well-worn reference. In using the book, perhaps you'll find that certain changes in the book might be warranted. You might find yourself making notes in the margins, or perhaps there is an example that you think might be nice to have, or perhaps you would like to see more or less detail on a specific topic. You might even find (gasp!) an error. In any case, please feel free to write me at dbaoracle@aol.com. I respond to all kind and civil e-mail as quickly as I can (and love each one), and dump the rest without reply. Also, if you ever find yourself at a conference that I'm attending, I'd love to meet you!

Finally, you can find lots of Oracle-related help in a number of places. There is Oracle-L (www.orafaq.com/maillist/newbies.htm) and Lazy DBA (www.lazydba.com). I tend to hang around in both of those places, as do some Oracle folks who are pretty sharp. Also, I'm a sysop on the Quest Oracle DBA Pipelines (www.quest-pipelines.com/pipelines/dba/index.asp), which has its own crop of Oracle smarties. On these web boards you will find the most active and well-known Oracle personalities, so stop by and interact with these large Oracle communities. Enjoy the book, and I hope that it comes in handy time and time again.

CHAPTER
1

DBA Cheat Sheet

s I mentioned in the introduction, this book is less about learning how to do something and more about actually doing it. As a beginner DBA and then, particularly, as an intermediate DBA, I found that I knew what I needed to do, such as create a tablespace. I knew the commands and most of the syntax on how to do it—use the **create tablespace** command, I knew there was a **datafile** clause, and so on. What I sometimes forgot was exactly how the command is supposed to be formatted, what order the different keywords are supposed to be in, and so on.

Certainly the documentation and syntax guides were available, but for beginners and intermediate DBAs (and even those of us older DBAs with foggy memories!), examples are really the key. For me, at least, examples are a much faster way of getting to what I want. They allow me to figure out the subtle order and method to do what I want to do, without having to sort through what can be long, and confusing, syntax diagrams.

With that in mind, I present in this chapter a cheat sheet of sorts. It contains examples of a number of the most commonly performed DBA activities. They are all listed in alphabetical order by the command being used, and then the activity being performed.

One note of caution: if you don't know what a specific keyword of a command does, don't use it without checking out its purpose. This is a reference for those who understand what something like **cascade constraints** means when associated with a **drop table** command. So, without further delay, let's get on with the examples!

alter cluster

```
ALTER CLUSTER pub_cluster SIZE 4K;
ALTER CLUSTER pub_cluster DEALLOCATE UNUSED KEEP 1M;
```

alter database: Alter a Data File

```
ALTER DATABASE DATAFILE 4 OFFLINE;
ALTER DATABASE DATAFILE '/opt/oracle/datafile/users01.dbf' OFFLINE;
ALTER DATABASE DATAFILE '/opt/oracle/datafile/users01.dbf'
RESIZE 100m;
ALTER DATABASE DATAFILE '/opt/oracle/datafile/users01.dbf'
AUTOEXTEND ON NEXT 100M MAXSIZE 1000M;
ALTER DATABASE DATAFILE 4 END BACKUP;
```

alter database: Alter a Tempfile

```
ALTER DATABASE TEMPFILE 4 RESIZE 100M;
ALTER DATABASE TEMPFILE 4
AUTOEXTEND ON NEXT 100M MAXSIZE 1000M;
ALTER DATABASE TEMPFILE 4 DROP INCLUDING DATAFILES;
ALTER DATABASE TEMPFILE 4 OFFLINE;
```

alter database: ARCHIVELOG Mode Commands

```
ALTER DATABASE ARCHIVELOG;
ALTER DATABASE NOARCHIVELOG;
```

```
ALTER DATABASE FORCE LOGGING;
ALTER DATABASE CLEAR LOGFILE '/opt/oracle/logfiles/redo01.rdo';
ALTER DATABASE CLEAR UNARCHIVED LOGFILE
'/opt/oracle/logfiles/redo01.rdo';
ALTER DATABASE ADD SUPPLEMENTAL LOG DATA;
ALTER DATABASE ADD SUPPLEMENTAL LOG DATA (PRIMARY KEY, UNIQUE);
ALTER DATABASE DROP SUPPLEMENTAL LOG DATA;
```

alter database: Control File Operations

```
ALTER DATABASE BACKUP CONTROLFILE TO TRACE;
ALTER DATABASE BACKUP CONTROLFILE TO TRACE
AS '/opt/oracle/logfile_backup/backup_logfile.trc'
REUSE RESETLOGS;
ALTER DATABASE BACKUP CONTROLFILE TO
'/opt/oracle/logfile_backup/backup_logfile.ctl';
```

alter database: Create a Data File

```
ALTER DATABASE CREATE DATAFILE
'/opt/oracle/datafile/users01.dbf' AS '/opt/oracle/datafile/users01.dbf';
ALTER DATABASE CREATE DATAFILE 4
AS '/opt/oracle/datafile/users01.dbf';
ALTER DATABASE CREATE DATAFILE
'/opt/oracle/datafile/users01.dbf' AS NEW;
```

alter database: Datafile Offline/Online
See alter database: Alter a Data File

alter database: Logfile Commands

```
ALTER DATABASE ADD LOGFILE GROUP 2
('/opt/oracle/logfiles/redo02a.rdo', '/opt/oracle/logfiles/redo02b.rdo')
SIZE 300M REUSE;
ALTER DATABASE ADD LOGFILE MEMBER
'/opt/oracle/logfiles/redo02c.rdo'
to GROUP 2;
ALTER DATABASE ADD LOGFILE thread 3 GROUP 2
('/opt/oracle/logfiles/redo02a.rdo', '/opt/oracle/logfiles/redo02b.rdo')
SIZE 300M REUSE;
ALTER DATABASE DROP LOGFILE GROUP 3;
ALTER DATABASE DROP LOGFILE MEMBER '/opt/oracle/logfiles/redo02b.rdo';
```

alter database: Mount and Open the Database

```
ALTER DATABASE MOUNT;
ALTER DATABASE OPEN;
```

alter database: Move or Rename a Database File or Online Redo Log

NOTE
The database must be mounted to rename or move online redo logs.
The database must be mounted or the data files taken offline to move
database data files.

```
ALTER DATABASE RENAME FILE '/ora/datafile/oldfile.dbf' TO '/ora/datafile/newfile.dbf';
```

alter database: Open the Database Read-Only

```
ALTER DATABASE OPEN READ ONLY;
```

alter database: Open the Database with resetlogs

```
ALTER DATABASE OPEN RESETLOGS;
```

alter database: Recover the Database

For database recovery, I recommend the use of the **recover** command instead. See the "recover" section, later in the chapter.

alter function: Recompile a Function

```
ALTER FUNCTION my_function COMPILE;
```

alter index: Allocate and Deallocate Extents

```
ALTER INDEX ix_my_tab ALLOCATE EXTENT;
ALTER INDEX ix_my_tab ALLOCATE EXTENT
DATAFILE '/ora/datafile/newidx.dbf';
ALTER INDEX ix_my_tab DEALLOCATE UNUSED;
ALTER INDEX ix_my_tab DEALLOCATE UNUSED KEEP 100M;
```

alter index: Miscellaneous Maintenance

```
ALTER INDEX ix_my_tab PARALLEL 3;
ALTER INDEX ix_my_tab NOPARALLEL;
ALTER INDEX ix_my_tab NOCOMPRESS;
ALTER INDEX ix_my_tab COMPRESS;
```

alter index: Modify Logging Attributes

```
ALTER INDEX ix_my_tab LOGGING;
ALTER INDEX ix_my_tab NOLOGGING;
```

alter index: Modify Storage and Physical Attributes

```
ALTER INDEX ix_my_tab PCTFREE 10 PCTUSED 40 INITRANS 5
STORAGE (NEXT 100k MAXEXTENTS UNLIMITED FREELISTS 10
BUFFER_POOL KEEP);
```

alter index: Partition – Add Hash Index Partition

```
ALTER INDEX ix_my_tab ADD PARTITION
TABLESPACE NEWIDXTBS;
```

alter index: Partition – Coalesce Partition

```
ALTER INDEX ix_my_tab COALESCE PARTITION;
```

alter index: Partition – Drop Partition

```
ALTER INDEX ix_my_tab DROP PARTITION ix_my_tab_jan_04;
```

alter index: Partition – Modify Default Attributes

```
ALTER INDEX ix_my_tab MODIFY DEFAULT ATTRIBUTES
FOR PARTITION ix_my_tab_jan_04
PCTFREE 10 PCTUSED 40 TABLESPACE newidxtbs
NOLOGGING COMPRESS;
```

alter index: Partition – Modify Partition

```
ALTER INDEX ix_my_tab MODIFY PARTITION ix_my_tab_jan_04
DEALLOCATE UNUSED KEEP 100M;
ALTER INDEX ix_my_tab MODIFY PARTITION ix_my_tab_jan_04
ALLOCATE EXTENT SIZE 100m;
ALTER INDEX ix_my_tab MODIFY PARTITION ix_my_tab_jan_04
PCTUSED 40 STORAGE(NEXT 50m) NOLOGGING;
```

alter index: Partition – Modify Subpartition

```
ALTER INDEX ix_my_tab MODIFY SUBPARTITION ix_my_tab_jan_04
DEALLOCATE UNUSED KEEP 100M;
ALTER INDEX ix_my_tab MODIFY SUBPARTITION ix_my_tab_jan_04
ALLOCATE EXTENT SIZE 100m;
ALTER INDEX ix_my_tab MODIFY SUBPARTITION ix_my_tab_jan_04
PCTUSED 40 STORAGE(NEXT 50m) NOLOGGING;
```

alter index: Partition – Rename

```
ALTER INDEX ix_my_tab RENAME
PARTITION ix_my_tab_jan_04 TO ix_my_tab_jan_05;
ALTER INDEX ix_my_tab RENAME
SUBPARTITION ix_my_tab_jan_04 TO ix_my_tab_jan_05;
```

alter index: Partition – Split

```
ALTER INDEX ix_my_tab SPLIT PARTITION ix_my_tab_jan_05
AT ('15-JAN-05') INTO PARTITION ix_my_tab_jan_05a
TABLESPACE myidxtbs
STORAGE (INITIAL 100m NEXT 50M FREELISTS 5);
```

alter index: Rebuild Nonpartitioned Indexes

```
ALTER INDEX ix_my_tab REBUILD ONLINE;
ALTER INDEX ix_my_tab REBUILD ONLINE
TABLESPACE idx_tbs_new PCTFREE 1
STORAGE (INITIAL 50M NEXT 50m FREELISTS 5)
COMPUTE STATISTICS PARALLEL 0;
```

alter index: Rebuild Partitions

```
ALTER INDEX ix_my_tab
REBUILD PARTITION ix_my_tab_jan_04 ONLINE;
ALTER INDEX ix_my_tab
REBUILD SUBPARTITION ix_my_tab_jan_04 ONLINE
PCTFREE 1 STORAGE (INITIAL 50M NEXT 50m FREELISTS 5)
COMPUTE STATISTICS PARALLEL 0;
```

alter index: Rename

```
ALTER INDEX ix_my_tab RENAME TO 'ix_my_tab_01';
```

alter index: Shrink

```
ALTER INDEX ix_my_tab SHRINK SPACE;
ALTER INDEX ix_my_tab SHRINK SPACE COMPACT CASCADE;
```

alter materialized view: Allocate and Deallocate Extents

```
ALTER MATERIALIZED VIEW mv_my_tab ALLOCATE EXTENT;
ALTER MATERIALIZED VIEW mv_my_tab DEALLOCATE UNUSED;
```

alter materialized view: Miscellaneous

```
ALTER MATERIALIZED VIEW mv_my_tab COMPRESS;
ALTER MATERIALIZED VIEW mv_my_tab PARALLEL 3;
ALTER MATERIALIZED VIEW mv_my_tab NOLOGGING;
ALTER MATERIALIZED VIEW mv_my_tab LOGGING;
ALTER MATERIALIZED VIEW mv_my_tab CONSIDER FRESH;
ALTER MATERIALIZED VIEW mv_my_tab ENABLE QUERY REWRITE;
```

alter materialized view: Physical Attributes and Storage

```
ALTER MATERIALIZED VIEW mv_my_tab
PCTFREE 5 PCTUSED 60
STORAGE (NEXT 100m FREELISTS 5);
```

alter materialized view: Refresh

```
ALTER MATERIALIZED VIEW mv_my_tab REFRESH FAST;
ALTER MATERIALIZED VIEW mv_my_tab REFRESH COMPLETE;
ALTER MATERIALIZED VIEW mv_my_tab REFRESH FAST ON DEMAND;
```

```
ALTER MATERIALIZED VIEW mv_my_tab REFRESH FAST ON COMMIT;
ALTER MATERIALIZED VIEW mv_my_tab REFRESH COMPLETE
START WITH sysdate;
ALTER MATERIALIZED VIEW mv_my_tab REFRESH COMPLETE
START WITH sysdate NEXT sysdate+1/24;
```

alter materialized view: Shrink Space

```
ALTER MATERIALIZED VIEW mv_my_tab SHRINK SPACE;
ALTER MATERIALIZED VIEW mv_my_tab
SHRINK SPACE COMPACT CASCADE;
```

alter materialized view log: Add Components

```
ALTER MATERIALIZED VIEW LOG ON my_tab ADD PRIMARY KEY;
ALTER MATERIALIZED VIEW LOG ON my_tab ADD (col1, col2)
INCLUDING NEW VALUES;
ALTER MATERIALIZED VIEW LOG ON my_tab ADD (col1, col2),
ROWID, SEQUENCE INCLUDING NEW VALUES;
```

alter materialized view log: Allocate and Deallocate Extents

```
ALTER MATERIALIZED VIEW LOG ON my_tab ALLOCATE EXTENT;
ALTER MATERIALIZED VIEW LOG ON my_tab DEALLOCATE UNUSED;
```

alter materialized view log: Miscellaneous

```
ALTER MATERIALIZED VIEW LOG ON my_tab PARALLEL 3;
ALTER MATERIALIZED VIEW LOG ON my_tab NOLOGGING;
ALTER MATERIALIZED VIEW LOG ON my_tab SHRINK SPACE;
```

alter materialized view log: Physical Attributes and Storage

```
ALTER MATERIALIZED VIEW LOG ON my_tab
PCTFREE 5 PCTUSED 60
STORAGE (NEXT 100m FREELISTS 5);
```

alter package: Compile

```
ALTER PACKAGE pk_my_package COMPILE;
ALTER PACKAGE pk_my_package COMPILE SPECIFICATION;
ALTER PACKAGE pk_my_package COMPILE BODY;
```

alter procedure: Compile

```
ALTER PROCEDURE pk_my_package COMPILE;
```

alter profile: Miscellaneous

```
ALTER ROLE my_role IDENTIFIED BY password;
ALTER ROLE my_role NOT IDENTIFIED;
```

alter profile: Modify Limits (Password)

```
ALTER PROFILE my_profile LIMIT FAILED_LOGIN_ATTEMPTS=3;
ALTER PROFILE my_profile LIMIT PASSWORD_LOCK_TIME=2/24;
ALTER PROFILE my_profile LIMIT PASSWORD_GRACE_TIME=5;
ALTER PROFILE my_profile LIMIT PASSWORD_LIFETIME=60;
ALTER PROFILE my_profile LIMIT PASSWORD_REUSE_TIME=365 PASSWORD_REUSE_MAX=3;
```

alter profile: Modify Limits (Resource)

```
ALTER PROFILE my_profile LIMIT SESSIONS_PER_CPU=10;
ALTER PROFILE my_profile LIMIT CONNECT_TIME=1000;
ALTER PROFILE my_profile LIMIT IDLE_TIME=60;
ALTER PROFILE my_profile LIMIT PRIVATE_SGA=1000000;
```

alter rollback segment: Online/Offline

```
ALTER ROLLBACK SEGMENT rbs01 OFFLINE;
ALTER ROLLBACK SEGMENT rbs01 ONLINE;
```

alter rollback segment: Shrink

```
ALTER ROLLBACK SEGMENT rbs01 SHRINK;
ALTER ROLLBACK SEGMENT rbs01 SHRINK TO 100M;
```

alter rollback segment: storage Clause

```
ALTER ROLLBACK SEGMENT rbs01 STORAGE(NEXT 50M OPTIMAL 100M);
```

alter sequence: Miscellaneous

```
ALTER SEQUENCE my_seq INCREMENT BY -5;
ALTER SEQUENCE my_seq INCREMENT BY 1 MAXVALUE 50000 CYCLE;
ALTER SEQUENCE my_seq NOMAXVALUE;
ALTER SEQUENCE my_seq CACHE ORDER;
ALTER SEQUENCE my_seq INCREMENT BY 1
MINVALUE 1 MAXVALUE 500 CYCLE;
```

alter session: Enable and Disable Parallel Operations

```
ALTER SESSION ENABLE PARALLEL DML PARALLEL 3;
ALTER SESSION ENABLE PARALLEL DDL;
ALTER SESSION DISABLE PARALLEL QUERY;
```

alter session: Resumable Space Management

```
ALTER SESSION ENABLE RESUMABLE TIMEOUT 3600;
ALTER SESSION DISABLE RESUMABLE;
```

alter session: Set Session Parameters

```
ALTER SESSION SET nls_date_format='MM/DD/YYYY HH24:MI:SS';
ALTER SESSION SET sort_area_size=10000000;
ALTER SESSION SET query_rewrite_enabled=TRUE;
ALTER SESSION SET resumable_timeout=3600;
ALTER SESSION SET skip_unusable_indexes=TRUE;
ALTER SESSION SET SQL_TRACE=TRUE;
```

alter system: Logfile and Archive Logfile Management

```
ALTER SYSTEM SWITCH LOGFILE;
ALTER SYSTEM ARCHIVE LOG START;
ALTER SYSTEM ARCHIVE LOG STOP;
ALTER SYSTEM ARCHIVE LOG ALL;
ALTER SYSTEM ARCHIVE LOG THREAD 1 ALL;
ALTER SYSTEM ARCHIVE LOG ALL TO 'C:\oracle\allarch';
```

alter system: Set System Parameters

```
ALTER SYSTEM SET db_cache_size=325M
COMMENT='This change is to add more memory to the system'
SCOPE=BOTH;
ALTER SYSTEM SET COMPATIBLE=10.0.0
COMMENT='GOING TO 10G!' SCOPE=SPFILE;
```

alter system: System Management

```
ALTER SYSTEM CHECKPOINT GLOBAL;
ALTER SYSTEM KILL SESSION '145,334';
ALTER SYSTEM ENABLE RESTRICTED SESSION;
ALTER SYSTEM DISABLE RESTRICTED SESSION;
ALTER SYSTEM SUSPEND;
ALTER SYSTEM QUIESCE RESTRICTED;
ALTER SYSTEM UNQUIESCE;
ALTER SYSTEM RESUME;
ALTER SYSTEM FLUSH SHARED_POOL;
ALTER SYSTEM FLUSH BUFFER_CACHE;
```

alter table: External Table Operations

```
ALTER TABLE ext_parts REJECT LIMIT 500;
ALTER TABLE ext_parts DEFUALT DIRECTORY ext_employee_dir;
ALTER TABLE ext_parts ACCESS PARAMETERS
(FIELDS TERMINATED BY ',');
ALTER TABLE ext_parts LOCATION ('PARTS01.TXT','PARTS02.TXT');
ALTER TABLE ext_parts ADD COLUMN (SSN NUMBER);
```

alter table: Move Table

```
ALTER TABLE parts move TABLESPACE parts_new_tbs PCTFREE 10 PCTUSED 60;
```

alter table: Table Column – Add

```
ALTER TABLE PARTS ADD (part_location VARCHAR2(20) );
ALTER TABLE PARTS ADD (part_location VARCHAR2(20), part_bin VARCHAR2(30) );
ALTER TABLE parts ADD (photo BLOB)
LOB (photo) STORE AS lob_parts_photo
(TABLESPACE parts_lob_tbs);
```

alter table: Table Column – Modify

```
ALTER TABLE PARTS MODIFY (part_location VARCHAR2(30) );
ALTER TABLE PARTS MODIFY
part_location VARCHAR2(30), part_bin VARCHAR2(20) );
ALTER TABLE parts modify (name NOT NULL);
ALTER TABLE parts modify (name NULL);
ALTER TABLE parts MODIFY LOB (photo) (STORAGE(FREELISTS 2));
ALTER TABLE parts MODIFY LOB (photo) (PCTVERSION 50);
```

alter table: Table Column – Remove

```
ALTER TABLE parts DROP (part_location);
ALTER TABLE parts DROP (part_location, part_bin);
```

alter table: Table Column – Rename

```
ALTER TABLE parts RENAME COLUMN part_location TO part_loc;
```

alter table: Table Constraints – Add Check Constraint

```
ALTER TABLE parts ADD (CONSTRAINT ck_parts_01 CHECK (id > 0) );
```

alter table: Table Constraints – Add Default Value

```
ALTER TABLE PARTS MODIFY (name DEFAULT 'Not Available');
ALTER TABLE PARTS ADD (vendor_code NUMBER DEFAULT 0);
ALTER TABLE PARTS MODIFY (part_description DEFAULT NULL);
```

alter table: Table Constraints – Add Foreign Key

```
ALTER TABLE parts ADD CONSTRAINT fk_part_bin
FOREIGN KEY (bin_code) REFERENCES part_bin;
```

alter table: Table Constraints – Add Primary and Unique Key

```
ALTER TABLE parts ADD CONSTRAINT pk_parts_part_id
PRIMARY KEY (id) USING INDEX TABLESPACE parts_index
STORAGE (INITIAL 100K NEXT 100K PCTINCREASE 0);
```

```
ALTER TABLE parts ADD CONSTRAINT uk_parts_part_bin
UNIQUE (part_bin)USING INDEX TABLESPACE parts_index
STORAGE (INITIAL 100K NEXT 100K PCTINCREASE 0);
```

alter table: Table Constraints – Modify

```
ALTER TABLE parts DISABLE UNIQUE (part_bin);
ALTER TABLE parts DISABLE CONSTRAINT uk_parts_part_bin;
ALTER TABLE parts DISABLE CONSTRAINT uk_parts_part_bin KEEP INDEX;
ALTER TABLE parts DISABLE CONSTRAINT fk_part_bin;
ALTER TABLE parts DISABLE CONSTRAINT fk_part_bin
DISABLE PRIMARY KEY KEEP INDEX;
ALTER TABLE parts ENABLE CONSTRAINT fk_part_bin;
ALTER TABLE parts ENABLE PRIMARY KEY;
ALTER TABLE parts ENABLE UNIQUE (part_bin);
ALTER TABLE parts ENABLE NOVALIDATE CONSTRAINT fk_part_bin;
ALTER TABLE parts ENABLE NOVALIDATE PRIMARY KEY;
ALTER TABLE parts ENABLE NOVALIDATE UNIQUE (part_bin);
ALTER TABLE parts ENABLE NOVALIDATE PRIMARY KEY
ENABLE NOVALIDATE CONSTRAINT fk_part_bin;
```

alter table: Table Constraints – Remove

```
ALTER TABLE parts DROP CONSTRAINT fk_part_bin;
ALTER TABLE parts DROP PRIMARY KEY;
ALTER TABLE parts DROP PRIMARY KEY CASCADE;
ALTER TABLE parts DROP UNIQUE (uk_parts_part_bin);
```

alter table: Table Partition – Add

```
ALTER TABLE store_sales ADD PARTITION sales_q1_04
VALUES LESS THAN (TO_DATE('01-APR-2004','DD-MON-YYYY'))
TABLESPACE data_0104_tbs UPDATE GLOBAL INDEXES;
ALTER TABLE daily_transactions ADD PARTITION;
ALTER TABLE daily_transactions
ADD PARTITION Alaska VALUES ('AK');
ALTER TABLE daily_transactions
add PARTITION SALES_2004_Q1 VALUES LESS THAN
        (TO_DATE('01-APR-2004','DD-MON-YYYY')) SUBPARTITIONS 4;
```

alter table: Table Partition – Merge

```
ALTER TABLE store_sales
MERGE PARTITIONS Oklahoma, texas
INTO PARTITION oktx;
```

alter table: Table Partition – Move

```
ALTER TABLE store_sales MOVE PARTITION sales_overflow TABLESPACE
new_sales_overflow STORAGE (INITIAL 100m NEXT 100m PCTINCREASE 0)
UPDATE GLOBAL INDEXES;
```

alter table: Table Partition – Remove

```
ALTER TABLE store_sales DROP PARTITION sales_q1_04 UPDATE GLOBAL INDEXES;
```

alter table: Table Partition – Rename

```
ALTER TABLE store_sales RENAME PARTITION sales_q1 TO sales_first_quarter;
```

alter table: Table Partition – Split

```
ALTER TABLE store_sales
SPLIT PARTITION sales_overflow AT
(TO_DATE('01-FEB-2004','DD-MON-YYYY') )
INTO (PARTITION sales_q4_2003,
      PARTITION sales_overflow)
UPDATE GLOBAL INDEXES;
ALTER TABLE composite_sales SPLIT PARTITION sales_q1
AT (TO_DATE('15-FEB-2003','DD-MON-YYYY'))
INTO (PARTITION sales_q1_01 SUBPARTITIONS 4
STORE IN (q1_01_tab1, q1_01_tab2, q1_01_tab3, q1_01_tab4),
PARTITION sales_q1_02 SUBPARTITIONS 4
STORE IN (q1_02_tab1, q1_02_tab2, q1_02_tab3, q1_02_tab4) )
UPDATE GLOBAL INDEXES;
```

alter table: Table Partition – Truncate

```
ALTER TABLE store_sales TRUNCATE PARTITION sales_overflow
UPDATE GLOBAL INDEXES;
```

alter table: Table Properties

```
ALTER TABLE parts PCTFREE 10 PCTUSED 60;
ALTER TABLE parts STORAGE (NEXT 1M);
ALTER TABLE parts PARALLEL 4;
```

alter table: Triggers – Modify Status

```
ALTER TABLE parts DISABLE ALL TRIGGERS;
ALTER TABLE parts ENABLE ALL TRIGGERS;
```

alter tablespace: Backups

```
ALTER TABLESPACE my_data_tbs BEGIN BACKUP;
ALTER TABLESPACE my_data_tbs END BACKUP;
```

alter tablespace: Data Files and Tempfiles

```
ALTER TABLESPACE mytbs
ADD DATAFILE '/ora100/oracle/mydb/mydb_mytbs_01.dbf' SIZE 100M;
```

```
ALTER TABLESPACE mytemp
ADD TEMPFILE '/ora100/oracle/mydb/mydb_mytemp_01.dbf'
SIZE 100M;
ALTER TABLESPACE mytemp AUTOEXTEND OFF;
ALTER TABLESPACE mytemp AUTOEXTEND ON NEXT 100m MAXSIZE 1G;
```

alter tablespace: Rename

```
ALTER TABLESPACE my_data_tbs RENAME TO my_newdata_tbs;
```

alter tablespace: Tablespace Management

```
ALTER TABLESPACE my_data_tbs DEFAULT
STORAGE (INITIAL 100m NEXT 100m FREELISTS 3);
ALTER TABLESPACE my_data_tbs MINIMUM EXTENT 500k;
ALTER TABLESPACE my_data_tbs RESIZE 100m;
ALTER TABLESPACE my_data_tbs COALESCE;
ALTER TABLESPACE my_data_tbs OFFLINE;
ALTER TABLESPACE my_data_tbs ONLINE;
ALTER TABLESPACE mytbs READ ONLY;
ALTER TABLESPACE mytbs READ WRITE;
ALTER TABLESPACE mytbs FORCE LOGGING;
ALTER TABLESPACE mytbs NOLOGGING;
ALTER TABLESPACE mytbs FLASHBACK ON;
ALTER TABLESPACE mytbs FLASHBACK OFF;
ALTER TABLESPACE mytbs RETENTION GUARANTEE;
ALTER TABLESPACE mytbs RETENTION NOGUARANTEE;
```

alter trigger

```
ALTER TRIGGER tr_my_trigger DISABLE;
ALTER TRIGGER tr_my_trigger ENABLE;
ALTER TRIGGER tr_my_trigger RENAME TO tr_new_my_trigger;
ALTER TRIGGER tr_my_trigger COMPILE;
```

alter user: Change Password

```
ALTER USER olduser IDENTIFIED BY newpassword;
ALTER USER olduser IDENTIFIED EXTERNALLY;
```

alter user: Password and Account Management

```
ALTER USER olduser PASSWORD EXPIRE;
ALTER USER olduser ACCOUNT LOCK;
ALTER USER olduser ACCOUNT UNLOCK;
```

alter user: Profile

```
ALTER USER olduser PROFILE admin_profile;
```

alter user: Quotas

```
ALTER USER olduser QUOTA UNLIMITED ON users;
ALTER USER olduser QUOTA 10000M ON USERS;
```

alter user: Roles

```
ALTER USER olduser DEFAULT ROLE admin_role;
ALTER USER olduser DEFAULT ROLE NONE;
ALTER USER olduser DEFAULT ROLE ALL EXCEPT admin_role;
```

alter user: Tablespace Assignments

```
ALTER USER olduser DEFAULT TABLESPACE users;
ALTER USER olduser TEMPORARY TABLESPACE temp;
```

alter view: Constraints

```
ALTER VIEW my_view
ADD CONSTRAINT u_my_view_01 UNIQUE (empno)
RELY DISABLE NOVALIDATE;
ALTER VIEW my_view DROP CONSTRAINT u_my_view_01;
ALTER VIEW my_view DROP PRIMARY KEY;
ALTER VIEW my_view MODIFY CONSTRAINT u_my_view_01 NORELY;
ALTER VIEW my_view MODIFY CONSTRAINT u_my_view_01 RELY;
```

alter view: Recompile

```
ALTER VIEW my_view RECOMPILE;
```

analyze: Analyze Cluster

```
ANALYZE CLUSTER my_cluster_tab COMPUTE STATISTICS FOR ALL ROWS;
ANALYZE CLUSTER my_cluster_tab
ESTIMATE STATISTICS SAMPLE 10000 ROWS FOR ALL ROWS;
```

analyze: Analyze Index

```
ANALYZE INDEX ix_tab_01 COMPUTE STATISTICS FOR ALL ROWS;
ANALYZE INDEX ix_tab_01
ESTIMATE STATISTICS SAMPLE 10000 ROWS FOR ALL ROWS;
```

analyze: Analyze Table

```
ANALYZE TABLE mytab COMPUTE STATISTICS
FOR ALL INDEXED COLUMNS SIZE 100;
ANALYZE TABLE mytab COMPUTE STATISTICS
FOR ALL INDEXES;
```

audit

```
AUDIT ALL ON scott.emp;
AUDIT UPDATE, DELETE ON scott.emp;
AUDIT SELECT on scott.emp WHENEVER NOT SUCCESSFUL;
AUDIT INSERT, UPDATE, DELETE ON DEFAULT;
```

comment

```
COMMENT ON TABLE scott.mytab IS
'This is a comment on the mytab table';
COMMENT ON COLUMN scott.mytab.col1 IS
'This is a comment on the col1 column';
COMMENT ON MATERIALIZED VIEW scott.mview IS
'This is a comment on the materialized view mview';
```

create cluster

```
CREATE CLUSTER pub_cluster (pubnum NUMBER)
SIZE 8K PCTFREE 10 PCTUSED 60 TABLESPACE user_data;
CREATE CLUSTER pub_cluster (pubnum NUMBER)
SIZE 8K HASHKEYS 1000 PCTFREE 10 PCTUSED 60
TABLESPACE user_data;
```

create control file

```
CREATE CONTROLFILE REUSE DATABASE "mydb"
NORESETLOGS NOARCHIVELOG
MAXLOGFILES 32    MAXLOGMEMBERS 3
MAXDATAFILES 200 MAXINSTANCES 1
MAXLOGHISTORY 1000
LOGFILE
   GROUP 1 ('/ora01/oracle/mydb/mydb_redo1a.rdo',
            '/ora02/oracle/mydb/mydb_redo1b.rdo') SIZE 500K,
   GROUP 2 ('/ora01/oracle/mydb/mydb_redo2a.rdo',
            '/ora01/oracle/mydb/mydb_redo2b.rdo') SIZE 500K
DATAFILE
   '/ora01/oracle/mydb/mydb_system_01.dbf ',
   '/ora01/oracle/mydb/mydb_users_01.dbf ',
   '/ora01/oracle/mydb/mydb_undo_01.dbf ',
   '/ora01/oracle/mydb/mydb_sysaux_01.dbf ',
   '/ora01/oracle/mydb/mydb_alldata_01.dbf ';
```

create database

```
CREATE DATABASE prodb
MAXINSTANCES 1 MAXLOGHISTORY 1
MAXLOGFILES 5 MAXLOGMEMBERS 3
MAXDATAFILES 100
```

```
DATAFILE 'C:\oracle\ora92010\prodb\system01.dbf'
SIZE 250M REUSE AUTOEXTEND ON NEXT 10240K
MAXSIZE UNLIMITED EXTENT MANAGEMENT LOCAL DEFAULT
TEMPORARY TABLESPACE TEMP
TEMPFILE 'C:\oracle\ora92010\prodb\temp01.dbf'
SIZE 40M REUSE AUTOEXTEND ON NEXT 640K MAXSIZE UNLIMITED
SYSAUX TABLESPACE
DATAFILE 'C:\oracle\ora92010\prodb\sysauxtbs01.dbf'
SIZE 300M REUSE AUTOEXTEND ON NEXT 5120K MAXSIZE UNLIMITED
UNDO TABLESPACE "UNDOTBS1"
DATAFILE 'C:\oracle\ora92010\prodb\undotbs01.dbf'
SIZE 200M REUSE AUTOEXTEND ON NEXT 5120K MAXSIZE UNLIMITED
CHARACTER SET WE8MSWIN1252
NATIONAL CHARACTER SET AL16UTF16
LOGFILE
GROUP 1 ('C:\oracle\ora92010\prodb\redo01.log') SIZE 102400K,
GROUP 2 ('C:\oracle\ora92010\prodb\redo02.log') SIZE 102400K,
GROUP 3 ('C:\oracle\ora92010\prodb\redo03.log') SIZE 102400K;
```

create database link

```
CREATE DATABASE LINK my_db_link
CONNECT TO current_user
USING 'my_db';
CREATE PUBLIC DATABASE LINK my_db_link
CONNECT TO remote_user IDENTIFIED BY psicorp
USING 'my_db';
```

create directory

```
CREATE OR REPLACE DIRECTORY mydir AS
'/opt/oracle/admin/directories/mydir';
```

create function

```
CREATE OR REPLACE FUNCTION find_value_in_table
(p_value IN NUMBER,  p_table IN VARCHAR2,
p_column IN VARCHAR2)
RETURN NUMBER IS
v_found NUMBER;
v_sql VARCHAR2(2000);
BEGIN
    v_sql:='SELECT 1 FROM '||p_table||' WHERE '||p_column||
          ' = '||p_value;
    execute immediate v_sql into v_found;
    return v_found;
END;
/
```

create index: Function-Based Index

```
CREATE INDEX fb_upper_last_name_emp ON emp_info (UPPER(last_name) );
```

create index: Global Partitioned Indexes

```
CREATE INDEX ix_part_my_tab_01 ON store_sales (invoice_number)
GLOBAL PARTITION BY RANGE (invoice_number)
(PARTITION part_001 VALUES LESS THAN (1000),
 PARTITION part_002 VALUES LESS THAN (10000),
 PARTITION part_003 VALUES LESS THAN (MAXVALUE) );
CREATE INDEX ix_part_my_tab_02 ON store_sales
(store_id, time_id)
GLOBAL PARTITION BY RANGE (store_id, time_id)
(PARTITION PART_001 VALUES LESS THAN
     (1000, TO_DATE('04-01-2003','MM-DD-YYYY') )
     TABLESPACE partition_001
     STORAGE (INITIAL 100M NEXT 200M PCTINCREASE 0),
 PARTITION part_002 VALUES LESS THAN
     (1000, TO_DATE('07-01-2003','MM-DD-YYYY')  )
     TABLESPACE partition_002
     STORAGE (INITIAL 200M NEXT 400M PCTINCREASE 0),
 PARTITION part_003 VALUES LESS THAN (maxvalue, maxvalue)
     TABLESPACE partition_003 );
```

create index: Local Partitioned Indexes

```
CREATE INDEX ix_part_my_tab_01 ON my_tab
(col_one, col_two, col_three)
LOCAL (PARTITION tbs_part_01 TABLESPACE part_tbs_01,
PARTITION tbs_part_02 TABLESPACE part_tbs_02,
PARTITION tbs_part_03 TABLESPACE part_tbs_03,
PARTITION tbs_part_04 TABLESPACE part_tbs_04);
CREATE INDEX ix_part_my_tab_01 ON my_tab (col_one, col_two, col_three)
LOCAL STORE IN (part_tbs_01, part_tbs_02, part_tbs_03, part_tbs_04);
CREATE INDEX ix_part_my_tab_01 ON my_tab (col_one, col_two, col_three)
LOCAL STORE IN (
part_tbs_01 STORAGE (INITIAL 10M NEXT 10M MAXEXTENTS 200),
part_tbs_02,
part_tbs_03 STORAGE (INITIAL 100M NEXT 100M MAXEXTENTS 200),
part_tbs_04 STORAGE (INITIAL 1000M NEXT 1000M MAXEXTENTS 200));
```

create index: Local Subpartitioned Indexes

```
CREATE INDEX sales_ix ON store_sales(time_id, store_id)
    STORAGE (INITIAL 1M MAXEXTENTS UNLIMITED) LOCAL
    (PARTITION q1_2003,
     PARTITION q2_2003,
     PARTITION q3_2003
       (SUBPARTITION pq3200301, SUBPARTITION pq3200302,
        SUBPARTITION pq3200303, SUBPARTITION pq3200304,
        SUBPARTITION pq3200305),
     PARTITION q4_2003
       (SUBPARTITION pq4200301 TABLESPACE tbs_1,
        SUBPARTITION pq4200302 TABLESPACE tbs_1,
```

```
    SUBPARTITION pq4200303 TABLESPACE tbs_1,
    SUBPARTITION pq4200304 TABLESPACE tbs_1,
    SUBPARTITION pq4200305 TABLESPACE tbs_1,
    SUBPARTITION pq4200306 TABLESPACE tbs_1,
    SUBPARTITION pq4200307 TABLESPACE tbs_1,
    SUBPARTITION pq4200308 TABLESPACE tbs_1),
 PARTITION sales_overflow
   (SUBPARTITION pqoflw01 TABLESPACE tbs_2,
    SUBPARTITION pqoflw02 TABLESPACE tbs_2,
    SUBPARTITION pqoflw03 TABLESPACE tbs_2,
    SUBPARTITION pqoflw04 TABLESPACE tbs_2));
```

create index: Nonpartitioned Indexes

```
CREATE INDEX ix_mytab_01 ON mytab(column_1);
CREATE UNIQUE INDEX ix_mytab_01 ON mytab(column_1, column_2, column_3);
CREATE INDEX ix_mytab_01 ON mytab(column_1, column_2, column_3)
TABLESPACE my_indexes COMPRESS
STORAGE (INITIAL 10K NEXT 10K PCTFREE 10) COMPUTE STATISTICS;
CREATE BITMAP INDEX bit_mytab_01 ON my_tab(col_two)
TABLESPACE my_tbs;
```

create materialized view

```
CREATE MATERIALIZED VIEW emp_dept_mv1
TABLESPACE users BUILD IMMEDIATE
REFRESH FAST ON COMMIT WITH ROWID
ENABLE QUERY REWRITE AS
SELECT d.rowid deptrowid, e.rowid emprowid,
       e.empno, e.ename, e.job, d.loc
FROM dept d, emp e
WHERE d.deptno = e.deptno;
CREATE MATERIALIZED VIEW emp_dept_mv3
TABLESPACE users BUILD IMMEDIATE
REFRESH FAST ON COMMIT WITH ROWID
DISABLE QUERY REWRITE AS
SELECT d.rowid deptrowid, e.rowid emprowid,
       d.dname, d.loc, e.ename, e.job
FROM dept d, emp e
WHERE d.deptno (+) = e.deptno;
```

create materialized view: Partitioned Materialized View

```
CREATE MATERIALIZED VIEW part_emp_mv1
PARTITION BY RANGE (hiredate)
  (PARTITION month1
     VALUES LESS THAN (TO_DATE('01-APR-1981', 'DD-MON-YYYY'))
     PCTFREE 0 PCTUSED 99
     STORAGE (INITIAL 64k NEXT 16k PCTINCREASE 0)
     TABLESPACE users,
```

```
        PARTITION month2
            VALUES LESS THAN (TO_DATE('01-DEC-1981', 'DD-MON-YYYY'))
            PCTFREE 0 PCTUSED 99
            STORAGE (INITIAL 64k NEXT 16k PCTINCREASE 0)
            TABLESPACE users,
        PARTITION month3
            VALUES LESS THAN (TO_DATE('01-APR-1988', 'DD-MON-YYYY'))
            PCTFREE 0 PCTUSED 99
            STORAGE (INITIAL 64k NEXT 16k PCTINCREASE 0)
            TABLESPACE users)
BUILD IMMEDIATE REFRESH FAST ENABLE QUERY REWRITE AS
SELECT hiredate, count(*) as hires
FROM emp
GROUP BY hiredate;
```

create materialized view log

```
CREATE MATERIALIZED VIEW LOG ON emp
TABLESPACE users
WITH PRIMARY KEY, SEQUENCE,
(ename, job, mgr, hiredate, sal, comm, deptno)
INCLUDING NEW VALUES;
```

create package/create package body

```
CREATE OR REPLACE PACKAGE get_Tomdate_pkg IS
    FUNCTION  GetTomdate  RETURN DATE;
    PRAGMA RESTRICT_REFERENCES (GetTomdate, WNDS);
    PROCEDURE ResetSysDate;
END get_Tomdate_pkg;
/

CREATE OR REPLACE PACKAGE BODY get_Tomdate_pkg IS
    v_Sysdate   DATE := TRUNC(SYSDATE);
    FUNCTION GetTomdate RETURN DATE IS
    BEGIN
        RETURN v_sysdate+1;
    END GetTomdate;
    PROCEDURE ResetSysdate IS
    BEGIN
        v_Sysdate := SYSDATE;
    END ResetSysdate;
END get_Tomdate_pkg;
/
```

create pfile

```
CREATE PFILE FROM SPFILE;
CREATE PFILE='/opt/oracle/admin/mydb/pfile/initmybd.ora'
FROM SPFILE='/opt/oracle/admin/mydb/pfile/spfilemybd.ora';
```

create procedure

```
CREATE OR REPLACE PROCEDURE new_emp_salary
(p_empid IN NUMBER,  p_increase IN NUMBER)
AS
BEGIN
     UPDATE emp SET salary=salary*p_increase
     WHERE empid=p_empid;
END;
/
```

create profile

```
CREATE PROFILE development_profile
LIMIT
SESSIONS_PER_USER 2 CONNECT_TIME 100000 IDLE_TIME 100000
LOGICAL_READS_PER_SESSION 1000000
PRIVATE_SGA 10m
FAILED_LOGIN_ATTEMPTS 3
PASSWORD_LIFE_TIME 60
PASSWORD_REUSE_TIME 365
PASSWORD_REUSE_MAX 3
PASSWORD_LOCK_TIME 30
PASSWORD_GRACE_TIME 5;
```

create role

```
CREATE ROLE developer_role IDENTIFIED USING develop;
```

create rollback segment

```
CREATE ROLLBACK SEGMENT r01 TABLESPACE RBS
STORAGE (INITIAL 100m NEXT 100M MINEXTENTS 5 OPTIMAL 500M);
```

create sequence

```
CREATE SEQUENCE my_seq
START WITH 1 INCREMENT BY 1 MAXVALUE 1000000 CYCLE CACHE;
```

create spfile

```
CREATE SPFILE FROM PFILE;
CREATE SPFILE='/opt/oracle/admin/mydb/pfile/spfilemybd.ora'
FROM PFILE='/opt/oracle/admin/mydb/pfile/initmybd.ora';
```

create synonym

```
CREATE SYNONYM scott_user.emp FOR scott.EMP;
CREATE PUBLIC SYNONYM emp FOR scott.EMP;
```

create table

```
CREATE TABLE my_tab
(id NUMBER,  current_value VARCHAR2(2000) ) COMPRESS;
CREATE TABLE parts (id NUMBER, version NUMBER, name VARCHAR2(30),
Bin_code NUMBER, upc NUMBER, active_code VARCHAR2(1) NOT NULL
     CONSTRAINT ck_parts_active_code_01
     CHECK (UPPER(active_code)= 'Y' or UPPER(active_code)='N'),
     CONSTRAINT pk_parts PRIMARY KEY (id, version)
     USING INDEX TABLESPACE parts_index
     STORAGE (INITIAL 1m NEXT 1m) )
TABLESPACE parts_tablespace
PCTFREE 20 PCTUSED 60 STORAGE ( INITIAL 10m NEXT 10m PCTINCREASE 0);
```

create tablespace: Permanent Tablespace

```
CREATE TABLESPACE data_tbs
DATAFILE '/opt/oracle/mydbs/data/mydbs_data_tbs_01.dbf'
SIZE 100m;
CREATE TABLESPACE data_tbs
DATAFILE '/opt/oracle/mydbs/data/mydbs_data_tbs_01.dbf'
SIZE 100m FORCE LOGGING BLOCKSIZE 8k;
CREATE TABLESPACE data_tbs
DATAFILE '/opt/oracle/mydbs/data/mydbs_data_tbs_01.dbf'
SIZE 100m NOLOGGING
DEFAULT COMPRESS EXTENT MANAGEMENT LOCAL UNIFORM SIZE 1M;
CREATE TABLESPACE data_tbs
DATAFILE '/opt/oracle/mydbs/data/mydbs_data_tbs_01.dbf'
SIZE 100m NOLOGGING
DEFAULT COMPRESS EXTENT MANAGEMENT LOCAL AUTOALLOCATE
SEGMENT SPACE MANAGEMENT AUTO;
CREATE BIGFILE TABLESPACE data_tbs
DATAFILE '/opt/oracle/mydbs/data/mydbs_data_tbs_01.dbf'
SIZE 10G;
```

create tablespace: Temporary Tablespace

```
CREATE TABLESPACE temp_tbs
TEMPFILE '/opt/oracle/mydbs/data/mydbs_temp_tbs_01.tmp'
SIZE 100m;
```

create tablespace: Undo Tablespace

```
CREATE TABLESPACE undo_tbs
TEMPFILE '/opt/oracle/mydbs/data/mydbs_undo_tbs_01.tmp'
SIZE 1g RETENTION GUARANTEE;
```

create trigger

```
CREATE OR REPLACE TRIGGER emp_comm_after_insert
BEFORE INSERT ON emp FOR EACH ROW
DECLARE
    v_sal  number;
    v_comm number;
BEGIN
    -- Find username of person performing the INSERT into the table
    v_sal:=:new.salary;
    :new.comm:=v_sal*.10;
END;
/
```

create user

```
CREATE USER Robert IDENTIFIED BY Freeman
DEFAULT TABLESPACE users_tbs
TEMPORARY TABLESPACE temp
QUOTA 100M ON users_tbs
QUOTA UNLIMITED ON data_tbs;
```

create view

```
CREATE OR REPLACE VIEW vw_emp_dept_10 AS
SELECT * FROM EMP WHERE dept=10;
CREATE OR REPLACE VIEW vw_public_email AS
SELECT ename_first, ename_last, email_address
FROM EMP WHERE public='Y'
```

delete

```
DELETE FROM emp WHERE empid=100;
DELETE FROM emp e WHERE e.rowid >
(SELECT MIN (esub.ROWID) FROM emp esub
WHERE e.empid=esub.empid);
```

drop cluster

```
DROP CLUSTER scott.emp_cluster
INCLUDING TABLES CASCADE CONSTRAINTS;
```

drop database

```
DROP DATABASE;
```

drop database link

```
DROP DATABASE LINK my_db_link;
DROP PUBLIC DATABASE LINK my_db_link;
```

drop directory

```
DROP DIRECTORY mydir;
```

drop function

```
DROP FUNCTION find_value_in_table;
```

drop index

```
DROP INDEX ix_my_tab;
```

drop materialized view

```
DROP MATERIALIZED VIEW my_mview;
DROP MATERIALIZED VIEW my_mview PRESERVE TABLE;
```

drop materialized view log

```
DROP MATERIALIZED VIEW LOG ON mytab;
```

drop package/drop package body

```
DROP PACKAGE scott.my_package
DROP PACKAGE BODY scott.my_package;
```

drop procedure

```
DROP PROCEDURE my_proc;
```

drop profile

```
DROP PROFILE my_profile CASCADE;
```

drop role

```
DROP ROLE my_role;
```

drop rollback segment

```
DROP ROLLBACK SEGMENT rbs01;
```

drop sequence

```
DROP SEQUENCE my_seq;
```

drop synonym

```
DROP SYNONYM my_synonym;
DROP PUBLIC SYNONYM my_synonym;
```

drop table

```
DROP TABLE my_tab;
DROP TABLE my_tab CASCADE CONSTRAINTS;
DROP TABLE my_tab CASCADE CONSTRAINTS PURGE;
```

drop tablespace

```
DROP TABLESPACE my_tbs;
DROP TABLESPACE my_tbs INCLUDING CONTENTS;
DROP TABLESPACE my_tbs INCLUDING CONTENTS
AND DATAFILES CASCADE CONSTRAINTS;
```

drop trigger

```
DROP TRIGGER my_trigger;
```

drop user

```
DROP USER my_user CASCADE;
```

drop view

```
DROP VIEW my_view CASCADE CONSTRAINTS;
```

explain plan

```
EXPLAIN PLAN SET STATEMENT_ID='TEST' FOR
SELECT * FROM emp WHERE EMPID=100;
```

flashback database

```
FLASHBACK DATABASE TO SCN 10000;
FLASHBACK DATABASE TO TIMESTAMP SYSDATE - 1/24;
FLASHBACK DATABASE TO BEFORE TIMESTAMP SYSDATE - 1/24;
```

flashback table

```
FLASHBACK TABLE my_tab TO SCN 10000;
FLASHBACK TABLE my_tab TO TIMESTAMP SYSDATE - 1/24
ENABLE TRIGGERS;
FLASHBACK TABLE my_tab TO BEFORE DROP;
FLASHBACK TABLE my_tab TO BEFORE DROP RENAME TO rec_tab;
```

grants: Object Grants

```
GRANT SELECT ON scott.my_tab TO my_user;
GRANT INSERT, UPDATE, SELECT ON scott.my_tab TO my_user;
```

```
GRANT SELECT ON scott.my_tab TO my_user WITH GRANT OPTION;
GRANT SELECT ON scott.my_tab TO PUBLIC WITH GRANT OPTION;
```

grants: System Grants

```
GRANT CREATE TABLE to my_user;
GRANT CREATE ANY TABLE to my_user WITH ADMIN OPTION;
GRANT ALL PRIVILEGES to my_user WITH ADMIN OPTION;
```

insert

```
INSERT INTO dept VALUES (100, 'Marketing', 'Y');
INSERT INTO dept (deptid, dept_name, active)
VALUES (100, 'Marketing', 'Y');
INSERT INTO emp_history SELECT * FROM emp a
WHERE a.empid NOT IN (SELECT empid FROM emp_history);
INSERT INTO emp_pay_summary
SELECT empid, sum(gross_pay) FROM emp_pay_history
GROUP BY empid;
INSERT ALL
INTO store_sales (store_id, sales_date, deptid, sales_amt)
VALUES (store_id, start_date, deptid, mon_sales)
INTO store_sales (store_id, sales_date, deptid, sales_amt)
VALUES (store_id, start_date+1, deptid, tue_sales)
INTO store_sales (store_id, sales_date, deptid, sales_amt)
VALUES (store_id, start_date+2, deptid, wed_sales)
INTO store_sales (store_id, sales_date, deptid, sales_amt)
VALUES (store_id, start_date+3, deptid, thur_sales)
INTO store_sales (store_id, sales_date, deptid, sales_amt)
VALUES (store_id, start_date+4, deptid, fri_sales)
INTO store_sales (store_id, sales_date, deptid, sales_amt)
VALUES (store_id, start_date+5, deptid, sat_sales)
INTO store_sales (store_id, sales_date, deptid, sales_amt)
VALUES (store_id, start_date+6, deptid, sun_sales)
SELECT store_id, start_date, deptid, mon_sales, tue_sales,
wed_sales, thur_sales, fri_sales, sat_sales, sun_sales
FROM store_sales_load;
INSERT ALL
WHEN store_id < 100 THEN INTO east_stores
WHEN store_id >= 100 THEN INTO west_stores
ELSE INTO misc_stores
SELECT * FROM store_sales_load;
INSERT /*+ APPEND */ INTO emp VALUES (100,
'Jacob','Freeman',1000,20, null, 10, sysdate, 100,
sysdate+365);
```

lock table

```
LOCK TABLE my_table IN EXCLUSIVE MODE NOWAIT;
LOCK TABLE my_table IN ROW EXCLUSIVE MODE;
```

merge

```
MERGE INTO emp_retire A
USING (SELECT empno, ename_last, ename_first, salary
FROM emp WHERE retire_cd='Y') B
ON (a.empid=b.empid)
WHEN MATCHED THEN UPDATE SET
a.ename_last=b.ename_last,
a.ename_first=b.ename_first,
a.salary=b.salary
DELETE WHERE (b.retire_cd='D')
WHEN NOT MATCHED THEN INSERT
(a.empid, a.ename_last, a.ename_first, a.salary)
VALUES (b.empid, b.ename_last, b.ename_first, b.salary)
WHERE (b.retire_cd!='D');
```

noaudit

```
NOAUDIT ALL ON scott.emp;
NOAUDIT UPDATE, DELETE ON scott.emp;
NOAUDIT SELECT on scott.emp WHENEVER NOT SUCCESSFUL;
NOAUDIT INSERT, UPDATE, DELETE ON DEFAULT;
```

purge

```
PURGE TABLE my_tab;
PURGE INDEX ix_my_tab;
PURGE RECYCLEBIN;
PURGE DBA_RECYCLEBIN;
PURGE TABLESPACE data_tbs USER scott;
```

recover

```
RECOVER DATABASE;
RECOVER TABLESPACE user_data, user_index;
RECOVER DATAFILE
'/opt/oracle/admin/mydb/datafile/mydb_users_01.dbf';
RECOVER DATABASE UNTIL CANCEL USING BACKUP CONTROLFILE;
RECOVER DATABASE UNTIL CHANGE 94044;
RECOVER DATABASE UNTIL TIME '2004-08-01:22:00:04';
```

rename

```
RENAME my_table to my_tab;
```

revoke: Object Grants

```
REVOKE SELECT ON scott.my_tab FROM my_user;
REVOKE INSERT, UPDATE, SELECT ON scott.my_tab FROM my_user;
REVOKE SELECT ON scott.my_tab FROM my_user;
REVOKE SELECT ON scott.my_tab FROM PUBLIC;
```

revoke: System Grants

```
REVOKE CREATE TABLE FROM my_user;
REVOKE CREATE ANY TABLE FROM my_user;
REVOKE ALL PRIVILEGES FROM my_user;
```

rollback

```
ROLLBACK;
```

savepoint

```
SAVEPOINT alpha;
```

select

```
SELECT ename_last, dname
FROM emp a, dept b
WHERE a.deptid=b.deptid;
SELECT a.empid, b.dept_name
FROM emp a, dept b
WHERE a.deptid=b.deptid (+);
SELECT a.empid, b.dept_name
FROM emp a LEFT OUTER JOIN dept b
ON a.deptid=b.deptid;
SELECT * FROM dept WHERE EXISTS
(SELECT * FROM emp
 WHERE emp.deptid=dept.deptid
 AND emp.salary > 100);
SELECT ename_first, ename_last,
CASE deptid
WHEN 10 THEN 'Acounting' WHEN 20 THEN 'Sales'
ELSE 'None' END FROM emp;
SELECT empid, ename_last, salary, comm
FROM emp a
WHERE salary*.10 >  (SELECT AVG(comm) FROM emp z
WHERE a.deptid=z.deptid);
WITH avg_dept_sales AS (
SELECT a.deptid, avg(b.sales_amt) avg_sales
FROM emp a, dept_sales b
WHERE a.deptid=b.deptid
GROUP BY a.deptid),
emp_salaries AS
(SELECT empid, AVG(salary) avg_salary FROM emp
GROUP BY empid)
SELECT * FROM emp_salaries b WHERE avg_salary*.05 >
(SELECT avg_sales FROM avg_dept_sales);
SELECT /*+ INDEX (a, emp_last_name_ix) */ empid
FROM emp a WHERE ename_last='Freeman'
SELECT empid, TO_CHAR(retire_date, 'MM/DD/YYYY')
FROM emp
```

```
WHERE retire_date IS NOT NULL
ORDER BY retire_date
SELECT empid, COUNT(*)
FROM emp
GROUP BY empid
HAVING COUNT(*) > 1;
SELECT empid, salary FROM emp
AS OF TIMESTAMP(SYSTIMESTAMP - INTERVAL '1' DAY)
WHERE empid=20;
SELECT empid, salary FROM emp
VERSIONS BETWEEN
TIMESTAMP SYSTIMESTAMP - INTERVAL '1' DAY AND
SYSTIMESTAMP - INTERVAL '1' HOUR
WHERE empid=20;
```

set constraints

```
SET CONSTRAINTS ALL IMMEDIATE;
SET CONSTRAINTS ALL DEFERRED;
SET CONSTRAINT fk_my_tab DEFERRED;
```

set transaction

```
SET TRANSACTION USE ROLLBACK SEGMENT rbs01;
SET TRANSACTION READ ONLY;
SET TRANSACTION ISOLATION LEVEL SERIALIZABLE;
```

truncate

```
TRUNCATE TABLE my_tab;
TRUNCATE TABLE my_tab PRESERVE MATERIALIZED VIEW LOG;
TRUNCATE TABLE my_tab REUSE STORAGE;
TRUNCATE TABLE my_tab DROP STORAGE;
```

update

```
UPDATE emp SET salary=100 WHERE empid=100;
UPDATE emp SET salary=NULL, retire_date=SYSDATE
WHERE empid=100;
UPDATE emp SET salary=salary*1.10
WHERE deptid IN
(SELECT deptid FROM dept WHERE dept_name = 'Sales');
UPDATE emp a SET (salary, comm)=
(SELECT salary*1.10, comm*1.10
FROM emp b WHERE a.empid=b.empid);
INSERT INTO store_sales
PARTITION (store_sales_jan_2004) sa
SET sa.sales_amt=1.10 where store_id=100;
```

CHAPTER
2

Database Creation and Management

arefully planning the creation of your Oracle database is a critical factor in the overall long-term success of that database and in reducing the overall time you spend maintaining it. In this chapter, I first highlight database creation issues. I then provide a database creation checklist, followed by an error resolution table that you can use if you run into problems during the creation of your database. Next, I present some high-level database management functions supported via the **alter database** command. Finally, I describe the process of removing an existing database.

Introduction to Oracle Database Creation

Creation of an Oracle database takes more than just issuing the **create database** command. The Oracle RDBMS software must be installed first, of course. Then you have to perform a number of tasks before you ever get to the point of actually creating the database. I would like to share a few thoughts with you about the creation of Oracle databases at this point.

Please, Read the Instructions

Before you install a new version of the Oracle Database software, read the installation instructions. I know, they can read like stereo instructions, but reading them is important. Additionally, the readme files on the CD-ROMs are very helpful. They contain references to known bugs and database limitations. Also, with each release, Oracle provides a list of bug fixes that have been applied to that release. It's a good idea to read this document carefully.

Using the Database Configuration Assistant

The DBCA is a great tool for the creation, or re-creation, of your Oracle database. If you find yourself re-creating the same basic database structure often, I suggest you look into the DBCA and its ability to store database templates. These templates can be used to quickly create a database in a fraction of the time it would take to create it manually.

The DBCA will create your databases for you, and will also generate database creation scripts that allow you to manually create the database yourself. While this book isn't going to cover the DBCA in detail, I strongly advise you to become acquainted with it. The DBCA isn't just for neophyte database administrators.

The DBCA gets better with later versions of Oracle Database. In Oracle Database 10g, for example, the DBCA will create an Oracle Real Application Clusters (RAC) cluster for you as well as help you to configure Oracle Database 10g's new Automatic Storage Management (ASM).

Creating a Database: Prerequisites

You must complete a number of prerequisites before you can issue the **create database** command. Some operating systems (OSs) may have operating system–specific prerequisites (such as Windows, which requires the creation of a service for your Oracle database). A partial list of prerequisites includes the following:

- Proper allocation of server memory

- Configuration of the database instance and its subsequent startup

- Creation of database-related directory structures

In Oracle Database 10g, most of these checks are actually done during the install of the database software. You will need to manually ensure that all requirements are met when installing previous versions of Oracle. It is always a good idea to check with Oracle and your OS vendor to see if there are any other recommended patches that you should apply before installing the Oracle Database software. Patches are frequently released and it's recommended to be on the most current patch set in order to get the best support. A complete list of prerequisites to be completed is provided in the section "Creating a Database Manually: A Checklist," later in this chapter.

Creating a Database: The create database Command

The **create database** command is used to create an Oracle database. It is executed as a part of a long list of database creation operations that your team will need to execute to successfully create your Oracle database. This list includes work on the part of the system administrator, disk administrator, network administrator, and possibly other personnel as well. In this section we look at some parameter-specific information related to the **create database** command, and then we review the default settings employed by the **create database** command.

Parameter Information

There are a few things to note about the parameters of the **create database** command (you can find the syntax diagram for the **create database** command in Appendix C of this book):

- The **sys** and **system** password clauses can be used to set the **sys** and **system** passwords when creating a database (Oracle9*i* Database and later).

- The **controlfile reuse** clause allows you to reuse existing control files. This also protects you from accidental executions of the **create database** command since the default is to not reuse the existing control file.

- The **logfile** parameter allows you to define the groups and names of the online redo logs.

- The **maxlogfiles**, **maxlogmembers**, **maxloghistory**, **maxdatafiles**, and **maxinstances** parameters need to all be carefully set, though often the defaults are sufficient (except for in RAC environments, in which you normally need to increase these values). Once you have created the database, you need to re-create the control file to change any of these parameters, except for the **maxdatafiles** parameter.

- The **archivelog** and **noarchivelog** parameters allow you to create the database in the appropriate mode (ARCHIVELOG or NOARCHIVELOG).

- The **force logging** parameter (Oracle9*i* Database and later) prohibits any **nologging** operations.

- The **character set** parameter allows you to set the database character set.

- The **national character set** parameter allows you to set the national language support for the database.

- The **datafile** clause allows you to define the data files for the SYSTEM tablespace.

- The **extent management local** clause allows you to define the SYSTEM tablespace as a locally managed tablespace.

- The **default_temp_tablespace** clause allows you to define the database's default temporary tablespace.

- The **set_time_zone** clause allows you to set the current time zone for the database.

■ In Oracle Database 10g, the **set default** clause allows you to define whether the default tablespace type is a bigfile or smallfile tablespace.

■ In Oracle Database 10g, the **sysaux datafile** clause allows you to define the data file and tablespace associated with the SYSAUX tablespace. The SYSAUX tablespace is required in Oracle Database 10g.

■ In Oracle Database 10g, you can use the **default tablespace** clause to create a tablespace that will be assigned as the default tablespace to all newly created database users.

Default Settings
The following default settings apply when a database is created:

■ A tablespace called SYSTEM is created. If Oracle Managed Files (OMF, an Oracle9i Database new feature) parameters are configured, then the Oracle database will create the data file for the SYSTEM tablespace without it being listed in the body of the **create database** command. It is, however, a good practice to define the location of the SYSTEM tablespace.

■ The SYSTEM tablespace is the default tablespace for any database user unless a default tablespace is defined via the **default_tablespace** clause.

■ The SYSTEM tablespace is a dictionary-managed tablespace by default; the OS filenames, sizes, and locations are defined in the **create database** command by default. You can use OMF to allow the datafile name, location, and size to be automatically selected by the database. You can create the SYSTEM tablespace as a locally managed tablespace in Oracle9i Database Release 2 and later. The SYSTEM tablespace is locally managed by default if you are creating your database using the DBCA.

■ If the SYSTEM tablespace is locally managed and not created using OMF, you must also define a default temporary tablespace. This is done automatically if you use OMF.

■ The SYSAUX tablespace is created as a locally managed tablespace, using automatic segment space management.

■ The name and location of the online redo logs can be defined manually or they can be automatically created if OMF is enabled. By default, an OMF database creates two redo log groups. The number of members of each group that will be created depends on which OMF parameters are set. If OMF is not configured and the names of the log files are not defined manually, the database creates two online redo logfile groups with names and locations that are OS-specific.

■ Two users, SYS and SYSTEM, are created. Default passwords are assigned to these accounts by default, though the **user sys** and **user system** clauses can be used in Oracle9i Database and later to define the default passwords for these users. The default password for SYS is **change_on_install** and for SYSTEM is **manager**.

NOTE
*Oracle9i Database and later allows you to define the SYS and SYSTEM passwords as a part of the **create database** command. Use this feature to increase the security of your database.*

- The database is assigned a name that can be up to eight characters long. If this name is not included in the body of the **create database** statement, then the value of the **db_name** parameter will be used.

- An undo tablespace (Oracle9*i* Database and later only) named SYS_UNDOTBS is created by default if the parameter **undo_management** equals **auto** and OMF is enabled. You can define the location and name of the undo tablespace within the body of the **create database** statement using the **undo_tablespace** clause. If no data file is provided, the database will use a predefined, OS-specific, default value if OMF is not enabled. In either case, a SYSTEM rollback segment is created in the SYSTEM tablespace.

- Oracle Database 10*g* and later allows you to define tablespaces as bigfile or smallfile, and to define one of those tablespace types as a default value for the database. The default value is smallfile. A smallfile tablespace can consist of up to 1022 data files in Oracle Database 10*g*. Each data file can contain up to four million database blocks. Bigfile tablespaces consist of only one data file, but it can contain up to four million million database blocks.

- The database time zone setting (Oracle9*i* Database only) is set to that of the server, if that time zone is a valid time zone; otherwise, the time zone is set to UTC.

Creating a Database: Security Issues

Once you have created your database, make sure that you change the SYS and SYSTEM passwords (or you can assign the passwords to them directly in the **create database** statement in Oracle9*i* Database and later). Additionally, you should lock out any accounts that will not need user access. If you use the DBCA to create your database, it prompts you to record new SYS and SYSTEM passwords (Oracle9*i* Database and later). It also locks out most ancillary accounts that get created during database creation.

Something to be aware of is that any user with SYSDBA privileges can issue a **create database** statement. This could materialize into a particularly nasty reality should one of your junior DBAs decide now is a good time to figure out what this **create database** command is all about (some folks shoot first and read the documentation second; go figure). This is yet another reason to be cautious about the privileges you give someone.

Also, note that if you are going to re-create a database, replacing an existing database, you need to set the **remote_login_passwordfile** parameter to **exclusive**. Otherwise, the database will generate an error when trying to re-create the database.

You will want to create a password file for your database. This makes the database more secure and allows you to perform more remote administrative activities. You create a password file whenever you first create a database, and if you ever re-create a database. Also, any time ORACLE_HOME changes, you need to move or re-create the password file to the new ORACLE_HOME.

The location and name of the password file is port-specific. Generally, however, you use the **orapwd** utility to create the password file. The utility takes three arguments:

- **file**   Name of the password file to be created.

- **password**   The SYSDBA password for that database.

- **entries**   The number of entry spaces that will be created in the password file. This should represent the maximum number of user accounts that will be given SYSDBA rights.

Here is an example of the use of the **orapwd** utility:

```
c:\>orapwd file=c:\oracle\9203\database\pwdMYDB.ora
password=google entries=10
```

Note that the database demands that you use a password file only if you are trying to connect externally to the database using SYSDBA privileges. The **remote_login_password** parameter defines whether the database should check for an external password file. If set to **none**, then no password file is required, but remote, privileged access is lost. If set to **shared** or **exclusive**, then the database uses the password file and remote, privileged access is allowed. Also note that you cannot have spaces around the equal signs.

Creating a Database: Recommended Practices

Several database best practices exist, and should be followed at all times. These include the following:

- Generally, it is recommended to create a separate database for larger applications that include disparate data. Keep in mind that combining applications into a single database instance can make performance tuning that much more difficult. Because of the memory and process overhead of Oracle Database, sometimes, small database schemas can be combined into a single database instance. Also, if two larger applications are tightly coupled (e.g., share many of the same data objects), then it might make sense to have those applications share the same database. The bottom line is that for this particular question, there is no one best way. You need to analyze your needs, scalability issues, and resource requirements and then decide.

- Make the name that you assign to the database meaningful. It should identify the application associated with the database and provide the database designation (e.g., dev, prod, tst, etc.). I recommend that you use a five-character naming standard. The first four characters associate the database with the application or project, and the final character denotes the kind of database associated with the name, such as production (p), test (t), quality assurance (q), development (d), or some other form of database. While database names can be in upper- or lowercase, I prefer lowercase.

- Size the online redo logs such that you see log switches every 15 minutes or so at a minimum. This sizing may be difficult to gauge at first.

- Follow Optimal Flexible Architecture (OFA), Oracle's recommended file directory and placement recommendations.

- Script your entire database creation process, and create a log as it executes. You can also use the DBCA to generate a database creation script.

NOTE
I love using the DBCA to create the initial database creation scripts. This method ensures that all the needed steps for the creation of a database get done the first time. Generally, I prefer to run those scripts manually, but you might prefer to just allow the DBCA to create the database for you.

- Allocate enough memory to the SGA. With more memory allocated to the SGA (particularly the default buffer pool and the shared pool), the database creation process goes more quickly. Ensure that you don't allocate so much memory that you cause the system to start thrashing due to excessive swap activity.

- Be cautious of implementing any new features and functionality. This is generally a good practice because new features often can be troublesome in the initial phases of implementation.

The create database Command: Examples

This section provides some examples of the actual use of the **create database** command. This first example works only with Oracle9*i* Database and later. It assumes that you have enabled OMF and configured the required OMF-related settings (at a minimum, **db_create_file_dest**) in the database parameter file. Assuming you are going to name your database mydb, here is the **create database** statement you would use:

```
Create database mydb;
```

Normally, you want to exert a bit more control over your database creations. You want to define the name and location of the online redo logs, the SYSTEM tablespace, and other database items. Here is an example of a more complex **create database** command:

```
CREATE DATABASE prodb
MAXINSTANCES 1 MAXLOGHISTORY 1
MAXLOGFILES 5 MAXLOGMEMBERS 3
MAXDATAFILES 100
DATAFILE 'C:\oracle\ora92010\prodb\system01.dbf'
SIZE 250M REUSE AUTOEXTEND ON NEXT 10240K MAXSIZE UNLIMITED
EXTENT MANAGEMENT LOCAL
DEFAULT TEMPORARY TABLESPACE TEMP TEMPFILE
'C:\oracle\ora92010\prodb\temp01.dbf' SIZE 40M REUSE AUTOEXTEND ON
NEXT   640K MAXSIZE UNLIMITED
UNDO TABLESPACE "UNDOTBS1" DATAFILE
'C:\oracle\ora92010\prodb\undotbs01.dbf' SIZE 200M REUSE
AUTOEXTEND ON NEXT   5120K MAXSIZE UNLIMITED
CHARACTER SET WE8MSWIN1252
NATIONAL CHARACTER SET AL16UTF16
LOGFILE
  GROUP 1 ('C:\oracle\ora92010\prodb\redo01a.log',
          'D:\oracle\ora92010\prodb\redo01b.log') SIZE 102400K,
  GROUP 2 ('C:\oracle\ora92010\prodb\redo02.log',
          'D:\oracle\ora92010\prodb\redo02b.log') SIZE 102400K,
  GROUP 3 ('C:\oracle\ora92010\prodb\redo03.log',
          'D:\oracle\ora92010\prodb\redo02b.log') SIZE 102400K;
```

NOTE
*If you need some more good examples of database creation scripts, the DBCA is the place to go. It will generate all the scripts you need (including the **create database** command) to create your database. You can execute DBCA and have it generate a basic set of scripts, and then you can customize those scripts as you require and run them.*

Creating a Database Manually: A Checklist

This checklist is designed to act as a guide for you to use during the creation of your database. There may be OS-specific tasks that you will need to complete that are not listed in this checklist. Therefore, it's a good idea to check the installation manual for your OS and determine what OS-specific tasks are required.

Also note that different versions of the Oracle database require slightly different install procedures. Also, optional products require additional install steps. Having said this, some of these steps might not need to be performed if you are using these tools. Finally, note that some of my suggestions for file-naming conventions are extensions of OFA. I've found these additional extensions very handy from an administrative point of view, so I offer them to you here.

Creating a Database Manually, Step 1: Prerequisites

The following are considered prerequisite tasks that you must complete before you begin manual creation of an Oracle database:

1. Read the documentation.

2. Check with Oracle support (www.metalink.com) and ensure that the versions of the OS and hardware that you will be using are supported. Check for any bug patches that you might need to apply. Typically, there is at least one Oracle Database maintenance patch set that you will want to apply after you have installed the Oracle RDBMS software.

3. Install any OS or other patches that are required to install the Oracle RDBMS software. This may require a reboot.

4. Configure your OS parameters appropriately for Oracle Database. This might include adjusting kernel parameters and so on.

5. Set up the database environment variables. The following list defines the most commonly used environment variables:

   - **ORACLE_BASE**   Defines the base directory for the database install (example: /opt/oracle or c:\oracle). From here, directories such as the admin directory, Oracle RDBMS software directory, and application-level directories get created.

   - **ORACLE_HOME**   Defines the location of the Oracle software directory (example: /opt/oracle/ora-9.2.0.3 or c:\oracle\ora9203).

   - **LD_LIBRARY_PATH** (or equivalent OS-specific variable)   For UNIX only, used to define the location of the dynamic libraries that the database loads while executing (example: $ORACLE_HOME/lib).

6. Install the Oracle RDBMS software. Make sure you install database features that you are going to need, but be careful not to install or use features that you are not licensed for. Install any patches that are required.

NOTE
Oracle Database 10g will check that you have properly configured your system before it starts the installation process!

7. Create any directories that you will be defining in the database parameter file, such as the location for **user_dump_dest**. This operation includes the creation of the following directories (typically these directories will be created in a directory structure that is ORACLE_BASE/admin/<database_name>):

- **ADUMP**   Used for audit files.

- **ARCH**   Used for database archived redo logs.

- **BDUMP**   Used to store background dump files and the alert log.

- **CDUMP**   Used to store core dump files.

- **LOGBOOK**   Used to log all database changes. Generally, this is a text file that contains a record of all changes (such as new tables added, tablespaces resized, new data files added, and so on) and when those changes were made.

- **PFILE**   Used to store the database parameter file.

- **SCRIPTS**   Used to store database creation scripts.

- **UDUMP**   Used to store user trace files.

8. Determine what tablespaces your database will need. Determine the sizes of these tablespaces, and how you will distribute the I/O of these tablespaces onto your disks. Determine the naming convention that you will use for your database data files. I suggest that you use the following naming convention (note that this suggestion is a slight extension of OFA):

    dbnm_tbsnm_nn.dbf

where:

- *dbnm* is the name of the database (e.g., mydb).

- *tbsnm* is the name of the tablespace (e.g., data).

- *nn* is a monotonically increasing number that makes the datafile name unique (e.g., 01, 02, etc.). I suggest that this number be zero padded to two or three digits so that sorting on the number is easier.

So, the first data file for the database mydb, for the tablespace data, would be mydb_data_01.dbf. Common (and some required) tablespaces include

- **SYSTEM**   This is required and is created by the **create database** command.

- **SYSAUX**   Required in Oracle Database 10*g* and later. This tablespace stores ancillary objects that are related to other Oracle database tools such as RMAN or Ultra Search.

- **RBS** or **UNDO**   This tablespace is for rollback segments. This might be a tablespace created for manual rollback segment usage, or an UNDO tablespace (Oracle9*i* Database and later) used in concert with Automated Undo.

- **USERS**   Generally used as the default tablespace for user objects.

- **TEMP**   Generally defined as the temporary tablespace for the database.

9. Determine other file-naming conventions. I suggest the following (again, these deviate slightly from OFA):

Online redo logs: *dbnm_redo_gg_m_tt_rr*.rdo

where:

- *dbnm* is the name of the database (e.g., mydb).

- *gg* is the number of the redo log group. This is typically a monotonically increasing number (e.g., 01).

- *m* is the member identifier of the group. This is typically an alphabetical identifier (e.g., a).

- *tt* is the thread identifier (only required if using RAC).

- *rr* is the reincarnation number (Oracle Database 10*g* and later). This additional parameter makes it easier to perform recovery through a **resetlogs** operation.

So, an example of an online redo log would be mydb_redo_01_a_01.rdo.

NOTE
Wonder why I don't use .log in the online redo log filename? It might seem natural, but it's also natural for people to suffix other types of logs with a .log extension. Every once in a while you get a system administrator who is on a quest for disk space who decides to just wipe out anything with a .log extension. So guess what happens to your online redo logs in that case if they have a .log extension? Not a good day for the DBA.

Control files: *dbnm_ctrl_nn*.ctl

where:

- *dbnm* is the name of the database.

- ctrl simply identifies the file as a control file.

- *nn* is a monotonically increasing number that makes the filename unique (e.g., 01, 02, etc.).

So, an example of a control file would be mydb_cntrl_01.ctl.

Archived redo logs: *dbnm_arch_ss_tt*.arc

where:

- *dbnm* is the name of the database.

- *ss* is the log sequence number (this is assigned by the database automatically when the archived redo log is generated if the configuration file is properly set up).

- *tt* is the thread number (this is assigned by the database automatically when the archived redo log is generated if the configuration file is properly set up).

10. Create the directories that you require to store your database files. You need to create directories for database data files, online redo logs, and database control files. You should

   - Create the database datafile directories using OFA. This is an example of a database datafile directory for a database called mydb: `/u100/oracle/mydb/data`. Make sure that you sufficiently distribute the I/O onto enough disks that disk contention will not be an issue.

   - Create the directories that will contain the online redo logs. This is an example of a directory structure for the database online redo logs for a database called mydb: `/u100/oracle/mydb/redo`. Note that you will want to create at least three of these directories on three different devices. These devices should be on three different controllers if possible. When you create your database, you will create three members of each redo log group. One copy of each member will go in one of these directories.

   - Create the directories that will contain the control files for the database. This is an example of a directory structure that you might use for a database called mydb: `/u100/oracle/mydb/control`. Note that you will want to create at least three of these directories on three different devices. These devices should be on three different controllers if possible. When you create your database parameter file, you will define three different control files, one of which will be located in these directories.

NOTE
In these examples, I am using a single mount point to create all data files, control files, and redo logs in. This is because I am using a stripe and mirror everything (SAME) *approach to I/O. In other words, I have striped all of my disks, and I am placing all of my data on those striped disks. You may need to lay out I/O differently on your system depending on your hardware configuration, the size of your database, and the total amount of activity you will be experiencing.*

11. Create the database parameter file that you will use when creating the database.

12. On UNIX systems, add to the oratab file the new database instance to be created (or create the oratab if required).

13. On Windows operating systems (2000, Windows NT, and XP), create the service for the system using **oradim**.

NOTE
If you are on a Windows Oracle database platform, then see the Windows-specific documents for the use of **oradim***.*

14. Create your database's password file with the **orapwd** program located in `$ORACLE_HOME/bin`.

There are a few detailed areas that I want to cover with regard to the preceding prerequisite steps. Those areas are covered in the following sections.

More on Configuration of the OS for Oracle Databases   Most systems require some OS configuration before an Oracle database can be installed and a database can be created. Often, this step is completed incorrectly. In the rush to install the database, often, parameters that impact such things as the amount of total shared memory that is available or how many processes can be started at one time are not set correctly. Sit down with your systems administrator and discuss these settings, including how you will need them set in the long term, before you install the database software.

A nice feature in the Oracle Database 10*g* installer is that it will validate a number of OS-related factors for you before installing the Oracle Database 10*g* software for you. Items such as OS level settings, applied patches, and memory settings are checked before the install to make sure that it will go smoothly.

More on the Creation of the Database Parameter File   The creation of the database parameter file is an area in which you need to use caution. Make sure you use the correct database block size, and carefully check over other parameters such as listener configuration parameters. If you are copying an existing database parameter file for use on a new database, be even more cautious. I have seen unchanged listener settings for databases copied from a production system to a test system wreak havoc in the production environment.

Also, be careful of the default parameter settings that the Oracle database provides. They are pretty much never adequate. Again, consider the future needs of your database, not just the short-term needs.

Typically, in earlier versions of Oracle Database the parameter file was text based and managed by the DBA. Oracle9*i* Database and later offers an option of a server-managed parameter file (SPFILE). This parameter file is managed by the server itself, and the parameters are altered via the **alter system** command using the **scope** parameter, as shown in this example:

```
Alter system set db_cache_size=100m scope=spfile;
```

In this example, I have altered the **db_cache_size** parameter in the SPFILE associated with the database instance so that it will be 100m. In this case, the change will take effect after the database is cycled. While **db_cache_size** is a static parameter, some Oracle database parameters are dynamic in nature. The **alter system** command uses the **scope=both** parameter to change both the SPFILE and the current database setting dynamically. You can also use the **scope=memory** parameter settings to indicate that the scope of the change is just for the live database, and that the SPFILE should not be changed. In this case, whatever the initial setting was will be the setting used when the database is later restarted.

More on the Database Creation Scripts   With the release of each new version of Oracle Database, the database creation scripts seem to change just a little. Make sure you are running the correct data dictionary creation scripts when you create the database. With each new version, I like to allow the DBCA to create the first database (or the first scripts for that database creation). I can then review the database creation scripts it generates. They can be very telling.

If you are using Oracle9*i* Database or later, I suggest that you define a default temporary tablespace (and create that tablespace) when you create your database using the **default temporary tablespace** clause of the **create tablespace** command. After you do this, users that are created will be assigned to that default temporary tablespace rather than to the SYSTEM tablespace.

Also, in Oracle Database 10*g* and later, Oracle allows you to define a database-wide default user tablespace. It is a recommended practice that you take advantage of this feature.

More on the Creation of the Required Directory Structures Oracle databases have a number of physical components that need places to live. These components include

- Database data files

- Database control files

- Database redo logs (online and archived)

- Administrative files (e.g., the parameter file, alert log, etc.)

Every database requires that a number of different directory structures be created for these files to be located in, and these directories need to be created before the database itself can be created. We have talked about OFA already. One of the key base components of OFA is identified by the environment variable ORACLE_HOME. This is the location in which the Oracle database software is installed. Typically, ORACLE_HOME is mounted under a nondescript mount point, such as /u01, and is followed by a directory structure that includes the fully qualified version name of the version of the Oracle database you are installing. An example would be /u01/oracle/product/9.2.0.2.0.

The Oracle Universal Installer, by default, creates ORACLE_HOME in an OFA-compliant manner; however, on some operating systems (Windows for example), it does not use the full version number of the Oracle RDBMS version being installed (for example, Oracle Database uses 10.0.1 instead of 10.0.1.2). I suggest in these cases that you override the installer default and make sure you use the complete version number when installing the software.

You need to create the following directory structures on your system before you can create the database (this assumes that you have already installed the Oracle RDBMS software):

1. Create the admin base directory. If your ORACLE_HOME is /ora01/oracle/product/9.2.0.1.0, then you should create the admin directory base structure under /ora01/oracle (this particular structure is known as ORACLE_BASE, because it is the base of many of the other Oracle database and software-related directories, such as the product directory and now the admin directory). Typically, the admin directory would be called admin (go figure) and you would have a directory structure that looks like this: /ora01/oracle/admin.

2. Create a directory under the admin base directory for the database that you are creating. For example, if your database is to be called mydb, then you would create a directory under the admin base directory called mydb. An example of this would be /ora01/oracle/admin/mydb.

3. Create the directory structures under the database admin directory structure you created in Step 2. You will create the following directories:

   - **adump**   For auditing.

   - **arch**   For archived redo logs.

   - **bdump**   For the database alert log and other database-related trace files.

   - **cdump**   For database core dumps.

   - **create**   For the scripts that will be used to create the database.

- **logbook**   For files that contain a history of changes to the database (e.g., structural changes) or application-related changes (e.g., new PL/SQL code). The DBA manages these text files, making entries for each change to the database.

- **pfile**   For the database parameter file.

- **udump**   For user trace files.

I suggest that certain directory structures, such as adump, bdump, cdump, and udump, not be stored directly on the ORACLE_BASE file system. This way, you avoid the possibility of filling up ORACLE_BASE, and ORACLE_HOME, which sits below ORACLE_BASE. I like to create soft links (on OSs that support such things) to other file systems for these directory structures, and point the database to the admin directory location for that link. Thus, while the udump directory might be in a directory called /oramisc/oracle/mydb/udump, there is a link to that directory in /ora01/oracle/admin/mydb/udump; additionally, the database will be pointing to the admin directory structure link, not the other file system.

Also, I strongly suggest that the arch directory be created on a different file system and that a link for that directory be created as well. Of course, if you are running Windows, you will not be able to create database links, and you will simply have to create the directory in a separate location and configure the database to use that location.

4. Once you have created the admin directories, create the directories that will be used to store database files. Again, follow the OFA standard for this. Here are the steps to follow:

   a). Determine what mount-point naming convention you will use. OFA suggests that you use a nondescriptive naming convention such as /u100.

   b). Create the base database file structures. This includes the database name. Generally, it follows the standard /*mount_point*/oracle/*dbname*. For example, /u100/oracle/MYDB. Create this structure on each base file system that you will use. This may consist of one to many different file systems, depending on your disk layout.

   c). Under the base database file structures, create a directory for the database data files, called data. Also, create one directory each for the redo logs and the control files. Examples would be /ora100/oracle/mydb/redo for the redo logs and /ora100/oracle/mydb/ctrl for the control files.

Creating a Database Manually, Step 2: Create the Database

Now that you have done your preparation work, the fun is about to begin. Here is a checklist of items to follow when creating the database.

NOTE
These steps might vary slightly for each version of Oracle Database that you are using. As always, check the documentation if you have any questions.

1. Make sure the preparation work is done. Double-check everything, particularly the following:

   ■ All patches are applied.

   ■ The OS kernel settings are correct.

   ■ All the file paths and database names are correct for the database parameter file.

   ■ Your database creation script has no errors.

   ■ The ancillary files (oratab, tnsnames.ora, listener.ora) are set up as required.

   ■ You have determined what tablespaces your database will need, what sizes they should be, and where the physical data files for those tablespaces should reside.

2. In UNIX, set the Oracle database environment variable (e.g., use the Oracle program oraenv) to set the correct Oracle database environment. If you are using Windows, open a command window, and set ORACLE_SID to the name of the database that you are going to create.

3. In Windows, make sure that the database service is created and that it has been started.

4. Sign on to the database using the **sys as sysdba** login.

5. To start the instance, issue the **startup nomount** command. Once this command has completed, your database instance has been successfully started.

6. Create your database creation scripts. These scripts are used to create the database and should contain these components:

   ■ A **spool** command to cause the output to be recorded. Also, use the **set echo on** command so that all output will be generated, including the commands themselves.

   ■ The **create database** command, which is used to actually create the database. Typically, this command will create the SYSTEM and SYSAUX (Oracle Database 10*g*) tablespaces. Also, this command can create the UNDO tablespace if automated undo is configured for the instance.

   ■ Commands used to create the data dictionary. Typically, the commands used to build the data dictionary include

      ■ Execution of `catalog.sql`, which is in the directory `$ORACLE_HOME/rdbms/admin`.

      ■ Execution of `catproc.sql`, which is in the same directory as `catalog.sql`.

      ■ Execution of other administrative scripts. In Oracle Database 10*g* this might include the following scripts in `$ORACLE_HOME/rdbms/admin`: `catblock.sql`, `catoctk.sql`, `owminst.plb`. You need to run (as SYSTEM) `pupbld.sql`, located in `$ORACLE_HOME/sqlplus/admin`, and you will want to run `helpbld.sql` located in `$ORACLE_HOME/sqlplus/admin` to build the SQL*Plus help table.

- Execution of other SQL scripts as required for any special Oracle products you might be installing. Check the Oracle documentation for your specific product set for more information.

- Commands to create any remaining tablespaces assigned to the database (e.g., UNDO tablespaces).

- Commands to create manual rollback segments (if you are using them) and bring them online.

7. Execute the database creation scripts.

8. Once these scripts have been successfully executed, the database has been created and is ready for use.

Creating a Database Manually, Step 3: Post Database Creation Tasks

Once the database is created, your work is not really done. There are a number of things that you need to do to secure the database and prepare it for general use. Which tasks you should actually perform depends on your specific conditions, but here are a few of the tasks that you should consider after you create your database:

1. Change the SYS and SYSTEM passwords if the default values were used during database creation.

2. Lock out all accounts that you will not be using (e.g., WMSYS, OUTLN, and DBSNMP).

3. Configure any Oracle database networking that is required. This might include creation of a tnsnames.ora file for your server and your clients.

NOTE
If you use the Oracle DBCA to create your database for you, most, if not all, of the previous steps will be done for you. The DBCA is an easy-to-use GUI that can help beginning DBAs easily create databases.

Creating a Database: Error Resolution Table

Many different errors can occur as a result of a failed attempt to create a database. The following table lists the most common errors and provides some suggestions to help you solve the problem and successfully create your database.

Oracle Error Message	Text Description	Possible Causes and Solutions
LRM-00109	Could not open parameter file 'xyz'	You have used the **startup pfile** command and the pfile or ifile specified in the command could not be found. Accompanied with the ORA-01078 error message.
ORA-00200	Controlfile could not be created	The RDBMS was unable to create the control file. This may mean that the control file already exists, or it might be that the directory does not exist.
ORA-00213	Cannot reuse controlfile	Generally, you are re-creating a database that previously existed, or a previous database creation failed. Remove the control files, and try to create the database again. Exercise caution, and make sure you remove the correct control file. This error may indicate that you are trying to overwrite the control files of another database.
ORA-00215	Must be at least one controlfile	You do not have at least one control file listed in your database parameter file, which is required. Correct the parameter file and re-run.
ORA-00221	Error on write to controlfile	An error has occurred when trying to create the control file, or on subsequent writes to the control file. You should make sure that the file system can be written to by the Oracle database login account. Also make sure that a control file does not already exist.
ORA-01031	Insufficient privileges	Generally, some security violation has occurred. Check the following: If the **remote_login_passwordfile** parameter is not set, or is set to none: 1. Make sure you are logged in as the Oracle user (or equivalent) if you are running in UNIX. 2. Make sure you are logged in to a Windows account that is a member of the ORA_DBA group. If the **remote_login_passwordfile** parameter is set, then make sure you are logging in with the correct password. If you cannot remember the password for your database, you can 1. Use the **orapwd** utility to create an Oracle database password file. 2. Add the Windows user you are signed in as to the ORA_DBA group.
ORA-01078	Failure in processing system parameters	Several possible causes (generally followed by another error message): • The parameter file could not be opened (followed by an LRM-00109 error message). Check that the parameter file exists, and that it can be opened and read by the database executable. By default, the database expects the parameter file to be in ORACLE_HOME/dbs (this is port-specific, however; for example, Windows expects it to be in $ORACLE_HOME/database by default). • An unknown parameter may be included in the parameter file (error LRM-00101 also appears). Correct the unknown parameter and restart the database.
ORA-01079	ORACLE database was not properly created, operation aborted	An error occurred during the creation of the Oracle database. Generally, this is followed by other error messages. Reasons for this error message might include • Errors in the database initialization file. • Errors in the **create database** command. • Oracle RDBMS bugs.
ORA-01501	CREATE DATABASE failed	Several possible causes. Sometimes followed by a second error message: ORA-01100: database already mounted Indicates that you attempted to issue a **create database** statement, and a database of the name specified has already been mounted or opened. Also check whether your ORACLE_SID is correctly set.

Oracle Error Message	Text Description	Possible Causes and Solutions
ORA-01504	Database name does not match parameter name	The **db_name** parameter in the database parameter file does not match the name of the database in the database control file or in the **create database** statement. Determine why this is the case, and correct the **db_name** parameter as appropriate.
ORA-12560 (There are a number of TNS errors like ORA-12560.)	TNS:protocol adapter error	Several possible causes. Check the following items: • In Windows, make sure your service has been created and started. • Check the tnsnames.ora and the listener.ora files to ensure they are correctly configured.
ORA-1505	Error in adding log files	The database encountered an error when adding the online redo log files during database creation. Additional errors are included to provide more detail. Often, solving this error means checking that the redo log destination directories exist and that the database has the correct privileges to those directories. Check that sufficient space exists for the online redo logs. Also, make sure that you have sufficient privileges to create files of the size you are trying to create for your online redo logs.
ORA-1506	Missing or illegal database name	The **db_name** parameter is not set and the database name is not contained within the **create database** command. Check the init.ora file to ensure the **db_name** parameter is set. If it is not, then either set it or include the name of the database in the **create database** statement.
ORA-1508	Cannot create database...	A problem exists in the **create database** statement you are issuing. This may be caused by any number of factors, such as running out of disk space, incorrect directory permissions, memory errors, and so on. In general, more information will appear if this error occurs. Frequently the error indicates a SQL error in the **create database** command. So, after making sure that OS-related issues are not a problem, you should check the syntax of the statement. Generally, after you see this error and have corrected the problem, you should clean up any files that may have been created by the failed **create database** command (e.g., online redo logs, the SYSTEM tablespace, etc.). This will not be a problem if you are using the **reuse** keyword within the context of the file definitions in the **create database** command.
ORA-1530	A database already mounted by the instance	You tried to mount the database but it's already mounted. In several situations, the failure of the **create database** statement leaves the database mounted and you need to shut down the database before you can reissue the command.

Other Typical Errors Associated with the create database Command

Often, errors occur because of some mistaken settings in the database parameter file. Another common cause of problems is that directories that are defined within the database parameter file are not physically created. Incorrect directory listings (typographical mistakes) in the database parameter file or the **create database** command itself are typical problems as well.

Often, memory allocation errors occur on the first attempt to create a database. This can be due to incorrect shared memory settings on the server or incorrect memory settings in the database parameter file.

Another thing to look at is the configuration of asynchronous I/O on those systems that support this technology (which today is almost every UNIX system that supports an Oracle database). Incorrect asynchronous I/O settings can lead to bad performance and even errors during database creation or future database operations.

The alter database Command

The **alter database** command offers database management features and the ability to modify some aspects of your database. This section looks at the **alter database** command and highlights its uses.

Functions of the alter database Command

The **alter database** command supports the following functionality:

- *Move the database between ARCHIVELOG and NOARCHIVELOG mode.* ARCHIVELOG mode allows you to perform online backups of your database and point-in-time recovery. NOARCHIVELOG mode does not allow online backups and point-in-time recovery.

- *Alter the mode of the database.* You can move the database from one status (such as mounted) to another (such as open). You can also use the **resetlogs** option if this is required after a database recovery. You can also use the **alter database** command to open the Oracle database in read-only mode, which is useful for certain operations with standby databases and various database-related flashback operations in Oracle Database 10*g* and later.

- *Execute various database recovery commands.* Although you can execute various database recovery functions, these functions are typically executed via the **recover** command. You also use the **alter database create datafile** command to create empty data files for use in recovery situations where a lost data file is not available from backup and only the archived redo logs are available.

- *Manage Oracle standby databases.* You can manage standby database recovery operations, which includes activating standby databases, managing the database protection level, registering log files with the standby database, and managing log application services.

- *Manage database data files.* You can manage database data files and temporary data files, also known as tempfiles (for example, you can resize a data file or modify its **autoextend** clause). Also, the **alter database** command is used to rename data files.

- *Manage online redo logs.* The addition, removal, and clearing of online redo log files is accommodated with the **alter database** command. You also use the **alter database** command to manage online redo log threads for RAC instances.

- *Modify database default settings.* Certain default settings, such as the database character set, are provided by the **alter database** command.

- *Alter the database compatibility version to facilitate rollback of a database migration.* This allows you to reset the database version upon the next database instance startup. This is not supported in Oracle Database 10*g* or later.

■ *Alter the creation of supplemental logging.* Use the **supplemental_db_logging** clause to indicate if supplemental data should be included in the log stream. This is used for operations such as Oracle LogMiner. Supplemental logging is off by default.

■ *Manage database default settings (Oracle Database 10g and later).* The **default_settings_ clause** parameter allows you to set the database data file default type to smallfile or bigfile. You can also define the default tablespace that new users will be assigned to when they are created. Other default functionality includes management of the block change tracking facility, and the database flashback mode. Default related functionality available prior to Oracle Database 10g has been moved into the **default_settings_clause**, including the default temporary tablespace, time zone settings, and the setting of the global database name.

Common Tasks Accomplished with alter database

This section covers the most common DBA tasks performed with the **alter database** command:

■ Switching between ARCHIVELOG and NOARCHIVELOG mode

■ Changing the database state

■ Maintaining log files

■ Maintaining data files

■ Backing up control files

■ Managing default database settings (Oracle Database 10g only)

Switching Between ARCHIVELOG and NOARCHIVELOG Mode

You use the **alter database** command to move the database between ARCHIVELOG and NOARCHIVELOG mode. When in ARCHIVELOG mode, you can perform hot backups of the database, online recoveries of most database data files and tablespaces, and point-in-time recoveries of the database.

The database log mode is initially defined when the database is created with the **create database** command. If you want to change the log mode of the database, you need to shut down the database (e.g., use **shutdown immediate**) and then mount it with the **startup mount** command. You can then issue the **alter database archivelog** command, and then open the database for operations with the **alter database open** command. Here is an example of putting the database in ARCHIVELOG mode and then opening the database for normal operations:

```
SHUTDOWN IMMEDIATE;
STARTUP MOUNT;
ALTER DATABASE ARCHIVELOG;
ALTER DATABASE OPEN;
```

Next is an example of setting the database in NOARCHIVELOG mode:

```
SHUTDOWN IMMEDIATE;
STARTUP MOUNT;
ALTER DATABASE NOARCHIVELOG;
ALTER DATABASE OPEN;
```

NOTE
Before you can change the database log mode, you must have a
clean database shutdown using **shutdown**, **shutdown transactional**,
or **shutdown immediate**.

Be aware that if you are going to put the database in ARCHIVELOG mode, you need to set certain database parameters to support this mode of operations. The parameters that you need to set are shown in the following table.

Parameter Name	Purpose
log_archive_dest or log_archive_dest_*n*	Defines the archive log destination directories (up to ten).
log_archive_dest_state_*n*	Defines the state of the archive log destination. This can be enabled or disabled.
log_archive_format	Defines the format of the filenames used for the archived redo logs.
log_archive_max_processes	Defines the maximum number of ARCH processes that the database can start.
log_archive_min_succeed_dest	Defines the minimum number of logfile destination directories that must be successfully copied to in order for an online redo log to be available for reuse.
log_archive_start	Used to enable the database ARCH process.

Here are some examples in which the preceding parameters are set:

```
log_archive_dest_1= c:\oracle\admin\backup\arch
log_archive_dest_2= d:\net\oracle\admin\backup\arch
log_archive_dest_state_1=enable
log_archive_dest_state_2=disable
log_archive_max_processes=2
log_archive_min_succeed_dest=1
log_archive_start=TRUE
log_archive_format=mydb_ARCH_%s_%t
```

Many of these parameters can also be changed dynamically via the **alter system** command, as shown here:

```
ALTER SYSTEM SET
log_archive_dest_1='c:\oracle\admin\backup\arch' SCOPE=both;
```

The **scope** parameter is only available in Oracle9*i* Database and later versions. If you are using Oracle SPFILEs, then you can use the **alter system** command to change not only the current setting but also the setting in the database parameter file. The following table demonstrates the options for the **scope** parameter.

Value	Description	Example

both	Updates both the SPFILE and the current instance settings	`ALTER SYSTEM SET log_archive_dest_1=`
		`'c:\oracle\admin\backup\arch'`
		`SCOPE=both;`

memory	Updates only the current settings of the instance	`ALTER SYSTEM SET log_archive_dest_1=`
		`'c:\oracle\admin\backup\arch'`
		`SCOPE=memory DEFERRED;`

spfile	Updates only the database SPFILE	`ALTER SYSTEM SET log_archive_dest_1=`
		`'c:\oracle\admin\backup\arch'`
		`SCOPE=spfile`
		`COMMENT='Changed for new disk';`

Other options available (examples are included in the previous table) include **deferred**, which allows you to indicate that the change should affect all future sessions but not the current session. Also, the **comment** parameter allows you to associate a comment with the change; this comment will be stored in the SPFILE if the SPFILE is changed by the command.

Changing the Database State

You use the **alter database** command to change the database state. The database must first be in either **nomount** or **mount** mode (which is accomplished with the **startup** command). You can then use the **alter database** command to **mount** the database, or **open** it. Here is an example:

```
SQL> STARTUP NOMOUNT
ORACLE instance started.

Total System Global Area  135076724 bytes
Fixed Size                   453492 bytes
Variable Size             109051904 bytes
Database Buffers           25165824 bytes
Redo Buffers                 405504 bytes
SQL> ALTER DATABASE MOUNT;
Database altered.
SQL> ALTER DATABASE OPEN;
Database altered.
```

Maintaining Log Files

The **alter database** command is used to accomplish several different tasks with respect to online redo logs, including:

- Adding logfile groups
- Adding logfile group members
- Dropping a logfile group
- Dropping a logfile group member

Adding a Logfile Group   To add a new logfile group, use the **alter database** command, as in the following example:

```
ALTER DATABASE ADD LOGFILE GROUP 5
('c:\oracle\oradata\mydb\logfiles\mydb_logfile_05a.log',
'd:\oracle\oradata\mydb\logfiles\mydb_logfile_05b.log',
'e:\oracle\oradata\mydb\logfiles\mydb_logfile_05c.log') SIZE 100m;
```

Adding a Logfile Group Member   To add a new member to an existing logfile group, use the **alter database** command, as in this example:

```
ALTER DATABASE ADD LOGFILE MEMBER
'c:\oracle\oradata\mydb\logfiles\mydb_logfile_05d.log' TO GROUP 5;
```

The total number of logfile members that can be created is limited by the **create database** command parameter **maxlogfilemembers**. If you try to exceed this, the database will generate an error.

Dropping a Logfile Group   To drop an existing logfile group from your database, use the **alter database** command, as in this example:

```
ALTER DATABASE DROP LOGFILE GROUP 1;
```

Note that you cannot drop a logfile group if that will leave the database with less than two logfile groups.

Dropping a Logfile Group Member   To drop a member from an existing logfile group (but not drop the entire logfile group), use the **alter database** command, as in this example:

```
ALTER DATABASE DROP LOGFILE MEMBER 'c:\oracle\oradata\redo01a.log';
```

Note that you cannot drop the last member of any logfile group with this command; rather, you must drop the logfile group itself, as in this example:

```
ALTER DATABASE DROP LOGFILE GROUP 5;
```

Maintaining Data Files

You can use the **alter database** command to resize an Oracle database data file. You can increase or decrease the size of the data file as required; however, you can only parry down blocks in a data file that are not currently in use. Here is an example of using the **alter database** command with the **resize** parameter to resize your database data files up or down in size:

```
SQL> COLUMN BYTES FORMAT 9,999,999,999,999
SQL> SELECT file_id, tablespace_name, bytes FROM dba_data_files;
   FILE_ID TABLESPACE_NAME                              BYTES
---------- ------------------------------ ------------------
         1 SYSTEM                                  285,212,672
         2 JAN_TICKETS                              10,485,760
```

```
    3  INDX                        11,796,480
    4  TOOLS                       10,485,760
    5  USERS                      270,008,320
    6  TEMP_UNDO                   10,485,760
    7  PART1                       10,485,760
    8  PART2                       10,485,760
    9  OVF                         10,485,760
   10  FEB_TICKETS                 10,485,760
   11  MAR_TICKETS                 10,485,760
SQL> ALTER DATABASE DATAFILE 5 RESIZE 100M;
```

Backing Up Control Files

The **alter database** command also allows you to perform backups of the database control file. Oracle offers two different types of backups:

- Creation of a backup control file that is a binary copy of the control file to be used for database recovery

- Creation of a trace file that has the **create control file** statement required to re-create the control file

The backup control file is generally the preferred method of recovering your control file. This preserves more database-related information (such as RMAN backup information and archived redo log history information) that is not preserved by re-creating the control file via the **create control file** statement. The following sections provide more details on how to perform each of these operations.

NOTE
RMAN also provides methods of backing up and recovering the control file. You should consider using RMAN as an alternative to manually performing this operation.

Creating a Backup Control File   The backup control file is created using the **alter database** command, as shown in this example:

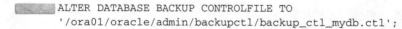
```
ALTER DATABASE BACKUP CONTROLFILE TO
'/ora01/oracle/admin/backupctl/backup_ctl_mydb.ctl';
```

Note that I give the database the location that I want the control file to be created in, as well as the name of the backup control file. If you are using a backup control file, you have to decide how to recover the database, because no script is created to perform this action for you.

Creating a Backup Trace File to Re-create the Control File   I use the **alter database** command to create a trace file that contains the required commands to re-create the control file and recover the database. Here is an example of the use of the **alter database** command to create the trace file:

```
ALTER DATABASE BACKUP CONTROLFILE TO TRACE;
```

Note that this command does not allow you to define the location of the trace file or its name. The database creates the trace file in the user dump destination directory of the database you are using. The database also uses the standard naming convention for Oracle trace files (which varies by platform). So, after creating this trace file, you might have to search through a few trace files to find it.

Managing Default Database Settings (Oracle Database 10g Only)

Oracle Database 10g allows you to establish some default settings within the Oracle database. For example, you can now designate a default tablespace (other than SYSTEM, as is the case in versions previous to Oracle Database 10g) to be assigned to all users when they are created. Here is an example:

```
ALTER DATABASE SET DEFAULT TABLESPACE users;
```

Oracle Database 10g offers block change tracking, a feature used by RMAN to reduce the size of incremental backups. You can enable or disable this feature via the **default_settings_clause** as well, as shown here:

```
ALTER DATABASE ENABLE BLOCK CHANGE TRACKING;
ALTER DATABASE DISABLE BLOCK CHANGE TRACKING;
```

Also, Oracle Database allows you to define the default tablespace type. Options are bigfile tablespaces or smallfile tablespaces. Bigfile tablespaces allow only one data file but can be sized upward of many terabytes (depending on the database block size), allowing the database as a whole to conceivably store several exabytes of data. Smallfile tablespaces are the old types of tablespaces that allow for the creation of many data files. However, smallfile tablespaces cannot hold nearly as much data as their bigfile brothers, given the same block size. You can define which type of tablespace you wish to use as a default (you can mix and match tablespace types in a database) via the **alter database** command:

```
ALTER DATABASE SET DEFAULT BIGFILE TABLESPACE;
```

Flashback Database is also a new feature in Oracle Database 10g. The **alter database** command allows you to either enable or disable flashback mode with the **flashback** mode clause, as shown here:

```
ALTER DATABASE FLASHBACK ON;
```

Error Messages Associated with the alter database Command

Several error messages may result from logfile maintenance. The following table lists several of these errors and possible causes and solutions.

Oracle Error Message	Text Description	Possible Causes and Solutions
ORA-00301	Error in adding logfile—file cannot be created	The log file could not be added. Generally, this means that the directory that you want to create the log file in does not exist or that the database does not have privileges to that directory.
ORA-00357	Too many members specified for logfile	You have exceeded the number of logfile members allowed for the logfile group you are adding to. You need to alter the **maxlogmembers** parameter by rebuilding the database control file.
ORA-00358	Too many file members	You have exceeded the total number of redo logfile members. Alter the **maxlogmembers** parameter setting by rebuilding the database control file.
ORA-00359	Logfile group does not exist	The logfile group you are trying to add a logfile member to does not exist.
ORA-00360	Not a logfile member	You attempted to drop a logfile member that does not exist.
ORA-00361	Cannot remove last log member	You tried to remove the last logfile member of a specific group. You need to remove the group instead.
ORA-01185	Logfile group number is invalid	The logfile group number you are attempting to create is invalid. This is generally because the **maxlogfiles** parameter is set to a value lower than the logfile group number that you are trying to create. For example, if **maxlogfiles** is set to 5 and you try to create logfile group 10 (even though there are only two other logfile groups), you will get this error. The solution is to either reduce the logfile group number, or increase the **maxlogfiles** parameter setting by re-creating the control file.
OR-01577	Cannot add log file—file already part of database	You have tried to add a log file that is already a part of the database. After making sure you really need an additional log file, choose a different filename for the log file, and try again.
ORA-00222	Operation would reuse name of a currently used controlfile	The **create control file** command tried to overwrite a control file that was currently in use by the database. Make sure you create the backup control file in a location other than the one in which the current control files reside. It's also a very good practice to name the backup control file differently than the current control files.
ORA-00905	Missing keyword	You spelled the command incorrectly. Often, the command is entered as **control file** (with a space) rather than **controlfile** (no space).
ORA-01580	Error creating control file backup file	Generally, the location that the database is trying to write to does not exist, or insufficient space exists. This is often followed by other error messages that clarify the nature of the errors.
ORA-1509	Specified name does not match actual	The name used in the **alter database** statement does not match the name of the database that is currently mounted.
ORA-1510	Error in deleting log files	The database could not drop an online redo log. Additional information will be included with this error to clarify the error.
ORA-1511 ORA-1512	Error renaming log/datafiles	An error occurred during an **alter database rename file** command. Additional error information will accompany this message. Often, this is a problem with misspelling the name of the data file or redo log, and the database doesn't think it exists.

Oracle Error Message	Text Description	Possible Causes and Solutions
ORA-1530	A database already mounted by the instance	You tried to mount the database but it's already mounted.
ORA-1531	A database already open by the instance	You tried to open the database but it's already open.

Removing Your Oracle Database

The task of removing an Oracle database differs based on what OS you are running on. For example, if you are running on UNIX, generally you must remove the related database files (database data files, online redo logs, and control files), files in the admin directories related to the database (database parameter files, trace files, etc.), and entries in ancillary database files such as the oratab, tnsnames.ora, and listener.ora files. If you are running on Windows, you need to make the same changes required on UNIX systems, but you also need to remove the database services for the database that you are removing. This will prevent errors from occurring when you start your Oracle database.

You can also use the DBCA to remove a database. The DBCA can be used to drop a database that you created with the DBCA or one that you manually created.

Oracle Database 10g offers a new command, **drop database**, that takes care of dropping your database for you. You still need to perform ancillary tasks, such as removing the database service and changing database files such as oratab, tnsnames.ora, and listener.ora.

Removing an Oracle database is quite different than removing the Oracle database software. If removing the software is your quest, you should first remove all Oracle databases on your system, and then use the Oracle Universal Installer to remove the Oracle RDBMS software. To completely remove the Oracle RDBMS software, you will probably have to manually remove files from the old ORACLE_HOME, as the installer is not always perfect in its removal process.

CHAPTER
3

Rollback/Undo
Segments, Control
Files, and Redo Logs

his chapter covers the management of three major database components: rollback/ undo segments, control files, and online redo logs. This chapter first describes what undo is, and then discusses automated undo management, a new feature introduced in Oracle9*i* Database. The manual creation, management, and removal of rollback segments is then described, followed by a discussion of issues revolving around control files. The chapter wraps up by looking at how to manage online redo logs.

Oracle Undo

Oracle generates undo as you make changes to the database. These changes are stored in database objects called *undo segments* or *rollback segments*. The undo that is generated allows Oracle to do the following:

- Rollback transactions that are not committed
- Provide a read-consistent image of database objects to other users
- Provide the ability to perform flashback queries

Thus, undo is used to reconstruct data as it looked at some point in the past. Oracle stores this data only for so long. At a minimum the undo is stored for the length of the transaction that the undo is related to. More often than not, you will want your undo to remain for a longer period of time. This can be controlled either by creating larger rollback segments when using manual rollback segments, or by manipulating database parameters when using automated undo.

When a database is created, a single rollback segment, called SYSTEM, is created in the database. You will create other rollback segments if manual rollback segments are to be used. Alternatively, if automated undo is to be used, you will create an undo tablespace and configure various parameters that Oracle will populate with undo segments. In the next sections we will look at the different types of undo management.

Automated Undo Management

Oracle9*i* Database introduced automated undo management in an effort to eliminate much of the management hassles of Oracle rollback segments. With automated undo management, you need to configure only a few database parameters and create a single tablespace, and Oracle manages the undo generated by the database. Note that a given instance can have only one active undo tablespace at any time. This does not preclude there being multiple defined undo tablespaces in the database (as might well be the case with an Oracle Real Application Clusters system).

So, let's first look at the undo tablespace and the management requirements for this beast. Once we are done with that, we will look at the different database parameters that you need to use to configure Oracle to use automated undo.

NOTE
With later versions of Oracle, it is likely that functionality of certain features will hinge more and more on automated undo. If you are running Oracle9i Database or later, I strongly recommend that you switch over to automated undo.

Configuration of Automated Undo Management

If you have decided to use automated undo management, you need to configure some database parameters. These parameters can be configured dynamically for the current instance via the **alter system** command:

```
ALTER SYSTEM SET UNDO_TABLESPACE=my_undotbs SCOPE=both;
```

Of course, you can use the different parameters for the **scope** command to set the value just for the current instance (SCOPE=memory) or you can just change the value in the server parameter file (SCOPE=spfile) if you prefer.

If you are not using an SPFILE and you want the settings to persist, then you need to update the settings in the database parameter file as well. Here is a list of the parameters that you should consider setting when configuring automated undo management:

Parameter Name	Type/Default	Options	Purpose
undo_tablespace	Dynamic/The first available undo tablespace in the database	List one or more undo tablespaces; only the first available is used by that instance	Defines the undo tablespace to be used by the instance. Only one undo tablespace can be defined per instance.
undo_management	Static/Manual	Manual or Auto	Determines if automated undo management is to be used or if normal rollback segments are to be used.
undo_retention	Dynamic/900 (seconds)	Any integer value from 0 to $2^{32}-1$	Determines the length of time that Oracle will attempt to maintain undo generated in the database after it has been committed. Setting this parameter higher can help eliminate "Snapshot to old" error messages. Additionally, Oracle features such as flashback query benefit from a higher setting. A higher setting, however, requires more tablespace space and results in larger undo segments, so be aware.
undo_suppress_errors	Dynamic/False	True or False	Enables users to suppress errors that might occur as the result of commands issued for manual undo management operations such as **alter rollback segment rbs1 online;**. Note this parameter is not available in Oracle Database 10g.

Managing the Undo Tablespace

There are four principle administrative activities that DBAs perform on undo tablespaces, each of which is described in turn in the sections that follow:

- Create the undo tablespace

- Drop the undo tablespace

- Alter the characteristics of the undo tablespace

- Manage the automated undo feature, which is mostly limited to setting a few database parameters

Creating the Undo Tablespace   Creating an undo tablespace is as simple as creating any other tablespace. You use the **create tablespace** command (this command is covered in Chapter 4) with the **undo** parameter, making the command **create undo tablespace**. Oracle always creates the tablespace as a locally managed tablespace (undo tablespaces cannot be dictionary managed). Beyond these issues, the **create** command for the undo tablespace looks much like a regular **create tablespace** command, as shown in this example:

```
CREATE UNDO TABLESPACE myundo1
DATAFILE 'c:\oracle\oradata\mydb\mydb_myundo1_01.dbf' SIZE 100m;
```

> **NOTE**
> *See the **create tablespace** command in Chapter 4 for more information on requirements and defaults when using the **create undo tablespace** command.*

You can also create an undo tablespace when you actually create your database. The **create database** command (see the syntax for this command in Chapter 2) contains a clause that allows you to create an undo tablespace when the database is created.

Dropping the Undo Tablespace   Dropping the undo tablespace is as easy as issuing the **drop tablespace** command (the syntax for this command can be found in Chapter 4), as shown in this example (note that the command is not **drop undo tablespace**):

```
DROP TABLESPACE my_undo_tbs;
```

In Oracle9*i* Database, you can include the **including contents and datafiles** clause to instruct Oracle to drop the data files associated with the tablespace:

```
DROP TABLESPACE my_undo_tbs INCLUDING CONTENTS AND DATAFILES;
```

Also note that if any transactions are still active in the undo tablespace, you will not be able to drop that tablespace. Also, if the undo tablespace is assigned to an instance, you cannot drop it. You can dynamically change which undo tablespace a given instance is using through the **alter system** command. Here is an example:

```
ALTER SYSTEM SET undo_tablespace=undo_tbs2;
```

After issuing this command, you can drop the old undo tablespace. Also, the **alter system set undo_tablespace** command allows you to add a new undo tablespace and then switch all future automated undo operations to that new tablespace. Any transactions started before the use of the **alter system set undo_tablespace** command use the old undo tablespace. Once those transactions are complete, you can drop the old undo tablespace.

Altering the Undo Tablespace   Maintenance operations on your undo tablespace are executed using the **alter tablespace** command (the syntax for this command can be found in Chapter 4). There are a limited number of operations that you can perform on an undo tablespace, including:

- Add a data file to the tablespace:

  ```
  ALTER TABLESPACE undo_tbs ADD DATAFILE
  '/ora101/oradata/mydb/mydb_undo_tbs_01.dbf' SIZE 100m;
  ```

■ Rename an existing data file:

```
ALTER TABLESPACE undo_tbs RENAME DATAFILE
'/ora101/oradata/mydb/mydb_undo_tbs_01.dbf' TO
'/ora102/oradata/mydb/mydb_undo_tbs_01.dbf';
```

■ Take offline or online a data file associated with the tablespace:

```
ALTER TABLESPACE undo_tbs DATAFILE 11 OFFLINE;
ALTER TABLESPACE undo_tbs DATAFILE 11 ONLINE;
```

■ Start or stop online backups of the tablespace:

```
ALTER TABLESPACE undo_tbs BEGIN BACKUP;
ALTER TABLESPACE undo_tbs END BACKUP;
```

■ Take offline or online an undo tablespace if the database is mounted but not open:

```
ALTER TABLESPACE undo_tbs OFFLINE;
ALTER TABLESPACE undo_tbs ONLINE;
```

NOTE
*See the **alter tablespace** command in Chapter 4 for more information on requirements and defaults when using the **alter tablespace** command.*

Using Automated Undo: Checklist

To start using automated undo management, you can follow this checklist to enable the feature in your database:

Step	Action
1.	Determine the name of the undo tablespace and the initial size that you wish to create it. How big should you create it? That's a hard number to initially quantify, and estimates generally tend to be way off the mark, for a number of reasons. I suggest that you create the tablespace using some reasonable size, and monitor the tablespace to ensure that it's performing well (which is covered later in this section).

2.	Create the undo tablespace:
	`CREATE TABLESPACE my_undotbs`
	`DATAFILE '/ora100/oradata/mydb/mydb_my_undotbs.dbf' SIZE 200m;`

3.	Edit the database initialization file. Set the following parameters:
	undo_tablespace　This is the name of the tablespace created in Step 2:
	`UNDO_TABLESPACE=my_undotbs`
	undo_retention　This is how long you wish to retain undo after the related transaction has been committed:
	`UNDO_RETENTION=1440`
	undo_management　This command actually enables automated undo management:
	`UNDO_MANAGEMENT=auto`
	If you are using an SPFILE, you need to set these parameters via the **alter system** command:
	`ALTER SYSTEM SET UNDO_TABLESPACE=my_undotbs SCOPE=spfile;`
	`ALTER SYSTEM SET UNDO_RETENTION=1440 SCOPE=spfile;`
	`ALTER SYSTEM SET UNDO_MANAGEMENT=auto SCOPE=spfile;`

4.	Shut down the database and restart it for automated undo to take effect. UNDO_MANAGEMENT is static, so you can't change it without a restart.

Manual Rollback Segment Administration

This section discusses the administration of manual rollback segments. Rollback segments have been around for much of Oracle's commercial life, and they have always been one of the thorns in the DBA's side. They are the cause of much grief, performance pains, and other woes. In this section, we cover rollback segment DBA issues. In the next few sections we will look at the creation, removal, and modification of rollback segments. We then look at monitoring your rollback segments. Finally, we look at error issues with rollback segments and how to correct those errors.

NOTE
The sys user owns all rollback segments, regardless of who created them (this is true of automated undo segments as well). The only exception to this is for public rollback segments associated with a RAC instance, which are owned by public.

Creating Rollback Segments

You should store all rollback segments in a tablespace dedicated to that purpose. If you are using manual rollback segments, you can actually create multiple rollback segment tablespaces if that is your desire. However one rollback segment tablespace is generally more than enough. Use the **create tablespace** command to create your rollback segment tablespace. Also, I suggest that you name the tablespace in such a way that it is clear that its intention is to store rollback segments (such as naming it RBS). Chapter 4 contains more information on the creation of tablespaces, but here is a quick example of the creation of a rollback segment tablespace:

```
CREATE TABLESPACE rbs
DATAFILE '/ora100/oracle/mydb/mydb_rbs_01.dbf' SIZE 100m;
```

Once you have created your rollback segment tablespace use the **create rollback segment** command to create a rollback segment. When creating a rollback segment, you must define the tablespace the rollback segment will be created in. Failure to do so will result in the rollback segment being assigned to the default tablespace of the user creating the rollback segment. Here is an example of the use of the **create rollback segment** command:

```
CREATE ROLLBACK SEGMENT rbs01 TABLESPACE rbs
STORAGE (INITIAL 100k NEXT 100k MINEXTENTS 10 OPTIMAL 1000k);
```

Privileges   In order to execute the **create rollback segment** command you must have the **create rollback segment** system privilege.

Parameter Information   There are only a few parameters that are used with the **create rollback segment** command. The **tablespace** clause defines the tablespace to create the rollback segment in. By default, this is the SYSTEM tablespace, so it's a good idea to define a tablespace that is specifically designed for rollback segments. It's also a good idea to create rollback segments in locally managed tablespaces. You have to use the **uniform** extent sizing policy because **autoallocate** is not supported for rollback segments.

The **storage** clause is also available for use in the **create rollback segment** command. In the previous example, we used the **storage** clause to define the **initial** and **next** extent size settings at 100KB. With rollback segments, it's very important to have the rollback segments within a given tablespace equi-sized. This eliminates problems with tablespace free space fragmentation. Also, in the previous example we forced Oracle to create ten initial extents for this rollback segment.

The **minextents** clause is only used during the initial creation of the rollback segment. After the initial creation of the database, the **optimal** parameter controls the actual amount of space that Oracle tries to maintain the rollback segment at. During the course of database operations, a given rollback segment will grow, of course. Frequently, the Oracle SMON process wakes up and looks at the rollback segments. If the extents are free, SMON tries to shrink the rollback segment down to the optimal setting for the rollback segment. In our example, Oracle will try to maintain the rollback segment at 1000KB, throughout the life of the rollback segment. Finally, note that the **pctincrease** parameter of the **storage** clause is not available for rollback segments.

Sizing Information   So, how much rollback segment space should you allocate? This really breaks down into two questions. The first is how large to make the rollback segment tablespace, and the second is how to size your rollback segments individually.

With regard to the initial creation of the rollback segment tablespace, I normally initially will create the tablespace such that it's sized at about 20 percent of the size of the data to be stored in the database. For larger or more active databases I might want to increase that, depending on concurrent usage, query vs. change volume, and length of queries (for example, how long reports will take to run). Also, this may be adjusted if there is one particularly large table, long-running reports, or based on some specific business requirement.

In spite of the best of numbers, it is often hard to estimate sizing of rollback segments at the beginning. Generally, I try to allocate no more than five users per rollback segment, so I take the maximum number of concurrent users and divide by five to get an idea of how many rollback segments to create. The size of rollback segments (and the performance as well) is also a factor of the redo generation rate, which is very hard to measure at the beginning. As a guide, I generally create rollback segments with ten initial extents all equi-sized. Then I create the extents sized such that they consume about 50 percent of the overall space allocated to the rollback segment tablespace.

Once you have created your rollback segment tablespace and your initial rollback segments, monitor your rollback segment usage, looking in particular at extents and the high watermark of the rollback segments as detailed in the V$ROLLSTAT view (discussed in more detail shortly). The WRITES column in this view provides a report of undo that has been generated. You can simply determine the total amount of undo written by reviewing the growth of the total number of writes over time, as seen in this example:

```
SELECT TO_CHAR(SYSDATE, 'mm/dd/yyyy hh24:mi:ss) the_date, SUM(writes)
FROM v$rollstat;
THE_DATE            SUM(WRITES)
------------------- -----------
04/26/2003 18:38:08    2328048
-- Run standard mix and load of transactions here
SELECT TO_CHAR(SYSDATE, 'mm/dd/yyyy hh24:mi:ss) The_Date, SUM(writes)
FROM v$rollstat;

THE_DATE            SUM(WRITES)
------------------- -----------
04/26/2003 19:38:08    3328048
```

In this example, we have had 1MB of undo generated in an hour. This nicely rounded number, coupled with other information, could then be used to determine how big we need to make our rollback segment tablespace, and the associated rollback segments. For example, if we knew we wanted to keep five days' worth of undo for flashback query purposes, we would need around 125MB (1MB * 24 hours * 5 days, assuming of course that the 1MB/hour generation rate is constant) of tablespace space allocated, plus some additional space for overhead and safety. Continue to monitor your rollback segments as your database continues to grow and new applications and users are added to it. Often, the initial usage footprint is very different than the usage footprint six months later.

Finalizing Rollback Segment Creation   Once you have created your rollback segment, you must bring it online with the **alter rollback segment online** command, as shown in this example:

```
ALTER ROLLBACK SEGMENT rbs01 ONLINE;
```

Oracle brings the rollback segment online for use at this point.

Once you have added rollback segments, you should also add them to the database parameter file, using the **rollback_segments** parameter:

```
ROLLBACK_SEGMENTS=rbs01, rbs02, rbs03
```

Configuring Rollback Segments: Checklist

Configuring manual rollback segments takes a bit of work. The following checklist hopefully will help you as you create them:

NOTE
The ugly truth about sizing rollback segments is that generally you make a good guess and then apply that guess and monitor.

Step	Action
1.	Determine how big you wish your rollback segment tablespace to be. Things to consider when calculating the size of the rollback segment tablespace include the following: • Length and number of transactions • Number of long-running transactions (both update and reporting) • Special needs for flashback query requirements

2.	Create your rollback segment tablespace:
	```CREATE TABLESPACE rbs```
	```DATAFILE '/ora010/oradata/mydb_rbs_01.dbf' SIZE 100m;```

3.	Determine the number and size of rollback segments. I suggest that you create a rollback segment for every five users. Sizes should be dependent on the sizes of database transactions as well as the velocity of operations. Finally, when determining a size, you should take into consideration the length of time you wish to have the generated undo available to other operations.

4.	Create your rollback segments:
	```CREATE ROLLBACK SEGMENT rbs01 TABLESPACE rbs STORAGE (INITIAL```
	```100K NEXT 100K MINEXTENTS 10 OPTIMAL 1000K);```
	```CREATE ROLLBACK SEGMENT rbs02 TABLESPACE rbs STORAGE (INITIAL```
	```100K NEXT 100K MINEXTENTS 10 OPTIMAL 1000K);```
	```CREATE ROLLBACK SEGMENT rbs03 TABLESPACE rbs STORAGE (INITIAL```
	```100K NEXT 100K MINEXTENTS 10 OPTIMAL 1000K);```

5.	Bring each rollback segment online:
	```ALTER ROLLBACK SEGMENT rbs01 ONLINE;```
	```ALTER ROLLBACK SEGMENT rbs02 ONLINE;```
	```ALTER ROLLBACK SEGMENT rbs03 ONLINE;```

6.	Modify the parameter file, or the database SPFILE. When modifying the database parameter file, set the **rollback_segments** parameter as shown here:
	```ROLLBACK_SEGMENTS=rbs01, rbs02, rbs03```
	When modifying the SPFILE, use the **alter system** command as shown here:
	```ALTER SYSTEM SET ROLLBACK_SEGMENTS=rbs01, rbs02, rbs03```
	```SCOPE=spfile;```

Dropping Rollback Segments

Rollback segments come and go, and to make them go you must drop them with the **drop rollback segment** command. A rollback segment can be dropped only if it's offline. Use the **alter rollback segment** command to perform this action. A checklist follows.

Dropping Rollback Segments: Checklist   Here is a checklist to follow when dropping a rollback segment:

Step	Action

1.	Determine if the rollback segment to be dropped is online:
	```SELECT a.name, b.status FROM v$rollname a, v$rollstat b```
	```WHERE a.usn=b.usn;```

2.	If the rollback segment status is showing ONLINE, then take the rollback segment offline with the following command: ```ALTER ROLLBACK SEGMENT xyz OFFLINE;```
3.	Drop the rollback segment using the **drop rollback segment** command: ```DROP ROLLBACK SEGMENT xyz;```

Changing Rollback Segments

If you want to change most attributes of a rollback segment, then use the **alter rollback segment** command. This command allows you to change a number of settings for rollback segments (e.g., **next**, **optimal**, **freelists**), take the rollback segment offline, or shrink a rollback segment if that is your desire. Here are some examples of the use of the **alter rollback segment** command (in no particular order):

```
ALTER ROLLBACK SEGMENT rbs01 ONLINE;
ALTER ROLLBACK SEGMENT rbs01 OFFLINE;
ALTER ROLLBACK SEGMENT rbs01 STORAGE (OPTIMAL 10M NEXT 1M MAXEXTENTS 100);
ALTER ROLLBACK SEGMENT rbs01 SHRINK TO 10M;
```

Monitoring Rollback Segments and Automated Undo

When you first configure automated undo management on your database, you will want to make sure that you have correctly set parameters such as **undo_retention** and that the size of the undo tablespace is set correctly. This is easily accomplished through the use of several data dictionary views.

The V$UNDOSTAT view is a historical representation of the state of your database with regard to undo. It can be used when you are using regular rollback segments, but is of particular use when using automated undo. Each row in the view represents a ten-minute snapshot of undo activity. You can use the V$UNDOSTAT view to determine the total amount of undo being generated in the database, as shown in this example:

```
SELECT TO_CHAR(begin_time, 'mm/dd/yyyy hh24:mi:ss') BEGIN,
TO_CHAR(end_time, 'mm/dd/yyyy hh24:mi:ss') END,
undoblks FROM v$undostat;
BEGIN                END                  UNDOBLKS
-------------------- -------------------- ----------
04/24/2003 21:18:00 04/24/2003 21:18:10           0
04/24/2003 21:08:00 04/24/2003 21:18:00         362
04/24/2003 20:58:00 04/24/2003 21:08:00         124
04/24/2003 20:48:00 04/24/2003 20:58:00           1
```

You can also determine if your undo tablespace is too small by querying the view and looking at the columns UNXPSTEALCNT, UNXPBLKRELCNT, and UNXPBLKREUCNT, as shown in this query:

```
SELECT TO_CHAR(begin_time, 'mm/dd/yyyy hh24:mi:ss') BEGIN,
TO_CHAR(end_time, 'mm/dd/yyyy hh24:mi:ss') END,
unxpstealcnt, unxpblkrelcnt, unxpblkreucnt, ssolderrcnt
FROM v$undostat;
```

High numbers in any of the latter three columns indicates that Oracle is stealing space from unexpired undo extents to satisfy current space requirements. This is not desirable, and you need to either adjust your **undo_retention** parameter down or increase the space available to the undo tablespace.

Note in the previous example the use of the SSOLDERRCNT column. This column provides a running count of ORA-01555 errors, which indicates that Oracle was not able to generate a read-consistent image from your rollback segments. Numbers in SSOLDERRCNT may indicate a problem with insufficient space in your undo tablespace or an **undo_retention** parameter that is set insufficiently.

The DBA_UNDO_EXTENTS view provides information on each extent in your undo tablespace. This view provides you information on the status of each undo extent and shows the commit time for each undo extent in the database.

CAUTION
Most of the V$ view statistics are reset after the database is restarted.
Be careful of this!

The V$ROLLSTAT view is useful in determining the effectiveness of manually allocated rollback segments. The values displayed in this view are cumulative and are reset at each database restart. There are a number of columns in the V$ROLLSTAT view, including:

- **USN**   Identifies each rollback segment.

- **EXTENTS**   Contains the number of extents currently allocated to the rollback segment.

- **RSSIZE**   Displays the current size of the rollback segment.

- **XACTS**   Displays the current number of transactions in the rollback segment.

- **WAITS**   Displays the total waits for the rollback segment. High numbers indicate contention for the rollback segment.

- **OPTSIZE**   Indicates the current optimal setting for the rollback segment.

- **HWMSIZE**   Indicates how large the rollback segment has grown.

- **SHRINKS**   Indicates how many shrink operations have occurred on the rollback segment. Each shrink operation may result in the removal of only a small number of extents, so for each individual extend operation, several shrink operations might occur.

- **WRAPS**   Displays the number of times the head of the rollback segment wrapped into a new extent.

- **EXTENDS**   Indicates the number of times that an extent had to be allocated to the rollback segment because the head of the rollback segment could not wrap into any available extent.

- **AVEACTIVE**   Indicates the average size of active rollback segments.

When looking at the V$ROLLSTAT view, perhaps the most important statistic comes from the EXTENDS column. Higher values in this column indicates your rollback segment had to have additional extents allocated to it in order for it to do its job. Allocating extents during a transaction is an expensive task for the database, and it's better if they are already there. Thus, if you see a large number of extents, you should consider either increasing the **initial** and **next** storage parameters of the rollback segments or increasing the number of extents allocated to each rollback segment.

Oracle Errors Associated with Rollback Segments and Automated Undo

A number of rollback segment–related errors might be encountered in Oracle. The following table lists a number of these errors and provides some resolution guidance:

Oracle Error Message	Text Description	Possible Causes and Solutions
ORA-0376	File *string* cannot be read at this time	This error, if it is associated with a rollback segment data file, generally indicates that a rollback segment with active transactions is not available after a database restart. You probably need to recover the rollback segment tablespace.
ORA-0601	Cleanup lock conflict	This error may appear in the alert log, but can safely be ignored.
ORA-1534	Rollback segment doesn't exist	An operation (**alter** or **drop**) on a rollback segment failed because the rollback segment didn't exist. Check the spelling of the rollback segment in the command. Also ensure that the rollback segment actually exists by checking the DBA_ROLLBACK_SEGS view.
ORA-1535	Rollback segment already exists	The rollback segment you are trying to create already exists. You can verify this with the DBA_ROLLBACK_SEGS view.
ORA-1544	Cannot drop system rollback segment	What are you doing? You can't drop the system rollback segment!
ORA-1545	Rollback segment specified not available	The operation you are attempting cannot be completed because the rollback segment is not available. It may be for a number of reasons: • The tablespace that the rollback segment is in is offline. • You or the database tried to bring the rollback segment online and it's already online. Check the database parameter **rollback_segments** to ensure that there is not a duplicate entry for that rollback segment. • You tried to drop a rollback segment that is online. You must offline the rollback segment first (see the earlier section "Dropping Rollback Segments"). • You tried to online a rollback segment that is corrupted. The rollback segment may need to be recovered or it may be listed in the **_corrupted_rollback_segments** parameter and need to be removed. (Be careful of underscore parameters, as they are unsupported and largely undocumented by Oracle!)
ORA-1548	Active rollback segment found, terminate dropping tablespace	You are trying to drop a tablespace that contains one or more active rollback segments. Offline the rollback segments and then try the operation again.
ORA-1551	Extended rollback segment, pinned blocks released	This error may appear in the alert log, but can safely be ignored.
ORA-1552	Cannot use the system rollback segment for non-system tablespace	This error is received any time you generate undo that is from a tablespace other than the system tablespace, and the system rollback segment is the only rollback segment available.

Oracle Error Message	Text Description	Possible Causes and Solutions
ORA-1555	Snapshot too old	There are several issues that can cause this error to occur. Generally the solution is one of the following: • Try to tune any long-running report to reduce its run time. Reducing the run time has a number of benefits. • If using manual rollback segments, increase the size of the initial and next extents of your rollback segments. Also consider increasing the setting of **optimal** or even removing **optimal**. • Remove, as much as possible, inner process commits, as these can lead to ORA-1555 errors. • Rebalance your transactions so long-running transactions run as much in isolation as possible. • If running automated undo, increase the **undo_retention** database parameter.
ORA-1556 ORA-1559	[MINEXTENTS or MAXEXTENTS] for rollback segment must be greater than 1	You are trying to create a rollback segment with the parameter **minextents** set to 1 or **maxextents** set to less than 2. Modify the DDL so that **minextents** or **maxextents** is larger and retry the creation.
ORA-1557	Rollback segment extents must be at least _n_ blocks	You have tried to create a rollback segment that is sized too small. Increase **initial** and **next** and retry your operation.
ORA-1558	Out of transaction IDs in rollback segment	The rollback segment listed has run out of transaction IDs. This is an inherent limitation of Oracle and is very rare, but can happen. You need to shut down the database and restart it. Once it's open, offline the rollback segment listed and then drop it.
ORA-1562	Failed to extend rollback segment	This error implies that your rollback segment could not extend. Additional error messages that accompany this message should make the reason clearer. Often, you may need to increase **maxextents** for your rollback segments or increase the size of the tablespace.
ORA-1575	Timeout waiting for space managed resource	This error may appear in the alert log, but can safely be ignored.
ORA-1578	Oracle data block corrupted	This error, if associated with a rollback segment tablespace, indicates that at least one block in the tablespace has been detected as corrupted. There are several solutions to this problem, depending on whether the corrupted block is in an active rollback segment or an inactive one. You may well be able to use RMAN to recover this corrupted block with minimal outage. I strongly suggest you contact Oracle support if you receive this error.
ORA-1581	Attempt to use rollback segment new extent that is being allocated	Should be very rare. If you are using manual rollback segments, you might consider increasing the size of the extents (**initial** and **next**) and unset **optimal**. If this error persists, contact Oracle.
ORA-1593	Rollback segment optimal size is smaller than the computed initial size	You are trying to create a rollback segment and you have set **optimal** to a size that is smaller than the cumulative size of the initial extents to be created for the rollback segments. Increase **optimal** so that it is equivalent to the initial size of the rollback segment.

Oracle Error Message	Text Description	Possible Causes and Solutions
ORA-1594	Attempt to wrap into rollback segment that is being freed	This error may indicate that your rollback segments are too small, and that you might need to adjust **initial**, **next**, or **optimal** settings if you are using manual rollback segments.
ORA-1595	Error freeing extent of rollback segment	This error may indicate that your rollback segments are too small, and that you might need to adjust **initial**, **next**, or **optimal** settings if you are using manual rollback segments.
ORA-1597	Cannot alter system rollback segment online or offline	You are trying to alter the system rollback segment online or offline. These are unsupported operations.
ORA-1598 ORA-1627	Rollback segment is not online	An attempt was made to force the use of a rollback segment that is not online or to offline a rollback segment that is not online. Check the status of the rollback segment via the V$ROLLSTAT view.
ORA-1608	Cannot bring rollback segment online	The rollback segment is already online.
ORA-1628	Max # extents reached for rollback segment	An attempt to extend a rollback segment beyond its **maxextents** setting failed. Raise the rollback segment **maxextents** setting or adjust your SQL code so that excessive undo is not generated.
ORA-1634	Rollback segment number is about to go offline	You have tried to force the use of a rollback segment that is still active but is scheduled to go offline once all activity is complete. Online the rollback segment if you wish to use it (**alter rollback segment rbs1 online;**).
ORA-1635	Rollback segment specified is not available	You are attempting an operation on a rollback segment that is offline. This might include trying to drop a rollback segment that contains active transactions.
ORA-1636	Rollback segment is already online	You tried to online a rollback segment that is already online in this, or another, instance.
ORA-1637	Rollback segment is being used by another instance	You attempted to use a rollback segment that is in use by another instance in your RAC cluster. This may be because the rollback segment is contained in the database parameter file for your instance and needs to be removed.
ORA-1650	Unable to extend rollback segment in tablespace	The rollback segment listed is trying to grow, but you have run out of tablespace space. Before just adding space to the rollback segment tablespace, try to determine why so much rollback segment space is needed. It may be a new process that is looping or creating some other form of havoc on your database.
ORA-1651 ORA-1652	Unable to extend save undo segment	This can occur when taking a tablespace offline. Bring the tablespace online again, allow the undo to be applied, and then take the tablespace offline again.
ORA-30012	Undo tablespace does not exist or of wrong type	Indicates that the automated undo tablespace listed in the **undo_tablespace** parameter does not exist. Check that the tablespace exists and that the name listed in the **undo-tablespace** parameter is correct.
ORA-30013	Undo tablespace is currently in use	You are trying to modify an undo tablespace (e.g., **drop tablespace**) that is in use by another instance. This is generally an RAC error message. Go to the instance that the tablespace is assigned to, and modify the tablespace as required.

Oracle Error Message	Text Description	Possible Causes and Solutions
ORA-30014	Operation only is supported in Automatic Undo Management mode	You have tried to execute an operation that is only supported in Automated Undo Management mode. Review why you are wanting to execute the operation, and also make sure you are on the correct database. It is also possible that the database did not start in Automated Undo Management mode.
ORA-30015	Previously offlined undo tablespace is still pending	Often appears when trying to drop an undo tablespace. This error indicates that there are transactions in that tablespace that are still active. You need to wait until all active transactions are complete before you can complete the operation.
ORA-30016	Undo tablespace is already in use by this instance	This tablespace is already in use. You might have typed in the wrong tablespace name in your command (e.g., **alter system set undo_tablespace**). It's also possible that your command is just incorrect.
ORA-30019	Illegal rollback segment operation in Automatic Undo mode	The command you tried to execute is not compatible with Automatic Undo mode. Review why you want to use the command, given that you are running in Automatic Undo mode.
ORA-30020	UNDO_MANAGEMENT= AUTO needs compatibility or greater	You tried to start the instance with Automated Undo Management mode enabled, but the **compatible** parameter is not set correctly. Check the **compatible** parameter and reset it to 9.0 or greater if you wish to enable AUM.
ORA-30021 Also related: ORA-30022	Operation not allowed on undo tablespace, or Cannot create segments in undo tablespace	The operation you are trying to execute is not allowed on an undo tablespace.
ORA-30024	Invalid specification for CREATE UNDO TABLESPACE	Your **create undo tablespace** statement has an error. Review the statement and determine what the error is. Correct the error and re-execute the statement. Generally this error implies that a clause used in the statement is not valid with the **create undo tablespace** command.
ORA-30026	Undo tablespace has unexpired undo with (sec) left, Undo_retention=(sec)	Occurs during a **drop undo** statement. Indicates that the undo tablespace you are trying to drop has unexpired undo information in it. You need to either wait until the undo has expired or change the **undo_retention** parameter.

Control File Administration

Every Oracle database has at least one control file. It a very good practice to actually have two or more control files for each database. These different control files (which will be named differently) should be located on different file systems to better protect them. The control file of the Oracle database contains a great deal of information. Oracle periodically updates the control file during the lifetime of your database. Events such as startup, shutdown, checkpoints, and log switches all cause activity to occur on the database control file.

Generally, there is little you will do with the control file except define its location and back it up. There may be cases in which you need to restore the control file, or you might need to rename your database, which requires a control file modification. We cover all of these topics in this section.

Control File Backups

There are two different methods of creating control file backups:

- Create a backup control file—this results in the creation of a backup control file. This is an exact copy of the backup control file, with some internal structures configured to allow its use during recovery using a backup control file.

- Create a text-based trace file, which contains the commands to re-create the control file via the SQL **create controlfile** command.

To create a backup control file, use the **alter database backup control file** command, as shown in this example:

```
ALTER DATABASE BACKUP CONTROLFILE TO
/ora01/backup/controlfile.ctl';
```

This command results in the creation of a file called controlfile.ctl in the /ora01/backup directory. The controlfile.ctl file will be a backup control file that you can use to perform recovery. Note that this is an actual control file (with some internal differences that make it usable for recovery), and thus is not editable or readable by the DBA.

An alternate method of backing up the control file is through the creation of a trace file, which will contain a set of SQL commands (like **create control file**) that can be used if your control file is lost. The script re-creates the control file and then recovers your database for you. Here is an example of the creation of this type of control file backup:

```
ALTER DATABASE BACKUP CONTROLFILE TO TRACE;
```

Note that in this case you are not given the option of defining the name or location of the backup file being created. The result of this command is a trace file contained in the directory defined via the database **user_dump_dest** parameter. The resulting output is in text, human-readable, format. You need to edit the file to actually be able to use it. See the upcoming section "Restoring the Control File" for more information on this operation. (Also, see Chapter 11 for more on database and control file backup and recovery.)

NOTE
In most cases, if you can recover from a backup control file, that is the preferable method. The backup control file leaves RMAN and archive redo log information intact. If you re-create the control file with the ***create controlfile*** *command, then this information will be lost.*

Moving the Control File

The location of the database control file(s) is contained in the database parameter file or SPFILE, depending on which you are using. If you wish to move one or more of your control files, you need to edit these files. Of course, the parameter file is a text-based file, so all you need to do is edit it with your favorite editor, and change the **control_files** parameter.

Changing the SPFILE is a bit different. In this case, you need to use the **alter system** command. Since the control file location cannot be changed dynamically, use the **scope=spfile** parameter to just update the SPFILE and prevent an Oracle-generated error. Here is an example of an operation that changes the control file location in the database SPFILE:

```
ALTER SYSTEM SET CONTROL_FILE="c:\oracle\oradata\control\control01.ctl,
c:\oracle\oradata\control02.ctl" SCOPE=spfile;
```

Once you have reset the location of the control files, you need to physically move them. To do this, you first need to shut down the database, and then physically move the control files. Here is a checklist of steps that you can use to move a control file:

Step	Action
1.	Determine the location(s) that you wish to move the control file(s) to.
2.	The database instance should be started, at a minimum. These steps can be completed with the database mounted or open as well.
3.	If a database parameter file is in use, modify the parameter file parameter **control_files** to reflect the new control file locations.
4.	If you are using an SPFILE, then use the **alter system** command to reset the **control_files** parameter. Make sure you use the **scope=spfile** parameter: ALTER SYSTEM SET CONTROL_FILES= "c:\oracle\oradata\control\control01.ctl, d:\oracle\oradata\control02.ctl" SCOPE=spfile;
5.	Shut down the database. This operation can be done at any time after the previous steps. Note that if the database shuts down for any reason, it will not restart until you have actually moved the control files.
6.	Move the control file(s) to the new locations.
7.	Restart the database.

NOTE
*When using the **alter system** command to change the location of the control files, make sure you include the location of all control files, including those you are not moving.*

Restoring the Control File

If you have lost one or more control files, there are a number of recovery options. The following checklist walks you through the different options, from the most desirable to the least:

Step	Action
1.	If one or more of the control files have survived the loss/failure, do the following: **a).** Shut down the database, if it is still running. SHUTDOWN ABORT **b).** Copy the surviving control file to the location of the control files that were lost. If these locations were permanently lost, then copy the control file to a new location so that you have at least no fewer than two control file copies. cp -p /ora100/oradata/control/control01.ctl /ora100/oradata/control/control02.ctl **c).** Start up the database instance using the **startup nomount** command from SQL*Plus: STARTUP NOMOUNT **d).** Modify the database parameter file (refer to the preceding section, "Moving the Control File") so that it is pointing to the new control file locations. **e).** Open the database (this assumes that the database data files are intact): ALTER DATABASE MOUNT; ALTER DATABASE OPEN;

Step	Action
2.	If none of the control files has survived, if you have a control file backup via RMAN, then use RMAN to restore the control file. Refer to Oracle Press's *Oracle9i RMAN Backup & Recovery* (McGraw-Hill/Osborne, 2002) for more detailed information on RMAN control file backups and recovery.
3.	If you are not using RMAN, then restore the control file using a backup control file, following these instructions:

a). Shut down the database, if it's still running (which is doubtful!):
```
SHUTDOWN IMMEDIATE
```
b). Copy the backup control file to each control file location. Rename it with each copy to the name of the control file at that location. In this example, the backup control file (control_back.ctl) has been copied to two different locations, using the unique names of the control files at that location:
```
cp -p /ora01/backup/control_back.ctl
/ora100/oradata/control/control01.ctl
cp -p /ora01/backup/control_back.ctl
/ora200/oradata/control/control02.ctl
```
c). Mount the database:
```
ALTER DATABASE MOUNT;
```
d). Open the database:
```
ALTER DATABASE OPEN USING BACKUP CONTROLFILE;
```
Recovery situations may vary if, for example, you have lost your online redo logs, lost individual data files, and experienced other permutations.

4.	If you do not have a backup control file, but you have a trace file that was created via the **alter database backup controlfile to trace** command, then you can use this trace file to re-create the database control file. You first need to edit the trace file, because it contains header information that you do not want to use. Once you have edited the trace file correctly, execute it from a SQL session. It should successfully re-create the control file for you.
5.	If all else fails, the last option is to manually create a control file by using the **create controlfile** command. To successfully create this command, you need to know the following information:

• The name of the database
• The location and name of at least one member of each redo log group
• The name and location of all database-related data files

NOTE
Detailed backup and recovery coverage is a complex topic and a book in its own right. Check out the Oracle Press books Oracle9i RMAN Backup & Recovery *and* Oracle Backup & Recovery 101 *(McGraw-Hill/Osborne, 2002) for more in-depth information on backup and recovery of your Oracle database.*

Renaming the Database

If you want to rename your database, you need to rebuild the control file using the **create controlfile** command. First, create the **create controlfile** command by issuing a **alter database backup controlfile to trace** command. Then, you need to edit the resulting trace file so that it performs a rename operation. Finally, you execute the trace file, which creates a new control file. Here is a checklist for the database rename operation:

Step	Action
1.	Create the backup control file trace file:

```
ALTER DATABASE BACKUP CONTROLFILE TO TRACE;
```

Step	Action
2.	Locate the resulting trace file in the location defined by USER_DUMP_DEST. You can determine the location of USER_DUMP_DEST in several ways:

• From SQL*Plus, use the command **show parameter USER_DUMP_DEST** to locate the value of the parameter:

```
SQL> SHOW PARAMETER USER_DUMP_DEST
NAME                    TYPE      VALUE
---------------    -------    ---------------------------
user_dump_dest     string   C:\oracle\admin\testdb\udump
```
• Query the V$PARAMETER view:
```
SELECT name, value FROM v$parameter
WHERE name = 'user_dump_dest';
NAME                  VALUE
--------------    ----------------------------
user_dump_dest    C:\oracle\admin\testdb\udump
```
• Simply open the parameter file and determine the likely value for the setting.

Step	Action
3.	In the USER_DUMP_DEST directory, find the trace file that you created in Step 1.
4.	Copy the trace file to a backup file with a .sql extension. Edit this backup file found in Step 3. Specifically, make the following changes:

a). Remove the header information in the trace file. This is all lines from the first line up to but not including the first line that reads **create control file**.

b). At the end of the first **create control file** statement (there will be more than one in later versions of Oracle), remove all remaining text from the trace file.

c). At the top of the SQL statement, replace the words **reuse database** with **set database**.

d). After **set database**, you will see the name of the old database listed in quotes. Replace this name with the name of the new database.

e). If you are renaming any directory names (as you should), then modify the directory name entries that will be changed in the control file. For example, for your data files, if you were to change your database data file `c:\oracle\oradata\devdb\devdb_system_01.dbf` to `c:\oracle\oradata\testdb\testdb_system_01.dbf`, you would want to change this entry in the create control file definition of testdb_system_01.dbf.

f). In the end, your SQL statement should look similar to the following example, in which the database name has been set to TESTDB:

```
CREATE CONTROLFILE SET DATABASE "TESTDB" NORESETLOGS
ARCHIVELOG MAXLOGFILES 5 MAXLOGMEMBERS 3 MAXDATAFILES 100
MAXINSTANCES 1 MAXLOGHISTORY 226
LOGFILE GROUP 1 'C:\ORACLE\ORADATA\TESTDB\TESTDB_REDO01.LOG'
SIZE 100M,
GROUP 2 'C:\ORACLE\ORADATA\TESTDB\TESTDB_REDO02.LOG'   SIZE 100M,
GROUP 3 'C:\ORACLE\ORADATA\TESTDB\TESTDB_REDO03.LOG'   SIZE 100M
DATAFILE
   'C:\ORACLE\ORADATA\TESTDB\TESTDB_SYSTEM_01.DBF',
   'C:\ORACLE\ORADATA\TESTDB\TESTDB_UNDOTBS_01.DBF',
   'C:\ORACLE\ORADATA\TESTDB\TESTDB_INDX_01.DBF',
   'C:\ORACLE\ORADATA\TESTDB\TESTDB_TOOLS_01.DBF',
   'C:\ORACLE\ORADATA\TESTDB\TESTDB_USERS_01.DBF'
CHARACTER SET WE8MSWIN1252;
```
g). Save the SQL file.

Step	Action
5.	Shut down the database.
6.	Back up the database before any operation. This includes a backup of the control file.

Note: This can be an online or offline backup, whichever you prefer.

Step	Action
7.	Rename the directories and data files in the database as you did in the SQL file created in Step 4.

Step	Action
8.	Start the instance: `STARTUP NOMOUNT`
9.	Execute the modified SQL script you created in Step 4.
10.	Issue a **recover database** command: `RECOVER DATABASE;` In most cases, Oracle should indicate that media recovery is complete without any additional user interaction being required.
11.	Open the database: `ALTER DATABASE OPEN RESETLOGS;` Your database will be renamed.
12.	Change the global name of the database: `ALTER DATABASE RENAME GLOBAL NAME TO testdb.mydomain.com;`
13.	Perform a full database backup.

NOTE

When you execute this operation, you lose all RMAN and archivelog history that is contained in the control file. This makes recovering your database much harder. You should make sure you have a good backup of the database and a copy of the old control file before you execute this operation. Also, be sure to back up your database immediately after this operation.

Oracle Errors Associated with Control Files

A number of control file–related errors might be encountered in Oracle. The following table lists a number of these errors and provides some resolution guidance:

Oracle Error Message	Text Description	Possible Causes and Solutions
ORA-0200	Controlfile could not be created	You attempted to create a control file and the operation failed. Check that there is sufficient disk space, and that permissions on the file system are correct. Make sure that you are not overwriting an existing, active control file.
ORA-0201	Controlfile version incompatible with Oracle version	You are either: • Starting Oracle with an incorrect version of the database software. • Using the wrong control file. • Experiencing corruption in the control file. Locate and use the correct control file or recover by using a backup control file or using the **create controlfile** command.
ORA-0203	Using the wrong controlfiles	Make sure that you are using the correct control files for your instance.
ORA-0204	Error in reading of controlfile	Some form of I/O failure has occurred and the control file cannot be read. Check the disk system for errors, and correct any errors found.

Oracle Error Message	Text Description	Possible Causes and Solutions
ORA-0205	Error in identifying controlfile	Some failure occurred as Oracle tried to identify the control file. Make sure that the **control_files** entry in the database parameter file is correct. Also make sure the control file exists and has the correct permissions. If only one of the control files is affected, remove its listing from the **control_files** parameter and restart the database.
ORA-0206	Error in writing of controlfile	An error occurred during a write operation against the control file. Generally this implies a disk system failure.
ORA-0207	Controlfiles are not for the same database	You have used the wrong control file for your database (the **control_files** parameter is likely set incorrectly). Point to the correct control file and continue operations.
ORA-0208	Number of controlfile names exceeds limit	You have too many control files defined for your database. Shut down the database and reduce the number of control files present in the database.
ORA-0209	Control file blocksize mismatch	The **db_block_size** initialization parameter and the block size setting in the control file are mismatched. Correct the **db_block_size** parameter and retry the operation.
ORA-0210	Cannot open the specified controlfile	The control file cannot be opened by Oracle. Check the accessibility and file permissions on the control file. If the control file is missing, then restore it with a backup control file or use the **create controlfile** command.
ORA-0213	Cannot reuse controlfile	You have tried to re-create the control file over an existing control file. This attempt failed because you did not use the **reuse** clause or because you did not remove the preexisting control file.
ORA-0214	Controlfile version inconsistent with file	The control files are inconsistent. You have mixed and matched control files, data files, or online redo logs from another database. Find the correct files and make the database files consistent.
ORA-0215	Must be at least one controlfile	No control file was found. Either the **control_files** parameter is not set or the control file cannot be accessed.
ORA-0218	Block size of controlfile does not match db_block_size	The block size in the control file does not match the **db_block_size** parameter. Either correct the **db_block_size** parameter, if that is in error, or restore the control file.
ORA-0221	Error on write to controlfile	An error occurred when trying to write to the control file. Additional messages should indicate the nature of the problem.
ORA-0225	Expected size of controlfile differs from actual size	Generally this indicates a corrupted control file. Restore the control file.
ORA-0227	Corrupt block detected in controlfile	Restore the control file from backup or using the **create controlfile** command.
ORA-1580 ORA-1582 ORA-1583 ORA-1584 ORA-1585 ORA-1586 ORA-1587	Varies	These errors indicate a problem creating a backup control file. These errors are accompanied with other error messages to assist you in determining the problem. Check for file permissions on the destination directory. Also check to ensure that if the backup control file exists already, it can be overwritten. The problem might be with the source control file. Make sure that the permissions on the control file have not been changed such that Oracle cannot read it.

Oracle Error Message	Text Description	Possible Causes and Solutions
ORA-1665	Controlfile is not a standby controlfile	You are trying to start a standby database without a standby control file. Use the **alter database create standby controlfile** command on the primary database to create a standby database control file. Move that control file to the standby database and try your operation again.
ORA-1669	Standby database controlfile not consistent	You are recovering your standby database with a control file that is not consistent. Re-create the standby control file on the primary database and retry the operation.
ORA-1671	Controlfile is a backup, cannot make a standby controlfile	You are trying to create a standby control file, but you have not completed recovery of your database so the current control file is a backup control file. Complete recovery of your database, open the database, and then try the operation again.

Online Redo Log Administration

Although online redo logs are one of the most important components in an Oracle database, they sometimes tend to get overlooked from an administration point of view. This section focuses on DBA tasks that revolve around online redo logs. First, we look at online redo log basics. We then move on to how to perform tasks such as creating and dropping online redo log groups and members and resizing online redo logs. Finally, we discuss monitoring online redo logs and look at errors you might see that are associated with online redo logs.

The Basics of Online Redo Logs

As your Oracle database does work, it records the essence of that work in memory first, in the online redo log buffer, in the form of redo. When that work is committed by the user (and when other conditions occur that require the redo log buffer to be flushed), the contents of the online redo log buffer are flushed to operating system files called online redo logs. These log files are generally created when the database is first created, though they may be added or removed during the life of the database as required.

During database recovery operations, these online redo logs are used to reconstitute the database to the point of failure. Alternatively, they can be used to recover the database to a point in time other than that of the failure. Without these files, this type of recovery is next to impossible; thus, loss of these critical files almost guarantees data loss in many database outage situations. This is why it is critical to locate these files on different file systems, on different disks, on different controllers, and so on. In summary, remove all single points of failure, if at all possible.

Online redo logs are created in groups. An Oracle instance writes to only one online redo log group at a time. The group that is being written to is the current online redo log group. Each online redo log group may contain several different mirrored members. Oracle writes to these mirrored members in parallel. If one online redo log member is lost, no data loss occurs and the database continues to function.

If you are running RAC, each RAC instance has its own redo log groups assigned to it. A given redo log group can be assigned to only a single RAC instance. Thus, if you created online redo log group 1 on RAC node 1, you could not create redo log group 1 on RAC node 2. Note also that in an RAC environment, you must define which thread (or instance) the redo log group belongs to when you create it. This is done via the **thread** parameter of the **alter database** command. So, for example, in a two-node RAC configuration, online redo logs belonging to node 1 will be thread 1, and those belonging to thread 2 will be thread 2.

Oracle requires all databases to have a minimum of two online redo log groups for each instance, with a single member in each group. I strongly recommend that you create at least four online redo log groups per instance to begin with, and that you create at least two or more members for each group. Separate each group member physically such that there is no single point of failure. That is, make sure they sit on different file systems, disks, controllers, and so on.

Oracle usually writes to the online redo logs in round-robin fashion (there are always exceptions, of course). That is, it writes to one online redo log, and when that log is filled, it closes that online redo log and moves on to the next one in order and starts writing to it. As Oracle opens and begins to write to an online redo log, the log is assigned a log sequence number. That number remains assigned to the redo contained within that log for the logical life of the database (if it is archived, that is).

Once the online redo log fills, Oracle closes the log file and searches for another available log file to open and write to. In the meantime, a couple of things might happen to the old online redo log:

- If the database is in ARCHIVELOG mode, the ARCH process is signaled to move the online redo log to any and all defined and enabled archived redo log destinations.

- If the database is in NOARCHIVELOG mode, all that is required is that DBWR write out all data changes to the data files before the online redo log can be reused. This is required in ARCHIVELOG mode as well. If this does not happen, then the database stops until DBWR can catch up.

If the database is in ARCHIVELOG mode, Oracle is unable to reuse a closed archived redo log until ARCH has completed its job of copying that online redo log to the archived redo log destinations. This means that if ARCH is behind and has not completed its copies, and there are no archived online redo logs available to switch into, the database halts until ARCH frees an online redo log. As a result, there may be cases where you need several online redo logs available to prevent system stoppage.

A common question is, "How big should I make my redo logs?" I like to size the online redo logs in such a way that log switches occur every 15 minutes. With new databases, it's hard to determine how much redo will be actually generated, so often you just have to create the online redo logs at some arbitrary size and monitor log switches. Log switches appear in the alert log of the database, which is stored in the location pointed to by the **background_dump_dest** database parameter. If the log switches are occurring in intervals of less than every 15 minutes, then increase the size of the online redo log such that the average switch intervals are every 15 minutes. If the switches are occurring more often than every 15 minutes, reduce the size.

Creating New Redo Log Groups

You create your initial redo log groups when you create the database. If you need to create additional online redo logs, use the **alter database** command. Here is an example of this operation:

```
ALTER DATABASE ADD LOGFILE THREAD 2 GROUP 4
('c:\oracle\oradata\mydb\mydb_logfile_4_2_a.log',
 'd:\oracle\oradata\mydb\mydb_logfile_4_2_b.log') SIZE 100m;
```

This command is creating a new redo log group (assigned as group 4) to thread 2. Two redo log members are assigned to the group, each sized at 100MB. This example is creating a redo log group for the second node of an RAC clustered database (as evidenced by the use of the **thread** parameter). Use of the **thread** parameter is perfectly valid in a non-RAC environment (the value should always be set to 1). You can also just remove the **thread** parameter completely in a non-RAC environment, so your command would look like this:

```
ALTER DATABASE ADD LOGFILE GROUP 4
('c:\oracle\oradata\mydb\mydb_logfile_4_1_a.log',
'd:\oracle\oradata\mydb\mydb_logfile_4_1_b.log') SIZE 100m;
```

Creating New Redo Log Members

Sometimes you may want to add an additional redo log member to an existing group. This requires the **alter database** command using the **add logfile** member clause, as shown in this example:

```
ALTER DATABASE ADD LOGFILE MEMBER
'd:\oracle\oradata\mydb\mydb_redo_1_1_a.log' TO GROUP 1;
```

NOTE
In the case of an RAC environment, you do not need to define a thread, since each group is unique to a specific thread.

Dropping an Online Redo Log Group

If you need to drop an online redo log group, simply use the **alter database** command. Oracle does not allow you to drop the current online redo log group, so you have to force a log switch with the **alter system** command if the online redo log group that you want to drop is the current online redo log group. Here is a checklist to follow for dropping an online redo log:

Step	Action
1.	Determine if the online redo log group you wish to drop is the current online redo log:

```
SQL> SELECT group#, status FROM v$log;
    GROUP# STATUS
---------- ----------------
         1 CURRENT
         2 INACTIVE
         3 INACTIVE|
         4 UNUSED
```

2.	If the group to be dropped is the current online redo log, then force a log switch:

```
ALTER SYSTEM SWITCH LOGFILE;
```

3.	Force a checkpoint to ensure that the logfile group you wish to drop is marked as inactive in the database. You must do this because DBWR has to write out the changes contained in the online redo log before Oracle will allow you to drop it, to ensure that instance recovery is possible.

```
ALTER DATABASE CHECKPOINT;
```

4.	Recheck the status of the online redo log group you wish to drop:

```
SQL> SELECT group#, sequence#, status FROM v$log WHERE group#=1;
    GROUP# SEQUENCE# STATUS
---------- --------- ----------------
         1       119 INACTIVE
```

Step	Action

5. Wait until the log file group has been archived. You can check the V$ARCHIVED_LOG view to ensure that the sequence number has been archived:
```
SQL> SELECT sequence#, status FROM v$archived_log WHERE sequence#=119;
SEQUENCE# S
--------- -
      119 A
```

6. Drop the logfile group with the **alter database** command:
```
ALTER DATABASE DROP LOGFILE GROUP 1;
```

7. Check the V$LOG view again to ensure that the log file has been removed:
```
SQL> SELECT group#, status FROM v$log WHERE group#=1;
no rows selected
```

8. Physically remove the dropped online redo logs from your disk system. They are no longer needed.

Dropping an Online Redo Log Group Member

Dropping an online redo log member requires the use of the **alter database** command with the **drop logfile member** clause. Here is an example:

```
ALTER DATABASE DROP LOGFILE MEMBER
'c:\oracle\oradata\mydb\mydb_logfile_4_1_a.log';
```

Resizing Online Redo Logs

Resizing the online redo logs takes two steps. First, you must drop the online redo log that you wish to resize, because Oracle does not make provisions to resize an online redo log group directly. Once you have dropped the online redo log group that you want to resize, then re-create it. Directions for both the removal and re-creation of online redo logs are supplied in the previous sections.

Clearing an Online Redo Log

When you are in ARCHIVELOG mode, there are some rare occasions in which Oracle tries to archive an online redo log and is unsuccessful. Often this is because the data in the online redo log itself is corrupted. In this event, you need to clear the online redo log via the **alter database clear logfile group** command, as shown in this example:

```
ALTER DATABASE CLEAR LOGFILE GROUP 1;
```

In this case, one or more of the log files assigned to group 1 may be corrupt and cannot be archived. This command clears the log file. You should perform a backup immediately after executing the **alter database clear logfile** command because you will have a gap in your archived redo logs and will not be able to recover to any point beyond the time of the missing redo.

Monitoring Online Redo Logs

You need to monitor your online redo logs to make sure that they are working in the most efficient manner. Oracle provides several views to assist you in this effort, including the following:

- **V$LOGFILE**   Provides the status of the online redo log files themselves. This includes information such as the name of the online redo log and the group it is assigned to.

- **V$LOG**   Provides information about online redo log groups such as the status of the group with respect to its use in Oracle (e.g., if it is the current online redo log or if it's in an active or inactive state). This view also gives you the size of the online redo log, the number of members in the group, the log sequence number, and other like information.

- **V$LOG_HISTORY**   Provides you with history information about the online redo logs. For example, this view allows you to determine the frequency of log switches at various times during the day.

Archived Redo Logs

Chapter 2 covered ARCHIVELOG mode and archived redo logs. If the Oracle ARCH process is enabled and the database is in ARCHIVELOG mode, the ARCH process will copy the current online redo log to one of a number of archivelog destination directories after a log switch occurs. See Chapter 2 for more information on configuring ARCHIVELOG mode and enabling the use of archived redo logs.

NOTE
Failure to configure your database in ARCHIVELOG mode can result in the unexpected suspension of database activities.

Oracle Errors Associated with Online Redo Logs

A number of redo log–related errors might be encountered in Oracle. Many of the redo log–oriented operations listed above may suffer from the same errors, so I have consolidated the error list here. The following table lists a number of these errors and provides some resolution guidance:

Oracle Error Message	Text Description	Possible Causes and Solutions
ORA-1571	Redo version incompatible with Oracle version	This error may indicate that you have started your database with the incorrect version of Oracle, and some form of recovery is required. This can occur if you start a migration without shutting down the database in a normal fashion (e.g., by using **shutdown abort**).
ORA-1184	Logfile group already exists	You have tried to add an online redo logfile group that already exists.
ORA-0301	Error adding log file...file cannot be created	An error stack that clarifies the nature of the error will follow this error.
ORA-17610	File does not exist and no size specified	You have tried to create an online redo log but did not define a size for that log file. Oracle will not generate this error if an unused log file with the logfile name is used, or if OMF is in use.
ORA-1185 ORA-0302	Logfile group number is invalid or Limit of logs exceeded	You have exceeded the logfile group number ceiling established when you created your database. The parameter **maxlogfiles** defines the maximum number to be assigned to any logfile group.
ORA-1566	File specified more than once in drop logfile	You duplicated an online redo logfile name in the **drop logfile** statement. Remove the duplicate and try again.

Oracle Error Message	Text Description	Possible Causes and Solutions
ORA-1900	Logfile keyword expected	You didn't use the **logfile** keyword. Make sure you didn't use **log file** (with a space) instead!
ORA-0344	Unable to re-create online log	This error generally occurs either during a **resetlogs** operation or when the **alter database clear logfile** command is issued. Check to see if the directory that the log file is to be written to exists and that the correct permissions are set on it.
ORA-0302	Limit of logs exceeded	The maximum number of redo logs has been exceeded. You need to re-create the control file and increase the **maxlogfiles** parameter.
ORA-0357	Too many members specified for logfile	You have tried to add online redo log members and the operation would result in too many members being created. Retry the operation using fewer redo logfile members.
ORA-0359	Logfile group does not exist	The logfile group that you are trying to drop or add a member to does not exist.
ORA-0360	Not a logfile member	You have tried to drop an online redo logfile member that does not exist.
ORA-0361	Cannot remove last log member for group	You have tried to remove the last logfile member from a group. Drop the logfile group instead.

CHAPTER
4

Tablespaces

his chapter is about tablespaces. We first review what tablespaces are and what kinds of tablespaces there are in the Oracle Database world. Then we cover the various commands used with tablespaces: **create tablespace**, **alter tablespace**, and **drop tablespace**. Next, we look at errors that are commonly found when using tablespaces. Finally, we review some suggested naming standards to be applied when you create your tablespaces.

About Oracle Tablespaces

Tablespaces are where the logical world of the Oracle database meets the physical world of the operating system. Oracle databases store objects (tables, indexes, etc.) in tablespaces. There are different kinds of tablespaces in Oracle databases. There are smallfile tablespaces (the default tablespace type in all versions), bigfile tablespaces (available in Oracle Database 10*g* and later), temporary tablespaces, and undo tablespaces. In this section, we look at what a tablespace is and how it is physically constructed, and then we review the individual tablespace types.

The Oracle Tablespace

Oracle database tablespaces are a central structure in the Oracle Database landscape. They provide the place to store data, and limit the amount of data that can be stored. In this section, we look at a general overview of what tablespaces are first. We then look into the database data file and see how it relates to a tablespace. Finally, we review smallfile and bigfile tablespaces.

Overview of Oracle Tablespaces

A tablespace in an Oracle database provides the mechanism to store the data that the database engine manages. When you create objects such as tables and indexes, you define which tablespace they are created in (or they are allocated a default tablespace), as shown in this simple example:

```
CREATE TABLE MYTABLE(id number) TABLESPACE my_tbs
STORAGE (INITIAL 100m NEXT 100m);
```

In this example, the MYTABLE table is created and assigned to the tablespace MY_TBS. The Oracle database will attempt to allocate 100MB of storage from the MY_TBS tablespace for the creation of this object, thus the tablespace must have at least that much space available or this statement will fail. This also implies that space for objects within a tablespace is preallocated before that object is used.

The typical Oracle database contains several tablespaces. The most commonly found are the following:

Tablespace Name	Required	Purpose
SYSTEM	Y	Stores system objects
SYSAUX	Y (in Oracle Database 10*g* only)	Stores ancillary Oracle database schema objects such as the RMAN recovery catalog
USERS	N	Typical default tablespace assigned to all users
RBS	N	For manual rollback segments

Tablespace Name	Required	Purpose
UNDO	N (an UNDO tablespace is required if automated undo is used)	For automated undo segments
DATA	N	Used to store data
INDEX	N	Used to store indexes
TOOLS	N	Used to store schema objects for DBA-related tools

Tablespaces can be read-write in nature, or they can be made read-only. Read-only tablespaces are particularly useful in data warehouse environments, when the data in the tablespace is static. In this event, you can make the tablespace read-only and back it up. After that backup, there is no reoccurring need to back up that tablespace again.

In Oracle8*i* and Oracle9*i* Database, tablespaces can be transported between different databases through the transportable tablespace functionality. Various restrictions exist that vary by database version, with later versions being less restrictive. Transportable tablespaces can be very handy when moving data between an online transaction processing (OLTP) tablespace and a data warehouse, for example.

Oracle Database 10*g* removes a principle restriction that has previously existed on transportable tablespaces: you now can move tablespaces between most operating systems, which further enhances the usability of this database feature. In some cases, the tablespace set can be directly moved to the other hardware platform, whereas in other cases it may need to undergo conversion using RMAN. Check your OS-specific Oracle database documentation to determine what your specific platform requires.

While each database has a standard block size, Oracle9*i* Database and later allows you to create a tablespace with a block size other than the default block size. This can be useful when you need to transport tablespaces between databases of two different block sizes. See the "create tablespace Examples" section later in this chapter for an example of the creation of a tablespace with a nondefault block size.

The basic building block of the tablespace is the data file. In the next section we will look at the Oracle database datafile in more detail.

The Oracle Database Data File

The space allocated to tablespaces comes from the database data files that are either initially allocated to the tablespace during the execution of the **create tablespace** or are added later via the **alter tablespace** command. At least one data file must be defined when the tablespace is created. The overall available storage space, then, is the summed size of all the data files associated with that tablespace. The maximum number of data files that you can allocate to a tablespace is constrained by the OS and the version of Oracle database that you are running.

As the data files are allocated on the disk, the space in the database data files is then logically subdivided into database blocks. When an object is created, space in the form of one or more extents is allocated from the free space in the tablespace. Each extent comprises a collection of consecutive blocks within a single data file, thus extents themselves cannot span database data files. When an object is created, the size of its initial extent is defined with the **initial** parameter, and subsequent extent allocations are defined using the **next** parameter.

Space in data files underlying a tablespace is initially preallocated, so once you define those data files, physical space will be utilized on your devices. Adding space to a tablespace is as easy as adding additional data files, or resizing the existing data files so that they are larger. Of course, the available space in a tablespace can quickly fill, sometimes quicker than a DBA has time to respond. In most cases, if the tablespace fills up, the database fails the operation and returns an error to the user.

NOTE
Temporary tablespaces are a bit different in nature, as will be discussed later in this chapter in "Temporary Tablespaces."

You can avoid problematic tablespace space exhaustion by enabling the **autoextend** option for the data files associated with that tablespace. The **autoextend** option allows the database to dynamically resize individual data files. This is particularly important in production, where outages and error messages are not desirable.

If using **autoextend** does not appeal to you, another solution to the space exhaustion might be resumable space management (see Chapter 13). This feature causes the session that has run out of space to pause for a predefined length of time, allowing the DBA to dynamically add space to the tablespace.

You can resize data files to make them smaller, but you cannot reduce any data file beyond the last object-assigned block. Thus, if the data file is 1GB in size, and the last block fills the data file at the 500MB mark (data files are generally filled from the first block to the last block in sequential order), you can resize that data file only down to the 500MB mark, and no more.

Tablespaces come in different forms. First, there are bigfile and smallfile tablespaces. Also, you can create either dictionary-managed tablespaces or locally managed tablespaces. Additionally, you can create temporary tablespaces and undo tablespaces. Let's look at these different tablespace types in more detail.

Bigfile and Smallfile Tablespaces   Oracle database tablespaces come in two different flavors. The smallfile tablespace is the default tablespace flavor in Oracle Database 10*g*, and the only kind of tablespace available in earlier Oracle Database versions. The smallfile tablespace is created via the standard **create tablespace** command. A smallfile tablespace can include up to 1022 data files (in Oracle Database 10*g*), and the maximum size is constrained such that each data file can only contain 4,194,303 million blocks. Thus, the maximum size that a smallfile tablespace can grow to is based on the database block size, the maximum number of data files, and operating system restrictions. The following chart demonstrates the limitations of smallfile tablespaces based on the database block size:

Database Block Size	Storage Capacity of a Single Smallfile Tablespace
4K	16GB
8K	32GB
16K	64GB
32K	128GB

The second type of Oracle database tablespace, only available in Oracle Database 10*g*, is the bigfile tablespace. This tablespace type is also created using the **create tablespace** command, using the **bigfile** clause if the bigfile tablespace is not the default tablespace type. A bigfile tablespace only allows a single data file, but the single data file assigned to a bigfile tablespace can contain up to four million million blocks. This allows for a single bigfile tablespace to store much more data than a smallfile tablespace. The following table lists the storage capacity of a bigfile tablespace based on the block size:

Block Size	Storage Capacity of a Single Bigfile Tablespace
4K	16TB
8K	32TB
16K	64TB
32K	128TB

When you are creating an Oracle Database under Oracle Database 10g, you can define the default tablespace type for the database as smallfile or bigfile (the default is smallfile).

Dictionary-Managed Tablespaces   Dictionary-managed tablespaces were the only type of tablespace available in early Oracle Database versions. As the name suggests, dictionary-managed tablespaces use the data dictionary to manage space within the tablespace. This results in increased recursive SQL activities during database operations. For example, if a new extent is added to a table during database operations, the result is both data dictionary activity and undo generation, which has performance impacts on the database and can also make certain operations take a long time (like **truncate** operations on tables with many extents). In Oracle database versions prior to Oracle9i Release 2, the SYSTEM tablespace had to be dictionary managed. In version 9.2 and later the SYSTEM tablespace can be locally managed, as discussed next.

Locally Managed Tablespaces   Oracle8i Database introduced locally managed tablespaces, which work just like dictionary-managed tablespaces except that they track all extent information in the tablespace itself, using bitmaps in the datafile headers. Locally managed tablespaces eliminate the need for most data dictionary operations during tablespace space operations, thereby speeding up tablespace-related operations, reducing the overhead of those operations, and making certain Oracle database features, such as transportable tablespaces, possible. As of Oracle9i Release 2, the Database Creation Assistant creates the SYSTEM tablespace as a locally managed tablespace by default.

Temporary Tablespaces

Temporary tablespaces are used for the creation of temporary objects, such as sort segments. Temporary tablespaces can be created using either normal database data files or database tempfiles, and they can be either dictionary managed or locally managed. The following table provides some guidance into the creation of temporary tablespaces:

Tablespace Management Method	Creation Command/Clause	Allows Other Objects	Data Files or Tempfiles
Dictionary	**create tablespace**	Yes	Data files
Dictionary	**create tablespace** using the **temporary** clause	No	Data files
Locally (recommended)	**create temporary tablespace**	No	Tempfiles

One of the benefits of locally managed temporary tablespaces is that you do not need to back up or recover the physical files (tempfiles) associated with that tablespace. Rather, you just re-create the temporary files when you recover the database. Since temporary tablespaces tend to be large, this can reduce the overall time for backup and recovery.

Undo Tablespaces

Oracle9i Database makes automated undo available, replacing the traditional rollback segment. In order to use this feature, you must create an undo tablespace for the Oracle database to use. You do this via the **create undo tablespace** command. Undo tablespaces must be backed up, just as any regular tablespace should be.

Once the undo tablespace is created, you need to configure the database to use automated undo management. The following parameters are used to configure this feature:

Parameter	Default/Other Options	Purpose
undo_tablespace	The first available undo tablespace in the system/Any valid undo tablespace	Defines the undo tablespace assigned to the database
undo_retention	900/Any valid value up to the maximum value represented by 32 bits	Defines how long the database will attempt to keep undo in the database to allow for generation of read-consistent images and flashback query
undo_suppress_errors	False/True (this parameter is obsolete in Oracle Database 10g)	Causes the database to suppress errors that may be generated by space-management transactions when automated undo is enabled
undo_management	Manual/Auto	Defines the method of undo management used in the database

Creating Tablespaces

Use the **create tablespace** command to create tablespaces within your Oracle database. When you create a tablespace, one or more data files is generally defined and created. If you have configured and are using the Oracle Managed Files (OMF) feature, which is available in Oracle9i Database and later, you can choose not to define the data files and the database will perform that function for you automatically. Additionally, when using OMF you can have the database size the data files, using OMF sizing defaults.

You can also define the minimum size of any extent created within a locally managed tablespace via the **minimum_extent_clause**. This can be very helpful when you want to avoid freespace-fragmentation issues.

When you create a tablespace, you can define default settings for the tablespace. Once you create default settings, objects being created in the tablespace take on those default characteristics, unless the default setting are overridden manually. In addition to storage parameters, configurable tablespace default settings include the following (the default values are underlined):

■ **Force Logging** Used to cause objects to default to a force logging setting, when they are created. This should be configured if you are using database features like Data Guard.

- **Logging or nologging**   Indicates that, by default, objects in the tablespace should take on **logging** or **nologging** attributes. Setting this default impacts redo generation during certain database operations on those objects. This also impacts the recoverability of objects in that tablespace, if they take on that default characteristic, so use this cautiously.

- **Compress or nocompress**   This setting is used to indicate whether or not objects within the tablespace should, by default, use Oracle compression.

Two other clauses are also available in the Oracle database that define the type of tablespace being created and the nature of the objects being created within that tablespace. These clauses are **extent_management_clause** and **segment_management_clause**. Let's look at those in a bit more detail next.

extent_management_clause

The **extent_management_clause** allows you to define how extents are to be managed in a given tablespace. The Oracle database offers two options, **dictionary** and **local**. Use the **dictionary** keyword if you want the segment space within the tablespace to be managed within the data dictionary. This is the default in Oracle8*i* Database and is the default in Oracle9*i* Database if the **compatible** initialization parameter is set to less than 9.0.0.

If you use the **local** keyword, the database creates the tablespace as a locally managed tablespace. With locally managed tablespaces, all segment space is managed internally within the tablespace itself. Locally managed tablespaces can have positive impacts on performance of segment space operations such as adding new extents or adding new objects to the tablespace. Locally managed tablespaces are optional in Oracle8*i* Database and are the default in Oracle9*i* Database. One tablespace that cannot be locally managed until Oracle Database 9*i* Release 2 is the SYSTEM tablespace. Also, if the SYSTEM tablespace is locally managed, the use of dictionary-managed tablespaces is precluded.

When creating locally managed tablespaces, you must choose between two extent-allocation options: **uniform** or **autoallocate**. Choosing the **uniform** space-management option causes the database to create equi-sized segments of a size defined via the **size** parameter when the tablespace is created, or 1MB if the **size** parameter is not defined. Uniform space management eliminates freespace-fragmentation issues that can arise when nonuniform extent sizes are used.

If you choose the **autoallocate** space-management option, the database makes all of your space-management decisions for you. The database manages all extent sizing and ignores any user-defined settings.

If the **extent_management_clause** *is not used*, then the database defaults come into play. To determine which defaults must come into play, the database uses the following parameters to define the **extent_management_clause**:

- **Compatible**

- The **minimum_extent_clause** setting of the **create tablespace** command

- The **default_storage_clause** setting of the **create tablespace** command

In Oracle9*i* Database, the database creates a locally managed tablespace of type **autoallocate** by default, if there is no storage clause. The following table sets forth the conditions that define the default locally managed tablespace type:

Compatible, Storage Clause, and Parameter Settings in the create tablespace Command	Result in This Tablespace Type
Compatible setting (or database version) < 9.0	Dictionary managed
Database > 9*i* No storage clause and compatible >= 9.0	Locally managed autoallocate
Minimum extent = Initial = next and pctincrease=0	Uniform with uniform size set to initial
Initial=next and pctincrease =0	Uniform with uniform size set to initial
Initial != next or pctincrease!=0	Autoallocate

You need to consider a few other things. If you configure the **extent_management_clause** to **local uniform**, then you must ensure that each extent contains at least five database blocks. If the database block size is larger than 16K and you set the **extent_management_clause** to **local autoallocate**, then the database will create extents with a minimum size of five blocks, and rounded up to 64K.

segment_management_clause

Space management for objects within a permanent, locally managed tablespace can be defined in a couple of different ways. The first method, which is the default, uses the data dictionary to manage space within the object. The second method, available since the beginning of Oracle9*i* Database, is known as automatic segment space management (ASSM). ASSM lets you specify whether the database should track the used and free space in the segments in the tablespace using free lists or bitmaps.

The **segment_management_clause** allows you to define the type of segment management for the tablespace. All objects in that tablespace will be defined using either manual or automatic segment space management (ASSM) as the method of managing space within a given segment.

Security Requirements

To create a tablespace, the database should be open and operational. The account you are using to create the tablespace must have the **create tablespace** privilege. Additionally, the directories that the database data files are to be created in should be able to be written to by the database process. To see if the user you are logged in to has the **create tablespace** privilege, issue the following query, replacing USER_NAME with the name of the user who will be issuing the **create tablespace** command:

```
SELECT grantee, privilege FROM dba_sys_privs
WHERE privilege = 'CREATE TABLESPACE' AND grantee='USER_NAME';
```

Once a tablespace is created, you must grant users access to that tablespace. You do this by assigning a quota to the user via the **create user** or **alter user** command. You can assign a quota of any amount:

```
ALTER USER TED QUOTA 100M ON DATA
```

Or, you can assign an unlimited quota if you prefer:

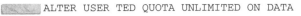

ALTER USER TED QUOTA UNLIMITED ON DATA

Alternatively, you can assign the system privilege **unlimited tablespace** to any user who needs unfettered access to all tablespaces.

NOTE
To use a nonsystem tablespace, you must have a rollback segment enabled beyond the SYSTEM rollback segment or have automated undo configured and enabled.

About OMF

Oracle Managed Files (OMF) is a feature that is available in Oracle9*i* Database and later that transitions much of the Oracle database file-management functions from the DBA to the database kernel. The DBA simply defines the directories that the files are to be created in via a database parameter, and the database takes care of the creation of the files. Further, OMF removes OMF data files associated with tablespaces when those tablespaces are dropped. The following table lists the parameters associated with OMF:

Parameter Name	Purpose
db_create_file_dest	Defines the directory in which to create database data files. If **db_create_online_log_dest** is not set, this directory is also the location in which all the online redo logs and the control file are created.
db_create_online_log_dest_*n*	Defines the directory in which to create the online redo logs and the database control files. You can define up to five different OMF file locations using this parameter. In this event, one member of each online redo log group will be created in each directory, and one copy of the control file will be created in each directory.

autoextend

The Oracle database preallocates space for data in the form of the database data files. Sometimes, however, the database grows at a rapid pace and the database data files fill up. If a space deficit occurs within a tablespace, Oracle sends an error to the user and fails the transaction, unless you have enabled the data files to use the **autoextend** functionality.

The **autoextend** option is available so that the database can dynamically expand those database data files as needed. Each data file has **autoextend** enabled or disabled, as you see fit. Through the use of the following parameters, you can control the growth and overall sizing of the data file:

- **next**   Defines how much additional space should be added each time the file requires an extension operation.

- **maxsize**   Allows you to define a maximum size that the data file should not exceed when extending. Once a data file has reached its **maxsize** threshold, it autoextends no more unless you adjust that threshold.

create tablespace Examples

This first example is the most elemental of tablespace creations. It assumes that OMF is configured.

```
CREATE TABLESPACE tbs;
```

This results in the creation of a tablespace called TBS, which will be created using OMF, if this is configured. If OMF is not configured or if this statement is run in Oracle Database versions prior to 9*i*, then this statement will fail.

The following example is the more typical **create tablespace** statement:

```
CREATE TABLESPACE tbs
DATAFILE '/ora100/oracle/mydb/mydb_tbs_01.dbf' SIZE 100m;
```

This example also creates a tablespace called TBS. The database will create a data file for the tablespace called mydb_tbs_01.dbf that will be 100MB in size. This tablespace takes on no defined storage characteristics, so the Oracle database defaults will be applied. These defaults vary based on the version of the database and the type of tablespace being created.

The next example creates a tablespace and causes the creation of two different data files during that process:

```
CREATE TABLESPACE tbs
DATAFILE '/ora100/oracle/mydb/mydb_tbs_01.dbf' SIZE 100m,
         '/ora200/oracle/mydb/mydb_tbs_01.dbf' SIZE 100m;
```

The next example creates a dictionary-managed tablespace and sets some tablespace default values for various parameters:

```
CREATE TABLESPACE tbs EXTENT MANAGEMENT DICTIONARY
STORAGE (INITIAL 100k NEXT 100k)
DATAFILE '/ora100/oracle/mydb/mydb_tbs_01.dbf' SIZE 100m;
```

NOTE
You cannot create a dictionary-managed tablespace if your system tablespace is locally managed!

In the preceding example, we defined default values for **initial** and **next** and used the **extent_management_clause** to define this as a dictionary-managed tablespace.

The following example demonstrates the creation of a locally managed tablespace using the uniform extent-allocation model:

```
CREATE TABLESPACE tbs EXTENT MANAGEMENT LOCAL UNIFORM 1M
STORAGE (INITIAL 2000K NEXT 1000K)
DATAFILE '/ora100/oracle/mydb/mydb_tbs_01.dbf' SIZE 100m;
```

In the final example, we need to create a tablespace with a block size that is smaller than the default block size of 16K. We need to do this so that we can transport tablespaces into our 16K data warehouse from our OLTP system that has 8K blocks. We first define an 8K memory cache in the database parameter file using the **db_8k_cache_size** parameter, as shown here:

```
DB_8K_CACHE_SIZE=100m
```

If we were using an SPFILE, we could also alter this parameter via the **alter system** command, and even dynamically configure the cache if memory were available to do so:

```
ALTER SYSTEM SET DB_8K_CACHE_SIZE=100M SCOPE=BOTH;
```

Finally, we create the tablespace, indicating via the **blocksize** parameter that it should be created with a nondefault 8K block size:

```
CREATE TABLESPACE oltp_import
BLOCKSIZE 8K
EXTENT MANAGEMENT LOCAL UNIFORM SIZE 10M
DATAFILE '/ora100/oracle/mydb/mydb_oltp_import_01.dbf' size 100m;
```

To enable a user to use space in the tablespaces that we have created, we would assign the user a quota:

```
ALTER USER ted QUOTA 100M ON users;
```

Altering Tablespaces

Managing tablespaces after they are created is accomplished with the **alter tablespace** command, with which you can do the following:

- Add data files to an existing tablespace

- Rename existing data files and tempfiles

- Add a tempfile to an existing temporary tablespace

- Modify default tablespace settings such as storage clause settings, minimum extent settings, and data compression settings

- Take a tablespace online or offline

- Put the tablespace in hot backup mode or take it out of hot backup mode

- Make the tablespace read-only or read-write

- Modify the tablespace to force logging

Security Requirements

The **alter tablespace** command is subject to two different system privileges. The lesser of these privileges is the **manage tablespace** privilege, which allows only the following operations:

- Take the tablespace online or offline

- Begin or end a backup of the tablespace

- Make the tablespace read-only or read-write

The **alter tablespace** system privilege allows the user to execute any **alter tablespace** command. To see which, if any, privileges your username has with regard to the **alter tablespace** command, issue the following query, replacing USER_NAME with the name of the user who will be issuing the **drop tablespace** command:

```
SELECT grantee, privilege FROM dba_sys_privs
WHERE privilege IN ('ALTER TABLESPACE', 'MANAGE TABLESPACE')
AND grantee='USER_NAME'
```

alter tablespace Examples

In the first example, we are going to add a data file to our tablespace:

```
ALTER TABLESPACE mytbs
ADD DATAFILE '/ora100/oracle/mydb/mydb_mytbs_01.dbf' SIZE 100M;
```

Note that we have defined the datafile name and size. If we had OMF enabled, we could perform the statement in this manner:

```
ALTER TABLESPACE mytbs ADD DATAFILE;
```

Or, if we wanted to define a size other than the default size (100MB) for the data file, we might do this:

```
ALTER TABLESPACE mytbs ADD DATAFILE SIZE 500M;
```

If you want to perform an online backup of a specific tablespace (or a set of tablespaces), you would want to put the tablespace in hot backup mode using the **alter tablespace** command as shown here:

```
ALTER TABLESPACE mytbs BEGIN BACKUP;
```

At this point, you could back up all the data files that are associated with the tablespace. Once the backup is complete, end the backup of the tablespace as shown here:

```
ALTER TABLESPACE mytbs END BACKUP;
```

Remember that you need to back up all the redo generated during this backup in order to be able to restore it.

In the event of a recovery situation, you may want to take a tablespace offline to perform the recovery. This is also done via the **alter tablespace** command:

```
ALTER TABLESPACE mytbs OFFLINE;
```

And to bring it back online:

```
RECOVER TABLESPACE mytbs;
ALTER TABLESPACE mytbs ONLINE;
```

Read-only tablespaces are commonly found in data-warehouse operations. To make a tablespace read-only, simply use the **alter tablespace** command as shown here:

```
ALTER TABLESPACE mytbs READ ONLY;
```

You want to back up the tablespace after all pending transactions in the tablespace have completed. Once you have backed up a read-only tablespace, there is little need to ever back it up again (except to provide for some media redundancy, since media does fail from time to time). Often, tablespaces that have been made read-only will be moved to other, longer-term media. This may require that you rename the data files associated with the tablespace using the **alter database rename file** command.

Should you wish to return the tablespace to read-write mode, a simple SQL statement is all that is needed:

```
ALTER TABLESPACE mytbs READ WRITE;
```

Dropping Tablespaces

When it's time to get rid of those old, unused tablespaces, you use the **drop tablespace** command. The **drop tablespace** command, without any additional clauses, removes an empty tablespace. If the tablespace was created via OMF, then the database removes the associated data files as well. If the tablespace was not created via OMF, then the data files are left in place unless you used the **including contents and datafiles** clause.

The **including contents** keywords indicate to the database that it's okay to drop the tablespace, even if it has objects in it as long as those objects are not active rollback segments. The database will not prompt you to make sure that you want to perform this action, so use **including contents** with care. Additionally, affix the **and datafiles** keywords to the **including contents** clause (Oracle9*i* Database and later) to cause the database to remove all data files from your operating system that are associated with the tablespace.

Finally, if you have tables in tablespaces outside the tablespace to be dropped that have references to objects within the tablespace you are dropping, you need to use the **cascade constraints** clause. The **cascade constraints** clause drops all referential integrity constraints from tables that are outside the tablespace you are dropping that reference primary and unique keys of the tables inside the tablespace you are dropping. Failure to use this clause in the event that referential integrity relationships are defined between objects within the tablespace to be dropped and other tablespaces will result in an error being generated.

Security Requirements

To use the **drop tablespace** command, you must have the **drop tablespace** system privilege. To see if you have that privilege, issue the following query, replacing USER_NAME with the name of the user who will be issuing the **drop tablespace** command:

```
SELECT grantee, privilege FROM dba_sys_privs
WHERE privilege = 'DROP TABLESPACE' AND grantee='USER_NAME'
```

drop tablespace Examples

The first example drops the tablespace MYTBS. In this case, the tablespace cannot contain any database objects or an error will appear.

```
DROP TABLESPACE mytbs;
```

Here, we drop the MYTBS tablespace and remove any objects that might be contained in it:

```
DROP TABLESPACE mytbs INCLUDING CONTENTS;
```

Next, we drop the MYTBS tablespace, removing any objects that might be contained in it. We also remove the database data files associated with that tablespace.

```
DROP TABLESPACE mytbs INCLUDING CONTENTS AND DATAFILES;
```

In this final example, we remove the tablespace, including all contents and all data files, and make sure that if there are any constraints between objects within and without the tablespace, they are removed as well:

```
DROP TABLESPACE mytbs INCLUDING CONTENTS AND DATAFILES CASCADE CONSTRAINTS;
```

Tablespace Data Dictionary Information

The Oracle database provides several different views that provide information on Oracle database tablespaces. The following table provides some details on these views, as well as information on the availability of the all and user varieties (e.g. **all_tablespaces** and **user_tablespaces**) of these views:

View Name	Description	All	User
DBA_TABLESPACES	Provides a list of all tablespaces in the database and the default settings associated with those tablespaces.	N	Y
DBA_DATA_FILES	Lists all data files associated with a given tablespace, including their location and configurations.	N	N

View Name	Description	All	User
DBA_SEGMENTS	Lists all segments (table, index, etc.) in the database, the segment type, and each segment's tablespace assignment.	N	Y
DBA_EXTENTS	Lists all extents in the table and the tablespace they are assigned to.	N	Y
V$TABLESPACE	Lists the tablespace number and name. This view is available when the database is mounted.	N/A	N/A
V$DATAFILE	Lists all database data files and the tablespace number that each data file is associated with. This view is available when the database is mounted.	N/A	N/A

Tablespace-Related Errors

As you manage tablespaces, you may run into various database errors. The following table lists the most common errors and provides some advice as to what to do in the event you run into those errors.

Oracle Error Message	Text Description	Possible Causes and Solutions
ORA-01119	Error in creating database file	Generally followed by other error messages (ORA-17610, for example) that provide more insight into the problem. When you get an ORA-01119 error message, check the following: • The file system and directory in which you are creating the data files actually exists. • You have access rights to the file system and directory where you are creating the data files. • There is sufficient space on the file system to write the data file.
ORA-1523 ORA-1537	Cannot add datafile – file already part of database	You tried to add a data file that already exists in the database. Often this is the result of cut and paste errors in SQL script files. Correct the datafile name and re-execute the statement. This message also appears if you try to use a file that belongs to a tablespace in another database.
ORA-00959	Tablespace does not exist	You tried to alter or drop a tablespace that does not exist. Check the tablespace name (reference DBA_TABLESPACES) and then try again.
ORA-00972	Identifier is too long	You tried to create a tablespace with a name that is too long. Reduce the name to 30 characters or less and try again.
ORA-02237	Invalid file size	You indicated an incorrect file size when trying to create your tablespace data files.

Oracle Error Message	Text Description	Possible Causes and Solutions
ORA-01144	File size exceeds maximum	The file size of the data file you are trying to create is too large. The size of an Oracle database data file is limited to the **db_block_size** parameter times 4,194,303 blocks. Refer to the tables in the "Bigfile and Smallfile Tablespaces" section earlier in this chapter for information on how big any given tablespace can be. If you must have larger data files, then you can either re-create the database with a larger block size or create the tablespace with a nondefault block size. Another option, if you are using Oracle Database 10g, is to create a bigfile tablespace.
ORA-29339	Tablespace block size does not match configured block sizes	You tried to create a tablespace using a specific nondefault block size. The statement is failing because you do not have a memory cache created that matches the block size for the tablespace you are trying to create.
ORA-00409	Compatible needs to be higher to use auto segment space management	You have not reset your **compatible** parameter before trying to use the ASSM feature of the Oracle database.
ORA-1123	Cannot start online backup; media recovery not enabled	You tried to issue an **alter tablespace begin backup** command but the database is in NOARCHIVELOG mode. The database must be in ARCHIVELOG mode to perform online backups.
ORA-1520	Number of data files to add exceeds limit	You tried to add more data files than allowed. This is a limit of the **maxdatafiles** parameter used when you created the database. You need to resize existing data files, add fewer data files, or re-create the control file.
ORA-1522	File to be renamed does not exist	You tried to rename a data file and the data file being renamed does not exist.
ORA-1533	Cannot rename file; file does not belong to tablespace	You tried to rename a file with the **alter tablespace** command but the file you listed does not belong to the tablespace.

Tablespace Naming Standards

All tablespaces should be named in such a way that the name describes the purpose of the tablespace or its association with the data within the tablespace. For example, if the tablespace contains data for an application called *trend*, you might call the tablespace TREND_DATA.

Often, DBAs create tablespaces for small-, medium-, and large-sized objects. In this case, you might call the trend application tablespaces TREND_SMALL, TREND_MEDIUM, and TREND_LARGE.

Another time that tablespace naming standards come into play is when they are used to store partitioned objects. A table or index can be partitioned into a number of different tablespaces. While it is common to use an intelligent naming schema for tablespace partitions, I prefer to use a nonintelligent solution. For example, if I am keeping 30 rolling partitions in 30 different tablespaces, I will name my tablespaces TREND_PART_01 to TREND_PART_30. This makes rolling partitions in and out of a given tablespace much easier. When I roll a partition, I just truncate the oldest partition of the table and then begin to write into the newly truncated partition (after I move any pertinent overflow data into it). Of course, your naming and partitioning strategy will have to take many different factors into account, which are beyond the scope of this book.

Datafile Naming Standards

I recommend that you name your data files using the following naming convention:

dddd_nnnnn_##.dbf

where:

- *dddd* is the name of the database.

- *nnnnn* is the name of the tablespace the data file is associated with.

- *##* is a monotonically increasing number that makes the data file unique for that tablespace.

   For example, a tablespace called DATA_LARGE in a database called perts would have data files that look as follows:

- perts_data_large_01.dbf

- perts_data_large_02.dbf

CHAPTER
5

Tables

ou built your Oracle database to store data. Tables are where that data gets stored. You create a table with the **create table** statement. In that statement you define the characteristics of that table. These characteristics include

- Characteristics of the table such as column names, data types, datatype storage, and precision specifications

- Storage specifications related to the overall table

- Constraints related to the table

- Properties associated with the table

- Any partitioning specifications associated with the table

- Associating special features with the table such as compression or disabling logging

In this chapter, we first cover some basic information about tables, including a review of the various Oracle database data types. We then review the different kinds of tables. Finally, we look at table-related information such as constraints, properties, and the **storage** clause.

Oracle Data Types

Each relational table in an Oracle database is made up of a number of columns. Each column is assigned a specific data type that defines the kinds of data stored in that column. The following table lists the principle data types that you will find in Oracle databases. Selected notes on some data types are provided in the next section.

Datatype Name	Description	Example
CHAR	Stores up to 2000 characters, or bytes, in fixed-length format. The default is to define the storage in characters. This data type is fixed length and pads blanks to the right.	`CREATE TABLE test` `(name char(20) )`
VARCHAR and VARCHAR2	Store up to 4000 bytes in a variable-length format, thus there is no blank padding. VARCHAR2 is preferred to VARCHAR, which remains in Oracle databases for compatibility reasons.	`CREATE TABLE test` `(name varchar2(20))`

NCHAR	This national language support (NLS) data type can store Unicode-only character sets as defined by the database NLS character set. It can hold up to 2000 bytes. NCHAR columns are blank-padded to the right.	`CREATE TABLE test`
		`(name Nchar(20) )`
		
		Note: This is a Unicode-only data type in Oracle9i Database and later.

Datatype Name	Description	Example

NVARCHAR2	The NLS equivalent of a VARCHAR2 data type. This data type holds up to 4000 bytes.	`CREATE TABLE test`
		`(name Nvarchar2(20))`
		
		Note: This is a Unicode-only data type in Oracle9i Database and later.

NUMBER	Stores zero, positive, and negative fixed and floating-point numbers.
	NUMBER data types allow you to define a level of precision and scale to the number in the format
	    NUMBER(p,s)
	where:
	p is the precision (1–38), which is the total number of digits that can be stored in the column.
	s is the scale, which is the number of digits to the right of the decimal. The scale can range from –84 to 127.
		`CREATE TABLE test`
		`(name number(5) )`
		Defines an integer with a precision of 5. (e.g., 12345).
		`CREATE TABLE test`
		`(name number(5,2) )`
		Defines a number with a precision of 5 and a scale of 2. Examples of value numbers in this data type are 123.45 and 12.34.

LONG	LONG columns store variable-length character strings containing up to 2GB. LONG columns have many of the characteristics of VARCHAR2 columns. You can use LONG columns to store LONG text strings. The LONG data type is provided for backward compatibility; it is recommended that you use the LOB data types instead.	`CREATE TABLE test` `(name long)`
DATE	Used to store the date and time in the database. The time is stored to a precision of 1/100th of a second. No time zone information is supported.	`CREATE TABLE test` `(name DATE )`

TIMESTAMP	Provides more granular support for date/time, with year, month, day, hour, minute, and second fields. Seconds are stored with a precision of up to nine digits (limited by support of the underlying OS). This data type has no time zone information. This data type is available in Oracle9i Database and later.	`CREATE TABLE test`
		`(timestamp_column`
		`    TIMESTAMP);`

TIMESTAMP WITH TIME ZONE	Contains the same fields as the TIMESTAMP data type with two additional fields, timezone_hour and timezone_minute. This data type includes support for time zone information. This data type is available in Oracle9i Database and later.	`CREATE TABLE test`
		`(timestamp_column`
		`    TIMESTAMP WITH`
		`    TIME ZONE);`

Datatype Name	Description	Example
TIMESTAMP WITH LOCAL TIME ZONE	Contains the same fields as TIMESTAMP, except it is normalized to the time zone stored in the database. When this column is selected, the date/time is adjusted to the session time zone. This data type is available in Oracle9i Database and later.	`CREATE TABLE test (timestamp_column TIMESTAMP WITH LOCAL TIME ZONE);`
INTERVAL YEAR TO MONTH	Used to store a period of time consisting of months and years. Requires 5 bytes of storage. This data type is available in Oracle9i Database and later.	`SELECT INTERVAL '01-05' YEAR TO MONTH - INTERVAL '01-02' YEAR TO MONTH FROM dual;`
INTERVAL DAY TO SECOND	Used to store a period of time consisting of days and seconds. Requires 11 bytes of storage. This data type is available in Oracle9i Database and later.	`SELECT INTERVAL '100 10:20:42.22' DAY(3) TO SECOND(2) - INTERVAL '101 10:20:42.22' DAY(3) TO SECOND(2) FROM dual`
RAW	Used to store raw, binary data. The maximum size is 2000 bytes. It is recommended that you use a BLOB instead.	`CREATE TABLE test (raw_column RAW(2000) );`
LONG RAW	Used to store raw, binary data up to 2GB in size. It is recommended that you use a BLOB instead.	`CREATE TABLE test (raw_column long RAW );`
ROWID	A string representation of the ROWID of the table. Use these data types to store values returned by the ROWID pseudo column.	`CREATE TABLE test (rowid_column ROWID);`
UROWID	Represents the logical address of a row in an index-organized table.	`CREATE TABLE test (urowid_column UROWID );`
CLOB	Used to store large character-based objects. The maximum size is limited to 4GB in Oracle9i Database. The maximum size is even higher in Oracle Database 10g, as it is now a factor of the database block size (~ 4GB * the database block size).	`CREATE TABLE test (clob_column CLOB );`
NCLOB	Can store Unicode-only character-based data using a character set defined by the database national character set. It can hold up to 4GB. The maximum size is even higher in Oracle Database 10g, as it is now a factor of the database block size (~ 4GB * the database block size).	`CREATE TABLE test (nclob_column NCLOB );`
BLOB	A binary large object that can store up to 4GB. The maximum size is even higher in Oracle Database 10g, as it is now a factor of the database block size (~ 4GB * the database block size).	`CREATE TABLE test (blob_column BLOB );`

Datatype Name	Description	Example

BFILE	Storage for a locator to an external file, stored outside the database. The external file can be a maximum of 4GB.	`CREATE TABLE test`
		`(bfile_column`
		`BFILE );`

BINARY_FLOAT	Floating-point data type based on the ANSI_ IEEE 754 standard, which defines a 32-bit, double-precision, floating-point number. This datatype requires 5 bytes of storage.	`CREATE TABLE test` `(b_float binary_float);`
BINARY_DOUBLE	Double-precision, floating-point data type based on the ANSI_IEEE 754 standard, which defines a 32-bit, double-precision, floating-point number. This data type requires 9 bytes of storage.	`CREATE TABLE test` `(b_float binary_double);`

Notes on Various Data Types

This section contains some notes about those data types in the preceding table that I feel will be helpful to you on a day-to-day basis. In this section, we specifically review details revolving around CHAR and VARCHAR2 data types and NUMBER data types. We end this section with notes on LONG data types, DATE data types, and TIMESTAMP- and INTERVAL-related data types.

Notes on CHAR and VARCHAR2 Data Types

The database character set determines the number of bytes that a specific CHAR, VARCHAR, or VARCHAR2 character will take. Characters in a multibyte character set can require from 1 to 4 bytes of storage. The size of a CHAR or VARCHAR2 data type can be determined based on either the number of bytes or number of characters that the data type can store. This is known as *character semantics*. By default, all storage is defined in bytes. If you are using a multibyte character set (most of the common Western character sets are single byte with the notable exception of UTF), you may want to define the storage in characters, as demonstrated in this example:

```
CREATE TABLE test
(name VARCHAR2(20 char) );
```

I recommend that you make sure that you create at the end of the table any columns that are likely to be NULL. By using this method, you eek out a savings of a few bytes with a VARCHAR2 that you would not get with a CHAR data type, because of the way the Oracle database stores contiguous NULL values in a row.

Oracle9*i* Database and later offers data compression, which should only be used in tables to be contained in a read-only tablespace (that is, no changes are going to be made to the data within the table). Data will be compressed only if it is loaded into the table via one of the following bulk-load operations:

- A table creation using a **create table as select** (CTAS) operation
- A direct mode **insert** operation or a parallel **insert** operation
- A SQL*Loader direct mode operation

NOTE
Compressed data blocks will be uncompressed if you modify the data
*with an **update** statement! Thus, a very small table can quickly grow*
very large.

You can compress data in an existing table through the use of the **alter table move**
command. Here is an example of creating a compressed table, and an example of compressing
an existing table:

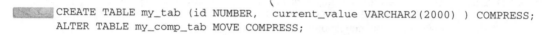

```
CREATE TABLE my_tab (id NUMBER,  current_value VARCHAR2(2000) ) COMPRESS;
ALTER TABLE my_comp_tab MOVE COMPRESS;
```

There is often a question with CHAR and VARCHAR2 data types as to which is best to use.
Here are some guidelines:

- Generally, VARCHAR2 data types are preferable in use over CHAR data types.

- If your data varies in size, VARCHAR2 data types save space in your database.

- If the data in a VARCHAR2 column is frequently updated, the VARCHAR2 column
  expansion may cause row chaining or migration to occur. In cases where you will use
  the entire size of the VARCHAR2 column eventually, you might want to consider the
  use of a CHAR data type instead.

NOTE
It is frequently suggested that use of VARCHAR2(1) is more
expensive than use of a CHAR(1). This is not the case.

Notes on NUMBER Data Types

The NUMBER data type is stored internally in a variable-length format using scientific notation.
One byte is used to store the exponent, with up to an additional 20 bytes (this number varies)
used to store the remaining part of the number. As a result of this storage scheme, NUMBER data
types are limited to 38 digits of precision.

If you want to determine the size that a given number will take up in bytes, you can use the
vsize function, as shown in this example:

```
SQL> SELECT VSIZE(100) FROM dual;
VSIZE(100)
----------
         2
```

The **vsize** function is used to determine the size of the number 100. It takes 2 bytes of storage,
1 byte for the digits and 1 byte for the exponent.

You can also use the **dump** function to determine the specific size of any column, as shown
in this example:

```
SQL> SELECT id, dump(id) did FROM test;
       ID DID
---------- ---------------
       123 Typ=2 Len=3: 194,2,24
       141 Typ=2 Len=3: 194,2,42
    123456 Typ=2 Len=4: 195,13,35,57
```

NUMBER data types can be defined in several ways. You can define numbers with or without precision and scale, as required. If you define a NUMBER column with a specific precision, the Oracle database will generate an error if you exceed that precision. For example, a NUMBER(6,2) will store a value of 1234.56 without any impact to the value being stored, but a number of 123.456 will be rounded and you will end up storing the number as 123.46. If you try to store a number 12345.67 in the same NUMBER data type, the database will generate an error since this would be a number with a precision of 7 rather than 6. Finally, you can also define a column as just a NUMBER data type with no precision. This indicates that the NUMBER column is to be treated as an integer, with no scale attributes possible.

Notes on LONG RAW Data Types

The LONG RAW data type is used to store binary data that is not to be interpreted by the database. This data type can store up to 2GB of data and its storage is variable. Oracle discourages the use of LONG RAW because this data type has been replaced by the BLOB data type. Oracle has provided, in Oracle9*i* Database and later, the ability to convert a LONG RAW column to its corresponding CLOB data type via the **alter table** command. You can also use the **to_lob** function to convert LONG RAW data into a BLOB data format.

Notes on LONG Data Types

LONG data types are used to store large amounts of character text. LONG data types can contain up to 2GB of data, within certain limitations. Oracle discourages the use of LONG because this data type has been replaced by the CLOB data type. Oracle has provided, in Oracle9*i* Database and later, the ability to convert a LONG column to its corresponding LOB data type via the **alter table** command. You can also use the **to_lob** function to convert LONG data into a CLOB data format.

LONG columns can be referenced in the following types of SQL statements:

- **select** lists
- In the **set** clause of an **update** statement
- In the **values** clause of an **insert** statement

The use of the LONG data type comes with a number of restrictions:

- Only one LONG column per table is allowed.
- You cannot create an object type with a LONG attribute.
- Oracle database **where** clauses or integrity constraints cannot reference a LONG data type. The only exception to this is that LONG data types can appear in NULL and NOT NULL constraints or as part of NULL or NOT NULL **where** clause predicates.

- You cannot index a LONG column.

- You cannot have distributed operations that involve LONG columns. All transactions involving LONG columns must be co-located in the same database.

- Replication does not support LONG data types.

- If the table you have created has both LONG and CLOB columns, you will not be able to bind more than 4000 bytes of data to both the LONG and CLOB columns in the same SQL statement. However, you can bind more than 4000 bytes of data to either the LONG or the CLOB column.

In addition to the previous restrictions, there are several restrictions on LONG columns when they are part of a SQL statement. To begin, the following operators do not support LONG columns:

- **group by**
- **order by**
- **connect by**
- **distinct**
- **unique**
- **group by**
- Any SQL built-in functions, expressions, or conditions
- Any **select** statement where the queries or subqueries are combined by the **union**, **intersect**, or **minus** operators

Further, the following DDL restrictions also exist with regard to LONG data types:

- A LONG column cannot be contained in the column list of a **create cluster** statement.

- A LONG column cannot be contained in select lists of **create table as select** statements.

- A LONG column cannot be contained in **alter table...move** statements.

- A LONG column cannot be contained in select lists in subqueries within the content of an **insert** statement.

The following restrictions also exist with reference to the use of LONG columns in PL/SQL program units and triggers:

- Variables in triggers cannot be declared using the LONG data type.

- Trigger variables **:new** and **:old** cannot be used with LONG columns.

- You cannot return a LONG from a stored PL/SQL function. However, a variable or argument of a PL/SQL program can use a LONG, although you cannot call such a PL/SQL unit from SQL.

Notes on DATE Data Types

The DATE data type is the native method of storing date and time within an Oracle database. When stored in the database, a DATE data type takes up 7 bytes of internal storage. These bytes store the century, year, month, day, hour, minute, and second details, respectively.

The default print format is generally OS-specific and dependent on various NLS parameter settings. Generally, the default for a date is **dd-mon-yy**, which represents the date, month, and a two-digit year, separated by dashes. As an example, the default format looks like this: 01-FEB-01. If you want to redefine the date format, set the **nls_date_format** variable in the database parameter file. You can also use the **alter session** command to set the **nls_date_format** for a specific session, to change the date format, as shown in this example:

```
SQL> SELECT sysdate FROM dual;
SYSDATE
---------
24-MAY-03
SQL> ALTER SESSION SET nls_date_format='mm/dd/yyyy hh24:mi:ss';
Session altered.
SQL> SELECT sysdate FROM dual;
SYSDATE
-------------------
05/24/2003 20:49:09
```

This example changes the date format mask to include the time in 24-hour format and to also give the year fully qualified with the century.

If you want all sessions on a specific system to use a different date format, you can set the NLS_LANG operating system environment along with setting NLS_DATE_FORMAT as an OS variable. This results in an **alter session** command being issued at each login. Note that the environment variable NLS_DATE_FORMAT will not take effect unless the environment variable NLS_LANG is also set.

NOTE
If you use Oracle Recovery Manager (RMAN), all dates reported will be in the default date format mask. You should set the NLS_LANG and NLS_DATE_FORMAT environment variable to the format mask you require before starting RMAN.

To change the format of the output within a SQL statement, you need to use the **to_char** built-in Oracle database function. If you have a character-based date that you wish to insert into a DATE column, you need to use the **to_date** function. An example of the conversion of a date format using the **to_char** function is shown here:

```
SQL> SELECT to_char(sysdate, 'mm/dd/yyyy hh24:mi:ss') the_date FROM dual;
          THE_DATE
-------------------
05/24/2003 20:41:36
```

This example converts the date format to include a four-digit year and the time in 24-hour format, with minutes and seconds.

Notes on TIMESTAMP and INTERVAL Data Types

Some of the new TIMESTAMP data types are dependent on the configuration of the proper time zone in the database. By default, the database is set to the time zone of the operating system. You can associate the database with a different time zone at creation time by using the **set time_zone** parameter in the **create database** command. You can also change the time zone of an existing database by using the **alter database set time_zone** command. You can alter time zone settings at the session level with the **alter session** command. You can define the time zone based on an hour offset from UTC, or using a named region such as CST or EST. Here are some examples of setting the database time zone:

```
ALTER DATABASE SET time_zone='CST';
ALTER DATABASE SET time_zone='-05:00';
```

Several conversion functions are available to be used with the TIMESTAMP and INTERVAL data types. These include **to_date**, **to_char**, **to_timestamp**, **to_timestamp_tz**, **to_yminterval**, and **to_dsinterval**. Also, the **nls_timestamp_format** and **nls_timestamp_tz_format** parameters are specifically associated with TIMESTAMP and INTERVAL data types.

Other built-in functions can be used when extracting data from a column with a TIMESTAMP data type. The **extract** function allows you to extract specific information from the TIMESTAMP column such as the hour or the minute. Here is an example (note the implicit conversion of the **sysdate** function to the TIMESTAMP datatype format):

```
CREATE TABLE my_tab(test_col TIMESTAMP);
INSERT INTO my_tab VALUES (sysdate);
SELECT test_col, EXTRACT(HOUR FROM test_col) FROM my_tab;
TEST_COL                                   HOUR
------------------------------- ----------
25-MAY-03 09.46.24.000000 AM            9
```

Table Types

Tables are created with the **create table** command and are the principle storage object within the Oracle database. Internally, when you create a table, the database allocates a chunk of contiguous blocks (the smallest unit of storage in an Oracle database) into logical entities called *extents*. One or more extents are then assigned to the table, as required.

Several types of tables are available for use in Oracle databases:

- Relational tables
- Temporary tables
- External tables
- Index-organized tables
- Object tables

The first four table types are described in the following sections. I decided not to give coverage in this text to Oracle's object features, such as object tables, in order to focus on more commonly used features.

Relational Tables

Relational tables are the default type of table that you create in the database. Relational tables consist of a set of columns. Each column is assigned a name, a data type, and, if appropriate to the data type, a width. Data within the table is stored in rows, each row making up a single record.

Temporary Tables

A temporary table is a special type of Oracle database table created with the **create global temporary table** command. Temporary tables are used to store data for a short period of time. The data in a temporary table is only visible to the session loading the data, and other operations such as **select**, **insert**, and **truncate** only impact your session's data. The lifetime of temporary table data is either transactional in nature (e.g., through a **commit**) or when the session ends (e.g, you exit SQL*Plus), and this is configured when the table is created.

External Tables

External tables (available in Oracle9*i* Database and later) allow you to access external data from within the database. When you create the external table with the **create table** statement, you define the format of the external data. You can then query the external data source from within an Oracle database with a **select** statement. You can perform joins to other Oracle database tables (including other external tables), use functions, and load the data into other Oracle database tables. Note that an external table itself requires no internal database space.

Oracle9*i* Database allows you only to read from an external table, not write to it. Oracle Database 10*g* enables you to write to an external table as well. Only the use of the **create table as select** command is supported for the creation and population of the external table. You cannot issue subsequent **insert**, **update**, or **delete** commands against that external table (though you can issue **select** statements against it).

When an external table is written to, it is written in an Oracle database proprietary format. This format is pretty easy to interpret, and thus the external file can be opened and read from with third-party bulk-load tools. This also implies that the file should always be secured if it contains sensitive data.

When you drop an external table with the **drop table** command, the files that were created by the external table are not dropped. Finally, the creation of the external table will fail if the files that it is to write to already exist.

Index-Organized Tables

An index-organized table (IOT) is really a B*Tree index dressed up to look like an Oracle database table. The result is that records are grouped together based on the primary key of the table (a defined primary key is required in the case of an IOT). An IOT can reduce the total number of logical reads required to access a given set of data, because an IOT can eliminate the need to access both the index and the associated table, assuming that the primary key is the typical predicate used on queries against the IOT. Also, Oracle databases allow for the creation of secondary indexes on IOTs.

Constraints

Oracle databases allow you to define a number of constraints, or integrity constraints, on tables and between tables. These constraints define specific rules that apply to the columns of a table, and between columns of multiple tables. The following table lists the different kinds of constraints available in Oracle databases:

Constraint Type	Description
Not null	Indicates that the column cannot contain a NULL value.
Foreign key	Used to enforce a parent-child relationship between columns within two different tables. To create a foreign key (FK), the columns of the FK must be part of the primary key, or a unique key, in the parent table.
Primary key	Represents a column or combination of columns that uniquely identifies each row within the table. Typically, the primary key constraint is enforced by a unique index, but this is not always the case. Each table can have only one primary key, and the primary key columns cannot be NULL.
Unique	Similar in nature to a primary key, the unique constraint defines a column, or combination of columns, that must be unique within the table for each row. Each table is allowed multiple unique constraints, and NULL values in the columns are allowed.
Check	Used to enforce specific data integrity/validity rules relating to a given column.

Table Attributes

When you create a table, you can associate specific attributes to that table with both the **physical_attributes** clause and the **storage** clause. Some of the more common table attributes that are set during the creation of a table (or an index) include

Attribute	Description	Default Value
pctfree	Determines how much of a block will be reserved for updates to existing rows. Once a block's usage is at or above **pctfree**, it is removed from the freelist and will not be used.	10
pctused	A block that has been removed from the freelist as a result of meeting or exceeding the **pctfree** threshold will be re-added to the list if its space utilization falls below that of **pctused**.	40
initrans	Defines the initial number of concurrent transaction entries that are allocated within each data block. The maximum value is dependent on the block size. You can change this value if you have a large number of concurrent operations, but the database will dynamically add transaction entries as required.	1

Attribute	Description	Default Value
maxtrans	Determines the maximum number of concurrent transactions allowed to update a given data block.	Varies based on block size

The **storage** clause is used to define storage parameters related to the object you are creating. When a table is created, the values used for the **storage** clause come from one of three sources, in this order:

1. The values established in the **storage** clause of the statement that created the object

2. The tablespace default storage values

3. Oracle database storage value defaults

The following table is provided as a quick reference for **storage** clause values that are commonly used when creating tables or indexes:

Parameter	Meaning
initial	Defines the size of the first extent of the table
next	Defines the size of the next extent of the table
minextents	Defines the minimum number of extents that should be assigned to the table
maxextents	Defines the maximum number of extents that should be assigned to the table
pctincrease	Defines the percentage that **next** should be increased after each extent operation
freelists	Defines the number of freelists to be allocated to the object
freelist groups	Defines the number of freelist groups to be allocated to the object
buffer_pool	Defines the Oracle database buffer pool (**keep**, **recycle**, or **default**) that the object should be assigned to

Parallel Processing

Certain operations, such as **select** statements, can be parallelized in Oracle databases. When you create a table, you can define default values for parallelization (or the *degree of parallelism*) for that table via the **parallel** clause. Parallelism for a given object can also be inherited when the object is created through tablespace defaults. Additionally, parallel operations can be indicated through the use of a hint in SQL code. When parallelism is defined, an Oracle database will try to parallelize access to the table based on those settings. When Oracle performs a parallel operation, a single controller process (called the *parallel query coordinator*) spawns off multiple slave processes, splitting up the work amongst those parallel processes. The slave processes perform their work and then return the row set (in the case of a query) to the parallel query coordinator. The coordinator process then collects all the result sets, combines and sorts them as required, and returns a result to the user process. Note that the sorts that are performed can also be done in parallel.

Oracle databases allow for parallel DML and DDL operations, so you can parallelize **select**, **insert**, **update**, and **delete** operations (there are limitations) as well as operations such as index builds and table creations (using the **create table as select** command, for example).

Partitioning

Oracle databases allow you to partition tables and indexes (see Chapter 5 for more details on partitioned tables and Chapter 6 for indexes). Four different partition methods are supported:

- **Range**   Partitions the table based on a range of values in one or more columns (the partition key).

- **Hash**   Partitions the table based on a derived hash value calculated on one or more columns (the partition key).

- **List**   Partitions the table based on a specific list of values based on the partition key. In Oracle9i Database, IOTs cannot be list partitioned. This restriction is removed in Oracle Database 10g.

- **Composite**   A combination of range-hash or range-list partitioning. Essentially, this is a method of creating a partitioned table, and then subpartitioning it further.

Partitioning offers a way of improving query performance, and easing administration on large tables. Performance improvements are largely gained through the elimination of reads on large numbers of rows via *partition pruning*. Partition pruning is the elimination during a read of partitions that contain data that does not need to be read. The Oracle database will determine if a partition can be pruned based on the *partition key* of the table. The partition key is the column or columns that the table is partitioned on.

Partition simplifies administration of tables through such things as partition-level truncate operations, partition-level analyze operations, and partition-level data-load operations.

Other Table-Related Features

A host of other features are available with tables in the Oracle database:

- **Table data compression**   You can compress data within your Oracle database tables. This is only available in Oracle9i Database Release 2 and later and should be used only for tables that have no **insert**, **update**, or **delete** activity on them.

- **Keep or recycle buffer pool assignments**   If a table is frequently accessed, it may be beneficial to pin it in the keep buffer pool. This buffer pool is designed for frequently accessed objects that you don't want aged out. If the object is infrequently read against, consider assigning it to the recycle buffer pool so that it will not have an inordinate impact on the default buffer cache.

- **Monitoring growth**   You can monitor your table's growth and the number of changes that take place in it by enabling the monitoring function. This functionality also allows you to quickly update the statistics on the table.

- **Object level statistics**   After you create your table and any related indexes, you will want to analyze these objects so that the optimizer has appropriate statistics for the object. See Chapter 12 for information on this Oracle database operation.

- **Disable logging**   A table can be defined as either **logging** (default) or **nologging**. This attribute allows you to indicate whether the creation of the table, along with any associated constraint-related indexes (but not any indexes created independently of the associated **create table** or **alter table** command), partitions, and LOB-related information should be stored in the online redo logs. After the creation of the table is complete, the **nologging** attribute determines whether subsequent Direct Loader (SQL*Loader) and direct-path INSERT operations against the table will be logged. This parameter also determines whether future changes to partitions, or LOB storage, are logged or not logged.

- **Shrinking and compacting of segments online**   This feature, available in Oracle Database 10g and later, allows you to manually shrink the overall size of a table, by removing unused space. You can also combine this operation with a compaction operation, which results in the resetting of the high-water mark of the table, potentially releasing more space to the tablespace for reuse.

Creating Tables

You create tables with the **create table** command. You can create a table without data, or you can use the **create table as select** version of the command to create a table and populate it with data at the same time. In this section we look in more detail at the specifics of the **create table** command. We look at the security requirements related to this command, and then look at several examples of the creation of tables in Oracle databases.

Security Requirements

Once a table is created, security access privileges must be assigned to other users via the **grant** command. Table-related security requirements come in two flavors:

- **DDL security requirements**   Related to the actual creation and management of a table
- **DML security requirements**   Related to accessing the table after it has been created

The DDL and DML requirements are described next, followed by a discussion of the use of roles for security, and then a look at how to determine who has rights to what.

DDL Security Requirements

To create a table in your own schema, you need the **create table** system privilege. You need the **create any table** system privilege to create a table in a schema other than the one you are logged into.

To create a table, you must have a quota on the tablespace you are creating the table in, or the **unlimited tablespace** system privilege. If the user doesn't have the appropriate quota, use the **alter user** command to correct the problem, as shown here:

```
ALTER USER scott QUOTA 100m ON prod_data;
```

If you are creating a table in another user's schema, then that user must have either a quota to the tablespace the table is being created in (via the **alter user** command) or the **unlimited tablespace** system privilege granted via the **grant** command (e.g., **grant unlimited tablespace to test**). Finally, to create an external table you must have the **read object** privilege on the directory where the external data resides.

To create an external table, you first define a directory with the **create directory** command. This is a security requirement that allows the DBA to control where objects like external tables can be created. Once the directory is created use the **grant** command to grant the **read** and **write** (Oracle Database 10g and later) privileges on the directory to the user who will create and use the external table. You also need the **create table** or **create any table** system privilege to be able to create an external table.

DML Security Requirements

To access a table often requires some security privileges. If you are in your own schema and you created the table in your own schema, then you have unfettered privileges to that table. Access to the table by other users requires that you use the **grant** command to define what access privileges they have. You can control access to the table as a whole, or to specific columns (only in the case of inserts, or updates). The following table provides a list of the security requirements that you need to access a table in another schema and includes examples of how to use the **grant** command to provide the associated access privileges:

DML Statement	Privilege Required	Example
select	You must have the **select** privilege on the table or the **select any table** system grant	`GRANT SELECT ON my_table TO my_user;` Or, to allow access to any table: `GRANT SELECT ANY TABLE TO my_user;`
insert	You must have the **insert** privilege on the table or the **insert any table** system grant	`GRANT INSERT ON my_table TO my_user;` Or, to control the ability to insert into a specific column: `GRANT INSERT (id) ON my_table TO my_user;` Or, to allow a user to insert into any table: `GRANT INSERT ANY TABLE TO my_user;`
update	You must have the **update** privilege on the table or the **update any table** system grant	`GRANT UPDATE ON my_table TO my_user;` Or, to control the ability to delete from a specific column: `GRANT UPDATE (id) ON my_table TO my_user;` Or, to grant the privilege globally: `GRANT UPDATE ANY TABLE TO my_user;`
delete	You must have the **delete** privilege on the table or the **delete any table** system grant	`GRANT DELETE ON my_table TO my_user;` Or, to grant the privilege globally: `GRANT DELETE ANY TABLE TO my_user;`

DML Statement	Privilege Required	Example
all	You can have all privileges on a given table through the use of the **grant all** system privilege	`GRANT ALL ON my_table TO my_user;`

Using Roles to Manage Security

Roles can be used to ease security administration. A role is much like a user, in that it is assigned rights and privileges. For example, if you have a group of 100 developers, it would be much easier to create a role called DEVELOPER, and grant that role the privileges that all 100 developers would need (such as **select any table**, and specific grants to specific tables). The alternative is to issue those grants individually to all users. Having created the role, you would then grant that role to developer user accounts as you create them. Here is an example of such an operation:

```
-- Create the role first
CREATE ROLE developer IDENTIFIED BY developer;
-- Now assign some privileges

GRANT INSERT, UPDATE, DELETE ON my_table TO developer;
GRANT CREATE SESSION TO developer;
-- Now, create a user and assign the developer role to it
CREATE USER dev_001 IDENTIFIED BY dev_001
DEFAULT TABLESPACE prod_data;
-- and grant the developer role
GRANT developer TO dev_001;
```

In this example, we create a role called DEVELOPER. We then **grant** DEVELOPER several privileges on the MY_TABLE table, including **select**, **insert**, **update**, and **delete**. Next, we **grant** the **create session** role to the DEVELOPER role. Finally, we create a new user, DEV_001, and grant the DEVELOPER role to that user. Now DEV_001 has the privileges assigned to the DEVELOPER role.

Note that there is a principle restriction on the use of roles. When you create PL/SQL program units, you must have direct grants to the objects being referenced by the PL/SQL program. Failure to have these privileges results in the failure of the PL/SQL program during its initial compilation.

Reporting on System and Object-Level Privileges

DBAs are sometimes not quite sure how to determine who has rights to what. Several views are available to help make that determination. Rights and privileges come in two principle forms: system privileges and object-level privileges. Let's look at each of these in a bit more detail.

Reporting on System Privileges   System privileges are reported via the view DBA_SYS_PRIVS. For example, if we want to know what system privileges the SCOTT account has, we would issue the following query:

```
SELECT grantee, privilege FROM dba_sys_privs WHERE grantee='SCOTT';
GRANTEE                          PRIVILEGE
```

```
-------------------------------  -------------------------
SCOTT                            UNLIMITED TABLESPACE
```

In this case, the SCOTT account has the **unlimited tablespace** system privilege. Of course, that doesn't tell the whole story, because SCOTT may well be assigned to a role or two, which may have system privileges. To determine if this is the case, we review the DBA_ROLE_PRIVS view to see if SCOTT is assigned to a role:

```
SELECT grantee, granted_role FROM dba_role_privs WHERE grantee='SCOTT';
GRANTEE                          GRANTED_ROLE
-------------------------------  ------------------------------
SCOTT                            DEVELOPER
```

Now, we need to determine what system privileges the DEVELOPER role has, so we return to our first query, slightly modified:

```
SQL> SELECT grantee, privilege FROM dba_sys_privs WHERE grantee='DEVELOPER';
GRANTEE                          PRIVILEGE
-------------------------------  ----------------------------------------
DEVELOPER                        CREATE SESSION
DEVELOPER                        SELECT ANY TABLE
```

And from this output we find that the DEVELOPER role has two privileges, **create session** and **select any table**. See Chapter 10 for more information on grants and how they work.

Reporting on Object-Level Privileges   Object-level privileges represent your ability to access specific objects. These privileges are given via the **grant** command and are removed through the **revoke** command. Both commands are covered in Chapter 10, but this section quickly summarizes how to determine if you have access to specific tables, and privileges to perform activities on those tables.

The view DBA_TAB_PRIVS provides the information you need to determine if you have access to a specific table, and what accesses you have. Here is an example:

```
select grantee, owner, table_name, grantor, privilege
from dba_tab_privs where grantee='SCOTT';
GRANTEE   OWNER       TABLE_NAME GRANTOR     PRIVILEGE
--------  ----------  ---------- ----------  ----------
SCOTT     PRODUCTION  ID_TABLE   PRODUCTION  SELECT
```

In this case, we find that SCOTT has **select** privileges on the table ID_TABLE in the schema PRODUCTION. It may be that SCOTT has these privileges through a role that was granted to him. In this case, we might try a join between DBA_ROLE_PRIVS and DBA_TAB_PRIVS to see what privileges SCOTT really has:

```
SELECT a.grantee, a.granted_role, b.table_name, b.privilege
FROM dba_role_privs a, dba_tab_privs b WHERE
a.grantee='SCOTT' AND b.grantee IN
(SELECT granted_role FROM dba_role_privs WHERE grantee='SCOTT');
```

GRANTEE	GRANTED_ROLE	PRIVILEGE	TABLE_NAME
SCOTT	DEVELOPER	SELECT	ID_TABLE

In this case we find that SCOTT is assigned the DEVELOPER role, and that the DEVELOPER role is granted **select** privileges. Finally, the DBA_COL_PRIVS table provides column-level grant information for a given table.

Sizing Tables Assigned to a Locally Managed Tablespace

What you see is not always what you get. For example, consider the **storage** clause and locally managed tablespaces (LMTs). When you use dictionary-managed tablespaces, you pretty much get the space allocated to you, in the sizes that you request (assuming the space is available). When dealing with LMTs, this isn't always the case. For example, if you have an LMT with a uniform size of 1M, and you create a table in it with a **storage** clause of **initial** 100K and **next** 100K and **minextents** 2, what is the result? Well, it's not two 100K extents, but rather one 1M extent. This is because Oracle databases combine the **storage** clause values together, which results in a uniform extent size (in this case, one extent of 1M) that is as close as possible to the initial storage request. The moral of the story is to be careful when creating your LMTs, and make sure that you don't define your uniform extent sizes too small or too large, as this can result in wasted space, or in objects that extend way too frequently.

Examples of Using the create table Command

This section contains a number of examples of how to use the **create table** command to create the following types of tables:

- Nonpartitioned tables, including index-organized tables
- Partitioned tables
- Global temporary tables
- External tables

Nonpartitioned Table Examples

Here is a basic example of the use of the **create table** command to create a relational table. In this example, we are using the Oracle Database tablespace defaults for storage, since there is no **storage** clause. We are also using the Oracle database defaults for the remaining table attributes.

```
CREATE TABLE parts (id NUMBER PRIMARY KEY,
name VARCHAR2(30), bin_code NUMBER, UPC  NUMBER);
```

This example also defines the ID column as the primary key of the table.

The following is a more complex example:

```
CREATE TABLE parts (id NUMBER NOT NULL, version NUMBER NOT NULL,
name VARCHAR2(30),Bin_code NUMBER NOT NULL, upc NUMBER NOT NULL)
TABLESPACE parts_tablespace
```

```
PCTFREE 20 PCTUSED 60
STORAGE ( INITIAL 10M NEXT 10M PCTINCREASE 0);
```

In this example, we have created a table called PARTS. Note that we assigned the table to the tablespace PARTS_TABLESPACE, and we assigned values to **pctfree**, **pctused**, and **pctincrease** so that we save some space in our blocks for updates and so that block growth will be consistent. Also note the use of the **not null** clause in the definition of several of the columns. This disallows the use of NULL values in those columns.

We also used the **storage** clause in the previous example, indicating that the **initial** extent should be 10MB and that each subsequent extent should be 10MB as well. In this example, we didn't assign a primary key to the table; we may be waiting to use the **alter table** command to do this (see coverage on the **alter table** command, later in this chapter, for information on how to do this).

The next example is even more complex:

```
CREATE TABLE parts (id NUMBER, version NUMBER, name VARCHAR2(30),
Bin_code NUMBER, upc NUMBER, active_code VARCHAR2(1) NOT NULL
    CONSTRAINT ck_parts_active_code_01
    CHECK (UPPER(active_code)= 'Y' or UPPER(active_code)='N'),
    CONSTRAINT pk_parts PRIMARY KEY (id, version)
    USING INDEX TABLESPACE parts_index
    STORAGE (INITIAL 1m NEXT 1m) )
TABLESPACE parts_tablespace
PCTFREE 20 PCTUSED 60 STORAGE ( INITIAL 10m NEXT 10m PCTINCREASE 0);
```

In this example, we have created our PARTS table again. We have also defined two different constraints. The first constraint is a check constraint to make sure that the ACTIVE_CODE is a Y or an N. The second constraint is a concatenated primary key constraint on the ID and VERSION columns, defining that the index for that primary key should be contained in the PARTS_INDEX tablespace and assigning a **storage** clause to that index.

The next example adds to the previous example by adding a foreign key to the **create table** statement. First, we create the table to be referenced by the foreign key, then we create the table and the foreign key within the same **create table** statement.

```
CREATE TABLE bin_codes (bin_code NUMBER PRIMARY KEY,
bin_description VARCHAR2(30) )
TABLESPACE parts_tablespace
STORAGE (INITIAL 100k NEXT 100k);

CREATE TABLE parts (id NUMBER, version NUMBER, name VARCHAR2(30),
Bin_code NUMBER, upc NUMBER, active_code VARCHAR2(1) NOT NULL
    CONSTRAINT ck_parts_active_code_01
    CHECK (UPPER(active_code)= 'Y' or UPPER(active_code)='N'),
    CONSTRAINT pk_parts PRIMARY KEY (id, version)
    USING INDEX TABLESPACE parts_index
    STORAGE (INITIAL 1m NEXT 1m),
    CONSTRAINT fk_parts_bin_codes FOREIGN KEY (bin_code)
    REFERENCES bin_codes(bin_code) )
```

```
TABLESPACE parts_tablespace
PCTFREE 20 PCTUSED 60 STORAGE ( INITIAL 10m NEXT 10m PCTINCREASE 0);
```

In this example, we have created two tables. The first is the BIN_CODE table, followed by the PARTS table. In the PARTS table, we have created a foreign key constraint between the BIN_CODE column within the PARTS table and the BIN_CODE column in the BIN_CODE table.

Sometimes you may want to create a table using data that already exists in the database (perhaps in another table or in an external table). You can use the **as select** clause in the **create table** command to perform such a task. Here is an example:

```
CREATE TABLE parts TABLESPACE parts_tablespace
PCTFREE 20 PCTUSED 60
STORAGE (INITIAL 100m NEXT 100m PCTINCREASE 0)
AS SELECT * FROM parts_external;
```

Configuring Tables to Use Oracle Parallel Query   If you feel that a table would generally benefit from parallel query, you can define the degree of parallelism that the Oracle database should consider using when creating the table. Use the **parallel** clause. For example, if you want to define a degree of parallelism of 4 for your table, you create the table thusly:

```
CREATE TABLE parts (id NUMBER PRIMARY KEY,
name VARCHAR2(30), bin_code NUMBER, UPC  NUMBER)
TABLESPACE parts_tablespace
PARALLEL 4;
```

Index-Organized Table Examples   The next example creates an IOT called PART_SERIAL_ NUMBER:

```
CREATE TABLE part_serial_number
(serial_number NUMBER PRIMARY KEY, date_of_manufacture DATE, start_date
DATE, worker_code VARCHAR2(5) )
ORGANIZATION INDEX STORAGE (INITIAL 10M NEXT 10M PCTINCREASE 0)
PCTFREE 10 TABLESPACE parts_tablespace
PCTTHRESHOLD 20 OVERFLOW TABLESPACE parts_overflow
PCTFREE 20 PCTUSED 60 STORAGE(INITIAL 10M NEXT 10M PCTINCREASE 0);
```

The first unique thing to note is the **organization index** clause, which defines this as an IOT. The next unique feature is the **pctthreshold** clause. This optional clause defines the percentage of the index block that will be allocated to the head of the row. Each row is split into a head and a tail. The head is stored in the IOT and the tail is stored in an overflow segment (which is covered in a moment). The database calculates the row size, and stores in the overflow segment any part of that row that is larger than **pctthreshold** times the database block size. In the preceding example, assuming that the database block size is 8096 bytes, no more than 1620 bytes would be stored in the IOT itself. A pointer to any remaining bytes will be stored in the IOT. That pointer represents the address of the remaining data in the overflow segment.

The *overflow segment* is defined with the use of the **overflow tablespace** clause. The overflow segment is a separately allocated segment, which is used to store the tail of any record inserted into the associated IOT. In the preceding example, we have defined an overflow segment and several physical properties.

Key compression of an IOT (see Chapter 6 for more information on key compression) is also possible, since an IOT is just a B*Tree index. Use the **organization index compress** parameter to key compress your IOT. Note one restriction to key compression is that you must have a multiple-column primary key defined. Here is an example:

```
CREATE TABLE worker_table (worker_code number PRIMARY KEY,
worker_name VARCHAR2(30) )
TABLESPACE parts_tablespace;
CREATE TABLE part_serial_number
(serial_number NUMBER, version NUMBER,
 date_of_manufacture DATE, start_date DATE, worker_code NUMBER,
CONSTRAINT pk_part_serial_number PRIMARY KEY (serial_number, version),
CONSTRAINT fk_part_serial_number_worker FOREIGN KEY (worker_code)
REFERENCES worker_table(worker_code) )
ORGANIZATION INDEX COMPRESS STORAGE (INITIAL 10M NEXT 10M PCTINCREASE 0)
PCTFREE 10 TABLESPACE parts_tablespace
PCTTHRESHOLD 20 OVERFLOW TABLESPACE parts_overflow
PCTFREE 20 PCTUSED 60 STORAGE(INITIAL 10M NEXT 10M PCTINCREASE 0);
```

Partitioned Table Examples
This section contains examples of how to create the following partitioned tables:

- Range-partitioned tables

- Hash-partitioned tables

- List-partitioned tables

- Composite-partitioned tables

Creation of Range-Partitioned Tables   This example of a range-partitioned table breaks the sales of a department store chain into partitions based on the store number:

```
CREATE TABLE store_sales
     ( Store_id       NUMBER(6), Dept_id       NUMBER
     , sales_date     DATE      , dept_sales    NUMBER(10,2)   )
PARTITION BY RANGE (sales_date)
  (PARTITION SALES_Q1 VALUES LESS THAN
   (TO_DATE('01-APR-2003','DD-MON-YYYY')),
   PARTITION SALES_Q2 VALUES LESS THAN
   (TO_DATE('01-JUL-2003','DD-MON-YYYY')),
   PARTITION SALES_Q3 VALUES LESS THAN
   (TO_DATE('01-OCT-2003','DD-MON-YYYY')),
   PARTITION SALES_Q4 VALUES LESS THAN
   (TO_DATE('01-JAN-2004','DD-MON-YYYY')),
   PARTITION SALES_OVERFLOW VALUES LESS THAN (MAXVALUE));
```

Creation of Hash-Partitioned Tables   In this example, we have created a table that is hash partitioned. This gives us the greatest distribution of our data within our table, helping to eliminate block contention in certain high-concurrency applications.

```
CREATE TABLE site_log
     ( operation_id        NUMBER,
       server_id           NUMBER,
       ts_of_action        TIMESTAMP,
       username            VARCHAR2(30),
       command             VARCHAR2(1),
       begin_time          TIMESTAMP,
       end_time            TIMESTAMP,
       CONSTRAINT command CHECK (command in ('A', 'D', 'M') ) )
PCTFREE 5 PCTUSED 70
STORAGE (INITIAL 100m NEXT 100m FREELISTS 10 FREELIST GROUPS 2)
PARTITION BY HASH (operation_id)
PARTITIONS 5
STORE IN (site_log_tbs1, site_log_tbs2, site_log_tbs3,
          site_log_tbs4, site_log_tbs5);
```

Creation of List-Partitioned Tables   In this example, we have created a list-partitioned table. We are storing our department store's sales information by state, rather than by store.

```
CREATE TABLE store_sales
     ( Store_id       NUMBER(6),   Dept_id       NUMBER
     , store_state    VARCHAR2(2), sales_date    DATE
     , dept_sales     NUMBER(10,2)   )
  PARTITION BY LIST (store_state) (
  PARTITION oklahoma VALUES ('OK'),
  PARTITION texas    VALUES ('TX'),
  PARTITION Kansas   VALUES ('KS') );
```

Creation of Composite-Partitioned Tables   In this example, we have created a range/hash composite-partitioned table. In this case, we have partitioned the table based on the sales date, and then subpartitioned it based on the TRANSACTION_ID.

```
CREATE TABLE composite_sales
     ( Store_id       NUMBER(6), Dept_id       NUMBER
     , transaction_id NUMBER   , sales_date    DATE
     , dept_sales     NUMBER(10,2),
       CONSTRAINT pk_parts PRIMARY KEY (store_id, transaction_id)
       USING INDEX TABLESPACE sales_index
       STORAGE (INITIAL 100m NEXT 100m) )
PARTITION BY RANGE (sales_date)
SUBPARTITION BY HASH (transaction_id)
  (PARTITION SALES_Q1 VALUES LESS THAN
       (TO_DATE('01-APR-2003','DD-MON-YYYY')) SUBPARTITIONS 4,
   PARTITION SALES_Q2 VALUES LESS THAN
```

```
        (TO_DATE('01-JUL-2003','DD-MON-YYYY')) SUBPARTITIONS 4,
    PARTITION SALES_Q3_1998 VALUES LESS THAN
        (TO_DATE('01-OCT-2003','DD-MON-YYYY')) SUBPARTITIONS 4,
    PARTITION SALES_Q4_1998 VALUES LESS THAN
        (TO_DATE('01-JAN-2004','DD-MON-YYYY'))
        (SUBPARTITION sub_one,  SUBPARTITION sub_two,
         SUBPARTITION sub_three, SUBPARTITION sub_four),
    PARTITION SALES_OVERFLOW VALUES LESS THAN (MAXVALUE)
        SUBPARTITIONS 4);
```

We have created five partitions in this example, with each partition split into four different subpartitions based on the hash value of the transaction_id. Note that in the next-to-last partition, for the last quarter, we have manually defined out partition names, whereas we allowed the database to name the partitions with default names. Finally, note that the overflow partition is defined to allow for values that do not have an associated partition definition.

Another form of composite partitioning is available in Oracle9i Database Release 2 and later. This is called range/list partitioning. This allows you to partition on a range value first, then partition on a list of values. Here is an example of such a partitioned table:

```
CREATE TABLE customers_part (customer_no          NUMBER,
    Store_id          NUMBER,
    Store_region      NUMBER,
    cust_first_name   VARCHAR2(20),
    cust_last_name    VARCHAR2(20),
    total_sales       NUMBER(9,2))
    PARTITION BY RANGE (total_sales)
    SUBPARTITION BY LIST (Store_id)
        SUBPARTITION TEMPLATE
            (SUBPARTITION Midwest VALUES (1, 2),
             SUBPARTITION south VALUES (3, 4),
             SUBPARTITION north values (5,6),
             SUBPARTITION other VALUES (DEFAULT))
     (PARTITION low_sales VALUES LESS THAN (1000) tablespace low_tbs,
      PARTITION moderate_sales VALUES LESS THAN (20000) tablespace mod_tbs,
      PARTITION high_sales VALUES LESS THAN (50000) tablespace high_tbs,
      PARTITION plat_cust VALUES LESS THAN (MAXVALUE) tablespace plat_tbs);
```

In this case, we first create a subpartition template using the **subpartition_template** clause. This defines the list of subpartitions before we actually create the partitions that they will be associated with. We then proceed to create the partitions that the subpartitions will be associated with.

Global Temporary Table Examples

Global temporary tables allow you to store temporary data in a normal table structure. In many respects global temporary tables can be treated like any other table (it can be indexed and so on); however, each session can only see its own data. There are some restrictions on the creation of a global temporary table including:

- A global temporary table cannot be partitioned, clustered, index-orgainzed and it can not have any foreign key constraints defined.

■ You cannot define the physical attributes of a global temporary table such as the tablespace, or the storage clause.

■ Distributed transactions and parallel operations are not supported on temporary tables.

You create a global temporary table using the **create table** command, adding the **global temporary** keywords. Data duration within a temporary table is controlled via the **on commit** clause. If you wish data to be preserved within a specific transaction, use the **on commit delete rows** clause. If you wish data to be preserved for the entire length of the session, use the **on commit preserve rows** clause. Here is an example of the creation of a global temporary table where rows will be removed at the end of a transaction:

```
CREATE GLOBAL TEMPORARY TABLE temporary_table
 (temporary_id  NUMBER,
 temporary_value  NUMBER )
ON COMMIT DELETE ROWS;
```

This example creates the same global temporary table, but this time, rows will be deleted only after the session disconnects:

```
CREATE GLOBAL TEMPORARY TABLE temporary_table
 (temporary_id  NUMBER,
 temporary_value  NUMBER )
ON COMMIT PRESERVE ROWS;
```

External Table Examples

External tables allow you to read from an external operating system file or write (in Oracle Database 10g and later only) to an external database file. This allows you to easily move data in and out of the Oracle database. To create an external table, you need to first use the **create directory** command to define what directories are available for it to access, and then grant access to those directories to the user who is creating the external table. In this first example, the user SCOTT is granted the privileges needed to create an external table in the c:\oracle\ external_tables\mydb\scott directory, and then the user SCOTT creates an external table that allows the user account to read the underlying flat file:

```
CREATE DIRECTORY external_directory_scott
AS 'c:\oracle\external_tables\mydb\scott';

GRANT READ ON DIRECTORY external_directory_scott to scott;

CONNECT scott/tiger
CREATE TABLE scott_import_data (sales_date date,
store_number number, dept_no number, amount number)
ORGANIZATION EXTERNAL
( type ORACLE_LOADER
  DEFAULT DIRECTORY external_directory_scott
  ACCESS PARAMETERS   (
    RECORDS DELIMITED BY NEWLINE FIELDS TERMINATED BY ','
```

```
      MISSING FIELD VALUES ARE NULL
      (sales_date CHAR date_format DATE MASK 'mm-dd-yyyy',
       store_number, dept_no, amount) )
   LOCATION ('scott_import_file.dat') );
```

In Oracle Database 10g, you can use the new Oracle Database 10g Data Pump driver to read from or write to an external table, as shown in this example:

```
CREATE DIRECTORY external_directory_scott AS '/oracle/directories/scott';
CREATE TABLE scott_import_data (sales_date,
store_number, dept_no, amount)
ORGANIZATION EXTERNAL
( type ORACLE_DATAPUMP
  DEFAULT DIRECTORY external_directory_scott
  LOCATION ('output_report.exp') )
PARALLEL
AS
SELECT * FROM scott_export_data;
```

In this case, the result will be an output file called output_report.exp. It is created in an Oracle database proprietary format. This format is not defined by Oracle, so it's somewhat difficult to write code to extract data from it. It is in a quasi-XML format, however, and if you have a need to extract that data from an external source, it should not be too difficult to figure out the format. However, the external file that is created can easily be imported into a database through the use of another external table, by using the Oracle Database 10g Data Pump driver.

Altering Tables

After you have created tables, you may need to modify them in some way. This is the purpose of the **alter table** command. With the **alter table** command, you can do the following:

- Add, modify, or remove table properties (e.g., **pctfree**, **pctused**, or the **storage** clause)

- Add, modify, or remove columns and column properties

- Add, modify, or remove constraints

- Add, modify, or remove table partitions

- Modify or remove external table settings

- Move a table to another tablespace, or rebuild the table

In this section, we look at specifics of the **alter table** command, including the security requirements related to the command and a number of different examples of its use.

Security Requirements

You can alter any table that is in your own schema. To use the **alter table** command on a table in another schema, you must have the **alter** privilege on that table, or you must have the **alter**

any table system privilege. Also, certain operations require that you have the **create any index** privilege if you do them in a schema other than your own.

If you need to drop or truncate a partition and you are not the owner of the table, you must have the **drop any table** privilege. If you wish to add, modify, move, or split a partition, you must have a quota in the tablespace that is sufficient for such an operation.

You need to have the privileges required to create an index on the table if you are going to create or enable a unique or primary key constraint, since these operations result in the creation of an index. Finally, if you are going to enable or disable triggers in a schema outside your own, you need the **alter any trigger** system privilege.

Altering Nonpartitioned Table Examples

This section provides a number of different examples of the **alter table** command that you will probably need to use in real life. We cover actions such as adding, modifying, and removing table columns, adding constraints to a table, and performing a number of other typical administrative activities.

Altering a Table to Add a Column

The following example demonstrates adding a column to an existing table:

```
ALTER TABLE PARTS ADD (part_location VARCHAR2(20) );
```

In this case we have added a column called PART_LOCATION to the PARTS table. If we wanted to add two columns, we could do this:

```
ALTER TABLE PARTS ADD (part_location VARCHAR2(20), part_bin VARCHAR2(30) );
```

Modifying a Column

Here are two examples of modifying a column:

```
ALTER TABLE PARTS MODIFY (part_location VARCHAR2(30) );
ALTER TABLE PARTS MODIFY
 (part_location VARCHAR2(30), part_bin VARCHAR2(20) );
```

Dropping a Column

Oracle9*i* Database and later allows you to drop a column as well:

```
ALTER TABLE PARTS DROP (part_location);
ALTER TABLE PARTS DROP (part_location, part_bin);
```

Renaming a Column

Renaming a column is easy when using Oracle9*i* Database and later:

```
ALTER TABLE PARTS RENAME COLUMN part_location TO part_loc;
```

If you are using a version earlier than Oracle9*i* Database then you will need to drop and re-create the table to rename a column.

Adding a Primary Key

Here is an example of using the **alter table** command to add a primary key constraint to a table:

```
ALTER TABLE parts
ADD CONSTRAINT pk_parts_part_id
PRIMARY KEY (id) USING INDEX
TABLESPACE parts_index
STORAGE (INITIAL 100K NEXT 100K PCTINCREASE 0);
```

Adding a Unique Key

Here is an example of using the **alter table** command to add a unique key constraint to a table:

```
ALTER TABLE parts
ADD CONSTRAINT uk_parts_part_bin
UNIQUE (part_bin)
USING INDEX
TABLESPACE parts_index
STORAGE (INITIAL 100K NEXT 100K PCTINCREASE 0);
```

Sometimes you may want to add a unique key to a column that exists but currently has duplicates. You need to perform a two-part operation to do this:

```
CREATE INDEX ix_parts_01 ON parts(part_bin);
ALTER TABLE parts
ADD CONSTRAINT uk_parts_part_bin
UNIQUE (part_bin)
ENABLE NOVALIDATE;
```

Note that the table still has the duplicates in it, but new rows that are added have to pass the uniqueness check; otherwise, an ORA-00001 error will appear, which indicates a unique constraint violation has occurred. If such an error appears, you need to determine what to do with the duplicate data and then dispose of it accordingly.

Adding a Foreign Key

After you have initially created your tables, you may find that you need to add additional foreign key constraints to them. This can be accomplished via the **alter table** command, as shown in this example:

```
ALTER TABLE parts ADD CONSTRAINT fk_part_bin
FOREIGN KEY (bin_code)
REFERENCES part_bin;
```

This example creates a foreign key constraint between the BIN_NUMBER column in the PARTS table and the same column in the PART_BIN table. Note that BIN_NUMBER must be the primary key or a unique key in the PART_BIN table, because a foreign key must reference primary key columns or unique key columns in the referenced table. If the referenced column name were different, then the statement would look slightly different, in that it would include the different name:

```
ALTER TABLE parts ADD CONSTRAINT fk_part_bin
FOREIGN KEY (bin_code)
REFERENCES part_bin (bin);
```

NOTE
It's generally a best practice to name related columns the same in your tables.

Adding a Check Constraint
The following SQL demonstrates the addition of a check constraint to an existing table via the **alter table** command:

```
ALTER TABLE parts ADD (CONSTRAINT ck_parts_01 CHECK (id > 0) );
```

Defining a Default Value for a Column
If you want to modify an existing column so that it has a default value, you could issue the following **alter table** statement:

```
ALTER TABLE PARTS MODIFY (name DEFAULT 'Not Available');
```

You can also add a column and define a default value at the same time:

```
ALTER TABLE PARTS ADD (vendor_code NUMBER DEFAULT 0);
```

To remove a default value, simply use the following:

```
ALTER TABLE PARTS MODIFY (part_description DEFAULT NULL);
```

Dropping a Constraint
Need to drop a constraint? Use the **alter table** command:

```
ALTER TABLE parts DROP CONSTRAINT fk_part_bin;
ALTER TABLE parts DROP PRIMARY KEY;
```

If you have foreign keys, then you need to use the **cascade** command when dropping a primary key:

```
ALTER TABLE parts DROP PRIMARY KEY CASCADE;
```

Dropping unique keys is just as easy:

```
ALTER TABLE parts DROP UNIQUE (uk_parts_part_bin);
```

Again, the **cascade** clause is available if needed:

```
ALTER TABLE parts DROP UNIQUE (uk_parts_part_bin) CASCADE;
```

Disabling Constraints

Sometimes you may just need to disable a particular constraint. You can disable a primary key:

```
ALTER TABLE parts DISABLE PRIMARY KEY;
```

Or you can disable a unique key. You can disable the unique key either by using the column that the key is built on or by referencing the constraint itself:

```
ALTER TABLE parts DISABLE UNIQUE (part_bin);
ALTER TABLE parts DISABLE CONSTRAINT uk_parts_part_bin;
```

By default, when you disable a constraint that is dependent on an index, that index will be removed. You can opt to keep the index by using the **keep index** clause, as shown here:

```
ALTER TABLE parts DISABLE CONSTRAINT uk_parts_part_bin KEEP INDEX;
```

You can also disable foreign keys:

```
ALTER TABLE parts DISABLE CONSTRAINT fk_part_bin;
```

You can also combine these statements:

```
ALTER TABLE parts DISABLE CONSTRAINT fk_part_bin
DISABLE PRIMARY KEY KEEP INDEX;
```

In some cases, it is desirable to keep the constraint valid but remove the associated index. In this case, use the **disable validate** clause:

```
ALTER TABLE parts DISABLE VALIDATE PRIMARY KEY;
```

Re-enabling Constraints

To re-enable constraints, you use the **alter table** statement. For smaller tables, just re-enabling the constraint is enough:

```
ALTER TABLE parts ENABLE CONSTRAINT fk_part_bin;
ALTER TABLE parts ENABLE PRIMARY KEY;
ALTER TABLE parts ENABLE UNIQUE (part_bin);
```

When keys are re-enabled, they are revalidated. Uniqueness is confirmed and/or relationship consistency is validated. This can take some time, and is often not required. If any of the rows in the tables violate the constraint, then the statement will fail. You can avoid these validations by using the **novalidate** command, as shown in these examples:

```
ALTER TABLE parts ENABLE NOVALIDATE CONSTRAINT fk_part_bin;
ALTER TABLE parts ENABLE NOVALIDATE PRIMARY KEY;
ALTER TABLE parts ENABLE NOVALIDATE UNIQUE (part_bin);
```

You can also combine these statements as well:

```
ALTER TABLE parts ENABLE NOVALIDATE PRIMARY KEY
ENABLE NOVALIDATE CONSTRAINT fk_part_bin;
```

NOTE
If you are going to enable a foreign key constraint, then the related primary key constraints must be enabled.

Disabling and Re-enabling Triggers
The **alter table** command allows you to enable and disable all triggers on a given table, as shown here:

```
ALTER TABLE parts DISABLE ALL TRIGGERS;
ALTER TABLE parts ENABLE ALL TRIGGERS;
```

Modifying a Column to NULL or NOT NULL
Sometimes you may need to modify a column so that it will allow NULL values, or disallow NULL values. You use the **alter table** command to perform this operation, as shown in the next example. Note that before you can change a column property to NOT NULL, you must ensure that all rows for that column are already NOT NULL or the command will fail.

```
ALTER TABLE parts MODIFY (name NOT NULL);
ALTER TABLE parts MODIFY (name NULL);
```

Changing a Table's Physical Attributes
If you need to change the physical attributes of the table, use the **alter table** command. Here are some examples:

```
ALTER TABLE parts PCTFREE 10 PCTUSED 60;
ALTER TABLE parts STORAGE (NEXT 1M);
```

Modifying a Table's Parallel Settings
Tables can be defined with a default level of parallelism. Occasionally, you may want to modify the default parallelism settings. Here is an example:

```
ALTER TABLE parts PARALLEL 4;
```

Rebuilding/Moving a Table
The **alter table** command, with the **move** parameter, can be used to move an existing table to another tablespace. This can also be used to rebuild a table when block usage is inefficient. Here is an example:

```
ALTER TABLE parts MOVE TABLESPACE parts_new_tbs PCTFREE 10 PCTUSED 60;
```

Converting a LONG to a LOB

LONG data types have been available for some time, but are being phased out in favor of LOBs. To ease the conversion from a LONG data type to a LOB data type, Oracle offers the **alter table modify** command:

```
ALTER TABLE parts MODIFY(part_comments CLOB);
```

Note that this command causes the entire table to be moved, which may require additional disk space and system resources. Also, VARCHAR and RAW data types cannot be converted using this method.

Adding a LOB Column

You might wish to add a new LOB column to your table. This example adds a BLOB column to the PARTS table:

```
ALTER TABLE parts ADD (photo BLOB)
LOB (photo) STORE AS lob_parts_photo
(TABLESPACE parts_lob_tbs);
```

Modifying the LOB Parameters and storage Clause

You might want to modify an existing LOB column in an existing table. The following examples demonstrate how to do this:

```
ALTER TABLE parts MODIFY LOB (photo) (STORAGE(FREELISTS 2));
ALTER TABLE parts MODIFY LOB (photo) (PCTVERSION 50);
```

Shrinking and Compacting Segments Online

If you have removed a number of rows from a table, you might want to compact that table and reset the high-water mark. In Oracle9*i* Database and earlier, you must either re-create the table or truncate it in order to perform this operation. In Oracle Database 10*g*, you can shrink and compact a given segment online using the **alter table shrink space cascade** command. This operation can be done on regular tables, partitioned tables, and index-organized tables, and on indexes as well. Here is an example of the use of this command:

```
ALTER TABLE test_table SHRINK SPACE CASCADE;
```

This command will cause the empty space in the TEST_TABLE to be coalesced, and compacted and causes the high-water mark to be reset. Also, the **cascade** parameter causes dependent objects, such as associated table indexes, to be compacted as well.

Before you can use the **alter table shrink space cascade** command on a table, you must enable row movement on the table by using the **alter table enable row movement** command.

Altering Partitioned Tables

One thing to keep in mind when doing partitioned table maintenance is the impact of these operations on global indexes. You should consider using the **update global indexes** clause during any partition operation that will involve physically altering the data within one or more partitions. Failure to do so will result in global index partitions becoming unusable, and you will then need to rebuild those indexes.

Adding a Partition or Subpartition
You may need to add a partition or subpartition to your partitioned table, as shown in this example:

```
ALTER TABLE store_sales add partition sales_q1_04
VALUES LESS THAN (TO_DATE('01-APR-2004','DD-MON-YYYY'))
TABLESPACE data_0104_tbs UPDATE GLOBAL INDEXES;
```

Dropping a Partition or Subpartition
Of course, if you need to add partitions, you probably need to remove them from time to time. Here is an example of such an operation:

```
ALTER TABLE store_sales DROP PARTITION sales_q1_04 UPDATE GLOBAL INDEXES;
```

Truncating a Partition or Subpartition
During normal partition maintenance operations, you may wish to truncate a partition. Here is an example of this operation:

```
ALTER TABLE store_sales TRUNCATE PARTITION sales_overflow
UPDATE GLOBAL INDEXES;
```

Moving a Partition or Subpartition
Sometimes you may need to move a partition to another tablespace, or perhaps you may want to reorganize the partition with new storage parameters. Here is an example of this type of operation:

```
ALTER TABLE store_sales MOVE PARTITION sales_overflow TABLESPACE new_sales_
overflow STORAGE (INITIAL 100m NEXT 100m PCTINCREASE 0)
UPDATE GLOBAL INDEXES;
```

Renaming a Partition or Subpartition
You may need to rename a partition in a partitioned table. Here is an example of just such a case:

```
ALTER TABLE store_sales RENAME PARTITION sales_q1 TO sales_first_quarter;
```

Splitting a Partition or Subpartition
Further dividing a partition, or splitting it, is also possible. This is handy when a specific partition is perhaps too large and you want to further partition it. Here are two examples of such an operation:

```
ALTER TABLE store_sales
SPLIT PARTITION sales_overflow AT (TO_DATE('01-FEB-2004','DD-MON-YYYY') )
INTO (PARTITION sales_q4_2003,
      PARTITION sales_overflow)
UPDATE GLOBAL INDEXES;
ALTER TABLE composite_sales SPLIT PARTITION SALES_Q1
AT (TO_DATE('15-FEB-2003','DD-MON-YYYY'))
```

```
INTO (PARTITION sales_q1_01 SUBPARTITIONS 4
STORE IN (q1_01_tab1, q1_01_tab2, q1_01_tab3, q1_01_tab4),
PARTITION sales_q1_02 SUBPARTITIONS 4
STORE IN (q1_02_tab1, q1_02_tab2, q1_02_tab3, q1_02_tab4) )
UPDATE GLOBAL INDEXES;
```

Merging a Partition or Subpartition

Okay...so you split the partition and now realize you made a mistake! Here is how you merge two (or more) partitions or subpartitions in a partitioned table. In this example, we have merged the Oklahoma and Texas partitions in the STORE_SALES table into one partition, oktx:

```
ALTER TABLE store_sales
MERGE PARTITIONS Oklahoma, texas
INTO PARTITION oktx;
```

Dropping Tables

The **drop table** SQL statement is used to drop tables (including external tables). When you drop a table, the database removes all rows from the table and drops all indexes, partitions, associated storage (e.g., LOB storage), and triggers. When you drop a table, you invalidate any stored procedures or views that reference that table. Materialized views based on the table to be dropped remain valid but cannot be refreshed.

You need to use the **cascade constraints** clause of the **drop table** command to drop any referential integrity constraints that might reference primary or unique keys in the dropped table. Failure to do so will result in an error if such constraints exist.

Security Requirements

To use the **drop table** command, the table should be in your own schema, or you must have the **drop any table** system privilege.

Examples

This command drops a table called PARTS:

```
DROP TABLE parts;
```

However, if PARTS has some foreign keys to other tables, this drop will fail.

The next command drops the table PARTS, regardless of the presence of foreign keys. In this case, the foreign keys are dropped as well.

```
DROP TABLE parts CASCADE CONSTRAINTS;
```

Table-Related Data Dictionary Information

Oracle databases provide several different views that provide information on Oracle database tables. The following table provides some details on these views, as well as information on the availability of the all and user varieties (e.g., **all_tables** and **user_tables**) of these views:

View Name	Description	All	User
DBA_TABLES	Provides detailed information on tables within the database.	Y	Y
DBA_TAB_COLUMNS	Provides detailed column-level information for all columns in database tables.	Y	Y
DBA_TAB_PARTITIONS	Provides information on individual partition configurations, including partition information, storage parameter information, logging attributes, and collected statistical information.	Y	Y
DBA_LOB_PARTITIONS	Provides information on all LOB partitions in the database, including specific LOB configuration information (e.g., PCTVERSION, IN_ROW, etc.).	Y	Y
DBA_LOB_SUBPARTITIONS	Provides information on all LOB subpartitions in the database, including specific LOB configuration information (e.g., PCTVERSION, IN_ROW, etc.).	Y	Y
DBA_PART_COL_STATISTICS	Provides column-level statistics for partitioned tables in the database.	Y	Y
DBA_PART_HISTOGRAMS	Provides histogram data for all histograms in partitioned tables in the database.	Y	Y
DBA_PART_KEY_COLUMNS	Provides partition key column information for all partitioned objects in the database.	Y	Y
DBA_PART_LOBS	Provides information for all partitioned LOBs in the database. Includes default attributes for LOB partitions.	Y	Y
DBA_PART_TABLES	Provides partitioning information for all partitioned tables in the database.	Y	Y
DBA_SUBPART_COL_STATISTICS	Provides column statistics for all subpartitions in the database.	Y	Y
DBA_SUBPART_HISTOGRAMS	Provides histogram data on all table subpartitions in the database.	Y	Y
DBA_TAB_SUBPARTITIONS	Provides information on table subpartitions for each partitioned table in the database. Includes the name of the subpartition and its related table and storage attributes.	Y	Y

Table-Related Errors

As you manage tables, you may run into various Oracle database errors. The following table lists the most common errors and provides some advice as to what to do in the event you run into those errors.

Oracle Error Message	Text Description	Possible Causes and Solutions
ORA-00901	Invalid CREATE command	You have issued an invalid **create table** statement. Check the statement for errors and rerun the command.
ORA-00906	Missing left parenthesis	There is a syntax error in your statement. Find the error in the SQL statement and re-execute the statement.
ORA-00904	Invalid identifier	You have issued a statement that references a column that does not exist in the referenced object. For example, you may have tried to modify a column in a table that does not exist. Often this is just a simple typo that needs to be corrected.
ORA-00942	Table or view does not exist	You have issued an **alter table** or **drop table** command against a table that does not exist. Often this occurs either because the command has a typo or because you are connected to the wrong database.
ORA-00955	Name is already used by an existing object	You are using a name that already exists in your namespace. Determine which object is using the name, and then determine if you should rename that object or the table being created.
ORA-00959	Tablespace does not exist	You have tried to create an object in a tablespace that does not exist. Check the tablespace name being used in the **create** statement, or create the tablespace.
ORA-01031	Insufficient privileges	You do not have privileges to perform the requested operation. The DBA needs to use the **grant** command to grant your user the appropriate privileges to the object.
ORA-01430	Column being added already exists in table	You have tried to add to a table a column that already exists in the table. Check to determine why the database thinks you already have this column in your table and correct the problem.
ORA-1451	Column to be modified to NULL cannot be modified to NULL	You have tried to alter a column to allow for NULL values but the column already allows NULL values.
ORA-01659	Unable to allocate MINEXTENTS beyond x in tablespace	You have tried to create a table but insufficient space exists in the tablespace. Make sure that you are sizing your table correctly. If so, you need to increase the size of the tablespace, or assign the table to another tablespace.
ORA-02149	Specified partition does not exist	You have referenced a partition that does not exist. Check to ensure that you are referencing a valid partition name and that the related table name is correct.
ORA-02203	INITIAL storage options not allowed	You cannot use the **initial** storage option in an **alter table** command. **initial** is only allowed when creating a table or moving the table.

Oracle Error Message	Text Description	Possible Causes and Solutions
ORA-02261	Such unique or primary key already exists in the table	You have tried to create with the **alter table** command a primary key or unique key that already exists. You may have already created the primary key or unique key. If you are trying to modify the primary or unique key, you may need to drop and re-create it.
ORA-02264	Name already used by an existing constraint	You have tried to create a constraint using a name that already exists. You may have already created the constraint or previously created a constraint with the same name.
ORA-02429	Cannot drop index used for enforcement of unique/ primary key	You have tried to drop an index that is associated with either a primary key or unique key constraint. Drop the constraint instead.
ORA-02449	Unique/primary keys in table referenced by foreign keys	You have tried to drop a table that has foreign key constraints to other tables. You need to remove those constraints either manually or by using the **drop table cascade constraints** command.
ORA-14048	A partition maintenance operation may not be combined with other operations	This error may be the result of a syntax error in your SQL statement. It may also indicate that you are trying to use an invalid set of combined partition operations in a single SQL statement.
ORA-14074	Partition bound must collate higher than that of the last partition	You have attempted to split a partition, but the partition boundary on which you have tried to split the partition is not within the boundary of the partition you have tried to split. Generally, this means that you are splitting based on an invalid date, and the date is greater than the partition boundary.
ORA-14310	VALUES LESS THAN or AT clause cannot be used with list partitioned tables	You have attempted an invalid operation on a list-partitioned table.
ORA-25150	ALTERING of extent parameters not permitted	In Oracle9*i* Database, if the object you are modifying is in a locally managed tablespace, you cannot alter extent sizing parameters. This includes parameters such as **next**, **maxextents**, and so on. If you have a need to perform such an operation, you can convert the tablespace to a dictionary-managed tablespace (subject to restrictions) via the Oracle database package **dbms_space_admin.tablespace_migrate_ from_local**.

Table-Related Recommended Standards

To close out this chapter, I would like to suggest some table-related standards and best practices that you may wish to consider using as you fire up your Oracle database creative juices:

- Name the tables plainly; describe what is being stored in the table. For example, if the table is going to store part components, name the table PART_COMPONENTS.

- Even though the Oracle database allows a table name to be 30 characters in length, make the name as compact as possible, while at the same time keeping it meaningful.

- You should make your table names plural in nature. For example, the table will be called PARTS rather than PART.

- Place tables in tablespaces based on the expected sizes of the tables. I recommend the following:

  - Place lookup (reference) tables in a common tablespace. These don't generally change often, and thus have common I/O characteristics.

  - Separate tables into different tablespaces based on the expected size of the tables. I create locally managed tablespaces using the uniform extent allocation method and assign tablespaces to one of three tablespaces. These tablespaces are designed to support small, midsize, and large tables. For example, small tables might be stored in an LMT with a uniform size of 1M, midsize tables might be stored in a tablespace with a uniform size of 10M, and large tables may be stored in a 100M tablespace.

  - Separate special, highly volatile tables into their own tablespaces. This makes it easier to deal with these important, and often most problematic, tables without impacting other tables in tablespaces.

CHAPTER

6

Indexes

ndexes are an indispensable part of an Oracle database. In many cases, indexes provide quick access to specific rows in your database, eliminating the need for full scans of tables. This chapter quickly reviews the basics of indexes, and then looks at the specifics of index-related DBA activities, including the **create index**, **alter index**, and **drop index** commands.

Indexing Overview

In this section, we quickly review some basic index information, including the different types of indexes that the Oracle database has available for use, the various options related to indexes, such as partitioning, and the different features that are available when using indexes.

Oracle Index Types

Oracle databases offers a number of different index options to suit the needs of the database designer:

- B*Tree indexes (the default)

- Reverse key indexes

- Bitmap indexes

- Bitmap join indexes

- Function-based indexes

- Domain indexes

Indexes will be used only if your SQL query includes a **where** clause. The database evaluates the **where** clause and determines whether it can use a given index to provide a faster access path to the data you are interested in. For example, assume you issue a SQL statement SELECT * FROM emp WHERE empno=100;. If there were an index on the EMPNO column, the database would likely choose that index to retrieve the data you were requesting. Let's look at each index type in a bit more detail.

B*Tree Indexes

A B*Tree index is the default index type in an Oracle database. B*Tree indexes are ordered lists of values. At the top of the index is the root block. The root block points to other, lower-level blocks known as branch blocks. These branch blocks can be multiple levels deep and lead finally to the leaf blocks, which contain the actual data values and the ROWIDs associated with these data values.

B*Tree indexes have a number of benefits:

- Access to unique values, or small ranges of values, within the index is quite fast. B*Tree indexes are particularly adept for range queries and queries that contain exact matching criteria.

- B*Tree indexes are automatically balanced.

■ Individual B*Tree indexes have a minimal impact on DML operations, though an excessive number of B*Tree indexes can impact DML operations.

■ In most cases, B*Tree index operations scale well as the amount of data grows.

By default, a B*Tree index allows for duplicate values in all the key columns. However, a B*Tree index can be created as a unique index, which requires that the data values in the index be unique. Adding indexes gives the Oracle database optimizer more options with regard to which execution plan it chooses to use. An Oracle database can perform the following operations on indexes:

Access Path	Description
Unique scan	A unique scan returns no more than one row. This type of scan is only possible with a primary key or unique index.
Range scan	This is a scan of an index that starts at a specific point within the index itself (as opposed to a full scan of an index). It can be either bounded or unbounded, depending on the associated **where** clause. A *bounded range scan* starts and stops at specific locations within the index. An *unbounded range scan* starts at a specific location within the index but reads the remaining leaf nodes of the index. A range scan may return multiple identical rows (if they exist in the table) and these will be sorted in ascending order by ROWID. Rows are returned in ascending order (and further sorting may occur if required by an **order by** clause). Range scans are not possible with reverse key indexes.
Range scan descending	Identical to a range scan except that the rows are returned in descending order. This is ignored in versions of Oracle Database earlier than 9*i*.
Fast full scan	A fast full scan is an alternative to a full table scan. It can be used if all columns in the query are present in the index, and at least one of those columns is NOT NULL. Fast full scans do not eliminate sorts, because the index key does not order the rows returned. Fast full scans use multiblock I/O (like full table scans) and can be parallelized. Thus, they may be faster than index full scans.
Index full scan	This is a full scan of the index and can be used to eliminate table accesses. Generally, this scan is used if all columns in the query are present in the index and at least one of those columns is NOT NULL. This type of index access can also eliminate sorts that might otherwise occur, but it does not eliminate table access. An index full scan does single-block I/O, thus it may be slower than a fast full scan (but the resulting sort of a fast full scan may negate this advantage).
Index skip scan	This is a scan of a composite index that skips one or more of the columns of the index, yet uses columns after that column as part of the index scan.
Index join	This is a hash join of two or more indexes that contain all the table columns referenced in the SQL query, thus eliminating table access. Sort operations are not eliminated.

Reverse Key Indexes

A reverse key index reverses the byte order of all the indexed columns in that index, with the exception of the ROWID. Reverse key indexes can help specific performance issues with indexes that involve columns that have values that are closely aligned (say, for example, repeating sequence numbers.) These aligned numbers will be placed on a small set of leaf blocks, which can lead to block contention during concurrent accesses. Additionally, high insert/delete rates of operations can cause the index to become horizontally "imbalanced" (though, in truth a B*Tree index does not become imbalanced at all). A reverse key index solves these problems by reversing the values of the columns of the index, and thereby spreading those values over more blocks. Reverse key indexes can also be helpful in certain types of RAC implementations where there are high concurrency requirements for individual blocks across RAC nodes. Access paths to reverse key indexes are limited to the following operations:

- Unique scans
- Full index scans

Bitmap Indexes

Bitmap indexes are designed to provide improved access to rows based on columns with a low number of distinct values. A bitmap index contains a bitmap relationship between the indexed values and the related ROWIDs in the table, with each bit indicating whether the value is present at a given ROWID.

Bitmap indexes tend to be much smaller than B*Tree indexes built on the same columns. They can offer enhanced performance over B*Tree indexes, particularly in data warehouse environments with infrequent data modification but heavy data query activity, particularly ad-hoc data queries. Bitmap indexes fare worse (often much worse) in OLTP applications because OLTP typically has heavy concurrent DML activity changing the data within the database. Heavy concurrent DML activity is a problem because of the way Oracle databases lock rows in a bitmap index: activity on one row can result in the locking of many rows within the bitmap index, which can cause serious locking contention.

Bitmap indexes are most efficient for equality type queries. Queries that involve range (greater than or less than) comparisons are not good candidates for bitmap indexes. Also, unlike B*Tree indexes, bitmap indexes include rows that contain NULL values, which can be quite helpful for certain types of SQL statements.

Bitmap indexes have the following limitations:

- Bitmap indexes are only available with the Enterprise Edition of the Oracle database.
- Bitmap indexes on partitioned tables must be local indexes.
- You cannot create a bitmap index as a secondary index on an IOT unless the IOT has a mapping table.
- A bitmap index cannot be defined as unique.

Bitmap Join Indexes

A bitmap join index is a bitmap index that joins the primary key columns of one table (generally a fact table) with one or more foreign key columns of other tables (which are generally dimension tables).

This provides improved join performance between these tables when you are joining using the columns of the bitmap join index.

Bitmap join indexes do come with some restrictions:

- Only one of the columns of the tables of the bitmap join index can be modified at a time, which means that during concurrent DML activity, other sessions will be blocked.

- You cannot create a bitmap join index on an IOT or a temporary table.

- Each column in the index must be a column that is in one of the dimension tables, thus the index represents a snowflake or star schema.

- Each column in the dimension tables that are in the index must be a primary key column or the columns must have unique constraints.

- You cannot join a table to itself in a bitmap join index.

- All restrictions that apply to normal bitmap indexes apply to bitmap join indexes.

Function-Based Indexes

A function-based index allows you to create an index on functions involving one or more columns of a table. When the function-based index is created, the value of the function is calculated and then stored in the index (which can be either a B*Tree or a bitmap index). Function-based indexes provide the benefits of index access when your **where** clause contains that function within it.

There are several restrictions on function-based indexes:

- Function-based indexes must be defined using a function that is deterministic. That is, it returns just one value.

- Function-based indexes must be defined using a function that returns a repeatable value. Functions returning variable values, such as **sysdate**, are not valid.

- Function-based indexes can be partitioned, but for globally partitioned function-based indexes the partition key cannot be the function that the function is based on.

- A function definition must be specified with parentheses, regardless if they actually have parameters or not. They will be interpreted as column names otherwise.

- The function that the index is based on cannot contain aggregate functions.

NOTE
insert and *update* statement performance does not benefit from a function-based index.

To use function-based indexes, you must have the parameter **query_rewrite_enabled** set to TRUE. Also, if a function that the function-based index is dependent on is removed, then that function-based index will be marked DISABLED, and any query attempting to use that index will fail.

Domain Indexes

"Domain index" is a generic term for an index created using the Oracle Extensibility framework. In a domain index, the mechanism used to store the values to be indexed, and to return the matching rows, is defined via the **create index type** command. A domain index allows you to create a user-defined index type rather than use the standard Oracle database B*Tree or bitmap indexes. The Oracle database itself uses this framework to create indexes for use with special types of data, such as text or spatial data.

Miscellaneous Index Features

In this section, we cover a variety of indexing features, including the following:

- Index attributes
- The **storage** clause
- Building indexes online
- Parallel processing
- Partitioning indexes
- Rebuilding indexes
- Coalescing indexes
- Analyzing indexes
- Index key compression
- Reverse key indexes
- The **nosort** option
- The **nologging** clause
- Monitoring index usage

Index Attributes

When you create an index, you can associate specific attributes to that index. The index attributes that you can set when creating an index include the following:

Attribute	Description	Default Value
pctfree	Determines how much of a block is reserved for updates to existing rows. Once a block's usage is at or above **pctfree**, it is removed from the freelist and will not be used.	10
pctused	A block that has been removed from the freelist as a result of meeting or exceeding the **pctfree** threshold will be re-added to the list if its space utilization falls below that of **pctused**.	40

Attribute	Description	Default Value
initrans	Defines the initial number of concurrent transaction entries that are allocated within each data block. The maximum value is dependent on the block size. Change this value if you have a large number of concurrent operations; however, the database dynamically adds transaction entries as required.	2
maxtrans	Determines the maximum number of concurrent transactions allowed to update a given data block.	Varies based on block size
storage clause	Determines the actual physical storage characteristics for the index.	See the next section.

The previous table mentions the **storage** clause. The **storage** clause is used to define storage parameters related to the object you are creating. When a table is created, the values used for the **storage** clause come from one of three sources, in this order:

1. The values established in the **storage** clause of the statement that created the object

2. The tablespace default storage values

3. Oracle database storage value defaults for the object type being created

The following table is a quick reference for **storage** clause values that are commonly used when creating indexes:

Parameter	Defines
initial	The size of the first extent of the index
next	The size of the next extent of the index
minextents	The minimum number of extents that should be assigned to the index
maxextents	The maximum number of extents that should be assigned to the index
pctincrease	The percentage that **next** should be increased after each extent operation
freelists	The number of freelists to be allocated to the index
freelist groups	The number of freelist groups to be allocated to the index
buffer_pool	The Oracle database buffer pool (keep, recycle, or default) that the index should be assigned to

Building Indexes Online

Normal index creation causes all DML operations to experience wait conditions until the index creation is complete. Use of the **online** clause of the **create index** command eliminates this problem and allows you to create the index with a minimum of interruption to base table DML.

Parallel DML is not supported during an online index build operation. Additionally online operations are not supported during bitmap index operations, and online operations are not supported if an index contains a UROWID column.

Parallel Processing

Creation of an index can occur in parallel in an Oracle database through the use of the **parallel** clause (examples of the use of the **parallel** clause are provided in "Creating Indexes Using Oracle Parallel Query" later in this chapter) or by issuing the **alter session force parallel ddl** command. When you use the **parallel** clause, you can choose to specify the degree of parallelism directly or you can allow the database to select the degree of parallelism for you. In the latter case, the database calculates the degree of parallelism as the number of CPUs available to the instance times the value of the database parameter **parallel_threads_per_cpu**.

The **alter index...rebuild** command can only parallelize the rebuild of a nonpartitioned index. You can rebuild individual partitions of an index in parallel with the **alter index....rebuild partition** command.

Some restrictions on parallel processing include the following:

- Parallel processing on an index that is being rebuilt online is not supported.

- A nonpartitioned index cannot be scanned in parallel.

Partitioning Indexes

Just as with tables, you can partition indexes. There are two principle types of partitioned indexes, local and global. Let's look at these types of indexes in a bit more detail.

Locally Partitioned Indexes   A locally partitioned index is always equi-partitioned with the underlying table. That is, the partition key of the index, the number of partitions, and the values stored in those partitions are just like the partitions of the underlying base table. You can assign names to the partitions of locally partitioned indexes, or the database will give the partitions system-assigned names. You can assign separate attributes and storage characteristics to index partitions, or you can choose to accept the default settings that the database derives for you, either from the defaults defined for the partitioned index or from the tablespace-level defaults.

Globally Partitioned Indexes   Globally partitioned indexes allow you to partition or subpartition an index in a different manner than the partitioning strategy for the underlying table. When the index is partitioned differently than the underlying table, it is said to be non-equi-partitioned. When creating a global index, the columns that the index is being built on must also be prefixed in the partition key. For example, if the index is to be built on COLUMN_ONE and COLUMN_TWO in a given table, then the partition boundaries of that index must begin with COLUMN_ONE and COLUMN_TWO.

Globally partitioned indexes in Oracle9*i* Database can only be range-partitioned indexes. In Oracle Database 10*g*, globally partitioned indexes can also be range or hash partitioned. When creating a global index, you need to define each individual partition and the partition range. You can assign separate attributes and storage characteristics to index partitions, or you can choose to take the default settings that the database derives for you, either from the defaults defined for the partitioned index or from the tablespace-level defaults.

Unusable Indexes   Both global and local partitioned indexes can become UNUSABLE due to various maintenance operations on the underlying tables of the index. Operations that can cause global and local indexes to become unusable include the following:

Operation	Local Index Unusable?	Global Index Unusable?
Operations that bypass local index maintenance (e.g., **imp** with **skip_unusable_indexes=y**)	Yes, but only impacted partitions	Yes
Failed direct path operations (e.g., SQL*Loader)	Yes, but only impacted partitions	Yes
alter table move	Yes	Yes
alter table move partition	Yes, but only impacted partitions	Yes
alter table truncate partition	Yes, but only impacted partitions	Yes
alter table add partition	No	No
alter table drop partition	Yes, if the partition being dropped is not empty or already marked unusable; the partition marked unusable will be the next partition in the local index	Yes
alter table split partition	Yes, but only impacted partitions	Yes
alter table modify partition	Yes, but only impacted partitions	Yes
alter index split partition	Yes, if the index is local, but only the impacted partition; no, if the index being split is global	Yes, if the index is local, but only the impacted partition; no, if the index being split is global

Here is a summary of the rules with regard to operations that will make indexes unusable:

- Operations that bypass local index maintenance will cause the affected local index partitions and entire global partitioned indexes to be marked unusable.

- Failure of direct load operations that cause the index to be out of synchronization with the underlying table will cause both affected local partitioned indexes and global indexes to be marked unusable.

- Any operation that can change ROWIDs will mark both local and global indexes UNUSABLE.

- Any partition maintenance operation that removes rows from the table will mark as unusable the impacted partitions in the local index and all partitions of global indexes.

- Any table partition maintenance operation that modifies the definition of the table partition will mark as unusable associated local index partitions.

- Index maintenance operations that modify the partition definition of the index partition will mark as unusable the index partition being changed and the associated global indexes.

You can look at the STATUS column in the DBA_INDEXES view to determine if a nonpartitioned index has been marked unusable, and the STATUS column in the DBA_PART_INDEXES view to determine if a partitioned index has been marked unusable. When an index is marked unusable, you must rebuild it.

If a partition in an index becomes unusable, then you must rebuild any partitions that are marked as unusable; however, the remaining partitions do not need to be rebuilt. Until the index or the index partitions are rebuilt, operations that involve those indexes will return an error in Oracle9*i* Database. See the next section for more information on rebuilding indexes. By default, Oracle Database 10*g* skips unusable indexes and index partitions when generating execution plans. You can disable this feature by setting the **skip_unusable_index** parameter to FALSE.

Another solution to the unusable index problem is to use the **rebuild unusable local indexes** and **update global indexes** clauses of the **alter table** command. This causes any indexes or index partitions that are invalidated as a result of the SQL command execution to be rebuilt during the execution of that command automatically. This causes the associated command to take longer to execute, since the index rebuilds must now also complete.

Rebuilding Indexes

For a variety of reasons, indexes need to be rebuilt. The most common reasons are the following:

- You need to move the index to a new tablespace.

- Block storage inside the index has become inefficient.

- You need to alter one of the attributes of the index, such as the **storage** clause.

You can rebuild an index in one of two ways. First, you can drop and re-create the index. This can be problematic, because you need the complete **create index** statement. Also, DML operations on the index will be blocked during the creation of the index. As an alternative, the Oracle database provides a very easy method of rebuilding an index, using the **alter index rebuild** command (or **alter index rebuild partition** or **alter index rebuild subpartition** for partitioned indexes). The **alter index rebuild** command allows you to rebuild the index, without having to drop it first. During normal operations, an exclusive lock is placed on the table that the index is being built on. This blocks all DML on the table that the index is associated with. You can avoid this locking situation by using the **alter index rebuild online** command to rebuild an index online.

With the **alter index rebuild** command, you can rebuild an index and, at the same time, move it to another tablespace, reset storage parameters, and alter physical attributes of the index. The **alter index rebuild** command can also be used to rebuild an index with an UNUSABLE status and make it usable again.

The ability to rebuild an index comes with a bucketful of restrictions:

- Indexes on temporary tables cannot be rebuilt.

- Bitmap indexes marked invalid must be dropped and re-created, because they cannot be dropped.

- If you wish to rebuild a partitioned (local or global) index, you must rebuild each individual partition with the **alter index rebuild partition** command.

- You cannot use the **deallocate unused** clause in the same statement as an index rebuild.

- If you are rebuilding a local index on a hash partition or subpartition, you can only specify the **tablespace** parameter in an **alter index rebuild partition** command.

- If the index is built on a list-partitioned table, you cannot rebuild it. You need to drop and re-create the partition.

Something interesting to note about the **alter index rebuild** command is that if you have pending transactions against the underlying table of the index that have not been committed, then the **alter index rebuild** command waits until those previous transactions have been committed.

Coalescing an Index

The **coalesce** option of the **alter index** command is an alternative to rebuilding an existing index. One of the issues with an index rebuild is that it is resource intensive. An index rebuild requires additional space during the rebuild process, because the old index and the new index must coexist during the rebuild process. In addition, a rebuild of an index requires space for sort operations. All in all, a rebuild can require a great deal of space.

The **alter table coalesce** option performs a logical scan of an index, combining adjacent blocks logically into a single block (if this operation is possible). The end result is that one block is populated with index data (and likely packed quite well) and the other block is returned to the freelist. In indexes with blocks that are sparsely populated, this can result in a significant reduction in the size of the index.

Restrictions on the **coalesce** option include the following:

- You cannot coalesce the primary key of an IOT with the **alter index** command (but you can with the **alter table** command).

- You cannot coalesce an index assigned to a temporary table.

- You can coalesce only a partition or subpartition, not the entire index.

Analyzing Indexes

For Oracle databases to efficiently generate execution plans under the Cost Based Optimizer (which you should be using in Oracle9*i* Database, because the Rule Based Optimizer is unsupported in Oracle Database 10*g*), you need to analyze any index that you create. Typically, you analyze tables and indexes together, but you may also want to just analyze an index (for example, after rebuilding the index or creating a new index). There are a number of ways to analyze an index:

- Analyze the index via the **analyze** command (not recommended in versions prior to Oracle8*i* Database), as shown in this example:

  ```
  ANALYZE INDEX ix_my_tb_01 COMPUTE STATISTICS;
  ```

- Analyze the associated table via the **analyze** command (recommended in Oracle8*i* and earlier versions), making sure that all indexes get analyzed as well. Here is an example:

  ```
  ANALYZE TABLE my_tb COMPUTE STATISTICS FOR ALL INDEXED COLUMNS;
  ```

- Analyze the index via the **dbms_stats** command (recommended in Oracle8*i* Database and later), as shown in this example:

  ```
  EXEC DBMS_STATS.GATHER_INDEX_STATS('MY_SCHEMA','IX_MY_TB_01', degree=>4);
  ```

- Analyze the table via the **dbms_stats** command, setting the **cascade** attribute to TRUE to ensure that the indexes get analyzed as well. Here is an example of this operation:

  ```
  EXEC DBMS_STATS.GATHER_TABLE_STATS('MY_SCHEMA','MY_TB',degree=>4,
  cascade=>TRUE);
  ```

NOTE
*The use of the **cascade** parameter is often missed by first-time users of the **gather_table_stats** procedure.*

■ Use the **compute statistics** clause to cause an index to be analyzed after a **create index** or **alter index** operation, as shown in this example:

```
ALTER INDEX ix_01_mytable REBUILD COMPUTE STATISTICS;
```

Index Key Compression
Indexes can be *key compressed*. When the index is compressed (using the **compress** keyword), the database eliminates repeated occurrences of the key column values, which can result in the reduction in the size of the index. If the index is unique, you can compress all but one column of the index. If the index is not unique, all columns may be compressed. You cannot compress a bitmap index, a partitioned unique index, or unique indexes that contain only one column.

Reverse Index
Oracle databases allow you to create an index in which the bytes are stored in reverse order (this does not impact the internal order of the rows in the index). Use the **reverse** clause of the **create index** or **alter index rebuild** command to build a reverse key index. You cannot build bitmap indexes or IOTs as reverse indexes.

Nosort Index Creation
The **create index** command allows you to speed up index creation by eliminating the sort operation that is associated with the index creation. If the data was loaded into the table already in order (e.g., presorted data loaded through SQL*Loader), then use the **nosort** clause of the **create index** command to speed up the creation of the index. Restrictions on **nosort** include the following:

■ The use of **nosort** and **reverse** are mutually exclusive.

■ The **nosort** clause does not support clusters, partitioned indexes, or bitmap indexes.

■ You cannot use the **nosort** clause on secondary indexes for IOTs.

The NoLogging Clause
Reduce redo log generation during index creation or rebuild operations with the **nologging** parameter of the **create index** or **alter index** logging clause (logging is the default). Additionally, **nologging** reduces the redo log generation that occurs during direct load operations.

If your index is partitioned, you can set the default logging value of all created partitions, and any partitions added in the future to the index, to **nologging** state by including **nologging** in the **create index** command. If you want a specific partition to be set to **nologging**, you can set that within the partition-specific attributes.

Of course, **nologging** has some recovery considerations. In particular, your **nologging** indexes will be **unusable** after a recovery and they will need to be rebuilt. This can have some impact on your overall mean time to recover.

Monitoring Index Usage

You may wish to determine whether or not an index is actually in use. You can do this through the use of the **monitoring usage** clause. When monitoring is enabled, you can check the USED column of the V$OBJECT_USAGE view to determine whether or not an index has been used. Note that you have to be connected as the owner of the index to be able to see the index usage in V$OBJECT_USAGE. Also, this information is only collected for execution plans created after the index monitoring is enabled, so any SQL statements already cached are not recorded.

Creating Indexes

To create indexes, you use the **create index** command, regardless of the type of index you wish to create. Various options of the **create index** command define the type of index that will be created (e.g., function-based) and the attributes and options that will be used when creating the index. In this section, we look first at the security requirements related to indexes, and then we consider some examples of index creation.

Security Requirements

If you wish to create an index in your own schema and the object exists in your schema, you need nothing more than a sufficient space quota in the tablespace that you will assign the index to. If the object is not in your schema, then you must have either the **index** object privilege on the object you wish to index or the **create any index** system privilege. Also, you should have sufficient quota on the tablespace the index is to be created in, or be granted the **unlimited tablespace** privilege.

To create a function-based index, you need **execute** object privileges on the function(s) that will be used in the function-based index. If you are going to create a function-based index in your own schema, then you need the **query rewrite** system privilege. You need the **global query rewrite** privilege if you wish to create the index in another schema.

Globally, to use function-based indexes, you need to set the **query_rewrite_enabled** parameter to TRUE and set the **query_rewrite_integrity** parameter to TRUSTED.

Examples Using the create index Command

In this section, we look at the creation of all sorts of indexes. We start with the creation of nonpartitioned indexes, and then we look at using parallel query when creating indexes. Then, we consider the creation of both local and global partitioned indexes.

Nonpartitioned Index Examples

Here is an example of the creation of a single-column, nonconcatenated index:

```
CREATE INDEX ix_mytab_01 ON mytab(column_1);
```

Also, we can create a concatenated index of two or more columns, concatenating up to 32 columns in one index (30 columns in a bitmap index). Here is an example of such an index:

```
CREATE INDEX ix_mytab_01 ON mytab(column_1, column_2, column_3);
```

Of course, we will probably want to define some attributes so that we can define how big our index is and where to store it. The following **create index** command does just that:

```
CREATE INDEX ix_mytab_01 ON mytab(column_1, column_2, column_3)
TABLESPACE my_indexes STORAGE (INITIAL 10K NEXT 10K PCTFREE 10);
```

You can also compute the statistics for the index at the same time you create the index through the use of the **compute statistics** clause of the **create index** command, as shown in this example:

```
CREATE INDEX ix_mytab_01 ON mytab(column_1, column_2, column_3)
TABLESPACE my_indexes STORAGE (INITIAL 10K NEXT 10K PCTFREE 10)
COMPUTE STATISTICS;
```

You can also key compress this index by using the **compress** keyword. Note that we have also made this a unique index.

```
CREATE UNIQUE INDEX ix_mytab_01 on mytab(column_1, column_2, column_3)
TABLESPACE my_indexes COMPRESS STORAGE (INITIAL 10K NEXT 10K PCTFREE 10)
COMPUTE STATISTICS;
```

Creating Bitmap Indexes

You can use the **create index** command to create a bitmap index, as shown in this example:

```
CREATE BITMAP INDEX bit_mytab_01 ON my_tab(col_two)
TABLESPACE my_tbs;
```

Creating Indexes Using Oracle Parallel Query

If you feel that a table would generally benefit from parallel query, you can define the degree of parallelism that the database should consider using when creating the table. The database also attempts to parallelize the index build operation when you use the **parallel** clause. For example, if you want to define a degree of parallelism of 4 for your index, you create the table thusly:

```
CREATE INDEX ix_parts on PARTS (id) TABLESPACE parts_tablespace
PARALLEL 4;
```

In this case, the index will be created using four parallel processes (in most cases), and the default degree of parallelism will be 4.

Partitioned Index Examples

As previously stated, Oracle databases allow two types of partitioned indexes, local and global. In this section, we look at the creation of a local partitioned index first, then a global partitioned index.

Creating a Local Partitioned Index   A local index is equi-partitioned with the underlying table. Thus, you do not define partition range information for a local index. You can define partition names, tablespace names, and partition attributes as required. Here is an example of the creation of a local partitioned index on a range-partitioned table:

```
CREATE INDEX ix_part_my_tab_01 ON my_tab (col_one, col_two, col_three)
LOCAL (PARTITION tbs_part_01 TABLESPACE part_tbs_01,
PARTITION tbs_part_02 TABLESPACE part_tbs_02,
PARTITION tbs_part_03 TABLESPACE part_tbs_03,
PARTITION tbs_part_04 TABLESPACE part_tbs_04);
```

If we had a hash-partitioned table, we would have created the index using the **store in** parameter, as shown in this example:

```
CREATE INDEX ix_part_my_tab_01 ON my_tab (col_one, col_two, col_three)
LOCAL STORE IN (part_tbs_01, part_tbs_02, part_tbs_03, part_tbs_04);
```

Each individual partition can have attributes defined for it, as shown in this local index that is created on a hash-partitioned table:

```
create index ix_part_my_tab_01 on my_tab (col_one, col_two, col_three)
LOCAL STORE IN (
part_tbs_01 storage (initial 10m next 10m maxextents 200),
part_tbs_02,
part_tbs_03 storage (initial 100m next 100m maxextents 200),
part_tbs_04 storage (initial 1000m next 1000m maxextents 200) );
```

If you have a composite-partitioned table, you will probably want to create indexes on that table. Here is an example of the creation of a locally managed index on a composite-partitioned table:

```
-- First, create the partitioned table that the index will be built on
CREATE TABLE store_sales
    ( store_id        NUMBER(6), invoice_number      NUMBER
    , time_id         DATE    , invoice_sale_amt    NUMBER(10,2) )
PARTITION BY RANGE (time_id)  SUBPARTITION BY HASH (invoice_number)
  (PARTITION SALES_Q1_2003
        VALUES LESS THAN (TO_DATE('01-APR-2003','DD-MON-YYYY')),
    PARTITION SALES_Q2_2003
        VALUES LESS THAN (TO_DATE('01-JUL-2003','DD-MON-YYYY')),
    PARTITION SALES_Q3_2003
        VALUES LESS THAN (TO_DATE('01-OCT-2003','DD-MON-YYYY'))
     (SUBPARTITION ch_c, SUBPARTITION ch_i,
      SUBPARTITION ch_p, SUBPARTITION ch_s, SUBPARTITION ch_t),
    PARTITION SALES_Q4_2003
        VALUES LESS THAN (TO_DATE('01-JAN-2004','DD-MON-YYYY'))
        SUBPARTITIONS 8,
    PARTITION SALES_OVERFLOW
        VALUES LESS THAN (MAXVALUE) SUBPARTITIONS 4);

-- Now create the index
CREATE INDEX sales_ix ON store_sales(time_id, store_id)
    STORAGE (INITIAL 1M MAXEXTENTS UNLIMITED) LOCAL
    (PARTITION q1_2003,
     PARTITION q2_2003,
```

```
     PARTITION q3_2003
       (SUBPARTITION pq3200301, SUBPARTITION pq3200302,
        SUBPARTITION pq3200303, SUBPARTITION pq3200304,
        SUBPARTITION pq3200305),
     PARTITION q4_2003
       (SUBPARTITION pq4200301 TABLESPACE tbs_1,
        SUBPARTITION pq4200302 TABLESPACE tbs_1,
        SUBPARTITION pq4200303 TABLESPACE tbs_1,
        SUBPARTITION pq4200304 TABLESPACE tbs_1,
        SUBPARTITION pq4200305 TABLESPACE tbs_1,
        SUBPARTITION pq4200306 TABLESPACE tbs_1,
        SUBPARTITION pq4200307 TABLESPACE tbs_1,
        SUBPARTITION pq4200308 TABLESPACE tbs_1),
     PARTITION sales_overflow
       (SUBPARTITION pqoflw01 TABLESPACE tbs_2,
        SUBPARTITION pqoflw02 TABLESPACE tbs_2,
        SUBPARTITION pqoflw03 TABLESPACE tbs_2,
        SUBPARTITION pqoflw04 TABLESPACE tbs_2));
```

Creating a Global Partitioned Index   Global indexes do not have to be equi-partitioned as do local indexes. Thus, global indexes offer more flexibility than local indexes, but with some added cost during certain maintenance operations and also potentially worse performance. With a global index, you define a partition key for that index as shown in this example:

```
CREATE TABLE store_sales
     ( store_id        NUMBER(6), invoice_number      NUMBER
     , time_id         DATE     , invoice_sale_amt    NUMBER(10,2) )
PARTITION BY RANGE (time_id)
   (PARTITION SALES_Q1_2003
        VALUES LESS THAN (TO_DATE('01-APR-2003','DD-MON-YYYY')),
    PARTITION SALES_Q2_2003
        VALUES LESS THAN (TO_DATE('01-JUL-2003','DD-MON-YYYY')),
    PARTITION SALES_Q3_2003
        VALUES LESS THAN (TO_DATE('01-OCT-2003','DD-MON-YYYY')),
    PARTITION SALES_Q4_2003
        VALUES LESS THAN (TO_DATE('01-JAN-2004','DD-MON-YYYY')),
    PARTITION SALES_OVERFLOW VALUES LESS THAN (MAXVALUE));

CREATE INDEX ix_part_my_tab_01 ON store_sales (invoice_number)
GLOBAL PARTITION BY RANGE (invoice_number)
(PARTITION part_001 VALUES LESS THAN (1000),
 PARTITION part_002 VALUES LESS THAN (10000),
 PARTITION part_003 VALUES LESS THAN (MAXVALUE) );
```

Of course, we can partition a global partitioned index on more than one column, as shown in this example:

```
CREATE INDEX ix_part_my_tab_02 ON store_sales (store_id, time_id)
GLOBAL PARTITION BY RANGE (store_id, time_id)
(PARTITION PART_001 VALUES LESS THAN
```

```
    (1000, TO_DATE('04-01-2003','MM-DD-YYYY') )
    TABLESPACE partition_001
    STORAGE (INITIAL 100M NEXT 200M PCTINCREASE 0),
PARTITION part_002 VALUES LESS THAN
    (1000, TO_DATE('07-01-2003','MM-DD-YYYY')  )
    TABLESPACE partition_002
    STORAGE (INITIAL 200M NEXT 400M PCTINCREASE 0),
PARTITION part_003 VALUES LESS THAN (maxvalue, maxvalue)
    TABLESPACE partition_003 );
```

Function-Based Index Examples

Often, you will find that you need to use a specific function in your SQL queries to locate data. Previous to the advent of function-based indexes, this meant that you had to execute a full table scan of your table. Now, with the function-based index, you can create an index on the function you need to use, and the query will use that index to speed the response to your query. Assume we have the following table:

```
CREATE TABLE EMP_INFO (last_name VARCHAR2(40),
                       first_name VARCHAR2(40),
                       hire_date DATE,
                       salary NUMBER);
```

Now, assume we want to use the following query in our application:

```
SELECT last_name, first_name, salary FROM emp_info
WHERE UPPER(last_name) LIKE 'THOMPSON';
```

Normally this query would not be able to take advantage of an index, but with a function-based index, it can. Here is how we create the index:

```
CREATE INDEX fb_upper_last_name_emp ON emp_info (UPPER(last_name) );
```

Once you have created the index, make sure you analyze it. Then, any query such as the previous example can take advantage of the index. If you are running Oracle Database 10g or later, the database will analyze the index automatically when you create it.

Altering Indexes

The **alter index** command allows you to manage existing indexes. You can use the **alter index** command to do the following:

- Deallocate unused extents from an existing index or index partition

- Allocate additional extents to an existing index or index partition

- Change the parallel attributes of an existing index or index partition

- Modify the physical attributes of an index (e.g., **pctfree**) or index partition

■ Modify the logging attributes of an index or index partition

■ Rebuild an existing index or index partition

■ Perform partition maintenance operations on an existing index

■ Enable or disable key compression on an existing index

Security Requirements

If the index is in your own schema, you require only a sufficient tablespace quota (if applicable) along with the ability to connect to the database. If the index is in another schema, then the **alter any index** system privilege is required. If you wish to use the **monitoring usage** clause, then the index must be in your own schema.

Nonpartitioned alter index Examples

This section provides a number of different examples of using the **alter table** command that you will probably need to use in real life. In this set of examples, we demonstrate the following:

■ Rebuilding an index

■ Modifying index attributes

■ Enabling parallel query

■ Renaming an index

■ Changing the logging clause

■ Changing the monitoring attributes

■ Coalescing an index

■ Deallocating unused space from an index

Rebuilding a Nonpartitioned Index

The following example rebuilds the PK_MYTABLE_01 index online, moving it to a new tablespace, NEW_PK_TBS:

```
ALTER INDEX pk_mytable_01 REBUILD ONLINE TABLESPACE new_pk_tbs;
```

The following example builds on the previous example. Here we are moving the index, and we are also resetting some storage parameters. We have also taken advantage of Oracle database parallel processing to speed up our index rebuild.

```
ALTER INDEX pk_mytable_01 REBUILD ONLINE TABLESPACE new_pk_tbs pctfree 20
STORAGE (INITIAL 1M NEXT 1M) PARALLEL;
```

Modifying Index Attributes

This example resets the number of freelists for a given index. Note that if you are using locally managed tablespaces, then there are actually few index attributes that can be changed (e.g., **next** and **pctfree** cannot be changed).

```
ALTER INDEX id_test_01 STORAGE (FREELISTS 5);
```

Enabling Parallel Query

The following **alter index** statement sets the **parallel** attribute for the given index:

```
ALTER INDEX id_test_01 PARALLEL;
```

Renaming an Index

Renaming an index is a nifty feature of the **alter index** command:

```
ALTER INDEX id_test_01 RENAME TO ix_test_01;
```

Changing the Logging Clause

If you wish to change the logging attribute of an index, use the **alter index** command with the **nologging** or **logging** parameter, as shown here:

```
-- Make the index nologging
ALTER INDEX ix_test_01 NOLOGGING;
-- Make the index logging again
ALTER INDEX ix_test_01 LOGGING;
```

Changing the Monitoring Attributes

To change the monitoring attributes of an index, use the **monitoring usage** or the **nomonitoring usage** clause, as shown in these examples:

```
-- Set the index to monitoring
ALTER INDEX ix_test_01 MONITORING USAGE;
-- Set it to nomonitoring
ALTER INDEX ix_test_01 NOMONITORING USAGE;
```

Coalescing an Index

The following example coalesces the IX_TEST_01 index:

```
ALTER INDEX ix_test_01 COALESCE;
```

Deallocating Unused Space from an Index

The **deallocate unused space** clause can be used to remove unneeded space from an index. Only space above the high-water mark is freed. Here is an example:

```
ALTER INDEX ix_test_01 DEALLOCATE UNUSED;
```

You can also instruct Oracle databases to keep a certain amount of space:

```
ALTER INDEX ix_test_01 DEALLOCATE UNUSED KEEP 10M;
```

If you issue this command against a partitioned index, then the command will apply to all partitions and subpartitions of the index.

Examples Using the Partitioned alter index Commands

This section provides examples of the different **alter index** commands related to partitioned indexes. In this set of examples, we demonstrate the following:

- Rebuilding a partition or subpartition

- Coalescing a partition or subpartition

- Modifying storage attributes for a partition or subpartition

- Modifying default attributes for a partition or subpartition

- Renaming partitions

- Splitting a partition or subpartition

- Dropping an index partition or subpartition

Rebuilding a Partition or Subpartition

This example allows you to rebuild a partition of an existing index:

```
Alter index ix_part_my_tab_01 rebuild partition tbs_part_01;
```

Here is an example of rebuilding a subpartition of a composite-partitioned index:

```
ALTER INDEX sales_ix REBUILD SUBPARTITION pq4200306 ;
```

Coalescing a Partition or Subpartition

The following example coalesces the TBS_PART_01 partition in the IX_PART_MY_TAB_01 partitioned index:

```
ALTER INDEX ix_part_my_tab_01 COALESCE PARTITION tbs_part_01;
```

Modifying Storage Attributes for a Partition or Subpartition

Modifying partitions or subpartition attributes is fairly easy, as shown in this example:

```
ALTER INDEX ix_part_my_tab_02 MODIFY PARTITION part_001
STORAGE (FREELISTS 5 BUFFER_POOL DEFAULT);
```

Here we have changed the number of freelists associated with the index to five and assigned the index to the default buffer pool. If the index were in a dictionary-managed tablespace, then you can issue statements to modify some of the storage settings, as shown next:

```
-- Only will work if the index is in a dictionary managed tablespace.
ALTER INDEX ix_part_my_tab_02 MODIFY PARTITION part_001
STORAGE (NEXT 10m FREELISTS 5 BUFFER_POOL DEFAULT);
```

Modifying Default Attributes for a Partitioned Index

When you create partitioned objects without any storage parameters, the default attributes of the underlying index are used to determine the storage settings. If default settings are not set for a partitioned object, then the system uses the tablespace default settings, followed by the Oracle RDBMS default settings. Here is an example of setting the defaults for an index:

```
ALTER INDEX ix_part_my_tab_02
       MODIFY DEFAULT ATTRIBUTES PCTFREE 10 STORAGE (INITIAL 200k NEXT 200K);
```

Renaming Partitions

Renaming an index partition is as simple as the following example:

```
ALTER INDEX ix_part_my_tab_02 RENAME PARTITION part_001 TO partition_001;
```

Renaming a subpartition is just as easy:

```
ALTER INDEX sales_ix RENAME SUBPARTITION pq3200301 to pq320301;
```

Splitting a Partition or Subpartition

If you have a global index, you may wish to split a partition within that index. Here is an example of such an operation:

```
ALTER INDEX ix_part_my_tab_01 SPLIT PARTITION part_002 AT (5000)
INTO (PARTITION partition_002_a, PARTITION partition_002_b);
```

Dropping an Index Partition or Subpartition

Finally, you can drop an index partition or subpartition, as shown in these examples:

```
ALTER INDEX ix_part_my_tab_01 DROP PARTITION partition_002_b;
```

Dropping Indexes

That which is created will eventually be destroyed. The **drop index** command is the grim reaper of the index world. The **drop index** command drops the specified index and all related partitions and subpartitions. This command also invalidates all execution plans that are dependent on the index being dropped, meaning that those SQL statements need to be reparsed.

Security Requirements

To be able to drop an index, the index must belong to the schema you are currently in, or the user you are logged into must have the **drop any index** system privilege.

Drop Index Example

Dropping an index is pretty straightforward, as shown in this example:

```
DROP INDEX ix_part_my_tab_01;
```

Index-Related Data Dictionary Information

Oracle databases provide several different views that provide a wealth of information on Oracle database indexes. The following list provides some details on these views, as well as information on the availability of the all and user varieties (e.g. **all_indexes** and **user_indexes**) of these views:

View Name	Description	All	User
DBA_INDEXES	Lists each individual index	Y	Y
DBA_IND_PARTITIONS	Lists each individual partition or subpartition of a partitioned index	Y	Y
DBA_IND_COLUMNS	Lists column details of all columns in a given index	Y	Y
DBA_IND_EXPRESSIONS	Provides all expressions associated with function-based indexes	Y	Y
DBA_IND_SUBPARTITIONS	Provides subpartition information for each partitioned index	Y	Y
DBA_JOIN_IND_COLUMNS	Describes the join conditions of bitmap join indexes within the database	Y	Y
DBA_PART_INDEXES	Describes partitioned indexes within the database	Y	Y

Index-Related Errors

As you manage indexes, you may run into various Oracle database related errors. The following table lists the most common errors and provides some advice as to what to do in the event you run into those errors.

Oracle Error Message	Text Description	Possible Causes and Solutions
ORA-00903	Invalid table name	You have tried to create an index on a table that does not exist. Determine what the correct table name is.
ORA-00904	Invalid identifier	You have tried to create an index on a column that does not exist. Check the column names in the table and determine what column name you should be using.
ORA-01408	Such column list already indexed	You have tried to create an index, and an index already exists with the same ordered column set. Make sure that you have the columns in the right order. If so, you don't need to create the index as it already exists.

Oracle Error Message	Text Description	Possible Causes and Solutions
ORA-00959	Tablespace does not exist	The tablespace you are trying to create the index in does not exist. Use the DBA_TABLESPACES or USER_TABLESPACES views to find the correct tablespace name.
ORA-01418	Specified index does not exist	You have tried to drop an index that does not exist. Check the ALL_INDEXES view to try to determine what the actual index name is of the index you wish to drop.
ORA-01631 ORA-01632	Max # extents reached in index	The index tried to extend beyond its **maxextents** setting, and the extend operation failed. You need to either increase the **maxextents** setting of the index or rebuild the index using larger **initial** and **next** settings.
ORA-01467	Sort key too long	The database has encountered a problem with a sort operation. You may be ordering on too many columns or perhaps using too many group functions. It is also possible that you are running into an Oracle database bug. Reduce the number of columns in your **order by** clause, if possible. You have to reduce the number of columns in the **order by** clause because some sort operations are limited by the block size of the database. Note that this error has nothing to do with the **sort_area_size** parameter.
ORA-01502	Index or partition of such index is in unusable state	The index listed, or a partition of that index, has been marked as UNUSABLE and needs to be rebuilt. Use the **alter index rebuild** or **alter index partition rebuild** command to rebuild the index.
ORA-01031	Insufficient privileges	You do not have the correct privileges to create the index. Make sure you have **create any index** privileges, if you are creating an index in a schema other than your own. If you are creating a function-based index, make sure you have **query rewrite** privileges.
ORA-01654	Unable to extend object in tablespace	The database has tried to add an additional extent to the index listed and was not able to. There are a number of reasons why this might occur: • The tablespace is out of free space. • Insufficient contiguous space in the tablespace data files exists. • **pctincrease** is set to a value that is incorrect. Solutions include adding space to the tablespace or resetting the **next** parameter value for the index.
ORA-02243	Invalid alter index or alter materialized view option	You have a syntax error in your **alter index** command. Check the command and correct the error.
ORA-02429	Cannot drop index used for enforcement of unique/primary key	You have tried to drop an index that is used to enforce a table's primary key or a unique key constraint. You need to disable the constraint, which will cause the index to be dropped at that time.
ORA-01452	Cannot create unique index	You are probably trying to create a unique index on a table, and the rows in the index are not unique. This can also occur when you try to rebuild an UNUSABLE index, and a failed data load has created duplicate keys.

Recommended Standards

This section presents recommended standards to employ with regard to indexes within your database.

Index Location Standards

It is a generally accepted practice to place indexes in tablespaces such that they are effectively separated from database tables onto different physical devices. This makes sense from an administrative point of view certainly. This also makes sense from a performance point of view in general (even separating heavily used tables and indexes into their own tablespaces and devices), particularly as a system scales and concurrent usage begins to take its toll.

In the storage area network (SAN) world, mixing indexes and tables in tablespaces is becoming a more common practice. This is because the SAN is supposed to effectively distribute the data onto multipule devices and because indexes and tables are not written or read from at the same time by a given process. Still, from an administrative point of view, separation of objects into common types of objects (e.g., big objects vs. small objects or fact tables vs. dimension tables) makes more sense.

Index Naming Standards

All indexes should follow a common naming convention. While there are a number of perfectly relevant ones, I recommend the following:

ix_*table_nn*

where:

- ■ ix indicates that this is an index.
- ■ *table* is the name of the table.
- ■ *nn* is a monotonically increasing number that makes the index name unique.

CHAPTER
7

Views

ften, more complex database applications and designs call for the use of complex SQL statements. These statements consist of multitable joins and join criteria that are quite complex and lengthy. These kinds of statements can lead to a number of problems, such as the following:

- Inconsistency in the way the SQL statements are written (should several developers require the same SQL in multiple pieces of code). This can lead to inconsistent and incorrect results as well as shared pool–related performance issues.

- Sub-par performance for some statements, while other similar statements perform fine because they have been tuned.

- Possible increased development costs if there is not a good method of providing information about the existence of SQL statements that are available for reuse.

The use of views solves these problems by making a standard definition of a SQL statement available, in the form of an Oracle database view, to anyone who is authorized to use it. A view provides for one central SQL statement, to be stored in the database. A view allows you to reuse SQL more efficiently, and allows you to use SQL that has already been tuned and optimized. Views reduce parsing time since the statement is always consistently the same. You can create additional joins around the view, and pass additional predicates (items in the **where** clause) as required. In many cases, the database can push the predicates down into the view definition itself, causing a new, and possibly more efficient, SQL execution plan to be created.

CAUTION
Be careful when using views built on other views. These structures quickly can become inefficient, and often predicate pushing will not occur within nested views.

Another common use of views in an Oracle database is to provide security. A view can be written for users to access, rather than having them access the underlying table(s) of the view. In creating the view, you can include or exclude columns as security requirements dictate. For example, you can create a view that contains just an employee's name and address for use by the marketing group, and exclude sensitive information about that employee in the view, such as their social security number.

The tables (or views or materialized views) that a view is based on are called the *base tables* of the view. The SQL that the view is based on is stored in the data dictionary of the database. Aside from the minimal amount of space that storing that SQL consumes, there are no other space requirements related to a view within the database.

Updateable Views

Views that are not created with the **with read only** clause are known as *updateable views*. Updateable views allow DML statements to be executed against the view (e.g., **insert**, **update**, or **delete** statements).

For a view to be updateable, the following rules apply:

- If the view is a multitable join view, only one table of the join can be modified in a given statement.

- If you wish to apply DML to any base table of a view, that base table must be *key preserved.* Columns in a view are updateable if the table they come from is key preserved. A table is key preserved in a join view if every primary key column of the base table (whether or not it is included in the **select** clause of the view) is also a key to the join contained within the SQL text of the view. In other words, to be key preserved means that a given row in each base table of the view will appear only once in the output of the view. You can determine if a column is updateable by querying the DBA_UPDATABLE_COLUMNS view.

- **delete** statements are allowed only in the case where there is exactly one key-preserved table in the SQL statement being executed. The view may contain many tables, but only one key-preserved table can be changed.

- **update** statements must map to columns of a **key-preserved table**.

- **insert** statements may not refer to the columns of a **table without a key**.

- If a view is defined with the **with check option** clause you cannot change the join columns of the base tables of the view.

Also, any join condition must uniquely identify any row of the table being modified (no Cartesian joins please!). Finally, all constraints of the underlying tables must adhere to some additional restrictions. Specifically, updateable views cannot contain the following:

- References to the ROWNUM pseudo column

- Hierarchical type queries such as **connect by**

- Set operations such as **union** and **minus**

- Grouping functions such as **distinct** and **group by**

- Math functions such as **count**, **sum**, or **avg**

NOTE
This chapter is about views, which should not be confused with materialized views.

Additionally, the following rules apply to views with single base tables:

- **update** and **delete** statements are not allowed on single-table join views if the view contains an expression, such as **decode**.

- No **inserts** are allowed on a view whose base table has a not null column that does not have a **default** value defined.

Sometimes you may wish to include a column in a view but give it a different (perhaps more user-friendly) name. You can do this by aliasing the column name in the **create view** statement. An example of this is shown later in the "Examples of Using the create view Command" section of this chapter.

Other View Considerations

Use the **force** keyword of the **create view** command if you want the database to create the view regardless of the presence of all objects referenced in the view. Note that if the base objects of the view are not present, an Oracle database error will be generated when a SQL statement attempts to access the view. Also note that the **create view ... force** command will fail if the base table does not exist and if the view definition contains any view constraints. A **create view** statement will also fail if the view contains a referenced object type that does not exist or if the view definition references a constraint that does not exist.

Finally, errors may occur when creating a view. If the database indicates that an error occurred while creating the view, you can determine the errors by using the **show errors** command in SQL*Plus, or query the DBA_ERRORS view after creating the view.

Security Benefits of Views

Views provide a number of benefits with regard to security. They allow you to abstract the source of the data being presented, keeping the source of the data hidden from the user. Further, views can be created on a subset of columns in a table. This capability can be used to allow users access to only specific table data. Of course, views can be used to limit access to specific rows of data as well.

All of the underlying security architecture of the base tables of a view remains in place, so a view really becomes a subset of the overall security architecture of the system.

View Triggers

Oracle databases allow you to create **instead of** triggers on a view. These triggers can be used to further control view access and the ability to change underlying data within the view. When an **instead of** trigger is created on a view, that trigger overrides the DML operation and performs the actions that the trigger is designed to execute. Here is an example of an **instead of** trigger on a view. In this example, inserts into the MYVIEW view will be intercepted by the **instead of** trigger tr_in_myview01. The trigger will take all insert attempts and record them in the EDITED_VIEW_ CHANGES table and then exit. The original insert will never actually occur.

```
CREATE TABLE mytab1 (col1 NUMBER PRIMARY KEY, col2 NUMBER, col3 NUMBER);
CREATE TABLE mytab2 (col1 NUMBER PRIMARY KEY,
                     cola NUMBER, colb NUMBER, colc NUMBER);
CREATE VIEW myview AS select a.col1, a.col2, b.cola
          FROM mytab1 a, mytab2 b
          WHERE a.col1=b.cola;
CREATE TABLE edited_view_changes (col1 NUMBER, col2 NUMBER, cola NUMBER);
CREATE OR REPLACE TRIGGER tr_in_myview01 INSTEAD OF INSERT ON myview
BEGIN
     INSERT INTO edited_view_changes (col1, col2, cola)
     VALUES (:new.col1, :new.col2, :new.cola);
END;
/
```

Creating Views

Views are created via the **create view** command (or you can use the **create or replace view** command). When you issue the **create view** command, the result will be the creation of the view definition in the database data dictionary, and the creator of the view will have access to that view (assuming no errors occur during the creation of that view). This section first reviews the security requirements for creating views and using views. It then provides a number of different examples of the use of the **create view** command.

NOTE
Partition views are an old, obsolete type of view available in the Oracle 7 days. These were replaced by Oracle partitioning and are not covered in this book.

Security Requirements

To be able to use the **create view** command and use the resulting view, you need specific security privileges. You need to grant privileges to other users as well. This section outlines the security grants that you need to execute the **create view** command, as well as those grants required to query the resulting view.

create view Security Requirements

Database user accounts need the **create view** system privilege to be able to create a view in their own schema. The **create any view** system privilege is required to create views in other users' schemas.

When creating a view, you must already have direct grants to the objects underlying that view. That means you cannot create a view on any object that you are granted access to through a role. Access to views themselves can be granted to roles, however.

Security Requirements Related to View Use

Once you have created the view, you need to grant to users access to the view. You can do this via a direct grant using the **grant** command. Alternatively, you can grant access to the view via a role, though assigning grants through a role entails certain restrictions (such as the ability to access the view through PL/SQL code). See Chapter 10 for more information on grants and roles.

If you wish to grant access to a view to others, the owner of that view has to have been granted access to the underlying base object of the view by using the **grant** option of the **grant** command or must have been granted the privilege with the **admin** option.

Examples of Using the create view Command

This section contains a number of examples of how to use the **create view** command, first to create some basic single-table views, then to create some multitable views, and finally to create some miscellaneous views.

Creation of Single-Table Views

Here is a basic **create view** command:

```
CREATE VIEW my_view
AS SELECT * FROM active_emp
UNION SELECT * FROM inactive_emp;
```

This command creates a view that provides a union between the ACTIVE_EMP table and the INACTIVE_EMP table. In this case, you must assume that the columns of both tables are the same. This is probably not a very safe assumption, so you might want to rewrite the view a little bit more clearly, as in this revised example:

```
CREATE VIEW my_view
AS SELECT emp_no, hire_date, birth_date FROM active_emp
UNION SELECT emp_no, hire_date, birth_date FROM inactive_emp;
```

This example clearly defines the columns of the underlying base tables that are presented when the view is queried. If either table had additional columns, you would be effectually hiding those columns from the user, as well as hiding the underlying source tables of the view. Also note that if the view already exists, you will get an error when you issue the **create view** command unless you use the **create or replace view** version of this command, as seen in this example:

```
CREATE OR REPLACE VIEW my_view
AS SELECT emp_no, hire_date, birth_date FROM active_emp
UNION SELECT emp_no, hire_date, birth_date FROM inactive_emp;
```

You may want to create a view that is not updateable. In this case, you would use the **create view** command with the **with read only** keyword:

```
CREATE VIEW my_view
AS SELECT emp_no, hire_date, birth_date FROM active_emp
UNION SELECT emp_no, hire_date, birth_date FROM inactive_emp
WITH READ ONLY;
```

Creation of Multitable Views

This first example creates a view using a two-table join:

```
CREATE VIEW my_view AS
SELECT a.empno, a.deptno, b.dname
FROM emp a, dept b
WHERE a.deptno=b.deptno;
```

This example joins the EMP and DEPT tables.

Sometimes tables have common column names, and you may want to display the values of both columns. This next example demonstrates such a view:

```
CREATE VIEW my_view AS
SELECT a.empno, a.deptno AS a_deptno, b.deptno AS b_deptno, b.dname
FROM emp a, dept b
WHERE a.deptno=b.deptno;
```

Note in this case that each of the common columns have been aliased. This allows them to exist in the view, albeit with different names.

View Constraints

Views can be created with *view constraints*. While these constraints are not enforced within the view, they enable the Oracle database optimizer to use query rewrite when generating execution plans. Here is an example of the creation of a view with a view constraint (in this case a primary key constraint) associated with the view:

```
CREATE VIEW my_view
        ( empno PRIMARY KEY RELY DISABLE NOVALIDATE, deptno, dname)
        AS SELECT a.empno, a.deptno, b.dname
        FROM emp a, dept b
        WHERE a.deptno=b.deptno;
```

Note the use of the keyword **rely disable novalidate**. All constraints to be created on views must use the **rely disable novalidate** keyword or **norely disable novalidate**; using any other combination will result in an Oracle database error.

Altering Views

The **alter view** command is used to add, remove, or modify a view constraint or recompile an existing view. You cannot modify the SQL associated with a given view with the **alter view** command; instead, you need to drop and re-create the view (or use the **create or replace view** command). In this section, we look at the security requirements associated with the **alter view** command, and then look at some examples of the **alter view** command.

Security Requirements

You can freely use the **alter view** command if the view is contained in your own schema. If the view is in a different schema, then the user needs to be granted the **alter any view** privilege either directly or via a grant.

alter view Examples

This example recompiles an existing view. Recompiling views is not often required, but can happen in cases, such as when you drop and re-create stored procedures:

```
ALTER VIEW my_view RECOMPILE;
```

You can also add constraints to existing views. Again, these constraints are not validated or enforced at any time, but are used by query rewrite and the optimizer to generate the best possible execution plans. Here is an example of adding a constraint to a view:

```
ALTER VIEW my_view
        ADD CONSTRAINT u_my_view_01 UNIQUE (empno) RELY DISABLE NOVALIDATE;
```

You can also drop the constraint:

```
ALTER VIEW my_view DROP CONSTRAINT u_my_view_01;
```

You can change view constraint conditions from RELY to NORELY and back again, as shown in this example:

```
ALTER VIEW my_view MODIFY CONSTRAINT u_my_view_01 NORELY;
ALTER VIEW my_view MODIFY CONSTRAINT u_my_view_01 RELY;
```

Dropping Views

You drop a view with the **drop view** command. If you have created view constraints, then you need to remove those constraints before you drop the view, or you can use the **cascade constraints** clause. This section quickly reviews the security considerations of the **drop view** command, and then provides an example.

Security Requirements

Within the confines of your own schema, you can drop any view that you own. If you want to drop a view owned by another user you need the **drop any view** system privilege.

drop view Examples

The first example drops the view MY_VIEW:

```
DROP VIEW my_view;
```

The next example drops the view MY_VIEW and removes any related view constraints:

```
DROP VIEW my_view CASCADE CONSTRAINTS;
```

View-Related Data Dictionary Information

Oracle databases provide several different views that provide information on Oracle database views. The following table provides some details on these views, as well as information on the availability of the all and user varieties (e.g., **all_views** and **user_views**) of these views:

View Name	Description	All	User
DBA_VIEWS	Provides a description of views in the database	Y	Y
DBA_CONSTRAINTS	Provides constraint information on view constraints	Y	Y
DBA_TAB_COLUMNS	Provides column-level information on columns within a view	Y	Y
DBA_UPDATABLE_COLUMNS	Lists all updateable columns in tables and views	Y	Y

View-Related Errors

As you manage views, you may run into various Oracle database errors. The following table lists the most common errors and provides some advice as to what to do in the event you run into those errors.

Oracle Error Message	Text Description	Possible Causes and Solutions
ORA-0922	Missing or invalid option	You have tried to create a view, using an invalid option. Check to make sure that you have defined any view constraint correctly, including use of the **disable novalidate** keyword.
ORA-0942	Table or view does not exist	You have tried to create a view on a table, and that table does not exist. Check the syntax of your **create view** statement.
ORA-1779	Cannot modify a column which maps to a non key-preserved table	You have tried to execute a DML statement on a view that is not key preserved. Check the view syntax and determine why it is not key preserved. Check that all tables of the view have a primary key. Rewrite and re-create the view and retry the statement.
ORA-2261	Such unique or primary key already exists in the table	You have tried to create a view constraint on a view, and a like constraint already exists.
ORA-2443	Cannot drop constraint – Nonexistent constraint	You have tried to drop a constraint that does not exist.
ORA-4031	Unable to allocate n bytes of shared memory	Indicates shared-pool issues. You probably need to add memory to the shared pool. You could also try flushing the shared pool.
ORA-4063	View view_name has errors	The view you are trying to use is invalid. Recompile the view and then use the **show errors** command to determine the cause of the problem. This may be a missing table, procedure, or function that is being called by the view.

View-Related Recommended Standards

I recommend that the following naming standards be applied to views:

- The view should be named in a manner that is plainly descriptive.

- Prefix view names with VW_. So, a view on the CARS table might be called VW_ALL_CARS.

CHAPTER
8

Clusters

I n Chapter 5, you looked at the **create table** command and its use. This chapter covers *clusters,* which allow you to tie two or more tables together. A cluster is a database structure in which you store two or more tables in the same data blocks or segment. Physically, the rows in each table that is participating in the cluster will be stored in the same block, as if the tables were joined on the cluster key. To get an idea of how this works, let's look at example with two tables, PUBLICATIONS and PUBLISHERS. The following is the PUBLICATIONS table:

```
SQL> SELECT * FROM publications;
ANUM TITLE                                AUTHOR       PUBNUM
---- ----------------------------------- ----------- ------
1001 On Procedures, Flushes, & Writes    T Kyte           20
1002 Oracle 9i New Features              R Freeman        10
1003 Oracle Database Changed the World   K Jacobs         20
1004 On Partitions, Lookups, & Integrity T Kyte           20
1005 Oracle9i RMAN Backup & Recovery     R Freeman        10
```

The PUBNUM column is the publisher number of the particular article. This column can be used to join to the PUBLISHER table, shown here:

```
SQL> SELECT * FROM publisher;
    PUBNUM PUBNAME              CITY                 STATE
---------- -------------------- -------------------- -----
        10 Oracle Press         Berkeley             CA
        20 Oracle Magazine      Redwood Shores       CA
```

While many joins perform well, others may need as much help as you can give them. Clusters enable you to give a boost to read performance on commonly joined tables, though at some cost to DML operations. In the case of the PUBLISHER table and the PUBLICATIONS table, you might want to place both tables in a cluster, joining the two tables on the PUBNUM column. In this case, the PUBNUM column would be known as the *cluster key.* Once the cluster is created, the data in the two tables will be joined together physically within the cluster.

Within the cluster, the cluster key is not repeated in the cluster structure for each table participating in the cluster. In the cluster described, the values in the PUBNUM column are only present once. If more than one column is needed to join the tables, a composite cluster key of up to 32 columns can be used. Additionally, you have a limit of 32 tables that can participate in the cluster. Also, LOB, LONG, and LONG RAW data types are not supported within a cluster.

There are two different kinds of clusters that you can create. The first is an *index cluster,* which is the default cluster type (and often just called a cluster). The second cluster type is a *hash cluster.* With a hash cluster, the cluster key is converted into a hash value and is stored in the cluster based on that hash value rather than on the cluster key value. The index cluster requires a cluster index be created on it, whereas a hash cluster does not.

Cluster Performance

The primary benefit of storing tables in a cluster is to improve the performance of any queries that will join the participating tables. In the example from the previous section, if the PUBLICATIONS and PUBLISHERS tables are frequently joined together, placing those tables in an index cluster stores the data in a pre-joined format. When a query is issued to join these two tables, disk I/O and access time are reduced.

The downside to storing tables in a cluster is that query performance can become worse when accessing one of the clustered tables individually. There is no way to pull data from the block of one table without also pulling the data for the joining rows of the other tables in the cluster. Performance can also suffer if any of the tables participating in the cluster undergo frequent DML activity. Appropriate indexing of the tables of the cluster can reduce these performance impacts.

Tables should be clustered only if SQL predicates will heavily use the cluster key of the cluster, and the tables of the cluster will not often be queried individually. When a clustered table is used, it is best to use index clusters when range scan and inequality predicates are used against the cluster key columns of the cluster. Hash clusters are generally a better cluster choice if equality predicates on the cluster columns are used.

Creating Clusters

Creating a cluster is essentially a two- or three-step process. First, you create the cluster with the **create cluster** command. Then, you create tables that will participate in the cluster with the **create table** command. If you are creating an index cluster, you then must create the cluster index. Let's look at the security consideration when creating clusters and then look at some examples of the creation of clusters.

Security Requirements

To create a cluster, you need the **create cluster** system privilege. To create a cluster in another schema, you need the **create any cluster** system privilege. The owner of the cluster must not have exceeded the quota on the tablespace that will hold the cluster. To create the index on the cluster key, you need the **create index** system privilege or the **create any index** system privilege if the cluster is in another schema.

create cluster Examples

The first step in creating a cluster is to use the **create cluster** command. With this command, you create the cluster, define the cluster key, and specify any storage parameters for the cluster. This first example creates an index cluster, which is the default cluster type:

```
CREATE CLUSTER pub_cluster (pubnum NUMBER)
SIZE 8K
PCTFREE 10 PCTUSED 60
TABLESPACE user_data;
```

This statement creates the PUB_CLUSTER and places it in the USER_DATA tablespace. Note the second line in the **create cluster** command. This defines the size of all rows for each cluster key. This optional **size** parameter helps Oracle determine how many cluster rows will be stored in each data block.

Since the previous cluster is an index cluster, you must create an index on the cluster key after the cluster is created, as shown in this example:

```
CREATE INDEX pub_cluster_idx
ON CLUSTER pub_cluster
TABLESPACE user_indexes;
```

We might want to create a hash cluster instead. In this case, the syntax of the **create cluster** command is somewhat different, as shown in this example:

```
CREATE CLUSTER pub_cluster (pubnum NUMBER)
SIZE 8K HASHKEYS 1000
PCTFREE 10 PCTUSED 60
TABLESPACE user_data;
```

This statement creates the PUB_CLUSTER hash cluster. The **hashkeys** parameter allows you to define how many hash values should be allocated to the table. This number should represent the maximum number of unique cluster key values that you expect in the cluster. Setting this number too low can result in key collisions, which can cause performance issues.

For either cluster type, we next need to create the tables that will participate in the cluster. In our example, let's add the PUBLISHER table to the cluster first:

```
CREATE TABLE publisher (
pubnum NUMBER,
pubname VARCHAR2(20),
city VARCHAR2(20),
state CHAR(2))
CLUSTER pub_cluster(pubnum);
```

The **cluster** clause in the **create table** command tells Oracle which cluster to place the table in. The column noted in the **cluster** clause will be the column that Oracle matches to the cluster key. Now, let's add the PUBLICATIONS table to the cluster:

```
CREATE TABLE publications (
articlenum NUMBER,
title VARCHAR2(50),
author VARCHAR2(50),
pubnum NUMBER)
CLUSTER pub_cluster(pubnum);
```

Note that you do not access data in a cluster directly. You issue statements against the tables in the cluster. Oracle will automatically use the cluster when DML statements are issued against the cluster.

Altering Clusters

After you have created clusters, you may need to modify them in some way. This is the purpose of the **alter cluster** command, which enables you to do the following:

- Alter the cluster's physical storage properties (e.g., **pctfree**, **pctused**, or the **storage** clause)
- Modify the average amount of size for the cluster rows (**size**) for an index cluster
- Modify the default degree of parallelism
- Allocate extents to an index cluster

- Deallocate unused extents from a cluster

- Enable cluster **cache** or **nocache** settings

In this section, we look at specifics of the **alter cluster** command, including the security requirements related to the command and a number of different examples of its use.

Security Requirements

You can alter any cluster that is in your own schema. To use the **alter cluster** command on a table in another schema, you must have the **alter cluster** privilege on that table, or you must have the **alter any cluster** system privilege.

Examples of Using the alter cluster Command

This section provides a couple of examples of using the **alter cluster** command that you will probably need to use in real life. The first example changes the number of cluster keys stored in an index cluster. The second example alters an index cluster to deallocate space within the cluster.

Altering the Number of Cluster Keys to Be Stored in an Index Cluster

The following example demonstrates how to modify the average size of the cluster row in an index cluster (this won't work for a hash cluster):

```
SQL> ALTER CLUSTER pub_cluster SIZE 4K;
```

Altering an Index Cluster to Deallocate Space

The following example demonstrates how to deallocate unused extents, but keep 1MB of unused space for future use:

```
SQL> ALTER CLUSTER pub_cluster DEALLOCATE UNUSED KEEP 1M;
```

Dropping Clusters

The **drop cluster** SQL statement is used to drop clusters. When you drop a cluster, you must first drop the tables that participate in the cluster or use the **including tables** clause. You cannot remove a table from an existing cluster.

Security Requirements

To use the **drop cluster** command, the table should be in your own schema, or you must have the **drop any cluster** system privilege.

drop cluster Example

This command drops a cluster and the tables that belong to that cluster:

```
SQL> DROP CLUSTER pub_cluster INCLUDING TABLES CASCADE
  CONSTRAINTS;
```

Cluster-Related Data Dictionary Information

Oracle provides several different views that provide information on Oracle clusters. The following list provides some detail on these views, as well as information on the availability of the all and user varieties (e.g., **all_cluster** and **user_cluster**) of these views:

View Name	Description	All	User
DBA_CLUSTERS	Provides detailed information on clusters within the database	Y	Y
DBA_CLU_COLUMNS	Provides detailed column-level information for all columns in database clusters	Y	Y

Cluster-Related Errors

As you manage clusters, you may run into various Oracle errors. The following table lists the most common errors and provides some advice as to what to do in the event you run into those errors.

Oracle Error Message	Text Description	Possible Causes and Solutions
ORA-00904	Invalid identifier	You have issued a statement that references a column that does not exist in the referenced object. For example, you have tried to create a cluster without a cluster key.
ORA-00906	Missing left parenthesis	There is a syntax error in your statement. Find the error and re-execute the statement.
ORA-00907	Missing right parenthesis	There is a syntax error in your statement. Find the error and re-execute the statement.
ORA-00941	Missing cluster name	You forgot to include the cluster name in your **create cluster** command.
ORA-00943	Cluster does not exist	You have issued an **alter cluster** or **drop cluster** statement against a cluster that does not exist.
ORA-00944	Insufficient number of clustered columns	You have created a table to participate in a cluster but did not include a sufficient number of columns to match the cluster key.
ORA-00945	Specified clustered column does not exist	You have created a table to participate in a cluster but did not specify the correct cluster column.
ORA-00951	Cluster not empty	You have tried to drop a cluster that is not empty. Either drop the participating tables or use the **including tables** clause.
ORA-00955	Name is already used by an existing object	You are using a name that already exists in your namespace. Determine which object is using the name, and then determine if you should rename that object or the table being created.
ORA-00959	Tablespace does not exist	You have tried to create an object in a tablespace that does not exist. Check the tablespace name being used in the **create** statement, or create the tablespace.

Oracle Error Message	Text Description	Possible Causes and Solutions
ORA-01031	Insufficient privileges	You do not have privileges to perform the requested operation. You (or your DBA) should use the **grant** command to give yourself the appropriate privileges.
ORA-01447	ALTER TABLE does not operate on clustered columns	You specified a column in your **alter table modify** command that is part of the cluster key. You are not allowed to modify columns that are part of the cluster key.
ORA-01655	Unable to extend cluster in tablespace	The cluster does not have enough space in the listed tablespace to allocate another extent. Allocate more room to the tablespace.
ORA-01656	Max # extents reached in cluster	The cluster has reached the maximum number of extents. Use the **alter cluster** command to modify the cluster's storage parameters to a higher number of maximum extents.
ORA-01701	A cluster is not appropriate here	The name of a cluster was specified in a statement in which clusters are not permitted. Change your statement.
ORA-01715	UNIQUE may not be used with a cluster index	You have tried to create a cluster index with the **unique** clause. This operation is not permitted.
ORA-01716	NOSORT may not be used with a cluster index	You have tried to create a cluster index with the **nosort** clause. This operation is not permitted.
ORA-01753	Column definition incompatible with clustered column definition	You have attempted to add a table to a cluster and the table's column data types are not the same as the cluster key's column data types. Use a different column or match the data type.
ORA-01769	Duplicate CLUSTER option specifications	You have attempted to specify more than one **cluster** clause when creating a table to participate in the cluster. Use only one **cluster** clause.
ORA-01770	CLUSTER option not allowed in CREATE CLUSTER command	You have added a **cluster** clause to the **create cluster** command. Remove this clause.
ORA-01771	Illegal option for a clustered table	During an **alter** or **create** of a clustered table, you have attempted to include one of the following options: **intrans**, **maxtrans**, **pctfree**, **pctused**, **storage**, **tablespace**. These options are allowed only on the **alter** or **create** of a cluster, not the table.
ORA-01782	UNRECOVERABLE cannot be specified for a cluster or clustered table	You have tried to create a cluster with the **unrecoverable** clause. This operation is not permitted.
ORA-01794	Maximum number of cluster columns is 32	You have tried to create a cluster with more than 32 columns in the cluster key. Use at most 32 columns.
ORA-02033	A cluster index for this cluster already exists	You have attempted to create an index on this cluster when one already exists.
ORA-2202	No more tables permitted in this cluster	You have attempted to add more than 32 tables to the cluster. Use at most 32 tables.
ORA-02227	Invalid cluster name	You have included an invalid cluster name in your statement. Use a valid cluster name.
ORA-02228	Duplicate SIZE specification	You have included more than one **size** clause in your statement. Use only one **size** clause.

Oracle Error Message	Text Description	Possible Causes and Solutions
ORA-02229	Invalid SIZE option value	You have specified an invalid **size** value. Use a correct value.
ORA-03292	Table to be truncated is part of a cluster	You have attempted to truncate a table that is part of a cluster. This operation is not permitted. Use **truncate cluster** instead.

CHAPTER
9

Sequences and Synonyms

equences and synonyms are commonly used in Oracle databases. Sequences allow you to generate unique numbers, whereas synonyms allow you to create named (public or private) aliases for database objects. In this chapter we look at sequences and synonyms.

Sequences

A sequence is used to generate a unique integer (not random) when requested by an application or user session. This section first addresses what sequences are, and then looks at the various commands used to create, alter, and drop sequences. Then, some examples are given of the use of sequences. Finally, we look at sequence data dictionary views, common errors, and best practices.

All About Sequences

As previously stated, a sequence generates a unique integer when an application or user session requests it. When created with the **create sequence** command, a sequence is assigned an initial starting number. As user sessions access the sequence to generate a sequence number, the sequence is incremented. How much the sequence number is incremented is dependent on the definition of the sequence.

Assignment of sequence numbers is independent of any rollback operations. Thus, once a sequence is assigned, it must be used or else it will be lost. This implies that you cannot use a sequence if you want to ensure that each and every number actually gets used. Sequences can be configured to roll over, in which case a given sequence number cannot be guaranteed to be unique. Assuming that a sufficient gap exists between the beginning and ending sequence numbers (or that the sequence is set to not cycle), no two concurrent users will ever acquire the same sequence number. Sequences are accessed via the use of several pseudo columns, including **currval** (which displays the current sequence value) and **nextval** (which increments the current sequence value), as you will see in the examples later in this chapter.

Creating Sequences

You use the **create sequence** command to create a sequence. When you define a sequence, you can assign a number of attributes to it:

- **start with**   Use to define the starting value of the sequence. You can use a number that is up to 28 digits in length. The default is to start with 1.

- **maxvalue**   Use to define the maximum value for the sequence. The default setting is the parameter **nomax**, which indicates there is no maximum value for the sequence.

- **increment**   Use to define the number to increment the sequence by. If you wish the sequence to be a descending sequence, then make this number a negative number.

- **minvalue**   Use to define the minimum value for the sequence. This is the number that the sequence resets itself to after it recycles. Also, if the **start with** parameter is less than **minvalue**, an error will occur. The default setting is the **nominvalue** parameter, which indicates that no minimum value is to be assigned.

- **cycle**   Use to cause the sequence to cycle back to 1 (or the value defined by **minvalue**) after a given sequence reaches **maxvalue**, or a number that is greater than 28 digits. The default setting is the **nocycle** parameter, which causes sequences to not cycle. Note that if you create a sequence using the **cycle** command, you must also use the **maxvalue** and **minvalue** parameters when you define the sequence.

- **cache**   Use to get faster access from your sequences, if you can afford to lose a sequence number now and then. This parameter causes Oracle to cache sequences in memory for quicker access. The default parameter, **nocache**, disables this feature. Note that any cached values stored in memory are lost if the database is recycled.

- **order**   Use to guarantee that sequence numbers are generated in the order in which they are requested. The default, **noorder**, indicates that sequence numbers will not be allocated in any specific order.

Security Requirements

If you want to create a sequence in your schema, you must have the **create sequence** privilege. If you want to create a sequence in another user's schema, you must have the **create any sequence** privilege.

create sequence Examples

This first example creates a simple sequence. It starts with a sequence number of 1, and will generate sequences up to 10000. Once 10000 is reached, the sequence will cycle:

```
CREATE SEQUENCE my_sequence START WITH 1 MAXVALUE 10000 CYCLE;
```

This next example creates a descending sequence number that starts with 10000 and cycles down until it hits 1, at which point it resets to 10000. Note that it is the use of the **increment by** parameter with a –1 value that causes the sequence to cycle in a descending manner. Also note that the **minvalue** parameter is included, which is required for descending sequences.

```
CREATE SEQUENCE my_sequence START WITH 10000
MAXVALUE 100000 MINVALUE 1
INCREMENT BY -1 CYCLE;
```

In this final example of the creation of a sequence, the sequence is being created with an increment of 5. Also, it is cached.

```
CREATE SEQUENCE my_sequence START WITH 1
INCREMENT BY 5 CACHE 20
MAXVALUE 10000 CYCLE;
```

Using Sequences

Sequences can be used in the **select** clause of most SQL statements. You use one of two pseudo columns available to extract sequences: use the **nextval** attribute to get the next sequence value for use, and use the **currval** attribute to get the current sequence value. Here are some examples:

```
SQL> SELECT my_sequence.NEXTVAL FROM dual;
   NEXTVAL
----------
        6
```

```
SQL> SELECT my_sequence.CURRVAL FROM dual;
   CURRVAL
----------
         6
SQL> SELECT my_sequence.NEXTVAL FROM dual;
   NEXTVAL
----------
         7
```

You cannot use sequences in the following places:

- In the **where** clause of a SQL **select** statement

- In a **group by** or **order by** clause of a SQL **select** statement

- In a **distinct** clause of a SQL **select** statement

- In a SQL statement that contains **union**, **intersect**, or **minus** directives

- In a SQL statement that contains a subquery

- In a subquery within an **update** or **delete** statement

- In either a view or snapshot

- In a **default** or **check** condition of a table definition

Altering Sequences

With the **alter sequence** command, you can change several of the attributes associated with a sequence. While you cannot use the **alter sequence** command to change the current number that the sequence is on, there is a little trick demonstrated later in this section that allows you to do this. The **alter sequence** command allows you to use the following parameters:

- **maxvalue**   Defines the maximum value for the sequence that is allowed.

- **increment by**   Defines the number to increment the sequence by. If you wish the sequence to be a descending sequence, then make this number a negative number.

- **minvalue**   Defines the minimum value for the sequence. This is the number that the sequence resets itself to after it recycles. Note that if the **start with** parameter is less than **minvalue**, an error will occur. You can also change a sequence to indicate that there is no minimum value with **nominvalue**.

- **cycle**   Allows the sequence to cycle. If **cycle** is set, then the sequence will cycle back to 1 (or the value defined by **minvalue**). If the sequence is already a cycling one, the **nocycle** parameter can be used to make the sequence not cycle. Note that if you use the **cycle** command to create a sequence, you must also use the **maxvalue** and **minvalue** parameters when you define the sequence.

- **cache**   Indicates that a sequence should be cached. If you wish faster access from your sequences, and if you can afford to lose a sequence number now and then (which can happen even if you don't use the cache parameter), use the **cache** parameter. This causes Oracle to cache sequences in memory for quicker access.

■ **nocache**   Disables the cache feature. Note that any cached values stored in memory will be lost if the database is recycled.

■ **order**   Used to guarantee that sequence numbers are generated in the order in which they are requested. Likewise, the **noorder** parameter indicates that sequence numbers will not be allocated in any specific order.

Security Requirements

You can alter any sequence in your own schema. To use the **alter sequence** command to manipulate a sequence in a schema other than your own schema, you must be assigned the **alter sequence** privilege. As an alternative, you can change any sequence if you have been granted the **alter any sequence** system privilege.

alter sequence Examples

This example of the **alter sequence** command changes the **increment** parameter of the sequence so that it starts incrementing by 5:

```
ALTER SEQUENCE my_sequence INCREMENT BY 5;
```

As previously indicated, you cannot reset a sequence value with the **alter sequence** command. For example, if the current value for a sequence is 2000, you cannot use a single **alter sequence** command to reset it to 1000. There are a couple of ways to work around this. The first is to drop and re-create the sequence. This is problematic because it invalidates related objects such as views and PL/SQL program units. Instead, you can use a combination of a couple of **alter sequence** commands and a call to the sequence to change the sequence value, as shown in this example:

```
SQL> CREATE SEQUENCE my_sequence START WITH 2000;
Sequence created.
SQL> SELECT my_sequence.NEXTVAL FROM dual;
   NEXTVAL
----------
      2000

SQL> ALTER SEQUENCE my_sequence INCREMENT  BY -1001;
Sequence altered.

SQL> SELECT my_sequence.NEXTVAL FROM dual;
   NEXTVAL
----------
       999
SQL> ALTER SEQUENCE my_sequence INCREMENT BY 1;
Sequence altered.

SQL> SELECT my_sequence.NEXTVAL FROM dual;
   NEXTVAL
----------
      1000
```

Dropping Sequences

When it's time to get rid of a sequence, the **drop sequence** command is the one to use. It's a pretty straightforward command.

Security Requirements

If the sequence exists in your own schema, you can drop the sequence without a problem. If the sequence is owned by another schema, you must have the **drop any sequence** system privilege.

drop sequence Example

Here is an example of the removal of the my_sequence sequence:

```
DROP SEQUENCE my_sequence;
```

Sequence-Related Data Dictionary Information

The following table provides a list of the data dictionary views you can use when dealing with sequences:

View Name	Description	All	User
DBA_SEQUENCES	Lists each individual sequence	Y	Y
DBA_OBJECTS	Lists each database object, including sequences	Y	Y

Sequence-Related Errors

As you manage sequences, you may run into various Oracle errors. The following table lists the most common errors and provides some advice as to what to do in the event you run into those errors.

Oracle Error Message	Text Description	Possible Causes and Solutions
ORA-00955	Name is already in use by an existing object	An object in the database namespace that you are using already has the name assigned to it that you are trying to assign to this sequence. Make sure that the sequence doesn't already exist.
ORA-04003	Sequence parameter START WITH exceeds maximum size allowed (28 digits)	Select a smaller **start with** parameter size.
ORA-08004	Sequence exceeds MAXVALUE and cannot be instantiated	You have used all available sequence numbers in the given sequence. Options are to drop and re-create the sequence, use the **alter sequence** command to increase the **maxvalue** setting for the sequence, or use the **alter sequence cycle** command to allow the index to cycle.
ORA-02287	Sequence number not allowed here	You have used a sequence number in SQL in a location that is not allowed. Check the SQL statement and find the illegal sequence number usage.
ORA-01722	Invalid number	This generally indicates that you have some incorrect syntax in your **create sequence** command. Check the command and make sure it is correct.

Oracle Error Message	Text Description	Possible Causes and Solutions
ORA-01031	Insufficient privileges	You do not have the required privileges to create the sequence. Have your DBA grant you the appropriate privileges and try again.
ORA-04014	Descending sequences that CYCLE must specify MINVALUE	You have defined a sequence that is descending, and have defined it as a **cycle** type sequence. You need to add the **minvalue** parameter so that the sequence knows when to cycle.
ORA-04015	Ascending sequences that CYCLE must specify MAXVALUE	You have defined a sequence that is ascending, and have defined it as a **cycle** type sequence. You need to add the **maxvalue** parameter so that the sequence knows when to cycle.

Sequence-Related Recommended Standards

I recommend that sequences use the following naming convention:

sq_*ssssssss*

where *sq* indicates that this is a sequence and *ssssssss* is a name that represents what the sequence is used for. For example, a sequence named sq_emp_num might represent a sequence that contains employee numbers.

Synonyms

The **create synonym** command allows you to define an alternate name and/or location for a number of different database objects, including tables, views, sequences, callable stored PL/SQL programs, materialized views, Java class schema objects, user-defined object types, or another synonym. This section looks at the mechanics of managing synonyms. First we will look at how to create synonyms, then we will look at how to drop synonyms. Finally, we will look at data dictionary information and error messages related to synonyms.

Creating Synonyms

You create a synonym with the **create synonym** command. Because dropping synonyms will cause other related database objects, such as views and stored PL/SQL programs, to become invalid, Oracle allows you to just replace a synonym with the **create or replace synonym** syntax, if that is your desire. You can create a synonym for an object in your own schema, for an object in another schema, and even for an object in another database via a database link.

When you issue the **create synonym** command, you create a private synonym, which is usable only by the schema that the synonym was created in. If you use the **create public synonym** option, then a public synonym is created, which is available to all schemas.

Be careful with public synonyms. First, there is a slight performance impact with the use of any synonym. With the use of public synonyms, the performance impact is about twice that of the use of private synonyms. This impact is very small and makes no measurable difference in most cases, but you should be aware of the potential for performance problems. Additionally, there are some potential security risks to the use of public synonyms. These risks come from the public nature of the synonym. Even if a user schema does not have a right to a given table, that schema can still see any public synonym. This is one potential method of engineering an attack against a database and should be taken as a serious threat. The bottom line is that you should avoid public synonyms in databases that are security sensitive or performance sensitive.

Yet another issue with public synonyms to be aware of involves what happens within a schema if you have a public synonym and an object (table, view, etc.) with the same name. Because synonyms use the same namespace as other database objects, you cannot have an object and a private synonym with the same name, in the same schema. However, public synonyms have their own namespace. Thus, you can have a public synonym called MY_TABLE and also a table called MY_TABLE, both within the same schema. In this event, an access request to the MY_TABLE table will first access the local table. If a local table is not available, then the access request will access the table pointed to by the public synonym. Be cautious about this type of behavior. Again, avoid public synonyms whenever possible. Also, references to an object via a database link will not use a synonym, and any object prefaced with a schema name will not use a database link.

Security Requirements

To access any object pointed to by a synonym, you must have the proper grants to that object. Creation of a synonym does not equate to granting of access rights to the object that the synonym points to. If you want to create a private synonym in your own schema, you must have the **create synonym** system privilege. If you wish to create a private synonym in a schema other than your own, you must have the **create any synonym** system privilege. Finally, if you wish to create a public synonym, you must have the **create public synonym** system privilege.

create synonym Examples

This example shows how synonyms can be used to facilitate easier access to objects within the database:

```
-- Connect to the scott user
SQL> CONNECT scott/tiger
-- Create a table to test with
SQL> CREATE TABLE test_table (id NUMBER);
-- Insert a row into the table
SQL> INSERT INTO test_table VALUES (1);
SQL> commit;
-- Grant access to the table to another user
SQL> GRANT ALL ON test_table TO dev_001;
-- Connect to that user
SQL> CONNECT dev_001/dev_001
-- Query test_table. This query fails.
SQL> SELECT * FROM test_table;
select * from test_table
               *
ERROR at line 1:
ORA-00942: table or view does not exist
-- This query works because we have prefixed the name of
-- the table with the name of the schema that owns the table.
SQL> SELECT * FROM scott.test_table;
        ID
----------
         1
```

```
-- Create a synonym for test_table so we don't have
-- to prefix it.
SQL> CREATE SYNONYM test_table FOR scott.test_table;
Synonym created.
-- Now query the table, we get no error this time.
SQL> SELECT * FROM test_table;
        ID
----------
         1
-- Note that you cannot create a table with the same
-- name in the schema where the private synonym was created.
SQL> CREATE TABLE test_table (id NUMBER);
CREATE TABLE test_table (id NUMBER)
             *
ERROR at line 1:
ORA-00955: name is already used by an existing object
```

You can also create a public synonym, which creates a synonym visible to the entire database:

```
-- Connect to the scott user
SQL> CONNECT scott/tiger
-- Create a table to test with
SQL> CREATE TABLE test_table (id NUMBER);
-- Insert a row into the table
SQL> INSERT INTO test_table VALUES (1);
SQL> COMMIT;
-- Grant access to the table to another user
SQL> GRANT ALL ON test_table TO dev_001;
-- Create the public synonym.
SQL> CREATE PUBLIC SYNONYM test_table FOR test_table;
-- Connect to our test user.
SQL> CONNECT dev_001/dev_001
-- This query works because we have prefixed the name of the
-- table with the name of the schema that owns the table.
SQL> SELECT * FROM scott.test_table;
        ID
----------
         1
-- Now query the table, we get no error since there is a public
-- synonym called test_table.
SQL> SELECT * FROM test_table;
        ID
----------
         1
-- Note that you can create a table with the same name as a public
-- synonym. BEWARE!!!
SQL> CREATE TABLE test_table (id NUMBER);
SQL> INSERT INTO test_table VALUES (2);
SQL> COMMIT;
```

```
-- Note that this query is retrieving rows from the local
-- table, NOT the table pointed to by the public synonym.
SQL> SELECT * FROM test_table;
        ID
----------
         2
```

It's also possible to create a synonym for an object in another database. When you create the synonym, you reference the object via a database link, as shown in this example:

```
CREATE OR REPLACE SYNONYM my_remote_table FOR my_remote_table@other_db;
```

Note also that this example uses the **create or replace synonym** syntax of the command. This helps to avoid the nasty impacts that dropping the synonym would have on stored objects such as views and stored PL/SQL program units.

Altering Synonyms

There is no **alter synonym** command available in Oracle. If you need to change a synonym, you need to re-create it with the **create or replace synonym** command or drop the synonym and re-create it with the **drop synonym** and **create synonym** commands.

Dropping Synonyms

The **drop synonym** command is used to drop synonyms from the database. If you need to remove a public synonym, then you need to add the **public** keyword to the command (**drop public synonym**). By default, if a synonym has dependent table or user-defined types, you cannot drop it. In this case, you can use the **force** keyword to remove the synonym. Be careful when doing this, because it can quickly invalidate a number of objects that are dependent on the synonym!

Security Requirements

If the synonym is a private synonym and it's in your own schema, you can drop it without a problem. If the private synonym is in another schema, you must have the **drop any synonym** system privilege. If the synonym is a public synonym, then you must have the **drop public synonym** privilege.

drop synonym Examples

Here are two examples, the first of which drops a private synonym and the second of which drops a public synonym:

```
DROP SYNONYM babylon;
DROP PUBLIC SYNONYM bester;
```

Synonym-Related Data Dictionary Information

The following table provides a list of the data dictionary views you can use when dealing with synonyms:

View Name	Description	All	User
DBA_SYNONYMS	Lists each individual synonym	Y	Y
DBA_OBJECTS	Lists each database object, including synonyms	Y	Y

Synonym-Related Errors

As you manage synonyms you may run into various Oracle errors. The following table lists the most common errors and provides some advice as to what to do in the event you run into those errors.

Oracle Error Message	Text Description	Possible Causes and Solutions
ORA-00942	Table or view does not exist	You have tried to access a table but either the table does not exist or the synonym for that table is not correctly defined.
ORA-00980	Synonym translation is no longer valid	Indicates that the object that the synonym was assigned to does not exist.
ORA-01031	Insufficient privileges	You do not have the required privileges to create the synonym. Have your DBA grant you the appropriate privileges and try again.

Synonym-Related Recommended Standards

Common practice is to name the synonym the same name as the object that it is pointing to. Often synonyms are not prefixed in any way that would identify them as synonyms. From a security-oriented approach, it may be better to name the synonym something other than the actual name of the base object, yet not in such a way as to readily be recognizable as a synonym.

CHAPTER
10

Users, Profiles, Roles, and Grants

his chapter covers the administration of users, profiles, roles, and grants in Oracle. Each section provides some detail about the topic and then specific administrative information that you need to know to make your job a little bit easier.

Administration of Users

Without users, there really isn't any need for a database. Users in Oracle own objects within the database such as tables, indexes, and the like. Additionally, users are granted specific system privileges, which allow them to perform specific actions in the database. Privileges are discussed in much more detail later in this chapter in the "Administration of System and Object Privileges" section.

Often in database circles, you will hear the terms "user" and "schema." Typically, a *user* is granted privileges within a database (such as the ability to query tables), whereas a *schema* owns specific objects. Within Oracle, users and schemas are basically the same thing. So in Oracle, when you create a user, you also create the schema associated with that user.

Associated with a user are a number of attributes. First is the user's password, which is required when the user logs in and protects the user account. User passwords can also be linked to the operating system (OS) account that is being logged into, and Oracle also has provisions for single sign-on.

Another attribute associated with a user is that user's default tablespace. This is defined when the user is created, and can be changed as required. By default, **system** is assigned as the user's default password. Oracle Database 10*g* allows you to define a database-wide user default tablespace that will be assigned to each user that is not specifically assigned a default tablespace.

A temporary tablespace is a tablespace that users are assigned to that is used for temporary segment storage (e.g., sort segments). As with a default tablespace, the temporary tablespace for a user is defined when the user is created, and the SYSTEM tablespace is the default temporary tablespace assignment. In Oracle9*i* and later, I recommend that you configure a default temporary tablespace for your database to avoid the assignment of the SYSTEM tablespace as the default.

To be able to create objects in a given tablespace (except a temporary tablespace), a user must either have a quota established for that tablespace or have the **unlimited quota** system privilege, which allows unlimited space usage in all tablespaces in the database.

A user can be assigned a profile when the user account is created, or assigned to a profile later if you desire. Profiles control a number of attributes, such as the ability to force password changes after a specific period of time, and provide the ability to enforce the use of strong passwords. Profiles are discussed later in this chapter in the "Administration of Profiles" section.

You can expire a user's password when you create an account, or you can alter the account later to expire the users' password, which forces the user to change the password before they can sign into the database again.

A user account can also be locked (or unlocked) at will. Accounts are commonly locked if they do not need to be accessed by users. Typically, these accounts are used just to store schema objects, such as tables. Users will log into other database user accounts to access these objects.

To create a user in the database, you use the **create user** command. You use the **alter user** command to modify user attributes, and use the **drop user** command to drop users. The following three sections describe in turn each of these commands in more detail.

Creating Users

Users are created with the **create user** command. The username assigned can be up to 30 characters long and cannot be an Oracle reserved word (such as **select**, or any keyword listed in V$RESERVED_WORDS) unless the username is enclosed in quotes (this is not a recommended practice, however).

Security Requirements

To use the **create user** command, you need the **create user** system privilege.

create user Examples

Here is an example of a basic **create user** command:

```
CREATE USER my_user IDENTIFIED BY my_password
DEFAULT TABLESPACE default_data
QUOTA UNLIMITED ON default_data
TEMPORARY TABLESPACE temp;
```

Here is a more complex **create user** command:

```
CREATE USER my_user IDENTIFIED BY my_password
DEFAULT TABLESPACE default_data
TEMPORARY TABLESPACE temp
QUOTA UNLIMITED ON default_data
QUOTA UNLIMITED ON my_data
QUOTA 100M ON all_data;
```

You might want to create a user account that is externally authenticated. Generally, this means that the user account is authenticated when you log into the operating system. Here is an example of such a command:

```
CREATE USER my_user IDENTIFIED EXTERNALLY
DEFAULT TABLESPACE default_data
TEMPORARY TABLESPACE temp;
```

You may want to create a user account that is initially locked out. Here is an example of such an operation:

```
CREATE USER my_user IDENTIFIED BY lockoutpwd
DEFAULT TABLESPACE default_data
TEMPORARY TABLESPACE temp
ACCOUNT LOCK;
```

Altering Users

There is always maintenance to be done it seems, and user account maintenance is no exception. With the **alter user** command, you can do the following:

- Alter the user's password
- Alter the user's temporary or default tablespaces

- Alter an existing quota or assign a new quota
- Alter the user's profile assignment
- Alter the user's default role
- Expire the user's password
- Lock or unlock the user's account

Security Requirements
To use the **alter user** command, you must have the **alter user** system privilege. Any user can change their own password without the **alter user** system privilege being assigned to them.

alter user Examples
Here is an example of an **alter user** command used to modify the password for the MY_USER user to the value of **george**:

```
ALTER USER my_user IDENTIFIED BY george;
```

Perhaps you want to lock the MY_USER account and change its default tablespace setting, as in this example:

```
alter user my_user DEFAULT tablespace default_two
ACCOUNT LOCK;
```

This example changes a user's tablespace quotas:

```
ALTER USER MYUSER QUOTA 100m ON USER_DATA
QUOTA UNLIMITED ON all_data;
```

This example removes a user's quota from a tablespace:

```
ALTER USER MYUSER QUOTA 0 ON USER_DATA;
```

You can also expire a user's password if you choose, as shown in this example:

```
Alter user myuser default tablespace default_two
password expire;
```

Dropping Users
You remove users with the **drop user** command. If the user schema contains objects, then you need to use the **cascade** parameter. The **cascade** parameter drops all objects owned by the user schema and then removes the user. Also, you cannot drop a user who is currently connected to the database.

Security Requirements
You need the **drop user** system privilege to use the **drop user** command.

drop user Examples

The simplest form of the **drop user** command can be used if the user's schema contains no objects:

```
Drop user my_user;
```

If the user schema has objects within it, you can either manually drop all of those objects, or use the **cascade** parameter, as shown here:

```
Drop user my_user cascade;
```

User-Related Data Dictionary Information

The following data dictionary views are used to manage user-related information:

View Name	Description	All	User
DBA_USERS	Lists individual users in the database	Y	Y
V$PWFILE_USERS	Lists all users in the password file listed as SYSDBA- or SYSOPER-level users	N	N
DBA_TS_QUOTAS	Lists all tablespaces and user quotas allocated on those tablespaces.	N	Y

User-Related Errors

As you manage users, you may run into various Oracle errors. The following table lists the most common errors and provides some advice as to what to do in the event you run into those errors.

Oracle Error Message	Text Description	Possible Causes and Solutions
ORA-01920	User name conflicts with another user or role name	The user you are trying to create already exists (either as another user or as a role).
ORA-00972	Identifier is too long	The name for the user that you chose is too long. Shorten the name and reissue the command.
ORA-00988	Missing or invalid password(s)	The password you have chosen is invalid, or you have issued the command without a password. Reissue the command with an appropriate password.
ORA-00959	Tablespace does not exist	The default tablespace, or temporary tablespace selected, does not exist (or you spelled it wrong). Reissue the command with the correct tablespace name(s).

Oracle Error Message	Text Description	Possible Causes and Solutions
ORA-02380	Profile does not exist	You have tried to assign a profile to a user, and that profile does not exist. Check to make sure the profile name is correct and that the profile actually exists in the database (using the DBA_PROFILES view).
ORA-1031	Insufficient privileges	You do not have sufficient privileges to issue the **create user** command. The account that is trying to issue the **create user** account needs to be granted the **create user** system privilege. Also may appear with **alter user** and **drop user** commands.
ORA-01936	Cannot specify owner when creating users or roles	You cannot include an owner name when creating a role. Remove the reference to the owner and try the statement again.

User-Related Recommended Standards

Common practices are to create centralized application-owning user accounts that own the objects related to the application. For the tightest security, lock out these accounts when direct access is not needed. Frequently, a second common "user" account is created that allows DML access to these objects. While this is a common practice, for a number of reasons, it is not a best practice, and this type of design should be avoided. Reasons for avoiding this design include

- Reduced user accountability for actions
- More limited auditing abilities
- Limits the use of certain Oracle features such as Virtual Private Database

I recommend that you use individual user accounts in your database and take advantage of functionality such as single sign-on to make the user experience more palatable. This type of design will make your database ultimately more secure.

Administration of Profiles

Profiles allow you to control the amount of system resources that an individual user can consume. When you create profiles, you can use the following parameters to control system resources:

- **sessions_per_user**   Limits the total number of concurrent sessions an individual user can start.
- **cpu_per_session**   Limits the total CPU that each user session is allowed to consume. Defined in hundredths of a second.

- **cpu_per_call**   Limits the total CPU consumption allowed per call. Defined in hundredths of a second.

- **connect_time**   Limits the total connect time allowed for a given session. Expressed in minutes.

- **idle_time**   Limits the total idle time allowed for a given session. Expressed in minutes. Note that if you have long-running operations (such as long-running report queries), they are not subject to this limitation.

- **logical_reads_per_session**   Limits the total number of logical reads allowed per session. Expressed in total number of block reads and includes reads from disk or memory.

- **logical_reads_per_call**   Limits the total number of logical reads allowed per call. Expressed in total number of block reads and includes reads from disk or memory.

- **private_sga**   Limits the maximum size of the private SGA, in bytes.

- **composite_limit**   Allows you to establish a composite limit, which is calculated based on a weighted average of the following factors: total CPU per session, total connect time, logical reads per session, and the maximum size of the private SGA.

When you create profiles, you can also use various password-related restrictions, including the following:

- **failed_login_attempts**   Allows you to establish a total number of allowable failed login attempts.

- **password_life_time**   Defines the total length of time that a password can be used before it must be changed.

- **password_reuse_time**   Defines the total number of days between which a given password cannot be reused. Must be set in conjunction with **password_reuse_max**.

- **password_reuse_max**   Defines the total number of password changes that are required before the current password can be reused. Must be set in conjunction with **password_reuse_time**.

- **password_lock_time**   Defines the total number of days an account will be locked after a given number of consecutive failed login attempts.

- **password_grace_time**   Defines the total number of days that you will be granted grace access to the account, after the password has expired, in order to change the password. If you do not change the password after the grace period expires, then you will be unable to access the account.

- **password_verify_function**   Defines a custom password verification function that allows you to define a PL/SQL function that can be used to validate user passwords. This function allows you to define custom password-validation routines.

To establish profiles, for users you must follow these steps:

1. Set the **resource_limit** parameter in the database parameter file. This parameter can be dynamically set with the **alter session** command as well. If you are going to use password resources, then you do not need to enable **resource_limit**.

2. Using the **create profile** command, create the profile that you wish to use.

3. After you create the profile, you can assign it to existing users with the **alter user** command using the **profile** keyword. You can also use the **profile** keyword with the **create user** command to assign profiles to new users.

When a profile limit is exceeded, one of the following will occur:

■ If the **connect_time** or **idle_time** resource limits are exceeded, then the transaction is rolled back and the session is ended.

■ If an operation is executed that exceeds a session resource limit (e.g., CPU), then the operation is aborted and rolled back. Additionally, Oracle returns an error. Note that the session is not ended by Oracle, so the user can decide to commit or roll back the operation. Once the session is rolled back or committed, the user must then end the session.

■ If the operation exceeds a single call limitation (e.g., **cpu_per_call**), then the operation is rolled back and Oracle returns an error. In this case, the current session is intact and the user can proceed to try to reissue the call, or another call.

To manage profiles, you use the **create profile**, **alter profile**, and **drop profile** commands, which are discussed in the following sections.

Creating Profiles

The **create profile** command is used to create profiles. After you create the profile, you can assign it to a user via the **create user** command or **alter user** command. This section first covers the security considerations of the **create profile** command and then provides examples of the use of the **create profile** command.

You can indicate that a resource limit should take on a default value through the use of the **default** keyword. You can also set these attributes to an unlimited setting via the **unlimited** keyword. Also, there is a profile called DEFAULT that is created when the database is created. You can modify this profile, just as you would any other profile. When you alter an attribute of the DEFAULT profile, that default attribute will be assigned to any attribute that is assigned a value of default. Note that all resource limit values are set to unlimited in the DEFAULT profile.

Security Requirements

To create a profile, you must have the **create profile system** privilege. Additionally, the **resource_limit** parameter must be set to enable non-password-related resource limits.

create profile Examples

Here is an example of the creation of a user profile that limits the number of concurrent user logins and limits the total amount of CPU that a given user call can consume:

```
Create profile production_profile limit
sessions_per_user 2 cpu_per_call 10000;
```

You can also define certain profile settings as unlimited, as shown in this example:

```
Create profile app_developer limit
sessions_per_user unlimited cpu_per_session 5000
connect_time unlimited;
```

And you can use the **default** keyword to accept the default values for various parameters:

```
Create profile app_developer limit
sessions_per_user unlimited cpu_per_session 5000
connect_time unlimited logical_reads_per_call default;
```

Setting password resource limits is easy as well, as shown in this example:

```
Create profile password_requirements limit
failed_login_attempts 3  password_life_time 45
password_reuse_max 30  password_reuse_time UNLIMITED
password_lock_time 1/24  password_grace_time 5
;
```

Finally, most profiles will probably combine both password management and resource constraints, as shown in this example:

```
Create profile all_resource_constraints limit
failed_login_attempts 3  password_life_time 45
password_reuse_max 30  password_reuse_time UNLIMITED
password_lock_time 1/24  password_grace_time 5
sessions_per_user unlimited cpu_per_session 5000
connect_time unlimited;
```

Altering Profiles

The **alter profile** command is used to add, modify, or remove profile attributes. See the previous section on the creation of profiles for more information on the attributes associated with profiles. Changes that are made via the **alter profile** command have an effect on user logins that occur after the **alter profile** command has been issued, and not the current session.

You can use the **alter profile** command to reset the various resource limits through the use of the **default** keyword. You can also set these attributes to an unlimited setting via the **unlimited** keyword.

Security Requirements
The **alter profile** system privilege is required to be able to use the **alter profile** command to change profile resource limits. If you wish to change password-related attributes, you need both the **alter profile** and the **alter user** system privileges.

alter profile Examples
This example of the use of the **alter profile** command limits users assigned to this profile to just two concurrent sessions:

```
Alter profile profile_users limit sessions_per_user 2;
```

Here is another example of the **alter profile** command that establishes password limitations:

```
Alter profile profile_managers limit
password_life_time 30
password_grace_time 10
```

Dropping Profiles
When you wish to remove a profile, use the **drop profile** command. You should use the **cascade** parameter to drop a profile that is assigned to a user. Any user that was assigned to the profile being dropped will be assigned to the default profile.

Security Requirements
To use the **drop profile** command, you must have the **drop profile** system privilege.

drop profile Example
Here is an example of the use of the **drop profile** command:

```
drop profile user_profile cascade;
```

Profile-Related Data Dictionary Information
Two views are available for managing profiles, as described in the following table:

View Name	Description	All	User
DBA_PROFILES	Lists individual profiles in the database. Note that any one profile will have multiple rows in this view.	N	N
DBA_USERS	Defines the profile that the user is assigned to.	Y	Y

Profile-Related Errors

Errors can occur related to profiles. The most common of these errors are seen in the following table:

Oracle Error Message	Text Description	Possible Causes and Solutions
ORA-02376	Invalid or redundant resource	You have tried to create or alter a profile using a resource that has not been defined, or you have tried to specify the same resource twice. Check that the resource name is spelled correctly and that it is not duplicated, and try again.
ORA-02378	Profile already exists	You have tried to create a profile with a name of an already existing profile. Check to make sure you really want to create the profile and, if so, rename it or drop the preexisting profile.
ORA-02380	Profile does not exist	You have attempted to assign a profile name to a user and that profile does not exist.
ORA-02381	Cannot drop PUBLIC DEFAULT profile	You have tried to drop the default profile. This is not allowed.

Administration of System and Object Privileges

The **grant** command is the means by which you allocate privileges to access objects within the database to users, roles, and to public. Grants also allow you to grant Oracle database system-level privileges to users and roles. Grants can also be used to grant roles to other users (see the discussion of roles later in this chapter).

Object Grants

Object grants allow you to grant different levels of access to specific objects (such as tables) within the database. This access can be very specific in its reach; for example, you can grant access to only specific columns of a table.

There are several different kinds of object grants, and they can be used on a variety of different kinds of objects. For example, the **alter grant** command can be used to grant the ability both to issue **alter table** commands on tables and to issue the **alter sequence** command on sequences.

You can grant all rights on a specific object to a user via the **all** parameter of the **grant** command. For example, if you want the user SCOTT to be able to perform all actions on the EMP table, you might issue the **grant all on emp to scott** command.

The following table lists the most commonly used Oracle object grants:

Object Grant	Description	Objects Supported
alter	Change the object definition	Tables, sequences

Object Grant	Description	Objects Supported
delete	Delete rows from the object	Tables, views, updateable materialized views
execute	Execute the object defined	Stored procedures, libraries, types
debug	Enable debugging on specific objects	Tables, views, stored procedures, types
flashback	Enable flashback operations on specific objects	Tables, views, materialized views
index	Create indexes on an object	Tables
insert	Enable the ability to insert into an object	Tables, views, updateable materialized views
on commit refresh	Allows an on-commit refreshable materialized view to be created on the table	Tables
query rewrite	Allows a materialized view to be created on the table that is query rewrite enabled	Tables
read	Allow a user to access a directory	Directories
references	Allows foreign key constraints to be created on the object	Tables, views
select	Allows the user to select from an object	Tables, views, sequences, materialized views
pdate	Allow the user to update the object	Tables, views, updateable materialized views
write	Allow the user to write to a directory	Directory

System Grants

System grants allow you to grant access to different functionality within the Oracle database, such as the ability to create a table or alter a session's parameter setting. Once a privilege is granted, it takes effect immediately. The following table lists the most commonly used system grants:

System Role	What It Allows You to Do
administer database trigger	Create a database trigger; requires the **create trigger** and **create any trigger** privileges
alter any cluster	Alter clusters in any schema
alter any dimension	Alter dimensions in any schema
alter any index	Alter indexes in any schema

System Role	What It Allows You to Do
alter any materialized view	Alter materialized views in any schema
alter any outline	Alter outlines
alter any procedure	Alter stored procedures, functions, or packages in any schema
alter any role	Alter any role in the database
alter any sequence	Alter any sequence in the database
alter any table	Alter any table or view in any schema
alter any trigger	Enable, disable, or compile database triggers in any schema
alter any type	Alter object types in any schema
alter database	Alter the database
alter profile	Alter profiles
alter rollback segment	Alter rollback segments
alter session	Use the **alter session** command
alter system	Use the **alter system** command
alter tablespace	Alter tablespaces
alter user	Alter any user
analyze any	Analyze any table, cluster, or index in any schema
audit any	Audit any object in any schema using the **audit** command
audit system	Issue **audit** statements
backup any table	Use the Export utility to incrementally export objects from the schema of other users
comment any table	Comment on any table, view, or column in any schema
create any cluster	Create a cluster in any schema
create any dimension	Create dimensions in any schema
create any directory	Create directory database objects
create any index	Create an index on any table in any schema
create any library	Create external procedure or function libraries in any schema
create any materialized view	Create materialized views in any schema
create any outline	Create public outlines in any schema
create any procedure	Create stored procedures, functions, and packages in any schema
create any sequence	Create sequences in any schema
create any synonym	Create private synonyms in any schema
create any table	Create tables in any schema

System Role	What It Allows You to Do
create any trigger	Create database triggers in any schema
create any type	Create object types and object type bodies in any schema
create any view	Create views in any schema
create cluster	Create clusters
create database link	Create private database links
create dimension	Create dimensions
create library	Create external procedure or function libraries
create materialized view	Create a materialized view
create procedure	Create stored procedures, functions, and packages
create profile	Create profiles
create public database link	Create public database links
create public synonym	Create public synonyms
create role	Create roles
create rollback segment	Create rollback segments
create sequence	Create sequences
create session	Connect to the database
create synonym	Create synonyms
create table	Create tables
create tablespace	Create tablespaces
create trigger	Create a database trigger
create type	Create object types and object type bodies
create user	Create users
create view	Create views in the grantee's schema
debug any procedure	Debug all PL/SQL and Java code in any database object
delete any table	Delete rows from tables, table partitions, or views in any schema
drop any cluster	Drop clusters in any schema
drop any dimension	Drop dimensions in any schema
drop any directory	Drop directory database objects
drop any index	Drop indexes in any schema
drop any library	Drop external procedure or function libraries in any schema
drop any materialized view	Drop materialized views in any schema
drop any outline	Drop outlines

System Role	What It Allows You to Do
drop any procedure	Drop stored procedures, functions, or packages in any schema
drop any role	Drop roles
drop any sequence	Drop sequences in any schema
drop any synonym	Drop private synonyms in any schema
drop any table	Drop or truncate tables or table partitions in any schema
drop any trigger	Drop database triggers in any schema
drop any type	Drop object types and object type bodies in any schema
drop any view	Drop views in any schema
drop profile	Drop profiles
drop public database link	Drop public database links
drop public synonym	Drop public synonyms
drop rollback segment	Drop rollback segments
drop tablespace	Drop tablespaces
drop user	Drop users
execute any procedure	Execute procedures or functions, either stand-alone or packaged; also, reference public package variables in any schema
execute any type	Use and reference object types and collection types in any schema
exempt access policy	Bypass fine-grained access control
flashback any table	Issue a SQL Flashback Query on any table, view, or materialized view in any schema; not required when using any **dbms_ flashback** procedures
force any transaction	Force the commit or rollback of any in-doubt distributed transaction in the local database
force transaction	Force the commit or rollback of the grantee's in-doubt distributed transactions in the local database
global query rewrite	Enable rewrite using a materialized view when that materialized view references tables or views in any schema
grant any object privilege	Grant any object privilege or revoke any object privilege that was granted by the object owner or by some other user with the **grant any object privilege** privilege
grant any privilege	Grant any system privilege
grant any role	Grant any role in the database
insert any table	Insert rows into tables and views in any schema
lock any table	Lock tables and views in any schema

System Role	What It Allows You to Do
manage tablespace	Take tablespaces offline and online and begin and end tablespace backups
on commit refresh	Create a refresh-on-commit materialized view on any table in the database; also, alter an existing materialized view from refresh-on-demand to refresh-on-commit
restricted session	Log on after the instance is started using the SQL*Plus **startup restrict** statement
resumable	Enable resumable space allocation
select any dictionary	Query any data dictionary object in the SYS schema
select any sequence	Reference sequences in any schema
select any table	Query tables, views, or materialized views in any schema
sysdba	Allows the user to **startup** or **shutdown** the database, to use most functions of the **alter database** command such as to open, mount, and backup the database. Also **sysdba** allows for the use of the **create database** and in Oracle Database 10*g* the **drop database** commands. Also allows for the use of the **create spfile** command and restricted session privileges.
sysoper	Allows the user to **startup** or **shutdown** the database, to use the **alter database** command to open, mount, and backup the database. Also use the **alter database** command to put the database in ARCHIVELOG mode, and to do complete database recovery. Also allows for the use of the **create spfile** command and restricted session privileges.
unlimited tablespace	Use an unlimited amount of any tablespace
update any table	Update rows in tables and views in any schema

Using the with admin option Clause

When granting system privileges, you will want to use the **with admin option** clause of the **grant** command in certain cases. These cases include

- You are granting a role to a user, and you wish that user to be able to grant that role to another user.

- You are granting a role to a user, and you wish that user to be able to revoke the role from another user.

- You are granting a role to a user, and you wish that user to be able to change the role's password authentication.

- You are granting a role to a user, and you wish that user to be able to drop the role.

Once you have granted a privilege using the **with admin option** clause, you cannot revoke the **privilege**; instead, you must revoke the grant and then reissue the grant without the **with admin option** clause. Any user who is granted a system privilege via the **with admin option** clause will not lose that grant should the grantor lose the privilege.

Using the with grant option Clause

When dealing with object grants, the **with grant option** clause allows the user who has been granted specific privileges to grant those privileges to other users. If the user who grants an object privilege later loses that privilege, then that grant revocation is cascaded to other users who were granted privileges via the revoked user. Note that the **with grant option** clause cannot be used when granting object privileges to a role.

If a user who was granted an object privilege with the **with grant option** clause privilege has that privilege revoked, the revoke will cascade through all users who were granted privileges by the user whose privileges were revoked.

Public Grants

On occasion, you may want to grant the entire database environment a specific privilege. The **public** grant allows this. Simply use the **public** keyword in place of a specific username when issuing your **grant** statement. To revoke the privilege from public, reverse the procedure with the **revoke** command, (discussed later).

Granting Privileges

The **grant** command is used to grant privileges (object or system level) to users, roles, or to public. This section looks at the security requirements associated with the use of the **grant** command. It then provides some examples of the use of the **grant** command.

Security Requirements

To use the **grant** command to grant a system privilege, you must meet one of the following criteria:

- You were granted the system privilege and the **with admin option** clause was used when the grant was issued.

- You were granted the **grant any privilege** system privilege.

If you wish to grant a role, then you must meet one of the following criteria:

- You created the role.

- You were granted the role and the **with admin option** clause was used when the grant was issued.

- You were granted the **grant any role** system privilege.

If you wish to grant an object privilege, then you must meet one of the following criteria:

- You own the object.
- You were granted access to the object and the **with grant option** clause was used when the grant was issued.
- You were granted the **grant any object privilege** system privilege.

grant Examples

This first example creates a user called APP_OWN and then uses the **grant** command to grant the **create session** privilege to APP_OWN:

```
Create user app_own identified by passwd;
Grant create session to app_own;
```

This next example uses the **grant** command to grant the **select any table** system privilege to the APP_OWN user, which allows APP_OWN to issue **select** commands from any table:

```
Grant select any table to app_own;
```

Assume now that the APP_OWN user owns a table called CLAIMS. You want to grant **select**, **insert**, **update**, and **delete** access to that table to the APP_USER user. Here is an example of such an operation:

```
Create table claims (claim_id number, claim_date date)
                tablespace data_tbs;
grant select, insert, update, delete on claims to app_user;
```

Now assume that you have decided that you need to grant access to CLAIMS and three other tables (CLAIM_DETAILS, CLAIM_PERSON, and CLAIM_CODES) to a number of users. This would result in at least four grants per user, which can result in a lot of **grant** statements. In this case, you can create a role called APP_USER_ROLE, grant the privileges to that role, and then grant the role to the users whom you wish to grant privileges to:

```
Create role app_user_role;
Grant select, insert, update, delete on
claims to app_user_role;
Grant select, insert, update, delete on
claim_details to app_user_role;
Grant select, insert, update, delete on
claim_person to app_user_role;
Grant select, insert, update, delete on
claim_codes to app_user_role;
Grant app_user_role to app_user_one;
Grant app_user_role to app_user_two;
Grant app_user_role to app_user_three;
```

This next example creates a user, called APP_ADMIN, that becomes the administrator for an application. After you create the APP_ADMIN user, you need to grant APP_ADMIN the **create session** system privilege, so that APP_ADMIN can log into the application. Note that the **with admin option** is used so that APP_ADMIN can grant the **create session** system privilege to other users. You then grant the **select**, **insert**, **update**, and **delete** privileges on the CLAIMS table to the APP_ADMIN user. The **with grant option** has been used so that APP_ADMIN can grant these privileges to other users.

```
CREATE USER app_admin IDENTIFIED BY passwd;
GRANT create session TO app_admin WITH ADMIN OPTION;
GRANT select, insert, update, delete ON CLAIMS TO app_admin WITH GRANT OPTION;
```

Revoking Privileges

The **revoke** command is used to revoke user, role, or public granted privileges.

Security Requirements

If you wish to revoke a system privilege, you must have been granted the privilege with the **admin option**. If you wish to revoke a role, you must also have been granted the role using the **admin option**.

To revoke an object privilege, one of the following must be true:

- You must have been granted the object privilege to the user you wish to revoke it from.

- You must have the **grant any object privilege** system privilege.

revoke Examples

The **revoke** command syntax is pretty basic. This example uses the **revoke** command to revoke the **select any table** system privilege from the APP_USER_ONE user:

```
Revoke select any table from app_user_one;
```

And this example removes the **create session** privilege from the APP_USER_ONE user:

```
revoke create session from app_user_one;
```

System and Object Privileges Data Dictionary Information

Several views are available that allow you to manage system and object privileges. These views are listed in the following table:

View Name	Description	All	User
DBA_COL_PRIVS	Describes any object grants in the database that are column specific	Y	Y
DBA_ROLE_PRIVS	Describes roles that are granted to users in the database as well as roles granted to other roles	N	Y
DBA_SYS_PRIVS	Describes the system privileges that have been granted to users and roles	N	Y

View Name	Description	All	User
DBA_TAB_PRIVS	Describes all object-related grants in the database	Y	Y
ROLE_ROLE_PRIVS	Describes roles that have been granted to other roles	N	N
ROLE_SYS_PRIVS	Describes system privileges that have been granted to roles	N	N
ROLE_TAB_PRIVS	Describes table privileges that have been granted to roles	N	N
SESSION_PRIVS	Describes the privileges that the user currently has access to	N	N

System and Object Privileges–Related Errors

There are a number of errors that can occur as a result of attempting activities that you are not authorized to perform. The following list provides some of the more common errors that might occur and solutions to those errors.

Oracle Error Message	Text Description	Possible Causes and Solutions
ORA-01031	Insufficient privileges	This error will occur if you have tried to change a user's password and you do not have privileges to do so.
ORA-01045	User lacks CREATE SESSION privilege; logon denied	You have tried to connect to a user that does not have the **create session** privilege, which allows it to be connected to. Grant the user the **create session** privilege, and try again.
ORA-01917	User or role does not exist	You have tried to grant object access, a role, or a system privilege to a user that does not exist. Check the user name and make sure it is correct.
ORA-01924	Role not granted or does not exist	You have tried to use the **set role** command to activate a role that you do not have privileges to or that does not exist. Check that the role exists and that the user is assigned that role.
ORA-01926	Cannot GRANT to a role WITH GRANT OPTION	You have tried to use the **with grant option** when granting a privilege to a role. This is not supported.
ORA-01927	Cannot REVOKE privileges you did not grant	You have attempted to revoke privileges from a user that you did not grant to the user. Connect as the user who granted the privileges or as a SYSDBA user.
ORA-01928	GRANT option not granted for all privileges	You have tried to grant a privilege that you do not have the right to grant. If you should be able to grant this privilege, have the administrator grant it to you with the **with grant option**.
ORA-01929	No privileges to GRANT	You have attempted to grant privileges using the **all** option, but you do not have the underlying privileges required to perform this grant.
ORA-01931	Cannot grant to a role	The privilege you are trying to grant cannot be granted to a role. It must be granted directly to the user.

Oracle Error Message	Text Description	Possible Causes and Solutions
ORA-01933	Cannot create a stored object using privileges from a role	You have tried to create a stored object based on privileges granted to you from a role. This is not supported. Have the administrator grant you direct privileges to the objects that the stored object needs access to and recompile the object.
ORA-01934	Circular role grant detected	You cannot grant roles in a circular fashion, and roles cannot be granted to themselves. Determine where the circular reference is occurring and correct it.
ORA-01935	Missing user or role name	The statement issued expected you to use the name of a user or a role, and none was found. Correct the statement and re-execute it.
ORA-1035	Oracle only available to users with RESTRICTED SESSION privilege	You have tried to log into an account that does not have the **restricted session** privilege while the database was open in restricted mode. Either take the database out of restricted session mode, or grant the user the **restricted session** privilege.
ORA-1039	Insufficient privileges on underlying objects of the view	You have attempted to execute an explain plan on a view, and you do not have privileges needed on the objects underlying the view. You will need direct access to the objects underlying the view to perform an explain plan on that view.

System and Object Privileges–Related Recommended Standards

It is always best, as much as possible, to grant privileges through roles to most users. This simplifies security in many ways. Often, roles are created for different groups of users, such as administrators, users, or those generating reports. Be cautious about granting the Oracle-supplied default roles such as CONNECT and RESOURCE, as they provide a number of privileges (for example, the RESOURCE role offers the **alter session** privilege, which can lead to security issues). It's better to create your own custom application roles using the base Oracle grants.

Administration of Roles

Larger database designs involve a number of security privileges, both system related and object related. Roles provide a user-like alias that you can assign object privileges and roles to. These roles can then be assigned to other users, who inherit the security grants assigned to the role. This simplifies the administration of security because you only need allocate multiple grants once, to the role. From then on, you only need grant the role to users. If objects are added later in the development cycle, then you only need grant access to those objects to the role, and those new grants will cascade to the users that are assigned to the role.

Roles can be granted either system privileges (such as **create table**) or object privileges (such as **select** or **insert** privileges on a specific table) or a combination of both. See "Granting Privileges" (the **grant** command), earlier in this chapter, for a list of valid system and object privileges.

Roles can be assigned to a user via the **grant** command, or the user can select a role via the **set role** command, if that role is assigned to them. A role can be associated with a password by using the **identified** clause of the **create role** command or **alter role** command. This password can be changed or removed via the **alter role** command. *Application roles* can be defined as well by defining a package that only the application can execute. External roles can also be defined that allow the user to be authenticated to the role externally. Roles are dropped via the **drop role** command.

There are a few restrictions that you need to be aware of with regard to roles. If a user tries to create a stored procedure, all objects accessed by that stored procedure must be granted directly to that user. Otherwise, the procedure will fail to compile. Also, the maximum number of roles that can be created in a given database is controlled by the parameter **max_enabled_roles**. This parameter is obsolete in later versions of Oracle but is still available and can cause problems within your database environment if it is set to a value that is too low.

Common Oracle-Provided Roles

The following table provides a list of the most commonly used Oracle-provided roles:

Role Name	Purpose
connect	Allocates basic privileges to a user account. It is not recommended that you grant this role without careful consideration to the privileges it contains.
resource	Allocates basic privileges to a user account. It is not recommended that you grant this role without careful consideration to the privileges it contains.
dba	Used to grant DBA-level privileges to a given user. It is not recommended that you grant this role without careful consideration to the privileges it contains.
select_catalog_role	Used to grant access to data dictionary views to users who must access the data dictionary and who are not DBAs. Also includes the **hs_admin** role.
execute_catalog_role	Allows execute privileges on data dictionary objects. Also includes the **hs_admin** role.
delete_catalog_role	Allows the user to delete records from the AUD$ table.
exp_full_database	Allows the user to perform full and incremental database exports.
imp_full_database	Allows the user to perform full and incremental database imports.
recovery_catalog_owner	Provides required privileges for the recovery catalog owner.
hs_admin	Allows access to the HS (Heterogeneous Services) data dictionary tables (grants **select**) and packages (grants **execute**).

Creating Roles

Roles are created via the **create role** command.

Security Requirements

To create a role, you must have the **create role** system privilege.

create role Examples

The **create role** command is pretty straightforward. This example creates a basic role called my_role:

```
Create role my_role;
```

You can also assign a password to the role. This example creates a role called my_role, assigning it a password of **my_pwd**:

```
Create role my_role identified by my_pwd;
```

Once the role is created, you can grant privileges as required. This example grants the **create any table** privilege to my_role along with **select** on a table called SCOTT.EMP:

```
Grant create any table to my_role;
Grant select on scott.emp to my_role;
```

Altering Roles

The **alter role** command is used to remove or change the password associated with a role.

Security Requirements

To use the **alter role** command to alter a role, you must have been granted the role with the **with admin option** clause or you must have the **alter any role** system privilege (of course, if you created it, you can probably alter it). If you wish to alter the role to an application role using the **identified globally** parameter of the **alter role** command, you must **revoke** all grants to that role except any grants to the user actually altering the role.

alter role Examples

Here is an example of removing the password from the my_role role:

```
Alter role my_role not identified;
```

And here is an example of changing the password of the my_role role to **my_new_pwd**:

```
Alter role my_role identified by my_new_pwd;
```

Dropping Roles

Roles are removed via the **drop role** command.

Security Requirements

To use the **drop role** command, you must have been granted the role using the **admin** option or you must have the **drop any role** system privilege.

drop role Example

This example drops the MY_ROLE role:

```
Drop role my_role;
```

Role-Related Data Dictionary Information

The following table lists role-related data dictionary views:

View Name	Description	All	User
DBA_ROLES	Lists defined roles in the database	N	N
DBA_ROLE_PRIVS	Lists roles granted to database users	N	Y
SESSION_ROLES	Lists roles enabled by the current user	N	N
ROLE_SYS_PRIVS	Lists roles granted to other roles.	N	N
ROLE_TAB_PRIVS	Lists table privileges that are granted to roles.	N	N
ROLE_ROLE_PRIVS	Lists system privileges that are granted to roles.	N	N

Role-Related Errors

As you manage roles, you may run into various Oracle errors. The following table lists the most common errors and provides some advice as to what to do in the event you run into those errors.

Oracle Error Message	Text Description	Possible Causes and Solutions
ORA-01924	Role not granted or does not exist	You have tried to use the **set role** command to activate a role that you do not have privileges to or that does not exist. Check that the role exists and that the user is assigned that role.
ORA-01925	Maximum of enabled roles exceeded	You have exceeded the maximum number of roles as defined by the parameter **max_enabled_roles**.
ORA-01933	Cannot create a stored object using privileges from a role	The user trying to create a stored object does not have direct grants to the database objects that the stored object needs access to. Ensure that direct grants are allocated to the user that is creating the stored object.
ORA-01934	Circular role grant detected	You have tried to create a circular role reference. You cannot grant a role to itself or grant a role to a role that has a grant to that role.
ORA-01935	Missing user or role name	You need to include the user or role name in your command. Check that the user or role actually exists.
ORA-01936	Cannot specify owner when creating users or roles	You cannot include an owner name when creating a role. Remove the reference to the owner and try the statement again.
ORA-28031	Maximum of enabled roles exceeded	You have exceeded the maximum number of roles as defined by the parameter **max_enabled_roles**.

CHAPTER
11

Miscellaneous Administrative Features

racle offers a number of additional features and utilities that DBAs use frequently, such as the following:

- The **imp** and **exp** utilities
- The Data Pump utilities
- Oracle built-in packages
- Backing up the database

This chapter provides essential reference information on these features and utilities.

Oracle Export Utility

The Oracle Export Utility (**exp**) is used to create logical exports of Oracle databases. You can export the entire database, a specific user, specific tables, or data within a specific tablespace. Also, the **exp** utility is used when moving tablespaces between databases via Oracle Transportable Tablespaces. This section first provides a quick reference to the parameters of the **exp** utility, and then provides examples of the use of this tool, including exports of the entire database, exports of specific tables, and other examples.

NOTE
exp and imp are obsolete in Oracle Database 10g and later. They can still be used, but you should use Oracle Data Pump Export and Import instead.

The exp Utility Command Line

The **exp** utility provides a number of different parameters that you can use. You can display the valid parameters by calling the **exp** utility with the **help=y** parameter, as shown in this example:

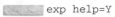
```
exp help=Y
```

If you do not use any parameters when calling **exp**, the program prompts you for the parameters that it requires to create an export file. These parameters include your username and password, the array fetch buffer size, the export filename, the type of export that you want to execute (entire database, user level, or table level), whether or not you want to export grants and table data, and whether or not you want to compress extents. The command line also provides a number of parameters that you can use, as described in the following table:

Parameter Name	Default Value Valid Values	Description
buffer	OS dependent	Specifies the size of the data buffer. In many cases you will want to set this value to a much higher number, particularly when dealing with LOBs. Buffers of 2M or larger are not uncommon.
compress	**y** or n	Causes Oracle to configure the output file such that when the object is imported in and re-created its initial size will be the size of the object that was exported.
consistent	**n** or y	Ensures, when set to **y**, that the export file data is consistent across all objects.
constraints	**y** or n	Indicates that constraints should be exported.
direct	**n** or y	Indicates if the data should be exported using direct path mode. This can improve performance.
feedback	**0** to any valid number	Displays progress every x rows.
file	EXPDAT.DMP or expdat.dmp depending on the OS	Identifies the name of the output export file or files to be created. Multiple output files can be defined, in comma-delimited fashion (see examples of this later in this section).
filesize	OS specific	Indicates the maximum size of each dump file.
flashback_scn	None	Indicates the SCN to be used to indicate which point in time you want the export to be consistent to.
flashback_time	None	Indicates the time used to indicate which point in time you want the export to be consistent to. Oracle rounds this to the nearest SCN value.
full	**n** or y	Indicates if the export is a full database export. Mutually exclusive with **owner** or **tables**. To perform a full export, the user that you connect to must be an administrative user or have the **exp_full_ database** privilege.
grants	**y** or n	Controls the export of grants.
indexes	**y** or n	Controls the export of indexes.
log	None	Indicates if a log file should be maintained during the export.
object_consistent	**n** or y	Indicates that the export should use the command SET TRANSACTION READ ONLY to ensure that the data being exported is consistent.
owner	None	Indicates that the export is an export of specific schema users. Multiple owners can be listed in comma-delimited format. Only objects in these schemas will be exported. Mutually exclusive with **full** or **tables**.

Parameter Name	Default Value Valid Values	Description
parfile	None	Identifies the parameter file filename.
query	None	Defines a set of predicates that restrict the row set being exported.
recordlength	OS dependent	Determines how much data is buffered before it is written to the export file. Generally recommended to set to the highest value, 64K.
resumable	**n** or y	Indicates that **exp** should use Oracle Resumable Space Management and suspend the export when a space-related error is encountered.
resumable_name	None	Indicates the name that should be used by Oracle to identify the resumable statement used by **exp**.
resumable_timeout	None	Specifies the time, if a resumable space event occurs, that Oracle should wait before the session fails with an error.
rows	**y** or n	Controls the export of actual data rows.
statistics	**estimate**, **computer**, or **none**	Indicates how object statistics should be generated.
tables	None	Indicates the schema and table names that should be exported. Commas should separate multiple table names. This parameter is mutually exclusive with **owner** or **full**.
tablespaces	None	Lists tablespace names that **exp** should export objects from. Used to move actual data or to transport tablespaces.
transport_ tablespace	**n** or y	Indicates that tablespace metadata should be exported for a transportable tablespace.
triggers	**y** or n	Indicates if triggers should be exported.
tts_full_check	None	Executes a transport tablespace dependency check.
userid	None	Indicates the username/password you wish to log into. The **exp** utility takes the username as the first parameter by default, and does not require the use of the **userid** parameter.

exp Utility Examples

This section provides a number of examples of the use of the **exp** utility. These include examples of exporting an entire database, exporting specific tables, exporting specific users, and exporting tables within a specific tablespace.

Using exp to Import an Entire Database

This first example exports the entire database. All default values are accepted. We are signing in using the sys account, and the dump file will be called myfull.dmp.

```
exp system/password full=y file=myfull.dmp
```

This example exports everything in the database, including data, table definitions, triggers, stored program objects (e.g., procedures), grants, and so on.

You can use various parameters to restrict the objects being exported. For example, if you wanted to export the database structure, but not the data, you would use this command:

```
exp system/password full=y rows=n file=myfull.dmp
```

Using exp to Export Specific Tables
The **exp** utility can also be used to export specific tables and the data in those tables, as shown in this example:

```
exp system/password tables=scott.emp, scott.dept
file=mytable.dmp
```

Note we could also have signed into the SCOTT account and exported the data. This allows users who only have access to limited accounts to still export their data. Here is an example of signing into SCOTT to export the EMP and DEPT tables:

```
exp scott/tiger tables=emp, dept file=myfull.dmp
```

Note that when a table-level export is performed, the only items backed up are the table definitions and the data in the tables.

Using exp to Export Specific Users
The **exp** command can also be used to export all objects owned by a specific user or users. Here is an example of exporting all objects from the SCOTT user:

```
exp scott/tiger owner=scott file=myuser.dmp
```

In this example, all objects owned by SCOTT will be exported, including views, synonyms, stored procedures, and so on.
You can also sign in from an administrator account and perform an owner-level export:

```
exp system/password owner=scott file=myuser.dmp
```

Using exp to Export Objects in Specific Tablespaces
You can use the **exp** utility to export objects that exist in a specific tablespace, as shown in this example:

```
exp system/password tablespace=users file=myfull.dmp
```

Other Examples of Using the exp Program
Here is an example of the use of the **exp** program using Resumable Space Management:

```
exp system/password tablespaces=users file=myfull.dmp resumable=Y resumable_timeout=3600
```

The **resumable** parameter indicates that the export should use Resumable Space Management. The **resumable_timeout** parameter defines the amount of time the database will wait if a space management issue occurs.

You can also use Flashback Query with the **exp** utility, as shown in this example:

```
exp system/robert tablespaces=users file=myfull.dmp
flashback_time="'2004-08-11 20:00:00'"
```

In this case, we used the **flashback_time** parameter to indicate the point in time we want the data being exported to be consistent to.

If you plan to use your export as a means of backup and recovery, you want to ensure that the backup data is consistent across all objects. Use the **consistent** parameter to perform this action, as shown in this example:

```
exp system/password tablespace=users file=myfull.dmp
consistent=Y
```

NOTE
Of course, recovery to point in time using archived redo logs is not possible.

Oracle Import Utility

The Oracle Import Utility (**imp**) is used to import export dumpfiles into Oracle databases. You can import the entire database, specific users, specific tables, or data from within a specific tablespace. Also, the **imp** utility is used when moving tablespaces between databases via Oracle Transportable Tablespaces. This section first provides a quick reference to the parameters of the **imp** utility, and then provides examples of the use of this tool.

The imp Utility Command Line

The Oracle Import Utility (**imp**) provides a number of different parameters that you can use. You can display the valid parameters by calling the **imp** utility with the **help=y** parameter, as shown in this example:

```
imp help=Y
```

If you do not use any parameters when calling the **imp** program, the program prompts you for the parameters that it requires to complete the import. The **imp** program prompts you for the username and password, the dump filename, the buffer size, whether or not you wish to just display the contents of the export file, whether or not you want to import the entire export file, and other information depending on the type of import you want to perform.

The command line also provides a number of parameters that you can use, as described in the following table:

Parameter Name	Default Value Other Valid Values	Description
buffer	OS dependent	Indicates the size of the data buffer.
commit	**n** or **y**	Allows for commit array inserts to occur. This can reduce the need for larger rollback segments.
compile	**y** or **n**	Causes procedures, packages, and functions to be compiled by the import process.
constraints	**y** or **n**	Allows you to determine if constraints should be imported.
destroy	**n** or **y**	If performing a full import, allows you to overwrite the tablespace data file during the import if it still exists.
feedback	**0**	Causes the **imp** utility to display progress as it performs the import.
file	OS dependent	Identifies a dump file created by the **exp** utility.
filesize	OS dependent	Indicates the size of the dump files to be imported.
fromuser	None	Allows you to copy objects in an export file from one user to another user. **fromuser** is used to indicate the name of the user to import from.
full	**n** or **y**	Causes a full import of the entire export file.
grants	**y** or **n**	Causes **imp** to import grants.
ignore	**n** or **y**	Causes **imp** to ignore create errors.
indexes	**y** or **n**	Causes **imp** to import indexes.
indexfile	None	Allows you to offload index creation statements into an output file.
log	None	Output to a log file.
parfile	None	Indicates the parameter filename that can contain parameters to be used during the import.
recordlength	OS dependent	Specifies the length of the I/O record.
resumable	**n** or **y**	Allows the use of Resumable Space Management.
resumable_name	None	Allows you to assign a name to the import session for use by Resumable Space Management.
resumable_timeout	7200 seconds	Specifies the timeout to be used if Resumable Space Management is used. The default is **0** if **resumable** is not enabled.
rows	**y** or **n**	Causes **imp** to import data rows.

Parameter Name	Default Value Other Valid Values	Description
show	**n** or **y**	Causes the **imp** utility to display only the contents of the dump file.
skip_unusable_indexes	**n** or **y**	Indicates that indexes that were set to an **unusable** state should not be rebuilt.
statistics	**always**, **none**, **safe**, or **recalculate**	Defines what should be done about statistics after the object it imported. **always** imports statistics from the dump file, **none** causes no action to be performed, **safe** allows optimizer statistics to be imported if they are not questionable, and **recalculate** causes the statistics to be recalculated.
tables	None	Allows you to import specific tables. Multiple tables are comma delimited.
touser	None	Allows you to copy objects in an export file from one user to another user. **touser** is used to indicate the name of the user to import to.
userid	None	Indicates the username/password to log in as.

imp Utility Examples

This section provides a number of examples of the use of the **imp** utility. These include examples of a full import, imports of users, and imports of tables. This section also looks at the use of some of the optional features of **imp**.

Using imp to Import an Entire Database

In this example, the **imp** program imports the entire contents of the export dump file into the database. This can include the creation of tablespaces, if they don't already exist, and the creation of all the objects to be imported, along with any ancillary objects such as indexes, grants, and sequences. Notice the use of the **ignore** parameter. Because the import attempts to create objects, these statements will fail if those objects already exist. The **ignore** parameter causes the **imp** program to ignore these errors. If the **ignore** parameter is not used, the import will error out in the event of an error caused by an attempt to create an object.

```
imp system/password full=y file=myfull.dmp ignore=y
```

Because a full export contains all the information required to re-create all objects in a database, it can be used as a means of logical database recovery, though it does not support point-in-time recovery and does not provide the means to recover the physical database.

Using imp to Import Specific Tables

You can use the **imp** utility to import specific tables from the dump file into the database. Here is an example of such an operation:

```
imp scott/tiger tables=emp file=mytable.dmp
```

You can also import tables into different database schemas by using the **fromuser** and **touser** parameters, as shown in this example:

```
imp system/password tables=emp fromuser=scott
touser=new_scott file=mytable.dmp
```

In this case, we are importing the EMP table in the dump file that belonged to the SCOTT user into the NEW_SCOTT user.

Using imp to Import Specific Users
To import all objects from a specific user in the dump file created by a full export, you use the **fromuser** and **touser** syntax used in the preceding example:

```
imp system/password tables=emp fromuser=scott
touser=new_scott file=mytable.dmp
```

If the export was created as a user-specific export, then the process of recovering the user objects follows this example:

```
imp scott/tiger tables=emp file=myuser.dmp
```

Other Examples Using imp and Its Parameters
The **imp** command comes with a number of helpful options. You can use Resumable Space Management (available in Oracle9*i* and later) when importing data to avoid failures. Here is an example of using Resumable Space Management during an import. We use the **resumable** parameter to indicate that we want to use Resumable Space Management, and we use the **resumable_timeout** parameter to set the timeout to 10 minutes (600 seconds).

```
imp scott/tiger tables=emp file=myuser.dmp resumable=y
resumable_timeout=600
```

If you are importing large objects, you might have some rollback segment issues. In this example, we use the **commit** parameter to indicate that **imp** should commit each time it completes importing data into the table:

```
imp scott/tiger tables=emp file=myuser.dmp commit=Y
```

Perhaps you want to restore from a full export, but you have already pre-created the database tables. Use the **ignore** command to ignore the errors that will occur when the **imp** program tries to create the tables:

```
imp scott/tiger full=y file=myfull.dmp ignore=y
```

You can also control how statistics are generated. Perhaps you don't want them generated at all. In this import, we use the **statistics** parameter to indicate that we don't want statistics calculated or imported. Also, we use the **feedback** parameter to indicate that Oracle should provide us with some feedback every time 1000 rows are imported into a table.

```
imp scott/tiger full=y file=myfull.dmp statistics=none
feedback=1000
```

Oracle Data Pump (Oracle Database 10*g*)

Oracle Data Pump replaces the old Oracle **imp** and **exp** utilities in Oracle Database 10*g*. This section introduces Data Pump Export, Data Pump Import, and Data Pump Interactive mode.

Oracle Data Pump Export

The Oracle Data Pump Export utility (**expdp**) works much like the **exp** utility does from a look and feel point of view. Features of **expdp** include the ability to estimate the size of the files that will result from the export operation, without actually having to write those files.

Oracle Data Pump Export makes managing your export much easier than it is using the old **exp** utility. **expdp** t allows you to suspend and resume an export job at will and attach or detach from a running export job at will. Also, you can restart many failed jobs from the point of failure.

Other functionality in **expdp** includes the ability to do fine-grained object selection when exporting. So, for example, you can choose to only export procedures and functions. **expdp** also provides for parallel processing and allows you to control the number of threads that will be used during the export operation.

expdp has two data access methods available to it. It can use either external tables (taking advantage of the new features associated with external tables in Oracle Database 10*g*, as discussed later in this chapter) or the direct path access method. The method used is selected automatically during the export process. **expdp** provides support for network mode operations, which allows you to load from another database, through a database link, directly.

expdp allows you to control the version of the object that is exported. This allows you to export data from one version of the Oracle database and ensure that it is compatible with a lower-level version of the database.

expdp offers three methods of database extraction. The first allows you to extract only database metadata (e.g., table and index creation statements). The second method allows you to extract only data from the database. The third method allows you to extract both database metadata and data at the same time.

Using Data Pump Export

Before you use **expdp**, you will want to create a directory object in the database that you will be exporting from. This is done with the **create directory** and **grant** commands, as shown in this example:

```
create directory pump_dir as 'c:\oracle\pump_dir';
grant read on directory pump_dir to scott;
```

When using **expdp**, the following order of operations is used to determine where the file will be written:

1. Oracle writes to a directory specifically listed as a part of the **dumpfile** specification in the **expdp** command line.

2. Oracle writes to the directory specified in the **directory** parameter setting in the **expdp** command line (note there still must be a database directory created for this directory).

3. Oracle writes to a location defined by the value of an environment variable that defines the default directory location (which is OS specific) on the client running the export, (again, a database directory by this name must be present).

If you are signing in as a user other than a SYSDBA user, that user must be granted the **exp_full_database** privilege in order to export data from a schema other than your own.

Pressing CTRL-C during an Oracle Data Pump operation causes Oracle to move the Data Pump operation into the background. Oracle then puts **expdp** in interactive mode, which allows you to either administer the job as it runs in the background or detach from the job completely while the job continues to run. Each Data Pump job is assigned a job name that allows you to track individual jobs, and to reconnect to those jobs. Either a default name is assigned or you can assign a job name when you start the export operation.

A number of parameters are available when using **expdp**, as listed and described in the following table:

Parameter	Description
attach	Indicates that **expdp** should attach to an existing job that is already running.
content	Allows you to control whether data or just database-related metadata is exported. Options: ALL, DATA_ONLY, and METADATA_ONLY.
directory	Defines the directory object to be used for the export dump files and log files. A directory of the same name must be created in the database that you are exporting or an error will occur.
dumpfile	Provides a list of destination dump files. Multiple dump files can be comma delimited. Also, a directory name can be included, separated from the filenames with a colon (:). Additionally, a substitution variable (**%u**) is available, which is a two-digit number from 01 to 99. This allows for the creation of multiple dump files. Note that **expdp** will not overwrite an existing file.
estimate	Tells the **expdp** process how to calculate the size of the resulting dump file. Options include **blocks** Calculate the dump file size based on the number of blocks of data times the database block size (default method). **sampling** Calculate the size based on a sample of the number of rows per table. **statistics** Base the size of the export on the current object statistics.
estimate_only	Causes **expdp** to determine the estimated size of the job, without actually doing the export.
exclude	Excludes certain metadata from the export operation. Note that for any object excluded, any dependent objects also are excluded. For example, exclusion of a table also excludes any indexes, triggers, constraints, and the related table data. You can also use wildcard characters and SQL statements to exclude specific ranges of objects.

Parameter	Description
filesize	Limits the size of the dump files being created. This parameter can be specified in bytes, or you can follow the size with the letter **B** (bytes), **K** (kilobytes), **M** (megabytes), or **G** (gigabytes).
flashback_scn	Allows you to use the Oracle Database flashback features when exporting the database. In this case, **expdp** uses the stated SCN to flashback to.
flashback_time	Allows you to use the Oracle Database flashback features when exporting the database. In this case, **expdp** will acquire the SCN nearest the stated time to flashback to.
full	If set to **y**, this parameter indicates that **expdp** should export the entire database. The default value for this parameter is **n**, which does not do a full export.
help	Allows you to display help messages and the syntax of **expdp**.
include	Allows you to define specific objects that you want exported. Only those objects, and dependent objects, are exported.
job_name	Defines the name of the export job. This name is used to manage the job (for example, via the **attach** command). By default, this name is system generated using the naming convention sys_*operation_mode_nn*. For example, a full export might take the job name sys_export_full_01.
logfile	Identifies the log file that is generated during the export operation. By default, it's called export.log and stored in the location defined by the directory parameter.
network_link	Allows for a network export through a remote database link to a predefined source system.
nologfile	Suppresses the writing of the **expdp** log file. Set to **n** by default.
parallel	Defines the maximum number of threads that can operate on behalf of the export job. This parameter allows you to adjust the level of parallelism, to provide a balance between system resource usage and time to create the export. This can be set when the export is started, and can also be changed via interactive mode (see "Oracle Data Pump Interactive Mode," later in this chapter). If the system resources allow, the number of parallel processes should be set to the number of dump files being created. The default for this setting is **1**.
parfile	Allows you to define an external parameter file for the **expdp** process. The parameter file is local to the client and does not use a database directory, as do the export dump files or log files.
query	Allows for the application of a SQL predicate to filter the database being exported. For example, this allows you to export from the STORE_SALES table the sales from store 100.

Parameter	Description
schemas	Defines the schemas you wish to export data from. The user must have the **exp_full_database** privilege to export any schema other than the schema that they have logged **expdp** into. Any table in the SYS.NOEXP$ table will not be exported in schema export mode.
status	Defines how frequently the job status should be updated, in seconds. Defaults to 0 seconds (which means it's constantly updated).
tables	Allows you to export specific tables only. Dependent objects are exported also.
tablespaces	Allows you to export objects listed in the specified tablespaces. All dependent objects in other tablespaces (e.g., indexes) also are exported.
transport_full_ check	During transportable tablespace operation, verifies that there are no dependencies between objects inside the transportable set and objects outside the transportable set.
transport_ tablespaces	Allows for the export of transportable tablespace metadata.
version	Restricts objects being exported to a specific version level of the database. This is designed to help with compatibility issues when moving database objects from a higher version of the database to a lower version.

Data Pump Export Examples

This section provides you with several examples of the use of Oracle Data Pump Export, including a full database export, a user data export, an export of specific tables, a tablespace export, and an export of only data. This section also describes how to estimate the size of the database export without actually running the export.

Full Database Export   In this first example, we do a dump of the entire database, data and all:

```
expdp system/tiger dumpfile=pump_dir:mydb_%U.dat filesize=100m nologfile=y
job_name=robert full=y estimate_only
```

This example demonstrates a number of things about **expdp**. First, we are creating a full database export, since we have included the **full** parameter. Also, we have limited each of the resulting dump files in size with the **filesize** parameter. Thus, **expdp** will limit the size of each dump file, and automatically create additional dump files as required.

The **dumpfile** parameter is of note in this example too. First, notice that we include the name of the Oracle Database directory to use (pump_dir). Also, we include the name of the dump file that should be created (mydb_%U.dat). That %U is a placeholder that is replaced by a unique sequence number. That way, if multiple dump files are created, each will be named uniquely.

In this example, we assigned a job name of ROBERT using the **job_name** parameter. This allows us to disconnect from the job and enter interactive mode. We can reconnect to the job at will by using the **attach** parameter. Interactive mode is covered later in this chapter. Finally, in this example, we have decided that we do not want a log file created, so we used the parameter **nologfile** to disable logging.

User Data Export   This example uses **expdp** to export just the SCOTT schema:

```
expdp system/tiger dumpfile=pump_dir:scott_%U.dat schemas=scott nologfile=y
job_name=just_scott
```

This example is much like the previous example of the full database export, except that we now are using the **schemas** parameter instead of the **full** parameter.

Export Specific Tables   In this example, we have chosen to export the EMP and DEPT tables from the SCOTT schema.

```
expdp system/tiger dumpfile=pump_dir:scott_tables_%U.dat
tables=scott.emp, scott.dept
nologfile=y job_name=just_scott
```

Again, this example is a lot like the first example, except that we are now using the **tables** parameter, and we are listing the tables we want to export.

Export Tablespace Data   In this example, we want to export data from a single tablespace, named USERS. So, we use the following command:

```
expdp system/tiger dumpfile=pump_dir:users_tbs_%U.dat tablespaces=users
nologfile=y job_name=users_tbs_exp
```

In this example, the **tablespace** parameter is used to indicate the name of the tablespace we want to export.

Using Other Data Pump Export Parameters

In this example, we want to export only database data for the entire database. We have also decided to create a log file, so we have included the **logfile** parameter. You might be asking why we didn't just allow **expdp** to create the default log file. The reason is that we did not define the default directory entry that **expdp** would be looking for, which is called PUMP_DIR in the database (PUMP_DIR needs to be created in the database with the **create directory** command). Thus, the **expdp** process would have failed in its attempt to create the directory.

```
expdp system/tiger dumpfile=pump_dir:mydb_%U.dat filesize=100m job_name=robert
full=y content=data_only
logfile=pump_log:mydb_exp_log
```

You can also use parameter files with **expdp**. In this next example, we create a parameter file that has individual **include** parameters. This export will export all database functions, procedures, and any table that has a name that starts with EMP.

```
INCLUDE=FUNCTION
INCLUDE=PROCEDURE
```

```
INCLUDE=TABLE:"LIKE 'EMP%'"
DUMPFILE=pump_dir:mydb_%U_objects.dat
NOLOGFILE=Y
JOB_NAME=specific_objects
FULL=y
```

Along with the preceding parameter file, we use the following command line to get just what we asked for:

```
expdp system/tiger parfile=c:\oracle\admin\mydb\exp\mypar.fil
```

Of course, we could have done all of this from the command line, too:

```
expdp system/tiger INCLUDE=FUNCTION INCLUDE=PROCEDURE
INCLUDE=TABLE:\"LIKE 'EMP%'\"
DUMPFILE=pump_dir:mydb_%U_objects.dat NOLOGFILE=Y
JOB_NAME=specific_objects FULL=y
```

By default, **expdp** estimates whether there is enough space for the dump file that it will create. You can also instruct **expdp** to only estimate whether there is enough space for a Data Pump export. Simply use the **estimate_only** parameter and you will get the estimate of how big the dump file will be without the actual creation of the dump file. Here is an example:

```
expdp scott/tiger full=y estimate_only=Y estimate=statistics nologfile=y
```

NOTE
Any account that will be exported from by Oracle Data Pump will need EXP_FULL_DATABASE.

Note the use of the **estimate** clause that allows us to choose the base for our size estimate. Oracle Data Pump Export allows you to use various bases for the estimate, including database statistics, a sample of blocks, or all the blocks. Using all the blocks is the default, and the most accurate and most restrictive. Using a sample of blocks is the middle ground, and using statistics is, well, only as good as the statistics.

Oracle Data Pump Import

The Oracle Data Pump Import utility (**impdp**) works much like the **imp** utility does from a look and feel point of view. Features of **impdp** include the ability to load data into the entire database, a specific schema, a specific tablespace, or specific tables. **impdp** is also used when transporting tablespaces into the database.

impdp supports the use of data filters that allow you to restrict the row sets that are loaded into the database and supports the use of metadata filters that allow you to control which object types (e.g., indexes, functions, or procedures) are imported.

impdp provides many administrative features, including the ability to suspend and resume an import job at will. Also, it allows you to attach or detach from a running import job at will, and you can often restart failed jobs from the point of failure.

Oracle Data Pump Import supports parallelism and allows you to assign a number of threads that will be used during the import operation. Oracle Data Pump Import also provides support for network mode operations, which allows you to load from another database directly.

Another feature of Oracle Data Pump is that it allows you to have control over the database-related version of the object that is imported. This enables you to import data from one version of the Oracle database and ensure that it is compatible with a lower-level version of the database.

Using Oracle Data Pump Import

To use **impdp**, you need to be aware of the privileges that are required. If creation of the export dump files you are using required **exp_full_database** rights, or if the import is done using the **full** parameter, then the user doing the import must have the **imp_full_database** privilege. In most other cases, the user need only have the same privileges as the user who created the dump file.

A number of parameters are available when using **impdp**, as listed and described in the following table.

Parameter	Description
attach	Indicates that **impdp** should attach to an existing job that is already running.
content	Allows you to control whether data or just database-related metadata is imported. Options: ALL, DATA_ONLY, and METADATA_ONLY.
directory	Defines the directory object to be used as the source of the dump files and log files. A directory of the same name must be created in the database that you are importing or an error will occur. A default value PUMP_DIR is used if directory is not defined.
dumpfile	Provides a list of the dump files to source the import from. Multiple dump files can be comma delimited. Also, a directory name can be included, separated from the filenames with a colon (:). Additionally, a substitution variable (%U) is available, which is a two-digit number from 01 to 99. This allows for the use of multiple dump files.
estimate	Tells the **impdp** process how to calculate the amount of data that will be generated and provides operation completion status information. If a dump file is being used, no estimate is needed.
exclude	Excludes certain metadata from the import operation. Note that for any object excluded, any dependent objects also are excluded. For example, exclusion of a table also excludes any indexes, triggers, constraints, and the related table data. You can also use wildcard characters and SQL statements to exclude specific ranges of objects.
flashback_scn	Allows you to use the Oracle Database flashback features when doing a network import directly from another source database. Used only in conjunction with the **network_link** parameter.
flashback_time	Allows you to use the Oracle Database flashback features when exporting the database. Used only in conjunction with the **network_link** parameter.

Parameter	Description
full	Indicates that **impdp** should import the entire database. The default for this parameter is **n**. If the **network_link** parameter is being used, or the creation of the source dump file set required the use of the **exp_full_ database** privilege, then the user account used to load the dump file must have the **imp_full_database** privileges.
help	Allows you to display help messages and the syntax of **impdp**.
include	Allows you to define specific objects that you want imported. Only those objects, and dependent objects, are imported.
job_name	Creates an import job. This name is used to manage the job (for example, via the **attach** command). By default, this name is system generated using the naming convention sys_*operation_mode_nn*. For example, a full import might take the job name sys_import_full_01.
logfile	Identifies the log file that is generated during the import operation. By default, it's called import.log and stored in the location defined by the **directory** parameter.
network_link	Allows for a network import through a remote database link to a predefined source system.
nologfile	Suppresses the writing of the **impdp** log file. This is set to **n** by default. Note that by default Oracle tries to create a log file in a directory called data_pump_dir. This must be created or the import will fail.
parallel	Defines the maximum number of threads that can operate on behalf of the import job. The default for this setting is **1**.
parfile	Allows you to define an external parameter file for the **impdp** process. The parameter file is local to the client and does not use a database directory as do the import dump files or log files.
query	Allows for the application of a SQL predicate to filter the data being imported.
remap_datafile	Allows you to redefine the datafile names and directories during the import.
remap_schema	Allows you to map objects destined for one schema to another schema.
remap_ tablespace	Allows you to map objects to tablespaces other than the ones the objects were originally assigned to.
reuse_datafiles	Allows for re-creation of the tablespace data files.
schemas	Defines the schemas you wish to import. Oracle Database 10*g* creates the schemas, and then the schemas are imported. The user must have the **imp_full_database** privilege to use this command, or only the objects within the schema will be restored (no schema definition is imported).
skip_unusable_ indexes	Indicates that the indexes that have an UNUSABLE status should not be created.

Parameter	Description
sqlfile	Extracts all SQL DDL that is imported to an output file.
status	Defines how frequently the job status should be updated, in seconds. Defaults to 0 seconds.
streams_ configuration	Indicates whether any general Oracle Streams metadata in the export dump file should be imported.
table_exists_ action	Determines the action to take if the table already exists. Options include **skip** Do not load the data (default) and move on to the next object. **append** Append to existing data already in the table. **replace** Drop the table, if it exists. Re-creates the table and loads the data. **truncate** Remove all rows before the load.
tables	Allows you to import specific tables only. Dependent objects are imported also.
tablespaces	Allows you to import objects listed in the specified tablespaces. All dependent objects in other tablespaces (e.g., indexes) also are imported.
transform	Allows you to alter the object creation DDL for either specific objects or all objects. This allows you to manipulate storage or physical attributes of objects.
transport_ datafiles	Defines the list of data files in the source database that are to be imported into the target system by the transportable mode import. Used with the **network_link** parameter.
transport_full_ check	During transportable tablespace operation, verifies that there are no dependencies between those objects inside the transportable set and those objects outside the transportable set. This is only valid when the **network_link** parameter is used.
transport_ tablespaces	Allows for the import of transportable tablespace metadata.
version	Restricts objects being imported to a specific version level of the database. This is designed to help with compatibility issues when moving database objects from a higher version of the database to a lower version of the database.

Data Pump Import Examples

This section provides you with several examples of the use of **impdp**, including a full database import, a tablespace import, an import that imports only data, and an import that imports only specific database object types.

Full Database Import   This first example demonstrates using **impdp** to perform a full database import. Note that we use the **full** parameter to indicate the full database dump. Also note the **dumpfile** parameter. We are using the name of the pump_dir directory, followed by a colon, and then the name of the dump file that should be read from. Also note the use of the **job_name** parameter, which allows us to connect and disconnect from the import session at will.

```
impdp scott/tiger dumpfile=pump_dir:mydb_%U.dat
nologfile=y job_name=robert full=y
```

Tablespace Import   In this example, we are importing data specific to the USERS tablespace into our database. In this example, we use the parameter **table_exists_action**. We have set **table_exists_action** to **truncate**, so the table will be truncated before the data is loaded into it.

```
impdp scott/tiger dumpfile=pump_dir:mydb_tbs_users_%U.dat
nologfile=y job_name=tablespace tablespaces=users
table_exists_action=truncate
```

Importing Only Specific Table Data   This next example uses the **content** parameter to indicate that only data should be imported into the database. Thus, if the table that the data is to be imported into does not exist, the import will fail. Also, if **content** is set to **data_only**, ancillary objects such as constraints, statistics, and the like will not be imported.

```
impdp scott/tiger dumpfile=pump_dir:mydb_%U_data.dat
content=data_only job_name=data_import
logfile=pump_log:mydb_imp.log tables=scott.emp
```

Importing Specific Database Object Types   In this example, we create a parameter file that has individual **include** statements. This imports all database functions, procedures, and any table that has a name that starts with EMP.

```
INCLUDE=FUNCTION
INCLUDE=PROCEDURE
INCLUDE=TABLE:"LIKE 'EMP%'"
DUMPFILE=pump_dir:mydb_%U_objects.dat
NOLOGFILE=Y
JOB_NAME=specific_objects
FULL=Y
```

Along with the preceding parameter file, we use the **parfile** parameter to indicate that **impdp** should use the parameter file we just created:

```
impdp scott/tiger parfile=c:\oracle\admin\mydb\exp\mypar.fil
```

Oracle Data Pump Interactive Mode

One of the nice new features available with Oracle Data Pump is that you can detach from a job and then reconnect to that job at a later time. This functionality is available with both **impdp** and **expdp**. To reconnect to a job, simply start the **impdp** or **expdp** utility using the **attach** parameter followed by the job name that you assigned to the job. If you are running an active import or export operation, all you need to do is press CTRL-C to exit client mode and enter interactive mode. The job will continue to run in the background until you kill it or it terminates in success or failure.

If you have exited to the command-line prompt, you can reconnect to the job by simply using the **attach** parameter of either the **impdp** or **expdp** command, which will put you into interactive mode.

Here is an example of exiting the client, and then reentering interactive mode using **expdp** (note that this output has been reformatted slightly to fit on the page):

```
expdp scott/tiger dumpfile=pump_dir:myd_%U.dat filesize=100m
nologfile=y job_name=robert full=y
<snip banner for brevity>
Starting "SCOTT"."ROBERT":  scott/********
dumpfile=pump_dir:myd_%U.dat filesize=100m nologfile=y
job_name=robert full=y
Estimate in progress using BLOCKS method...
<we hit ctrl-c at this point>
Export>
```

At this point, you are in interactive mode. You can immediately reattach to the job using the **continue_client** interactive mode command, as shown here:

```
Export> continue_client
```

Or, you can exit interactive mode with the **exit** command, leaving the job to run in the background:

```
Export> exit
```

If you wish to reattach to the session, use the **attach** parameter, along with the job name:

```
expdp scott/tiger attach=Robert
```

Once you have entered interactive mode, you can issue one of the valid interactive commands, such as the **status** command shown here:

```
Export> status
Job: ROBERT  Operation: EXPORT  Mode: FULL
State: EXECUTING  Degree: 1  Job Error Count: 0
 <snip remaining output for brevity>
```

Data Pump Export: Interactive Mode Parameters

Several commands are available from interactive mode, as listed and described in the following table:

Command	Description
add_file	Allows you to add a file to the list of dump files. Only available for exports.
continue_client	Returns you to client logging mode.
exit_client	Exits client logging mode without killing the job.

Command	Description
help	Provides help on all commands.
kill_job	Allows you to detach from and delete an existing job.
parallel	Allows you to change the number of active workers for the current job.
start_job	Allows you to start or resume the current job.
status	Defines the refresh frequency for monitoring a job, in seconds. The default is 0 seconds.
stop_job	Stops job execution and exits the client.

Data Pump–Related Data Dictionary Information

Oracle provides several data dictionary views that you can use to manage and monitor data pump operations. These views are listed in the following table, along with a description of their use:

View Name	Purpose/Description	All	User
DBA_DATAPUMP_JOBS	Displays information on running Data Pump jobs; also comes in the USER_DATAPUMP_JOBS variety	N	Y
DBA_DATAPUMP_SESSIONS	Provides session-level information on Data Pump jobs	N	N
DATAPUMP_PATHS	Provides a list of valid object types that you can associate with the **include** or **exclude** parameters of **expdp** or **impdp**	NA	NA
DBA_DIRECTORIES	Provides a list of defined directories	Y	N

Oracle Backups

All Oracle DBAs need to back up their databases. This section gives you quick notes on backing up your database. First, we look at cold backups, which require the database to be shut down and may or may not offer point-in-time recovery. Then, we look at hot backups, which allow you to back up the database while it is up and running, and offers point-in-time (or incomplete) recovery.

Oracle also offers RMAN as a backup and recovery solution. The final sections provide information on using RMAN for backups of your database. Finally, the examples of backups in this section are very basic; they are designed to get your database backed up quickly. Backups to media devices, scheduled backups, and other more complex backup strategies are beyond the scope of this book.

> **NOTE**
> *Check out* Oracle9i RMAN Backup & Recovery *(Oracle Press, McGraw-Hill/Osborne, 2002) for more on backing up your Oracle database.*

Oracle Database Cold Backups

Every DBA needs to know how to back up the database they manage. This section provides a quick reference to manual backups and using RMAN to perform a cold backup.

Manual Cold Backups

Here are the quick steps to completing a manual cold backup of your system:

Step	What to Do
1.	Perform a checkpoint on the database (optional, but this can reduce the overall outage): `SQL> alter system checkpoint`
2.	Shut down your database. Using **shutdown immediate** is preferred, but **shutdown abort** is allowed. `SQL> shutdown abort`
3.	Back up all files associated with the database. This includes • Data files (`SELECT file_name FROM dba_data_files;`) • Control files (`SELECT name FROM v$controlfile;`) • All online redo logs (`SELECT member FROM V$LOG;`) If your database is in ARCHIVELOG mode, back up any archived redo logs as well. You should also back up the archived redo logs on a regular basis to ensure point-in-time recovery is available.
4.	Restart the database; your backup is complete.

Manual Cold Backups with RMAN

Here are the quick steps to completing a manual cold backup of your system with RMAN:

Step	What to Do
1.	Start RMAN from the command prompt: `Rman target=/`
2.	Perform a checkpoint on the database (optional, but this can reduce the overall outage): `RMAN> SQL 'ALTER SYSTEM CHECKPOINT';`

3.	Shut down the database, and then mount it from RMAN:
	`RMAN>SHUTDOWN IMMEDIATE`
	`RMAN>STARTUP MOUNT`

4.	Back up the database and archived redo logs. Also back up the control file after the backup:
	Oracle9*i* and Oracle Database 10*g* if not using a flash recovery area:
	`RMAN>BACKUP DATABASE FORMAT`
	`'c:\oracle\dbbackup\back_%U.dbf' PLUS ARCHIVELOG;`
	`RMAN>BACKUP CURRENT CONTROLFILE FORMAT`
	`'c:\oracle\dbbackup\back_ctl_%U.dbf';`
	If using a flash recovery area in Oracle Database 10*g* and later (RMAN in Oracle Database 10*g* uses a configured flash recovery area by default):
	`RMAN>BACKUP DATABASE PLUS ARCHIVELOG;`
	`RMAN>BACKUP CURRENT CONTROLFILE;`

Step	What to Do
5.	Open the database: `RMAN>SQL 'ALTER DATABASE OPEN';`
6.	Exit RMAN; your backup is complete.

Oracle Database Hot Backups

Performing Oracle hot backups is only slightly more complex than performing cold backups. To perform hot backups, the database must be in ARCHIVELOG mode and generating archived redo logs properly. This section first provides a quick reference checklist for configuring the database for hot backups, and then walks you through the process of doing a hot backup.

Preparing for Hot Backups

The following table provides a list of steps to follow to configure your database for hot backups:

Step	What to Do
1.	Determine where you wish Oracle to copy archived redo logs to. This example uses the file system `/opt/oracle/admin/mydb/arch`.
2.	Set the following parameters if you are using Oracle9*i* and earlier to prepare for ARCHIVELOG mode. Also set these parameters if you are using Oracle Database 10*g* and will not be using RMAN backups: • Set **log_archive _dest_1** to the location defined in Step 1. • Set the **log_archive_start** parameter to **true**. If you are using Oracle Database 10*g* and later and you are using RMAN, you can optionally configure a flash recovery area using the following Oracle database parameters for ARCHIVELOG mode operations: • Set **db_recovery_file_dest** to the location defined in Step 1. • Set **db_recovery_file_dest_size** to a value large enough to hold at least one backup of your database, plus all archived redo logs that will be generated. • Set the **log_archive_start** parameter to **true**.

3.	Put the database in ARCHIVELOG mode. You must shut down the database to perform this action:
	`SQL>shutdown immediate`
	`SQL>startup mount;`
	`SQL>alter database archivelog;`
	`SQL>alter database open;`

4.	Confirm the database is in ARCHIVELOG mode: `SQL>archive log list` This command should show the Database log mode is Archive Mode and Automatic archival is Enabled. Also the archive destination should either show the location defined in Step 2 above, or if a flash recovery area was used (Oracle Database 10*g*). The archive destination should show a value of **use_db_recovery_file_dest**.

5.	If you are using RMAN, use the **configure** command to configure for automatic backups of control files and the SPFILE:
	`Rman target=/`
	`RMAN>configure controlfile autobackup on;`

Doing a Manual Hot Backup

Having set up the database for hot backups, as shown in the previous section, you can now perform a hot backup by following these steps:

Step	What to Do
1.	Generate a list of tablespaces to back up using DBA_TABLESPACES: `SELECT tablespace_name FROM dba_tablespaces;`
2.	Determine the location of all database data files to back up: `SELECT file_name FROM dba_data_files;`
3.	Put in hot backup mode, using the **alter tablespace begin backup** command, each tablespace found in Step 1: `ALTER TABLESPACE tablespace_name BEGIN BACKUP;` *Note: In Oracle Database 10g you can put the whole database in backup mode at once if you like with the* **alter database begin backup** *command.*
4.	Back up each data file listed in Step 2 to another disk, tape, or other media. This is your backup.
5.	Take out of hot backup mode, using the **alter tablespace end backup** command, each tablespace put in hot backup mode in Step 3: `ALTER TABLESPACE tablespace_name END BACKUP;` *Note: In Oracle Database 10g you can take the whole database out of backup mode at once if you like with the* **alter database end backup** *command.*
6.	Determine the location of the archived redo logs using the V$PARAMETER view: `SELECT name, value FROM v$parameter WHERE name IN ('log_archive_dest', 'log_archive_dest_1', 'db_recovery_file_dest');` Generally, only one location will appear.
7.	Back up all archived redo logs generated between Steps 3 and 5.

8.	Create a backup control file using two different **alter database backup controlfile** commands:
	`Alter database backup controlfile to trace;`
	`Alter database backup controlfile to 'your_backup_location';`
	You should copy these control file backups.

9.	Your backup is complete.

Using RMAN to Perform a Hot Backup

If you are using RMAN, then performing hot backups of your database is easy. Here are the steps to perform a hot backup with RMAN:

Step	What to Do
1.	Start RMAN from the command prompt: `Rman target=/`

Step	What to Do

2.	Use the RMAN **backup** command to back up the database and archived redo logs. Also back up the control file after the backup:
	Oracle9*i* and Oracle Database 10*g* if not using a flash recovery area:
	`RMAN>BACKUP DATABASE FORMAT`
	`'c:\oracle\dbbackup\back_%U.dbf' PLUS archivelog;`
	`RMAN>BACKUP CURRENT CONTROLFILE FORMAT`
	`'c:\oracle\dbbackup\back_ctl_%U.dbf';`
	If using a flash recovery area in Oracle Database 10*g* and later (RMAN in Oracle Database 10*g* uses a configured flash recovery area by default):
	`RMAN>BACKUP DATABASE PLUS ARCHIVELOG;`
	`RMAN>BACKUP CURRENT CONTROLFILE;`

3.	Exit RMAN; your backup is complete.

Other Oracle Backups

You will want to back up other things associated with your database. Specifically, you will want to back up your archived redo logs, your control files, your parameter/SPFILE files, and your Oracle database software. This section quickly covers how to back up these items.

Back Up Archived Redo Logs

Archived redo logs can be backed up manually or through RMAN. To back up archived redo logs manually, simply copy or move those files to the backup media. You can back up archived redo logs via RMAN either during a database backup operation (this is demonstrated in a previous section of this chapter) or separately as shown in this example:

```
RMAN>backup archivelog all;
```

Back Up Control Files

You need to back up your database control files. This is to protect the control files in the event they become unavailable or unusable. It's particularly important to back up control files after a backup has completed. This section looks at manual backups of control files and RMAN backups of control files.

Control File Manual Backups   You can back up control files manually using one of two methods. First, you can create a backup control file, which is an actual copy of the control file with some settings modified for recovery purposes, through the **alter database** command, as shown in this example:

```
ALTER DATABASE
BACKUP CONTROLFILE TO '/tmp/control_file.bkp';
```

You can also use the following statement to have Oracle create a trace file that contains the **create controlfile** statement. You can then use that file to recover your control file.

```
ALTER DATABASE BACKUP CONTROLFILE TO TRACE;
```

In this case, the trace file is created in a location defined by the parameter **user_dump_dest**.

Control File RMAN Backups   RMAN allows you to back up control files with the **backup current controlfile** command:

```
RMAN>BACKUP CURRENT CONTROLFILE;
```

RMAN also allows you to configure automatic backups of the control file after each backup by using the **configure controlfile autobackup on** command.

Back Up Parameter/SPFILE Files

You should back up your database parameter or SPFILE files on a regular basis. To do a manual backup of this file, simply copy it to the backup media. RMAN allows you to configure automatic backups of the SPFILE file after each backup by using the **configure controlfile autobackup on** command. If you are using regular parameter files, you still need to back them up manually.

Back Up the Oracle Database Software

You should back up the entire contents of $ORACLE_HOME on a regular basis. You should particularly back up $ORACLE_HOME after any patches have been applied, or after any specific configuration changes have been made to your system.

Database Recovery

Database recovery is a critical DBA function. In this section we will review recovering databases from manual cold backups, RMAN backups, and hot backups. We will then look at incomplete recovery of Oracle databases.

Recovering from a Manual Cold Backup (In NOARCHIVELOG Mode)

To recover using a manual cold backup when the database is not in ARCHIVELOG mode, follow these steps:

Step	What to Do
1.	If it is still up, shut down the database that you will be recovering: SQL> SHUTDOWN ABORT Note that this recovery will completely wipe out the current database and any data entered after the backup will be unrecoverable.
2.	Copy the database data files, online redo logs, and control files from the last database cold backup (see Step 3 in the section "Manual Cold Backups," earlier in this chapter). You might also need to recover the parameter file.
3.	Start up the database: SQL>STARTUP

Recovering from a Manual Cold Backup (In ARCHIVELOG Mode)

Recovery from a manual cold backup of a database in ARCHIVELOG mode is just like recovering from a hot backup. See the upcoming section "Recovering from a Manual Hot Backup" for those instructions.

Recovering from an RMAN Cold Backup (NOARCHIVELOG Mode)

If you used RMAN to perform a cold backup of your database, and the database was in NOARCHIVELOG mode, here are the steps to perform a hot backup with RMAN:

Step	What to Do
1.	Start RMAN from the command prompt: `rman target=/`
2.	Start the database instance: `RMAN>STARTUP NOMOUNT;`
3.	Recover the control file from the most recent control file backup: `RMAN>RECOVER CONTROLFILE FROM AUTOBACKUP;`
4.	Mount the database: `RMAN>SQL 'ALTER DATABASE MOUNT';`
5.	Recover the database: `RMAN>RECOVER DATABASE;`
6.	Open the database: `RMAN>SQL 'ALTER DATABASE OPEN';`
7.	Your database recovery is complete.

Recovering from an RMAN Cold Backup (In ARCHIVELOG Mode)

Recovery from an RMAN cold backup of a database in ARCHIVELOG mode is just like recovering from an RMAN hot backup. See the upcoming section, "Recovering from an RMAN Hot Backup," for those instructions.

Recovering from a Manual Hot Backup

To recover using a manual hot backup to the point of the failure when the database is not in ARCHIVELOG mode, follow these steps (note that the procedure assumes that the control file and at least one member of each online redo log group are intact):

Step	What to Do
1.	Determine what needs to be recovered. With a hot backup, you can choose to recover: • An individual data file • A tablespace • The entire database

Step	What to Do

Prepare for the Recovery

2.   If you are going to recover specific data files, then offline those data files:
   `ALTER DATABASE DATAFILE 'datafile_name' OFFLINE;`
   You can get the correct datafile name from the V$DATAFILE view or DBA_DATA_FILES view. Back up the data files you have just offlined.

3.   If you are going to recover a specific tablespace, then offline the tablespaces to be recovered:
   `ALTER TABLESPACE tablespace_name OFFLINE;`
   Tablespace names are available in V$TABLESPACE and DBA_TABLESPACES. Back up all data files associated with the tablespaces you have just offlined.

4.   If you are restoring the entire database, then shut down the database (if it is still available):
   `SQL>SHUTDOWN ABORT`

Restore the Required Backup Elements

5.   If you are recovering a specific data file, replace the data file you are restoring with a copy of the data file from the most current backup.

6.   If you are recovering a tablespace, replace all the existing data files with the data files from the most current backup.

7.   If you are recovering the entire database, then replace all the existing data files with the data files from the most current backup.

8.   Ensure that all archived redo logs are available in the correct archive log directory location. You can find the location where the archived redo logs need to be through this query:
   `SELECT name, value FROM v$parameter WHERE name IN`
   `('log_archive_dest','log_archive_dest_1',`
   `'db_recovery_file_dest');`

Perform the Recovery

9.   If you are recovering a data file, use the **recover datafile** command from the SQL prompt:
   `SQL> RECOVER DATAFILE datafile_name`
   Now, bring the data file online:
   `SQL>ALTER DATABASE DATAFILE 'datafile_name' ONLINE;`

10.   If you are recovering a tablespace, use the **recover tablespace** command from the SQL prompt:
   `SQL>RECOVER TABLESPACE tablespace_name;`
   And bring the tablespace online:
   `SQL>ALTER TABLESPACE tablespace_name ONLINE;`

Step	What to Do

11. If you are recovering the entire database, mount the database and recover it using the **recover database** command:
```
SQL>STARTUP MOUNT
SQL>RECOVER DATABASE;
SQL>ALTER DATABASE OPEN;
```

12. You have completed your database recovery.

Recovering from an RMAN Hot Backup

If you wish to recover from a hot backup taken with RMAN, follow these instructions:

Step	What to Do

1. Determine if you need to restore a data file, a tablespace, or the entire database.

2. Start RMAN:
```
rman target=/
```

Prepare for the Recovery

3. If you need to restore a data file, take the data file offline:
```
RMAN>SQL 'ALTER DATAFILE 'DATAFILE_NAME' OFFLINE';
```

4. If you need to restore a tablespace, take the tablespace offline:
```
RMAN>SQL 'ALTER TABLESPACE 'TABLESPACE_NAME' OFFLINE';
```

5. If you are restoring the database, and the database is still up, then you need to shut down the database and then mount it:
```
RMAN>SHUTDOWN ABORT
RMAN>STARTUP MOUNT
```

Perform the Restore

6. If you are recovering a data file, use the **restore datafile** command to retrieve the data file from the most recent backup:
```
RMAN>RESTORE DATAFILE 'datafile_name';
```

7. If you are restoring a tablespace, then use the **restore tablespace** command to retrieve the data files associated with the tablespace from the most recent backup:
```
RMAN>RESTORE TABLESPACE 'tablespace_name';
```

8. If you are restoring the database, use the **restore database** command to retrieve the data files associated with the tablespace from the most recent backup:
```
RMAN>RESTORE DATABASE;
```

Step	What to Do
	Recover the Data File, Tablespace, or Database

9. If you are recovering a data file, use the **recover datafile** command to perform recovery:
   RMAN>RECOVER DATAFILE '*datafile_name*';
   And put the data file online:
   RMAN>SQL 'ALTER DATAFILE 'datafile_name' ONLINE';

10. If you are recovering a tablespace, use the **recover tablespace** command to perform recovery:
    RMAN>RECOVER TABLESPACE '*tablespace_name*';
    And bring the tablespace online:
    RMAN>SQL 'ALTER TABLESPACE 'tablespace_name' ONLINE';

11. If you are recovering the entire database, use the **recover database** command:
    RMAN>RECOVER DATABASE;
    And open the database:
    RMAN>ALTER DATABASE OPEN;

Incomplete Database Recovery

Oracle also supports incomplete database recovery. This allows you to recover the database to any time after the time that any backup was taken, as long as the archived redo logs are available to support that recovery. To perform incomplete database recovery, you must recover the entire database to the same point in time; thus, you will have to restore all database data files by following the instructions provided earlier in this section. Once you have restored the database data files, use the **recover database until** clause if you are recovering the database manually. You can restore to a time, restore to a log sequence number, or indicate that you will manually cancel the recovery. All these options are shown in these examples:

```
SQL>RESTORE DATABASE UNTIL TIME '08-28-2004 04:00:00';
SQL>RESTORE DATABASE UNTIL CHANGE 4403023303;
SQL>RESTORE DATABASE UNTIL CANCEL;
```

Once you restore the database, you must open it using the **resetlogs** command.

If you are using RMAN, you use the **recover database** command using the **until time** or **until scn** clause, and then open the database with the **alter database open** command, as shown in this example:

```
RMAN> RECOVER DATABASE UNTIL TIME '07-30-2004 05:00:00';
RMAN> SQL 'ALTER DATABASE OPEN RESETLOGS';
```

Finally, if you are using a backup control file during your recovery (manual or RMAN), you need to use the **using backup controlfile** syntax when opening the database, as shown in this example:

```
ALTER DATABASE OPEN USING BACKUP CONTROLFILE;
```

Database Control File Recovery

Recovery of the control file may be required in certain cases. It might be part of a complete or partial database recovery, or it might be required due to the inadvertent loss or corruption of the control file. Recovery of the control file can be done manually or via RMAN. Let's look at each of these options.

Manual Control File Recovery

Manual recovery of a control file can come in two forms: use a pre-generated backup control file, or use the **create controlfile** command to create a control file. Generally, using a pre-generated backup control file is the preferred method of control file recovery. The next two sections highlight the methods used to perform these recoveries.

Recovering with a Backup Control File   Follow these steps to recover your database with a backup control file:

Step	What to Do
1.	If the database is still operating, shut it down.
2.	Note the name and location of each control file as defined in the database parameter or SPFILE file.
3.	Copy the backup control file to the locations discovered in Step 1. During this copy, rename the control file to the name of the control file found in Step 1.
4.	Mount the database: `SQL>STARTUP MOUNT`
5.	Recover the database using the backup control file: `SQL>RECOVER DATABASE USING BACKUP CONTROLFILE;`
6.	Open the database: `SQL>ALTER DATABASE OPEN;`

Recovering with the create controlfile Command   If you are recovering with a **create controlfile** command (which was likely generated as a result of the **alter database backup controlfile to test** command), follow these steps:

Step	What to Do
1.	Modify the script file you are going to use to issue the **create controlfile** command so that it is correct. Often, if you are using the trace file from the **alter database** command, you need to strip out the header portion, and determine if you need to recover using the **resetlogs** or **noresetlogs** command. Typically, if the online redo logs are available, then you can recover using the **noresetlogs** command.
2.	If the database is running, shut it down: `SQL>SHUTDOWN ABORT`

Step	What to Do
3.	Mount the database: `SQL>STARTUP NOMOUNT`
4.	Recover and open the database by running the script with the **create controlfile** statement. Typically, this script contains the **create controlfile** statement, the required recover database statement, and the **alter database open** statement.

Recovering the Control File with RMAN

If you are recovering your control file with RMAN you have a few options. The first is to recover the control file from an autobackup (Oracle9*i* and later). The second is if you are using a recovery catalog. The last option, which is to recover a control file from a backup set without a recovery catalog can be very complex. I recommend you look in *Oracle9i RMAN Backup & Recovery* for details on this procedure. Let's look at the first two options in more detail.

Recovering the Control File from an RMAN Autobackup   If you wish to recover from a hot backup taken with RMAN, follow these instructions:

Step	What to Do
1.	Start RMAN: `rman target=/`

2.	If the database is still running, shut it down and then mount it:
	`RMAN>SHUTDOWN ABORT`
	`RMAN>STARTUP MOUNT`

3.	Setup RMAN and then issue the **restore controlfile from autobackup** command:
	`RMAN> SET UNTIL TIME '23-JUN-2001 00:00:00';`
	`RMAN> SET CONTROLFILE AUTOBACKUP FORMAT FOR`
	`DEVICE TYPE disk TO 'c:\oracle\controlfiles';`
	`RMAN> ALLOCATE CHANNEL CHANNEL_1 DEVICE TYPE disk;`
	`RMAN> RESTORE CONTROLFILE FROM AUTOBACKUP;`

4.	Now, restart the database: `RMAN> SQL 'ALTER DATABASE OPEN RESETLOGS';`

Recovering the Control File via RMAN When Connected to a Recovery Catalog   If you wish to recover from a hot backup taken with RMAN and you are using a recovery catalog, follow these instructions:

Step	What to Do
1.	Start RMAN: `rman target=/ catalog=rman/rman@rcat`

2.	If the database is still running, shut it down and then mount it:
	`RMAN>SHUTDOWN ABORT`
	`RMAN>STARTUP MOUNT`

3.	Set up RMAN and then issue the **restore controlfile from autobackup** command:
	`RMAN> SET UNTIL TIME '23-JUN-2001 00:00:00';`
	`RMAN> ALLOCATE CHANNEL CHANNEL_1 DEVICE TYPE disk;`
	`RMAN> RESTORE CONTROLFILE;`

4.	Now, restart the database: `RMAN> SQL 'ALTER DATABASE OPEN RESETLOGS';`

CHAPTER
12

The Optimizer

he Oracle optimizer attempts to determine the best way to execute every query submitted to the system. The goal is to have the query execute in the fastest time possible. The optimizer needs the best information possible, in the form of statistics, to make good decisions about how to satisfy the query. While the optimizer has come a long way in making very good decisions, it occasionally needs to be nudged in one direction or another.

Optimizer Modes

Before a query can be satisfied, the Oracle database needs to determine how it will satisfy that request. Many times, there are multiple methods, or access paths, to return a result set. For example, if an index exists, using it could help return the data faster as opposed to reading every row in the table. If tables need to be joined to satisfy the query, the optimizer must choose from multiple join methods that are available.

As the Oracle database has grown through many versions, the manner in which the optimizer makes decisions has changed. The optimizer has gone from using a set of predefined rules to using statistics on the data to make informed decisions. In any case, the end goal is to return the query's results as soon as possible.

Rule Based Optimizer (RBO)

In Oracle's early days, the optimizer came with a predetermined set of rules. One of those rules stated that using an index was more preferable to reading every row in the table, called a full table scan (FTS). As new versions were introduced, more rules were added. The RBO is deprecated in Oracle 10*g*. It is still available, but the Cost Based Optimizer should be used instead. In versions prior to 10*g*, you can force the optimizer to use RBO by setting the **optimizer_mode** initialization parameter to **rule**. The following shows how to change your session to RBO mode:

```
ALTER SESSION SET optimizer_mode=RULE;
```

This command can be used to override the system-wide settings for the OPTIMIZER_MODE initialization parameter, just for your specific session.

Cost Based Optimizer (CBO)

In RBO, one of the rules stated that if an index is available, you must use it. This rule did not take into account the data itself. For instance, suppose I have an index on a column, and all 100,000 rows of that table contain the exact same value in that column. Reading blocks of an index, and then reading every row in the table, would require more work than just reading every row in the table. The problem with RBO is that it does not take data distribution into account. For this reason, CBO was introduced. CBO uses statistics on the data to help make better informed decisions than a canned set of rules could make. Prior to Oracle 10*g*, you could set the optimizer to run in RBO or CBO. To use CBO, you would set the **optimizer_mode** parameter to **choose**, and generate statistics on your tables and indexes. The following is an example on how to change your session's settings to use CBO mode instead of the systemwide settings:

```
ALTER SESSION SET optimizer_mode=CHOOSE;
```

If set to **choose**, the optimizer uses CBO if statistics are present on any table involved in the SQL statement. If no statistics are available, RBO is used instead.

Starting with Oracle 10g, the **optimizer_mode** settings of **rule** and **choose** are obsolete. In Oracle 10g, the only valid values of the **optimizer_mode** parameter are **first_rows_*n***, **first_rows**, and **all_rows**. The following examples show how to modify the **optimizer_mode** systemwide setting for the session:

```
ALTER SESSION SET optimizer_mode=ALL_ROWS;
ALTER SESSION SET optimizer_mode=FIRST_ROWS;
ALTER SESSION SET optimizer_mode=FIRST_ROWS_100;
```

SQL Tuning

The goal of SQL tuning is to have a query return results in an acceptable amount of time. In most cases, the CBO does a good job of determining an access path to the data that returns the results quickly. In other cases, the CBO needs some help. The CBO has become better at making decisions with each new version. When the CBO has not made a good decision, there are three goals to strive for, as described in the following sections.

Reduce the Work

In most cases where a SQL statement needs to be tuned, the CBO has chosen an access path that requires a lot of work. If the CBO can choose another path, the amount of resources required to satisfy the query can be significantly reduced, thus making the query return results faster. The three basic ways to help the CBO make better decisions are to generate better statistics, employ stored outlines, or use hints.

Balance the Work

Some queries operate on a very large amount of data, so you can expect that the results will take a long time to complete. In these cases, the query does not have to be run right at that moment. If possible, long-running queries should be scheduled as batch jobs to be run during low-volume usage of the database. You can use Oracle's Database Resource Manager to ensure that short transactions are given priority during peak usage times and long-running queries are given preference during low usage times.

Fine-Tune the Work

Each new release of Oracle brings new features that help long-running queries execute faster. These new features may need to be leveraged to improve certain SQL statement processing times. As data volumes increase, it may become impossible to tune the query adequately in one operation. Performing the query with parallel processing can break down a large job into multiple small jobs. Partitioning a table can eliminate most rows that will not participate in the query through partition pruning. Materialized views can pre-aggregate or pre-join tables for improved performance.

Identifying Poor SQL

So how do you determine which SQL statements need your attention? There are many tools at your disposal. The goal is to identify those SQL statements that take the most time to complete, use the most resources to return results, or cause the user to experience the most discomfort. This section will discuss views and other tools that you can use to identify poor SQL statements.

V$SQL View

The first view to look at is the V$SQL view. This view shows all the SQL statements in the shared pool along with statistics on their operation. This view is a good way to look at all SQL statements, systemwide. The following query shows the five queries that have been executed the most often:

```
SELECT sql_text,executions
FROM (SELECT sql_text,executions,
      RANK() OVER (ORDER BY executions DESC) exec_rank
      FROM v$sql )
WHERE exec_rank <= 5;
```

If a query executes too often, the application may be issuing the query too often. Decreasing the number of times a query executes can save system resources.

Another problem to look for is SQL statements that require a large number of costly disk reads to complete. The following query shows the top five SQL statements that require the most disk reads to complete:

```
SELECT sql_text,disk_reads
FROM (SELECT sql_text,disk_reads,
      DENSE_RANK() OVER
          (ORDER BY disk_reads DESC) disk_reads_rank
      FROM v$sql )
WHERE disk_reads_rank <=5;
```

Tuning statements that require a large number of disk reads can lead to faster query executions and lessen demand for system resources. Similarly, a query that consumes a high number of buffer gets (logical reads) can consume a large amount of resources. The following query shows the top five SQL statements that require the most logical reads:

```
SELECT sql_text,buffer_gets
FROM (SELECT sql_text,buffer_gets,
      DENSE_RANK() OVER
          (ORDER BY buffer_gets DESC) buffer_gets_rank
      FROM v$sql )
WHERE buffer_gets_rank <=5;
```

SQL Trace

While the V$SQL view shows those SQL statements that are consuming the most resources systemwide, it is often desirable to look at SQL statements particular to a session. The most common way to find these SQL statements is by using Oracle's SQL Trace facility. If you want to start a trace in your current session, issue the following command:

```
ALTER SESSION SET sql_trace=TRUE;
```

If you want to start a trace in another user's session, you first need to query V$SESSION to identify that session's SID and SERIAL#. To start a trace in another session, issue the following command:

```
EXEC SYS.dbms_session.set_sql_trace_in_session(sid,serial#,TRUE);
```

Substitute appropriate values for *sid* and *serial#*. To stop the trace at any time, execute one of the preceding statements with FALSE instead of TRUE.

When a trace is started in a session, a trace file will be generated. That trace file can be found in the directory specified by the **user_dump_dest** initialization parameter. In this directory, it can be difficult to identify the trace file for your specific session. The **tracefile_identifier** initialization parameter can be used to help you identify your trace file. Before starting a trace in your session, issue a command similar to the following:

```
ALTER SESSION SET tracefile_identifier='scotts_trace';
```

When looking in the **user_dump_dest** directory, the trace file will have the identifier you specified above in the file name. The raw trace files can be difficult to read. Oracle includes a utility called **tkprof**, which formats this trace file into readable output. The following is an example of using tkprof to convert the raw trace file to a format that is more readable:

```
tkprof ora76492.trc trace_output.txt
```

The resulting text file contains all SQL statements that were executed while the trace was running. It also includes statistics on the performance of those SQL statements.

Statspack

Statspack is a utility that you use to monitor system performance between two time intervals. If Statspack has been set up in your database, you can generate a Statspack report with the ORACLE_HOME/rdbms/admin/spreport script. The Statspack report will contain a couple of listings of poorly performing SQL statements similar to the queries against the V$SQL view, described earlier in the chapter.

Automatic Database Diagnostic Monitor

The Automatic Database Diagnostic Monitor (ADDM) utility is a new utility for Oracle 10g. The ADDM makes recommendations for correcting performance problems. These recommendations can be viewed in the Oracle Enterprise Manager or in the DBA_ADVISOR_RECOMMENDATIONS view. ADDM is turned on when the **statistics_level** parameter is set to TYPICAL or ALL. ADDM also includes a new report that is similar to the Statspack report. Like the Statspack report, ADDM can report those SQL statements that consume large amounts of resources. ADDM also reports possible solutions.

Tuning Advisors

Oracle 10*g* includes many new advisors to help with performance tuning. Some of these advisors help in tuning different memory structures like the buffer cache or shared pool. Two new advisors help with tuning SQL statements. The SQL Tuning Advisor will make recommendations on using specific SQL profiles, gathering optimizer statistics, or rewriting a query to make it perform better. The SQL Access Advisor will suggest new indexes or materialized views to help SQL statements perform better. These advisors can be run against the most resource-intensive SQL statements in the shared pool, or against supplied queries.

Optimizer Statistics

The CBO needs good statistics to make the best decisions it can on the most appropriate access path. Without any statistics, the CBO must make guesses regarding which access paths are the best. In many cases, absence of statistics leads the CBO to poor choices. It is imperative that the CBO has a good set of statistics to work with. The statistics that are gathered include statistics on tables (number of rows, number of blocks, average row length), statistics on columns (number of distinct values, number of NULLs, data distribution or histogram), statistics on indexes (number of blocks, index height, clustering factor), and statistics on system performance. There are two methods used to collect statistics, the **analyze** command and the **dbms_stats** supplied package. These two methods are discussed in the following sections.

analyze Command

The original method used to calculate statistics was to use the **analyze** command. The **analyze** command could be used to calculate statistics on table, indexes, or clusters. The **analyze** command should be used to calculate statistics only if you are running Oracle8*i* or earlier. If you are running Oracle9*i* or Oracle Database 10*g*, consider using the **dbms_stats** supplied package instead. The **dbms_stats** package has more features and fully supports the CBO.

For Oracle8*i* or earlier, you use the **analyze** command to calculate statistics. You have two choices on how much data to analyze. You can calculate statistics on all data in a table. However, if the table is large, it can take a very long time to calculate statistics on all rows of data. The second choice is to estimate the statistics based on a sampling of rows. You must own the object being analyzed or have the **analyze any** system privilege. To compute statistics on all rows of data in a table, use a command similar to the following:

```
ANALYZE TABLE emp COMPUTE STATISTICS;
```

To estimate statistics for 20 percent of the rows in the table, the command would be as follows:

```
ANALYZE TABLE emp ESTIMATE STATISTICS SAMPLE 20 PERCENT;
```

To estimate statistics using 10,000 rows of data in the table, the command would be as follows:

```
ANALYZE TABLE emp ESTIMATE STATISTICS SAMPLE 10000 ROWS;
```

If the **sample** clause is not specified when estimating statistics, Oracle samples 1064 rows of data. The following table shows additional clauses for the **analyze** command:

Clause	Meaning
for table	Restricts statistics collection to the table only.
for columns	Restricts statistics collection to the columns only.
for all columns	Collects column statistics for all columns.
for all indexed columns	Collects column statistics for those columns that have indexes.
for all indexes	Restricts statistics collection to indexes of a table.
size	Specifies the maximum number of buckets in a histogram. The default value is 75. The minimum value is 1 and the maximum value is 254.

dbms_stats Package

The supplied **dbms_stats** package is the preferred method to calculate statistics for the CBO. In Oracle 10*g*, statistics can still be computed with the **analyze** command. In future versions, the **dbms_stats** package will be the only way to calculate statistics. The **dbms_stats** package also has advantages over the **analyze** command, as the following table illustrates.

Advantage	Description
Parallelization	Can use parallel processing to calculate statistics much quicker.
Transfer statistics	Can transfer statistics from the data dictionary to a statistics table, and back again. Once in a table, statistics can be moved with Oracle's **exp/imp** utilities.
Manually set statistics	Can manually define statistics instead of calculating based on the data.
Gather stale statistics	Can save time by calculating statistics on new objects, or those objects that have changed significantly. If the object has not changed much, the current statistics should be fine.
External tables	Can calculate statistics on external tables.
System statistics	Can calculate statistics on system performance.

The **dbms_stats** package can be used to calculate statistics or remove statistics. Only those statistics in the data dictionary are used by the CBO. The **dbms_stats** package does let you store statistics in other tables so that you can maintain and experiment with multiple sets of statistics. The **dbms_stats** package includes export and import utilities for transport to another system. The sections that follow highlight many of the procedures in the **dbms_stats** package.

create_stat_table Procedure

The **create_stat_table** procedure is used to create a table that is capable of holding statistics. Statistics in these tables are not used by the CBO. But you can store multiple sets of statistics with these tables and then switch the statistics in the data dictionary to ones that you have stored. You can even export these tables to other systems. The following is an example of creating a table to hold statistics:

```
EXEC DBMS_STATS.CREATE_STAT_TABLE('scott','scotts_stats','user_data');
```

This example creates a table called SCOTT_STATS owned by the user SCOTT. The table will be placed in the USER_DATA tablespace. The tablespace parameter is optional.

delete_column_stats Procedure

The **delete_column_stats** procedure is used to remove column-related statistics. The statistics may be in the data dictionary or in a user table. The following is an example of deleting statistics on a column:

```
EXEC DBMS_STATS.DELETE_COLUMN_STATS('scott','emp','empno');
```

This example removes the statistics on the EMPNO column of the SCOTT.EMP table.

delete_dictionary_stats Procedure

Oracle9*i*R2 was the first version to fully support statistics on data dictionary objects. These objects are owned by SYS, SYSTEM, and RDBMS component schemas. The **delete_dictionary_stats** procedure removes statistics for data dictionary objects. To remove data dictionary statistics, you must have the **sysdba** privilege or the **analyze any dictionary** and **analyze any** system privileges. The following examples show how to delete statistics on data dictionary objects:

```
EXEC DBMS_STATS.DELETE_DICTIONARY_STATS();
EXEC DBMS_STATS.DELETE_DICTIONARY_STATS(statown=>'scott', -
stattab=>'scotts_stats');
```

The first example removes statistics from the data dictionary on data dictionary tables. The second example removes statistics on data dictionary tables that are stored in the SCOTT.SCOTTS_STATS table.

delete_fixed_object_stats Procedure

The **delete_fixed_object_stats** procedure is used to remove statistics of all fixed tables. The statistics can be in the data dictionary or in a user table. The following examples show how to remove fixed table statistics:

```
EXEC DBMS_STATS.DELETE_FIXED_OBJECTS_STATS;
EXEC DBMS_STATS.DELETE_FIXED_OBJECTS_STATS(ownname=>'scott', -
    stattab=>'scotts_stats');
```

The first example removes statistics on fixed tables from the data dictionary. The second example removes those statistics from the SCOTT.SCOTTS_STATS statistics table.

delete_index_stats Procedure

The **delete_index_stats** procedure is used to remove statistics on an index. The statistics can be in the data dictionary or in a user table. The following examples show how to remove statistics on an index:

```
EXEC DBMS_STATS.DELETE_INDEX_STATS('scott','emp_pk');
EXEC DBMS_STATS.DELETE_INDEX_STATS(ownname=>'scott', -
    indname=>'emp_pk',stattab=>'scotts_stats');
```

The first example removes the statistics on the SCOTT.EMP_PK index from the data dictionary. The second example removes the statistics on the same index, but from the SCOTTS_STATS statistics table instead. Since the table's owner was not specified, it is assumed that the SCOTTS_STATS table is owned by SCOTT.

delete_schema_stats Procedure

The **delete_schema_stats** procedure is used to remove statistics on all objects in the given schema. The statistics can be in the data dictionary or in a user table. The following example shows how to remove all statistics on all objects owned by SCOTT from the data dictionary:

```
EXEC DBMS_STATS.DELETE_SCHEMA_STATS('scott');
```

delete_table_stats Procedure

The **delete_table_stats** procedure is used to remove statistics on a table. The statistics can be in the data dictionary or in a user table. The following examples show how to remove statistics on tables:

```
EXEC DBMS_STATS.DELETE_TABLE_STATS('scott','emp');
EXEC DBMS_STATS.DELETE_TABLE_STATS(ownname=>'scott', -
    tabname=>'emp', cascade_columns=>TRUE, cascade_indexes=>FALSE);
```

Both examples remove statistics on the SCOTT.EMP table from the data dictionary. The second example also removes statistics on the table's columns (with the **cascade_columns** parameter) while leaving the statistics on the table's indexes (with the **cascade_indexes** parameter).

drop_stat_table Procedure

The **drop_stat_table** procedure is used to remove a statistics table. This table was created with the **create_stat_procedure** procedure. You must own the table or have the **drop any table** system privilege. The following is an example of dropping a statistics table:

```
EXEC DBMS_STATS.DROP_STAT_TABLE('scott','scotts_stats');
```

export_column_stats Procedure

The **export_column_stats** procedure retrieves the statistics for a specific column and places them in a user's statistics table. This table was created with the **create_stat_table** procedure. This procedure does not create a dump file with the statistics in it. Once the statistics are exported to the statistics table, the Oracle **exp** utility can be used to create a dump file. The following is an example of copying a column's statistics to a statistics table:

```
EXEC DBMS_STATS.EXPORT_COLUMN_STATS(ownname=>'scott', -
     tabname=>'emp', colname=>'empno', stattab=>'scotts_stats');
```

This example copies the statistics of the EMPNO column of the SCOTT.EMP table to the SCOTT.SCOTTS_STATS statistics table.

export_fixed_object_stats Procedure

The **export_fixed_object_stats** procedure retrieves the statistics for all fixed tables and places them in a user's statistics table. This table was created with the **create_stat_table** procedure. This procedure does not create a dump file with the statistics in it. Once the statistics are exported to the statistics table, the Oracle **exp** utility can be used to create a dump file. The following is an example of copying fixed table statistics to a statistics table:

```
EXEC DBMS_STATS.EXPORT_FIXED_OBJECTS_STATS(ownname=>'scott', -
     stattab=>'scotts_stats');
```

Since the owner of the statistics table was not specified, the current schema is used.

export_index_stats Procedure

The **export_index_stats** procedure will retrieve the statistics for a specific index and place them in a user's statistics table. This table was created with the **create_stat_table** procedure. This procedure does not create a dump file with the statistics in it. Once the statistics are exported to the statistics table, the Oracle **exp** utility can be used to create a dump file. The following is an example of copying an index's statistics to a statistics table:

```
EXEC DBMS_STATS.EXPORT_INDEX_STATS(ownname=>'scott', -
     indname=>'emp_pk', stattab=>'scotts_stats');
```

This example copies the statistics of the EMP_PK index to the SCOTT.SCOTTS_STATS statistics table.

export_schema_stats Procedure

The **export_schema_stats** procedure retrieves the statistics for all objects in a schema and places them in a user's statistics table. This table was created with the **create_stat_table** procedure. This procedure does not create a dump file with the statistics in it. Once the statistics are exported to the statistics table, the Oracle **exp** utility can be used to create a dump file. The following example shows how to export all statistics for a schema into a statistics table:

```
EXEC DBMS_STATS.EXPORT_SCHEMA_STATS(ownname=>'hr', -
     statown=>'scott',stattab=>'scotts_stats');
```

This example copies all the statistics for the HR schema from the data dictionary into the SCOTT.SCOTTS_STATS statistics table. Normally, the SCOTT user would not be able to export another user's statistics. The SCOTT user would need the **analyze any** system privilege to be able to run the above command. However, another user with the **analyze any** system privilege could run this command provided they have the privileges required to insert data into the SCOTT.SCOTTS_ STATS table.

export_table_stats Procedure

The **export_table_stats** procedure retrieves the statistics for a specific table and places them in a user's statistics table. This table was created with the **create_stat_table** procedure. This procedure does not create a dump file with the statistics in it. Once the statistics are exported to the statistics table, the Oracle **exp** utility can be used to create a dump file. The following examples show how to copy table statistics from the data dictionary to a statistics table:

```
EXEC DBMS_STATS.EXPORT_TABLE_STATS(ownname=>'scott', -
     tabname=>'emp',statab=>'scotts_stats');
EXEC DBMS_STATS.EXPORT_TABLE_STATS(ownname=>'scott', -
     tabname=>'emp', stattab=>'scotts_stats', cascade=>FALSE);
```

Both examples copy the statistics of the SCOTT.EMP table to the SCOTTS_STATS table. The second example will not copy column and index statistics of the table. The default for **cascade** is TRUE.

gather_database_stats Procedure

The **gather_database_stats** procedure calculates statistics for all objects in the database. The statistics can be placed in the data dictionary or in a user's statistics table. In order to use this procedure, you will need the **analyze any** system privilege. The following example shows how to calculate statistics for all database objects:

```
EXEC DBMS_STATS.GATHER_DATABASE_STATS(estimate_percent=>NULL, -
method_opt=>'FOR ALL COLUMNS', degree=>4, cascade=>FALSE, -
gather_sys=>TRUE);
```

In this example, the statistics will be computed, not estimated. If **estimate_percent** is NULL, then compute is performed. If **estimate_percent** is non-NULL, then statistics are estimated using that percentage. The **method_opt** parameter specifies to calculate statistics on all columns as well. The **degree** of parallelization is 4. The **cascade** parameter defines whether statistics are also calculated on indexes. The **gather_sys** parameter defines whether statistics are also calculated on data dictionary objects.

gather_fixed_object_stats Procedure

The **gather_fixed_object_stats** procedure calculates statistics for all fixed objects (dynamic performance tables) in the database. The statistics can be placed in the data dictionary or in a user's statistics table. The following example shows how to calculate statistics for all database objects:

```
EXEC DBMS_STATS.GATHER_FIXED_OBJECTS_STATS;
EXEC DBMS_STATS.GATHER_FIXED_OBJECTS_STATS(statown=>'scott', -
     stattab=>'scotts_stats');
```

The first example calculates statistics on fixed objects and places them in the data dictionary. The second example places those statistics in the SCOTT.SCOTTS_STATS statistics table.

gather_index_stats Procedure

The **gather_index_stats** procedure calculates statistics for a specific index. The statistics can be placed in the data dictionary or in a user's statistics table. The following example shows how to use the **gather_index_stats** procedure:

```
EXEC DBMS_STATS.GATHER_INDEX_STATS(ownname=>'scott', -
     indname=>'emp_pk', estimate_percent=>20);
```

In this example, statistics are estimated using 20 percent of the rows on the SCOTT.EMP_PK index.

gather_schema_stats Procedure

The **gather_schema_stats** procedure calculates statistics for all objects in a given schema. The statistics can be placed in the data dictionary or in a user's statistics table. The following example shows how to use this procedure:

```
EXEC DBMS_STATS.GATHER_SCHEMA_STATS(ownname=>'scott', -
statown=>'scott',stattab=>'scotts_stats');
```

This example computes statistics on the SCOTT schema and stores them in a statistics table.

gather_table_stats Procedure

The **gather_table_stats** procedure calculates statistics for a specific table. The statistics can also be generated for the table's columns and indexes. The statistics can be placed in the data dictionary or in a user's statistics table. The following examples show how to use this procedure:

```
EXEC DBMS_STATS.GATHER_TABLE_STATS('scott','emp');
EXEC DBMS_STATS.GATHER_TABLE_STATS(ownname=>'scott', -
     tabname=>'emp',estimate_percent=>10, -
method_opt=>'FOR ALL INDEXED COLUMNS');
```

The first example calculates statistics on the SCOTT.EMP table and stores them in the data dictionary. The second example does the same, but estimates the statistics on 10 percent of the rows, and computes statistics on all columns that have indexes.

import_column_stats Procedure

The **import_column_stats** procedure retrieves the statistics for a specific column from a user's statistics table and places them in the data dictionary. This procedure does not import from a dump file. Instead, import the user table containing the statistics and then run this procedure. The following example shows how to use this procedure:

```
EXEC DBMS_STATS.IMPORT_COLUMN_STATS(ownname=>'scott', -
tabname=>'emp',colname=>'empno',stattab=>'scotts_stats');
```

This example retrieves the statistics on the EMPNO column of the SCOTT.EMP table from the SCOTTS_STATS statistics table and places them in the data dictionary.

import_dictionary_stats Procedure

The **import_dictionary_stats** procedure retrieves the statistics for data dictionary objects from a user's statistics table and places them in the data dictionary. This procedure does not import from a dump file. Instead, import the user table containing the statistics and then run this procedure. The following example shows how to use this procedure:

```
EXEC DBMS_STATS.IMPORT_DICTIONARY_STATS('scotts_stats');
```

This example copies data dictionary stats from the current user's SCOTTS_STATS statistic table into the data dictionary. You must have the **sysdba** or both the **analyze any** and **analyze any dictionary** system privileges to execute this procedure.

import_fixed_object_stats Procedure

The **import_fixed_object_stats** procedure retrieves the statistics for fixed table objects from a user's statistics table and places them in the data dictionary. This procedure does not import from a dump file. Instead, import the user table containing the statistics and then run this procedure. The following example shows how to use this procedure:

```
EXEC DBMS_STATS.IMPORT_FIXED_OBJECTS_STATS('scotts_stats');
```

This example copies data dictionary stats from the SCOTTS_STATS statistics table. Since the table owner was not specified, it is assumed to be in the current schema.

import_index_stats Procedure

The **import_index_stats** procedure retrieves the statistics for a specific index from a user's statistics table and places them in the data dictionary. This procedure does not import from a dump file. Instead, import the user table containing the statistics and then run this procedure. The following shows how to use this procedure:

```
EXEC DBMS_STATS.IMPORT_INDEX_STATS(ownname=>'scott', -
indname=>'emp_pk',stattab=>'scotts_stats');
```

import_schema_stats Procedure

The **import_schema_stats** procedure retrieves the statistics for all objects of a given schema from a user's statistics table and places them in the data dictionary. This procedure does not import from a dump file. Instead, import the user table containing the statistics and then run this procedure. The following example shows how to use this procedure:

```
EXEC DBMS_STATS.IMPORT_SCHEMA_STATS('scott','scotts_stats');
```

This example copies the statistics of all of SCOTT's objects from the SCOTTS_STATS statistics table to the data dictionary.

import_table_stats Procedure

The **import_table_stats** procedure retrieves the statistics for a specific table from a user's statistics table and places them in the data dictionary. This procedure does not import from a dump file.

Instead, import the user table containing the statistics and then run this procedure. The following example shows how to use this procedure:

```
EXEC DBMS_STATS.IMPORT_TABLE_STATS(ownname=>'scott', -
tabname=>'emp', stattab=>'scotts_stats',cascade=>FALSE);
```

This example copies the statistics of the SCOTT.EMP table from the SCOTTS_STATS statistics table to the data dictionary. By specifying FALSE for the **cascade** parameter, no column or index statistics are copied with this operation. The default is TRUE.

set_column_stats Procedure
The **set_column_stats** procedure can be used to explicitly define your own statistics on a particular column. These statistics can be placed in a statistics table or in the data dictionary. The following is an example of explicitly stating your own statistics for a column:

```
EXEC DBMS_STATS.SET_COLUMN_STATS(ownname=>'scott', -
        tabname=>'emp',colname=>'empno',distcnt=>12, nullcnt=>1,avgclen=>9);
```

This example explicitly sets statistics for the EMPNO column of the SCOTT.EMP table. The number of distinct values (**distcnt**) is 12. The number of null values (**nullcnt**) is 1. The average column length (**avgclen**) is 9 bytes.

set_index_stats Procedure
The **set_index_stats** procedure can be used to explicitly define your own statistics on a specific index. These statistics can be placed in a statistics table or in the data dictionary. The following is an example of explicitly stating your own statistics for an index:

```
EXEC DBMS_STATS.SET_INDEX_STATS(ownname=>'scott', -
        indname=>'emp_pk', numrows=>12, numlblks=>2, indlevel=>1);
```

This example explicitly sets statistics for the EMP_PK index. The number of row entries (**numrows**) in the index is 12. The number of leaf blocks (**numlblks**) in the index is 2. The height of the index (**indlevel**) is 1.

set_table_stats Procedure
The **set_table_stats** procedure can be used to explicitly define your own statistics on a specific table. These statistics can be placed in a statistics table or in the data dictionary. The following is an example of explicitly stating your own statistics for a table:

```
EXEC DBMS_STATS.SET_TABLE_STATS(ownname=>'scott', -
        tabname=>'emp', numrows=>13, numblks=>1, avgrlen=>108);
```

This example explicitly sets statistics for the EMP table. The number of rows (**numrows**) in the table is 13. The number of blocks (**numblks**) in the table is 1. The average length of each row (**avgrlen**) is 108 bytes.

Automatic Statistics Gathering

In versions prior to Oracle 10*g*, the DBA would have to automate the task of calculating statistics on database objects. Oracle 10*g* introduces the capability to automate this task. Automated statistics gathering is enabled by default when an Oracle 10*g* database is created or a prior version is upgraded to Oracle 10*g*. The automated statistics gathering job is called **gather_stats_job** and can be seen in the DBA_SCHEDULER_JOBS view. The automated statistics gathering job needs to know when database objects have been modified. This requires the **statistics_level** initialization parameter to be set to either TYPICAL (the default value) or ALL.

In many cases, you may want to lock down certain statistics to prevent them from being changed by automatic statistics gathering. The **dbms_stats** package provides the **lock_schema_stats** and **lock_table_stats** stored procedures. When statistics are locked, they can be overwritten if the **force** parameter in most of the **dbms_stats** procedures is set to TRUE. To unlock statistics, use the **unlock_schema_stats** and **unlock_table_stats** procedures of the **dbms_stats** package. The following are examples of these procedures:

```
EXEC DBMS_STATS.LOCK_SCHEMA_STATS('scott');
EXEC DBMS_STATS.UNLOCK_SCHEMA_STATS('scott');
EXEC DBMS_STATS.LOCK_TABLE_STATS('scott','emp');
EXEC DBMS_STATS.UNLOCK_TABLE_STATS('scott','emp');
```

Execution Plans

When you submit a query to the database, it is up to the optimizer to determine the best plan to execute the query. Armed with statistics that have been generated on the database objects, the optimizer tries to execute the query with the lowest cost possible. The optimizer takes into account any hints (discussed later in this chapter) as suggestions on the most optimal path to take. There are many different ways to retrieve the data, called *access paths.* When multiple tables are involved, there are many different ways to join the tables together.

Access Paths

Access paths are how the database retrieves data from a table. Many times, there can be more than one access path to the same data. This section discusses the different access paths to the data.

Full Table Scans

Full table scans (FTSs) read all rows of data from the table. Every block below the table's high-water mark is read, even if the block does not contain any rows of data. As each block is read, any rows that will not participate in the query are filtered out. When an FTS is performed, Oracle reads **db_file_multiblock_read_count** blocks in one I/O operation. FTSs are beneficial when reading a large percentage of rows in the table, or if the table is small. If a small percentage of rows in the table are needed, an index scan may be preferable. If there is no index on the table, an FTS is the only option.

Index Scans

An index scan uses an index on columns of data to quickly find the row that matches those columns' values. The leaf blocks of the index contain the ROWID of the row of data. Once the

ROWID has been determined, a ROWID scan may be performed. If a small percentage of rows from the table needs to be returned, an index scan is preferable to a FTS. If a large percentage of rows needs to be returned, using an index can lead to excessive I/O.

Index Range Scans

If a range of data needs to be returned, and there is an index on the column, a more efficient method of using an index can be used to access the data. When an index range scan is employed, the index is searched for the first value in the range. The leaf nodes contain a pointer to the previous and the next leaf node in the tree. This means that the branch blocks do not need to be traversed, reducing costly I/O operations. The most typical means to cause an index range scan is to employ the **between** or **order by** operator in the query. Less than, greater than, less than or equal, and greater than or equal operators can also force an index range scan. Index Range Scans can proceed in an ascending or descending order.

ROWID Lookups

A ROWID uniquely identifies each row by denoting the exact data file, object, block, and row in the block to find the row of data. If the ROWID is known in advance, the ROWID lookup is the fastest way to access a row of data. Generally, the ROWID is not known in advance.

Index Skip Scans

Introduced in Oracle9*i*, index skip scans improve performance when using nonprefixed columns. Prior to Oracle9*i*, the **where** clause must have the leading columns in a composite index (an index on more than one column) in order to be used. The index skip scan access method means that you do not necessarily need to have all the leading columns of a composite index in order to use that index.

Fast Full Index Scans

If an index contains all of the data that needs to be returned, then the data block in the table never needs to be visited. A fast full index scan reads only blocks of the index and does not touch the data in the table. This speed of accessing the data is only possible because only the columns of the index appear in the **select** and **where** clauses.

Index Join

An index join is not a table join. Rather, multiple indexes are joined together and used in a similar fashion as a fast full index scan. Only those columns in the indexes can be used in the query; otherwise, the table needs to be accessed.

Joins

When multiple tables participate in the query, those tables need to be joined together in some fashion. You can tell if a join is required by the presence of more than one table in the **from** clause. There are four basic methods used to join tables together: the Cartesian join, the nested loops join, the sort merge join, and the hash join. A join operation joins only two tables together. If a third table is present in the **from** clause, the *results of the join* of the first two tables are joined to the third table. This process continues until all tables have been joined together to form one result set.

Cartesian Joins

To create a Cartesian join (sometimes called a Cartesian product), every row from one table is matched with every row in the other table. This requires an FTS on both tables. Many times, a Cartesian join is not intended. You can spot a Cartesian join by the absence of a join condition in the **where** clause. Occasionally, the optimizer may choose to perform a Cartesian join on two very small tables and then eliminate nonparticipating rows.

Nested Loop Join

A nested loop join is one of the oldest join methods around. This join method starts with one of the tables in the join as the driving table, or outer table. The other table in the join is the inner table. Every row in the outer table is read. For each row in the outer table, the inner table is searched to see if there is a match. The outer table is accessed with an FTS. The inner table can use any other access method. A nested loop join is preferred when the outer table is small, and the inner table can be quickly searched (ideally through an index) for matches.

Sort Merge Joins

The sort merge join first sorts the two tables into order. After they are sorted, the results are merged together to find matching rows of data. Typically, hash joins and nested loop joins are preferable to sort merge joins. However, the sort merge join works nicely if the data is already sorted or if a non-equi-join is required.

Hash Join

To process a hash join, the smaller of the two tables is run through a hash function. This hash function builds a table in which data can be found very quickly. The larger of the two tables is then run through the same hash function. If a row from the second table matches a row from the first table, it is found very quickly. The hash join works best when there is enough memory to hold the smaller table entirely in memory. In order for a hash join to be possible, an equi-join (searching for records in two tables that are equivalent) must be performed.

Outer Join

In the previous join methods, rows from a table are included in the result set only if there is a match in the other table, and vice versa. In an outer join, all rows of data from one table participate in the join, even if there is no match in the other table.

Optimizer Hints

The optimizer does not always make the best decisions. You may find that you know a better way to process the SQL statement. Optimizer hints let you give directives to the optimizer on a different, hopefully better, way to execute a query.

Specifying Hints

You specify hints by enclosing the hint within a comment in the query. There can be only one comment in the query, but this comment can contain multiple hints. The comment must follow the **select**, **update**, **merge**, **insert**, or **delete** keyword. The comment must contain the **+** sign at the start of the comment; otherwise, the optimizer will not know that a hint is contained within the comment. If the hint is not specified correctly, the hint will be ignored and no errors or warnings will be generated. A hint is specified as follows:

```
SELECT /*+ hint [text] [hint [text]] … */ ….
```

or as follows:

```
SELECT –+ hint [text] [hint [text]] …  ….
```

In the preceding syntax examples, the **update**, **merge**, **insert**, or **delete** keywords can also be used. If there are multiple hints, each hint must be separated by a space.

An example of a hint might be as follows:

```
SELECT empid,ename /*+ INDEX( e emp_pk) */
FROM emp e
WHERE empid IN (1001, 1002);
```

In this example, the INDEX hint is used to suggest a specific index to the optimizer. Normally, a table name is denoted to define which table's index to use. But in this example, the table was aliased; therefore, the hint must use the table's alias. If the table was aliased in the **from** clause, and the table name was used in the hint, the hint would be ignored.

Optimizer Mode Hints

The **optimizer_mode** parameter can be used to determine the optimizer method for the entire database or just for the session. To change the optimizer mode for just one query, use an optimizer hint. The following table shows the optimizer hints:

Optimizer Hint	Meaning
ALL_ROWS	Return all rows as fast as possible
FIRST_ROWS(n)	Return the first n rows as fast as possible, where n is 1, 10, 100, or 1000
RULE	Use RBO

The RULE optimizer hint is desupported in Oracle 10g.

Access Path Hints

Access path hints suggest certain access paths to the optimizer. The optimizer will only choose the access path if it is possible. If the suggested access path is not possible, the hint is ignored. The access path hints are listed and described in the following table:

Hint	Meaning	Example

FULL	Suggests an FTS	`SELECT ename /*+ FULL(e) */`
		`FROM emp e`
		`WHERE empno=1001;`

INDEX	Suggests a specific index to use	`SELECT ename /*+ INDEX(e) */` `FROM emp e WHERE empno=1001;`
NO_INDEX	Suggests not using an index	`SELECT * /*+ NO_INDEX(e) */` `FROM emp e WHERE empno=100;`

INDEX_ASC	Suggests using an index in ascending mode	`SELECT * /*+ INDEX_ASC(e) */`
		`FROM emp e`
		`WHERE empno BETWEEN 1 AND 10;`

INDEX_DESC	Suggests using an index in descending mode	`SELECT * /*+ INDEX_DESC(e) */`
		`FROM emp e`
		`WHERE empno BETWEEN 10 AND 1;`

INDEX_JOIN	Suggests using an index join access method	`SELECT * /*+ INDEX_JOIN */`
		`FROM emp`
		`WHERE empno=1001`
		`AND ename='JONES';`

INDEX_FFS	Suggests using an index full fast scan	`SELECT empno /*+ INDEX_FFS(e) */`
		`FROM emp e`
		`WHERE empno=1001;`

NO_INDEX_FFS	Suggests not using an index full fast scan	`SELECT * /*+ NO_INDEX_FFS */`
		`FROM emp`
		`WHERE empno=1001;`

INDEX_SS	Suggests using an index skip scan	`SELECT * /*+ INDEX_SS(e) */`
		`FROM emp e`
		`WHERE ename='Jones';`

INDEX_SS_ASC	Suggests using an index skip scan in ascending mode	`SELECT * /*+ INDEX_SS_ASC(e) */`
		`FROM emp e`
		`WHERE ename='Jones';`

INDEX_SS_DESC	Suggests using an index skip scan in descending mode	`SELECT * /*+ INDEX_SS_DESC(e) */`
		`FROM emp e`
		`WHERE ename='Jones';`

NO_INDEX_SS	Suggests not using an index skip scan	`SELECT * /*+ NO_INDEX_SS(e) */`
		`FROM emp e`
		`WHERE ename='Jones';`

Join Hints

The join hints suggest a specific join algorithm be used to process a join. The join hints are listed and described in the following table:

Hint	Meaning	Example
USE_NL	Suggests using a nested loop join method	SELECT ename, dname /*+ USE_NL(e d) */ FROM emp e, dept d WHERE e.deptno=d.deptno;
NO_USE_NL	Suggests not using a nested loop join method	SELECT ename, dname /*+ NO_USE_NL(e d) */ FROM emp e, dept d WHERE e.deptno=d.deptno;
USE_NL_WITH_INDEX	Suggests using a nested loop join method with an index	SELECT ename, dname /*+ USE_NL_WITH_INDEX(e d) */ FROM emp e, dept d WHERE e.deptno=d.deptno;
USE_MERGE	Suggests using a sort merge join method	SELECT ename, dname /*+ USE_MERGE(e d) */ FROM emp e, dept d WHERE e.deptno=d.deptno;
NO_USE_MERGE	Suggests not using a sort merge join method	SELECT ename, dname /*+ NO_USE_MERGE(e d) */ FROM emp e, dept d WHERE e.deptno=d.deptno;
USE_HASH	Suggests using a hash join method	SELECT ename, dname /*+ USE_HASH(e d) */ FROM emp e, dept d WHERE e.deptno=d.deptno;
NO_USE_HASH	Suggests not using a hash join method	SELECT ename, dname /*+ NO_USE_HASH(e d) */ FROM emp e, dept d WHERE e.deptno=d.deptno;

Parallel Hints

Certain operations can take advantage of being performed in parallel on multiple processors. The following hints suggest parallel operations to the optimizer:

Hint	Meaning	Example
PARALLEL(*n*)	Suggests performing the operation in parallel. The degree of parallelization, *n*, can be specified.	SELECT * /* PARALLEL(4) */ FROM emp ORDER BY empno;
NO_PARALLEL	Suggests not performing the query in parallel. This overrides the PARALLEL(*n*) specification for a table.	SELECT * /* NO_PARALLEL */ FROM emp ORDER BY empno;
PARALLEL_INDEX(*n*)	Suggests parallelizing the index range scan. The degree of parallelization, *n*, can be specified.	SELECT * /*+ PARALLEL_INDEX */ FROM emp WHERE empno BETWEEN 1001 AND 2002;
NO_PARALLEL_INDEX	Suggests not parallelizing the index range scan.	SELECT * /*+ NO_PARALLEL_INDEX */ FROM emp WHERE empno BETWEEN 1001 AND 2002;

Miscellaneous Hints

The hints that follow do not fall under any of the previous categories. These hints do not have any parameters.

Hint	Meaning	Example
APPEND	Enables Direct Path insert mode so that data is appended to the end of the table.	INSERT /*+ APPEND */ INTO emp SELECT * FROM my_emp;
NOAPPEND	Disables Direct Path insert mode.	INSERT /*+ NOAPPEND */ INTO emp SELECT * FROM my_emp;
CACHE	Blocks accessed with this query are placed on the most recently used end of the LRU list.	SELECT * /*+ CACHE(e) */ FROM emp e;
NOCACHE	Blocks accessed with this query are placed on the least recently used end of the LRU list.	SELECT * /*+ NOCACHE(e) */ FROM emp e;

Hint	Meaning	Example

PUSH_SUBQ	Causes subqueries to be evaluated at the earliest possible time.	`SELECT e.ename,d.dname`
		`/*+ PUSH_SUBQ */`
		`FROM emp e,`
		`(SELECT * FROM dept`
		`  WHERE deptno=10) d`
		`WHERE e.deptno=d.deptno;`

NO_PUSH_SUBQ	Causes subqueries to be evaluated at the last possible time.	`SELECT e.ename,d.dname`
		`/*+ NO_PUSH_SUBQ */`
		`FROM emp e,`
		`(SELECT * FROM dept`
		`  WHERE deptno=10) d`
		`WHERE e.deptno=d.deptno;`

DRIVING_SITE	Causes another database in a distributed query to be the driving site for the query.	`SELECT e.ename,d.deptno`
		`/*+ DRIVING_SITE(d) */`
		`FROM emp e,`
		`    dept@prod d`
		`WHERE e.deptno=d.deptno;`

explain plan Command

The **explain plan** command is used to show the optimizer's intended execution plan of a query. In addition to the **explain plan** command, you can get the execution plan of a query in V$SQL by joining the contents of that view to the V$SQL_PLAN view.

Running explain plan

Before you can run the **explain plan** command, you must have a table in which to store the results. This table is called PLAN_TABLE. If you are running Oracle 10*g*, then the plan table is created automatically for you as a global temporary table. Prior to Oracle 10*g*, the plan table was created by running the `ORACLE_HOME/rdbms/admin/utlxplan.sql` script.

Now that the plan table is set up, you can populate it with the **explain plan** command. The **explain plan** command should define a statement identifier for the SQL statement you want explained. It will also contain the SQL statement you want explained. The following is an example of the **explain plan** command:

```
EXPLAIN PLAN SET statement_id='emp_query_1'
FOR SELECT * FROM emp WHERE empno=1005;
```

The **set** clause defines the STATEMENT_ID for this plan. By defining the STATEMENT_ID, you can have multiple plans in the same plan table. The **for** clause defines the SQL statement you want explained.

Displaying explain plan Output

If you query the plan table directly, the data might not make much sense. Luckily, there are scripts available to display the **explain plan** results in readable format. These scripts are in the ORACLE_HOME/rdbms/admin directory:

- ■ **utlxpls.sql** Displays the plan results for queries executed serially
- ■ **utlxplp.sql** Displays plan results for queries executed with parallel processing

Additionally, the **dbms_xplan.display** stored procedure can be used to display the results.

Interpreting explain plan Output

For the uninitiated, the output generated from the preceding queries can be a little difficult to read. This section gives some hints on how to read **explain plan** output. The biggest hint is to start from the inside out (right to left), and read from top to bottom. The following output from the utlxpls.sql script helps explain this concept a little more (I have reformatted the output just a bit to make it more readable):

```
PLAN_TABLE_OUTPUT
-----------------------------------------------------------------
| Id  | Operation                   | Name  | Rows  | Bytes | Cost  |
-----------------------------------------------------------------
|   0 | SELECT STATEMENT            |       |     1 |    87 |     1 |
|   1 |   TABLE ACCESS BY INDEX ROWID| EMP  |     1 |    87 |     1 |
|   2 |     INDEX RANGE SCAN        | EMP_PK|    1 |       |     1 |
-----------------------------------------------------------------
```

In the OPERATION column, go down and to the right until you cannot go down and right any more. This leaves us with an INDEX RANGE SCAN. The NAME column tells us the EMP_PK index was used. Since we can't go down and right any more, go up one row and to the left. This tells us that the table was accessed by using an index on the EMP table. The EMP__PK index was first read and then the table was accessed. Finally, the **select** statement was processed to trim any unnecessary columns from the result set. Overall, one row of data was processed, which was 87 bytes.

Let's look at a more complex example:

```
PLAN_TABLE_OUTPUT
-----------------------------------------------------------------
| Id  | Operation               | Name  | Rows  | Bytes  | Cost  |
-----------------------------------------------------------------
|   0 | SELECT STATEMENT        |       |    82 |   4510 |     4 |
|   1 |   HASH JOIN             |       |    82 |   4510 |     4 |
|   2 |     TABLE ACCESS FULL   | EMP   |    82 |   2706 |     1 |
|   3 |     TABLE ACCESS FULL   | DEPT  |    82 |   1804 |     2 |
-----------------------------------------------------------------
```

In this plan, we first go down and to the right. Our first line is TABLE ACCESS FULL of the DEPT table. An FTS was performed on the DEPT table. We can go up and stay the same distance to the right to see that an FTS was performed on the EMP table. Since we cannot go to the right any more, we return to the next level to the left. This tells us that a hash join was performed. What tables did the hash join method operate on? On the two tables accessed previously. A hash join occurred on the EMP and DEPT tables.

We'll look at one more complex example:

```
PLAN_TABLE_OUTPUT
-----------------------------------------------------------------
| Id  | Operation               | Name      | Rows | Bytes | Cost  |
-----------------------------------------------------------------
|   0 | SELECT STATEMENT        |           |      |       |       |
|   1 |  SORT GROUP BY          |           |      |       |       |
|   2 |   MERGE JOIN            |           |      |       |       |
|   3 |    SORT JOIN            |           |      |       |       |
|   4 |     TABLE ACCESS FULL|RESULTS|      |       |       |
|   5 |    SORT JOIN            |           |      |       |       |
|   6 |     TABLE ACCESS FULL|WAIT_STATS|  |       |       |
```

Going down and to the right, we come to TABLE ACCESS FULL on the RESULTS table in line 4. This operation is then taken up one level where the results are sorted in line 3. Now that the RESULTS table has been accessed and sorted, we can still go down and to the right to line 6, where we perform an FTS on the WAIT_STATS table. The results of this table access are sorted on line 5. We now take the sorted results from line 3 and line 5 and go up and to the left to line 2, where a merge operation takes place. All of these steps show us the sort merge join operation. Next, we take the results of the joined table to line 1, where another sort operation is performed, this time due to a **group by** clause. Finally, the results are passed to the **select** operation.

Hopefully, the examples in this section have taken the mystery out of reading the output from **explain plan** commands. With practice, it doesn't take too long to understand the operations that the optimizer takes to satisfy the query. The access paths discussed earlier in this chapter become really important when reading **explain plan** output.

dbms_xplan Package

The **dbms_xplan** package is new in Oracle 10g. The main purpose of this package is to display the results of **explain plan**. It can even display the execution plan of a statement stored in the Automatic Workload Repository (AWR). The **dbms_xplan** package has three procedures, **display**, **display_cursor**, and **display_awr**, each of which is discussed in the sections that follow.

display Procedure

The **display** procedure is used to quickly display the results of the **explain plan** command. This procedure runs with the permissions of the calling user. The following is an example of this procedure:

```
EXPLAIN PLAN FOR SELECT * FROM emp;
SELECT * FROM table(DBMS_XPLAN.DISPLAY);
```

After the **explain plan** command is issued, the **dbms_xplan.display** procedure is called. The results of the **select** statement show the execution plan.

display_cursor Procedure

The **display_cursor** procedure displays the execution plan for the last executed statement in the session. This, in effect, bypasses the need for the explicit **explain plan** command. This procedure requires **select** privileges on the VSQL_PLAN, VSESSION, and V$SQL_PLAN_STATISTICS_ALL views. The privileges are granted automatically with the SELECT_CATALOG role. The follow is an example of following a SQL statement with the **display_cursor** procedure:

```
SELECT * FROM emp WHERE empno=1001;
SELECT * FROM table(DBMS_XPLAN.DISPLAY_CURSOR);
```

This procedure can also be used to display the execution plan of any cursor in the SQL area.

display_awr Procedure

The **display_awr** procedure displays the execution plan of any SQL statement in the AWR. This procedure requires **select** privileges on the DBA_HIST_SQL_PLAN, DBA_HIST_SQLTEXT, and V$DATABASE views. The privileges are granted automatically with the SELECT_CATALOG role. The following is an example of this procedure:

```
SELECT * FROM table(DBMS_XPLAN.DISPLAY_AWR('peawch7pnlkkp',NULL,NULL,'ALL'));
```

This example displays the execution plan for the SQL statement identified by **sql_id** 'peawch7pnlkkp' in the AWR. The second optional parameter is **plan_hash_value**. The third optional parameter is **database_id**. The fourth optional parameter specifies the level of detail. The allowed values are BASIC, TYPICAL, SERIAL, and ALL. The BASIC level displays the minimum amount of information, i.e. the operation identifier, the object name, and the operation option. The TYPICAL level displays the BASIC level information as well as partition and parallelism information, if applicable. The TYPICAL level is the default level. The SERIAL level displays the same information as the TYPICAL level without any parallel information, even if the plan executes in parallel. The ALL level displays every bit of detail possible.

Plan Stability

During the course of a database's life, the database undergoes a great amount of change. Certain initialization parameters that influence the CBO change. The statistics generated on database objects change. The database may be upgraded to a new version. These changes can cause the CBO to make different decisions in the future than it does today. Sometimes, those changes hamper application performance.

Plan stability prevents the CBO from responding to these changes, which could be of vital importance to the application users. Plan stability preserves execution plans for queries in something called a *stored outline,* which is a set of optimizer hints associated with a particular query. When the database is issued this query, the optimizer automatically uses these hints when processing the query. The performance of third-party applications, for which you cannot modify the application code, can be tuned using these stored outlines. If you are an application developer for a third-party application, you can ship stored outlines with your application so that your customer's application will perform as expected. Oracle stores these outlines in the OL$, OL$HINTS, and OL$NODES tables, accessible through the USER_OUTLINES and USER_ OUTLINE_HINTS data dictionary views.

Creating Outlines

Before you can create a stored outline, you must have the **create any outline** system privilege. Creating an outline is very easy. You can use the **create outline** command or set the **create_ stored_outlines** session parameter. The following is an example of the **create outline** command, which creates the outline for the given query:

```
CREATE OR REPLACE OUTLINE emp_outline
FOR CATEGORY appl_X_outlines
ON
SELECT empno, ename FROM emp WHERE empno IN (1001, 1002);
```

The same outline can be created as follows:

```
ALTER SESSION SET create_stored_outlines=appl_X_outlines;
SELECT empno, ename FROM emp WHERE empno IN (1001, 1002);
ALTER SESSION SET create_stored_outlines=FALSE;
```

Notice that the parameter was set to the category name. If you set the parameter to TRUE, the category is the DEFAULT category. By setting the **create_stored_outlines** parameter to FALSE, outlines were stopped from being stored.

So what hint was stored for the preceding query? The hint that was used depends on the execution plan for the query. If the query used an index on the EMPNO column, then the outline will generate a hint to use that index. If the query did an FTS, then the outline will generate a hint to perform an FTS. You may have to play with parameters or statistics to get the appropriate execution plan.

Using Outlines

Now that you have created and stored outlines for many queries, you can implement outlines with the **use_stored_outlines** initialization parameter. This parameter is both system and session modifiable. When you set this parameter, any outlines in the category you specify, or the DEFAULT category if you don't specify one, will be used. The following is an example of setting a session to use a specific set of stored outlines:

```
ALTER SESSION SET use_stored_outlines=appl_x_outlines;
```

To turn off the use of stored outlines, set the parameter to FALSE:

```
ALTER SESSION SET use_stored_outlines=FALSE;
```

When you enable stored outlines, the optimizer searches for your named category for any outlines for a given query. If the optimizer does not find any outlines for the query in that category, the optimizer looks in the DEFAULT category for an outline.

To tell if an outline is being used, query the V$SQL view. The OUTLINE_CATEGORY column of the V$SQL view for the specific SQL statement is non-NULL if an outline is used. The value in this column will be the outline's category.

Moving Outlines

Since outlines are stored in tables, they can be moved quite easily. The outline tables, OL$, OL$HINTS, and OL$NODES, are owned by the OUTLN user. If you wish to move all outlines from one database to another, you need to export the OL$ and OL$HINTS tables and import them in another database:

```
exp userid=outlln/outln file=outln.dmp tables=(ol$,ol$hints)
```

Now transport the dump file to the new database's server, drop those tables, and import them from the dump files. If you want to move outlines for only a specific category, you can still use the export method, as follows:

```
exp userid=outln/outln file=outln.dmp tables=(ol$,ol$hints)
         query="where category='APPL_X_CATEGORY'"
```

The resulting dump file contains outlines from the outline tables, but only for a specific category.

Managing Outlines

Now that you have created outlines, you may have to perform management tasks like renaming the outline, changing the category, or dropping the outline. Simple DDL commands can be used to manage the outlines. For instance, to change a category, use the **alter outline** command, as follows:

```
ALTER OUTLINE emp_outline CHANGE CATEGORY TO appl_ZZ_outln;
```

The **alter outline** command can also be used to rename the outline:

```
ALTER OUTLINE emp_outline RENAME TO hr_outline;
```

The outline can be dropped with the **drop outline** command.

```
DROP OUTLINE hr_outline;
```

CHAPTER
13

Miscellaneous Commands

his chapter covers miscellaneous Oracle database commands that didn't neatly fit into other chapter subject areas. In this chapter, you will find discussion of the **alter system** command, the **alter session** command, and the **create directory** and **drop directory** commands. This chapter also covers the **comment**, **lock table**, **purge**, **rename**, **set constraints**, **set transaction**, **create database link**, and **drop database link** commands.

The alter system Command

The **alter system** command is used to modify Oracle instance settings. This command is used to perform such actions as the following:

- Start the ARCH background process.

- Control archiving activities via the **archive_log** clause. This includes such activities as forcing archival of the online redo logs.

- Control redo log switches via the **switch logfile** command.

- Cause a checkpoint to occur via the **checkpoint** clause.

- Check data files via the **check_datafiles** clause.

- Enable or disable restricted session mode via the **restricted_session** clause.

- Quiesce the database with the **quiesce** clause.

- Control database activity with the **suspend** and **resume** commands.

- Shut down a dispatcher with the **shutdown_dispatcher** clause.

- Alter system settings with the **set** and **reset** commands along with the **alter_system_set** and **alter_system_reset** clauses.

- Flush the shared pool or the database buffer cache.

- Kill other database sessions.

- Register the system with the listener.

Security Requirements

You must have the **alter system** privilege to use the **alter system** command.

alter system Examples

This example uses the **alter system** command to force a log switch:

```
ALTER SYSTEM SWITCH LOGFILE;
```

You can also use the **alter system** command to start or stop the ARCH process, as shown in these examples:

```
ALTER SYSTEM ARCHIVE LOG START;
ALTER SYSTEM ARCHIVE LOG STOP;
```

Note that using the **alter system archive log stop** command does not take the database out of ARCHIVELOG mode; you must use the **alter database** command to do this. This means that the database will stop once it has filled up all the online redo logs unless you archive them.

The **archive log** clause of the **alter system** command also allows you to force Oracle to archive all unarchived redo logs with the **alter system** command, as shown in this example:

```
ALTER SYSTEM ARCHIVE LOG ALL;
```

You can also force archiving across a RAC cluster by using the **thread** parameter:

```
ALTER SYSTEM ARCHIVE LOG THREAD 1 ALL;
```

The **alter system archive log all to** command allows you to direct the ARCH process to archive filled online redo logs to a specific location, as shown in this example:

```
ALTER SYSTEM ARCHIVE LOG ALL TO 'C:\oracle\allarch';
```

You can use the **alter system checkpoint** command to force the database to perform a checkpoint. With this command, you can force a local or, if you are using RAC, a global checkpoint. Both options are shown in these examples:

```
ALTER SYSTEM CHECKPOINT;
ALTER SYSTEM CHECKPOINT GLOBAL;
```

You can also use the **alter system** command to disconnect sessions from the database. The **alter system kill session** command allows you to end a user session, resulting in a rollback of any uncommitted DML operations and a release of any locks that the session might have acquired. You must issue the **alter system kill session** command from the same instance that the session is operating on.

The **alter system kill session** command takes two parameters, the SID of the session to be killed and the associated SERIAL# of that session. These parameters are enclosed in single quotes, and separated by a comma. You can retrieve the SID and SERIAL# from the V$SESSION view. In the following example, we query V$SESSION to find the user connected to the SCOTT account. We then use the **alter system kill session** command to kill the user, who is assigned to SID 145.

```
SELECT sid, serial#, username FROM v$session
WHERE username='SCOTT';
      SID    SERIAL# USERNAME
----- ----- ---------------
      145        334 SCOTT

ALTER SYSTEM KILL SESSION '145,334';
```

The **alter system** command comes with a number of options that make the DBA's life a little easier. The **alter system** command enables you to restrict all users from logging into the database unless they have the **restricted session** system privilege. Use the **alter system enable restricted session** command to restrict access, and use the **alter system disable restricted session** command to allow users to once again use the system. Note that enabling restricted session mode impacts only new user logins; existing logins are not impacted. Also, the command has an impact only on the instance that it is executed on. Here are examples of using the **alter system** command to enable and disable restricted sessions:

```
ALTER SYSTEM ENABLE RESTRICTED SESSION;
ALTER SYSTEM DISABLE RESTRICTED SESSION;
```

Want even more power? Use the **alter system suspend** and **alter system resume** commands to stop all database activity. This is handy if you want to do some form of database backup that involves disk mirrors and breaking those disk mirrors (Oracle requires that you put tablespaces in hot backup mode before you suspend the database for a backup of any kind, however). Here are examples:

```
ALTER SYSTEM SUSPEND;
ALTER SYSTEM RESUME;
```

The **alter system quiesce restricted** and **alter system unquiesce** commands allow you to quiesce the database, so that you can perform maintenance activities without having to bring the database down, kill sessions, or put the database in restricted mode. This command is very handy if you have a high-activity database and you need to perform some action that requires acquisition of exclusive locks (for example, the removal of an index). Here are examples:

```
ALTER SYSTEM QUIESCE RESTRICTED;
ALTER SYSTEM UNQUIESCE;
```

You must have enabled the Database Resource Manager in order to use this functionality. Once you issue the **alter system quiesce restricted** command, Oracle prevents any new non-SYS or -SYSTEM transactions from starting (they will not generate errors, however). Oracle then waits for existing transactions to complete. Once these transactions are complete, Oracle quiesces the system, enabling you to perform the maintenance activities required. Issue the **alter system unquiesce** command to reverse the process.

The **alter system register** command causes the Oracle database to register itself with the listener indicated in the database parameter file. This command is handy if you have changed listener information or if the listener has been stopped and restarted for some reason.

The **alter system set** command is used to modify Oracle database parameters. This clause can be used to change the setting of a database parameter, either temporarily or permanently. Here is an example of using the **alter system set** clause to change a database parameter dynamically, and permanently:

```
ALTER SYSTEM SET db_cache_size=325M
COMMENT='This change is to add more memory to the system'
SCOPE=BOTH;
```

In this example, the **db_cache_size** parameter is changed to 325MB. Note that this change is systemwide, not just for the session (session-level parameters can be changed via the **alter session** command). So, be careful about setting parameters like **sort_area_size** with the **alter system** command. Note that the **scope** parameter of the **alter system set** clause is used to define the scope of the change. Valid values are as follows:

- **BOTH**   Changes both the current system setting and the database SPFILE.
- **SPFILE**   Changes just the database SPFILE. The current database settings are unaffected.
- **MEMORY**   Changes the current database system settings. The SPFILE is unaffected.

You can use the BOTH and SPFILE options only if you are using a database SPFILE. Also, not all database parameters can be set dynamically. See Appendix A for a list of parameters, and to determine if the ones that you want to use can be set dynamically. You can also include comments with parameter changes by using the **comment** keyword.

You can also indicate via the **deferred** keyword that the change applies to only new connections, not existing ones, although many parameters are deferred by default. In some cases, you must include the **deferred** keyword in the **alter system set** command. If the ISSYS_MODIFIABLE column of the V$PARAMETER view is set to DEFERRED, then this is required. If the column is set to FALSE, then you cannot defer the change. If it is set to IMMEDIATE, then you can opt to use the **deferred** keyword to defer the change.

The V$PARAMETER view is helpful in determining a number of attributes about database parameters. You can determine such things as the name of the parameter, its current setting, whether it can be modified immediately or can only be changed in a deferred manner, and other information.

Here are some examples of changing system parameters with the **alter system set** clause:

```
ALTER SYSTEM SET COMPATIBLE=10.0.0 COMMENT='GOING TO 10G!'
SCOPE=SPFILE;
ALTER SYSTEM SET JOB_QUEUE_PROCESSES=10 SCOPE=MEMORY;
```

If you are using RAC, you can use the **alter system set** clause to manage instance SPFILEs from any instance in the cluster. Use the **sid** parameter of the **alter system set** clause to indicate which session ID (SID) the change applies to. If you do not indicate the SID to change, Oracle changes all instances if they were started with SPFILEs. Dynamic parameter settings will affect only the local instance that the **alter system set** command is executed on if that instance was started with a normal server parameter file. You can reset server parameter files by using the **alter_system_reset** clause of the **alter system** command.

If you are running RAC, you may occasionally want to quickly update the status of a given data file in all the control files of the cluster (the Oracle database will eventually do this on its own, of course). The **check_datafiles** clause of the **alter system** command is used for this operation. As with checkpointing, you can execute the check on just the local instance, or globally as shown in this example:

```
ALTER SYSTEM CHECK DATAFILES GLOBAL;
```

The **alter system** command allows you to enable or disable restricted recovery, as shown in these examples:

```
ALTER SYSTEM ENABLE DISTRIBUTED RECOVERY;
ALTER SYSTEM DISABLE DISTRIBUTED RECOVERY;
```

The **alter system** command can be used to flush the shared pool and, in Oracle Database 10g, the database buffer cache, as shown in these examples:

```
ALTER SYSTEM FLUSH SHARED_POOL;
ALTER SYSTEM FLUSH BUFFER_CACHE;
```

alter system–Related Data Dictionary Information

Oracle provides several different views that provide information associated with the **alter system** command:

View Name	Description	All	User
V$PARAMETER V$PARAMETER2 V$SPPARAMETER	Provides a list of all parameters in the database. Useful when setting database parameters, to determine if they can be dynamically modified by the **alter system** command and if they can be deferred (ISSYS_MODIFIABLE column). Also, contains current values, indicates if the current values are the Oracle database default values, and provides other information.	N	N
V$SYSTEM_ PARAMETER	Displays information on parameters currently in effect for the instance. All new sessions inherit these parameters when they start.	N	N
V$DATABASE	Provides database-specific information.	N	N
V$INSTANCE	Provides instance-specific information.	N	N
V$THREAD	Provides thread-specific information.	N	N
V$LOGFILE	Provides information on the database redo logs.	N	N
V$LOG	Provides information on the database redo logs.	N	N
V$SESSION	Provides information on database sessions.	N	N
V$PROCESS	Provides process information for database sessions.	N	N

alter system–Related Errors

You may run into various Oracle errors when using the **alter system** command. The following table lists the most common errors and provides some advice as to what to do in the event you run into those errors.

Oracle Error Message	**Text Description**	**Possible Causes and Solutions**
ORA-00026	Missing or invalid session ID	You have tried to kill a session with the **alter system kill session** command and likely used an invalid format for the SID or SERIAL#. Check the format of the command and insure the SID and SERIAL# are correct.
ORA-00027	Cannot kill current session	You have tried to use the **alter system** command to kill your current session. This is not allowed.
ORA-00028	Your session has been killed	Your session was killed by the **alter system kill session** command.
ORA-00029	Session is not a user session	The session you have tried to kill is not a user session. It is likely a background session, and should not be killed.
ORA-00030	User session ID does not exist	You have tried to kill a session with the **alter system kill session** command and passed either an incorrect SID or SERIAL# parameter. Check V$SESSION for the correct SID and SERIAL# values and reissue the command.
ORA-00031	Session marked for kill	The session you have tried to kill with the **alter system kill session** command could not be killed immediately. Oracle marks the session to be killed and will kill the session when possible.
ORA-00254	Character limit exceeded by archive destination string	You have tried to use the **alter system archive log start** command to start the ARCH process, but the destination string was too long. Shorten the string if possible.
ORA-00256	Cannot translate archive destination string	You have tried to use the **alter system archive log start** command to start the ARCH process, but the destination string could not be interpreted. Reissue the command after correcting the string.
ORA-00271	There are no logs that need archiving	You have tried to archive logs with the **alter system** command, but there are no logs that need archived.
ORA-02096	Specified initialization parameter is not modifiable with this option	You have tried to modify a parameter by using an invalid option. For example, you might have tried to use the **deferred** keyword when modifying the parameter **job_queue_processes**, which is not allowed.

Oracle Error Message	Text Description	Possible Causes and Solutions
ORA-16178	Incremental changes not allowed with SPFILE	You have tried to change a **log_archive_dest_*n*** parameter in the SPFILE. This failure actually indicates that you have not specified all the attributes that are required to set the parameter **log_archive_dest_*n*** with the **alter system** command. Reissue the command using the location or service attributes and any other attributes that might be required.
ORA-25506 ORA-25507	Resource manager has not been continuously on (in some instances)	You cannot quiesce the system because the Database Resource Manager has not been enabled for all database instances since they were started. If you want to use the **alter system quiesce** command, you need to enable the Database Resource Manager.
ORA-32001	Write to SPFILE requested but no SPFILE specified at startup	You did not open the database with an SPFILE, thus activity requiring an SPFILE is restricted.

The alter session Command

The **alter session** command is used to alter various session-level conditions and settings for your session, and these changes take effect immediately. Changes include the ability to modify session-related environmental settings, enable parallel operations, and enable or disable Resumable Space Management. This section looks at security issues revolving around the **alter session** command. It then provides a number of examples of the use of the **alter session** command, along with a discussion of the examples being presented. Finally, this section presents the data dictionary views and error messages associated with the **alter session** command.

Security Requirements

You do not need any special privileges to use the **alter session** command, though specific commands that can be issued using the **alter session** command require privileges. If you want to use the **alter session** command to use Resumable Space Management, then you need the **resumable** system privilege. If you want to use the **alter session** command to control the SQL trace facility, then you need the **alter session** system privilege.

Examples of Using the alter session Command

The **alter session** command is used for a number of things. It is often used to set session-level parameters, which is covered first in this section. Examples for other uses of the **alter session** command follow after that.

Setting System Parameters

Probably the number one use of the **alter session** command is to set session-level parameters. The syntax for such a command is much like the **alter system** command, but only a subset of parameters can be changed at the session level. Here is an example of using the **alter session** command to change the **sort_area_size** of the current session:

```
ALTER SESSION SET SORT_AREA_SIZE=10000000;
ALTER SESSION SET HASH_AREA_SIZE=1000000;
```

The **alter session set** command changes two different kinds of parameters. Many of the parameters found in Appendix A can be changed at the session or system level. Additionally, the session-specific parameters in the following table can be set only by the **alter session** command.

Parameter Name	Settings [Default]	Comments
constraint[s]	**[Immediate]**, **deferred**, or **default**.	Used to control when constraint enforcement occurs.
current_schema	N/A	Changes the current schema to the one defined.
error_on_overlap_time	**True** or **[false]**	Determines how the database handles ambiguous datetime values.
flagger	**Entry**, **intermediate**, **[full]**, **off**	Causes an error to be generated when a SQL statement is issued that is an extension of ANSI SQL92.
instance	*n*	Used in a RAC environment to allow you access to another instance as if it were your own instance.
isolation_level	**Serializable**, **[read committed]**	Defines whether transactions should be handled in serializable mode or read committed mode.
time_zone	**+hh:mm** or **–hh:mm**, **[local]**, **dbtimezone**, or a valid time zone region	Defines the time zone for the session. Valid time zone regions are in the TZNAME column of the V$TIMEZONE_NAMES view.
use_private_outlines	**True**, **[false]**, category_name	Allows for the use of private outlines. This is a mutually exclusive parameter when **use_stored_outlines** is set.
use_stored_outlines	**True**, **[false]**, category_name	Allows the use of stored public outlines. This is a mutually exclusive parameter when **use_private_outlines** is set.

NOTE
*Several parameters that were session level–only parameters were converted into system level parameters in Oracle Database 10g. These include **plsql_debug**, **skip_unusable_indexes** and **sql_trace**. See Appendix A for more information on these parameters.*

The following example sets the **time_zone** parameter for the session so that it is set for the central time zone:

```
ALTER SESSION SET TIME_ZONE='CST';
```

Also, you can change the date display format for the session with the **alter session set** command, as shown in this example:

```
Alter session set nls_date_format='mm/dd/yyyy hh24:mi:ss';
```

Chapter 14 contains a list of valid date format masks that can be used under the **to_char** command.

Other Examples

You can use the **alter session** command to control how a remote database will handle a transaction executed by the session should the transaction become in doubt. You can advise a rollback, commit, or nothing. Note that advising a rollback or a commit does not roll back or commit the transaction on the distributed site. Here is an example of the use of the **alter session** command to advise a rollback of a statement should the transaction become in doubt:

```
UPDATE emp@test SET sal=1000.00 WHERE empno=1010;
ALTER SESSION ADVISE COMMIT;
UPDATE emp@test SET comm=100.00 WHERE empno=1010;
ALTER SESSION ADVISE ROLLBACK;
COMMIT;
```

You can disable the ability of PL/SQL programs to issue **commit** or **rollback** statements by using the **alter session disable commit in procedure** command. Reenable this functionality with the **alter session enable commit in procedure** command. When **commits** are disabled, an error will be raised in the event of a **commit** or **rollback**.

Parallelism of DML, DDL, and queries can be disabled, enabled, or forced, and the degree of parallelism can be defined via the **alter session** command. You can issue the **alter session enable parallel** command only at the start of a transaction.

If parallel DML is enabled via the **alter session enable parallel DML** command, then session-level DML statements will execute in parallel if either a **parallel** hint is used or the **parallel** clause is used in the DML statement.

If the **alter session enable parallel DDL** command is issued, DDL statements execute in parallel if the **parallel** clause is used in any subsequent DDL statement. Also, the **alter session**

enable parallel query command enables parallel query operations for **select** statements (but parallel query operations for **select** statements are enabled by default). Use the **alter session disable parallel** command to disallow parallelism of DML, DDL, or **select** statements.

The **alter session parallel** clause also provides a **force** clause, which forces parallel execution of SQL statements in the session as long as such an operation is valid. You can also specify the degree of parallelism when using the **force** option to override the parallel settings associated with subsequently issued statements, or the **degree** setting for a given table. SQL **parallel** hints override the **degree** setting. Here is an example of enabling parallel DML with the **alter session** command:

```
ALTER SESSION ENABLE PARALLEL DML;
```

You can also enable parallel DDL, as shown in this example:

```
ALTER SESSION ENABLE PARALLEL DDL;
```

You can force the execution of a parallel DML operation with the **force** clause, as shown in this example, which also forces the use of four parallel servers if the statement is capable of being parallelized:

```
ALTER SESSION FORCE PARALLEL DML PARALLEL 4;
```

NOTE
*Restrictions on parallel operations vary widely on different versions of Oracle. Use of the **alter session** command to force parallelism may or may not actually result in a parallel operation. Please check your specific version documentation to see if parallelism is supported for the operations you are planning.*

Resumable Space Management, available since Oracle9*i* Database, allows Oracle to suspend operations if they run into out-of-space situations, and then resume those operations once the out-of-space condition is resolved. To enable Resumable Space Management for your session, use the **alter session enable resumable** command. Using the **timeout** parameter, you can define the length of time that Oracle will suspend the session. Once that time period has expired, if the out-of-space condition is not resolved, the operation will fail and be rolled back.

NOTE
*The initialization parameter **resumable_timeout** is available in Oracle Database 10g and later, and it defaults to 0. The **resumable_timeout** parameter allows for Resumable Space Management to be enabled by default at a global level. You can alter the default **resumable_timeout** setting with the **alter session enable resumable** command.*

alter session–Related Data Dictionary Information

The **alter session** command has several data dictionary views that are related to its use. These views are found in the following table:

View Name	Description	All	User
V$PARAMETER V$PARAMETER2	Provide a list of all parameters in the database. This is useful when setting database parameters, to determine whether they can be dynamically modified by the **alter session** command and whether the parameter setting can be deferred (ISSYS_ MODIFIABLE column). Also contain current values, indicate if the current values are the Oracle database default values, and provide other information.	N	N
V$SYSTEM_ PARAMETER	Displays information on parameters currently in effect for the instance. All new sessions will inherit these parameters when they start.	N	N

alter session–Related Errors

Several errors might occur as a result of the **alter session** command. Here are the most common:

Oracle Error Message	Text Description	Possible Causes and Solutions
ORA-00034	Cannot commit in current PL/SQL session	You have tried to run a PL/SQL procedure that contains either a **commit** or a **rollback** statement in it. This has caused an error because the **alter session disable commit in procedure** command has been executed.
ORA-00922	Missing or invalid option	The **alter session** command syntax is incorrect. Check the syntax and correct it.
ORA-02248	Invalid option for alter session	The **alter session** command issued is invalid. Check the syntax for the command, correct the error, and reissue the command.
ORA-12705	Invalid or unknown NLS parameter value specified	You have tried to change an NLS parameter with the **alter session set** command, but the parameter value that you used was invalid. Check the value and try again.
ORA-30072	Invalid time zone value	You have tried to use an invalid time zone value in the **alter session** command. Correct the **alter session** command, using a valid time zone. You can find valid time zone names in the V$TIMEZONE_NAMES view.

The create directory/ drop directory Commands

A directory is an Oracle object that, once defined, can be used by Oracle features such as BFILES or external tables to define locations on the local disk that those features can access. This section presents the commands that you use to manage directories, namely the **create directory** and **drop directory** commands.

Security Requirements

To use the **create directory** command, you must have the **create any directory** system privilege. You can issue this grant as shown in this example:

```
GRANT CREATE ANY DIRECTORY TO my_user;
```

The schema that the directory is created in will have read and write privileges to the directory by default. If you wish to allow other users access to the directory, you must grant read and write privileges on that directory by using the **grant** command with the **on directory** keywords, as shown in this example:

```
GRANT read, write ON DIRECTORY my_directory TO george;
```

Since a directory points to a file system on an operating system, Oracle must have the appropriate privileges to that directory in order to be able to write to it.

If you wish to drop a directory, then you need the **drop any directory** privilege.

create directory Examples

The **create directory** command is pretty straightforward. You simply define the location of the directory within the body of the command, as shown in this example:

```
CREATE OR REPLACE DIRECTORY my_directory AS
'c:\oracle\directory\my_directory';
```

Note that this example also includes the optional **or replace** keywords, which instructs Oracle to replace the directory my_directory, if it already exists, or create a new one if it does not exist. If the **or replace** keywords are not included, then the command fails if the directory already exists. If you create a directory, no error is returned if the file system the directory points to does not exist and you can only create a directory for the user you are logged in as. You cannot create a directory for another user, unless you can connect as that user.

drop directory Example

Use the **drop directory** command to drop directories. Note that when you drop a directory, the operating system files associated with that directory are not removed. To drop a directory, you will need the **drop any directory** privilege. Here is an example of using the **drop directory** command:

```
DROP DIRECTORY my_directory;
```

create directory– /drop directory–Related Data Dictionary Information

The following table lists data dictionary views that are associated with directories:

View Name	Description	All	User
DBA_DIRECTORIES	Provides a list of all directories	Y	N
DBA_SYS_PRIVS	Indicates if the specific user has been assigned the **create directory** privilege	N	Y
DBA_ROLE_PRIVS	Indicates if the specific role has been assigned the **create any directory** or **drop any directory** privilege	N	Y

create directory– /drop directory–Related Errors

Here are some common error messages associated with the use of the **create directory** and **drop directory** commands:

Oracle Error Message	Text Description	Possible Causes and Solutions
ORA-00955	Name is already used by an existing object	The directory name you have tried to create is already in use. Either change the name of the directory you are trying to create or use the **create or replace directory** command syntax instead.
ORA-01031	Insufficient privileges	You have either tried to create a directory with the **create directory** command or tried to **grant** the **create any directory** privilege, but you do not have the privileges required to perform either action. To perform either action, you must use the **grant** command and grant the **create any directory** privilege with the **admin** option.
ORA-04043	Object does not exist	The directory you have tried to drop does not exist. Check the command and make sure it's correct. Then, check the user and make sure it has the correct privileges to drop the directory in question.

The comment Command

The **comment** command allows you to store comments on tables, columns, materialized views, and other Oracle database objects. This section shows you how to use the **comment** command, and then how to find the comments you have saved. Finally, this section looks at the errors you might encounter with the **comment** command.

Security Requirements

If the table, materialized view, or view is in your own schema, you do not need any additional privileges to be able to use the **comment** command. To be able to create a comment on a table, materialized view, or view in another schema, you must have the **comment any table** system privilege.

comment Examples

You create a comment on a table or view by using the **comment on table** command, followed by the **is** keyword and then the comment in single quotes, as shown in this example:

```
COMMENT ON TABLE scott.emp IS
'This is a comment, don''t forget to use double quotes!';
```

Note that double quotes are used within the body of the comment to indicate that it should interpret the double quote as a quote and not the end of the comment.

Use the **comment on column** command to create a comment associated with a column in a given table, view, or materialized view. In this command, you include the name of the schema, the name of the table, and the name of the column, as shown in this example:

```
COMMENT ON column scott.emp.empid
IS 'This is the employee id.';
```

To create a comment on a materialized view, use the **comment on materialized view** command, which is much like the **comment on table** command, as shown in this example:

```
COMMENT ON MATERIALIZED VIEW scott.emp_mv
IS 'This is a comment!';
```

You drop comments from objects by issuing the **comment** command and then just using two single quotes to define a blank comment, as shown in this example:

```
COMMENT ON MATERIALIZED VIEW scott.emp_mv
IS '';
```

comment-Related Data Dictionary Information

Data dictionary views can be used to view comments, as shown in the following table:

View Name	Description	All	User
DBA_TAB_COMMENTS	Displays comments on tables, views, or materialized views	Y	Y
DBA_COL_COMMENTS	Displays comments on columns within a table, view, or materialized view	Y	Y

comment-Related Errors

Here are some common error messages associated with the use of the **comment** command:

Oracle Error Message	Text Description	Possible Causes and Solutions
ORA-00942	Table or view does not exist	Either the table, view, or materialized view you have tried to comment on does not exist, the SQL statement is misspelled, or you do not have access to the object you are trying to comment on.
ORA-01031	Insufficient privileges	You do not have privileges required to create a comment on the object. You need to have the **comment any table** system privilege.
ORA-01756	Quoted string not properly terminated	This most often happens when you have not put two single quotes in a word that has an apostrophe, like the word "don't." Check the comment and add double quotes so that don't becomes don''t. It is also possible that you did not include a closing quote in the comment string.

The lock table Command

The **lock table** command allows you to manually lock a database object in a specific mode. Oracle allows you to lock tables, table partitions, table subpartitions, and views with the **lock table** command. The lock remains in place until you have completed the transaction or have rolled back the operation beyond the point that you locked the table.

Security Requirements

You can use the **lock table** command on any table, table partition or subpartition, or view in your own schema. If you wish to lock an object in another schema, you must have the **lock any table** system privilege. Alternatively, you can use the **lock table** command on an object if you have any object-specific privilege on that object.

lock table Examples

The **lock table** command is pretty straightforward. You simply indicate the object you wish to lock, and the lock mode you wish to lock it in. For example, if you wanted to lock the EMP table in exclusive mode, you would issue the following command:

```
LOCK TABLE emp IN EXCLUSIVE MODE;
```

By default, Oracle waits to acquire the lock against the table. This can take a long time in certain cases. If you don't want to wait to acquire the lock, then you can use the optional **nowait** keyword, as shown in this example:

```
LOCK TABLE emp IN EXCLUSIVE MODE NOWAIT;
```

You can also lock specific table partitions and subpartitions by using the **partition** and **subpartition** keywords, as shown in these examples:

```
LOCK TABLE store_sales PARTITION (sales_overflow)
IN EXCLUSIVE MODE NOWAIT;
LOCK TABLE composite_sales SUBPARTITION (sub_two)
IN EXCLUSIVE MODE NOWAIT;
```

Oracle supports a number of different lock modes, as shown in the following tables:

Lock Mode	Description
Row share and share update	Prevents users from taking an exclusive lock against a table. Concurrent DML access to the table is allowed, however.
Row exclusive	Has the attributes of a row share lock, and also prohibits locking the table in share mode. This type of lock is automatically taken during an **update**, **insert**, or **delete** operation.
Share	Disallows updates on the table but allows queries.
Share row exclusive	Prohibits locking the table in share mode or updating rows. Allows concurrent access to rows in the table.
Exclusive	Allows queries to be executed, but other activities are restricted.

lock table–Related Data Dictionary Information

Data dictionary views can be used to view current locks taken out against specific tables. Here is a list of those views:

View Name	Description	All	User
DBA_DDL_LOCKS	Provides a list of any locks held in the database as a result of DDL requests	N	N
DBA_DML_LOCKS	Provides a list of any locks held in the database as a result of DML operation requests	N	N

View Name	Description	All	User
DBA_LOCKS	Provides a list of all locks held in the database	N	N
V$LOCK	Lists all locks taken in the database and provides information on blocking locks.	n/a	n/a
DBA_BLOCKERS	Lists sessions that are blocking other sessions	N	N

lock table–Related Errors

Here are some common error messages associated with the use of the **lock table** command:

Oracle Error Message	Text Description	Possible Causes and Solutions
ORA-00054	Resource busy and acquire with NOWAIT specified	Another process has locked the table in an incompatible mode. You have used the **nowait** option of the **lock table** command, so this error is returned.
ORA-00069	Cannot acquire lock – table locks disabled	The table you have tried to lock has had table locks disabled. Use the **alter table enable table lock** command to enable locks on the table and then retry the command.
ORA-00942	Table or view does not exist	Either the table, view, or materialized view you have tried to lock does not exist, the SQL statement is misspelled, or you do not have access to the object you are trying to lock.

The purge Command

The **purge** command is used in Oracle Database 10*g* and later to purge the recycle bin. When you drop most segments in Oracle Database 10*g*, the segment is retained in the recycle bin. These segments are assigned a new system-generated name. This prevents naming conflicts that might otherwise occur. Each schema has its own recycle bin, and all of the user recycle bins can be combined into a systemwide recycle bin for the purposes of the **purge** command.

Security Requirements

You can purge any object within your own schema from your own recycle bin. To purge an object in another schema, you must have the **drop any** privilege associated with that object, such as **drop any table**. Also, if your user has the SYSDBA privilege, then it can purge any object in the database.

purge Examples

In its simplest form, you just indicate the name of the object to purge with the **purge** command, as shown in this example:

```
PURGE TABLE emp;
```

In this case, Oracle purges the EMP table, if it exists, from the recycle bin. If multiple copies of EMP exist, then the oldest copy will be purged. You can also purge an object based on its recycle bin ID (which can be found in the data dictionary views listed later in this section), as shown in this example:

```
PURGE TABLE "BIN$K0CYybxBQVe71iTNWxGNyg==$0";
```

Note in this example that the table name is enclosed in double quotes. This is a requirement in many cases, because the system-generated name can sometimes throw off the SQL interpreter when it's not enclosed in quotes. You can also purge indexes that have been dropped, as shown in this example:

```
PURGE INDEX ix_gold_supply_01;
```

Note that indexes get moved to the recycle bin only if their associated tables are dropped. An index that is dropped with the **drop index** command does not go to the recycle bin.

Oracle also allows you to purge the entire recycle bin with the **purge recyclebin** command, as shown in this example:

```
PURGE RECYCLEBIN;
```

You can remove all recycle bin entries with the **dba_recyclebin** purge option, as shown here:

```
PURGE DBA_RECYCLEBIN;
```

You can also opt to remove all tablespace-specific objects from the recycle bin with the **purge tablespace** command:

```
PURGE TABLESPACE USERS;
```

You can also purge specific users from a tablespace by adding the **users** clause:

```
PURGE TABLESPACE EC_DATA USER SCOTT;
```

purge-Related Data Dictionary Information

Data dictionary views can be used to view the recycle bin. Here is a list of those views:

View Name	Description	All	User
RECYCLEBIN	Displays items in the recycle bin	N	N
DBA_RECYCLEBIN	Displays items in the recycle bin	N	Y

purge-Related Errors

Here are some common error messages associated with the use of the **purge** command:

Oracle Error Message	Text Description	Possible Causes and Solutions
ORA-00933	SQL command not properly ended	You are probably using the recycle bin object name rather than the original object name. Enclose the recycle bin object name in double quotes and try again.
ORA-01031	Insufficient privileges	You are trying to purge an object that is owned by another user and you do not have the correct access rights. Grant yourself the correct access rights.
ORA-38302	Invalid purge option	You have used an invalid option with the **purge** command. Correct the syntax and try again.
ORA-38307	Object not in RECYCLE BIN	The object you have tried to purge does not exist in the recycle bin. Check the RECYCLEBIN data dictionary view and make sure the object is there. Check the command and ensure that the object's name is spelled correctly.

The rename Command

The **rename** command allows you to rename a table, view, sequence, or private synonym. All associated objects (indexes, constraints, grants, etc.) are transferred to the new object. Note that renaming an object invalidates dependent database objects. You cannot rename a materialized view, and a **rename** operation cannot be rolled back.

> **NOTE**
> The **rename** command is not used to rename indexes (use the **alter index rename** command), column names, or constraints (use the **alter table** command to rename those objects). You cannot rename a public synonym with the **rename** command.

Security Requirements

You can rename only objects in your own schema. Within your own schema, you can rename any table without restriction.

rename Examples

The **rename** command is very easy to use. Simply indicate the current name of the table and what you wish the new name to be. This example renames GOLD_TABLE to SILVER_AND_ GOLD_TABLE:

```
RENAME gold_table TO silver_and_gold_table;
```

rename-Related Data Dictionary Information

Data dictionary views can be used to view table-related information, which can be used by the **rename** command:

View Name	Description	All	User
DBA_TABLES	Lists owners and table names in the database	Y	Y
DBA_VIEWS	Lists owners and view names in the database	Y	Y
DBA_SEQUENCES	Lists owners and sequence names in the database	Y	Y
DBA_SYNONYMS	Describes all synonyms in the database	Y	Y

rename-Related Errors

Here are some common error messages associated with the use of the **rename** command:

Oracle Error Message	Text Description	Possible Causes and Solutions
ORA-00903	Invalid table name	The table name that you have tried to rename is invalid. Check the name of the table in the command and make sure it is correct.
ORA-01765	Specifying table's owner name is not allowed	You cannot rename a table across schemas.
ORA-04043	Object does not exist	The table you have tried to rename does not exist.

The set constraints Command

The **set constraints** command allows you to define the state of constraints for a given transaction. Constraints by default are set to be immediate, but the **set constraint** command allows you to alter constraint enforcement to be deferred if it was defined as deferrable when it was created. When the **set constraints** command is used to set constraints to deferred condition, the constraints will not be validated until the transaction is completed.

Security Requirements

You must either own the table that owns the constraint when using the **set constraint** command or have the **select** privilege on the table that owns the constraint.

set constraints Examples

The **set constraint** command is simple to use. Simply indicate the name of the constraint you wish to set to deferrable, as shown in this example:

```
SET CONSTRAINTS fk_emp_dept DEFERRED;
```

All deferrable constraints can be set to deferred with the **set constraints** command, as shown in this example:

```
SET CONSTRAINTS ALL DEFERRED;
```

You can alter deferrable constraints to immediate by using the **immediate** clause of the **set constraints** command:

```
SET CONSTRAINTS ALL IMMEDIATE;
SET CONSTRAINTS fk_emp_dept IMMEDIATE;
```

When constraints are set to immediate with the **set constraints** command, the database checks all constraints. Errors will occur if constraint violations occur.

set constraints–Related Data Dictionary Information

Data dictionary views can be used to view constraints and the tables they are assigned to. Here is a list of those views:

View Name	Description	All	User
DBA_CONSTRAINTS	Lists information on constraints, including whether they can be deferred and whether they are currently deferred	Y	Y
DBA_CONS_COLUMNS	List column-level constraint information	Y	Y

set constraints–Related Errors

Here are some common error messages associated with the use of the **set constraint** command:

Oracle Error Message	Text Description	Possible Causes and Solutions
ORA-02447	Cannot defer a constraint that is not deferrable	You have tried to set a constraint state to deferred, but it was not created as deferrable. You need to drop and re-create the constraint if you wish to be able to defer it.
ORA-02448	Constraint does not exist	The constraint you have tried to defer does not exist. Check the name of the constraint in the **set constraints** command and make sure it is correct.

The set transaction Command

The **set transaction** command can be used only at the beginning of a transaction. It can be used to make the transaction read-only (read-write is the default), define a specific isolation level, or assign the transaction to a specific rollback segment if you are using manual rollback segments. The settings configured with the **set transaction** command revert to the default settings after the transaction is completed via a **commit** or if a **rollback** command is issued.

Security Requirements

The **set transaction** command can be used in any transaction, and there are no special security considerations. It must be the first statement in the transaction.

set transaction Examples

Here is an example of using the **set transaction** command to set the current transaction to read-only:

```
COMMIT;
SET TRANSACTION READ ONLY;
```

The **set transaction** command also allows you to use a specific rollback segment if you are using manual rollback segments. The next example sets the transaction to use the RBSBIG rollback segment:

```
COMMIT;
SET TRANSACTION USE ROLLBACK SEGMENT rbsbig;
```

In Oracle9*i* Database, an error appears if you try to use the **set transaction** command to assign a rollback segment to a transaction unless the parameter **undo_suppress_errors** is set to TRUE. This parameter is obsolete in Oracle Database 10*g*, and the use of the **set transaction** command to assign a rollback segment to a transaction will be ignored.

set transaction–Related Errors

Here are some common error messages associated with the use of the **set transaction** command:

Oracle Error Message	Text Description	Possible Causes and Solutions
ORA-01453	SET TRANSACTION must be first statement of transaction	You can use the **set transaction** command only when it is the first statement of a transaction. Issue a **commit** or **rollback**, depending on which is correct, and try the statement again.
ORA-01534	Rollback segment does not exist	The rollback segment you have tried to force the use of with the **set transaction** statement does not exist. Check the name of the rollback segment in the command and make sure the rollback segment has been created and is online.
ORA-30019	Illegal rollback segment operation in Automatic Undo mode	You have tried to use the **set transaction** command to assign a rollback segment to the transaction but you are running in automatic undo mode. This error will appear in Oracle9*i* Databases only. Remove the **set transaction** statement or use the parameter **undo_suppress_ errors** to correct this problem.

The create database link/drop database link Commands

You can use a database link to create an access path to objects in another database. You create a database link via the **create database link** command, assigning an alias name to the database link being created. Oracle supports direct database links to other Oracle databases by default, or to other, non-Oracle systems with the optional use of Oracle Heterogeneous Services.

Once the database link is created, you can, with few restrictions, issue DML commands against the objects in a remote database as you would in a local Oracle database. DDL operations are not allowed for the most part. Some Oracle database features, such as materialized views and advanced replication, commonly use database links.

Database links come in the form of a private database link or a public database link. A private database link is accessible only by the user who created the link, whereas the public database link is accessible by all users.

Security Requirements

Creation of a private database link requires that you have the **create database link** system privilege. Creation of a public database link requires the **create public database link** system privilege. Additionally, the user account on the remote system that the database link will be connecting to must have the **create session** system privilege. Note that you also must have Oracle networking configured correctly to use database links.

You can drop a private database link in your own schema without special permissions. You can drop a public database link through the **drop database link** command if you have the **drop public database link** system privilege.

create database link/drop database link Examples

By default, database links that are created are private and only accessible when logged into your schema. The **create database link** command is used to create the database link, as shown in this example:

```
CREATE DATABASE LINK my_db_link
CONNECT TO current_user
USING 'my_db';
```

The next example creates a public database link called MY_DB_LINK by using the **create database link** command with the optional **public** keyword:

```
CREATE PUBLIC DATABASE LINK my_db_link
CONNECT TO current_user
USING 'my_db';
```

In the last example, we have defined a shared public database link called MY_DB_LINK that points to the database defined by the MY_DB service. When you access the MY_DB_LINK database through the database link, the username and password that will be used when connecting to the remote system will be the same as the username and password as the account of the local database that you are on. This is because we used the **connect to current_user** syntax. Thus, if you are signed on as scott/tiger and you issue this command:

```
INSERT INTO emp@my_db_link
(empid, ename_last, ename_first, salary)
VALUES (10030, 'Peel','Emma', 1000.00);
```

The local database will try to connect to scott/tiger on the database defined by the MY_DB_LINK database link (which is the database defined by the service MY_DB defined in the first example).

It is frequently desirable to have access to a remote database connect through a single account. You can define the account that a database link should connect through when issuing the **create database link** command, as shown in this example:

```
CREATE PUBLIC DATABASE LINK my_db_link
CONNECT TO remote_user IDENTIFIED BY psicorp
USING 'my_db';
```

Dropping private database links is quite easy. Just use the **drop database link** command as seen in this example:

```
DROP DATABASE LINK my_db_link;
```

You can also drop public database links as seen in this example:

```
DROP PUBLIC DATABASE LINK my_db_link;
```

create database link– /drop database link–Related Data Dictionary Information

Data dictionary views can be used to view current database links available in the database. Those views are:

View Name	Description	All	User
DBA_DB_LINKS	Describes each database link	Y	Y
SYS.LINK$	Describes each database link	N	N

create database link–Related Errors

Here are some common error messages associated with the use of the **create database link** command:

Oracle Error Message	Text Description	Possible Causes and Solutions
ORA-02020	Too many database links in use	You have tried to open more database links than allowed by the **open_links** database parameter. Reset the parameter and try again.
ORA-02021	DDL Operations are not allowed on a remote database	You have tried a DDL operation through a database link, which is not a supported operation.
ORA-02024	Database link not found	The database link you have tried to use cannot be found. You may have misspelled the database link or it was never created.
ORA-02086	Database name is too long	The database link name you have tried to create is too long. Shorten the link name to less than 128 characters and try again.

CHAPTER
14

Built-in Functions

racle includes many SQL functions built right into the database. These functions can be used in a variety of ways in SQL and PL/SQL. These functions can take any number of parameters, and always return a result of a specifically defined data type. The functions discussed in this chapter are included in the database and are not to be confused with user-defined functions. In this chapter we will look at Oracle Database built-in functions.

Introducing Oracle Built-in Functions

Oracle's built-in functions take one or more parameters as input and return one and only one value. The input parameters and the return value can be any of Oracle's built-in data types. The built-in functions can be single-row functions, aggregate functions, analytic functions, object reference functions, or model functions. You can also have functions that are multiples of these types.

Single-Row Functions

Single-row functions return a single row as a result, for every row in the query's result set. Single-row functions can appear in the **select**, **where**, **connect by**, or **having** clauses. Single-row functions can be further classified into other groups:

- Numeric functions

- Character functions that return character values

- Character functions that return numeric values

- Date/time functions

- Conversion functions

- Collection functions

- XML single-row functions

- LOB single-row functions

- Miscellaneous functions

Numeric Single-Row Functions

Numeric single-row functions accept numbers as input and return a number. Most numeric functions return a number that is accurate to 38 digits. The numeric functions are as follows:

abs	Returns the absolute value of a number	**mod**	Returns the remainder of m divided by n, mod(m,n)
acos	Returns the arc cosine of a number	**nanvl**	Returns n if m is not a number, nanvl(m,n)
asin	Returns the arc sine of a number	**power**	Returns m raised to the nth power, power(m,n)

atan	Returns the arc tangent of a number	**remainder**	Returns the remainder of m divided by n. Same as mod except uses round instead of floor
atan2	Returns the arc tangent of n and m, atan2(n,m) = atan(n/m)	**round**	Returns a number rounded to the specified number of decimal places
bitand	Returns the bitwise AND operation on two numbers	**sign**	Returns −1 if $n < 0$, 0 if $n = 0$, and 1 if $n > 0$
ceil	Returns the smallest integer greater than or equal to the given number	**sin**	Returns the sine of a number
cos	Returns the cosine of an angle expressed in radians	**sinh**	Returns the hyperbolic sine of a number
cosh	Returns the hyperbolic cosine of a number	**sqrt**	Returns the square root of a number
exp	Returns e raised to the given number, where e = 2.71828183...	**tan**	Returns the tangent of a number
floor	Returns the largest integer less than or equal to the given number	**tanh**	Returns the hyperbolic tangent of a number
ln	Returns the natural logarithm of the given number, greather than zero	**trunc**	Returns the number n truncated to m decimal places, trunc(n,m)
log	Returns the logarithm, base m, of n. log(m,n)	**width_bucket**	Returns a bucket number the given expression would fall in

Character Single-Row Functions That Return Characters

These character single-row functions accept character input and return character output. The maximum number of characters returned is the limit of the data type returned. If the output exceeds this limit, the return value is truncated without error. The character functions that return character values are as follows:

chr	Returns the char represented by the given number	**regexp_substr**	Returns substrings of the given string using regular expression searches
concat	Returns the string formed by concatenating the two given strings	**replace**	Returns the string with every occurrence of a set of chars replaced with other chars
initcap	Returns the given string with the first letter of each word capitalized	**rpad**	Returns the given string right padded with characters

lower	Returns the given string converted to all lower case	**rtrim**	Returns the string with the right characters trimmed off
lpad	Returns the given string left padded with characters	**soundex**	Returns the phonetic expression of a given string
ltrim	Returns the given string with the left characters trimmed off	**substr**	Returns a portion of the given string
nls_initcap	Returns the given string with the first letter of each word capitalized according to the NLS settings	**translate**	Returns the given string with all occurrences of some characters replaced with other characters
nls_lower	Returns the given string with all letters lower case according to the NLS settings	**treat**	Changes the type of an expression
nlssort	Returns the string of bytes used to sort the given string, according to the NLS settings	**trim**	Returns the given string with characters trimmed from the right and left sides
nls_upper	Returns the given string with all letters upper case, according to the NLS settings	**upper**	Returns the given string converted to all upper case
regexp_replace	Replaces characters in the given string using regular expressions		

Character Single-Row Functions That Return Numbers

Some character single-row functions return numbers:

ascii	Returns the decimal representation of the given character	**length**	Returns the length of the given string
instr	Returns the location of the given substring within the given string	**regexp_instr**	Returns the location of the given substring within the given string using regular expression searches

Date/Time Functions

The date/time functions accept DATE, TIMESTAMP, and INTERVAL data types. The output values will be DATE, TIMESTAMP, or INTERVAL data types. The following are the date/time functions:

add_months	Returns the given date with the number of months added to it	**round**	Returns the given date rounded
current_date	Returns the current date in the session time zone	**sessiontimezone**	Returns the time zone of the current session
current_timestamp	Returns the current timestamp in the session time zone	**sys_extract_utc**	Returns the Universal Time Coordinate (UTC) from a datetime value
dbtimezone	Returns the database time zone	**sysdate**	Returns the current date and time
extract	Returns the specified datetime field from the given expression	**systimestamp**	Returns the current date and time as the TIMESTAMP datatype
from_tz	Converts a timestamp and given timezone to a TIMESTAMP WITH TIMEZONE datatype	**to_char**	Converts a date and time to a string value
last_day	Returns the date of the last day of the month	**to_timestamp**	Converts a string to a TIMESTAMP value
localtimestamp	Returns the current timestamp of the session's time zone	**to_timestamp_tz**	Converts a string to a TIMESTAMP WITH TIME ZONE value
months_between	Returns the number of months between two dates	**to_dsinterval**	Converts a string to an INTERVAL DAY TO SECOND value
new_time	Returns the date and time in the new time zone	**to_yminterval**	Converts a string to an INTERVAL YEAR TO MONTH value
next_day	Returns the date of the first weekday of the given date	**trunc**	Returns the date truncated to the specified precision
numtodsinterval	Converts the number to an INTERVAL DAY TO SECOND datatype	**tz_offset**	Returns the time zone offset
numtoyminterval	Converts the number to an INTERVAL YEAR TO MONTH datatype		

Conversion Functions

Conversion functions are used to convert a value from one data type to another data type. The conversion functions are as follows:

asciistr	Converts a string to its ASCII version	**to_binary_float**	Converts to a single-precision floating point number
bin_to_num	Converts a bit vector to its number	**to_char**	Converts to a character string
cast	Converts a value to a new datatype	**to_clob**	Converts to CLOB datatype
chartorowid	Converts string to a ROWID type	**to_date**	Converts to DATE datatype
compose	Converts a string to a Unicode string	**to_dsinterval**	Converts to INTERVAL DAY TO SECOND datatype
convert	Converts a string to a new character set	**to_lob**	Converts LONG or LONG RAW to LOB datatypes
decompose	Converts a string to a Unicode string after decomposition	**to_multi_byte**	Converts string to multi-byte string
hextoraw	Converts a hex string to a RAW datatype	**to_nchar**	Converts to National Character Set string
numtodsinterval	Converts a number to an INTERVAL DAY TO SECOND datatype	**to_nclob**	Converts to CLOB using National Character Set
numtoyminterval	Converts a number to an INTERVAL YEAR TO MONTH datatype	**to_number**	Converts to a NUMBER datatype
rawtohex	Converts a RAW datatype to its hex number	**to_single_byte**	Converts multi-byte string to single-byte string
rawtonhex	Converts a RAW datatype to its hex number NVARCHAR2 datatype	**to_timestamp**	Converts to TIMESTAMP datatype
rowidtochar	Converts a ROWID to VARCHAR2 datatype	**to_timestamp_tz**	Converts to TIMESTAMP WITH TIME ZONE datatype

rowidtonchar	Converts a ROWID to NVARCHAR2 datatype	**to_yminterval**	Converts to INTERVAL YEAR TO MONTH datatype
scn_to_timestamp	Converts SCN to TIMESTAMP datatype	**translate..using**	Converts from character set to National Character Set
timestamp_to_scn	Converts TIMESTAMP to SCN value	**unistr**	Converts to National Character Set
to_binary_double	Converts number to double-precision floating point number		

Collection Functions

The collection functions take collections (nested tables or varrays) as input. The collection functions are as follows:

cardinality	Returns number of elements in the nested table	**powermultiset_ by_cardinality**	Returns a nested table of nested tables using cardinality
collect	Returns a nested table from the input	**set**	Converts nested table into a set
powermultiset	Returns a nested table of nested tables		

XML Single-Row Functions

With the rise of XML, it became necessary to create functions that work with XML. The following are the XML functions:

extract	Returns XMLType instance containing an XML fragment	**xmlforest**	Converts arguments to XML
sys_xmlagg	Aggregates all XML fragments into one XML document	**xmlcolattval**	Creates XML fragment where each fragment has name *column* and value *name.*
sys_xmlgen	Generates XMLType instance from a row and column	**xmlconcat**	Concatenates XMLType instances
updatexml	Updates XMLType instances	**xmlsequence**	Returns varray of top-level nodes of XMLType
xmlagg	Aggregates all XML fragments into one XML document without formatting	**xmltransform**	Applies style sheet to XMLType instance and returns XMLType instance

Large Object Single-Row Functions

Single-row functions were created to handle support for large objects (BLOB, CLOB, BFILE). The large object single-row functions are as follows:

bfilename	Returns BFILE locator to physical file	**empty_clob**	Returns empty CLOB locator used to populate CLOB column or initialize CLOB variable
empty_blob	Returns empty BLOB locator used to populate BLOB column or initialize BLOB variable		

Miscellaneous Single-Row Functions

Aside from the preceding single-row functions, there are some single-row functions that do not necessarily fall into any categories:

coalesce	Returns first non-null expression in the list	**ora_hash**	Returns a hash value for given expression
cv	Returns current value of dimension column	**path**	Returns relative path leading to specified resource
decode	Returns value from search list depending on input value	**presentnnv**	Returns specified values depending on existence of *cell_reference* if it is not NULL
depth	Returns number of levels in the path	**presentv**	Returns specified values depending on existence of *cell_reference*
dump	Returns the internal representation of the input	**previous**	Returns the value of *cell_reference* at beginning of each iteration
existsnode	Determines if traversal of XML document results in a node	**sys_connect_by_path**	Returns the path from root to node
extractvalue	Returns the value of a node in a XML document	**sys_context**	Returns the value of *parameter* for the context *namespace*
greatest	Returns the largest of a list of arguments	**sys_dburigen**	Returns URL of type DBURIType to retrieve XML document
least	Returns the smallest of a list of arguments	**sys_extract_utc**	Returns the Universal Time Coordinate from datetime value

lnnvl	Determines if one or both operands is NULL	**sys_guid**	Returns a Globally Unique Identifier (GUID)
nls_charset_ decl_len	Returns the declaration length of NCHAR value	**sys_typeid**	Returns the type identifier
nls_charset_id	Returns the character set id number of the given name	**uid**	Returns a unique identifier of the session's user
nls_charset_ name	Returns the character set name of the given id	**user**	Returns the session's username
nullif	Returns NULL if two expressions are equal, else returns first expression	**userenv**	Returns information about current session
nvl	Returns a specified value if given expression is NULL	**vsize**	Returns the number of bytes for the internal representation of the expression
nvl2	Returns a specified value if given expression is NULL; otherwise, returns a different specified value		

Aggregate Functions

Aggregate functions return a single-row result for a group of rows in the queried table. Aggregate functions can appear in the **select**, **order by**, or **having** clauses. The aggregate function either must be applied to all rows in the table or must be accompanied by a **group by** clause; otherwise, an error is raised. Many aggregate functions can use the **distinct** operator to limit the input values to unique values only, or you can use **all** values, including duplicates. The default is **all** values. All aggregate functions ignore NULL values, except for **count(*)** and **grouping**. The following are the aggregate functions:

avg	Returns average value of expression	**rank**	Returns the rank of the value
collect	Returns a nested table out of input values	**regr**	Returns linear regression values
corr	Returns the coefficient of correlation of number pairs	**stats_binomial_ test**	Exact probability test with two possible values
count	Returns the number of rows returned by query	**stats_crosstab**	Returns crosstabulation of two variables
covar_pop	Returns the population covariance of number pairs	**stats_f_test**	Tests whether two variances are significantly different
covar_samp	Returns the sample covariance of number pairs	**stats_ks_test**	Kolmogrov-Smirnov function to compare two samples

cume_dist	Returns cumulative distribution of values	**stats_mode**	Returns the value that occurs with greatest frequency
dense_rank	Returns dense ranking in the group of rows	**stats_mw_test**	Mann Whitney test on null hypothesis
first	Returns first ranked row	**stats_one_ way_anova**	One way analysis of variance function
group_id	Returns duplicate groups	**stats_t_test**	Measures the significance of a difference of means
grouping	Distinguishes super-aggregate rows from regular grouped rows	**stats_wsr_test**	Wilcoxon Signed Ranks test or paired samples
grouping_id	Returns number corresponding to GROUPING bit vector	**stddev**	Returns the standard deviation of a set of numbers
last	Returns final ranked row	**stddev_pop**	Returns the population standard deviation
max	Returns maximum value	**stddev_samp**	Returns the cumulative sample standard deviation
median	Returns middle value	**sum**	Returns the sum of values
min	Returns minimum value	**var_pop**	Returns the population variance
percentile_cont	Returns value that falls in the given percentile using continuous distribution model	**var_samp**	Returns the sample variance
percentile_disc	Returns value that falls in the given percentile using discrete distribution model	**variance**	Returns the variance
percentile_rank	Similar to cume_dist, but can return zero		

Analytic Functions

Analytic functions return an aggregate value based on a group of rows. Analytic functions differ from aggregate functions in that they can return multiple rows for each group of rows. The group of rows is a *window* that can move through the input rows of data. Analytic functions appear in the **select** or the **order by** clause. The analytic functions are as follows:

avg	Returns the average of values	**ntile**	Divides ordered set into buckets and assigns bucket number to each row
corr	Returns the coefficient of correlation of a set of number pairs	**percent_rank**	Similar to cume_dist, but can return zero
covar_pop	Returns the population covariance of number pairs	**percentile_cont**	Returns value that falls in the given percentile using continuous distribution model
covar_samp	Returns the sample covariance of number pairs	**percentile_disc**	Returns value that falls in the given percentile using discrete distribution model
count	Returns the number of rows returned by query	**rank**	Returns the rank of the value
cume_dist	Returns cumulative distribution of values	**ratio_to_report**	Returns the ratio of a value to the sum of a set of values
dense_rank	Returns dense ranking in the group of rows	**regr**	Returns linear regression values
first	Returns first ranked row	**row_number**	Returns unique number to each returned row
first_value	Returns the first value in an ordered set of values	**stddev**	Returns the standard deviation of a set of numbers
lag	Allows access to rows of a table without a self join	**stddev_pop**	Returns the population standard deviation
last	Returns final ranked row	**stddev_samp**	Returns the cumulative sample standard deviation
last_value	Returns the last value in an ordered set of values	**sum**	Returns the sum of values
lead	Provides access to more than one row of a table at the same time without a self join	**var_pop**	Returns the population variance
max	Returns the maximum value of the expression	**var_samp**	Returns the sample variance
min	Returns the minimum value of the expression	**variance**	Returns the variance

Object Reference Functions

Object reference functions manipulate REFs, which are pointers to objects of different object types. Those object types can be user-defined or Oracle-defined object types. The object reference functions are the following:

deref	Returns the object reference of the given argument	**reftohex**	Converts expression to hexadecimal equivalent
make_ref	Create a REF to a row of object	**value**	Returns object instances
ref	Returns REF value for the object instance		

Model Functions

Model functions are used for interrow calculations. You can use model functions only in the **model** clause of the **select** statement. The model functions are as follows:

cv	Returns current value of dimension column	**presentv**	Returns specified values depending on existence of *cell_reference*
iteration_number	Returns the completed iteration through the model rules	**previous**	Returns the value of *cell_reference* at beginning of each iteration
presentnnv	Returns specified values depending on existence of *cell_reference* if it is not NULL		

Examples of Commonly Used Functions

Now that you have been introduced to the different kinds of functions out there, this section provides a quick-lookup reference to the most commonly used functions. For each function, a description of the usage of the function and an example of it being used are provided. You will also find the format masks for numeric and date conversions contained later in these sections.

abs
Usage: abs(*n*)
The **abs** function returns the absolute value of the argument *n*.

```
SELECT ABS(-5) FROM dual;
```

ascii
Usage: ascii(*char*)

The **ascii** function returns the decimal value of the *char* argument. The value returned is dependent on the character set of the database.

```
SELECT ASCII('A') FROM dual;
```

avg

Usage: avg([DISTINCT,ALL], *expr*)

The **avg** function returns the average value of the given expression, *expr*. This function can optionally use just **distinct** values in the expression. The default is to use **all** values in the expression. This function can be an aggregate or an analytic function.

```
SELECT AVG(salary) FROM emp;
```

The **avg** function can be used both as a single-row, number function and as an analytic function. The preceding example shows **avg** as a single-row function. The following example shows how **avg** might be used as an analytic function:

```
SELECT manager, ename_last, salary,
AVG(sal) OVER
(PARTITION BY mgr ORDER BY sal DESC) AS moving_avg
FROM emp;
```

bfilename

Usage: bfilename('*directory*', '*filename*')

The **bfilename** function returns a BFILE locator to the physical file on the server's file system. This locator is used to access the large object. The **bfilename** function takes two parameters:

- *directory* – A directory is created with the **create directory** command. This is the location of the BFILE.

- *filename* – This is the name of the file on the database server.

Before you can use this function, you should create the directory and make sure the physical file is in place:

```
CREATE DIRECTORY my_dir AS '/ora01/app/sec/pics';
INSERT INTO emp_sec (emp_id, graphic_pic)
VALUES (3000, bfilename('MY_DIR', 'robert.jpg'));
```

cast

Usage: cast(*expr* or **multiset**(*subquery*) **as** *type_name*)

The **cast** function converts a given datatype value into another datatype value. For example, you can convert a **number** data type to a **char**. **long**, **long raw**, **lob**, and Oracle-supplied types are not supported by the **cast** function. The following table lists the different **cast** conversions that are possible:

Converting from	Can Convert to
binary_float or **binary_double**	**binary_float, binary_double, char, varchar2, nchar, nvarchar2**
char	**binary_float, binary_double, char, varchar2, number, date, timestamp, interval, raw, rowid, urowid**
varchar2	**binary_float, binary_double, char, varchar2, number, date, timestamp, interval, raw, rowid, urowid**
number	**binary_float, binary_double, char, varchar2, number, date, timestamp, interval, raw, rowid, urowid**
date (includes **date, timestamp, timestamp with timezone, interval day to second,** and **interval year to month**)	**binary_float, binary_double, char, varchar2, number,** interval, nchar, nvarchar2
raw	char, varchar2, raw, nchar, nvarchar2
rowid	char, varchar2, raw, rowid, urowid
urowid	char, varchar2, raw, rowid, urowid
nchar	**binary_float, binary_double, number, nvarchar2**
nvarchar2	**binary_float, binary_double, number, nchar**

```
SELECT CAST('01-JUN-04' AS TIMESTAMP) FROM dual;
SELECT CAST('12' AS NUMBER) FROM dual;
```

ceil
Usage: ceil(*n*)
   The **ceil** function returns the smallest integer value, or ceiling, greater than or equal to *n*.

```
SELECT CEIL(1.5),CEIL(2.0) FROM dual;
```

chartorowid
Usage: chartorowid(*char*)
   The **chartorowid** function is used to convert a character-based ROWID representation to an actual ROWID data type.

```
SELECT empid FROM emp
WHERE ROWID = CHARTOROWID(AAAADDAABAAAAHSAAA');
```

chr
Usage: chr(*n* {using nchar_cs})

The **chr** function takes a **number** argument and returns the character that is equivalent to the binary value passed into the function. The value is returned as a VARCHAR2 equivalent in the database character set or the NLS character set if the **using nchar_cs** keywords are used.

```
SELECT CHR(66) FROM dual;
```

concat
Usage: **concat**(*string1*, *string2*)
The **concat** function returns a string formed by concatenating the two input strings, *string1* with *string2*.

```
SELECT CONCAT('he','llo') FROM dual;
```

The **concat** function as just specified can be unwieldy to use. Instead, many people use the **concat** operator (||). The same example has been written here using the **concat** operator:

```
SELECT 'he'||'llo' FROM DUAL;
```

convert
Usage: **convert**(*char, dest_char_set, {source_char_set}*)
The **convert** function converts a character string value from one character set to another. The *char* argument represents the value to be converted. It can be a CHAR, VARCHAR2, NCHAR, NVARCHAR2, CLOB, or NCLOB data type. The *dest_char_set* argument is the name of the character set that you wish *char* to be converted to. By default, the conversion of the data is based on the database character set. You can use the *source_char_set* parameter to name a character set other than the database character set for the source data character set.

```
SELECT CONVERT('aeiou', 'US7ASCII','WE8EBCDIC500') FROM dual;
```

count
Usage: **count**([DISTINCT|ALL] *expr*)
The **count** function returns the number of rows defined by the expression. The count of rows can be an aggregate or an analytic function. This function never returns NULL.

```
SELECT COUNT(*) FROM emp;
```

decode
Usage: **decode**(*expr, search1, result1,* [*search2, result2, ..., searchn, resultn*] [*default*])
The **decode** function is a little like a **case** operation. It looks at the given expression, *expr,* and if it matches a search condition, *search1,* it returns the given result, *result1.* If the expression does not match the search condition, the next search condition, if present, is examined. If the expression does not match any of the search conditions, the *default* value is returned, if present. There can be a maximum of 255 components in the **decode** statement.

```
SELECT loc,
DECODE(loc,'DALLAS','SOUTHWEST','CHICAGO','MIDWEST','EASTERN')
FROM dept;
```

The preceding example uses the **decode** function to return a geographical location depending on the location in the DEPT table. Dallas is in the Southwest region, and Chicago is in the Midwest region. If the LOC value is neither of these two cities, then the default of the Eastern region is used.

floor

Usage: floor(*n*)

The **floor** function returns the largest integer less than or equal to the argument *n*.

```
SELECT FLOOR(3.14) FROM dual;
```

greatest

Usage: greatest(*expr,expr,...*)

The **greatest** function takes a list of one or more expressions and returns the greatest of those expressions. If the expressions are numbers, the value returned is the largest number in the list. If the expressions are non-numeric, the expressions are all converted to the datatype of the first expression. The character comparison is based on the database character set to find the largest value. The return type is the type of the first expression of the function.

```
SELECT GREATEST('Robert','Jacob','Elizabeth') FROM dual;
```

initcap

Usage: initcap(*string*)

The **initcap** function takes the character input *string* and returns the same string with the initial letter of each word in the string in uppercase, and all other letters in lowercase.

```
SELECT INITCAP('CONVERT ME') FROM dual;
```

instr

Usage: instr(*string, substring* [*,position* [*,occurrence*]])

The **instr** function searches for an occurrence of the given *substring* in the given input *string*. **instr** returns a number denoting the position of the substring within the string. If the substring is not found in the string, then **instr** returns 0. Optionally, the search of the substring can begin in a certain *position* of the string. If *position* is negative, the search starts at the end of the string and goes backward. If *occurrence* is optionally specified, then **instr** searches for that number of occurrences of the substring before returning a value.

```
SELECT INSTR('Hello world','o') FROM dual;
```

least

Usage: least(*expr,expr,...*)

The **least** function takes a list of one or more expressions and returns the least of those expressions. The return type is the type of the first expression of the function.

```
SELECT LEAST('Robert','Jacob','Elizabeth') FROM dual;
```

length
Usage: length(*string*)
> The **length** function returns the number of characters that make up the input *string*.

```
SELECT LENGTH('Hello world') FROM dual;
```

lower
Usage: lower(*string*)
> The **lower** function returns the *string* with all characters converted to lowercase.

```
SELECT LOWER('Hello WORLD') FROM dual;
```

length, lengthb, lengthc, length2, and length4
Usage: length(*char*)
> The **length** function returns the number of characters in *char* in the form of a NUMBER data type. **length** calculates length using characters as defined by the database character set. The other versions of the function use different code sets:

- **lengthb** uses bytes instead of characters.
- **lengthc** uses Unicode complete characters.
- **length2** uses UCS2 code points.
- **length4** uses UCS4 code points.

```
SELECT LENGTH('This is a test') FROM dual;
```

lower
Usage: lower(*char*)
> The **lower** function returns the *char* expression in lowercase. The data type returned is the same data type as the *char* argument.

```
SELECT LOWER('THIS IS A TEST') FROM dual;
```

lpad
Usage: lpad(*expr1, n* [,*expr2*])
> The **lpad** function returns the input string, *expr1*, left padded with characters so that the string becomes *n* characters in length. If the optional second expression, *expr2*, is specified, then *expr1* is left padded with *expr2*. If *expr2* is not specified, then *expr1* is left padded with blank spaces. If *expr1* is longer than *n* characters, then **lpad** returns *expr1* truncated to *n* characters.

```
SELECT LPAD('Hello world',20,'+-') FROM dual;
```

ltrim
Usage: ltrim(*string* [,*set*])

The **ltrim** function returns a string where the left portion of *string* has been trimmed. If the trim *set* is not specified, then **ltrim** removes all spaces on the left side of the input *string*. If the trim *set* is specified, then **ltrim** removes the set of characters from the left side of the input *string*.

```
SELECT LTRIM('+-+-+-Hello World','+-') FROM dual;
```

max
Usage: **max**([DISTINCT|ALL] *expr*)

The **max** function returns the maximum value of the input expression, *expr*. This function can be an aggregate or an analytic function. If the optional **distinct** parameter is specified, then only distinct values are considered. The default is **all**.

```
SELECT MAX(salary) FROM emp;
```

min
Usage: **min**([DISTINCT|ALL] *expr*)

The **min** function returns the minimum value of the input expression, *expr*. This function can be an aggregate or an analytic function. If the optional **distinct** parameter is specified, then only distinct values are considered. The default is **all**.

```
SELECT MIN(salary) FROM emp;
```

mod
Usage: **mod**(*m,n*)

The **mod** function returns the modulus, or remainder, of dividing *m* by *n*. If *n* is 0, then **mod** returns *m*.

```
SELECT MOD(13,2) FROM dual;
```

months_between
Usage: **months_between**(*date1*, *date2*)

The **months_between** function returns the number of months that separate *date1* and *date2*.

```
SELECT MONTHS_BETWEEN(SYSDATE, SYSDATE-60) FROM dual;
```

nullif
Usage: **nullif**(*expr1*, *expr2*)

The **nullif** function returns NULL if the two input expressions, *expr1* and *expr2*, are equal. If the two expressions are not equal, **nullif** returns *expr1*.

```
SELECT NULLIF(empno, mgr) FROM emp;
```

nvl
Usage: **nvl**(*expr1*, *expr2*)

The **nvl** function is used to supply a value in replacement of a NULL value. If *expr1* is NULL, then *expr2* is returned. If *expr1* is not NULL, then **nvl** returns *expr1*.

```
SELECT NVL(mgr,'No Manager') FROM emp;
```

power
Usage: power(*m*, *n*)

The **power** function returns a number where *m* is raised to the nth power. The input parameters can be any numbers. If *m* is negative, then *n* must be an integer.

```
SELECT POWER(2,3) FROM dual;
```

regexp_instr
Usage: regexp_instr(*search_string*, pattern [, position [, occurrence [, *return_option* [, *match_option*]]]]);

The **regexp_instr** function is an extension of the **instr** operator. It searches the input string for the regular expression pattern. Based on the **return_option** setting, the function then returns an integer indicating the position where the match either began or ended. The input value can be any of the following data types: CHAR, VARCHAR2, NCHAR, NVARCHAR2, CLOB, or NCLOB. The regular expression will be converted to the same data type as search value. If the regular expression is a NULL value then the function returns an unknown value.

The usage syntax for **regexp_instr** is shown at the beginning of this section. The function has several parameters including:

- *search_string* is the search value.

- **pattern** is the regular expression to be used; limited to 512 bytes.

- **position** is a positive integer that indicates where the search should begin. This value defaults to 1.

- **occurrence** defines the occurrence of the pattern to search for. The default is 1, meaning that Oracle Database 10g will search for the first occurrence.

- *return_option* is a numeric value that indicates which value should be returned by the function. This can be the beginning position of the match (defined by a zero value) or a non-zero option indicates that the ending position (the position after the character found) should be returned.

- *match_option* is a literal text string that allows you to change the matching behavior of the function. This parameter can consist of one or more of the values, described in the following table:

match_option Value	Description
C	Case-sensitive matching (the default).
I	Case-insensitive matching.
N	Allows the period (.) to match any the newline character.
M	Treats the source string as if it contains multiple lines. This causes Oracle Database 10g to interpret the ^ and $ characters as the start and end for any line anywhere in the source string, rather than treating the entire source string as one big line.

So, let's look at some examples of this function in use. We will use the table TEST_
EXPRESSIONS again. Here is our first example:

```
SELECT * FROM test_expressions
WHERE REGEXP_INSTR(char_value,'b',1, 2, 0) > 0;
```

In this example we are looking for the second occurrence of the character b in the CHAR_
VALUE column.

Of course, we are really not using a regular expression in the preceding example, so let's
do so in the next:

```
SELECT * FROM test_expressions
WHERE REGEXP_INSTR(char_value,'[b-c]',1, 2, 0) > 0;
```

In this example, we have looked for the second occurrence of the character b or c in the
CHAR_VALUE column, which gives us two results. Let's look at another example:

```
SQL> SELECT REGEXP_INSTR('This is a test','[^ ]+', 1, 2)
FROM dual;
```

Note in this example that the function returns the character position after the end of the search
string, not the position of the last character in the search string.

regexp_replace
Usage: regexp_replace(*search_string*, pattern [,replacestr [, position [, occurrence [, *match_
option*]]]]);

The **regexp_replace** function is an extension of the **replace** function. It allows you to search
the input string for the regular expression and, as an output, replace those characters with a
replacement string. The input string value can be any of the following data types: CHAR,
VARCHAR2, NCHAR, NVARCHAR2, CLOB, or NCLOB. The regular expression will be
converted to the same data type as search value.

The usage syntax for **regexp_replace** is shown at the beginning of this section. The function
has several parameters including:

- *search_string* is the search value.

- **pattern** is the regular expression to be used; limited to 512 bytes.

- **replacestr** can be any character type and is the string that will be used to replace the
  search string.

- **position** is a positive integer that indicates where the search should begin. This value
  defaults to 1.

- **occurrence** defines the occurrence of the pattern to search for. The default is 1, meaning
  that Oracle Database 10g will search for the first occurrence.

- *match_option* is a literal text string that allows you to change the matching behavior of
  the function. This parameter can consist of one or more of the values, described in the
  following table:

match_option Value	Description
C	Case-sensitive matching (the default).
I	Case-insensitive matching.
N	Allows the period (.) to match any the newline character.
M	Treat the source string as if it contains multiple lines. This causes Oracle Database 10*g* to interpret the ^ and $ characters as the start and end for any line anywhere in the source string, rather than treating the entire source string as one big line.

So, let's look at some examples of this function in use. Our first example is pretty basic, demonstrating how the function works. In this case, we replace the string "This is the wild west west" with the string "This is the wild west dude":

```
SELECT REGEXP_REPLACE
('this is the wild west west',
'west$','dude') FROM dual;
```

This next example is a bit more complex. It converts existing phone numbers with dashes into a decimal format:

```
Select regexp_replace('206-555-1212',
'([[:digit:]]{3})\-([[:digit:]]{3})\-([[:digit:]]{4})','\1.\2.\3') from dual;
```

In this example, we used what is known as a character class definition (called [:digit:]) to indicate that the range of expressions indicated are digits. So, the first part of the example [[:digit:]]{3} basically patterns three digits and is the same as [0-9]{3}. This convention (which is POSIX compliant) makes it easier to deal with character classes such as lowercase letters or only numeric values.

regexp_substr
Usage: **regexp_substr**(*search_string*, pattern [, position [, occurrence [, *match_option*]]]);

The **regexp_substr** function is an extension of the **substr** function. It allows you to search the input string for the regular expression, and the output is the replacement string. In this way, it is much like the **regexp_instr** function, except that **regexp_substr** returns the actual string rather than a starting or ending position. The input string value can be any of the following data types: CHAR, VARCHAR2, NCHAR, NVARCHAR2, CLOB, or NCLOB. The regular expression will be converted to the same data type as search value.

The usage syntax for **regexp_substr** is shown at the beginning of this section. The function has several parameters including:

- *search_string* is the search value.

- **pattern** is the regular expression to be used; limited to 512 bytes.

- **position** is a positive integer that indicates where the search should begin. This value defaults to 1.

■ **occurrence** defines the occurrence of the pattern to search for. The default is 1, meaning that Oracle Database 10g will search for the first occurrence.

■ *match_option* is a literal text string that allows you to change the matching behavior of the function. This parameter can consist of one or more of the values seen in the following table:

match_option Value	Description
C	Case-sensitive matching (the default).
I	Case-insensitive matching.
N	Allows the period (.) to match any the newline character.
M	Treat the source string as if it contains multiple lines. This causes Oracle Database 10g to interpret the ^ and $ characters as the start and end for any line anywhere in the source string, rather than treating the entire source string as one big line.

So, let's look at some examples of this function in use. In this first example, we are looking for any record that has a b in it as the second occurrence:

```
SQL> SELECT REGEXP_SUBSTR(char_value,'b',1, 2)
  2  FROM test_expressions
  3* WHERE REGEXP_INSTR(char_value,'b',1,2) > 0;
```

In the next example, we want to find all character values with either the letter b or c in them, and then we want to only print out characters in those strings that have b, c, or d values:

```
SQL> SELECT char_value,
  2  REGEXP_SUBSTR(char_value,'([b-d]+/?) {0,5}/?')
  3  FROM test_expressions
  4  WHERE REGEXP_INSTR(char_value,'[b-c]',1,2) > 0;
```

replace
Usage: **replace**(*string, search_string* [,*replacement_string*])
   The **replace** function returns a string where every occurrence of the *search_string* in the input *string* is replaced by the *replacement_string*. If the *replacement_string* parameter is not specified, then **replace** removes all occurrences of the *search_string* in the input *string*.

```
SELECT REPLACE('Todd knows Codd','odd','had') FROM dual;
```

round
Usage: **round**(*n* [,*integer*])
   round(*date,* {*fmt*})
   The **round** function has two different functions. The first returns a number where *n* is rounded to *integer* places to the right of the decimal point. If *integer* is not specified, then **round** returns an integer. The second function rounds the date found in the *date* parameter to the nearest day, or to

the value defined by the date format parameter *fmt*. See the **trunc** function for a table of valid values for *fmt*.

```
SELECT ROUND(3.14) FROM dual;
```

rpad
Usage: rpad(*expr1*, *n* [,*expr2*])
    The **rpad** function returns the input string, *expr1*, right padded with characters so that the string becomes *n* characters in length. If the optional second expression, *expr2*, is specified, then *expr1* is right padded with *expr2*. If *expr2* is not specified, then *expr1* is right padded with blank spaces. If *expr1* is longer than *n* characters, then **rpad** returns the *expr1* truncated to *n* characters. One common usage of **rpad** is to make a simple chart.

```
SELECT salary,RPAD(' ',salary/1000,'*') FROM emp;
```

rowidtochar
Usage: rowidtochar(*rowid*)
    The **rowidtochar** function converts a *rowid* to a character value. The result is always 18 characters in length.

```
SELECT ROWIDTOCHAR(rowid) FROM emp;
```

rpad
Usage: rpad(*expr1*, *n*, {*expr2*})
    The **rpad** function returns *expr1*, which can be a CHAR, VARCHAR2, NCHAR, NVARCHAR2, CLOB, or NCLOB. The return value is returned as a VARCHAR2, which is right padded to a length of *n* with characters from *expr2*.

```
SELECT RPAD(empid,10,'-' ) FROM emp;
```

rtrim
Usage: rtrim(*string* [,*set*])
    The **rtrim** function returns a string where the right portion of *string* has been trimmed. If the trim *set* is not specified, then **rtrim** removes all spaces on the right side of the input *string*. If the trim *set* is specified, then **rtrim** removes the set of characters from the right side of the input *string*.

```
SELECT RTRIM('Hello World!!!!!','!') FROM dual;
```

sign
Usage: **sign**(*n*)
    The **sign** function returns a value denoting the sign of the number *n*. If *n* is negative, then **sign** returns –1. If *n* is 0, then **sign** returns 0. If *n* is positive, then **sign** returns 1.

```
SELECT SIGN(salary-1500) AS over_under_1500 FROM emp;
```

substr

Usage: substr(*string, position* [*,substring_length*])

The **substr** function returns a portion of the given input *string*. The portion of *string* returned starts at character *position* and is *substring_length* characters long. If *substring_length* is not specified, then all characters from *position* to the end of the input *string* are returned. If *position* is positive, then the **substr** function starts counting from the beginning of the *string*. If *position* is negative, then the function starts counting from the end of the *string*, going backward.

```
SELECT SUBSTR('Hello World',7) FROM dual;
```

sum

Usage: sum([DISTINCT|ALL,] *expr*)

The **sum** function returns a number denoting the summation, or addition, of all values in the given input expression, *expr*. If **distinct** is used, then only distinct values in the expression participate in the **sum** operation. The default is to use **all** values. The **sum** function can be an aggregate function or an analytic function.

```
SELECT SUM(salary) AS total_pay FROM emp;
```

sysdate

Usage: sysdate

The **sysdate** function returns the current date and time for the operating system that is running the Oracle database. The return value is of the DATE data type.

```
SELECT SYSDATE FROM dual;
```

to_char

Usage: to_char(*expr*)

The **to_char** function returns a character string for the given expression, *expr*. The *expr* expression can be a character value, a date, or a number. If the input expression is a date, then you can optionally include a format mask. The following tables list and describe the most common format models that are available:

Number Formats:

Format Model	Example	Description
, or .	9,999	Causes the listed value to be displayed in the position defined. Multiple commas are supported.
$	$999.99	Returns a leading dollar sign.
0	0999.99 or 99990	Returns leading or trailing 0's.
999	999.99	Returns the number of digits specified. A negative space is listed if the number is negative; a leading space appears for a positive number.
EEEE	9.9EEEE	Causes the number to be returned using scientific notation.

Format Model	Example	Description
MI	9,999MI	Returns the number with a trailing minus sign.
RN or rn	RN or rn	Returns the values as a roman number in uppercase or lowercase (supports 1 to 3999).
S	S999 or 999S	Causes a positive or negative sign to be placed at the leading or trailing end of the number.

Most Common Datetime Format Models:

Format Model	Meaning
AD or A.D.	Prints the AD indicator with or without periods.
AM or A.M.	Prints the AM indicator with or without periods.
BC or B.C.	Prints the BC indicator with or without periods.
CC or SCC	Prints the century.
D	Returns the numeric day of the week.
DAY	The name of the day of the week (9 characters).
DD	Day of the month.
DDD	Day of the year.
DY	Name of the day.
FF [up to 9]	Fractional seconds. Use numbers 1 to 9 to indicate the precision. Example: ss.ff6.
HH and HH12	Hour of the day (12-hour format).
HH24	Hour of the day (24-hour format).
IW	Week of the year.
IYYY	Four-digit year based on the ISO standard.
J	Julian date, which is the number of days since 1/1/4712 BC.
MI	Minute.
MM	Month (January = 01).
MON	Abbreviated month name.
MONTH	Full name of the month.
PM and P.M.	PM indicator with or without periods.
Q	Quarter of the year.
RM	Roman numeral month.

Format Model	Meaning
RR	Allows for the storage of dates using only two digits. If two digits are between '00' and '49', then current century is assumed. If two digits are between '50' and '99', then previous century is assumed.
SS	Second.
SSSSS	Seconds past midnight.
TZD	Returns daylight savings time information.
TZH or TZM	Returns the time zone hour or minute.
TZR	Returns the time zone region.
WW	Week of the year.
W	Returns the week of the month.

```
SELECT TO_CHAR(hire_date,'MON DD, YYYY') AS hire_date
FROM emp;
SELECT TO_CHAR(salary,'$999,999') FROM emp;
```

to_date
Usage: to_date(*string* [,*format*])

The **to_date** function takes the given input *string* and converts it to a DATE data type. If the *format* is not specified, then the *string* must be in the default date format. If the given *string* is not in the default date format, then you must specify a format that the given *string* is in.

```
SELECT TO_DATE('12/13/1966','MM/DD/YYYY') FROM dual;
```

translate
Usage: translate(*string, from_string, to_string*)

The **translate** function returns the input *string* where all occurrences of *from_string* in *string* are replaced with *to_string*. Any characters in *string* that are not in *from_string* are not replaced.

```
SELECT TRANSLATE('Get*rid*of*asterisks','*',' ') FROM dual;
```

trunc
Usage: trunc(*n* [,*m*])
    trunc(*date*, {*fmt*})

The **trunc** function comes in two flavors. The first returns a number where *n* is truncated to *m* decimal places. If *m* is not specified, then *n* is truncated to an integer value. The second format for the **trunc** function involves the truncation of DATE data types. The *date*, with no specified format model, is truncated to the nearest day, or you can use a format model in the *fmt* parameter to specify how the date should be truncated. The following table contains the valid format models:

Format Model	Result of Truncation
CC or SCC	The resulting date is one greater than the first two digits of a four-digit year.
SYYYY or YYYY or YEAR or SYEAR or YYY or YY or Y	Rounds to the nearest year. Rounds down before July 1.
IYYY or IY or I	Rounds to the ISO year.
Q	Rounds to the nearest quarter. Rounds down before the 16th of the month.
MONTH or MON or MM or RM	Rounds to the month with the 16th of the month being the point at which it rounds down.
WW	Rounds to the same week as the first day of the year.
IW	Rounds to the same week as the first day of the ISO year.
W	Rounds to the same day of the week as the first day of the month.
DDD or DD or J	Rounds to the nearest day.
DAY or DY or D	Rounds to the starting day of the week
HH or HH12 or HH24	Rounds to the nearest hour.
MI	Rounds to the nearest minute.

```
SELECT TRUNC(3.14) FROM dual;
```

upper
Usage: upper(*string*)

The **upper** function returns a string where all characters in the given input *string* are converted to uppercase.

```
SELECT UPPER('Hello World') FROM dual;
```

user
Usage: user

The **user** function returns the username of the current session.

```
SELECT user FROM dual;
```

CHAPTER
15

DML Commands

his chapter covers Oracle DML commands—**insert**, **update**, **delete**, **merge**, **commit**, **rollback**, **savepoint**, and **truncate**. And even though it really isn't a DML command, I have included the **select** command in this chapter as well. The final section of the chapter explains how to write readable DML statements.

The select Command

The **select** command is used to query data from a table, view, or materialized view. A **select** statement contains a number of different elements, which can make it very long and complex. This section describes the most basic elements of a **select** statement, and then presents other elements of the **select** statement. Then, the security requirements relevant to the **select** statement are provided. Finally, this section reviews the error messages that are associated with the **select** statement.

Security Requirements

You can use the **select** command to select data from a table, view, or materialized view if one of the following is true:

- The object is in your own schema.

- You have been granted the **select** privilege on that object.

- You have been granted the **select any table** privilege.

Additionally, if you are selecting from a view, you only need privileges on the view itself. You do not need privileges on the objects underlying the view.

Common Elements in a select Command

The most elemental **select** command frequently contains the following components:

- The **select** list

- The **from** clause

- The **where** clause

The end of the **select** command is terminated, as are other SQL commands, with a semicolon or a forward slash. The preceding fundamental components are presented next in a bit more detail.

The select List

The **select** list provides the list of comma-delimited columns that should be returned by the **select** statement. The columns listed in the **select** list can be prefixed either by the name of the object that the column is derived from or by an alias assigned to that object in the body of the **from** clause (discussed next). Alternatively, you can use an asterisk (*) to indicate that all columns of the object being queried should be returned. All column names can also be aliased as well, by placing the alias name directly after the name of the column. The **select** clause can also contain aggregate functions that allow you to aggregate results.

The elements of the **select** list can be acted upon by functions, and you can control the distinctness of the columns returned by using the **distinct** and **unique** keywords. When using the **distinct** and/or **unique** keywords, the **select** list is limited to a size slightly smaller than the block size of the database. Also, you cannot use the **distinct** keyword if you have any LOB columns in your **select** list.

Within the **select** list, you can also indicate the uniqueness of the records that should be returned. If you have a number of duplicate records, then you can use the **distinct** and/or **unique** keywords to filter out duplicate rows.

The from Clause

The **from** clause allows you to define the objects that the **select** statement will return data from. In a typical **from** clause, each object is listed, delimited by commas. Objects can be aliased by providing the alias immediately following the object name. If two tables contain common column names, and one of the common column names is to be used in the **select** list, then you must alias those tables, and alias the duplicate column names in the **select** list. The **from** clause also allows you to define subqueries in the place of a table. When this is done, the subqueries are much like views and allow for much more complex **select** statements. You can also specify the use of specific partitions within the confines of the **from** clause by using the **partition** or **subpartition** clause. Database links can also be used within the context of the **from** clause to allow for access to remote database data. The database link must be defined before it can be used.

Finally, Oracle9*i* and later supports the use of the ANSI standard join clause within the **from** clause. This includes the **natural join**, **inner join**, **cross join**, and **outer join** keywords.

The where Clause

The **where** clause contains one or more predicates (or conditions) that help determine what rows should be returned by the DML statement being executed. Predicates are expressions and/or Boolean operators that, when applied, restrict the rowset being returned by the database. The **where** clause also provides the join criteria used in the DML statement. The next two sections look at the most important parts of the **where** clause—predicates and joins—in more detail.

Predicates   Several different conditions can be applied within the confines of the **where** clause of a **select** statement. Some Oracle database add-on products, such as Oracle Text, add additional conditions that can be used. The following table provides a list of the most common condition types and examples of each:

Condition Type and Associated Expressions	Notes and Examples
Comparison conditions: =, !=, <, >, >=, <=, **any**, **some**, and **all**	Used to compare two expressions, the comparison resulting in either a true, false, or null. This expression returns any row in the EMP table that has an EMPNO value of 2500: `SELECT * FROM emp WHERE empid=2500;`
	The next example returns all rows from the DEPT table where the DEPT_ID column is not 20: `SELECT * FROM dept WHERE deptid != 20;`

Condition Type and Associated Expressions	**Notes and Examples**
Floating-point conditions: **is nan**, **is not nan**, **is infinite**, and **is not infinite** You can also use the literals **binary_float_nan**, **binary_float_infinity**, **binary_double_nan**, and **binary_double_infinity**	Used to determine if the special floating-point conditions **nan** and **infinite** are present. The first example queries the EMP table for all rows where the SALARY column does not contain the special NAN (not a number) identifier: `SELECT * FROM emp` `WHERE salary IS NOT NAN;` The second example searches for all rows in the EMP table where the SALARY column does not use the special INFINITE identifier: `SELECT * FROM emp` `WHERE salary IS NOT INFINITE;` The next example assumes that the SALARY column is a BINARY_FLOAT and uses the BINARY_FLOAT_INFINITY literal to look for SALARIES that are less than BINARY_FLOAT_INFINITY: `SELECT * FROM emp` `WHERE SALARY < BINARY_FLOAT_INFINITY;`
Logical conditions and compound conditions: **not**, **and**, and **or**	This is a logical conditional expression that searches for all records in EMP where the DEPTID column is not between 10 and 30: `SELECT * FROM emp` `WHERE NOT` `(deptid BETWEEN 10 AND 30);` The following is a logical conditional expression, but it is also a compound conditional expression that uses the **and** operator, to combine two logical conditions in the **where** clause. In this case, we want to find all rows in the EMP table with ENAME_LAST='Freeman' and ENAME_FIRST='Jake': `SELECT empid FROM emp` `WHERE` `ename_last='Freeman'` `AND ename_first='Jake';` The next example is a logical conditional expression, but it is also a compound conditional expression that uses the **or** operator to combine two logical conditions in the **where** clause. In this case, we want to find all rows in the EMP table where the ENAME_LAST column is either 'Freeman' or 'Trezzo': `SELECT * FROM emp WHERE` `ename_last='Freeman' OR` `ename_last='Trezzo';`

Condition Type and Associated Expressions	Notes and Examples

Range conditions: **(not) between** x **and** y	A range expression allows you to determine if an expression is greater than or equal to one condition and less than or equal to another condition. This allows you to determine if a value is contained within a given range of values. This next example is a range expression, which limits EMPID column values in the EMP table to values between 100 and 1000:
	`SELECT * FROM emp`
	`WHERE empid NOT BETWEEN`
	`100 AND 1000;`
	
	In this case, Oracle checks that the EMPID column is greater than or equal to 100, and less than or equal to 1000. Note that this query would give incorrect results if the 100 and 1000 were reversed in the **between** condition.

NULL conditions: **is (not) null**	The NULL condition is used to test for NULL values and is the only condition that should be used to test for NULL values. This query uses a NULL condition that rejects all RETIRE_DATE columns that are NULL:
	`SELECT * FROM emp`
	`WHERE retire_date IS NULL;`

exists	The **exists** condition checks for the existence of rows within a subquery and returns a true if at least one row is returned. This example uses an **exists** expression that will determine if a DEPTID in DEPT exists in the EMP table:
	`SELECT deptid FROM dept d`
	`WHERE EXISTS`
	`(SELECT * FROM emp e`
	`WHERE d.deptid=e.deptid);`

in	The **in** condition checks for membership in a list. This list can be a literal list or derived from a subquery. Here is an example of an **in** list using a literal list. In this case. we want all rows where the DEPTID column in the EMP table is either 10 or 20:
	`SELECT * FROM emp`
	`WHERE deptid IN (10, 20);`
	
	Of course, you can use the **not in** option to achieve the opposite result, as shown in this example:
	`SELECT * FROM emp`
	`WHERE deptid NOT IN (10, 20);`
	
	A subquery can be used in place of the list, as shown in this example:
	`SELECT * FROM emp`
	`WHERE deptid IN`
	`(SELECT deptid FROM dept`
	`WHERE active='Y');`

Condition Type and Associated Expressions	Notes and Examples

like, **likec**, **like2**, and **like4**	The **like** conditions are used to do pattern matching, allowing for more flexible conditional evaluations. **like** uses the input character set, **likec** uses Unicode characters, **like2** uses the UCS2 code points, and **like4** uses the UCS4 code points.
	
	Within a **like** condition, you can use an underscore character to match one character in the value, and you can use a percent sign to match zero or more characters, but not NULL values. Here is an example of using the **like** condition using the % pattern-matching character to find all employees in the EMP table whose name starts with the letters FR and end with any other combination of characters:
	`SELECT empid FROM emp`
	`WHERE ename_last LIKE '%Fr%';`
	
	The next example uses the underscore character to "fill in the blanks":
	`SELECT empid FROM emp`
	`WHERE ename_first LIKE 'J__e';`
	In this case, the query would return values like Jake and Jude.

regexp_like	The **regexp_like** condition is available in Oracle Database 10*g*. It is similar to the **like** condition except that it allows regular expression pattern matching using the POSIX regular expression standard and the Unicode Regular Expression Guidelines. This example looks for all employees with a last name that starts with RIC and ends with S:
	`SELECT ename_last`
	`FROM emp`
	`WHERE regexp_like`
	`(UPPER(ename_last), '^RIC[[:alpha:]]+S$');`
	Note that this condition is only available in Oracle Database version 10*g*. The stored procedure **owa_pattern** is available as an alternative.
	
	*Note: See Chapter 14 for more on the **regexp_instr**, **regexp_substr**, and **regexp_replace** functions.*

NULL and Three-Valued Logic   Be aware of the impact of three-valued logic on conditional expressions. You can end up with results that you might not expect. Take this query as an example:

```
SELECT deptid FROM dept WHERE deptid NOT IN (20, 30, NULL);
```

You might expect to see rows where DEPTID is equal to 10 or perhaps 40, if they exist in the table. Instead, this query returns no rows, because the **not in** clause is evaluated like this:

```
Deptid!=20 AND deptid!=30 AND deptid!=NULL
```

which always evaluates to false, and as a result, no rows.

The correct way to write the preceding query is like this:

```
SELECT deptid FROM dept WHERE deptid NOT IN (20, 30)
AND deptid IS NOT NULL;
```

Conditions have a level of precedence that must be considered. Operators are ordered in the following manner:

- All SQL operators are evaluated before SQL conditions are evaluated. SQL operator precedence is in this order:

  - \+ and – (used as unary operators), **prior**, and **connect_by_root** SQL operators

  - * and **/** SQL operators

  - \+ and – (used as binary operators) and | | SQL operators

- The operators =, !=, <, >, <=, and >=

- The operators **null** and **not null**, **between** and **not between**, **in** and **not in**, and **exists**

- The **not** operator

- The **and** operator

- The **or** operator

Other Elements in a select Command

Now that you are familiar with the basics of the **select** command, this section presents the various other elements that may appear in a **select** command, such as set operators, joins, and expressions.

Set Operators

Set operators are designed to combine the result sets from two or more **select** statements, producing a single result set. When using a set operator, the order, number, and data types of each column in the **select** list must be the same. The names of the columns may differ in each statement, in which case Oracle uses the name of the column in the first statement before the set operator as the default name.

There are four set operators, described in the following table:

Operator Name	Description	Example

union	Joins the two result sets. Duplicate rowsets are eliminated.	`SELECT empid`
		`FROM emp`
		`UNION`
		`SELECT empid`
		`FROM temp_emp;`

union all	Joins the two result sets. Duplicate rowsets are retained.	`SELECT empid`
		`FROM emp`
		`UNION ALL`
		`SELECT empid`
		`FROM temp_emp;`

Operator Name	Description	Example

intersect	Returns only those rows that appear in both queries.	`SELECT empid`
		`FROM emp`
		`INTERSECT`
		`SELECT empid`
		`FROM temp_emp;`

minus	Returns rows that were returned in the first query, but were not returned in the second query.	`SELECT empid`
		`FROM emp`
		`MINUS`
		`SELECT empid`
		`FROM temp_emp;`

There are some restrictions on the use of set operators:

- You cannot use set operators on BLOB, CLOB, BFILE, VARRAY, or nested table columns. Additionally, LONG columns are only supported when using the **union all** operator.

- You must include column aliases for any column that contains an expression if you wish to use the **order by** clause in the SQL statement.

- The **for update** clause is not supported when using set operators.

- You cannot use the **order by** clause within a subquery of any SQL statement that uses operators.

Joins

A query that combines rows from more than one table is known as a join. A join generally involves the following:

- Columns from multiple tables in the join list

- Multiple tables in the **from** clause

- Column comparisons in the **where** clause, known as a *join condition*

When the query is executed, Oracle combines the rows in each table, based on the join condition. The following example joins the EMP table and the DEPT table by the DEPTID column, in order to print each employee name and the department name that the employee is assigned to:

```
SELECT ename_last, dept_name
FROM emp a, dept b
WHERE a.deptid=b.deptid;
```

If the tables you are joining to have common column names, you need to alias those columns, as shown in this example where the DEPTID column is present in both the EMP and DEPT tables:

```
SELECT ename_last, a.deptid, dept_name
FROM emp a, dept b
WHERE a.deptid=b.deptid;
```

More complex joins may involve multiple tables and multiple join criteria. Also, failure to properly define the join conditions in a query can result in a Cartesian product where each row of each table is joined together. There are a number of different join types, as shown in the following table:

Join Type	Description and Example

Equi-join (or inner join)	This is a join of all rows in one table to matching rows in another table. If matching rows are not found, then neither row will be displayed. Here is an example of an equi-join that joins equivalent rows in the EMP table to those in the DEPT table:
	
	`SELECT a.ename_last, a.ename_first, b.dept_name`
	`FROM emp a, dept b`
	`WHERE a.deptid=b.deptid;`
	
	This join is based on the DEPTID column. If there are rows in the EMP table that do not have a matching DEPT record, they will not be displayed. Likewise, if there are rows in the DEPT table without related rows in the EMP table, they will not be displayed. This can have unexpected consequences on your queries, as rows you might expect to appear might not.
	
	Oracle also supports the ANSI standard **join** clause, as shown in this example:
	
	`SELECT a.ename_last, a.ename_first, b.dept_name`
	`FROM emp a JOIN dept b`
	`ON a.deptid=b.deptid;`

Self join	A self join involves a join of a table to itself. The table appears at least twice in the **from** clause in a self join, and the **where** clause contains the criteria that define the join condition. Here is an example of a self join:
	
	`SELECT a.ename_last emp_last_name,`
	`a.ename_first emp_first_name,`
	`b.ename_last mgr_last_name,`
	`b.ename_first mgr_first_name`
	`FROM emp a, emp b`
	`WHERE a.manager=b.empid;`

Outer join using the (+) clause	An outer join is a superset of a regular join in that it returns all rows that satisfy the join conditions from one table as a part of the overall join operation. The result is that some of the join columns may be NULL in the result set. A join can be a right outer join, a left outer join, or a full join.
	
	Oracle provides two different types of syntax for outer joins. The first is the (+) operator, which is applied to the join condition in the **where** clause. This operator supports both left and right outer joins, but not a full join. The second syntax is the ANSI outer join syntax, which is covered in the next two rows of this list.
	
	To use the (+) operator, apply the operator to the join conditions associated with the table that you wish all the rows to be returned from, as in this example:
	
	`SELECT a.empid, b.dept_name`
	`FROM emp a, dept b`
	`WHERE a.deptid=b.deptid (+);`
	
	In this example, you will see all employees in the EMP table, including those not assigned to a department.

Join Type	Description and Example

Outer join using the **outer join** clause	Oracle9*i* and later also supports the ANSI **outer join** syntax, which is supported by the **right outer join** and **left outer join** clauses.
	
	These clauses provide a much more robust ability than the **(+)** join clause to perform outer joins within Oracle, and Oracle recommends the use of the **outer join** clause instead. Here is an example of using the **left outer join** clause in a query:
	`SELECT a.empid, b.dept_name`
	`FROM emp a LEFT OUTER JOIN dept b`
	`ON a.deptid=b.deptid;`
	In this case, the outer join is performed on the DEPT table, the result of which will be a NULL value in the DEPT_NAME column for any employee that is not assigned to a department.

Full join	Available in Oracle9*i* and later, full joins allow for a two-sided outer join where rows from both tables that are not returned as a result of the inner join are preserved and displayed in the query using NULL values. Here is an example of a full join:
	`SELECT a.empid, b.dept_name`
	`FROM emp a FULL OUTER JOIN dept b`
	`ON a.deptid=b.deptid;`
	The result of this join is the display of all EMPID records, including those not assigned to a department. Also included will be any department that is not assigned to any employee.

Antijoin	An antijoin is performed using the **not in** clause, in the predicate of a SQL statement. It is used to remove rows from the result set when there are no corresponding rows contained as a result of the **not in** clause. Here is an example of an antijoin:
	`SELECT empid FROM emp`
	`WHERE deptid NOT IN`
	`(SELECT deptid FROM dept`
	`WHERE active!='N');`
	In this example, Oracle returns all employee IDs that are assigned to an invalid department ID. Antijoins are not possible if they are part of an **or** branch within a **where** clause.

Semijoin	A semijoin involves the use of an **exists** clause that provides a list of rows where the right side of the predicate has multiple rows that match a single row on the left side:
	`SELECT * FROM dept WHERE EXISTS`
	`(SELECT * FROM emp`
	` WHERE emp.deptid=dept.deptid`
	` AND emp.salary > 100);`

NOTE
See Chapter 14 for more information on built-in functions that you can use in Oracle DML statements.

Expressions

Oracle supports the use of expressions. An expression allows you to evaluate the combination of values, operators, and functions. Expressions can be used in a number of places, including the following:

- In the **select** list of a **select** statement
- In one or more conditions of a **where** clause
- Within the **having** clause
- Within the **connect by** clause
- Within the **start with** clause
- Within the **order by** clause
- In the **values** clause of an **insert** statement
- In the **set** clause of an **update** statement

There are a number of different kinds of expressions within Oracle, including:

- Simple expressions
- Compound expressions
- Case expressions
- Date/time expressions
- Function expressions
- Interval expressions
- Scalar subquery expressions

The following sections look at these types of expressions in a bit more detail.

Simple Expressions   Simple expressions define a column, pseudo column, Oracle-defined constant, sequence number, or a NULL. The following are some examples of the use of simple expressions. The first example is a text simple expression:

```
SELECT 'This is a simple text expression' FROM dual;
```

Simple expressions include pseudo columns such as ROWNUM and ROWID, as shown in this example:

```
SELECT rowid, empid FROM emp WHERE ROWNUM < 5;
```

Oracle provides a number of pseudo columns that you can use. The following table lists the valid pseudo columns and their purpose:

Pseudo Column Name	Purpose
CONNECT BY ISCYCLE	When used in a hierarchical query, this pseudo column returns a 0 if the current row does not have a child that is also its ancestor.
CONNECT BY ISLEAF	When used in a hierarchical query, this pseudo column returns a 0 if the current row is not a leaf of the tree defined via the **connect by** condition. You can use this pseudo column to determine if a given row can be expanded to show more of the hierarchy.
LEVEL	When used in a hierarchical query, this pseudo column returns a 1 for a root row, a 2 for a child of a root, and subsequent numbers for children at lower levels.
CURRVAL	Used to return the current value assigned to a sequence.
NEXTVAL	Used to increment the sequence and return the next value.
VERSIONS_STARTTIME	Returns the timestamp of the first version of the queried row. Valid only when using Oracle Flashback Version Query in Oracle Database 10*g*.
VERSIONS_STARTSCN	Returns the SCN of the first version of the queried row. Valid only when using Oracle Flashback Version Query in Oracle Database 10*g*.
VERSIONS_ENDTIME	Returns the timestamp of the first version of the queried row. Valid only when using Oracle Flashback Version Query in Oracle Database 10*g*.
VERSIONS_ENDSCN	Returns the SCN of the last version of the queried row. Valid only when using Oracle Flashback Version Query in Oracle Database 10*g*.
VERSIONS_XID	Returns the transaction ID (which is a RAW number) of the transaction that created that row version. Valid only when using Oracle Flashback Version Query in Oracle Database 10*g*.
VERSIONS_OPERATION	Returns a single character representing the operation that caused the row version for each row. Values returned include I – **insert** operation U – **update** operation D – **delete** operation
OBJECT_ID	Returns the OID of the column of an object table or view. This pseudo column is used as the primary key of an object table.
OBJECT_VALUE	Returns system-generated names for the columns of an object table.
ORA_ROWSCN	Returns the upper-bound system change number of the most recent change to the row. This allows you to roughly determine when the row was last updated.
ROWID	This is an address that is unique to each row.
ROWNUM	Each row in a result set has a **ROWNUM** associated with it. This value indicates the order of the row when Oracle selects it from either the table or the join rowset. Note that clauses such as **order by** affect the **ROWNUM** order of rows in a rowset.
XMLDATA	Allows you to access XML-related information.

Compound Expressions   A compound expression allows you to combine string expressions or perform calculations. The following are examples of valid compound expressions:

```
SELECT 10+20 FROM dual;
SELECT ename_first||' '||ename_last FROM emp;
```

Case Expressions   Case expressions allow you to apply an if-then-else logic to a SQL statement in a non-procedural way. Oracle provides two different types of case expressions, the simple case expression and a searched case expression.

When using a simple case expression, you pass the expression a single value. Oracle searches the case expression for a match to that value and assigns the resulting expression. For example, the query

```
SELECT ename_first, ename_last,
CASE deptid
WHEN 10 THEN 'Acounting'
WHEN 20 THEN 'Sales'
ELSE 'None'
END FROM emp;
```

tests the DEPTID column (which is a simple expression) for a value of 10 and, if it has a value of 10, returns the value Accounting.

A searched case expression allows you to pass a condition, and then tests that condition, returning the results of that test. For example, the query

```
SELECT ename_first, ename_last,
CASE WHEN deptid > 20
     THEN 'department ID is greater than 20'
ELSE 'None'
END from emp;
```

checks the department ID to determine if it is greater than 20. If it is, text will be returned indicating that the department ID is greater than 20, otherwise the **else** clause displays a message indicating that the department ID is less than or equal to 20.

Date/Time Expressions   A date/time expression allows you to convert a given date/time datatype value into new date/time values. Using the **time zone** clause, you can convert the local date into a date/time based on another time zone. For example, to query the current system date at eastern standard time, you could use the **at time zone** expression as follows:

```
SELECT TO_TIMESTAMP(SYSDATE)
AT TIME ZONE 'EST' FROM dual;
```

Of course, the default is the current session time zone. The **at time zone** clause also allows you to use the database time zone setting (using the **dbtimezone** keyword), or you can use the session time zone setting (using the **sessiontimezone** keyword) to cause the time to be displayed based on the time zone setting of the session. Here are examples of these two clauses in use:

```
SELECT TO_TIMESTAMP(SYSDATE)
AT TIME ZONE DBTIMEZONE FROM dual;
SELECT TO_TIMESTAMP(SYSDATE)
AT TIME ZONE SESSIONTIMEZONE FROM dual;
```

You can also indicate a time zone offset from UTC by using the + or − symbol along with the offset value, as shown in this example:

```
SELECT TO_TIMESTAMP(SYSDATE) AT
TIME ZONE '+02:00' FROM dual;
```

You can combine date/time expressions with interval expressions to derive a new date/time value. Date/times and intervals can be combined in a number of different ways, as shown in this table:

Operator	Expression	Result
+	Date/time+interval or interval+date/time	Date/time
+	Interval+interval	Interval
−	Date/time–interval	Date/time
−	Date/time–date/time	Interval
−	Interval–interval	Interval
*	Numeric*interval	Interval
/	Interval/numeric	Interval

Here are some examples of date/time calculations:

```
SELECT TO_TIMESTAMP(SYSDATE)+ INTERVAL '1' DAY FROM dual;
SELECT TO_TIMESTAMP(SYSDATE)+ INTERVAL '1' HOUR FROM dual;
SELECT INTERVAL '1' HOUR+INTERVAL '1' DAY FROM dual;
```

Function Expressions   You can use Oracle built-in functions or user-defined functions as expressions in Oracle SQL statements. These are known as function expressions. See Chapter 14 for a list of Oracle built-in functions that you can use in function expressions.

Interval Expressions   An interval expression allows you to return a value as either a year-to-month interval or a day-to-second interval. For example, if you want to know how many years and months have passed since a given employee retired, you might use this query:

```
SELECT (SYSTIMESTAMP - retire_date) YEAR TO MONTH
FROM emp WHERE retire_date IS NOT NULL;
```

Scalar Subquery Expressions   A scalar subquery expression is a subquery contained in the **select** list that is used to return a single value. Here is an example of a scalar subquery expression:

```
SELECT (SELECT MAX(salary) max_salary FROM emp) max_sal,
empid, ename_last, salary
FROM emp;
```

This query displays the maximum salary paid to any employee beside each specific employee salary record.

Expression Lists

An expression list allows you to combine multiple expressions into a single expression. These expressions can appear in comparison conditions, in membership conditions, and in the **group by** clause in a query or subquery. You can include up to 1000 comma-delimited expressions, as in this example:

```
SELECT empid FROM emp
WHERE (ename_first, ename_last, manager) IN
( ('Robert', 'Freeman',NULL), ('Jake','Freeman', 1) );
```

Subqueries

More complex queries may well require subqueries to solve them. Thus, a subquery is a query that is nested within the text of a query and that is used to provide information needed by the calling (parent) query. Subqueries are used to define rowsets or values for a number of different types of statements, including **insert**, **update**, **delete**, and **select** statements. Subqueries can be found in the **from** clause, where they act much like a view, in the **where** clause, where they provide values for the predicates in the **where** clause, or in the body of the statement, such as with the **create table as select** statements. Here is an example of a subquery:

```
SELECT empid
FROM emp
WHERE deptid IN (SELECT deptid FROM dept WHERE active='Y');
```

In this example, the subquery is contained within the parentheses. The subquery executes first, returning all valid rows to the **where** clause of the query.

A correlated subquery is executed when a subquery nested in the body of a query references one or more columns in the table being referenced in the parent query. Correlated subqueries can be nested very deeply, and are evaluated once for each row processed by the parent statement. Here is an example of a correlated subquery:

```
SELECT empid, ename_last, salary, comm
FROM emp a
WHERE salary*.10 >  (SELECT AVG(comm) FROM emp z
WHERE a.deptid=z.deptid);
```

The subquery-factoring clause (available in Oracle9*i* and later) allows you to define a subquery block at the beginning of a statement, and then you can reference that subquery block later in the SQL statement. This clause is available in both parent-level **select** statements and any subqueries that might be nested within the parent query. The scope of the block is from the query that the block is defined in down to any children.

The subquery factoring clause occurs at the beginning of a **select** statement with the use of the **with** clause, followed by an assigned variable and the associated subquery. Here is an example of the use of a subquery factoring clause:

```
WITH avg_dept_sales AS (
SELECT a.deptid, avg(b.sales_amt) avg_sales
FROM emp a, dept_sales b
WHERE a.deptid=b.deptid
GROUP BY a.deptid),
emp_salaries AS
(SELECT empid, AVG(salary) avg_salary FROM emp
GROUP BY empid)
SELECT * FROM emp_salaries b WHERE avg_salary*.05 >
(SELECT avg_sales FROM avg_dept_sales);
```

Hints

A **select** statement (and other DML statements as well) can contain hints. These hints are used to help the Oracle optimizer produce the most efficient execution plan for the query. There are a number of different hints available for use in Oracle. See Chapter 12 for more information on hints and how to use them. Here is an example of the use of a hint within a **select** statement:

```
SELECT /*+ INDEX (a, emp_last_name_ix) */ empid
FROM emp a WHERE ename_last='Freeman';
```

Sorting Clauses

The **order by** clause is used to sort the result set before it is output to the user. For most queries, you can use the column names within the confines of the **order by** clause to define which columns you wish to sort by, as shown in this example:

```
SELECT empid, TO_CHAR(retire_date, 'MM/DD/YYYY')
FROM emp
WHERE retire_date IS NOT NULL
ORDER BY retire_date;
```

The **order by** clause comes with a few options to consider. You can sort in either ascending (**asc** keyword, the default) or descending (**desc** keyword) order, and you can choose to sort NULL values either at the top of the rowset or at the bottom of the rowset.

Grouping Clauses

Grouping, or aggregating, of data is generally performed using the **group by** clause. Oracle groups the rows based on the grouping expressions used in the **select** statement (such as **sum**, **avg**, or **count**) and return a single row for the defined group. Grouping can be multidimensional if either the **cube** or **rollup** clause is used. Note that the **group by** clause has no interest in ordering of the result set—that is the job of the **order by** clause. Here is an example of a **select** statement using the **group by** clause:

```
SELECT deptid, AVG(salary) avg_salary
FROM emp
GROUP BY deptid;
```

The **having** clause is a handy option to the **group by** clause that allows you to restrict the result set to only those rows that meet a specific criteria. For example, if you are looking for duplicate rows in your EMP table, you might issue this query:

```
SELECT empid, COUNT(*)
FROM emp
GROUP BY empid
HAVING COUNT(*) > 1;
```

The result of this query is that only those employee IDs that appear more than once will be displayed.

You can also perform a rollup to derive subtotal values for the rows of your query. The next example does just that, rolling up sales by department, state, and finally region:

```
SELECT a.store_id, b.deptid, a.state, a.region, SUM(b.sales_amt)
FROM stores a, store_sales b
WHERE a.store_id=b.store_id
GROUP BY ROLLUP(a.store_id, b.deptid, a.state, a.region);
```

You can also roll up on a partial column list, as shown in this example, which rolls up sales only by region and state:

```
SELECT a.store_id, b.deptid, a.state, a.region, SUM(b.sales_amt)
FROM stores a, store_sales b
WHERE a.store_id=b.store_id
GROUP BY a.store_id, b.deptid, rollup(a.state, a.region);
```

Another option is to use the **group by cube** syntax, which results in generation of all possible subtotals that could be calculated for a given data cube's dimensions. For example, if you cube state and region, the result is all the results you would get using the rollup grouping, plus additional combinations. Here is an example of using the **group by cube** clause:

```
SELECT a.store_id, b.deptid, a.state, a.region, SUM(b.sales_amt)
FROM stores a, store_sales b
WHERE a.store_id=b.store_id
GROUP BY CUBE(a.store_id, b.deptid, a.state, a.region);
```

In this example, you will find many more combinations displayed than with the **rollup** clause. The result is a ready-made multidimensional summary of all the possible combinations of data derived from the query.

Hierarchical Queries

Oracle provides some unique syntax to allow you to select rows in a hierarchical order within a table. Oracle provides a number of Oracle-specific (i.e., not ANSI compliant) keywords, expressions, and operators that make hierarchical queries easier to manage. The following table provides documentation of these:

Expression	Use
start with	Defines the parent row of the hierarchy.
connect by	The **connect by** expression defines the relationship between the parent and child rows in the hierarchical query. The **connect by** expression contains two or more conditions, at least one of which must contain the **prior** operator (multiple **prior** operators are allowed). The **prior** keyword indicates to Oracle which column Oracle should use as the parent in the hierarchical relationship.
nocycle	This optional parameter allows Oracle to return rowsets even if there are circular relationships within the hierarchy. If this parameter is not used, the query will fail if there are circular relationships.

Oracle also provides specific functions and pseudo columns that you can use within hierarchical queries:

Name	Purpose
connect_by_iscycle	Returns a 0 if the current row is not a child that is also its ancestor. This is useful if there is a looping structure built into the data being queried. This pseudo column should be used when the **connect by nocycle** syntax is used.
sys_connect_by_path	Returns the hierarchal path of the row from the root to the row being displayed. Each step in the path is delimited by a value defined in the pseudo column.
connect_by_isleaf	Returns a 0 if the current row is not a child record as determined by the **connect by** condition. Otherwise a 1 is returned. A value of 1 essentially indicates the hierarchical relationship can go deeper.
connect_by_root	Returns the root value of the hierarchy for that row.
level	Returns the depth of the row being returned from the root row. The root is always at level one, and subsequent children records start at a level of two and higher.
siblings	This keyword, used within the **order by** clause, causes Oracle to preserve the order of the rows within the hierarchy. Thus, the first level of the hierarchy appears at the top of the query, then the second level (ordered by the columns in the **order by** clause), then the third level, and so forth.

The following are some examples of hierarchical queries in action. The first example has a table called PARTS. In the PARTS table there are component parts, and parts made up of those component parts. This example takes part number 100 and explodes out its individual component parts:

```
SELECT part_id, description, master_component, level
FROM parts
START WITH part_id=100
CONNECT BY PRIOR part_id= master_component
ORDER SIBLINGS BY part_id;
```

The following shows an example of how to use the **nocycle** parameter to code a query to handle a suspected recursive looping condition:

```
SELECT part_id, description, master_component, level
FROM parts
START WITH part_id=100
CONNECT BY NOCYCLE PRIOR part_id= master_component
ORDER SIBLINGS BY part_id;
```

The model Clause

The **model** clause, available in Oracle Database 10g and later, allows you to treat Oracle result sets like a spreadsheet. With the **model** clause, you can cause Oracle to do interrow calculations within the SQL statement. The **model** clause allows you to define cell assignments. You can then assign rules that cause calculations to occur on specific cells or ranges of cells. You can create views and materialized views using the **model** clause as well.

Flashback Elements

Flashback query allows you to query data within an Oracle table as it looked at a specific point in time. The **flashback_query** clause is available in Oracle Database 10g. It is also available in Oracle9i in a somewhat less functional version.

In Oracle9i, you could indicate that a given **select** statement should return rows as of a specific SCN or timestamp by using the **flashback_query** clause. Use of the **flashback_query** clause also requires that the user have the **flashback** object privilege or the **flashback any table** privilege. You cannot issue flashback queries on remote objects (though you can join local flashback objects to remote objects in a non-flashback mode). Here is an example of the use of a flashback query using the **flashback_query** clause:

```
SELECT empid, salary FROM emp
AS OF TIMESTAMP(SYSTIMESTAMP - INTERVAL '1' DAY)
WHERE empid=20;
```

In the previous example, we want to find out what the value of the SALARY column for EMPID 20 was a day ago. This example uses the **flashback_query** clause (in the form of the **as of timestamp** keywords) to indicate the time to flash back to.

In Oracle Database 10g the **flashback_query_clause** contains the same elements as the **flashback_query** clause, plus the addition of the **versions between** keywords, as shown in the following example. The **versions between** keywords allow you to look at data as it existed within a specific period of time.

```
SELECT empid, salary FROM emp
VERSIONS BETWEEN
TIMESTAMP SYSTIMESTAMP - INTERVAL '1' DAY AND
SYSTIMESTAMP - INTERVAL '1' HOUR
WHERE empid=20;
```

Note that flashback query is very sensitive to the availability of undo to reconstruct the records that you desire. This implies that you need to set the **undo_retention** parameter high enough to allow Oracle to generate a consistent image needed for the flashback query.

The sample Clause

The **sample** clause allows you to generate a random sample of data from a table. This can be handy if you wish to create a test database with a subset of data. You can have Oracle perform either random row sampling (the default) or random block sampling (by including the **block** keyword). The **sample_percent** clause indicates the percentage of data you wish Oracle to return. Valid values for **sample_percent** are .000001 to any value less than 100. If you want to eliminate much of the variability in the rows returned, use the **seed** keyword to cause Oracle to use the same seed value for each execution using the **seed** keyword. While there may be some variability (particularly if the data is changing), using the **seed** keyword will reduce it a great deal. Note that if you select a small percentage, you may end up getting no rows returned.

In this example, we sample 10 percent of the rows in the EMP table:

```
SELECT * FROM emp SAMPLE (10);
```

Partitioned Outer Joins

Data tends to be sparse at times. For example, if you have a store and it's closed on Sundays, there is no sales data for Sunday to query. Sometimes, though, you may not want your data to be queried in sparse format; instead, you may want Oracle to "fill in the gaps." That is what a partitioned outer join is for. Using the **partition by** clause, you can cause Oracle to partition your rows logically in the query, and return those rows that don't have values associated with the join criteria.

In the following example, we want to make sure that we have sales numbers for every day for every store, even though some of our stores are closed on Sundays. We use a partitioned outer join to fill in the missing data from the stores that are closed on Sundays. First, we use the **partition by** clause to indicate that we want to partition this data by STORE_ID; that is, we want to make sure that for every STORE_ID, we get a sales record for that store, even if the store is closed on Sunday, in which case a NULL value is returned. We then use the **right outer join** keyword to create a join to the STORE_SALES table again, this time to get the distinct sales dates that are present in the STORE_SALES table. This allows Oracle to fill in the missing data. Of course, if no stores were open on Sunday, and no Sunday dates were in the STORE_SALES table, we would still have missing Sunday dates.

```
SELECT z.sales_date, s.store_id, s.sales_amt
FROM store_sales s
PARTITION BY (s.store_id)
RIGHT OUTER JOIN
(SELECT DISTINCT sales_date FROM store_sales
 WHERE sales_date BETWEEN SYSDATE AND SYSDATE - 10) z
ON (s.sales_date=z.sales_date)
ORDER BY z.sales_date;
```

The for update Clause   The **for update** clause allows you to lock the rows selected by your query in preparation for a later update of some or all of those selected rows. The lock is released at the end of the transaction. You can use the **for update of** clause to indicate which tables you wish to lock if your query is a join. You can also use the **nowait** or **wait** option to indicate whether or not you wish the **select** statement to wait for row-level locks held by other sessions to be released. Here is an example that queries the EMP table in preparation for salary updates:

```
SELECT a.empid, a.ename_last, b.dept_name, a.salary
FROM emp a, dept b
WHERE sal_review_dt < sysdate - 180
AND a.deptid=b.deptid
FOR update of a.salary;
```

This statement can be used in combination with the **where current of** clause in PL/SQL code blocks to create a cursor that can be fetched from and modified.

Materialized Views   If a materialized view is available that matches (or, in some cases, closely matches) the **select** statement being issued, then Oracle will try to use that materialized view instead of the **select** statement. This process is called query rewrite, and is subject to a number of restrictions.

Select Statement Performance   Performance of **select** statements is sensitive to a number of factors:

- The optimizer being used
- Statistics gathered for the tables being queried
- Available performance structures, such as indexes
- Physical issues such as slow disk response times
- Database configuration such as the buffer cache or the shared pool

It is important to tune your database and your SQL statements so that they are as efficient as possible. Oracle Press has a number of good books on tuning Oracle databases and SQL statements that you will want to reference, such as *Oracle Wait Interface: A Practical Guide to Performance Diagnostics & Tuning* (McGraw-Hill, 2004) and *Oracle9i Performance Tuning Tips & Techniques* (McGraw-Hill, 2003).

select Command–Related Error Messages

As you use the **select** command, you may run into various Oracle errors. The following table lists the most common errors and provides some advice as to what to do in the event you run into those errors.

Oracle Error Message	Text Description	Possible Causes and Solutions
ORA-00904	Invalid identifier	You have used a column name that does not exist. Check the spelling of the column name, and make sure that it actually exists in the object being queried. Certain types of syntax errors in your **select** statement can also cause this.
ORA-00905	Missing Keyword	There is an error in your **select** statement. Correct the error and try again.
ORA-00923	FROM keyword not found where expected	This is most often caused by a syntax error in the **select** clause of your SQL statement. Review the **select** clause of the SQL statement and correct the error. Often this can be because of errant characters in the **select** clause, or missed characters.

Oracle Error Message	Text Description	Possible Causes and Solutions
ORA-00933	SQL Command not properly ended	You did not end the **select** statement with a semi-colon or with a forward slash. This message can also be caused by syntax errors in the **select** command itself.
ORA-00942	Table or view does not exist	You have tried to query a table that does not exist in your schema. You might also have tried to query a table or view that is in another schema that you do not have access rights to. Check to make sure that the object you are trying to access really exists. If it does, make sure that your SQL statement is correct. If it is, make sure you actually have access to that object.
SP2-0734	Unknown command…rest of line ignored	You likely have misspelled the **select** keyword. Check your SQL command and correct the error.

The insert Command

The **insert** command can be used to add rows to a table (partitioned or nonpartitioned) or to the base table of a view. The rows inserted are not visible to other users until the **commit** command (or an implied commit) is issued.

Security Requirements

To use the **insert** command to insert a row into a table, the table must be in your own schema. If the table is not in your own schema, you must have had the **insert** object privilege granted to the schema you are using, or you must have the **insert any table** system privilege. You can also insert rows into one of the base tables of a given view through the view. To do so, you must either own the view and the base tables or have the **insert** object privilege on the view and the base table being inserted into.

Specifics of the insert Command

This section contains specific information on the formation of the **insert** command. In this section, we look at basic **insert** statements and then look at more complex **insert** statements.

Basic insert Statement

A basic **insert** statement inserts one row into an object. More advanced forms of the **insert** statement can insert many rows into an object. The basic **insert** statement contains the **insert** command, any hints that might be needed, the **insert into** clause, and then the **values** clause. The result is something like this:

```
INSERT INTO dept (deptid, dept_name, active)
VALUES (100, 'Marketing', 'Y');
```

In this case, we are inserting a record into an object called DEPT, which might be a table, view, or materialized view. In the **insert into** clause, we define the columns where we are inserting our data; in this example, we are inserting it into the DEPTID, DEPT_NAME, and ACTIVE columns.

The **values** clause then defines the data values we are inserting into the rows; in this case, the data values are 100, Marketing, and Y.

The **insert into** clause need not contain the names of the columns if you are inserting into each column of the table, and the values are being inserted in the same order of the columns in the table. Thus, the previous **insert** statement could be rewritten like this:

```
INSERT INTO dept VALUES (100, 'Marketing', 'Y');
```

Note that it is often considered a best practice to list each column you are inserting into.

More Complex insert Statements
You can, of course, have much more complex **insert** statements:

- **insert** statements can contain subqueries that define the data to be inserted.

- **insert** statements can insert data into multiple tables.

- If default values have been defined for a table, you can write the **insert** statement to indicate that the default values should be used using the **default** keyword.

- Values can actually be returned from an **insert** statement by using the **returning** clause.

- If you are inserting into a partitioned table, you can define the partition and subpartition of that table to insert data into.

- **insert** statements can take advantage of Oracle's direct mode insert option.

The following sections describe these additional **insert** features in some more detail.

Using Subqueries in Your insert Command   You can use subqueries in your **insert** command to cause data to be moved from one database object (table, view, etc.) to the object you are inserting into. The subquery can also be used to transform the data during the move process. Here is an example of using a subquery in an **insert** statement:

```
INSERT INTO emp_history SELECT * FROM emp a
WHERE a.empid NOT IN (SELECT empid FROM emp_history);
```

This statement inserts into the EMP_HISTORY table any records from the EMP table that do not already exist in the EMP_HISTORY table. Note that the number of columns in the **select** list of the subquery must match the number of columns listed in the **insert** command. For example, consider this SQL statement:

```
INSERT INTO emp_history (empid)
SELECT * FROM emp a
WHERE a.empid NOT IN (SELECT empid FROM emp_history);
```

This statement will fail if the EMP table has more than one column in it, since the **select** list contains the * wildcard character, which will cause the subquery to return all rows in the EMP table.

It is often a better practice to write **insert** statements using subqueries that return the exact column names, as shown in this example:

```
INSERT INTO emp_history (empid)
SELECT empid FROM emp a
WHERE a.empid NOT IN (SELECT empid FROM emp_history);
```

Subqueries can contain aggregate functions, model expressions, or hierarchical clauses (all of which were discussed earlier in this chapter), as shown in this example:

```
INSERT INTO emp_pay_summary
SELECT empid, sum(gross_pay) FROM emp_pay_history
GROUP BY empid;
```

Multitable Inserts Multitable **insert** statements allow you to insert rows into one or more tables. This is quite handy if you wish to insert the contents of a denormalized structure into a more normalized structure. You can use an unconditional multitable insert by using the **all** clause of the **insert** command or you can use the **when** clause (up to 127 are allowed) followed by specific conditions to determine whether or not a specific insert should occur. Optional clauses are provided for. These include the **else** clause, which provides for a default action if none of the **when** clause criteria is met, and the **first** clause, to indicate that only the first **when** clause criteria that is met should be executed (other **when** clauses will be skipped).

Multitable inserts have the following limitations:

- Multitable inserts are supported only on tables; they cannot be performed on views or materialized views.

- Multitable inserts are not supported for remote operations.

- You cannot use more than 999 target columns in all of the **insert into** clauses.

- The subquery that you use in the multitable insert cannot use any sequence numbers.

- You cannot parallelize a multitable insert in a RAC environment.

- Multitable inserts will fail if the table that is the destination of the **insert** operation is an index-organized table or if the table being inserted into has a bitmap index.

The following are some examples of multitable insert operations. The first example moves data from a flattened, denormalized table called STORE_SALES_LOAD to a normalized table called STORE_SALES. In STORE_SALES_LOAD, all the sales for a given store for a given week are on one row. You can see the structure of the table in the following output:

```
SQL> desc store_sales_load
 Name                                      Null?    Type
 ----------------------------------------- -------- -------
 STORE_ID                                           NUMBER
 MON_SALES                                          NUMBER
 TUE_SALES                                          NUMBER
```

```
WED_SALES                                    NUMBER
THUR_SALES                                   NUMBER
FRI_SALES                                    NUMBER
SAT_SALES                                    NUMBER
SUN_SALES                                    NUMBER
START_DATE                                   DATE
END_DATE                                     DATE
DEPTID                                       NUMBER
```

In the following example, we want to process a single row that contains a week's worth of sales data and **insert** seven separate records into the STORE_SALES table, one for each day of the week. We use a multitable insert to perform this action, as shown here:

```
INSERT ALL
INTO store_sales (store_id, sales_date, deptid, sales_amt)
VALUES (store_id, start_date, deptid, mon_sales)
INTO store_sales (store_id, sales_date, deptid, sales_amt)
VALUES (store_id, start_date+1, deptid, tue_sales)
INTO store_sales (store_id, sales_date, deptid, sales_amt)
VALUES (store_id, start_date+2, deptid, wed_sales)
INTO store_sales (store_id, sales_date, deptid, sales_amt)
VALUES (store_id, start_date+3, deptid, thur_sales)
INTO store_sales (store_id, sales_date, deptid, sales_amt)
VALUES (store_id, start_date+4, deptid, fri_sales)
INTO store_sales (store_id, sales_date, deptid, sales_amt)
VALUES (store_id, start_date+5, deptid, sat_sales)
INTO store_sales (store_id, sales_date, deptid, sales_amt)
VALUES (store_id, start_date+6, deptid, sun_sales)
SELECT store_id, start_date, deptid, mon_sales, tue_sales,
wed_sales, thur_sales, fri_sales, sat_sales, sun_sales
FROM store_sales_load;
```

Multitable inserts also allow you to determine which table you wish to **insert** records into based on various conditions. For example, we could have performed a conditional multitable insert using the **when** clause of the **insert** command. In this example, we are going to store total store sales in two different tables, EAST_STORES and WEST_STORES, depending on the location of the store (which is determined by the store number). Also note that we use the **else** condition to catch anything that might not fit into east or west categories (perhaps we have temporary kiosks or some such thing):

```
INSERT ALL
WHEN store_id < 100 THEN
INTO east_stores
WHEN store_id >= 100 THEN
INTO west_stores
ELSE
INTO misc_stores
SELECT * FROM store_sales_load;
```

The returning Clause   The **returning** clause allows you to retrieve values affected by the **insert** statement. Typically, the **returning** clause is used in PL/SQL, but it can also be used in normal SQL statements, as shown in this example:

```
SET AUTOPRINT ON
VAR e NUMBER;
INSERT INTO emp VALUES
(100, 'Willard','Joseph',100,10,NULL,10,sysdate,
1000, sysdate+365)
RETURNING empid INTO :e;
PRINT e;
```

Direct vs. Conventional Path Inserts   Oracle offers two options on how the data is physically inserted into the database when using the **insert** command: the conventional path insert (default) and the direct path insert. The conventional path insert uses the Oracle kernel to move the rows into the database data files. Oracle also reuses (if possible) existing free space within the object, and referential integrity constraints are validated at the time the rows are inserted.

Direct path mode, in contrast, directly inserts data into the data files, circumventing the Oracle internal buffer cache. This can result in much faster insert times. The data is appended to the high-water mark of the table; thus, reusable space below the high-water mark is left unused, so a direct mode insert can potentially waste a great deal of space. Also, referential integrity is not checked until the **insert** operation is complete, at which time the entire operation will be rolled back. Here is an example of an **insert** statement performing a direct mode insert:

```
INSERT /*+ APPEND */ INTO emp VALUES (100,
'Jacob','Freeman',1000,20, null, 10, sysdate, 100,
sysdate+365);
```

Note the use of the **append** hint in the preceding **insert** statement. This instructs Oracle to perform a direct path insert. You can also use the **append** hint in a subquery, right after the select keyword is used:

```
INSERT INTO emp
SELECT /*+ APPEND */ * FROM temp_emp;
```

insert Command–Related Error Messages

As you issue **insert** commands, you may run into various Oracle errors. The following table lists the most common errors and provides some advice as to what to do in the event you run into those errors.

Oracle Error Message	Text Description	Possible Causes and Solutions
ORA-00942	Table or view does not exist	You have tried to insert into a table that does not exist in your schema. You might also have tried to insert into a table or view that is in another schema that you do not have access rights to. Check to make sure that the object you are trying to access really exists. If it does, make sure that your SQL statement is correct. If it is, make sure you actually have access to that object.

Oracle Error Message	Text Description	Possible Causes and Solutions
ORA-01031	Insufficient privileges	You have insufficient privileges to insert a row into the table contained in the **insert** command. Check the ALL_TAB_PRIVS view to determine what privileges you have been assigned to the table in question. Assign the required privileges to the user account issuing the statement and try again.

The update Command

The **update** command is used to update values that already exist in a table, base table of a view, or a materialized view. In this section, we look at the specifics of the **update** command, followed by examples of the use of the **update** command. Finally, we look at errors associated with the **update** command.

Security Requirements

To use the **update** command to update data in a table, the table must be in your own schema. If the table is not in your own schema, you must have had the **update** object privilege granted to the schema you are using, or you must have the **update any table** system privilege. You can also update rows into one of the base tables of a given view through the view. To do so, you must either own the view and the base tables or have the **update** object privilege on the view being updated into. If the view and its base tables are owned by different schemas, then the schema that owns the view you wish to update must have the **update** object privilege on the base tables of the view as well.

Specifics of the update Command

The **update** command is fairly straightforward. First you use the **update** keyword, followed by any hints. You define what you want to update via the **dml_table_expression** clause or by just including the name of the table that is being updated. Following that is the **update_set** clause, which indicates which columns to update and the values that you wish to update them to. Finally, you can include a **where** clause, which allows you to control which rows are updated, and the **returning** clause, which allows you to return values back to the calling SQL statement. The following sections look at each of these items in a bit more detail.

The dml_table_expression Clause of the update Command

The **dml_table_expression** clause defines the table, view, or materialized view that you wish to update. You can alias this table, which might be required in certain **update** statements that involve subqueries in the **update_set** clause. Also, you can optionally indicate specific partitions that you wish to update, which in certain cases can aide performance of the **update** statement.

The update_set Clause of the update Command

The **update_set** clause is used to set specific column values in the **update** statement. In this clause, you define the column you wish to update, and then define the value you wish to update the value with. The update value can be a literal or it can be in the form of a subquery. If a subquery is used, that subquery must return exactly one row. The subquery should return as many columns as are being updated in the **update** statement. In Oracle Database 10*g*, you can also use the **flashback_query** clause within the subquery to update the table with data as it existed at a specific point in time in the database. The **flashback_query** clause was discussed earlier in this chapter, in the section "Flashback Elements."

The where Clause of the update Command

The **where** clause is used to determine which rows you wish to actually update. Refer to the section "The where Clause," earlier in the chapter, for a detailed treatment of the **where** clause.

The returning Clause of the update Command

The **returning** clause returns specific values from the rows that are changed by the **update** statement. Refer to "The returning Clause" section, earlier in the chapter, for more details on the **returning** clause.

update Command Examples

This section provides you with some examples of the use of the **update** command. The first example is a simple update of a single column value:

```
UPDATE emp SET salary=100 WHERE empid=100;
```

This example updates the EMP table by setting the SALARY column equal to 100 for every row where EMPID is equal to 100.

You can set multiple columns in the **update** statement as well. This next example appears to be retiring employee number 100:

```
UPDATE emp SET salary=NULL, retire_date=SYSDATE
WHERE empid=100;
```

Perhaps you want to set salaries for all employees in department 10, as shown in this example:

```
UPDATE emp SET salary=100 WHERE deptid=10;
```

Note that the **where** clause looks just like the **where** clause in the **select** statement. It can contain multiple predicates, as in this example:

```
UPDATE emp SET salary=salary*1.10
WHERE deptid=10 AND sal_review_dt > sysdate-180;
```

This example references the current value of the SALARY column in the clause and increases it by 10 percent (salary*1.10). The **update** clause allows you to reference the old column value and use that to determine the new column value.

As you might suspect, the **where** clause can contain a subquery as well, as shown in this example, where everyone in the sales department is given a 10 percent raise:

```
UPDATE emp SET salary=salary*1.10
WHERE deptid IN
(SELECT deptid FROM dept WHERE dept_name = 'Sales');
```

And you can combine subqueries and predicates, as in this example:

```
UPDATE emp SET salary=salary*1.10
WHERE deptid IN
(SELECT deptid FROM dept WHERE dept_name = 'Sales')
AND retire_date IS NOT NULL;
```

You can actually use subqueries in the **update_set** clause to define the value of the column being set, as shown in this example, which derives the department ID from the value of the department name:

```
UPDATE emp SET deptid=
(SELECT deptid FROM dept WHERE dept_name='Sales')
WHERE empid=100;
```

You can also set multiple column values using a single subquery, as shown in this example, which not only gives employees a raise but also gives them a higher commission:

```
UPDATE emp a SET (salary, comm)=
(SELECT salary*1.10, comm*1.10
FROM emp b WHERE a.empid=b.empid);
```

Note that in this example it is critical that the subquery return only one row for each row to be updated. Because the EMPID is likely to be unique, this query would work. However, if duplicate employee IDs existed, then this query would fail.

You can also indicate a specific partition to **insert** into, as shown in this example:

```
UPDATE store_sales
PARTITION (store_sales_jan_2004) sa
SET sa.sales_amt=1.10
WHERE store_id=100;
```

update Command–Related Error Messages

As you use the **update** command, you may run into various Oracle errors. The following table lists the most common errors and provides some advice as to what to do in the event you run into those errors.

Oracle Error Message	Text Description	Possible Causes and Solutions
ORA-00942	Table or view does not exist	You have tried to update a table that does not exist in your schema. You might also have tried to update a table or view that is in another schema that you do not have access rights to. Check to make sure that the object you are trying to access really exists. If it does, make sure that your SQL statement is correct. If it is, make sure you actually have access to that object.
ORA-01031	Insufficient privileges	You have insufficient privileges to update a row into the table contained in the **update** command. Check the ALL_TAB_PRIVS view to determine what privileges you have been assigned to the table in question. Assign the required privileges to the user account issuing the statement and try again.

Oracle Error Message	Text Description	Possible Causes and Solutions
ORA-01427	Single-row subquery returns more than one row	A subquery in the **set** clause of the **update** statement is returning more than one row. Review the query and rewrite the statement so that it only returns a single row, if that is possible. Otherwise, you may need to rewrite the SQL statement.

The delete Command

The **delete** command is used to remove one or more rows from a specific table. In this section, we look at the specifics of the **delete** command, followed by examples of the use of the **delete** command. Finally, we look at how to deal with errors associated with the use of the **delete** command.

Security Requirements

To use the **delete** command to delete data from a table, the table must be in your own schema. If the table is not in your own schema, you must have had the **delete** object privilege granted to the schema you are using, or you must have the **delete any table** system privilege. You can also delete rows into one of the base tables of a given view through the view. To do so, you must either own the view and the base tables or have the **delete** object privilege on the view being updated into. If the view and its base tables are owned by different schemas, then the schema that owns the view you wish to delete must have the **delete** object privilege on the base tables of the view as well.

Specifics of the delete Command

The **delete** command syntax is much like that of the **update** command. It includes the **delete** command and any associated hints, followed by the **from** keyword. Following that is the **dml_table_expression** clause, which indicates the object that the **delete** is occurring on. The **where** clause is next, which is followed by the **returning** clause.

The dml_table_expression Clause of the delete Command

The **dml_table_expression** clause defines the table, view, or materialized view that you wish to delete rows from. You can alias this table, which might be required in certain **delete** statements that involve subqueries in the **dml_table_expression** clause. Also, you can optionally indicate a specific partition that you wish to delete from, which in certain cases can aide performance of the **delete** statement.

The where Clause of the update Command

The **where** clause is used to determine which rows you wish to actually delete. Refer to the section "The where Clause," earlier in the chapter, for a detailed treatment of the **where** clause.

The returning Clause of the update Command

The **returning** clause returns specific values from the rows that are removed by the **delete** statement. Refer to the section "The returning Clause," earlier in the chapter, for more details on the **returning** clause.

delete Command Examples

Our first example is a rather straightforward **delete** command where we remove one row from the EMP table based on the EMPID column value:

```
DELETE FROM emp WHERE empid=100;
```

delete commands can be complex as well. One common case in which a complex **delete** command is required is when you need to delete duplicate rows from a table. This might be because a data load program failed and accidentally loaded duplicate records into a table while the primary key constraint was disabled. Here is a **delete** statement that removes all duplicate rows from a table where there are duplicates on the EMPID column:

```
DELETE FROM emp e WHERE e.rowid >
(SELECT MIN (esub.ROWID) FROM emp esub
WHERE e.empid=esub.empid);
```

This example includes pretty much every possible option. It uses the ROWID pseudo column, subqueries, and aliases.

delete Command–Related Error Messages

As you issue the **delete** command, you may run into various Oracle errors. The following table lists the most common errors and provides some advice as to what to do in the event you run into those errors.

Oracle Error Message	Text Description	Possible Causes and Solutions
ORA-00942	Table or view does not exist	You have tried to delete a row from a table that does not exist in your schema. You might also have tried to delete from a table or view that is in another schema that you do not have access rights to. Check to make sure that the object you are trying to access really exists. If it does, make sure that your SQL statement is correct. If it is, make sure you actually have access to that object.
ORA-01031	Insufficient privileges	You have insufficient privileges to delete a row from the table contained in the **delete** command. Check the ALL_TAB_PRIVS view to determine what privileges you have been assigned to the table in question. Assign the required privileges to the user account issuing the statement and try again.
ORA-01427	Single-row subquery returns more than one row	A subquery in the **set** clause of the **delete** statement is returning more than one row. Review the query and rewrite the statement so that it only returns a single row, if that is possible. Otherwise, you may need to rewrite the SQL statement.

The merge Command

The **merge** command allows you to consolidate multiple **insert**, **update**, and **delete** operations into a single table with one command. With the **merge** command, you select rows from one data source and, based on conditions that you define, insert or update those rows into a destination table. Further, you can define conditions that will cause data to be deleted in the destination table. This section discusses the security requirements regarding the **merge** command and the specifics of how the **merge** command works. It then provides examples of the **merge** command, and looks at errors related to the **merge** command.

Security Requirements

The requirements for the use of the **merge** command are straightforward. You first must be able to select the data from the source table or view. Then, to be able to use the **when matched then update** clause, you must have the same privileges required to update the table (see the "Security Requirements" section for the **update** command, earlier in this chapter, for more details). To be able to use the **when not matched then insert** clause, you must have the same privileges required to insert into a table (see the "Security Requirements" section for the **insert** command, earlier in this chapter). Finally, if you wish to be able to use the **delete where** clause, you must have the same privileges required to delete from the table (see the "Security Requirements" section for the **delete** command, earlier in this chapter).

Specifics of the merge Command

The **merge** command starts with the use of the **merge** command keyword. Following that you use the **into** keyword to indicate which table you wish to merge the data into. The **using** keyword is then used to define the table that contains the source data. The **on** condition follows, and is used to define the conditions where the **merge** operation will either update or insert the data being processed. The **on** condition determines whether the **merge** command executes the **merge_update** clause or the **merge_insert** clause. The **merge_update** clause defines how the **merge** command should update the table, and the **merge_insert** clause defines how the data should be inserted into the table. In Oracle Database 10*g* the **merge_update** clause also provides the capability to delete data based on specific defined criteria.

There are a some restrictions on the use of the **merge** command. First, the **merge** command cannot be used if the table is an index-organized table. Also, if you are using security policies on your destination tables, the **merge** command cannot be used on destination tables.

merge Command Examples

In this example, I'm going to use the **merge** command to maintain the RETIRED_EMP table. In this case, I want the SQL statement to either insert newly retired employees and update existing retired employees in the RETIRED_EMP table.

```
MERGE INTO retired_emp R
USING (SELECT empid, ename_first, ename_last, salary*.20 AS salary,
retire_date, hire_date, ssn, status
FROM emp WHERE retire_date IS NOT NULL) E
```

```
ON (R.ssn=E.ssn)
WHEN MATCHED THEN UPDATE
SET R.status=E.status, R.retire_payment_amt=E.salary
DELETE WHERE (R.status='D')
WHEN NOT MATCHED THEN INSERT
(R.empid, R.ename_last, r.ename_first, r.retire_payment_amt, r.retire_date,
r.hire_date, R.ssn, R.status)
VALUES (E.empid, E.ename_last, E.ename_first, E.salary*.20, E.retire_date,
E.hire_date, E.ssn, E.status);
```

In this example, I use the **merge** command to indicate that I want to merge the data into the table RETIRED_EMP. Note that I ailased the RETIRED_EMP table with an *R*. Then I define the records to be merged into the RETIRED_EMP table through a query defined in the **using** clause. In this case, I select records from the EMP table, where the RETIRE_DATE column is not NULL, which presumably implies that the employee has retired.

Note a couple of things in the **select** command in the **using** clause. In the case of the SALARY column, the retirees get 20 percent of their salary as a pension benefit, so I multiply the SALARY column by .20. Also note the **using** clause is ailased with an *E*.

Next, the **on** clause is used to define the join criteria that exists between the records of the two tables. In this case, the SSN column. Next, are the update, delete and insert activities. First, the **when matched then update** clause is executed if there is a match on the SSN column. The **when matched then update** clause will set the current status of the retiree, and their payment amount (if it has changed).

Note the **delete where** statement, which is part of the **when matched then update** clause and is only available in Oracle Database 10*g* and later. Using the **delete where** statement, I have indicated that if the STATUS column of the EMP table is set to *D*, the column should be removed from the RETIRED_EMP table. Finally, if there is not a match on the key defined in the **on** clause, then the **when not matched then insert** clause will be executed. This clause looks much like a regular **insert** statement, defining the rows to be inserted into the RETIRED_EMP table.

merge Command–Related Error Messages

As you issue the **merge** command, you may run into various Oracle errors, many of which will be common errors associated with **insert**, **update**, and **delete** commands. In these cases, refer to their respective sections in this chapter for the proper error resolutions. In some cases, errors specific to the **merge** command might occur. The following table lists the most common errors and provides some advice as to what to do in the event you run into those errors.

Oracle Error Message	Text Description	Possible Causes and Solutions
ORA-28132	Merge into syntax does not support security policies	The **merge** command does not support defined security policies (for example, VPD) if they are defined on the destination table. If you are using security policies, you need to use normal **insert** and **update** commands.
ORA-28673	Merge operation not allowed on an index-organized table	You cannot perform a merge operation on an index-organized table.

The commit Command

The **commit** command is used to end the current transaction. All changes made in that transaction are made permanent and cannot be rolled back. A **commit** should be explicitly executed after DML statements to ensure that the changes are made permanent. Implicit **commit** commands occur when any DDL activity occurs, such as the use of the **truncate** command, use of the **create table** command, or the use of other DDL commands. The **commit** command can also be used to force a commit of a distributed in-doubt transaction.

Security Requirements

There are no specific security requirements pertaining to the use of the **commit** command except when using it to force commit an in-doubt transaction. In this case, you must have the **force transaction** system privilege if you originally committed the transaction, or you must have the **force any transaction** system privilege if another user committed the transaction.

commit Command Examples

The **commit** command's use is quite basic:

```
COMMIT;
```

If you are trying to force a commit of an in-doubt distributed transaction, determine the local or global transaction ID of the transaction from the DBA_2PC_PENDING view. Use this transaction ID with the **commit** command to force the transaction to complete, as shown in this example:

```
COMMIT FORCE '66.24.44';
```

The savepoint Command

Use the **savepoint** command to establish markers at different points within a transaction that you can roll back to at a later time. No security requirements exist for the use of the **savepoint** command. Simply use the **savepoint** command and a unique identifier for each savepoint, as shown in this example:

```
SAVEPOINT Point_A;
```

The rollback Command

Use the **rollback** command to roll back a transaction either to the beginning of the transaction or to a savepoint. The **rollback** command can also be used to undo work involved in in-doubt distributed transactions.

Security Requirements

There are no specific security requirements pertaining to the use of the **rollback** command except when using it to force a rollback of an in-doubt transaction. In this case, you must have the **force**

transaction system privilege if you originally committed the transaction, or you must have the **force any transaction** system privilege if another user committed the transaction.

rollback Command Examples

This example uses the **rollback** command to roll back all changes to the beginning of the transaction:

```
ROLLBACK;
```

This example uses the **rollback** command to roll back to an established savepoint:

```
ROLLBACK TO savepoint point_a;
```

If you are trying to force a rollback of an in-doubt distributed transaction, determine the local or global transaction ID of the transaction from the DBA_2PC_PENDING view. Use this transaction ID with the **rollback** command to force the transaction to complete, as shown in this example:

```
ROLLBACK FORCE '66.24.44';
```

The truncate Command

The **truncate** command is used to remove all rows from a table or a cluster. Oracle will also deallocate all space used, to the point defined by the **minextents** storage parameter by default. It will also reset the **next** storage parameter to the size of the last extent that was removed from the object, and reset the high-water mark.

Security Requirements

To use the **truncate** command, you must have the **drop any table** system privilege or the object must be in your own schema.

Specifics of the truncate Command

Use the **truncate table** command to truncate a table, and use the **truncate cluster** command to truncate a cluster. Temporary tables and index-organized tables can be truncated. Indexes associated with the table are also truncated, and UNUSABLE indicators on local partitioned indexes are reset. Note that nonpartitioned indexes and global partitioned indexes will be marked UNUSABLE. Partitions and any UNUSABLE indicators are reset as well.

You cannot truncate individual tables of a cluster and you cannot truncate a parent table that is involved in an enabled foreign key relationship unless the relationship is a self-referential relationship.

The **truncate** command can result in better space management than the **delete** command in certain cases. For example, when using direct load, Oracle will load data at the high-water mark. Since the **delete** command doesn't reset this high-water mark, direct loads can cause tables to grow. Using the **truncate** command before a direct load can alleviate this problem. Using the **reuse storage** command, you can indicate that the **truncate** command should not deallocate extents and reset the high-water mark.

truncate Command Examples

This example truncates the TEMP_EMP table:

```
TRUNCATE TABLE temp_emp;
```

This example truncates the LOAD_EMP table, but preserves the current storage attributes of that table:

```
TRUNCATE TABLE temp_emp REUSE STORAGE;
```

truncate Command–Related Error Messages

As you use the **truncate** command, you may run into various Oracle errors. The following table lists the most common errors and provides some advice as to what to do in the event you run into those errors.

Oracle Error Message	Text Description	Possible Causes and Solutions
ORA-02266	Unique/primary keys in table referenced by enabled foreign keys	You have tried to truncate a table that is a parent table in a foreign key relationship. Check the USER_CONSTRAINTS view to determine what that constraint is. You must disable the constraint or remove it before you will be able to truncate the table.
ORA-03290	Invalid truncate command – missing CLUSTER or TABLE keyword	Check your **truncate** command and make sure that the syntax is correct.
ORA-03291	Invalid truncate option – missing STORAGE keyword	The storage keyword is missing from the **truncate** command when it was expected. Check the syntax of the command and try again.
ORA-03292	Cluster to be truncated is part of a cluster	You cannot truncate a table that is part of a cluster.
ORA-03293	Cluster to be truncated is a HASH CLUSTER	You cannot truncate a hash cluster.
ORA-14072 ORA-14073	Fixed table may not be truncated or Bootstrap or cluster may not be truncated	You have tried to truncate a fixed (system) table.

Writing Readable DML Statements

As you might expect, SQL DML statements can get quite long. It is a good idea to employ some of the following standards when writing your SQL statements in order to make them more readable. Note that some of these conventions are not followed in this book, to ensure that the book is not unreasonably long.

- Separate keywords into their own lines. For example, instead of this:

```
DELETE FROM emp WHERE empid> 100 AND retire_date IS NOT NULL;
```

write the statement like this:

```
DELETE FROM emp
WHERE empid>100
AND retire_date IS NOT NULL;
```

■ Use uppercase for keywords and lowercase for non-keywords. All of the code examples in this book follow this convention. For example, insert should be INSERT.

■ Indent continuation lines three to five spaces after the keyword. Indent subqueries three to five spaces as well. For example:

```
SELECT empid, ename_last, ename_first, retire_date, salary,
comm, manager, deptid, hire_date, sal_review_dt
FROM emp WHERE empid>100
AND retire_dt IS NOT NULL AND deptid IN
(SELECT deptid FROM dept WHERE dept_name='Sales');
```

is easier to read if rewritten this way:

```
SELECT empid, ename_last, ename_first, retire_date, salary,
comm, manager, deptid, hire_date, sal_review_dt
FROM emp
WHERE empid>100
AND retire_dt IS NOT NULL
AND deptid IN (SELECT deptid
               FROM dept
               WHERE dept_name='Sales');
```

■ If you are going to be changing a statement quite a bit (for example, during its development) It is often easier to have each column of a **select** statement on its own line, with the comma in front of the column or expression, as shown in the example below. Some might find this format harder to read, but it is easier to comment out, add or drop columns when the statement is written in this way:

```
SELECT empid
, ename_last
, ename_first
, retire_date
, salary
, comm
, manager
, deptid
, hire_date
, sal_review_dt
FROM emp
WHERE empid>100
AND empid IS NOT NULL
AND deptid IN (SELECT deptid
               FROM dept
               WHERE dept_name='Sales');
```

APPENDIX
A

Initialization
Parameters

nitialization parameters are used to control the behavior of the database. They define many different aspects of the database, including database resource limits, user and process limits, and performance aspects. Many initialization parameters have default values. Some initialization parameters are derived from other initialization parameters. You can choose to override the derived initialization parameters if you need to. Many parameters are operating system–dependent, meaning that their allowable values vary from platform to platform.

Parameter Files

The values of nondefault initialization parameters are stored in a file called a parameter file. When the database starts, or initializes, a parameter file is read. Any parameters defined in this file are set to the values in that file on database startup. If a parameter is not located in the parameter file, then the parameter is set to its default value. There are two types of parameter files. Each of these is discussed in turn in the next two sections.

Initialization Parameter File

In the earliest versions of the Oracle database, this parameter file was the only one available. This file is a text file, which can be easily modified with any text editor. Often, this file is called a pfile. When you start up a database, you can define which pfile you wish to use to start the database with by using the **pfile** parameter, as follows:

```
STARTUP PFILE=/my_directory/initorcl.ora
```

The filename is typically of the form init*sid*.ora, where *sid* is the database identifier. For this reason, this file is also commonly referred to as the init.ora file. The default location of the **pfile** is operating system–specific, although it can be in any directory on the database server and referenced similar to the preceding example.

Parameters are specified in the **pfile** in the form *parameter=value*. A pound sign (#) denotes a comment in the parameter file. The parameters can be specified in any order. If you have the same parameter specified more than once in the parameter file, the value specified last in the parameter file is used. To change the values of parameters in this file, or to add new parameters, modify the file's contents with a text editor. If you manually change the parameters in the init.ora file, these changes will not take effect until the database is restarted. You can still change any dynamic parameters with the **alter sytem** or **alter session** commands, and by using the **scope=memory** setting, as described in the next section.

Server Parameter Files

Server parameter files were introduced in Oracle9*i*. These files are binary files, which should not be modified with any editor. A server parameter file is often called a spfile. This filename is typically of the form spfile*sid*.ora, where *sid* is the database identifier. The location of the spfile is operating system–specific.

There are only two approved methods of modifying a parameter in the spfile. The first method is to use the **alter system** command with the **scope** set to either **both** or **spfile**. The following is an example of changing a parameter with the **alter system** command:

```
ALTER System SET db_buffer_cache=200M SCOPE=spfile;
```

This example modifies the **db_buffer_cache** parameter to be 200MB. Since the **scope** is **spfile**, only the value in the server parameter file is changed. If the **scope** were set to **memory**, then only the database's memory would be changed, and not the contents of the server parameter file. This would mean that a database restart would lose the parameter change. If **scope** is set to **both**, then the parameter's value is changed in both the database's memory and the spfile.

The second method to change the contents of a server parameter file is to create an init.ora file from the **spfile**, use a text editor to modify its contents, and then create the **spfile** from the init.ora file. You should not need to use this method very often, but there are rare occasions when it is nice to be able to do.

To create an init.ora file from the contents of the SPFILE, use the following command:

```
CREATE PFILE FROM SPFILE;
```

The **pfile** will be found in the database's default location. Modify its contents with any text editor. Once done, re-create the **spfile** as follows:

```
CREATE SPFILE FROM PFILE;
```

You need to restart the database for the changes to take effect. You can also include file names in the commands as in this example:

```
CREATE SPFILE='c:\oracle\spfile\spfilemydb.ora' FROM
PFILE='c:\oracle\pfile\initpfile.ora';
```

Displaying Parameter Values

If you are using the old text-based init.ora file, you can always look at the contents of this file to determine a parameter's value. This approach does have its drawbacks. Any parameters that are not explicitly set are not in this file. Some parameters can be modified while the database is running. If a parameter has been modified since instance startup, its new value is not shown in the init.ora file. There are many ways to determine the value of a parameter from within the database itself and we will discuss this in the next section. These methods include using the **show parameter** command from SQL*Plus, and using various database views including V$System_PARAMETER, V$PARAMETER, V$PARAMETER2, and V$SPPARAMETER views.

show parameter

The SQL*Plus **show parameter** command can be used to show the current values of initialization parameters. By itself, the **show parameter** SQL*Plus command shows the current values of all parameters. If the command is followed by a string, all parameters with that string in their name are displayed. The following displays all parameters and their values with the word "block" in their name:

```
SHOW PARAMETER block
```

V$System_PARAMETER

The V$System_PARAMETER view shows information about all the current parameter settings for the database instance. New sessions inherit these settings when the session starts. The following shows a common query of this view:

```
SELECT name,value,isdefault,isses_modifiable,issys_modifiable
FROM v$system_parameter;
```

This example shows the parameter's NAME, its current VALUE, whether its current value is the default value (ISDEFAULT), whether the parameter is modifiable in the session (ISSES_MODIFIABLE), and whether the parameter is modifiable for the system (ISSYS_MODIFIABLE). The ISSYS_MODIFIABLE column will have one of the following three values:

- **immediate** Means that an **alter system** command can modify this parameter regardless of the initialization file used. The change takes effect immediately.

- **deferred** Means that an **alter system** command can modify this parameter regardless of the initialization file used. The change takes effect for subsequent sessions.

- **false** Means that the parameter cannot be modified with the **alter system** command unless an **spfile** was used to start the instance.

V$PARAMETER

The V$PARAMETER view shows information about all the current parameter settings for the current session. A new session inherits its parameters from the instance-wide values. The columns in this view are very similar to those in the V$System_PARAMETER view.

V$PARAMETER2

The V$PARAMETER view shows information about all the current parameter settings for the current session. A new session inherits its parameters from the instance-wide values. The columns in this view are very similar to those in the V$System_PARAMETER view. The V$PARAMETER2 view also displays the database default values for each parameter, so you can easily compare the two values.

V$SPPARAMETER

The V$SPPARAMETER view is the window into the contents of the spfile. Querying this view may be easier than creating a pfile from the spfile, just to see the parameter's values. The following is an example of a common query against this view:

```
SELECT name,value,isspecified FROM v$spparameter;
```

In this example, the NAME of the parameter and its VALUE in the spfile are returned. If the parameter is explicitly specified in the spfile, the ISSPECIFIED column contains TRUE; otherwise, it contains FALSE. If no SPFILE was used to start the database, all rows of the view contain FALSE for the ISSPECIFIED column.

The Parameters

The remainder of this appendix gives information about each initialization parameter. For each parameter, a description of the parameter is given. The default value, range of values, and derived value are shown, if applicable. If the parameter is modifiable with the **alter session** or **alter system** command, that is noted as well.

active_instance_count   Defines one cluster in a two-cluster environment as the primary cluster.

Default Value	Modifiable	Range of Values	Session or System Mod.
None	No	1 or >= num instances	No

aq_tm_processes   Defines the number of time-management processes that are started to manage Advanced Queues.

Default Value	Modifiable	Range of Values	Session or System Mod.
0	Yes	1–10	System

archive_lag_target   Specifies the number of seconds of data that can be lost in a standby database.

Default Value	Modifiable	Range of Values	Session or System Mod.
0	Yes	0, 60–7200 (in seconds)	System

asm_diskgroups   Lists the names of disk groups that are to be mounted by the ASM instance.

Default Value	Modifiable	Range of Values	Session or System Mod.
None	Yes	Varies	System

asm_diskstring   Specifies a value used by ASM to limit the set of disks used for recovery.

Default Value	Modifiable	Range of Values	Session or System Mod.
NULL	Yes	No	System

asm_power_limit   Specifies the maximum power for ASM for disk rebalancing.

Default Value	Modifiable	Range of Values	Session or System Mod.
1	Yes	1–11	Both

audit_file_dest   Specifies the disk location for audit trail records.

Default Value	Modifiable	Range of Values	Session or System Mod.
ORACLE_HOME/rdbms/audit	Yes	No	System

audit_sys_operations   Determines whether or not operations by the user SYS are audited.

Default Value	Modifiable	Range of Values	Session or System Mod.
FALSE	No	TRUE or FALSE	No

audit_trail   Controls database auditing. If set to OS, the audit trail is written to disk. If set to DB or TRUE, the audit trail is written to the SYS.AUD$ table.

Default Value	Modifiable	Range of Values	Session or System Mod.
None	No	DB, OS, NONE, TRUE, FALSE, or DB_EXTENDED	No

background_core_dump   Determines whether core dumps include the full or partial contents of the SGA.

Default Value	Modifiable	Range of Values	Session or System Mod.
PARTIAL	No	PARTIAL or FULL	No

background_dump_dest   Specifies the location on disk where background process (SMON, PMON, DBWn, etc.) trace files and the alert log are written.

Default Value	Modifiable	Range of Values	Session or System Mod.
OS dependent	No	No	No

backup_tape_io_slaves   Denotes whether or not server processes are used for tape devices for RMAN.

Default Value	Modifiable	Range of Values	Session or System Mod.
FALSE	No	TRUE or FALSE	No

bitmap_merge_area_size   Specifies the amount of memory a session process can use to merge bitmaps in query processing.

Default Value	Modifiable	Range of Values	Session or System Mod.
1MB	No	OS dependent	No

blank_trimming   Determines whether or not a source character string can be larger than the destination column or variable by removing trailing blanks.

Default Value	Modifiable	Range of Values	Session or System Mod.
FALSE	No	TRUE or FALSE	No

circuits   Specifies the total network circuits available for network traffic.

Default Value	Modifiable	Range of Values	Session or System Mod.
None	No	No	No

cluster_database   Determines whether or not the database is clustered in a RAC environment.

Default Value	Modifiable	Range of Values	Session or System Mod.
FALSE	No	TRUE or FALSE	No

cluster_database_instances   Specifies the number of database instances in the cluster in a RAC environment.

Default Value	Modifiable	Range of Values	Session or System Mod.
1	No	Any integer > 0	No

cluster_interconnects   Defines the cluster interconnects in a RAC environment.

Default Value	Modifiable	Range of Values	Session or System Mod.
None	No	One or more IP addresses	No

commit_point_strength   Determines the commit point node for distributed transactions.

Default Value	Modifiable	Range of Values	Session or System Mod.
1	No	0–255	No

compatible   Determines which version of Oracle to be compatible with. Enables version's features.

Default Value	Modifiable	Range of Values	Session or System Mod.
Version	No	Oracle version number	No

control_file_record_keep_time   Specifies the minimum number of days that reusable records in the control must be kept.

Default Value	Modifiable	Range of Values	Session or System Mod.
7	Yes	0–365	System

control_files   Explicitly names the control files. Needed for database startup.

Default Value	Modifiable	Range of Values	Session or System Mod.
OS dependent	No	1 to 8 filenames	No

core_dump_dest   Determines the disk location where core dumps are written.

Default Value	Modifiable	Range of Values	Session or System Mod.
ORACLE_HOME/dbs	Yes	Any valid directory	System

cpu_count   Specifies the number of CPUs available to the database.

Default Value	Modifiable	Range of Values	Session or System Mod.
Number of CPUs	No	0 to unlimited	No

create_bitmap_area_size   Specifies how much memory a session is allocated to create bitmaps.

Default Value	Modifiable	Range of Values	Session or System Mod.
8MB	No	OS dependent	No

create_stored_outlines   Directs the session to create stored outlines of SQL statements.

Default Value	Modifiable	Range of Values	Session or System Mod.
None	Yes	TRUE, FALSE, or *category*	Both

cursor_sharing   Determines how SQL statements share cursors in the shared pool.

Default Value	Modifiable	Range of Values	Session or System Mod.
EXACT	Yes	SIMILAR, EXACT, or FORCE	Both

cursor_space_for_time   Determines whether or not more space will be used for cursors, to save time.

Default Value	Modifiable	Range of Values	Session or System Mod.
FALSE	NoS	TRUE or FALSE	No

db_*n*k_cache_size   Specifies the size of the buffer cache that holds blocks that are *n*K in size, where *n* is a value (OS dependent) of 2, 4, 8, 16, or 32, but not equal to the default block size.

Default Value	Modifiable	Range of Values	Session or System Mod.
0	Yes	0 to OS dependent	System

db_block_buffers   Specifies the number of blocks in the database buffer cache.

Default Value	Modifiable	Range of Values	Session or System Mod.
The default is calculated as db_block_buffers= 48M/db_block_size	No	50 to OS dependent	No

db_block_checking   Determines whether or not the database checks blocks to help prevent corruption.

Default Value	Modifiable	Range of Values	Session or System Mod.
FALSE	Yes	TRUE or FALSE	Both

db_block_checksum   Determines whether or not DBW*n* calculates a checksum on database blocks.

Default Value	Modifiable	Range of Values	Session or System Mod.
TRUE	Yes	TRUE or FALSE	System

db_block_size   Specifies the default block size. This parameter is set at the time the database is created and cannot be changed.

Default Value	Modifiable	Range of Values	Session or System Mod.
8192	No	2048, 4096, 8192, 16384, or 32768	No

db_cache_advice   Specifies if advice data for sizing the database buffer caches will be generated. If set to READY, the advisor will be turned off, but the memory for the advisor will be allocated, and the advisor can be turned on. If the database is started with the parameter set to OFF, then the advisor cannot be started dynamically.

Default Value	Modifiable	Range of Values	Session or System Mod.
ON	Yes	ON, OFF, or READY	System

db_cache_size   Specifies the memory size of the default buffer cache. The Oracle database will round up the value of this parameter to the multiple of the granule size (see following). This parameter can be adjusted up or down while the database is operating as long as the current amount of SGA memory is less than the value of SGA_MAX_SIZE.

The granule size on most platforms is dependent on the size of the SGA. If the total SGA size is less than or equal to 1GB, then granule size is 4MB. If the SGA is larger than 1GB, then the granule size is 16MB. There are OS platform exceptions to this rule.

Default Value	Modifiable	Range of Values	Session or System Mod.
48M	Yes	Varies	System

db_create_file_dest   Specifies the default location for Oracle Managed Files.

Default Value	Modifiable	Range of Values	Session or System Mod.
None	Yes	Any valid directory	Both

db_create_online_log_dest_*n*   Specifies the locations for OMF control files and redo log files.

Default Value	Modifiable	Range of Values	Session or System Mod.
None	Yes	Any valid directory	Both

db_domain   Specifies the logical location in a network of distributed databases.

Default Value	Modifiable	Range of Values	Session or System Mod.
None	No	No	No

db_file_multiblock_read_count   Specifies how many blocks to read as one I/O operation during sequential (full table) scans.

Default Value	Modifiable	Range of Values	Session or System Mod.
8	Yes	OS dependent	Both

db_file_name_convert Defines how to convert filenames from the primary to the standby database file structure.

Default Value	Modifiable	Range of Values	Session or System Mod.
None	Yes	No	SESSION

db_files Specifies the maximum number of data files the database can open.

Default Value	Modifiable	Range of Values	Session or System Mod.
200	No	OS dependent	No

db_flashback_retention_target Specifies the amount of time to be able to flashback the database.

Default Value	Modifiable	Range of Values	Session or System Mod.
1440	Yes	0 to $2^{32} - 1$	System

db_keep_cache_size Determines how much memory is allocated to the KEEP buffer pool.

Default Value	Modifiable	Range of Values	Session or System Mod.
0	Yes	0 to OS dependent	System

db_name Specifies the database name.

Default Value	Modifiable	Range of Values	Session or System Mod.
None	No	No	No

db_recovery_file_dest Specifies the default location for the flash recovery area.

Default Value	Modifiable	Range of Values	Session or System Mod.
None	Yes	No	System

db_recovery_file_dest_size Specifies how much memory to be used by recovery files in the flashback recovery area.

Default Value	Modifiable	Range of Values	Session or System Mod.
None	Yes	0 or OS dependent value in K, M, or G	System

db_recycle_cache_size   Specifies the size of the RECYCLE buffer pool.

Default Value	Modifiable	Range of Values	Session or System Mod.
0	Yes	0 to OS dependent	System

db_unique_name   Specifies a globally unique name for the database.

Default Value	Modifiable	Range of Values	Session or System Mod.
db_name	No	No	No

db_writer_processes   Determines how many DBW*n* background processes to start.

Default Value	Modifiable	Range of Values	Session or System Mod.
1 or **cpu_count/8**	No	1–20	No

dbwr_io_slaves   Determines how many slave processes will be started to assist DBWR.

Default Value	Modifiable	Range of Values	Session or System Mod.
0	No	0 to OS dependent	No

ddl_wait_for_locks   Determines whether DDL statements wait for locks to be released or do not wait and raise an exception.

Default Value	Modifiable	Range of Values	Session or System Mod.
FALSE	Yes	TRUE or FALSE	Both

dg_broker_config_file*n*   Specifies the names for Data Guard broker configuration files.

Default Value	Modifiable	Range of Values	Session or System Mod.
OS dependent	Yes	One filename	System

dg_broker_start   Specifies whether or not the Data Guard DMON process should be started.

Default Value	Modifiable	Range of Values	Session or System Mod.
FALSE	Yes	TRUE or FALSE	System

disk_asynch_io   Determines whether or not I/O operations are performed asynchronously.

Default Value	Modifiable	Range of Values	Session or System Mod.
TRUE	No	TRUE or FALSE	No

dispatchers   Specifies the number of dispatcher processes in the shared server architecture.

Default Value	Modifiable	Range of Values	Session or System Mod.
'(PROTOCOL=tcp)'	No	No	No

distributed_lock_timeout   Specifies the time (in seconds) for a distributed transaction to wait for lock release.

Default Value	Modifiable	Range of Values	Session or System Mod.
60	No	1 to unlimited	No

dml_locks   Specifies the maximum number of DML locks.

Default Value	Modifiable	Range of Values	Session or System Mod.
.4*transactions	No	20 to unlimited	No

enqueue_resources   Specifies the maximum number of resources that can be locked.

Default Value	Modifiable	Range of Values	Session or System Mod.
None	No	10 to unlimited	No

fal_client   Specifies the Fetch Archive Log (FAL) client used by the FAL service.

Default Value	Modifiable	Range of Values	Session or System Mod.
None	Yes	No	System

fal_server   Specifies the FAL server in the standby database.

Default Value	Modifiable	Range of Values	Session or System Mod.
None	Yes	No	System

fast_start_io_target   Specifies the number of I/O operations that are needed during crash recovery.

Default Value	Modifiable	Range of Values	Session or System Mod.
All buffers	Yes	1000 to all buffers	System

fast_start_mttr_target   Specifies a target time (in seconds) needed for crash or instance recovery.

Default Value	Modifiable	Range of Values	Session or System Mod.
0	Yes	0–3600	System

fast_start_parallel_rollback   Specifies the maximum number of processes to be used for parallel rollback.

Default Value	Modifiable	Range of Values	Session or System Mod.
LOW	Yes	HI, LOW, or FALSE	System

file_mapping   Specifies whether file mapping is enabled or disabled.

Default Value	Modifiable	Range of Values	Session or System Mod.
FALSE	Yes	TRUE or FALSE	System

fileio_network_adapters   Specifies the network adapters to be used to access disk storage.

Default Value	Modifiable	Range of Values	Session or System Mod.
None	No	No	No

filesystemio_options   Specifies how the database performs file I/O operations.

Default Value	Modifiable	Range of Values	Session or System Mod.
None	Yes	NONE, SETALL, DIRECTION, or ASYNCH	Both

fixed_date   Specifies a fixed valued that **sysdate** will always return.

Default Value	Modifiable	Range of Values	Session or System Mod.
None	Yes	Any valid date value	System

gc_files_to_locks   Defines the mapping of PCM locks to files in RAC environments.

Default Value	Modifiable	Range of Values	Session or System Mod.
None	No	Varies	No

gcs_server_processes   Specifies initial number of GCS processes for RAC environments.

Default Value	Modifiable	Range of Values	Session or System Mod.
0	No	1–20	No

global_context_pool_size   Determines the amount of memory in the SGA for global application context data.

Default Value	Modifiable	Range of Values	Session or System Mod.
1MB	No	Any integer value, in MB	No

global_names   Specifies whether or not a database link needs to have the same name as the database it connects to.

Default Value	Modifiable	Range of Values	Session or System Mod.
FALSE	Yes	TRUE or FALSE	Both

hash_area_size   Specifies how much memory in a session to reserve for hash joins.

Default Value	Modifiable	Range of Values	Session or System Mod.
2***sort_area_size**	Yes	0 to OS dependent	Session

hi_shared_memory_address   Specifies the starting address of the SGA.

Default Value	Modifiable	Range of Values	Session or System Mod.
0	No	No	No

hs_autoregister   Specifies whether or not Heterogeneous Services agents automatically register.

Default Value	Modifiable	Range of Values	Session or System Mod.
TRUE	Yes	TRUE or FALSE	System

ifile   Specifies a parameter file to include in this parameter file.

Default Value	Modifiable	Range of Values	Session or System Mod.
None	No	Valid parameter files	No

instance_groups   Specifies which instances to limit parallel queries to for RAC.

Default Value	Modifiable	Range of Values	Session or System Mod.
None	No	Valid parameter files	No

instance_name   Specifies the name of the instance.

Default Value	Modifiable	Range of Values	Session or System Mod.
Database SID	No	Any alphanumeric characters	No

instance_number   Specifies a unique number for the instance in RAC environments.

Default Value	Modifiable	Range of Values	Session or System Mod.
Lowest available	No	1 to maximum number of instances	No

instance_type   Specifies the type of instance that is running.

Default Value	Modifiable	Range of Values	Session or System Mod.
RDBMS	No	RDBMS or ASM	No

java_max_sessionspace_size   Specifies the maximum memory for the Java session space.

Default Value	Modifiable	Range of Values	Session or System Mod.
0	No	0–(2GB – 1)	No

java_pool_size   Specifies the amount of memory to allocate for the Java Pool.

Default Value	Modifiable	Range of Values	Session or System Mod.
0	Yes	0 to OS dependent	System

java_soft_sessionspace_limit   Specifies a warning threshold for the Java session space.

Default Value	Modifiable	Range of Values	Session or System Mod.
0	No	0–(2G – 1)	No

job_queue_processes   Specifies the maximum number of processes to handle scheduled jobs.

Default Value	Modifiable	Range of Values	Session or System Mod.
0	Yes	0–1000	System

large_pool_size   Specifies the amount of memory to reserve for the Large Pool.

Default Value	Modifiable	Range of Values	Session or System Mod.
0	Yes	300K to OS specific	System

ldap_directory_access   Specifies how the database refers to the OID for authentication.

Default Value	Modifiable	Range of Values	Session or System Mod.
None	Yes	NONE, PASSWORD, or SSL	System

license_max_sessions   Specifies the maximum number of concurrent sessions allowed.

Default Value	Modifiable	Range of Values	Session or System Mod.
0	Yes	0 to unlimited	System

license_max_users   Specifies the maximum number of users you can create in the database.

Default Value	Modifiable	Range of Values	Session or System Mod.
0	Yes	0 to unlimited	System

license_sessions_warning   Specifies the threshold for a warning if the number of sessions is too high.

Default Value	Modifiable	Range of Values	Session or System Mod.
0	Yes	0 to **license_max_ sessions**	System

local_listener   Specifies the name of the listener for this instance.

Default Value	Modifiable	Range of Values	Session or System Mod.
(ADDRESS = (PROTOCOL=TCP) (HOST=your_host) (PORT=1521))	Yes	No	System

lock_name_space   Specifies the namespace that the DLM uses to generate locks.

Default Value	Modifiable	Range of Values	Session or System Mod.
None	No	Up to 8 alphanumeric characters	No

lock_sga   Determines whether or not the instance locks the entire SGA in memory.

Default Value	Modifiable	Range of Values	Session or System Mod.
FALSE	No	TRUE or FALSE	No

log_archive_config   Determines if redo logs can be sent or received in Data Guard. Syntax for this parameter is

```
LOG_ARCHIVE_CONFIG = { [ SEND or NOSEND ] [ RECEIVE or NORECEIVE ]
  [ DG_CONFIG=(remote_db_unique_name1
      [, ... remote_db_unique_name9)
| NODG_CONFIG ] }
```

where:

- **Send** allows redo logs to be sent to remote destinations.

- **Nosend** prevents redo logs from being sent to remote destinations.

- **Receive** allows receipt of remotely archived redo logs.

- **Noreceive** disables receipt of remotely archived redo logs.

- **dg_config** allows you to define up to nine unique database names (defined with the **db_unique_name** initialization parameter) for all of the databases in the Data Guard configuration.

- **nodg_config** removes the list of service provider names previously specified with the **dg_config** parameter.

Default Value	Modifiable	Range of Values	Session or System Mod.
SEND, RECEIVE, NODG_CONFIG	Yes	Numerous	System

log_archive_dest   Specifies the archive location for redo logs.

Default Value	Modifiable	Range of Values	Session or System Mod.
NULL	Yes	Any valid directory	System

log_archive_dest_*n*   Specifies up to ten destinations for the archived redo logs. Syntax for this parameter is

```
LOG_ARCHIVE_DEST_n
(where n is a numeric value 1 through 9)=
( null_string or  ( LOCATION=path_name or SERVICE=service_name )
<( MANDATORY | OPTIONAL ) > < REOPEN[=seconds] | NOREOPEN >
< DELAY[=minutes] | NODELAY >
< REGISTER[=template] | NOREGISTER >
< TEMPLATE=template] | NOTEMPLATE >
< ALTERNATE=destination | NOALTERNATE >
< DEPENDENCY=destination | NODEPENDENCY >
< MAX_FAILURE=count | NOMAX_FAILURE >
< QUOTA_SIZE=blocks | NOQUOTA_SIZE >
< QUOTA_USED=blocks | NOQUOTA_USED > < ARCH | LGWR >
< SYNC[=PARALLEL|NOPARALLEL] | ASYNC[=blocks] >
< AFFIRM | NOAFFIRM > < NET_TIMEOUT=seconds | NONET_TIMEOUT >
< VALID_FOR=(redo_log_type,database_role) >
< DB_UNIQUE_NAME | NODB_UNIQUE_NAME > < VERIFY | NOVERIFY > )
```

The various parameter meanings are

- The **service** parameter defines a standby destination. This should relate to a service name defined in the tnsnames.ora.

- The **location** parameter defines a local file system destination. If log archiving is to be enabled then this parameter must be defined for at least one destination.

- The **mandatory** parameter indicates that archiving to the destination must succeed before the redo log file can be reused.

- The **optional** parameter indicates that successful archiving to the destination is not required before the redo log file can be reused. This is the default value.

- The **reopen** parameter defines the minimum number of seconds before the archiver process (ARC*n*, foreground, or log writer process) should try again to access a previously failed destination. The default value is 300 seconds.

Default Value	Modifiable	Range of Values	Session or System Mod.
None	Yes	Any valid directory	Both

log_archive_dest_state_*n*   Determines the availability state of the destination specified by **log_archive_dest_*n***. Value meanings are

- A value of **enabled** indicates that a valid log archive destination can be used for archiving. This is the default.

- A value of **defer** indicates that the destination is excluded from archiving operations.

- A value of **alternate** indicates that the log archive destination is not enabled but will become enabled if the ability to archive to another destination fails.

Default Value	Modifiable	Range of Values	Session or System Mod.
ENABLE	Yes	ALTERNATE, RESET, DEFER, or ENABLE	Both

log_archive_duplex_dest　Specifies a second location for the **log_archive_dest** location.

Default Value	Modifiable	Range of Values	Session or System Mod.
None	Yes	Any valid directory	System

log_archive_format　Specifies the filename format of archived redo logs.

Default Value	Modifiable	Range of Values	Session or System Mod.
OS dependent	No	Any valid string	No

log_archive_local_first　Specifies whether or not the archiver transmits the redo to the standby.

Default Value	Modifiable	Range of Values	Session or System Mod.
TRUE	Yes	TRUE or FALSE	System

log_archive_max_processes　Specifies the number of archiver processes (ARC*n*).

Default Value	Modifiable	Range of Values	Session or System Mod.
2	Yes	1–10	System

log_archive_min_succeed_dest　Specifies the minimum number of archive destinations that the redo log must successfully be archived to.

Default Value	Modifiable	Range of Values	Session or System Mod.
1	Yes	1 to number of destinations	Both

log_archive_trace　Determines the level of tracing for the archiver process.

Default Value	Modifiable	Range of Values	Session or System Mod.
0	Yes	0, 1, 2, 4, 8, 16, 32, 64, or 128	System

log_buffer　Specifies the amount of memory to allocate to the redo log buffer.

Default Value	Modifiable	Range of Values	Session or System Mod.
512K or 128K***cpu_count**	No	OS dependent	No

log_checkpoint_interval   Defines the frequency of checkpointing based on the number of redo log file blocks that can exist between two incremental checkpoints.

Default Value	Modifiable	Range of Values	Session or System Mod.
0	Yes	Unlimited (in redo log file blocks)	System

log_checkpoint_timeout   Specifies the amount of time between incremental checkpoints.

Default Value	Modifiable	Range of Values	Session or System Mod.
1800	Yes	0 to unlimited (in seconds)	System

log_checkpoints_to_alert   Specifies whether or not to write checkpoint information in the alert log.

Default Value	Modifiable	Range of Values	Session or System Mod.
FALSE	Yes	TRUE or FALSE	System

log_file_name_convert   Specifies whether or not log files are converted from the primary to the standby.

Default Value	Modifiable	Range of Values	Session or System Mod.
None	Yes	TRUE or FALSE	SESSION

logmnr_max_persistent_sessions   Specifies the maximum number of persistent Log Miner sessions.

Default Value	Modifiable	Range of Values	Session or System Mod.
1	No	1 to **license_max_ sessions**	No

max_commit_propagation_delay   Specifies the amount of time before the SCN is refreshed for RAC.

Default Value	Modifiable	Range of Values	Session or System Mod.
700	No	0–90000 (in seconds)	No

max_dispatchers   Specifies the maximum number of dispatcher processes that can be started.

Default Value	Modifiable	Range of Values	Session or System Mod.
None	Yes	dispatchers<max_ dispatchers<processes	System

max_dump_file_size   Determines the maximum size of trace files, excluding the alert log.

Default Value	Modifiable	Range of Values	Session or System Mod.
UNLIMITED	Yes	0 to UNLIMITED	Both

max_enabled_roles   Specifies the maximum number of roles that a session can enable.

Default Value	Modifiable	Range of Values	Session or System Mod.
30	No	0–148	No

max_shared_servers   Specifies the maximum number of shared server processes that can be started.

Default Value	Modifiable	Range of Values	Session or System Mod.
None	Yes	Less than processes	System

nls_calendar   Determines which calendar system the session uses.

Default Value	Modifiable	Range of Values	Session or System Mod.
None	Yes	Any valid calendar format	SESSION

nls_comp   Specifies how comparisons in the **where** clause are handled.

Default Value	Modifiable	Range of Values	Session or System Mod.
BINARY	Yes	BINARY or ANSI	SESSION

nls_currency   Specifies the local currency symbol.

Default Value	Modifiable	Range of Values	Session or System Mod.
Derived	Yes	Any valid string	SESSION

nls_date_format   Specifies the default date format.

Default Value	Modifiable	Range of Values	Session or System Mod.
Derived	Yes	Any valid format mask	SESSION

nls_date_language   Specifies how to spell the day and month names and abbreviations.

Default Value	Modifiable	Range of Values	Session or System Mod.
Derived	Yes	Any **nls_language** value	SESSION

nls_dual_currency   Specifies the dual currency symbol.

Default Value	Modifiable	Range of Values	Session or System Mod.
Derived	Yes	Any valid format	SESSION

nls_iso_currency   Specifies the default international currency symbol.

Default Value	Modifiable	Range of Values	Session or System Mod.
Derived	Yes	Any **nls_territory** value	SESSION

nls_language   Specifies the default language of the database or session.

Default Value	Modifiable	Range of Values	Session or System Mod.
OS Dependent	Yes	Any valid language	SESSION

nls_length_semantics   Determines the default length meaning of character data types.

Default Value	Modifiable	Range of Values	Session or System Mod.
BYTE	Yes	BYTE or CHAR	Both

nls_nchar_conv_excp   Determines whether or not an exception is raised when data is lost during conversion between NCHAR/NVARCHAR and CHAR/VARCHAR2 data types.

Default Value	Modifiable	Range of Values	Session or System Mod.
FALSE	Yes	TRUE or FALSE	Both

nls_numeric_characters   Specifies the characters to use as a group separator and decimal character.

Default Value	Modifiable	Range of Values	Session or System Mod.
Derived	Yes	Any valid characters	SESSION

nls_sort   Specifies collation sequence for sorting.

Default Value	Modifiable	Range of Values	Session or System Mod.
Derived	Yes	Any valid linguistic name	SESSION

nls_territory   Specifies the name of the territory of the database or session.

Default Value	Modifiable	Range of Values	Session or System Mod.
OS dependent	Yes	Any valid territory	SESSION

nls_timestamp_format   Specifies the default timestamp format.

Default Value	Modifiable	Range of Values	Session or System Mod.
Derived	Yes	Any valid format mask	SESSION

nls_timestamp_tz_format   Specifies the default timestamp with timezone format.

Default Value	Modifiable	Range of Values	Session or System Mod.
Derived	Yes	Any valid format mask	SESSION

o7_dictionary_accessibility   Determines how the **select any table** privilege behaves with SYS objects.

Default Value	Modifiable	Range of Values	Session or System Mod.
FALSE	No	TRUE or FALSE	No

object_cache_max_size_percent   Specifies the percentage of the optimal object cache size that the session can grow past the optimal size.

Default Value	Modifiable	Range of Values	Session or System Mod.
10	Yes	0 to OS dependent	Both

object_cache_optimal_size   Specifies the size the object cache will shrink to.

Default Value	Modifiable	Range of Values	Session or System Mod.
100K	Yes	10K to OS dependent	Both

olap_page_pool_size   Specifies the size of the OLAP pool.

Default Value	Modifiable	Range of Values	Session or System Mod.
32M	Yes	32M–2G	Both

open_cursors   Specifies the maximum number of cursors a session can hold.

Default Value	Modifiable	Range of Values	Session or System Mod.
50	Yes	1–(4G – 1)	System

open_links   Specifies the maximum number of database links opened.

Default Value	Modifiable	Range of Values	Session or System Mod.
4	No	0–255	No

open_links_per_instance   Specifies the maximum number of database links opened globally for each instance.

Default Value	Modifiable	Range of Values	Session or System Mod.
4	No	0–(4G – 1)	No

optimizer_dynamic_sampling   Determines the level of dynamic sampling performed by the optimizer.

Default Value	Modifiable	Range of Values	Session or System Mod.
2	Yes	0–10	Both

optimizer_features_enable   Determines which features are available to the optimizer.

Default Value	Modifiable	Range of Values	Session or System Mod.
10.0.0	Yes	8.0.0, 8.0.3, 8.0.4, 8.0.5, 8.0.6, 8.0.7, 8.1.0, 8.1.3, 8.1.4, 8.1.5, 8.1.6, 8.1.7, 9.0.0, 9.0.1, 9.2.0, or 10.0.0	Both

optimizer_index_caching   Instructs the optimizer what the percentage chance that an index block will be found in the buffer cache.

Default Value	Modifiable	Range of Values	Session or System Mod.
0	Yes	0–100	Both

optimizer_index_cost_adj   Instructs the optimizer on the cost of using an index.

Default Value	Modifiable	Range of Values	Session or System Mod.
100	Yes	1–10000	Both

optimizer_mode   Determines how the optimizer behaves, by default.

Default Value	Modifiable	Range of Values	Session or System Mod.
ALL_ROWS	Yes	ALL_ROWS, FIRST_ROWS, or FIRST_ROWS_*n*	Both

os_authent_prefix   Specifies the prefix to affix to the username when using OS authentication.

Default Value	Modifiable	Range of Values	Session or System Mod.
OP$	No	Any valid characters	No

os_roles   Determines if Oracle or the OS manages roles. If set to TRUE then the OS will manage roles; otherwise, Oracle manages them.

Default Value	Modifiable	Range of Values	Session or System Mod.
FALSE	No	TRUE or FALSE	No

parallel_adaptive_multi_user   Determines whether or not an adaptive algorithm is used to improve performance of parallel operations in a multiuser environment.

Default Value	Modifiable	Range of Values	Session or System Mod.
TRUE	Yes	TRUE or FALSE	System

parallel_automatic_tuning   Determines whether or not default parallel parameters are automatically established.

Default Value	Modifiable	Range of Values	Session or System Mod.
FALSE	No	TRUE or FALSE	No

parallel_execution_message_size   Specifies the size of messages for parallel execution.

Default Value	Modifiable	Range of Values	Session or System Mod.
OS dependent	No	2148–65535 (in bytes)	No

parallel_instance_group   Determines if parallel operations are allowed in the instance group. If no instances are listed, then RAC will not parallelize operations among instances in the cluster.

Default Value	Modifiable	Range of Values	Session or System Mod.
All current instances	Yes	Any group in **instance_groups**	Both

parallel_max_servers   Determines the maximum number of parallel execution processes.

Default Value	Modifiable	Range of Values	Session or System Mod.
Derived	Yes	0–3599	System

parallel_min_percent   Specifies the minimum percentage of parallel execution processes required in order to perform parallel operations.

Default Value	Modifiable	Range of Values	Session or System Mod.
0	Yes	0–100	SESSION

parallel_min_servers   Determines the minimum number of parallel processes to start when the instance is started.

Default Value	Modifiable	Range of Values	Session or System Mod.
0	Yes	0 to **parallel_max_servers**	System

parallel_threads_per_cpu   Determines the default degree of parallelism for the instance.

Default Value	Modifiable	Range of Values	Session or System Mod.
OS dependent	Yes	> 0	System

pga_aggregate_target   Specifies the target PGA memory size of all server processes for the instance.

Default Value	Modifiable	Range of Values	Session or System Mod.
20% of SGA size	Yes	10M–(4096G – 1)	System

plsql_code_type   Specifies the compilation mode for PL/SQL blocks.

Default Value	Modifiable	Range of Values	Session or System Mod.
INTERPRETED	Yes	INTERPRETED or NATIVE	Both

plsql_compiler_flags   Specifies compiler directives for the PL/SQL compiler.

Default Value	Modifiable	Range of Values	Session or System Mod.
INTERPRETED, NON_DEBUG	Yes	DEBUG/NON_DEBUG, INTERPRETED, or NATIVE	Both

plsql_debug   Determines whether or not PL/SQL blocks are compiled for debugging.

Default Value	Modifiable	Range of Values	Session or System Mod.
FALSE	Yes	TRUE or FALSE	Both

plsql_native_library_dir   Defines the name of a directory where the shared objects produced by the native compiler are stored.

Default Value	Modifiable	Range of Values	Session or System Mod.
None	Yes	Any valid directory	System

plsql_native_library_subdir_count   Specifies the number of subdirectories in the **plsql_native_library_dir** parameter.

Default Value	Modifiable	Range of Values	Session or System Mod.
0	Yes	$0–(2^{32} – 1)$	System

plsql_optimize_level   Specifies the optimization level when compiling PL/SQL blocks.

Default Value	Modifiable	Range of Values	Session or System Mod.
0	Yes	0–2	Both

plsql_v2_compatibility   Determines whether or not PL/SQL allows some Version 8 abnormalities.

Default Value	Modifiable	Range of Values	Session or System Mod.
FALSE	Yes	TRUE or FALSE	Both

plsql_warnings   Determines which warning messages are generated by the PL/SQL compiler. The syntax for the parameter is as follows:

```
( ENABLE or DISABLE or ERROR ):
( ALL or SEVERE or INFORMATIONAL or PERFORMANCE or
( integer or (integer [, integer ] ...) ) )
```

Default Value	Modifiable	Range of Values	Session or System Mod.
DISABLE:ALL	Yes	Various (see syntax)	Both

pre_page_sga   Determines whether or not the entire SGA is read into memory on startup.

Default Value	Modifiable	Range of Values	Session or System Mod.
FALSE	No	TRUE or FALSE	No

processes   Determines the maximum number of processes that can connect to the instance.

Default Value	Modifiable	Range of Values	Session or System Mod.
Derived	No	6 to OS dependent	No

query_rewrite_enabled   Determines whether or not queries are rewritten to use features such as materialized views and function-based indexes. Meanings of the range of values (see the following table) are

- **false**   Oracle will not use query rewrite.
- **true**   Oracle will include query rewrite in its cost calculations and rewrite the query if the cost justifies the rewrite.
- **force**   Oracle will always rewrite a rewritable query, regardless of the cost.

Default Value	Modifiable	Range of Values	Session or System Mod.
TRUE	Yes	TRUE, FALSE, or FORCE	Both

query_rewrite_integrity   Determines the degree to which the query is rewritten.

Default Value	Modifiable	Range of Values	Session or System Mod.
ENFORCED	No	ENFORCED, TRUSTED, or STALE_TOLERATED	No

rdbms_server_dn   Specifies the distinguished name of the database.

Default Value	Modifiable	Range of Values	Session or System Mod.
None	No	Valid distinguished names	No

read_only_open_delayed   Determines when files for READ ONLY tablespaces are accessed.

Default Value	Modifiable	Range of Values	Session or System Mod.
FALSE	No	TRUE or FALSE	No

recovery_parallelism   Determines the number of parallel processes to aid in instance recovery.

Default Value	Modifiable	Range of Values	Session or System Mod.
OS dependent	No	OS dependent	No

remote_archive_enable   Determines if a redo log can be sent or received from a remotely archived redo.

Default Value	Modifiable	Range of Values	Session or System Mod.
TRUE	No	RECEIVE, SEND, FALSE, or TRUE	No

remote_dependencies_mode   Specifies how to handle dependencies on remote PL/SQL stored procedures.

Default Value	Modifiable	Range of Values	Session or System Mod.
TIMESTAMP	Yes	TIMESTAMP or SIGNATURE	Both

remote_listener   Specifies the address of listeners that are not local to the database server.

Default Value	Modifiable	Range of Values	Session or System Mod.
None	Yes	Any valid network name	System

remote_login_passwordfile   Determines if a password file is used and, if so, how it is used.

Default Value	Modifiable	Range of Values	Session or System Mod.
NONE	No	NONE, SHARED, or EXCLUSIVE	No

remote_os_authent   Determines whether or not OS authentication can be performed from remote servers.

Default Value	Modifiable	Range of Values	Session or System Mod.
FALSE	No	TRUE or FALSE	No

remote_os_roles   Determines whether or not OS roles are allowed for remote clients.

Default Value	Modifiable	Range of Values	Session or System Mod.
FALSE	No	TRUE or FALSE	No

replication_dependency_tracking   Determines whether or not dependency tracking is available.

Default Value	Modifiable	Range of Values	Session or System Mod.
TRUE	No	TRUE or FALSE	No

resource_limit   Determines whether or not resource limits are enforced in database profiles.

Default Value	Modifiable	Range of Values	Session or System Mod.
FALSE	Yes	TRUE or FALSE	System

resource_manager_plan   Specifies the top-level resource plan to use for the instance.

Default Value	Modifiable	Range of Values	Session or System Mod.
None	Yes	Any valid string	System

resumable_timeout   Specifies the amount of time a resumable space transaction can be suspended before it times out.

Default Value	Modifiable	Range of Values	Session or System Mod.
0	Yes	0 to $2^{31} - 1$ (in seconds)	Both

rollback_segments   Determines which rollback segments to bring online on database startup.

Default Value	Modifiable	Range of Values	Session or System Mod.
None	No	Any valid rollback segments	No

serial_reuse   Determines which cursors can use the serial-reusable memory feature.

Default Value	Modifiable	Range of Values	Session or System Mod.
DISABLE	No	DISABLE, SELECT, DML, PLSQL, or ALL	No

service_names   Specifies the service names that the instance registers with the listener.

Default Value	Modifiable	Range of Values	Session or System Mod.
db_name.db_domain	Yes	Any character string	System

session_cached_cursors   Specifies the number of cursors to cache for a session.

Default Value	Modifiable	Range of Values	Session or System Mod.
0	Yes	0 to OS dependent	SESSION

session_max_open_files   Specifies the maximum number of BFILEs that can be opened in one session.

Default Value	Modifiable	Range of Values	Session or System Mod.
10	No	1 to **max_open_files**	No

sessions   Specifies the maximum number of sessions that can be concurrently connected to the instance at any one time.

Default Value	Modifiable	Range of Values	Session or System Mod.
Derived	No	1 to 2^{31}	No

sga_max_size   Determines the maximum size of the SGA.

Default Value	Modifiable	Range of Values	Session or System Mod.
Total SGA size	No	0 to OS dependent (in bytes, K, M, or G)	No

sga_target   Specifies a target size of the SGA.

Default Value	Modifiable	Range of Values	Session or System Mod.
0	Yes	64 to OS dependent (In bytes, K, M, or G)	System

shadow_core_dump   Determines whether the SGA is included in core dump files and, if so, how much is included.

Default Value	Modifiable	Range of Values	Session or System Mod.
PARTIAL	No	PARTIAL, FULL, or NONE	No

shared_memory_address   Specifies the starting address of the SGA.

Default Value	Modifiable	Range of Values	Session or System Mod.
0	No	Any valid address	No

shared_pool_reserved_size   Specifies the amount of the shared pool that is reserved for large requests of shared pool memory.

Default Value	Modifiable	Range of Values	Session or System Mod.
5%***shared_ pool_size**	No	5000–50%***shared_ pool_size** (in bytes, K, M, or G)	No

shared_pool_size   Specifies how much memory to allocate for the shared pool.

Default Value	Modifiable	Range of Values	Session or System Mod.
32M or 84M	Yes	1 granule to OS dependent	System

shared_server_sessions   Specifies the maximum number of shared server sessions to allow.

Default Value	Modifiable	Range of Values	Session or System Mod.
None	Yes	0 to sessions	System

shared_servers   Determines the number of shared servers to create at instance startup.

Default Value	Modifiable	Range of Values	Session or System Mod.
0	Yes	0 to **max_shared_servers**	System

skip_unusable_indexes   Determines whether or not tables with unusable indexes are reported.

Default Value	Modifiable	Range of Values	Session or System Mod.
TRUE	Yes	TRUE or FALSE	Both

smtp_out_server   Specifies the SMTP host to use for sending mail through the **utl_mail** supplied package.

Default Value	Modifiable	Range of Values	Session or System Mod.
None	No	*host_name*[:*port*]	No

sort_area_retained_size   Specifies the memory in the PGA to retain after a sort completes.

Default Value	Modifiable	Range of Values	Session or System Mod.
Derived	Yes	Two blocks to sort_area_size	Both

sort_area_size   Specifies the maximum amount of memory to be used in sorting operations. If a sort operation exceeds **sort_area_size**, then the sort must be performed on disk in temporary tablespaces. This parameter is obsoleted with the **pga_aggregate_target** parameter.

Default Value	Modifiable	Range of Values	Session or System Mod.
65536 bytes	Yes	OS dependent	Both

spfile   Specifies the server parameter file to use to start the database. This parameter is defined in the PFILE.

Default Value	Modifiable	Range of Values	Session or System Mod.
ORACLE_HOME/ dbs/spfile.ora	No	Any valid SPFILE	No

sql_trace   Determines whether or not tracing SQL statements in a session is enabled.

Default Value	Modifiable	Range of Values	Session or System Mod.
FALSE	Yes	TRUE or FALSE	Both

sql92_security   Specifies whether or not a user who issues an **update** or **delete** statement against a table and references column values in the **where** or **set** clause must have **select** privileges on that table.

Default Value	Modifiable	Range of Values	Session or System Mod.
FALSE	No	TRUE or FALSE	No

sqltune_category   Specifies the default category name to use by sessions.

Default Value	Modifiable	Range of Values	Session or System Mod.
DEFAULT	Yes	Any valid category	Both

standby_archive_dest   Specifies the location of archived redo logs from the primary database.

Default Value	Modifiable	Range of Values	Session or System Mod.
OS specific	Yes	Any valid directory	System

standby_file_management   Determines whether or not the standby database automatically manages files.

Default Value	Modifiable	Range of Values	Session or System Mod.
MANUAL	Yes	MANUAL or AUTO	System

star_transformation_enabled   Determines if a cost-based query transformation is applied to star queries.

Default Value	Modifiable	Range of Values	Session or System Mod.
FALSE	Yes	TRUE, FALSE, or TEMP_DISABLE	Both

statistics_level   Specifies the level of collection for database and operating system statistics.

Default Value	Modifiable	Range of Values	Session or System Mod.
TYPICAL	Yes	ALL, TYPICAL, or BASIC	Both

streams_pool_size   Specifies the size of the Streams pool, used to process Oracle Streams.

Default Value	Modifiable	Range of Values	Session or System Mod.
0	Yes	0 to OS dependent	System

tape_asynch_io   Specifies whether or not I/O operations to sequential devices are asynchronous.

Default Value	Modifiable	Range of Values	Session or System Mod.
TRUE	No	TRUE or FALSE	No

thread   In RAC, defines the thread number for the instance.

Default Value	Modifiable	Range of Values	Session or System Mod.
0	No	0 to maximum enabled threads	No

timed_os_statistics   Specifies the interval (in seconds) for the database to collect OS statistics.

Default Value	Modifiable	Range of Values	Session or System Mod.
Derived	Yes	Unlimited	Both

timed_statistics   Determines whether or not timing information is collected with statistics.

Default Value	Modifiable	Range of Values	Session or System Mod.
Derived based on **statistics_level**	Yes	TRUE or FALSE	Both

trace_enabled   Specifies whether or not tracing of the execution history of the instance is enabled.

Default Value	Modifiable	Range of Values	Session or System Mod.
TRUE	Yes	TRUE or FALSE	System

tracefile_identifier   Specifies an identifier that will become part of the trace file's name.

Default Value	Modifiable	Range of Values	Session or System Mod.
None	Yes	Any valid filename	SESSION

transactions   Specifies the maximum number of concurrent transactions allowed in the instance at any given time.

Default Value	Modifiable	Range of Values	Session or System Mod.
Derived	No	4–2^{32}	No

transactions_per_rollback_segment   Specifies the expected number of transactions a rollback segment should be able to handle.

Default Value	Modifiable	Range of Values	Session or System Mod.
5	No	1 to OS dependent	No

undo_management   Determines the method in which undo is managed in the database. If set to MANUAL, then undo is managed in traditional rollback segments. If set to AUTO, then undo is managed in an UNDO tablespace.

Default Value	Modifiable	Range of Values	Session or System Mod.
MANUAL	No	MANUAL or AUTO	No

undo_retention   Determines how long undo information should be kept in the undo tablespace, if there is space in the tablespace.

Default Value	Modifiable	Range of Values	Session or System Mod.
900	Yes	0 to $2^{32} - 1$	System

undo_tablespace   Specifies the undo tablespace to use in the database.

Default Value	Modifiable	Range of Values	Session or System Mod.
First undo tablespace	Yes	Any valid undo tablespace	System

use_indirect_data_buffers   Enables or disables the use of the extended buffer cache algorithm for 32-bit platforms that can support more than 4GB of memory.

Default Value	Modifiable	Range of Values	Session or System Mod.
FALSE	No	TRUE or FALSE	No

user_dump_dest   Specifies the location where user process trace files are stored.

Default Value	Modifiable	Range of Values	Session or System Mod.
OS dependent	Yes	Any valid directory	System

utl_file_dir   Specifies one or more directories that the **utl_file** supplied package can read or write to.

Default Value	Modifiable	Range of Values	Session or System Mod.
None	No	Any valid directory	No

workarea_size_policy   Specifies the policy for working areas, used for sorting, hashing, creating bitmap indexes, or merging bitmap indexes. If set to AUTO, the **pga_aggregate_target** parameter should also be set.

Default Value	Modifiable	Range of Values	Session or System Mod.
AUTO	Yes	AUTO or MANUAL	Both

APPENDIX
B

Data Dictionary Views

he data dictionary gives detailed information about every aspect of the database. The base data dictionary tables are owned by SYS and reside in the SYSTEM tablespace. These tables should not be accessed directly. Instead, the information should be accessed through a number of views, which are covered in this appendix.

USER_, ALL_, and DBA_

Many of the data dictionary views start with a prefix of USER_, ALL_, and DBA_. The prefix to the view details the scope of information presented in that view:

- **USER_**   Views that show information from the schema of the current user. For instance, USER_TABLES shows information on all tables that the current user owns.

- **ALL_**   Views that show information from the schema of the current user, as well as information from other schemas if the current user has appropriate privileges for that information. For example, ALL_TABLES shows information on all tables that the current user owns and information on the tables that the current user can access.

- **DBA_**   Views that show information for the entire database. Continuing the example, the DBA_TABLES view shows information on all tables in the database.

Typically, only the DBA has access to the DBA_ family of views. Any user in the database has access to the ALL_ and USER_ views, but the information presented in those views may vary from user to user. If a non-DBA needs access to the DBA_ views, they can be granted the SELECT CATALOG role.

DBA_ View

This section describes each of the DBA_ views, including the purpose of each view and whether a corresponding ALL_ or USER_ view exists for that view. Note that these views are from Oracle Database 10g, and they may or may not exist in earlier versions of the database.

View Name	All	User	Displays
DBA_2PC_NEIGHBORS			Incoming and outgoing connections for pending transactions
DBA_2PC_PENDING			Distributed transactions that need recovery
DBA_ADVISOR_ACTIONS		Y	Recommendations in the database from advisors
DBA_ADVISOR_COMMANDS			Information about commands in the database from advisors
DBA_ADVISOR_DEFINITIONS			Properties of all advisors
DBA_ADVISOR_FINDINGS		Y	The findings from all advisors
DBA_ADVISOR_JOURNAL		Y	Journal entries for all advisors
DBA_ADVISOR_LOG		Y	All advisor tasks
DBA_ADVISOR_OBJECT_TYPES			All object types used by advisors in the database

View Name	All	User	Displays
DBA_ADVISOR_OBJECT		Y	All objects referenced by all advisors in the database
DBA_ADVISOR_PARAMETERS		Y	Parameters and their values for advisor tasks in the database
DBA_ADVISOR_RATIONALE		Y	The rationale behind all recommendations in the database
DBA_ADVISOR_RECOMMENDATIONS		Y	The recommendations of all advisors in the database
DBA_ADVISOR_SQLA_REC_SUM		Y	The rollup information from the Access Advisor
DBA_ADVISOR_SQLA_WK_MAP		Y	The workload references from the Access Advisor
DBA_ADVISOR_SQLA_WK_STMTS		Y	The workload statements from the Access Advisor
DBA_ADVISOR_SQLW_JOURNAL		Y	The journal entries for workload objects
DBA_ADVISOR_SQLW_PARAMETERS		Y	All the workload parameters and their values in the database
DBA_ADVISOR_SQLW_STMTS		Y	All statements in the workload for the database
DBA_ADVISOR_SQLW_SUM		Y	An aggregated summary of all workload objects in the database
DBA_ADVISOR_SQLW_TABLES		Y	The workload statements and the tables they reference
DBA_ADVISOR_SQLW_TEMPLATES		Y	Aggregate information on workload templates in the database
DBA_ADVISOR_TASKS		Y	All advisor tasks
DBA_ADVISOR_TEMPLATES		Y	All advisor templates
DBA_ADVISOR_USAGE			The usage of each advisor
DBA_ALERT_HISTORY			A history of alerts
DBA_ALL_TABLES	Y	Y	All object tables and relational tables in the database
DBA_APPLICATION_ROLES			All roles that have authentication policies
DBA_APPLY	Y		All SQL Apply processes
DBA_APPLY_CONFLICT_COLUMNS	Y		All conflict handlers
DBA_APPLY_DML_HANDLERS	Y		All DML handlers
DBA_APPLY_ENQUEUE	Y		The SQL Apply enqueue
DBA_APPLY_ERROR	Y		Any errors generated by the SQL Apply process
DBA_APPLY_EXECUTE	Y		The SQL Apply execute actions
DBA_APPLY_INSTANTIATED_GLOBAL			Information about those databases with an instantiation SCN
DBA_APPLY_INSTANTIATED_OBJECTS			Information about those objects with an instantiation SCN
DBA_APPLY_INSTANTIATED_SCHEMAS			Information about those schemas with an instantiation SCN

View Name	All	User	Displays
DBA_APPLY_KEY_COLUMNS	Y		All substitute key columns
DBA_APPLY_PARAMETERS	Y		Parameters for the SQL Apply process
DBA_APPLY_PROGRESS	Y		The progress of the SQL Apply process
DBA_APPLY_TABLE_COLUMNS	Y		Information about the destination table's columns
DBA_AQ_AGENT_PRIVS		Y	The privileges of AQ agents
DBA_AQ_AGENTS			All registered AQ agents
DBA_ASSOCIATIONS	Y	Y	All user-defined statistics
DBA_ATTRIBUTE_TRANSFORMATIONS		Y	Information about transform functions
DBA_AUDIT_EXISTS			Audit trail entries produced by **audit exists** and **audit not exists**
DBA_AUDIT_OBJECT		Y	Audit trail entries for all audited objects
DBA_AUDIT_POLICIES	Y	Y	All fine-grained audit policies
DBA_AUDIT_POLICY_COLUMNS	Y	Y	All fine-grained audit columns
DBA_AUDIT_SESSION		Y	Audit trail entries for **connect** and **disconnect** operations
DBA_AUDIT_STATEMENT		Y	Audit trail entries for **grant**, **revoke**, **audit**, **noaudit**, and **alter system** statements
DBA_AUDIT_TRAIL		Y	Audit trail entries
DBA_AW_PS	Y	Y	Analytic workspace page spaces
DBA_AWS	Y	Y	All analytic workspaces
DBA_BAE_TABLE_MVIEWS	Y	Y	Information on materialized views using logs
DBA_BLOCKERS			Those sessions blocking other sessions
DBA_CAPTURE	Y		All streams capture processes
DBA_CAPTURE_EXTRA_ATTRIBUTES	Y		Information on extra attributes for all streams capture processes
DBA_CAPTURE_PARAMETERS	Y		Information on the parameters for all streams capture processes
DBA_CAPTURE_PREPARED_DATABASE	Y		Information about when the local database was instantiated
DBA_CAPTURE_PREPARED_SCHEMAS	Y		Information about schemas prepared for instantiation
DBA_CAPTURE_PREPARED_TABLES	Y		Information about all tables ready for instantiation
DBA_CATALOG	Y	Y	Information on all indexes, tables, views, clusters, synonyms, and sequences
DBA_CLU_COLUMNS		Y	The columns of all clusters
DBA_CLUSTER_HASH_EXPRESSIONS	Y	Y	The hash function information for hash clusters
DBA_CLUSTERS	Y	Y	Information on all clusters

View Name	All	User	Displays
DBA_COL_COMMENTS	Y	Y	All comments on any columns of all tables and views
DBA_COL_PRIVS	Y	Y	Privileges on any columns of all tables and views
DBA_COLL_TYPES	Y	Y	All collection types
DBA_COMMON_AUDIT_TRAIL			All standard and fine-grained audit trail entries
DBA_CONS_OBJ_COLUMNS	Y	Y	Constraints on object columns
DBA_CONSTRAINTS	Y	Y	Information on all constraints
DBA_CONTEXT	Y		All context namespace information
DBA_DATA_FILES			All database data files
DBA_DATAPUMP_JOBS		Y	All Data Pump jobs
DBA_DATAPUMP_SESSIONS			All Data Pump sessions
DBA_DB_LINKS	Y	Y	All database links
DBA_DDL_LOCKS			All held DDL locks
DBA_DEPENDENCIES	Y	Y	All dependencies between database objects
DBA_DIM_ATTRIBUTES	Y	Y	Attribute information on all dimensions
DBA_DIM_CHILD_OF	Y	Y	Hierarchical children on all dimensions
DBA_DIM_HIERARCHIES	Y	Y	Hierarchical relationships on all dimensions
DBA_DIM_JOIN_KEY	Y	Y	All joins for all dimensions
DBA_DIM_LEVEL_KEY	Y	Y	The columns for all dimension levels
DBA_DIM_LEVELS	Y	Y	All the dimension levels
DBA_DIMENSIONS	Y	Y	Information on all dimensions
DBA_DIRECTORIES	Y		All directory objects
DBA_DML_LOCKS			All held DML locks
DBA_DMT_FREE_SPACE			All free extents in dictionary-managed tablespaces
DBA_DMT_USED_EXTENTS			All used extents in dictionary-managed tablespaces
DBA_ENABLED_AGGREGATIONS			Information about enabled on-demand aggregations
DBA_ENABLED_TRACES			All enabled SQL traces
DBA_ERRORS	Y	Y	All errors for compiled objects
DBA_EVALUATION_CONTEXT_TABLES	Y	Y	All rule evaluation contexts
DBA_EVALUATION_CONTEXT_VARS	Y	Y	Variable information for all rule evaluation contexts
DBA_EVALUATION_CONTEXTS	Y	Y	All rule evaluation contexts
DBA_EXP_FILES			Information on export files
DBA_EXP_OBJECTS			Information on exported objects for incremental exports

View Name	All	User	Displays
DBA_EXP_VERSION			Version number information for exports
DBA_EXTENTS		Y	All extents for all segments
DBA_EXTERNAL_LOCATIONS	Y	Y	The locations for all external tables
DBA_EXTERNAL_TABLES	Y	Y	All external tables
DBA_FEATURE_USAGE_STATISTICS			Information about feature usage statistics
DBA_FGA_AUDIT_TRAIL			Audit trail entries for fine-grained auditing
DBA_FREE_SPACE		Y	All free extents in the database
DBA_FREE_SPACE_COALESCED			Information on the coalesced space in the database
DBA_HIGH_WATER_MARK_STATISTICS			Statistics for high-water marks for all tables
DBA_HIST_ACTIVE_SESS_ACTIVITY			The history for recent session activity
DBA_HIST_BASELINE			System baselines
DBA_HIST_BG_EVENT_SUMMARY			The historical background summary information
DBA_HIST_BUFFER_POOL_STAT			The historical information for buffer pools
DBA_HIST_CR_BLOCK_SERVER			The historical statistics for consistent read blocks for Cache Fusion
DBA_HIST_CURRENT_BLOCK_SERVER			The historical statistics for current blocks for Cache Fusion
DBA_HIST_DATABASE_INSTANCE			The historical statistics for the database instance
DBA_HIST_DATAFILE			The historical statistics for database data files
DBA_HIST_DB_CACHE_ADVICE			The historical information for database cache advice
DBA_HIST_DLM_MISC			Miscellaneous RAC historical statistics
DBA_HIST_ENQUEUE_STAT			The historical statistics on lock requests
DBA_HIST_EVENT_NAME			Historical information on wait events
DBA_HIST_FILEMETRIC_HISTORY			Historical statistics on file metrics
DBA_HIST_FILESTATXS			Historical statistics on file read/write operations
DBA_HIST_INSTANCE_RECOVERY			Historical statistics for instance recovery
DBA_HIST_JAVA_POOL_ADVICE			Historical statistics on Java Pool advice
DBA_HIST_LATCH			Historical statistics on latches
DBA_HIST_LATCH_CHILDREN			Historical statistics on child latches
DBA_HIST_LATCH_MISSES_SUMMARY			Historical statistics on latch misses
DBA_HIST_LATCH_NAME			Latch names
DBA_HIST_LATCH_PARENT			Historical statistics on parent latches
DBA_HIST_LIBRARYCACHE			Historical statistics on the library cache
DBA_HIST_LOG			Historical statistics on log files
DBA_HIST_METRIC_NAME			Historical statistics on metric names
DBA_HIST_MTTR_TARGET_ADVICE			Historical metrics on MTTR target advice

View Name	All	User	Displays
DBA_HIST_OPTIMIZER_ENV			Historical information on the optimizer environment
DBA_HIST_OSSTAT			Historical statistics on the OS
DBA_HIST_OSSTAT_NAME			Names of the OS statistics
DBA_HIST_PARAMETER			The initialization parameters that were in effect
DBA_HIST_PARAMETER_NAME			The parameter names
DBA_HIST_PGA_TARGET_ADVICE			Historical statistics on advice for the PGA aggregate target
DBA_HIST_PGASTAT			Historical statistics on the PGA memory usage
DBA_HIST_RESOURCE_LIMIT			Historical statistics on resource limits
DBA_HIST_ROLLSTAT			Historical statistics on rollback segments
DBA_HIST_ROWCACHE_SUMMARY			Historical statistics on the data dictionary cache
DBA_HIST_SEG_STAT			Historical statistics on segments
DBA_HIST_SEG_STAT_OBJ			The segment names
DBA_HIST_SERVICE_NAME			The names of services
DBA_HIST_SERVICE_STAT			Historical statistics on services
DBA_HIST_SERVICE_WAIT_CLASS			Historical statistics on wait class information
DBA_HIST_SESSMETRIC_HISTORY			Historical statistics on session metrics
DBA_HIST_SGA			Historical statistics on the System Global Area
DBA_HIST_SGASTAT			Historical statistics on the SGA
DBA_HIST_SHARED_POOL_ADVICE			Historical information on advice for the shared pool
DBA_HIST_SNAP_ERROR			Historical information on snapshot errors
DBA_HIST_SNAPSHOT			Historical information on snapshots
DBA_HIST_SQL_PLAN			Historical SQL execution plan information
DBA_HIST_SQL_SUMMARY			Historical SQL summary information
DBA_HIST_SQL_WORKAREA_HSTGRM			Historical work area execution statistics
DBA_HIST_SQLBIND			Historical bind variable information
DBA_HIST_SQLSTAT			Historical information on SQL statistics
DBA_HIST_SQLTEXT			Historical SQL text information
DBA_HIST_STAT_NAME			Historical statistics names
DBA_HIST_SYS_TIME_MODEL			Historical system time model statistics
DBA_HIST_SYSMETRIC_HISTORY			Historical system metric statistics
DBA_HIST_SYSMETRIC_SUMMARY			Summarized historical system metric statistics
DBA_HIST_SYSSTAT			Historical system statistics
DBA_HIST_SYSTEM_EVENT			Historical system event information
DBA_HIST_TABLESPACE_STAT			Historical tablespace statistics
DBA_HIST_TBSPC_SPACE_USAGE			Historical tablespace usage statistics

View Name	All	User	Displays
DBA_HIST_TEMPFILE			Historical statistics on tempfiles
DBA_HIST_TEMPSTATXS			Historical read/write statistics on tempfiles
DBA_HIST_THREAD			Historical statistics on threads
DBA_HIST_UNDOSTAT			Historical statistics on undo segments
DBA_HIST_WAITCLASSMET_HISTORY			Historical statistics on wait class metrics
DBA_HIST_WAITSTAT			Historical statistics on block contention
DBA_HIST_WR_CONTROL			Historical control information for the Workload Repository
DBA_IND_COLUMNS	Y	Y	The columns of all indexes
DBA_IND_EXPRESSIONS	Y	Y	The expressions for all function-based indexes
DBA_IND_PARTITIONS	Y	Y	All index partitions
DBA_IND_STATISTICS	Y	Y	Optimizer statistics for all indexes
DBA_IND_SUBPARTITIONS	Y	Y	All index subpartitions
DBA_INDEXES	Y	Y	All indexes
DBA_INDEXTYPE_ARRAYTYPES	Y	Y	Array type information on all indextypes
DBA_INDEXTYPE_COMMENTS	Y	Y	Comments on all indextypes
DBA_INDEXTYPE_OPERATORS	Y	Y	Operators of all indextypes
DBA_INDEXTYPES	Y	Y	All indextypes
DBA_INTERNAL_TRIGGERS	Y	Y	All internal triggers
DBA_JAVA_ARGUMENTS	Y	Y	Arguments for all Java classes
DBA_JAVA_CLASSES	Y	Y	All Java classes
DBA_JAVA_DERIVATIONS	Y	Y	All derived Java classes
DBA_JAVA_FIELDS	Y	Y	Fields for all Java classes
DBA_JAVA_IMPLEMENTS	Y	Y	Interface implementation information for all Java classes
DBA_JAVA_INNERS	Y	Y	All inner Java classes
DBA_JAVA_LAYOUTS	Y	Y	Class layouts for all Java classes
DBA_JAVA_METHODS	Y	Y	Methods for all Java classes
DBA_JAVA_NCOMPS	Y	Y	ncomp-related information for all Java classes
DBA_JAVA_POLICY		Y	Security policies for all Java classes
DBA_JAVA_RESOLVERS	Y	Y	All resolvers for all Java classes
DBA_JAVA_THROWS	Y	Y	Exception information for all Java classes
DBA_JOBS	Y	Y	All scheduled jobs
DBA_JOBS_RUNNING			Running jobs
DBA_JOIN_IND_COLUMNS	Y	Y	Columns of all join indexes
DBA_KGLLOCK			Locks and pins on KGL objects
DBA_LIBRARIES	Y	Y	All libraries

View Name	All	User	Displays
DBA_LMT_FREE_SPACE			Free extents for all LMTs
DBA_LMT_USED_EXTENTS			All extents in LMTs
DBA_LOB_PARTITIONS	Y	Y	All LOB partitions
DBA_LOB_SUBPARTITIONS	Y	Y	All LOB subpartitions
DBA_LOB_TEMPLATES	Y	Y	All LOB subpartition templates
DBA_LOBS	Y	Y	Information on LOBs
DBA_LOCK			Locks and latches held in the database
DBA_LOCK_INTERNAL			Locks and latches held in the database
DBA_LOCKS			Synonym for **dba_lock**
DBA_LOG_GROUP_COLUMNS	Y	Y	All columns that are specified for log groups
DBA_LOG_GROUPS	Y	Y	Definitions for all log groups
DBA_LOGMNR_LOG			Archived logs registered with LogMiner
DBA_LOGMNR_PURGED_LOG			Archived logs no longer needed by LogMiner
DBA_LOGMNR_SESSION			All active LogMiner sessions
DBA_LOGSTDBY_EVENTS			Information on the events of the logical standby databases
DBA_LOGSTDBY_LOG			Information about the logs registered for the logical standby databases
DBA_LOGSTDBY_NOT_UNIQUE			Tables that do not have primary keys or non-null unique indexes
DBA_LOGSTDBY_PARAMETERS			Parameters used by standby apply process
DBA_LOGSTDBY_PROGRESS			Progress of standby apply process
DBA_LOGSTDBY_SKIP			Tables skipped by standby apply process
DBA_LOGSTDBY_SKIP_TRANSACTION			Skip settings chosen for logical standby
DBA_LOGSTDBY_UNSUPPORTED			Objects with unsupported data types
DBA_METHOD_PARAMS	Y	Y	Method parameters for all object types
DBA_METHOD_RESULTS	Y	Y	Method results for all object types
DBA_MVIEW_AGGREGATES	Y	Y	Grouping functions in MVIEW select statements
DBA_MVIEW_ANALYSIS	Y	Y	Displays MVIEWs that support query rewrite
DBA_MVIEW_COMMENTS	Y	Y	Comments on MVIEWs
DBA_MVIEW_DETAIL_RELATIONS	Y	Y	Detail relations on all MVIEWs
DBA_MVIEW_JOINS	Y	Y	Columns that are joined to satisfy the MVIEW
DBA_MVIEW_KEYS	Y	Y	Columns that MVIEWs are based on
DBA_MVIEW_LOG_FILTER_COLS			All columns being logged for MVIEWs
DBA_MVIEW_LOGS	Y	Y	All MVIEW logs
DBA_MVIEW_REFRESH_TIMES	Y	Y	Refresh times of all MVIEWs
DBA_MVIEWS	Y	Y	All materialized views

View Name	All	User	Displays
DBA_NESTED_TABLE_COLS	Y	Y	All the columns of nested tables
DBA_NESTED_TABLES	Y	Y	All nested tables
DBA_OBJ_AUDIT_OPTS		Y	All object auditing options
DBA_OBJ_COLATTRS	Y	Y	All columns and attributes for all tables
DBA_OBJECT_SIZE		Y	All PL/SQL object sizes
DBA_OBJECT_TABLES	Y	Y	All object tables
DBA_OBJECTS	Y	Y	All objects in the database
DBA_OPANCILLARY	Y	Y	All operator binding ancillary information
DBA_OPARGUMENTS	Y	Y	All operator binding arguments
DBA_OPBINDINGS	Y	Y	All operator binding functions and methods
DBA_OPERATOR_COMMENTS	Y	Y	Comments on user-defined operators
DBA_OPERATORS	Y	Y	User-defined operators
DBA_ORPHAN_KEY_TABLE			Key values from underlying base tables that have corruption
DBA_OUTLINE_HINTS	Y	Y	Hints for all outlines
DBA_OUTLINES	Y	Y	All outlines
DBA_OUTSTANDING_ALERTS			All outstanding alerts
DBA_PART_COL_STATISTICS	Y	Y	Column statistics for all partitions
DBA_PART_HISTOGRAMS	Y	Y	Histograms for all partitions
DBA_PART_INDEXES	Y	Y	All partitioned indexes
DBA_PART_KEY_COLUMNS	Y	Y	The partition key columns for all partitioned objects
DBA_PART_LOBS	Y	Y	All partitioned LOBs
DBA_PART_TABLES	Y	Y	All partitioned tables
DBA_PARTIAL_DROP_TABS	Y	Y	All tables that have partially completed the **drop column** operation
DBA_PENDING_CONV_TABLES	Y	Y	All pending conversion tables in the database
DBA_PENDING_TRANSACTIONS			All unresolved transactions
DBA_PLSQL_OBJECT_SETTINGS	Y	Y	Compiler settings for all PL/SQL objects
DBA_POLICIES	Y	Y	All security policies
DBA_POLICY_CONTEXTS	Y	Y	All driving contexts
DBA_POLICY_GROUPS	Y	Y	All policy groups
DBA_PRIV_AUDIT_OPTS			All currently audited system privileges
DBA_PROCEDURES	Y	Y	All stored procedures and functions
DBA_PROFILES			All profiles and their limits
DBA_PROPAGATION	Y		All Streams propagations
DBA_PROXIES		Y	All proxy connections
DBA_PUBLISHED_COLUMNS	Y	Y	All published source columns

View Name	All	User	Displays
DBA_QUEUE_SCHEDULES		Y	All schedules for propagating messages
DBA_QUEUE_TABLES	Y	Y	All message queue tables
DBA_QUEUES	Y	Y	All message queues
DBA_RCHILD			All children in any refresh group
DBA_RECYCLEBIN		Y	All recycle bins
DBA_REDEFINITION_ERRORS			Online redefinition errors
DBA_REDEFINITION_OBJECTS			Online redefinition objects
DBA_REFRESH	Y	Y	All refresh groups
DBA_REFRESH_CHILDREN	Y	Y	All objects in all refresh groups
DBA_REFS	Y	Y	All ref columns
DBA_REGISTERED_ARCHIVED_LOG			All registered archive logs
DBA_REGISTERED_MVIEW_GROUPS			All registered MVIEW groups
DBA_REGISTERED_MVIEWS	Y	Y	All registered MVIEWs
DBA_REGISTRY		Y	All loaded components
DBA_REGISTRY_HIERARCHY			All loaded components in hierarchical format
DBA_REPAIR_TABLE			All corruptions found by **dbms_repair.check_object**
DBA_RESUMABLE		Y	All resumable operations
DBA_REWRITE_EQUIVALENCES	Y	Y	All query rewrite equivalences
DBA_RGROUP			All refresh groups
DBA_ROLE_PRIVS		Y	All roles granted to users and other roles
DBA_ROLES			All roles
DBA_ROLLBACK_SEGS			All rollback segments
DBA_RSRC_CONSUMER_GROUP_PRIVS		Y	All resource consumer group privileges
DBA_RSRC_CONSUMER_GROUPS			All resource consumer groups
DBA_RSRC_GROUP_MAPPINGS			Mapping between consumer groups and sessions
DBA_RSRC_MANAGER_SYSTEM_PRIVS		Y	Users and roles that have been granted **administer_resource_manager** privileges
DBA_RSRC_MAPPING_PRIORITY			All resource consumer group mapping priorities
DBA_RSRC_PLAN_DIRECTIVES			All resource plan directives
DBA_RSRC_PLANS			All resource plans
DBA_RULE_SET_RULES	Y	Y	Rules in all rule sets
DBA_RULE_SETS	Y	Y	All rule sets
DBA_RULES	Y	Y	All rules
DBA_SCHEDULER_JOB_ARGS	Y	Y	Arguments of all Scheduler jobs
DBA_SCHEDULER_JOB_CLASSES	Y		Classes of all Scheduler jobs
DBA_SCHEDULER_JOB_LOG	Y	Y	Log of all Scheduler jobs

View Name	All	User	Displays
DBA_SCHEDULER_JOB_RUN_DETAILS	Y	Y	Run details of Scheduler jobs
DBA_SCHEDULER_JOBS	Y	Y	All Scheduler jobs
DBA_SCHEDULER_PROGRAM_ARGS	Y	Y	Arguments of all Scheduler programs
DBA_SCHEDULER_PROGRAMS	Y	Y	All Scheduler programs
DBA_SCHEDULER_RUNNING_JOBS	Y	Y	All running Scheduler jobs
DBA_SCHEDULER_SCHEDULES	Y	Y	All Scheduler schedules
DBA_SCHEDULER_WINDOW_DETAILS	Y		Log details for all Scheduler windows
DBA_SCHEDULER_WINDOW_GROUPS	Y		Information on all Scheduler window groups
DBA_SCHEDULER_WINDOW_LOG	Y		Log information for all Scheduler windows
DBA_SCHEDULER_WINDOWS	Y		All Scheduler windows
DBA_SCHEDULER_WINGROUP_MEMBERS	Y		The members of all Scheduler window groups
DBA_SEC_RELEVANT_COLS	Y	Y	Relevant columns of all security policies
DBA_SEGMENTS		Y	All segments
DBA_SEQUENCES	Y	Y	All sequences
DBA_SERVER_REGISTRY			All loaded components
DBA_SERVICES	Y		All services
DBA_SOURCE	Y	Y	Source code for stored objects
DBA_SOURCE_TABLES	Y	Y	All source tables
DBA_SQL_PROFILES			All SQL profiles
DBA_SQLJ_TYPE_ATTRS	Y	Y	Attributes of all SQLJ object types
DBA_SQLJ_TYPE_METHODS	Y	Y	Methods of all SQLJ object types
DBA_SQLJ_TYPES	Y	Y	All SQLJ object types
DBA_SQLSET		Y	Displays SQL tuning sets
DBA_SQLSET_BINDS		Y	Bind variables for SQL tuning sets
DBA_SQLSET_REFERENCES		Y	If SQL tuning sets are active
DBA_SQLSET_STATEMENTS		Y	Displays SQL statements for all SQL tuning sets
DBA_SQLTUNE_BINDS		Y	Bind variables for all tuned SQL statements
DBA_SQLTUNE_PLANS		Y	Execution plans for all tuned SQL statements
DBA_SQLTUNE_RATIONALE_PLAN		Y	Rationale for execution plans for all tuned SQL statements
DBA_SQLTUNE_STATISTICS		Y	Statistics for all tuned SQL statements
DBA_STMT_AUDIT_OPTS			Current auditing options
DBA_STORED_SETTINGS	Y	Y	Parameter settings for PL/SQL units
DBA_STREAMS_ADMINISTRATOR			Users who are Streams administrators
DBA_STREAMS_GLOBAL_RULES	Y		Global rules for all Streams processes
DBA_STREAMS_MESSAGE_CONSUMERS	Y		Information on Streams messaging clients
DBA_STREAMS_MESSAGE_RULES	Y		Displays Streams messaging rules

View Name	All	User	Displays
DBA_STREAMS_NEWLY_SUPPORTED	Y		Information on tables that are newly supported by Streams
DBA_STREAMS_RULES	Y		Rules used by Streams
DBA_STREAMS_SCHEMA_RULES	Y		Schema rules used by Streams
DBA_STREAMS_TABLE_RULES	Y		Table rules used by Streams
DBA_STREAMS_TRANSFORM_FUNCTION	Y		Rule-based transformation functions used by Streams
DBA_STREAMS_UNSUPPORTED	Y		Tables unsupported by Streams
DBA_SUBPART_COL_STATISTICS	Y	Y	Column statistics for subpartitions
DBA_SUBPART_HISTOGRAMS	Y	Y	Histograms for subpartitions
DBA_SUBPART_KEY_COLUMNS	Y	Y	Key columns for subpartitions
DBA_SUBPART_TEMPLATES	Y	Y	Subpartition templates
DBA_SUBSCRIBED_COLUMNS	Y	Y	Columns of source tables for subscribers
DBA_SUBSCRIBED_TABLES	Y	Y	Source tables for subscribers
DBA_SUBSCRIPTIONS	Y	Y	All subscriptions
DBA_SYNONYMS	Y	Y	All synonyms
DBA_SYS_PRIVS		Y	System privileges granted to users and roles
DBA_TAB_COL_STATISTICS	Y	Y	Statistics on table columns
DBA_TAB_COLS	Y	Y	Columns of all tables
DBA_TAB_COLUMNS	Y	Y	Columns of all tables but excludes hidden columns
DBA_TAB_COMMENTS	Y	Y	Comments on all tables
DBA_TAB_HISTOGRAMS	Y	Y	Histograms on all tables
DBA_TAB_MODIFICATIONS	Y	Y	Modifications to all tables since statistics were last gathered
DBA_TAB_PARTITIONS	Y	Y	Partitions on all tables
DBA_TAB_PRIVS	Y	Y	Object privileges granted to all users and roles
DBA_TAB_STATISTICS	Y	Y	Statistics on all tables
DBA_TAB_SUBPARTITIONS	Y	Y	Subpartitions on all tables
DBA_TABLES	Y	Y	All tables in the database
DBA_TABLESPACE_GROUPS			All tablespace groups
DBA_TABLESPACES		Y	All tablespaces
DBA_TEMP_FILES			All temporary files
DBA_THRESHOLDS			All thresholds
DBA_TRANSFORMATIONS		Y	All transformations
DBA_TRIGGER_COLS	Y	Y	Columns used by all triggers in the database
DBA_TRIGGERS	Y	Y	All triggers in the database
DBA_TS_QUOTAS		Y	Quotas on all tablespaces for all users
DBA_TUNE_MVIEW		Y	Results from **dbms_advisor.tune_mview**

View Name	All	User	Displays
DBA_TYPE_ATTRS	Y	Y	Attributes of all object types
DBA_TYPE_METHODS	Y	Y	Methods of all object types
DBA_TYPE_VERSIONS	Y	Y	Versions of all object types
DBA_TYPES	Y	Y	All object types in the database
DBA_UNDO_EXTENTS			All undo extents
DBA_UNUSED_COL_TABS	Y	Y	All tables containing unused columns
DBA_UPDATABLE_COLUMNS	Y	Y	All columns in a join view that can be updated
DBA_USERS	Y	Y	All users in the database
DBA_USTATS	Y	Y	All user-defined statistics
DBA_VARRAYS	Y	Y	All varrays in the database
DBA_VIEWS	Y	Y	All views in the database
DBA_WAITERS			All processes waiting on locks to be released
DBA_WARNING_SETTINGS	Y	Y	Warning parameters
DBA_XML_SCHEMAS	Y	Y	All registered XML schemas
DBA_XML_TAB_COLS	Y	Y	The columns of all XML tables
DBA_XML_TABLES	Y	Y	All XML tables
DBA_XML_VIEW_COLS	Y	Y	The columns of all XML views

Miscellaneous Views

There are a number of data dictionary views that are not DBA_ views or V$ views, but are still quite useful. This section lists and describes the most commonly used of these miscellaneous data dictionary views.

View	Displays
CHAINED_ROWS	Output for the **analyze list chained rows** command
COLS	Synonym for **user_tab_columns**
DATABASE_PROPERTIES	Permanent database properties
DICTIONARY	Data dictionary views
EXCEPTIONS	Integrity constraint exceptions
GLOBAL_NAME	The database's global name
INDEX_STATS	Information from the **analyze index validate structure** command
PLAN_TABLE	Execution plan from the **explain plan** command
RECYCLEBIN	Synonym for **user_recyclebin**
SESSION_CONTEXT	Current session context information
TABS	Synonym for **user_tables**

V$ Views

The V$ views are dynamic performance-tuning views. The contents of these views are continuously updated to reflect the performance of the instance. The V$ views are not based on actual tables. Instead, they are gateways into the allocated memory structures of the Oracle instance. As such, when the instance is shut down, all historical information in the V$ views is lost. Use caution with V$ views, because read consistency is not guaranteed.

The actual V$ views really start with the V_$ prefix and are owned by SYS. Public synonyms with the prefix V$ are then created. For instance, there is a view called SYS.V_$SESSION with a public synonym called V$SESSION. References to the V$ views are made to the synonym rather than to the actual view name.

There are a number of GV$ views, or global V$ views. The GV$ views are useful in Real Application Cluster environments. Most V$ views simply query the associated GV$ view for the current instance. The GV$ views have one additional column, INST_ID, representing an instance identifier. In single-instance environments, V$ views still query from the associated GV$ view.

View	Displays
V$ACCESS	Objects that are currently locked and sessions accessing them
V$ACTIVE_INSTANCES	Instance names and numbers
V$ACTIVE_SERVICES	Active services
V$ACTIVE_SESS_POOL_MTH	Active session pool resource allocation methods
V$ACTIVE_SESSION_HISTORY	Historical session activity
V$ALERT_TYPES	Alert type information
V$AQ	Advanced queuing statistics
V$ARCHIVE	Redo log files that need archiving
V$ARCHIVE_DEST	Archive log destination information
V$ARCHIVE_DEST_STATUS	Archive log destination status
V$ARCHIVE_GAP	Gaps in archive logs in the standby database
V$ARCHIVE_PROCESS	State of ARCHn processes
V$ARCHIVED_LOG	Archived log information
V$ASM_ALIAS	Aliases for disk groups in ASM
V$ASM_CLIENT	Databases using ASM
V$ASM_DISK	Disks used by ASM
V$ASM_DISKGROUP	Disk groups used by ASM
V$ASM_FILE	ASM files
V$ASM_OPERATION	ASM long-running operations
V$ASM_TEMPLATE	ASM diskgroup templates
V$BACKUP	File backup status
V$BACKUP_AYNC_IO	Performance information on RMAN backups and restores

View	Displays
V$BACKUP_CORRUPTION	Corrupt blocks from backups
V$BACKUP_DATAFILE	Files in backup sets from the control file
V$BACKUP_DEVICE	Supported backup devices
V$BACKUP_FILES	RMAN backup files
V$BACKUP_PIECE	RMAN backup pieces from the control file
V$BACKUP_REDOLOG	Archived redo logs in RMAN backup sets
V$BACKUP_SET	RMAN backup sets from the control file
V$BACKUP_SPFILE	SPFILES in backup sets from the control file
V$BACKUP_SYNC_IO	Performance information about RMAN backups and restores
V$BGPROCESS	Background processes
V$BH	Buffer header information
V$BLOCK_CHANGE_TRACKING	Block change tracking information
V$BUFFER_POOL	Information on the buffer pools
V$BUFFER_POOL_STATISTICS	Stats on the buffer pools
V$BUFFERED_PUBLISHERS	Information on buffered publishers
V$BUFFERED_QUEUES	Information on buffered queues
V$BUFFERED_SUBSCRIBERS	Information on buffered subscribers
V$CACHE	Block header information for RAC
V$CACHE_LOCK	Lock manager IDs for block header information for RAC
V$CACHE_TRANSFER	Blocks that have been pinged at least once, for RAC
V$CIRCUIT	Information on virtual circuits
V$CLIENT_STATS	Client statistics
V$CONTEXT	Attributes of current session
V$CONTROLFILE	Names of the control files
V$CONTROLFILE_RECORD_SECTION	Information on each control file record section
V$COPY_CORRUPTION	Information on datafile copy corruptions
V$CR_BLOCK_SERVER	Consistent read statistics on Cache Fusion processes
V$CURRENT_BLOCK_SERVER	Current statistics on Cache Fusion processes
V$DATABASE	Information on the database from the control file
V$DATABASE_BLOCK_CORRUPTION	Corrupt blocks from the last backup
V$DATABASE_INCARNATION	Information on all database incarnations
V$DATAFILE	Information on database files from the control file
V$DATAFILE_COPY	Datafile copy information from the control file
V$DATAFILE_HEADER	Datafile header information from the control file
V$DATAGUARD_CONFIG	Data Guard configuration information
V$DATAGUARD_STATUS	Data Guard status

View	Displays
V$DB_CACHE_ADVICE	Advice on sizing buffer cache
V$DB_OBJECT_CACHE	Objects cached in the library cache
V$DB_PIPES	Pipes in the shared pool
V$DBFILE	Data files; use V$DATAFILE instead
V$DBLINK	Open database links
V$DELETED_OBJECT	Information on deleted RMAN objects from the control file
V$DISPATCHER	Information on the dispatcher processes
V$DISPATCHER_CONFIG	Configuration information on the dispatcher processes
V$DISPATCHER_RATE	Rate statistics on the dispatcher processes
V$ENABLEDPRIVS	Those privileges that are enabled
V$ENQUEUE_LOCK	Locks owned by enqueue objects
V$ENQUEUE_STAT	Statistics on enqueue objects
V$EVENT_HISTOGRAM	Histogram statistics on wait events
V$EVENT_NAME	Wait event names and parameters
V$EVENTMETRIC	Wait event metrics
V$EXECUTION	Information on parallel execution
V$FALSE_PING	Buffers getting false pings in RAC
V$FAST_START_SERVERS	Information on recovery slaves performing parallel transaction recovery
V$FAST_START_TRANSACTIONS	Information on the progress of recovering transactions
V$FILE_HISTOGRAM	Histogram on single block reads on data files
V$FILEMETRIC	File metrics
V$FILEMETRIC_HISTORY	History of file metrics
V$FILESTAT	I/O statistics on data files
V$FIXED_TABLE	All dynamic performance views
V$FIXED_VIEW_DEFINITION	Definitions of fixed views
V$FLASHBACK_DATABASE_LOG	Flashback information on the database
V$FLASHBACK_DATABASE_STAT	Flashback statistics on the database
V$GC_ELEMENT	Global Cache elements for RAC
V$GC_ELEMENT_WITH_COLLISIONS	GC elements for RAC, including collisions
V$GES_BLOCKING_ENQUEUE	Locks known to the Lock Manager in RAC
V$GES_CONVERT_LOCAL	Convert time enqueue operations for local RAC instance
V$GES_CONVERT_REMOTE	Convert time enqueue operations for remote RAC instance
V$GES_ENQUEUE	Locks known to the Lock Manager in RAC
V$GES_RESOURCE	Resources known to the Lock Manager in RAC
V$GES_STATISTICS	Miscellaneous GES statistics for RAC
V$GLOBAL_BLOCKED_LOCKS	Global blocked locks

View	Displays
V$GLOBAL_TRANSACTION	Information on global transactions
V$HS_AGENT	Heterogeneous Services agents
V$HS_PARAMETER	Heterogeneous Services parameters
V$HS_SESSION	Heterogeneous Services sessions
V$HVMASTER_INFO	Master instances of GES for RAC
V$INDEXED_FIXED_COLUMN	Columns in fixed tables that are indexed
V$INSTANCE	Information on the current instance
V$INSTANCE_RECOVERY	Mechanisms to limit recovery I/O
V$JAVA_LIBRARY_CACHE_MEMORY	Information on the memory in the library cache allocated to Java namespaces
V$JAVA_POOL_ADVICE	Advice on sizing the Java Pool
V$LATCH	Statistics on latches
V$LATCH_CHILDREN	Statistics on child latches
V$LATCH_MISSES	Misses on latches
V$LATCH_PARENT	Statistics on parent latches
V$LATCHHOLDER	Information on the session holding the latch
V$LATCHNAME	Latch names
V$LIBRARY_CACHE_MEMORY	Information on library cache memory
V$LIBRARYCACHE	Statistics on the library cache
V$LICENSE	License limits
V$LOADISTAT	Errors updating indexes on Direct Path loads
V$LOADPSTAT	Statistics on loading partitions using Direct Path loads
V$LOCK	Information on current locks
V$LOCKED_OBJECT	Locked objects
V$LOG	Information for online redo logs
V$LOG_HISTORY	Historical information for online redo logs
V$LOGFILE	Online redo logfile names
V$LOGHIST	Historical information for online redo logs; use V$LOG_HISTORY instead
V$LOGMNR_CONTENTS	Contents of LogMiner session
V$LOGMNR_DICTIONARY	LogMiner dictionary contents
V$LOGMNR_LOGS	Logs used in LogMiner session
V$LOGMNR_PARAMETERS	Parameters used in LogMiner session
V$LOGSTDBY	Log apply information for Standby
V$LOGSTDBY_STATS	Log apply statistics for Standby
V$MANAGED_STANDBY	Status information for Standby

View	Displays
V$MAP_COMP_LIST	Displays supplementary information for element mapping structures
V$MAP_ELEMENT	Element mapping structures
V$MAP_EXT_ELEMENT	Supplementary mapping structures
V$MAP_FILE	File mapping structures
V$MAP_FILE_EXTENT	File extent mapping structures
V$MAP_FILE_IO_STACK	Hierarchical storage containers for files
V$MAP_LIBRARY	List of all mapping libraries
V$MAP_SUBELEMENT	List of all mapping subelements
V$METRICNAME	Metrics and their names
V$MTTR_TARGET_ADVICE	Advice for achieving MTTR target
V$MVREFRESH	Information on MVIEWs being refreshed
V$MYSTAT	Statistics on current session
V$NLS_PARAMETERS	Current NLS parameters
V$NLS_VALID_VALUES	Valid values of NLS parameters
V$OBJECT_DEPENDENCY	Display objects dependent on other objects
V$OBJECT_USAGE	Usage of indexes
V$OBSOLETE_BACKUP_FILES	Obsolete RMAN backup files
V$OBSOLETE_PARAMETER	Obsolete initialization parameters
V$OFFLINE_RANGE	Offline datafile information
V$OPEN_CURSOR	Session's open cursors
V$OPTION	Installed database options
V$OSSTAT	OS statistics
V$PARALLEL_DEGREE_LIMIT_MTH	Parallel degree resource limit allocation methods
V$PARAMETER	Initialization parameter settings for the current session
V$PARAMETER2	Initialization parameter settings for the current session
V$PGA_TARGET_ADVICE	Advice on setting **pga_aggregate_target**
V$PGA_TARGET_ADVICE_HISTOGRAM	Advice in histogram form for setting **pga_aggregate_target**
V$PGASTAT	Statistics on PGA performance
V$PQ_SESSTAT	Parallel query session statistics
V$PQ_SLAVE	Information on parallel query slaves
V$PQ_SYSSTAT	Parallel query system statistics
V$PQ_TQSTAT	Parallel query execution statistics
V$PROCESS	Information on all database processes
V$PROPAGATION_RECEIVER	Information on queue propagation receivers
V$PROPAGATION_SENDER	Information on queue propagation senders

View	Displays
V$PROXY_ARCHIVEDLOG	Archived log backups taken with Proxy Copy
V$PROXY_DATAFILE	Datafile backups taken with Proxy Copy
V$PWFILE_USERS	Users in the password file
V$PX_PROCESS	Processes running parallel execution
V$PX_PROCESS_SYSSTAT	System statistics on parallel execution
V$PX_SESSION	Sessions running parallel execution
V$PX_SESSTAT	Session statistics on parallel execution
V$QUEUE	Information on shared server message queues
V$QUEUEING_MTH	Information on queueing resource allocation methods
V$RECOVER_FILE	Information on files needing recovery
V$RECOVERY_FILE_DEST	Information on disk quota and disk usage in flashback recovery area
V$RECOVERY_FILE_STATUS	Status on disk quota and disk usage in flashback recovery area
V$RECOVERY_LOG	Information on archived logs for recovery
V$RECOVERY_PROGRESS	Progress on recovery operations
V$RECOVERY_STATUS	Status on recovery operations
V$REPLPROP	Replication properties
V$REPLQUEUE	Information on the replication queue
V$REQDIST	Information on dispatcher request times
V$RESERVED_WORDS	All reserved words in the database
V$RESOURCE	Information on all resources
V$RESOURCE_LIMIT	Resources and their limits
V$RMAN_CONFIGURATION	RMAN persistent settings
V$RMAN_OUTPUT	RMAN output messages
V$RMAN_STATUS	Status of RMAN jobs
V$ROLLNAME	Names of rollback segments
V$ROLLSTAT	Statistics on rollback segments
V$ROWCACHE	Statistics on the data dictionary cache
V$ROWCACHE_PARENT	Information on parent objects in the data dictionary cache
V$ROWCACHE_SUBORDINATE	Information on subordinate objects in the data dictionary cache
V$RSRC_CONSUMER_GROUP	Information on resource consumer groups
V$RSRC_CONSUMER_GROUP_PU_MTH	Resource consumer group CPU methods
V$RSRC_PLAN	Information on resource plans
V$RSRC_PLAN_CPU_MTH	Resource plan CPU methods
V$RULE	Statistics on rules
V$RULE_SET	Statistics on rule sets

View	Displays
V$RULE_SET_AGGREGATE_STATS	Aggregate statistics on rule sets
V$SEGMENT_STATISTICS	Statistics on segment usage
V$SEGSTAT	Segment-level statistics
V$SEGSTAT_NAME	Segment-level statistics names
V$SERVICE_EVENT	Statistics on service events
V$SERVICE_STATS	Statistics on services
V$SERVICE_WAIT_CLASS	Wait class statistics on services
V$SERVICEMETRIC	Metrics for services
V$SERVICEMETRIC_HISTORY	Service metric history
V$SERVICES	Services in the database
V$SES_OPTIMIZER_ENV	Optimizer environment for each session
V$SESS_IO	Session I/O statistics
V$SESS_TIME_MODEL	Session accumulated time for various operations
V$SESSION	Information on all database sessions
V$SESSION_CONNECT_INFO	Network connection information for database sessions
V$SESSION_CURSOR_CACHE	Information on session cursor usage
V$SESSION_EVENT	Statistics on wait events for each session
V$SESSION_LONGOPS	Statistics on session's long-running operations
V$SESSION_OBJECT_CACHE	Object cache statistics for current session
V$SESSION_WAIT	Wait statistics for current session
V$SESSION_WAIT_CLASS	Statistics for current session wait classes
V$SESSION_WAIT_HISTORY	Last ten wait events for each session
V$SESSMETRIC	Metric values for each session
V$SESSTAT	Session statistics
V$SGA	Information on System Global Area
V$SGA_CURRENT_RESIZED_OPS	Information on current SGA resize operations
V$SGA_DYNAMIC_COMPONENTS	Information on SGA dynamic components
V$SGA_DYNAMIC_FREE_MEMORY	Information on free memory in SGA
V$SGA_RESIZE_OPS	Last 400 SGA resize operations
V$SGAINFO	Info on the SGA
V$SGASTAT	Detailed information on the SGA
V$SHARED_POOL_ADVICE	Advice on sizing the shared pool
V$SHARED_POOL_RESERVED	Statistics to tune the SGA reserved pool
V$SHARED_SERVER	Information on shared server processes

View	Displays
V$SHARED_SERVER_MONITOR	Information to tune shared servers
V$SORT_SEGMENTS	Information on sorting segments
V$SPPARAMETER	Contents of server parameter file
V$SQL	Shared SQL area contents
V$SQL_BIND_CAPTURE	Bind variable information for SQL cursors
V$SQL_BIND_DATA	Bind variable data for SQL cursors
V$SQL_BIND_METADATA	Bind variable metadata for SQL cursors
V$SQL_CURSOR	Debugging information for SQL cursors
V$SQL_OPTIMIZER_ENV	Optimizer environment for SQL cursors
V$SQL_PLAN	Execution plan for SQL cursors
V$SQL_PLAN_STATISTICS	Execution statistics for SQL cursors
V$SQL_PLAN_STATISTICS_ALL	Memory usage statistics for SQL cursors
V$SQL_REDIRECTION	SQL cursors that are redirected
V$SQL_SHARED_CURSOR	Information about why a shared cursor is not shared
V$SQL_SHARED_MEMORY	Child shared memory snapshots
V$SQL_WORKAREA	Information on work areas for SQL cursors
V$SQL_WORKAREA_ACTIVE	Active work areas for SQL cursors
V$SQL_WORKAREA_HISTOGRAM	Histograms on SQL work areas
V$SQLAREA	Statements in shared SQL area
V$SQLTEXT	Actual text for SQL cursors
V$SQLTEXT_WITH_NEWLINES	Text with newline characters
V$STANDBY_LOG	Information about Standby logs
V$STATISTICS_LEVEL	Status of advisories controlled by the **statistics_level** parameter
V$STATNAME	Names of statistics
V$STREAMS_APPLY_COORDINATOR	Information about apply process coordinators
V$STREAMS_APPLY_READER	Information about apply process readers
V$STREAMS_APPLY_SERVER	Information about apply process servers
V$STREAMS_CAPTURE	Information about capture process
V$SUBCACHE	Information about subordinate caches in the library cache
V$SYS_OPTIMIZER_ENV	Information on the optimizer environment for the instance
V$SYS_TIME_MODEL	System-wide time model statistics
V$SYSAUX_OCCUPANTS	SYSAUX tablespace occupants
V$SYSMETRIC	System metric values
V$SYSMETRIC_HISTORY	System metric historical values
V$SYSMETRIC_SUMMARY	Aggregated system metric values
V$SYSSTAT	System-wide statistics

View	Displays
V$SYSTEM_CURSOR_CACHE	Information on system cursor usage
V$SYSTEM_EVENT	Totals on system-wide wait events
V$SYSTEM_PARAMETER	System initialization parameters
V$SYSTEM_PARAMETER2	System initialization parameters
V$SYSTEM_WAIT_CLASS	System-wide wait class statistics
V$TABLESPACE	Information on tablespaces from the control file
V$TEMP_EXTENT_MAP	Status of temporary extents in LMTs
V$TEMP_EXTENT_POOL	Stats of temporary extents
V$TEMP_HISTOGRAM	Histogram of tempfile reads
V$TEMP_SPACE_HEADER	Information on tempfile usage
V$TEMPFILE	Information on tempfiles from control files
V$TEMPORARY_LOBS	Information on temporary LOBs
V$TEMPSEG_USAGE	Information on temporary segment usage
V$TEMPSTAT	Tempfile I/O statistics
V$THREAD	Information on threads from control file
V$THRESHOLD_TYPES	Information on threshold types
V$TIMER	Elapsed time in 1/100 of a second
V$TIMEZONE_NAMES	Time zone names
V$TRANSACTION	Information on all active transactions
V$TRANSACTION_ENQUEUE	Locks owned by transaction objects
V$TRANSPORTABLE_PLATFORM	TTS platform names
V$TYPE_SIZE	Sizes of database components
V$UNDOSTAT	Undo usage statistics
V$VERSION	Component version information
V$VPD_POLICY	FGAC policy information
V$WAITCLASSMETRIC	Metric values for wait classes
V$WAITCLASSMETRIC_HISTORY	Historical metric values for wait classes
V$WAITSTAT	Block contention statistics

APPENDIX
C

Oracle SQL Syntax

Oracle SQL Syntax

The Oracle Database comes with a number of SQL commands and clauses. This section lists the syntax for those commands and clauses for quick reference. The common DDL clauses are listed first, followed by the syntax for SQL DML commands, and then the syntax for SQL DDL commands.

alter cluster

Format:

alter_cluster::=

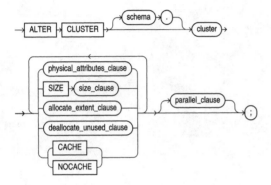

physical_attributes_clause::=

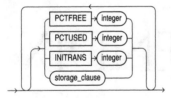

allocate_extent_clause::=

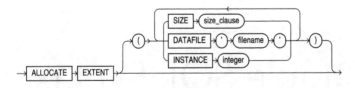

deallocate_unused_clause::=

size_clause::=

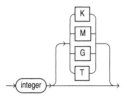

parallel_clause::=

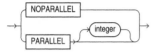

alter database

Format:

alter_database::=

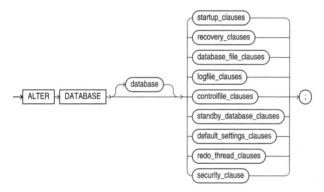

startup_clauses::=

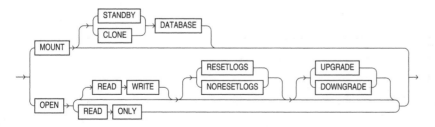

recovery_clauses::=

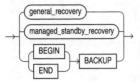

general_recovery::=

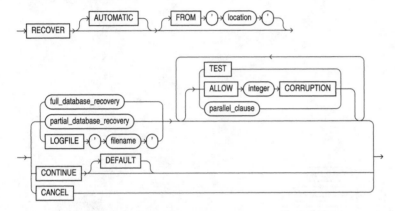

full_database_recovery::=

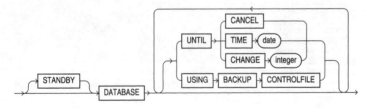

partial_database_recovery::=

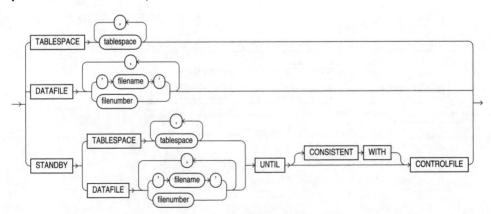

parallel_clause::=

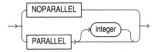

managed_standby_recovery::=

recover_clause::=

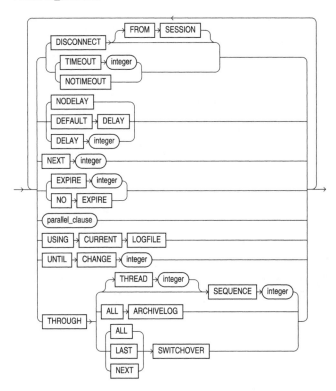

cancel_clause::=

finish_clause::=

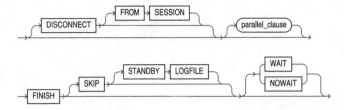

database_file_clauses::=

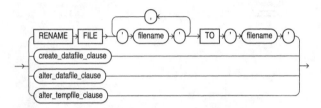

create_datafile_clause::=

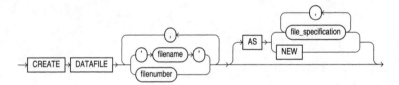

alter_datafile_clause::=

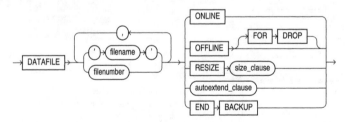

size_clause::=

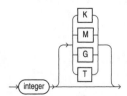

alter_tempfile_clause::=

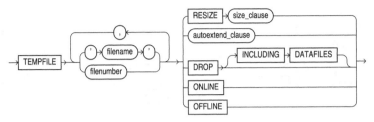

autoextend_clause::=

maxsize_clause::=

logfile_clauses::=

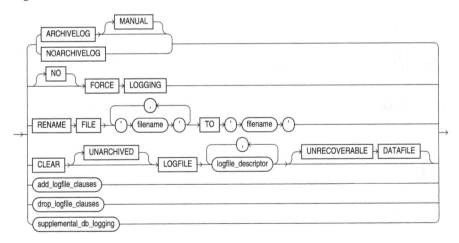

add_logfile_clauses::=

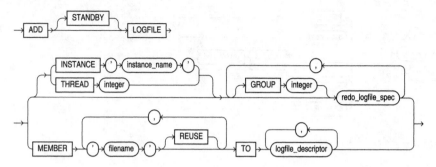

drop_logfile_clauses::=

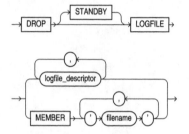

supplemental_db_logging::=

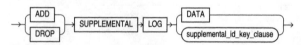

supplemental_id_key_clause::=

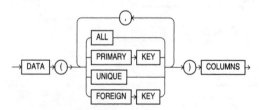

logfile_descriptor::=

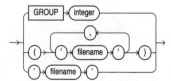

controlfile_clauses::=

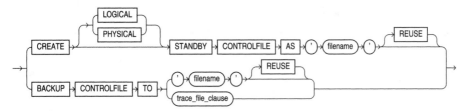

trace_file_clause::=

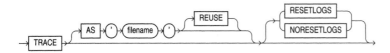

standby_database_clauses::=

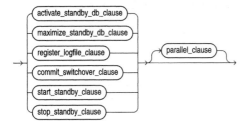

activate_standby_db_clause::=

maximize_standby_db_clause::=

register_logfile_clause::=

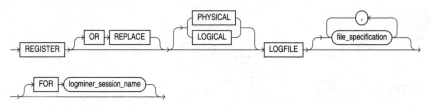

commit_switchover_clause::=

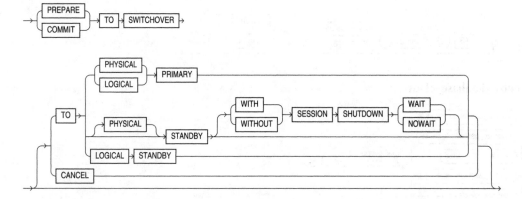

start_standby_clause::=

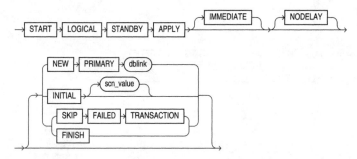

stop_standby_clause::=

default_settings_clauses::=

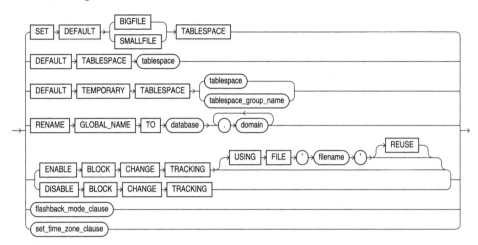

set_time_zone_clause::=

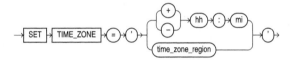

flashback_mode_clause::=

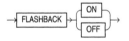

redo_thread_clauses::=

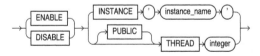

security_clause::=

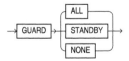

alter dimension

<u>Format:</u>

alter_dimension::=

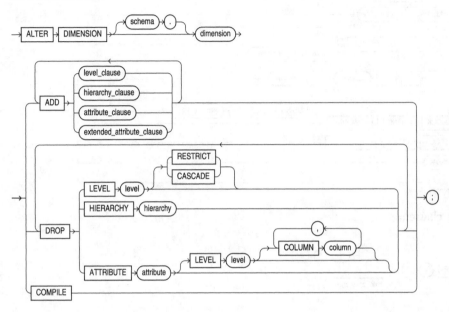

level_clause::=

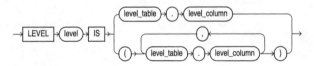

hierarchy_clause::=

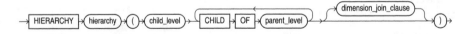

dimension_join_clause::=

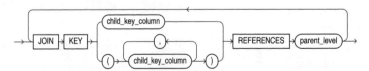

attribute_clause::=

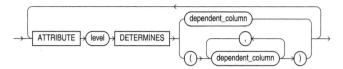

extended_attribute_clause::=

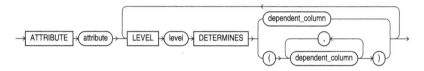

alter diskgroup

Format:

alter_diskgroup::=

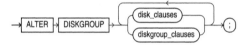

disk_clauses::=

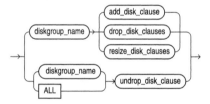

diskgroup_clauses::=

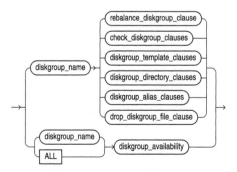

add_disk_clause::=

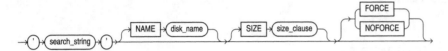

qualified_disk_clause::=

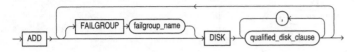

size_clause::=

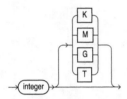

drop_disk_clauses::=

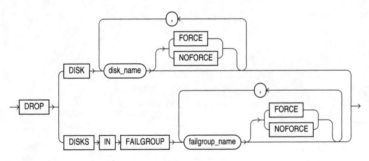

resize_disk_clauses::=

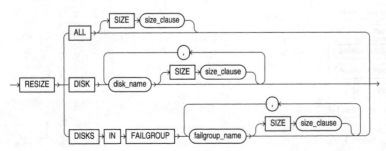

undrop_disk_clause::=

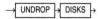

rebalance_diskgroup_clause::=

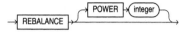

check_diskgroup_clauses::=

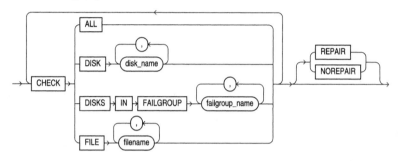

diskgroup_template_clauses::=

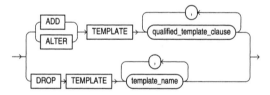

qualified_template_clause::=

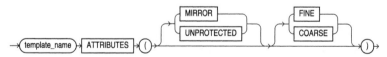

diskgroup_directory_clauses::=

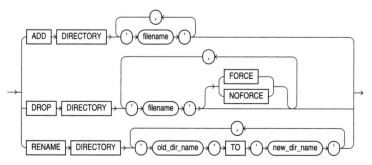

diskgroup_alias_clauses::=

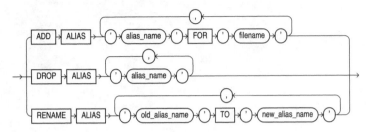

drop_diskgroup_file_clause::=

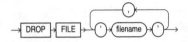

diskgroup_availability::=

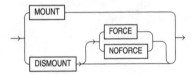

alter function

<u>Format:</u>

alter_function::=

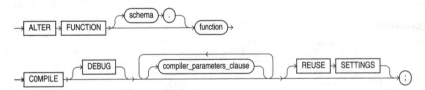

compiler_parameters_clause::=

alter_index::=

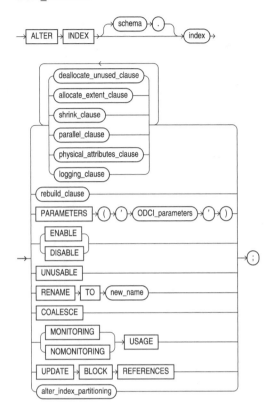

alter index

Format:

deallocate_unused_clause::=

allocate_extent_clause::=

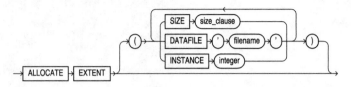

size_clause::=

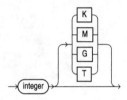

shrink_clause::=

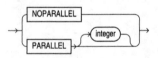

parallel_clause::=

physical_attributes_clause::=

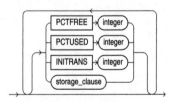

logging_clause::=

rebuild_clause::=

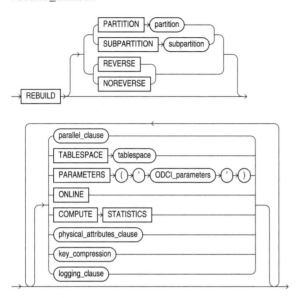

key_compression::=

alter_index_partitioning::=

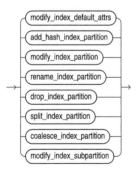

modify_index_default_attrs::=

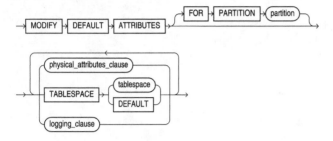

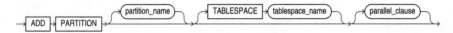

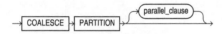

add_hash_index_partition::=

coalesce_index_partition::=

modify_index_partition::=

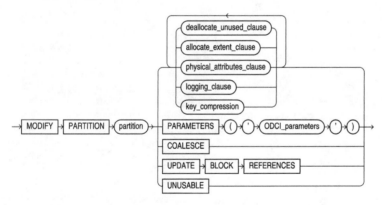

rename_index_partition::=

drop_index_partition::=

split_index_partition::=

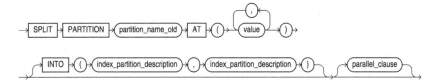

index_partition_description::=

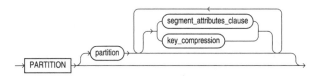

segment_attributes_clause::=

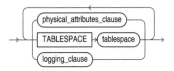

modify_index_subpartition::=

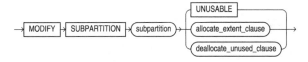

alter indextype

Format:

alter_indextype::=

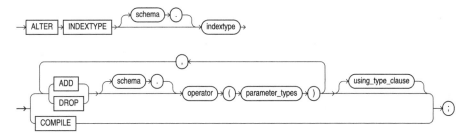

using_type_clause::=

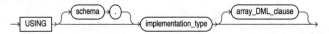

array_DML_clause::=

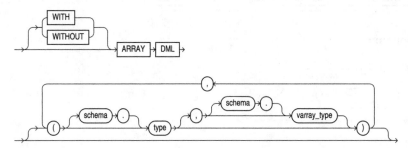

alter java

Format:

alter_java::=

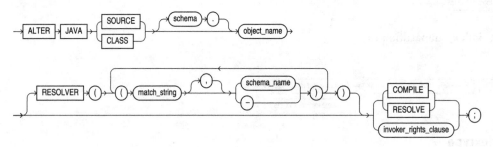

invoker_rights_clause::=

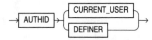

alter materialized view

Format:

alter_materialized_view::=

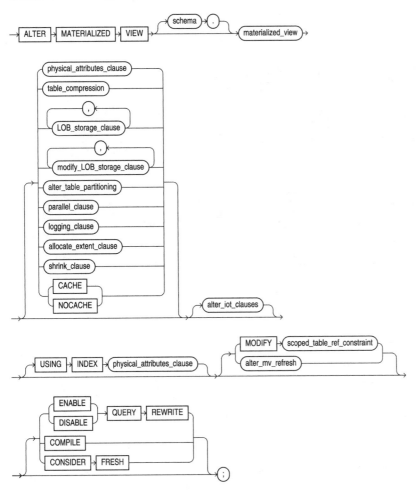

physical_attributes_clause::=

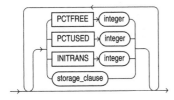

table_compression::=

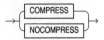

LOB_storage_clause::=

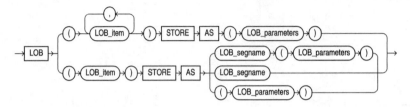

LOB_parameters::=

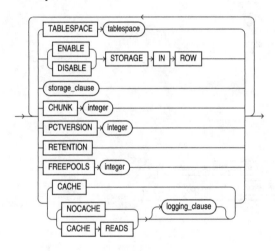

modify_LOB_storage_clause::=

modify_LOB_parameters::=

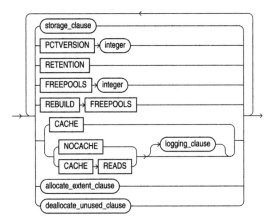

parallel_clause::=

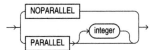

logging_clause::=

allocate_extent_clause::=

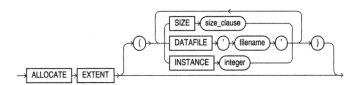

deallocate_unused_clause::=

size_clause::=

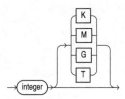

shrink_clause::=

alter_iot_clauses::=

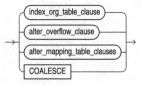

index_org_table_clause::=

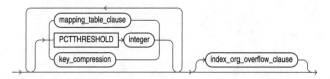

index_org_overflow_clause::=

alter_overflow_clause::=

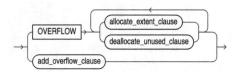

add_overflow_clause::=

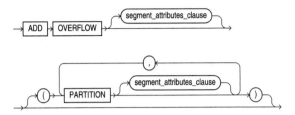

scoped_table_ref_constraint::=

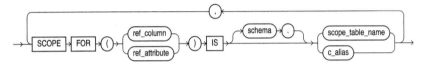

alter_mv_refresh::=

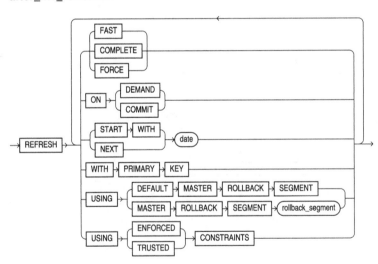

alter materialized view log

Format:

alter_materialized_view_log::=

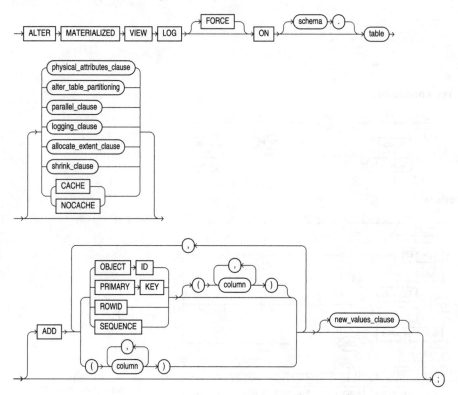

new_values_clause::=

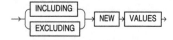

physical_attributes_clause::=

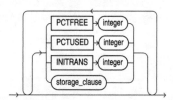

allocate_extent_clause::=

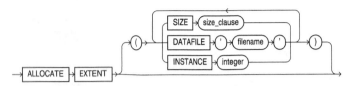

size_clause::=

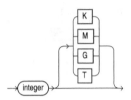

shrink_clause::=

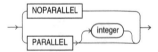

parallel_clause::=

alter operator

Format:

alter_operator::=

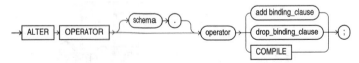

add_binding_clause::=

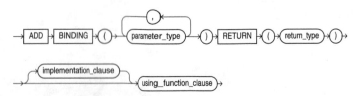

implementation_clause::=

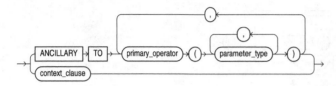

context_clause::=

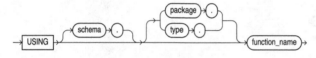

using_function_clause::=

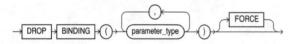

drop_binding_clause::=

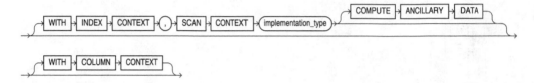

alter outline

Format:

alter_outline::=

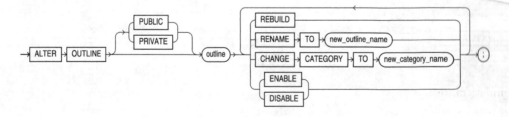

alter package

Format:

alter_package::=

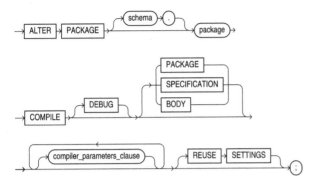

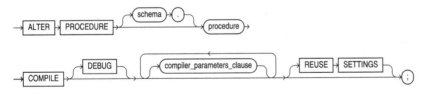

compiler_parameters_clause::=

alter procedure

Format:

alter_procedure::=

compiler_parameters_clause::=

alter profile

Format:

alter_profile::=

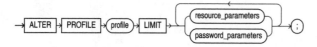

resource_parameters::=

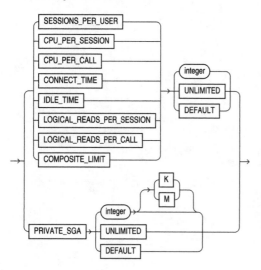

password_parameters::=

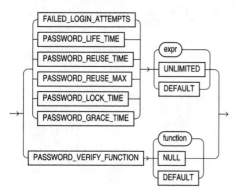

alter resource cost

Format:

alter_resource_cost::=

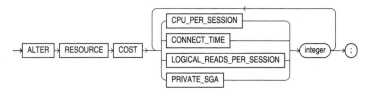

alter role

Format:

alter_role::=

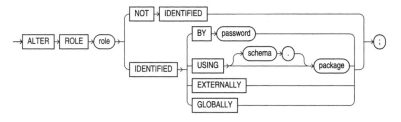

alter rollback segment

Format:

alter_rollback_segment::=

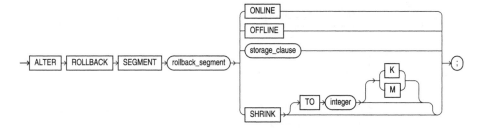

alter sequence

Format:
alter_sequence::=

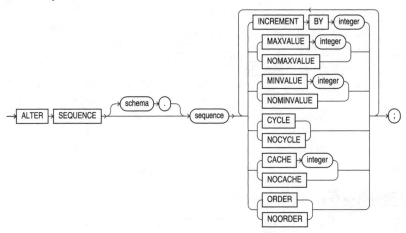

alter session

Format:
alter_session::=

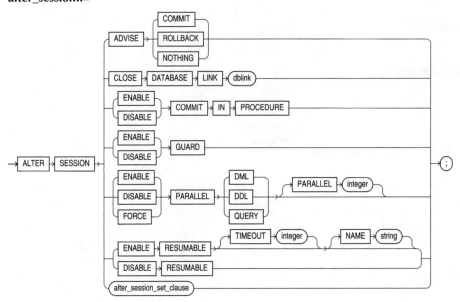

alter_session_set_clause::=

alter system

Format:

alter_system::=

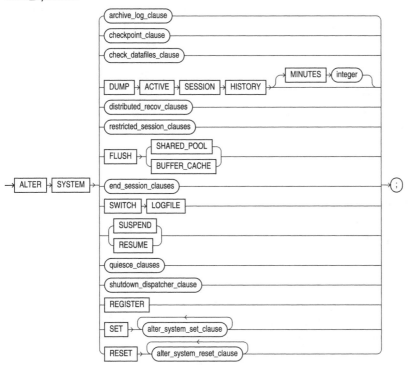

archive_log_clause::=

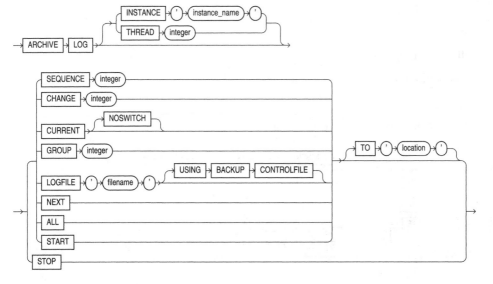

checkpoint_clause::=

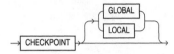

check_datafiles_clause::=

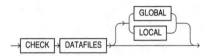

distributed_recov_clauses::=

restricted_session_clauses::=

end_session_clauses::=

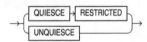

quiesce_clauses::=

shutdown_dispatcher_clause::=

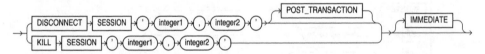

alter_system_set_clause::=

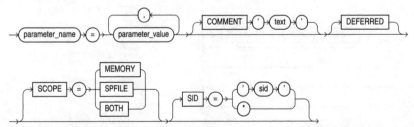

alter_system_reset_clause::=

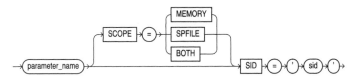

alter table

Format:
alter_table::=

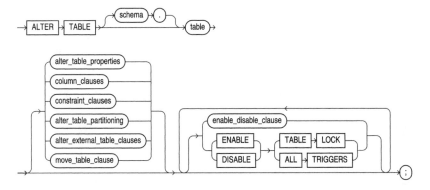

alter_table_properties::=

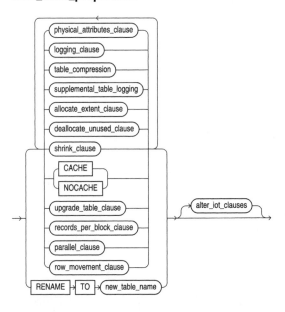

physical_attributes_clause::=

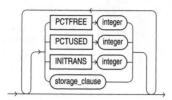

logging_clause::=

table_compression::=

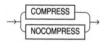

supplemental_table_logging::=

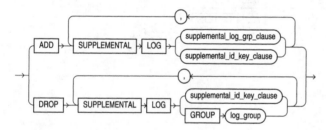

supplemental_log_grp_clause::=

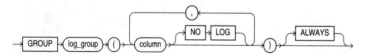

supplemental_id_key_clause::=

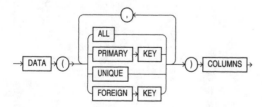

allocate_extent_clause::=

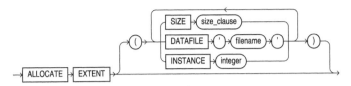

deallocate_unused_clause::=

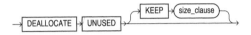

size_clause::=

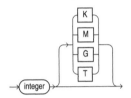

shrink_clause::=

upgrade_table_clause::=

records_per_block_clause::=

parallel_clause::=

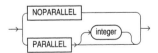

row_movement_clause::=

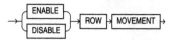

alter_iot_clauses::=

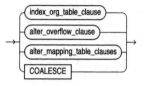

index_org_table_clause::=

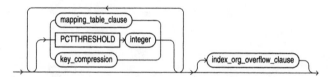

mapping_table_clauses::=

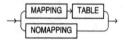

key_compression::=

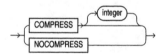

index_org_overflow_clause::=

segment_attributes_clause::=

alter_overflow_clause::=

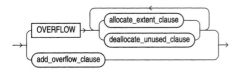

add_overflow_clause::=

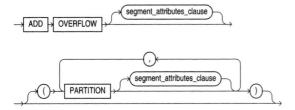

alter_mapping_table_clauses::=

column_clauses::=

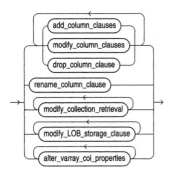

add_column_clause::=

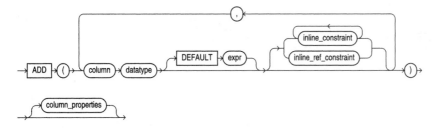

modify_column_clauses::=

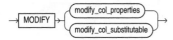

modify_col_properties::=

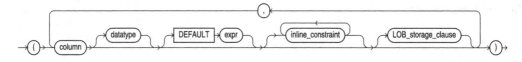

modify_col_substitutable::=

drop_column_clause::=

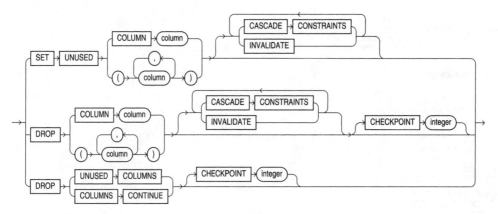

rename_column_clause::=

modify_collection_retrieval::=

constraint_clauses::=

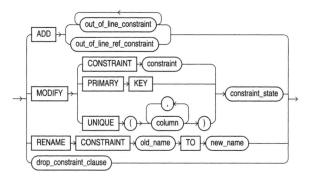

drop_contraint_clause::=

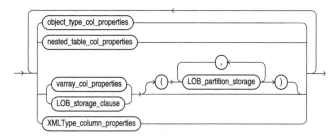

column_properties::=

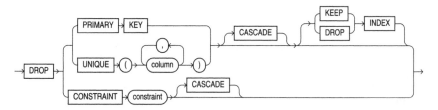

object_type_col_properties::=

substitutable_column_clause::=

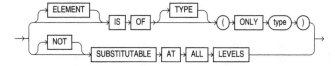

nested_table_col_properties::=

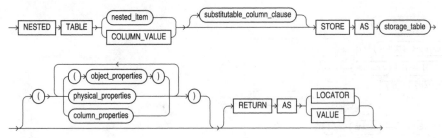

object_properties::=

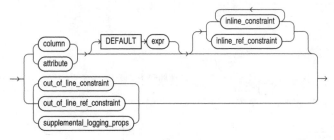

supplemental_logging_props::=

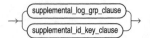

physical_properties::=

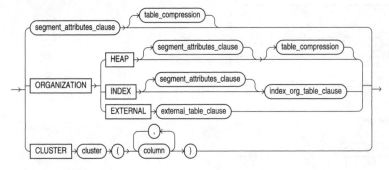

varray_col_properties::=

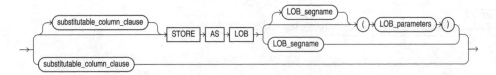

LOB_storage_clause::=

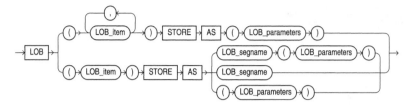

LOB_parameters::=

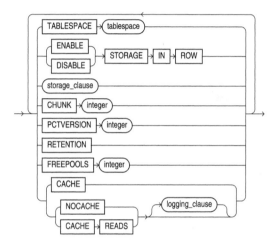

modify_LOB_storage_clause::=

modify_LOB_parameters::=

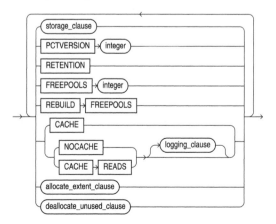

alter_varray_col_properties::=

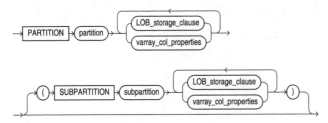

LOB_partition_storage::=

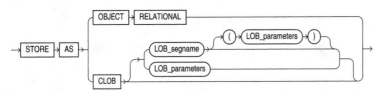

XMLType_column_properties::=

XMLType_storage::=

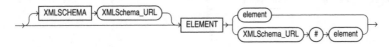

XMLSchema_spec::=

alter_external_table_clauses::=

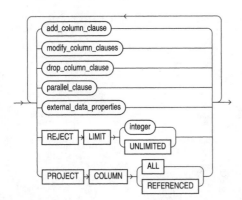

external_data_properties::=

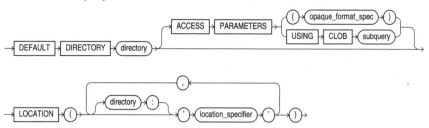

alter_table_partitioning::=

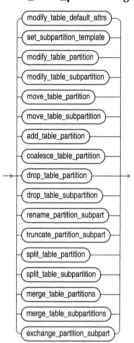

modify_table_default_attrs::=

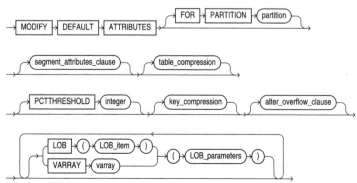

set_subpartition_template::=

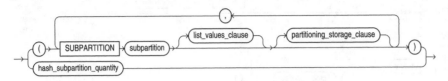

modify_table_partition::=

modify_range_partition::=

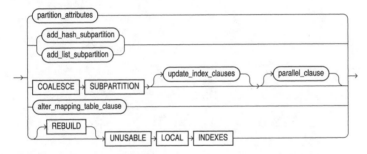

modify_hash_partition::=

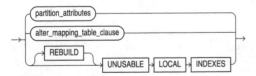

modify_list_partition::=

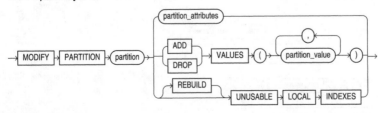

modify_table_subpartition::=

move_table_partition::=

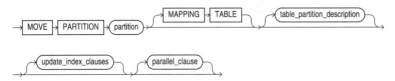

move_table_subpartition::=

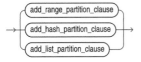

add_table_partition::=

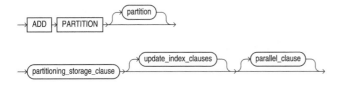

add_range_partition_clause::=

add_harsh_partition_clause::=

add_list_partition_clause::=

coalesce_table_partition::=

drop_table_partition::=

drop_table_subpartition::=

rename_partition_subpart::=

truncate_partition_subpart::=

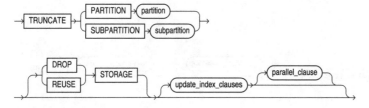

split_table_partition::=

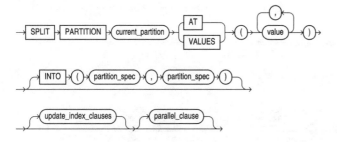

split_table_subpartition::=

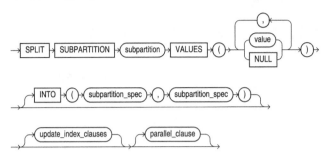

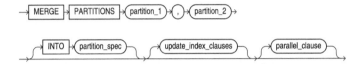

merge_table_partitions::=

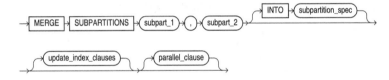

merge_table_subpartitions::=

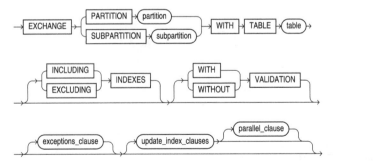

exchange_partition_subpart::=

exceptions_clause::=

list_values_clause::=

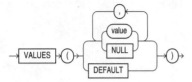

range_values_clause::=

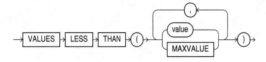

partitioning_storage_clause::=

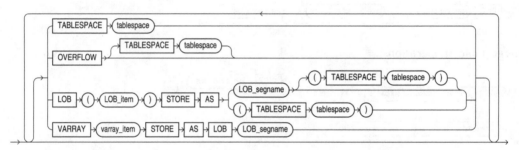

partition_attributes::=

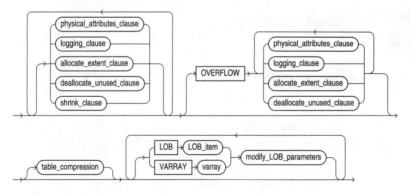

add_hash_subpartition::=

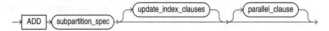

add_list_subpartition::=

modify_hash_subpartition::=

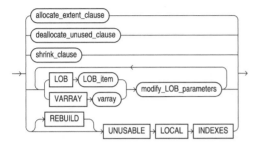

modify_list_subpartition::=

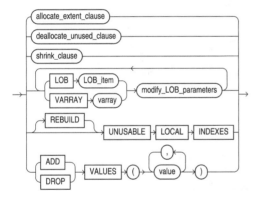

table_partition_description::=

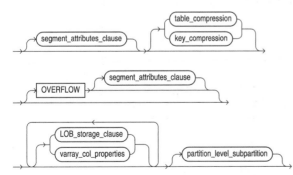

partition_level_subpartition::=

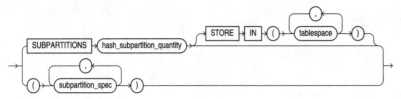

partition_spec::=

subpartition_spec::=

update_index_clauses::=

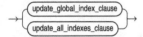

update_global_index_clause::=

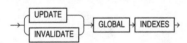

update_all_indexes_clause::=

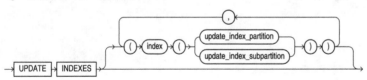

update_index_partition::=

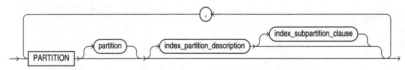

update_index_subpartition::=

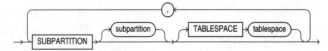

index_partition_description::=

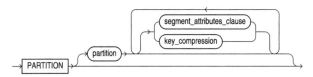

index_subpartition_clause::=

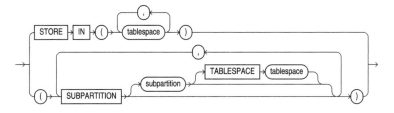

parallel_clause::=

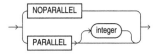

move_table_clause::=

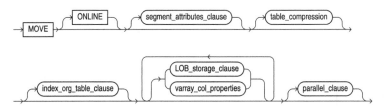

enable_disable_clause::=

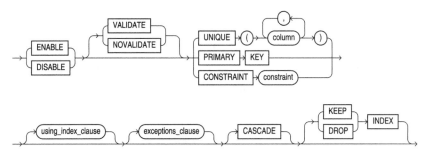

using_index_clause::=

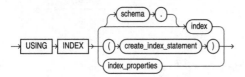

index_properties::=

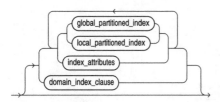

index_attributes::=

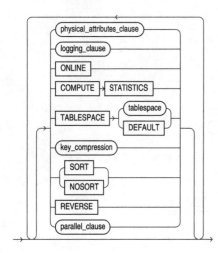

alter tablespace

Format:

alter_tablespace::=

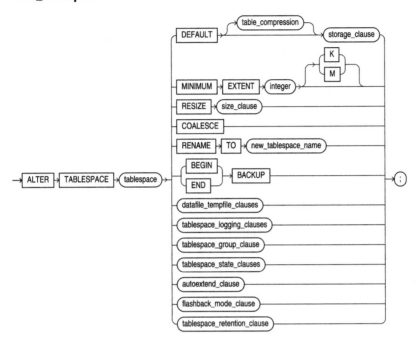

size_clause::=

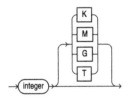

datafile_tempfile_clauses::=

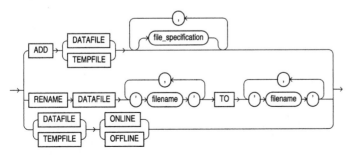

tablespace_logging_clauses::=

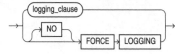

tablespace_group_clause::=

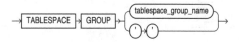

tablespace_state_clauses::=

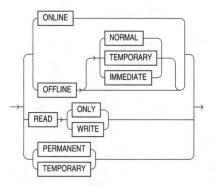

autoextend_clause::=

maxsize_clause::=

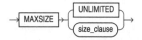

flashback_mode_clause::=

tablespace_retention_clause::=

alter trigger

Format:

alter_trigger::=

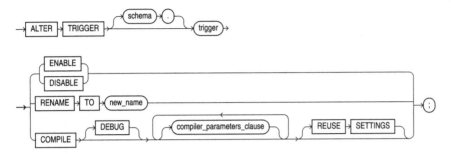

compiler_parameters_clause::=

alter type

Format:

alter_type::=

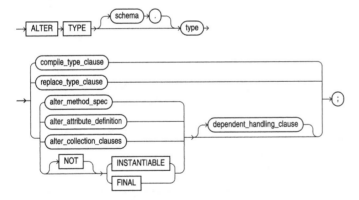

compile_type_clause::=

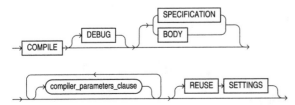

compiler_parameters_clause::=

replace_type_clause::=

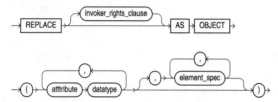

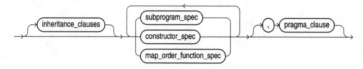

invoker_rights_clause::=

element_spec::=

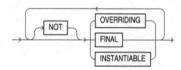

inheritance_clauses::=

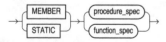

subprogram_spec::=

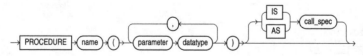

procedure_spec::=

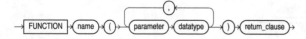

function_spec::=

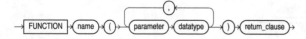

constructor_spec::=

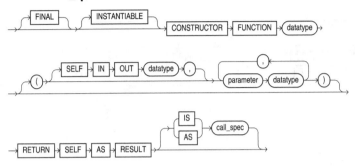

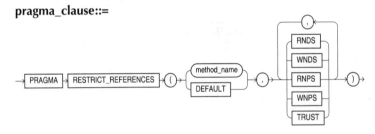

map_order_function_spec::=

pragma_clause::=

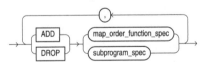

alter_method_spec::=

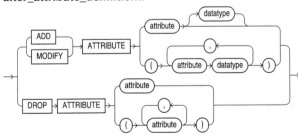

alter_attribute_definition::=

alter_collection_clauses::=

dependent_handling_clause::=

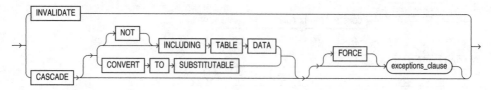

exceptions_clause::=

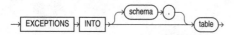

alter user

Format:

alter_user::=

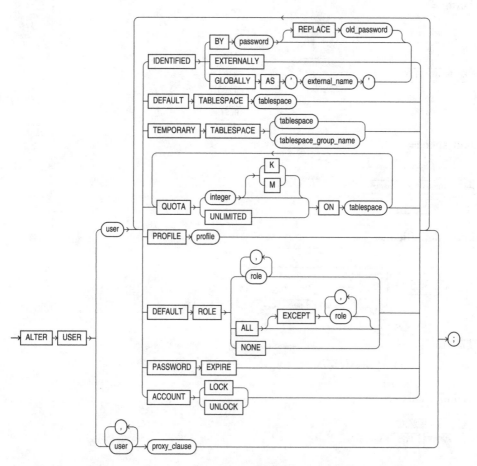

proxy_clause::=

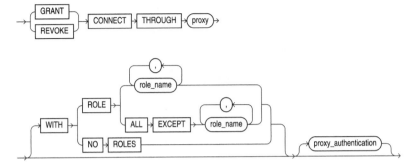

proxy_authentication::=

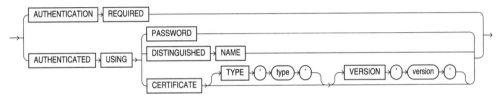

alter view

Format:

alter_view::=

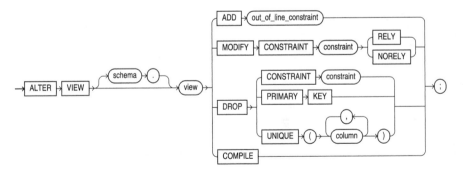

analyze

Format:
analyze::=

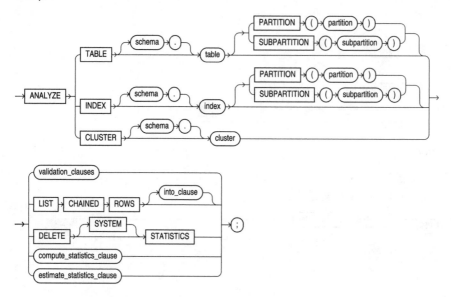

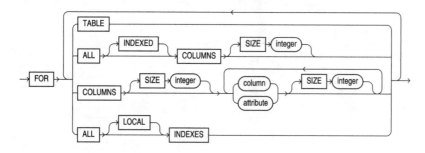

validation_clauses::=

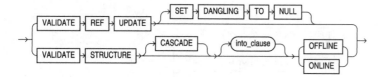

for_clause::=

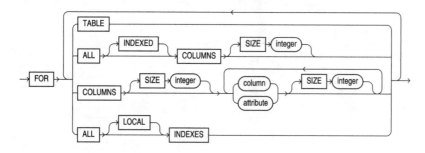

into_clause::=

compute_statistics_clause::=

estimate_statistics_clause::=

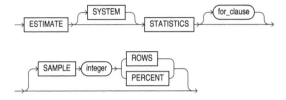

associate statistics

Format:

associate_statistics::=

column_association::=

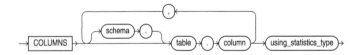

function_association::=

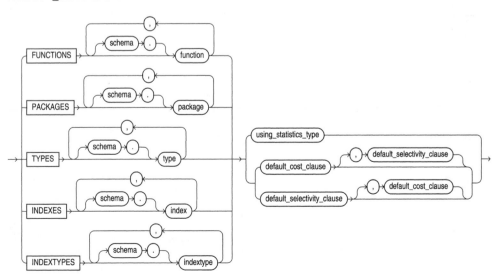

using_statistics_type::=

default_cost_clause::=

default_selectivity_clause::=

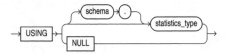

audit

Format:
audit::=

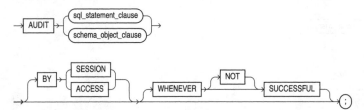

sql_statement_clause::=

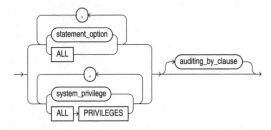

auditing_by_clause::=

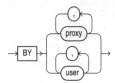

schema_object_clause::=

auditing_on_clause::=

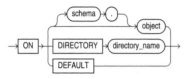

Additional Information   You can use the **audit** command to audit statements executed by users and statements that access specific objects. The statement options are as follows:

Option	Audits
cluster	Create, alter, drop, or truncate cluster
context	Create or drop context
database link	Create or drop database link
dimension	Create, alter, or drop dimension
directory	Create or drop directory
index	Create, alter, or drop index
materialized view	Create, alter, or drop materialized view
not exists	SQL statements that fail because an object does not exist
procedure	Create or drop procedure, function, library, or package; create package body
profile	Create, alter, or drop profile
public database link	Create or drop public database link
public synonym	Create or drop public synonym
role	Create, alter, drop, or set role
rollback segment	Create, alter, or drop rollback segment
sequence	Create or drop sequence
session	Logon attempts
synonym	Create or drop synonym
system audit	Audit or noaudit of SQL statements

Option	Audits
system grant	Grant or revoke system privileges and roles
table	Create, drop, or truncate table
tablespace	Create, alter, or drop tablespace
trigger	Create, alter, or drop trigger; alter table with **enable|disable all triggers**
type	Create, alter, or drop type or type body
user	Create, alter, or drop user
view	Create or drop view

The following are additional statement-level options that are available:

Option	Commands Audited
alter sequence	**alter sequence**
alter table	**alter table**
comment table	**comment on table**—*table, view, materialized view* **comment on column**—*table.column, view.column, materialized view.column*
delete table	**delete from** *table, view*
execute procedure	**call** Execution of any procedure or function or access to any variable, library, or cursor inside a package
grant directory	**grant** *privilege* **on** *directory* **revoke** *privilege* **on** *directory*
grant procedure	**grant** *privilege* **on** *procedure, function, package* **revoke** *privilege* **on** *procedure, function, package*
grant sequence	**grant** *privilege* **on** *sequence* **revoke** *privilege* **on** *sequence*
grant table	**grant** *privilege* **on** *table, view, materialized view* **revoke** *privilege* **on** *table, view, materialized view*
grant type	**grant** *privilege* ON *type* **revoke** *privilege* ON *type*
insert table	**insert into** *table, view*
lock table	**lock table** *table, view*
select sequence	Any statement containing *sequence*.CURRVAL or *sequence*.NEXTVAL
select table	**select from** *table, view, materialized view*
update table	**update** *table, view*

Auditing information is written to a table named SYS.AUD$ and accessed via data dictionary views.

call

Format:
call::=

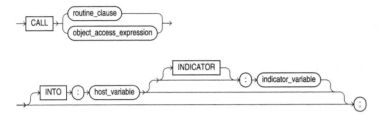

routine_clause::=

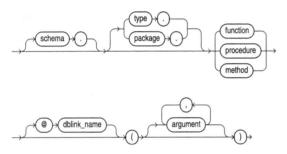

object_access_expression::=

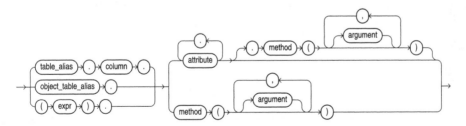

comment

Format:

```
COMMENT ON
{ TABLE [schema .] { table | view | materialized view }
| COLUMN [schema .] { table . | view . | materialized view . } column
| OPERATOR [schema .] operator
```

```
| INDEXTYPE [schema .] indextype
}
IS 'text';
```

commit (Form 1—Embedded SQL)

Format:

```
EXEC SQL [AT { database| :host variable}] COMMIT [WORK]
 [ [COMMENT 'text' ] [RELEASE]
 | FORCE 'text' [, integer ]]
```

commit (Form 2—PL/SQL Statement)

Format:

```
COMMIT [WORK] [ COMMENT 'text' | FORCE 'text' [, integer] ];
```

connect by

Format:

```
SELECT expression [,expression]...
  FROM [user.]table
 WHERE condition
CONNECT BY [PRIOR] expression = [PRIOR] expression
 START WITH expression = expression
 ORDER BY expression
```

constraints

Format:

constraint::=

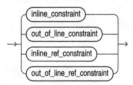

inline_constraint::=

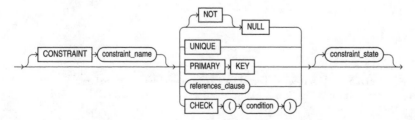

out_of_line_constraint::=

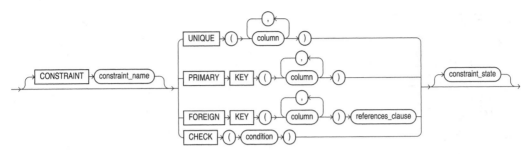

inline_ref_constraint::=

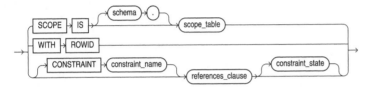

out_of_line_ref_constraint

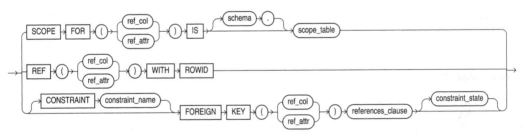

references_clause::=

constraint_state::=

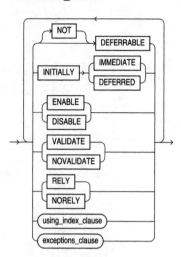

using_index_clause::=

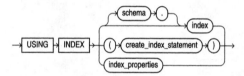

index_properties::=

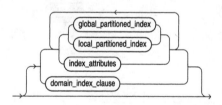

index_attributes::=

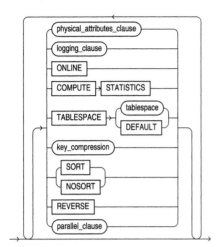

exceptions_clause::=

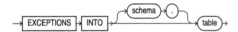

create cluster

Format:
create_cluster::=

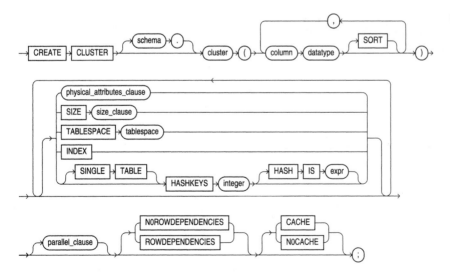

physical_attributes_clause::=

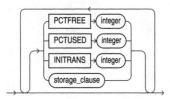

size_clause::=

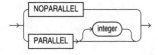

parallel_clause::=

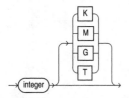

create context

Format:

```
CREATE [OR REPLACE] CONTEXT namespace USING [schema .] package
[ INITIALIZED { EXTERNALLY | GLOBALLY }
| ACCESSED GLOBALLY ] ;
```

create controlfile

Format:

create_controlfile::=

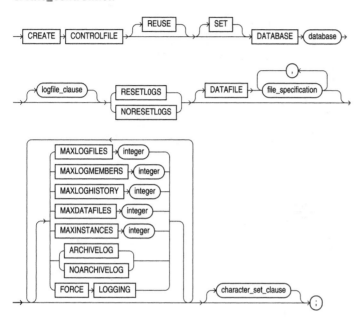

logfile_clause::=

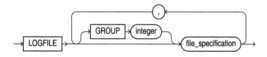

character_set_clause::=

create database

Format:
create_database::=

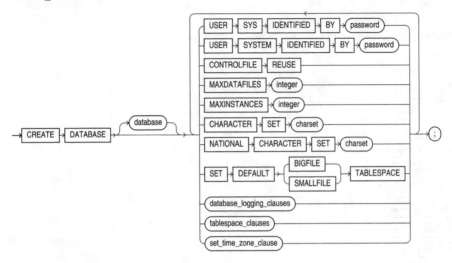

database_logging_clauses::=

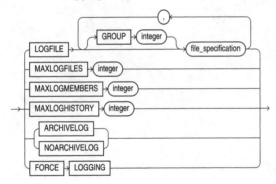

tablespace_clauses::=

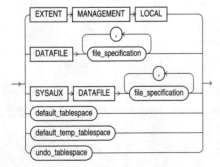

default_tablespace::=

default_temp_tablespace::=

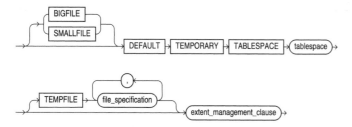

extent_management_clause::=

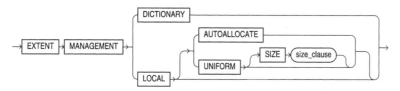

size_clause::=

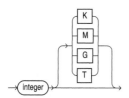

undo_tablespace::=

set_time_zone_clause::=

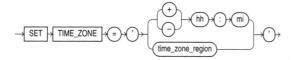

create database link

Format:

```
CREATE [SHARED] [PUBLIC] DATABASE LINK dblink
[ CONNECT TO { CURRENT_USER | user IDENTIFIED BY password
[AUTHENTICATED BY user IDENTIFIED BY password] }
 | AUTHENTICATED BY user IDENTIFIED BY password]
[USING 'connect_string'];
```

create dimension

Format:
create_dimension::=

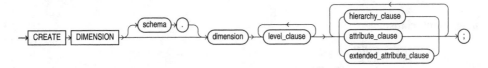

level_clause::=

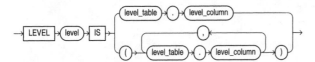

hierarchy_clause::=

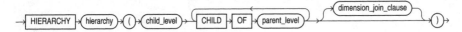

dimension_join_clause::=

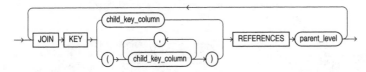

attribute_clause::=

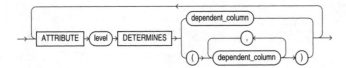

extended_attribute_clause::=

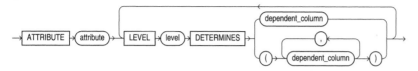

create directory

Format:

```
CREATE [OR REPLACE] DIRECTORY directory AS 'path_name';
```

create diskgroup

Format:
create_diskgroup::=

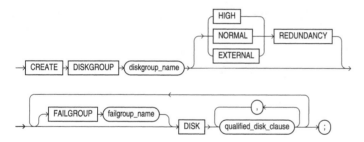

qualified_disk_clause::=

size_clause::=

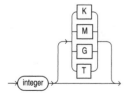

create function

Format:
create_function::=

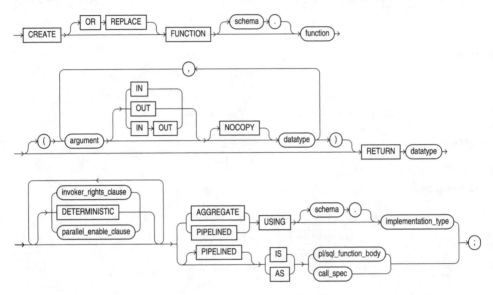

invoker_rights_clause::=

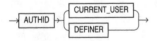

parallel_enable_clause::=

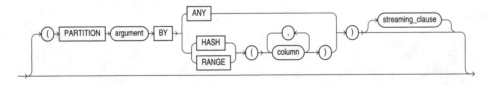

streaming_clause::=

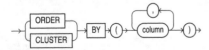

call_spec::=

Java_declaration::=

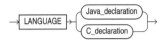

C_declaration::=

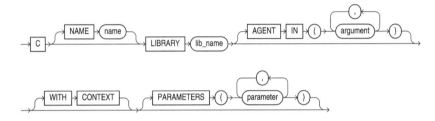

create index

Format:
create_index::=

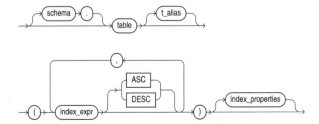

cluster_index_clause::=

table_index_clause::=

bitmap_join_index_clause::=

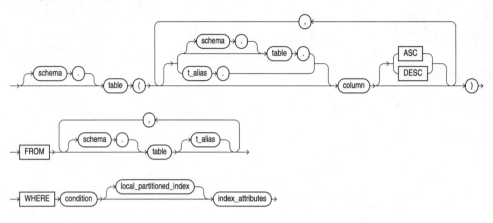

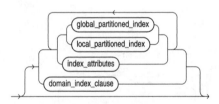

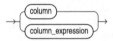

index_expr::=

index_properties::=

index_attributes::=

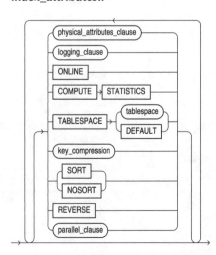

physical_attributes_clause::=

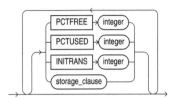

logging_clause::=

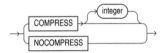

key_compression::=

domain_index_clause::=

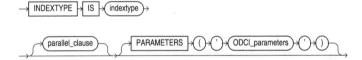

global_partitioned_index::=

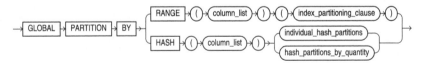

individual_hash_partitions::=

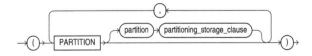

partitioning_storage_clause::=

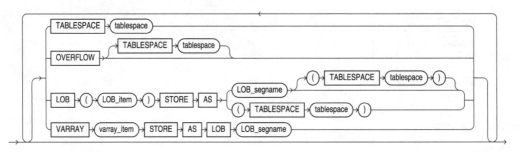

hash_partitions_by_quantity::=

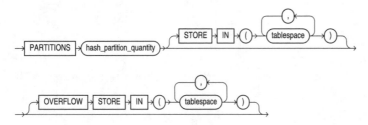

index_partitioning_clause::=

local_partitioned_index::=

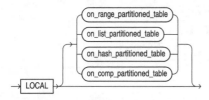

on_range_partitioned_table::=

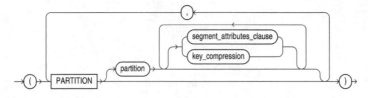

on_list_partitioned_table::=

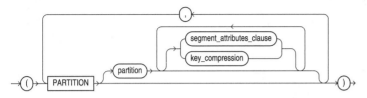

segment_attributes_clause::=

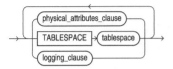

on_hash_partitioned_table::=

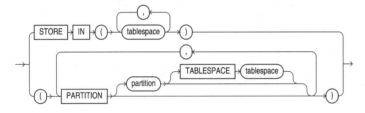

on_comp_partitioned_table::=

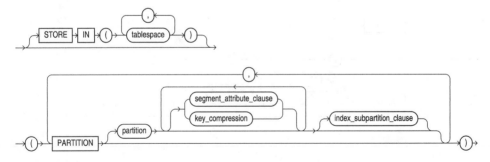

index_subpartition_clause::=

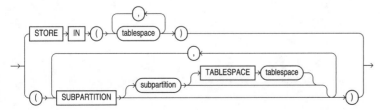

parallel_clause::=

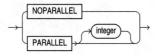

create indextype

Format:

create_indextype::=

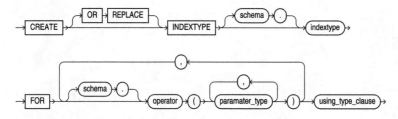

using_type_clause::=

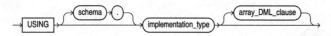

array_DML_clause::=

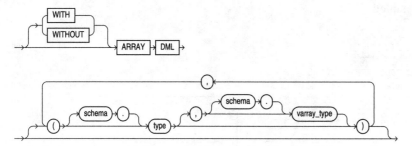

create java

Format:

create_java::=

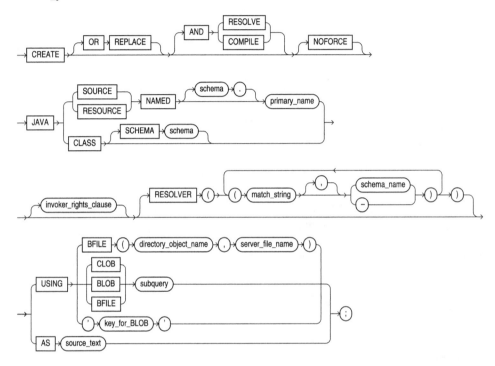

invoker_rights_clause::=

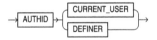

create library

Format:

```
CREATE [OR REPLACE] LIBRARY [schema .] libname
{ IS | AS } 'filespec' [AGENT 'agent_dblink'];
```

create materialized view

create_materialized_view::=

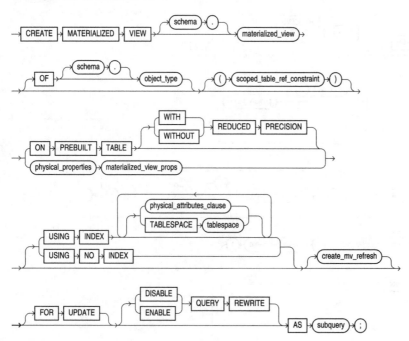

physical_properties::=

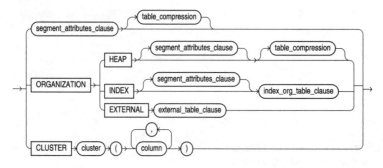

materialized_view_props::=

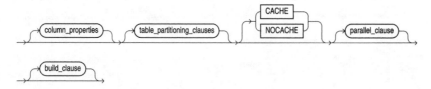

scoped_table_ref_constraint::=

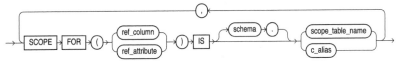

index_org_table_clause::=

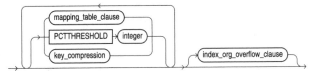

key_compression::=

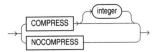

index_org_overflow-clause::=

create_mv_refresh:=

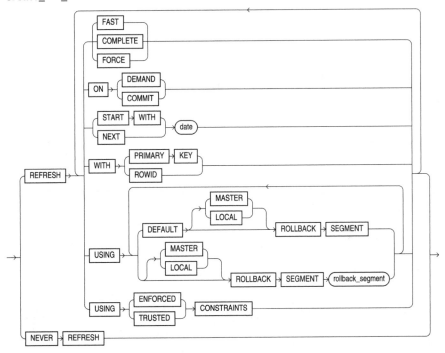

segment_attributes_clause::=

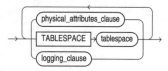

physical_attributes_clause::=

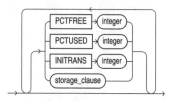

logging_clause::=

table_compression::=

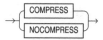

column_properties::=

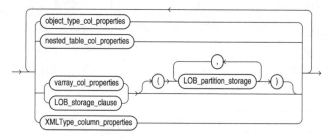

object_type_col_properties::=

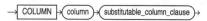

substitutable_column_clause::=

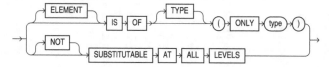

nested_table_col_properties::=

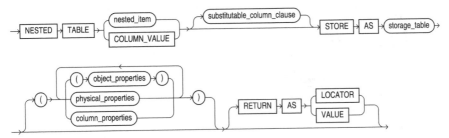

varray_col_properties::=

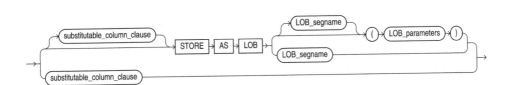

LOB_storage_clause::=

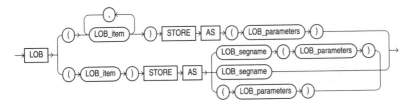

LOB_parameters::=

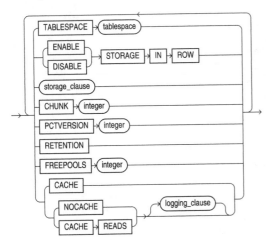

LOB_partition_storage::=

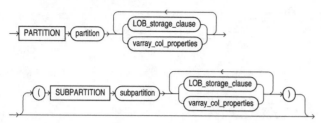

parallel_clause::=

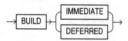

build_clause::=

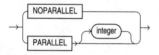

create materialized view log

Format:

create_materialized_vw_log::=

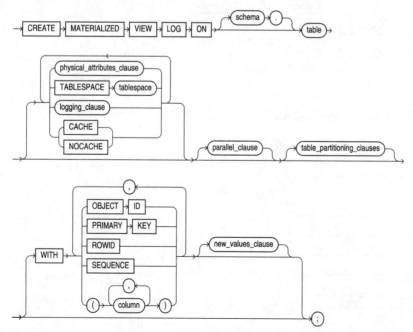

physical_attributes_clause::=

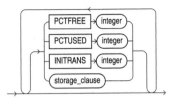

logging_clause::=

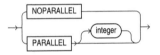

parallel_clause::=

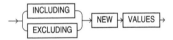

new_values_clause::=

create operator

Format:

create_operator::=

binding_clause::=

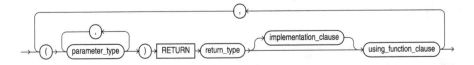

implementation_clause::=

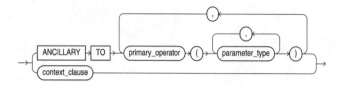

context_clause::=

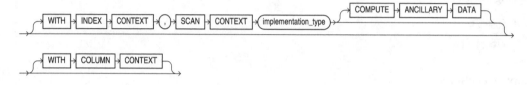

using_function_clause::=

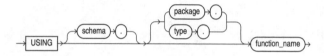

create outline

Format:

```
CREATE [OR REPLACE] [ PUBLIC | PRIVATE ] OUTLINE [outline]
[FROM [ PUBLIC | PRIVATE ] source_outline]
[FOR CATEGORY category]
[ON statement];
```

create package

Format:

```
CREATE [OR REPLACE] PACKAGE [schema .] package
[AUTHID { CURRENT_USER | DEFINER }]
{ IS | AS } pl/sql_package_spec;
```

create package body

Format:

```
CREATE [OR REPLACE] PACKAGE BODY [schema .] package
{ IS | AS } pl/sql_package_body;
```

create pfile

Format:

```
CREATE PFILE [= 'pfile_name'] FROM SPFILE [= 'spfile_name'];
```

create procedure

Format:
create_procedure::=

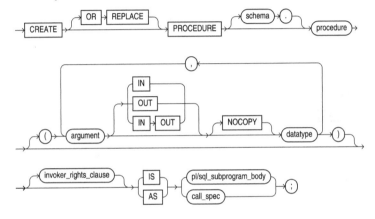

invoker_rights_clause::=

call_spec::=

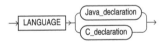

Java_declaration::=

C_declaration::=

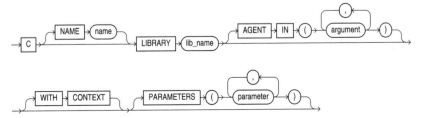

create profile

Format:

create_profile::=

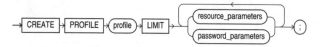

resource_parameters::=

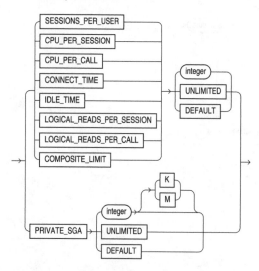

password_parameters::=

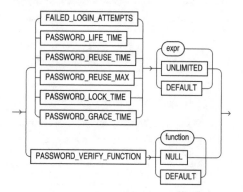

create role

Format:

```
CREATE ROLE role
[ NOT IDENTIFIED
| IDENTIFIED { BY password |
  USING [schema .] package | EXTERNALLY | GLOBALLY }];
```

create rollback segment

Format:

```
CREATE [PUBLIC] ROLLBACK SEGMENT rollback_segment
[{ TABLESPACE tablespace | storage_clause }
[ TABLESPACE tablespace | storage_clause ]...];
```

create schema

Format:

```
CREATE SCHEMA AUTHORIZATION schema
{ create_table_statement | create_view_statement | grant_statement }
[ create_table_statement | create_view_statement | grant_statement ]...;
```

create sequence

Format:

```
CREATE SEQUENCE [schema .] sequence
[{ { INCREMENT BY | START WITH } integer
  | { MAXVALUE integer | NOMAXVALUE }
  | { MINVALUE integer | NOMINVALUE }
  | { CYCLE | NOCYCLE }
  | { CACHE integer | NOCACHE }
  | { ORDER | NOORDER }
  }
  [ { INCREMENT BY | START WITH } integer
  | { MAXVALUE integer | NOMAXVALUE }
  | { MINVALUE integer | NOMINVALUE }
  | { CYCLE | NOCYCLE }
  | { CACHE integer | NOCACHE }
  | { ORDER | NOORDER }  ]... ];
```

create spfile

Format:

```
CREATE SPFILE [= 'spfile_name'] FROM PFILE [= 'pfile_name'];
```

create synonym

Format:

```
CREATE [PUBLIC] SYNONYM [schema .] synonym
    FOR [schema .] object [@ dblink];
```

create table

Format:
create_table::=

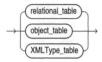

relational_table::=

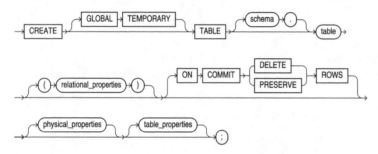

object_table::=

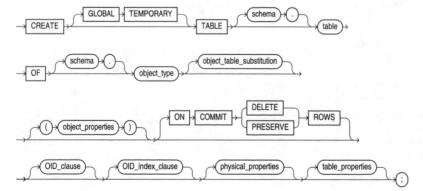

XMLType_table::=

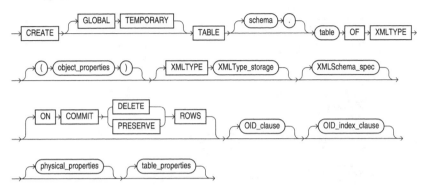

relational_properties::=

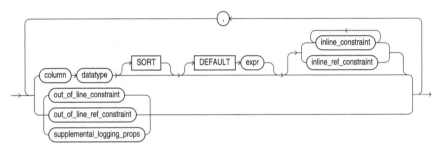

object_table_substitution::=

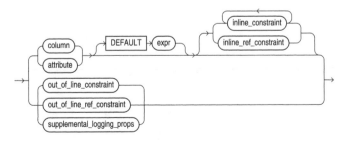

object_properties::=

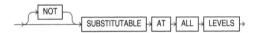

oid_clause::=

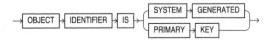

oid_index_clause::=

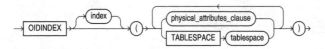

physical_properties::=

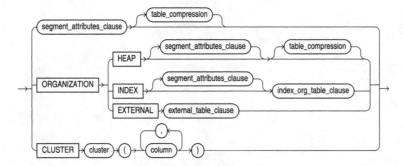

segment_attributes_clause::=

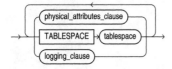

physical_attributes_clause::=

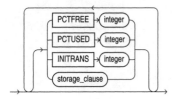

table_compression::=

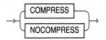

table_properties::=

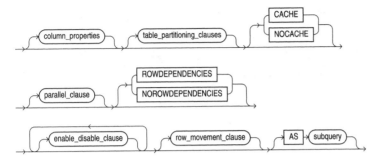

column_properties::=

object_type_col_properties::=

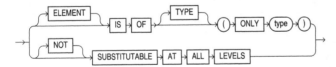

substitutable_column_clause::=

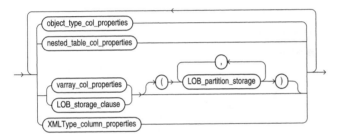

nested_table_col_properties::=

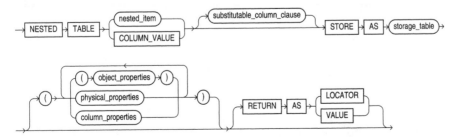

varray_col_properties::=

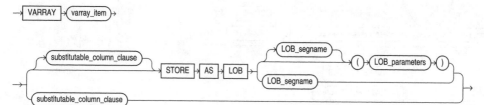

LOB_storage_clause::=

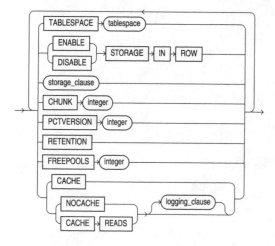

LOB_parameters::=

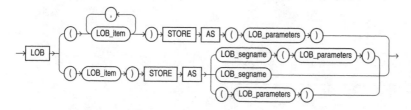

logging_clause::=

LOB_partition_storage::=

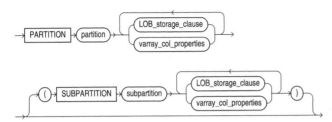

XMLType_column_properties::=

XMLType_storage::=

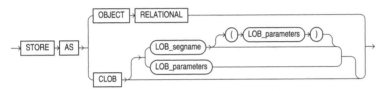

XMLSchema_spec::=

row_movement_clause::=

index_org_table_clause::=

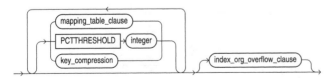

mapping_table_clauses::=

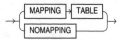

key_compression::=

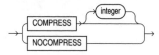

index_org_overflow_clause::=

supplemental_logging_props::=

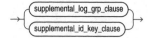

supplemental_log_grp_clause::=

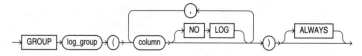

supplemental_id_key_clause::=

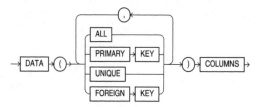

external_table_clause::=

external_data_properties::=

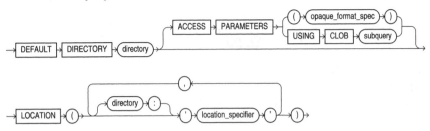

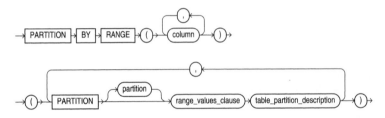

table_partitioning_clauses::=

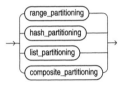

range_partitioning::=

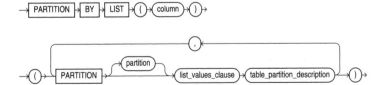

hash_partitioning::=

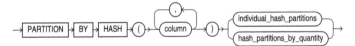

list_partitioning::=

composite_partitioning::=

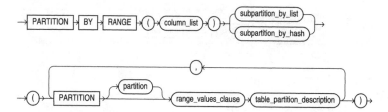

subpartition_by_hash::=

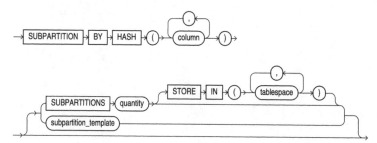

individual_hash_partitions::=

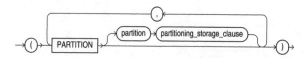

hash_partitions_by_quantity::=

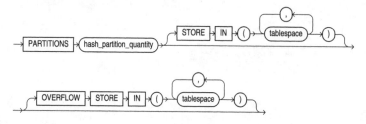

subpartition_by_list::=

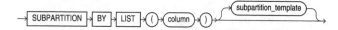

subpartition_template::=

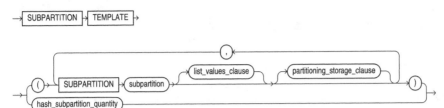

range_values_clause::=

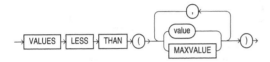

list_values_clause::=

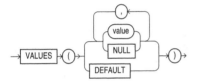

table_partition_description::=

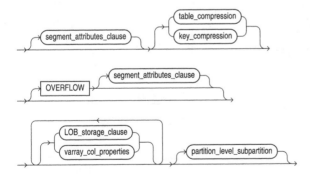

partition_level_subpartition::=

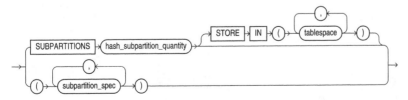

subpartition_spec::=

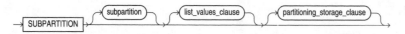

partitioning_storage_clause::=

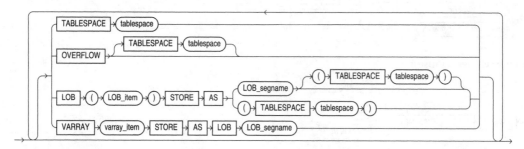

parallel_clause::=

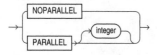

enable_disable_clause::=

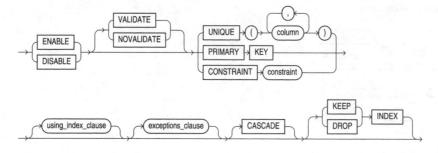

using_index_clause::=

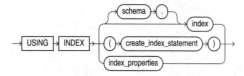

index_properties::=

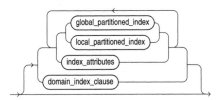

index_attributes::=

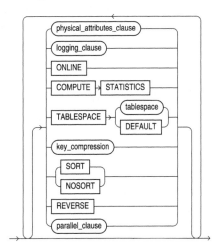

create tablespace

Format:

create_tablespace::=

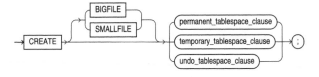

permanent_tablespace_clause::=

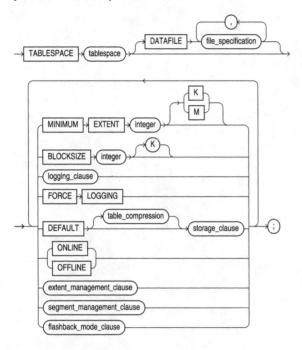

logging_clause::=

table_compression::=

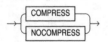

extent_management_clause::=

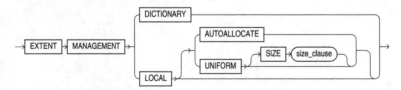

size_clause::=

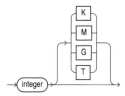

segment_management_clause::=

flashback_mode_clause::=

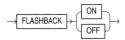

temporary_tablespace_clause::=

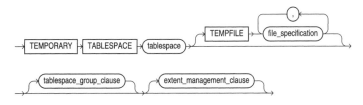

tablespace_group_clause::=

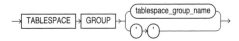

undo_tablespace_clause::=

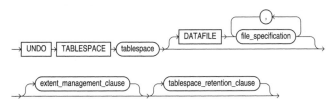

tablespace_retention_clause::=

create trigger

Format:
create_trigger::=

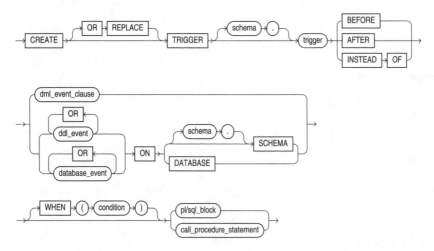

DML_event_clause::=

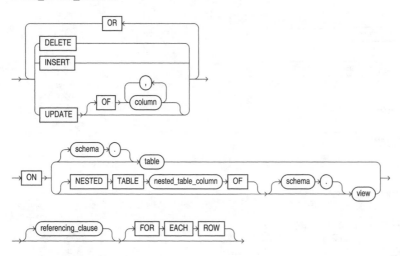

referencing_clause::=

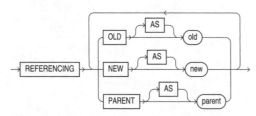

create type

Format:

create_type::=

create_incomplete_type::=

create_object_type::=

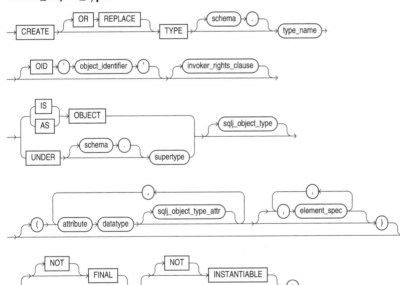

invoker_rights_clause::=

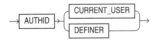

sqlj_object_type::=

sqlj_object_type_attr::=

element_spec::=

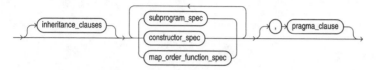

inheritance_clauses::=

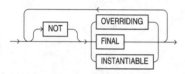

subprogram_spec::=

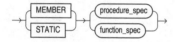

procedure_spec::=

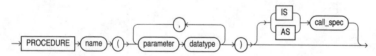

function_spec::=

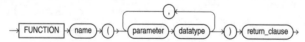

constructor_spec::=

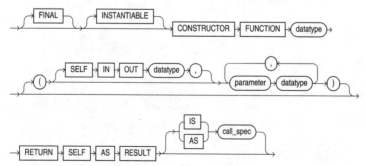

map_order_function_spec::=

return_clause::=

sqlj_object_type_sig::=

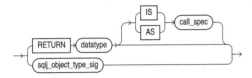

pragma_clause::=

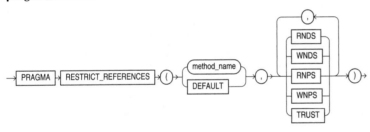

call_spec::=

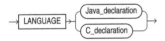

Java_declaration::=

C_declaration::=

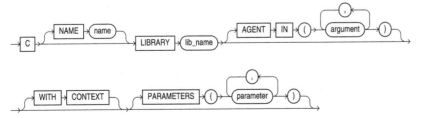

create_varray_type::=

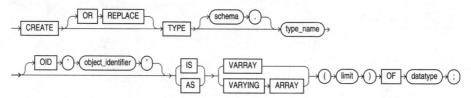

create_nested_table_type::=

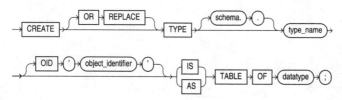

create type body

Format:

create_type_body::=

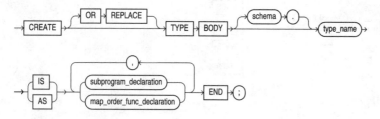

subprogram_declaration::=

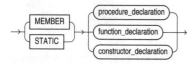

procedure_declaration::=

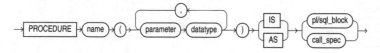

function_declaration::=

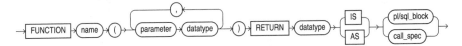

constructor_declaration::=

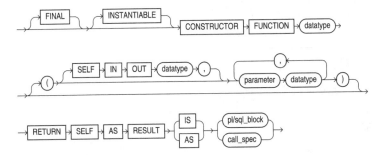

map_order_func_declaration::=

call_spec::=

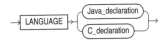

Java_declaration::=

C_declaration::=

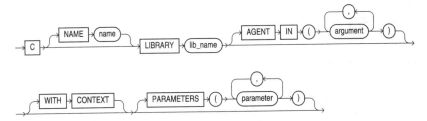

create user

Format:
create_user::=

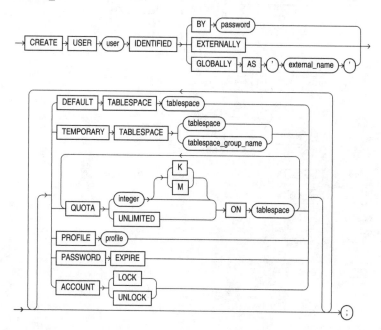

create view

Format:
create_view::=

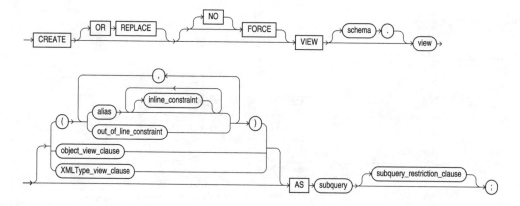

object_view_clause::=

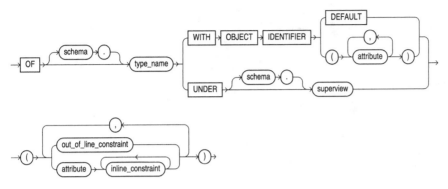

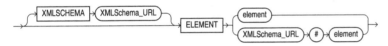

XMLType_view_clause::=

XMLSchema_spec::=

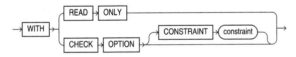

subquery_restriction_clause::=

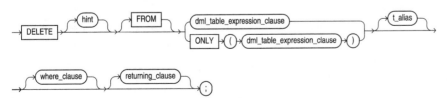

delete (SQL Command)

<u>Format:</u>

delete::=

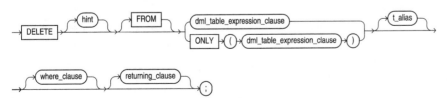

DML_table_expression_clause::=

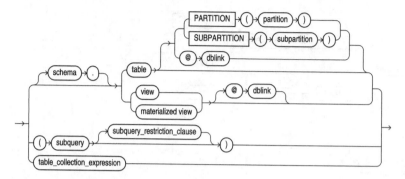

subquery_restriction_clause::=

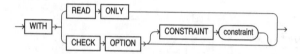

table_collection_expression::=

where_clause::=

returning_clause::=

delete (Embedded SQL)

Format:

```
EXEC SQL [AT {db_name | :host_variable} ] [FOR :host_integer | integer]
 DELETE [FROM]
 [ (subquery)
 | [user.] {table | view } [@dblink |PARTITION (partition_name)] ]
[alias] [WHERE {condition | CURRENT OF cursor} ]
[{ RETURN | RETURNING } expr [, expr]... INTO
 :host_variable [[INDICATOR] :ind_variable]
 [, :host_variable [[INDICATOR] :ind_variable]]...]
```

disassociate statistics

Format:

disassociate_statistics::=

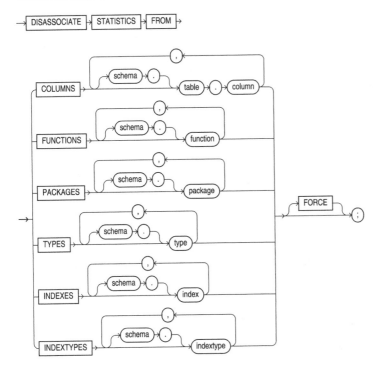

drop cluster

Format:

```
DROP CLUSTER [schema .] cluster
[INCLUDING TABLES [CASCADE CONSTRAINTS]];
```

drop context

Format:

```
DROP CONTEXT namespace;
```

drop database (Oracle Database 10g and later only)

Format:

```
DROP DATABASE ;
```

drop database link

Format:

```
DROP [PUBLIC] DATABASE LINK link;
```

drop dimension

Format:

```
DROP DIMENSION [schema .] dimension;
```

drop directory

Format:

```
DROP DIRECTORY directory_name;
```

drop diskgroup

Format:

```
DROP DISKGROUP diskgroup_name [ {INCLUDING | EXCLUDING} CONTENTS ];
```

drop function

Format:

```
DROP FUNCTION [schema .] function_name;
```

drop index

Format:

```
DROP INDEX [schema .] index [FORCE];
```

drop indextype

Format:

```
DROP INDEXTYPE [schema .] indextype [FORCE];
```

drop java

Format:

```
DROP JAVA { SOURCE | CLASS | RESOURCE } [schema .] object_name;
```

drop library

Format:

```
DROP LIBRARY library_name;
```

drop materialized view

Format:

```
DROP MATERIALIZED VIEW [schema .] materialized_view [PRESERVE TABLE];
```

drop materialized view log

Format:

```
DROP MATERIALIZED VIEW LOG ON [schema .] table;
```

drop operator

Format:

```
DROP OPERATOR [schema .] operator [FORCE];
```

drop outline

Format:

```
DROP OUTLINE outline;
```

drop package

Format:

```
DROP PACKAGE [BODY] [schema .] package;
```

drop procedure

Format:

```
DROP PROCEDURE [schema .] procedure;
```

drop profile

Format:

```
DROP PROFILE profile [CASCADE];
```

drop role

Format:

```
DROP ROLE role;
```

drop rollback segment

Format:

```
DROP ROLLBACK SEGMENT rollback_segment;
```

drop sequence

Format:

```
DROP SEQUENCE [schema .] sequence_name;
```

drop synonym

Format:

```
DROP [PUBLIC] SYNONYM [schema .] synonym [FORCE];
```

drop table

Format:

```
DROP TABLE [schema .] table [CASCADE CONSTRAINTS] [PURGE];
```

drop tablespace

Format:

```
DROP TABLESPACE tablespace
[INCLUDING CONTENTS [AND DATAFILES] [CASCADE CONSTRAINTS]];
```

drop trigger

Format:

```
DROP TRIGGER [schema .] trigger;
```

drop type

Format:

```
DROP TYPE [schema .] type_name [ FORCE | VALIDATE ];
```

drop type body

Format:

```
DROP TYPE BODY [schema .] type_name;
```

drop user

Format:

```
DROP USER user [CASCADE];
```

drop view

Format:

```
DROP VIEW [schema .] view [CASCADE CONSTRAINTS];
```

explain plan

Format:

```
EXPLAIN PLAN [SET STATEMENT_ID = 'name']
[INTO [schema .] table [@ dblink]]
FOR statement;
```

NOTE
Use the `utlxplan.sql` *script to create the plan table that the* **explain plan** *command uses.*

file_specification

Format:
file_specification::=

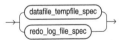

datafile_tempfile_spec::=

redo_log_file_spec::=

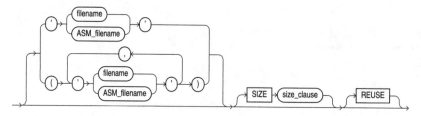

size_clause::=

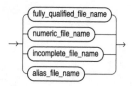

ASM_filename::=

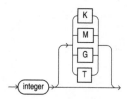

fully_qualified_file_name::=

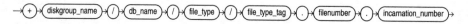

numeric_file_name::=

incomplete_file_name::=

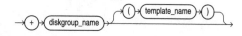

alias_file_name::=

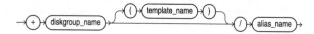

autoextend_clause::=

maxsize_clause::=

flashback database

<u>Format:</u>

flashback_database::=

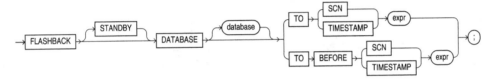

flashback table

<u>Format:</u>

flashback_table::=

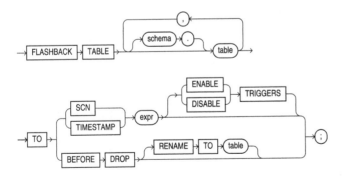

grant

<u>Format:</u>

grant::=

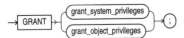

grant_system_privileges::=

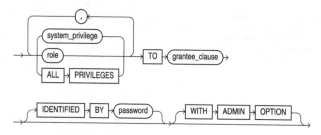

grant_object_privileges::=

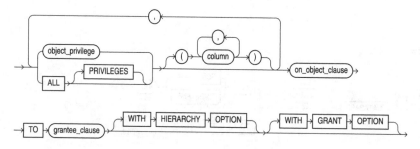

on_object_clause::=

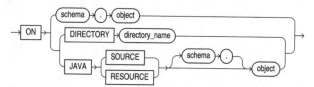

grantee_clause::=

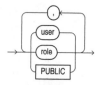

group by

Format:

```
SELECT expression [,expression]...
 GROUP BY expression [,expression]...
HAVING condition
    ...
```

insert - PL/SQL

Format:

```
INSERT INTO [user.]table[@db_link] [(column [,column]...)]
   VALUES (expression [,expression]...) | query...);
```

insert - SQL

Format:
insert::=

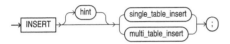

single_table_insert::=

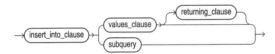

insert_into_clause::=

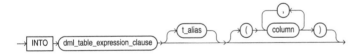

values_clause::=

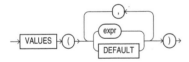

returning_clause::=

multi_table_insert::=

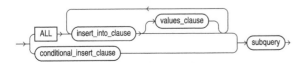

conditional_insert_clause::=

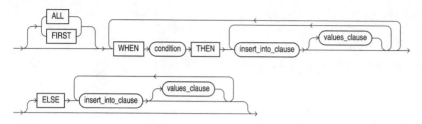

DML_table_expression_clause::=

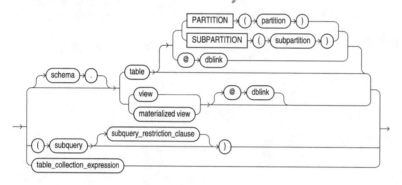

subquery_restriction_clause::=

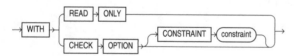

table_collection_expression::=

lock table

Format:

```
LOCK TABLE
[schema .] { table | view }
[ { PARTITION ( partition ) | SUBPARTITION ( subpartition ) }
| @ dblink ]
[, [schema .] { table | view }
 [ { PARTITION ( partition ) | SUBPARTITION ( subpartition ) }
 | @ dblink ] ]...
IN lockmode MODE [NOWAIT];
```

noaudit

Format:

noaudit::=

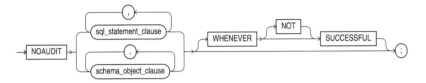

sql_statement_clause::=

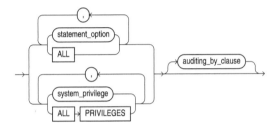

auditing_by_clause::=

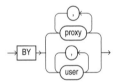

schema_object_clause::=

auditing_on_clause::=

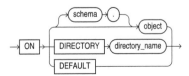

recover (SQL*Plus Command)

recover is a clause within the **alter database** command.

Format:

```
RECOVER {general | managed | BEGIN BACKUP | END BACKUP}
```

where the **general** clause has the following syntax:

```
[AUTOMATIC] [FROM location]
{ {full_database_recovery | partial_database_recovery |LOGFILE filename}
[ {TEST | ALLOW integer CORRUPTION | parallel_clause }
[TEST | ALLOW integer CORRUPTION | parallel_clause]...]
|CONTINUE [DEFAULT]|CANCEL}
```

where the **full database recovery** clause has the following syntax:

```
[STANDBY] DATABASE
[ {UNTIL {CANCEL | TIME date | CHANGE integer} | USING BACKUP CONTROLFILE}
[UNTIL {CANCEL | TIME date | CHANGE integer} | USING BACKUP CONTROLFILE]...]
```

where the **partial database recovery** clause has the following syntax:

```
{TABLESPACE tablespace [, tablespace]... | DATAFILE datafilename [,
datafilenumber]...
| STANDBY
{TABLESPACE tablespace [, tablespace]... | DATAFILE datafilename [,
datafilenumber]...}
UNTIL [CONSISTENT WITH] CONTROLFILE }
```

and the **parallel** clause has the following syntax:

```
{NOPARALLEL | PARALLEL [integer]}
```

and the **managed** clause has the following syntax:

```
MANAGED STANDBY DATABASE recover_clause | cancel_clause | finish_clause
```

and the **recover** clause has the following syntax:

```
{{DISCONNECT [FROM SESSION]|{TIMEOUT integer | NOTIMEOUT}}
 |{NODELAY | DEFAULT DELAY | DELAY integer} | NEXT integer
 |{EXPIRE integer | NO EXPIRE} | parallel_clause
 | USING CURRENT LOGFILE | UNTIL CHANGE integer
 | THROUGH {[THREAD integer] SEQUENCE integer
     | ALL ARCHIVELOG | {ALL|LAST|NEXT} SWITCHOVER}}
[DISCONNECT [FROM SESSION] | {TIMEOUT integer | NOTIMEOUT}
  | {NODELAY|DEFAULT DELAY|DELAY integer}| NEXT integer
  | {EXPIRE integer | NO EXPIRE}| parallel_clause
```

```
| USING CURRENT LOGFILE | UNTIL CHANGE integer
| THROUGH {[THREAD integer]SEQUENCE integer
  | ALL ARCHIVELOG | {ALL|LAST|NEXT} SWITCHOVER}}
```

and the **cancel** clause has the following syntax:

```
CANCEL [IMMEDIATE] [WAIT | NOWAIT]
```

and the **finish** clause has the following syntax:

```
[DISCONNECT [FROM SESSION]][parallel_clause]
FINISH [SKIP [STANDBY LOGFILE]][WAIT|NOWAIT]
```

rename

Format:

```
RENAME old TO new;
```

revoke

Format:
revoke::=

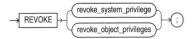

revoke_system_privileges::=

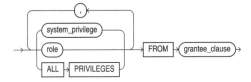

revoke_object_privileges::=

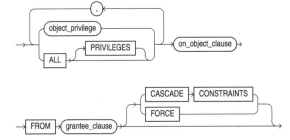

grantee_clause::=

on_object_clause::=

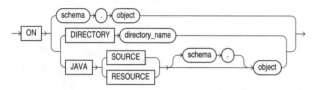

rollback

Format:

```
ROLLBACK [WORK] [ TO [SAVEPOINT] savepoint | FORCE 'text' ];
```

NOTE
*If **set autocommit** is ON, every **insert**, **update**, or **delete** immediately
and automatically commits the changes to the database. Typing the
word **rollback** will produce a 'ROLLBACK COMPLETE' message, but
this message won't mean anything since **rollback** only rolls back to
the last **commit**.
Also, note that all DDL commands cause an implicit commit.*

savepoint

Format:

```
SAVEPOINT savepoint;
```

select

Format:
select::=

subquery::=

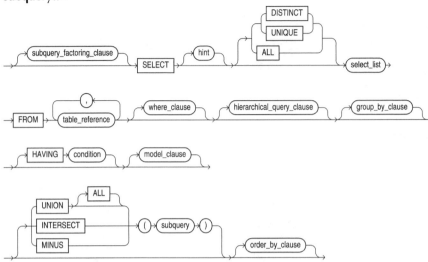

subquery_factoring_clause::=

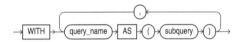

select_list::=

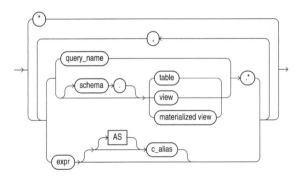

table_reference::=

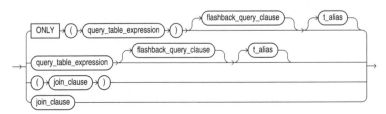

flashback_query_clause::=

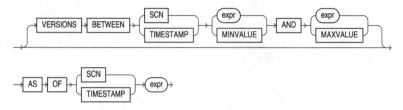

query_table_expression::=

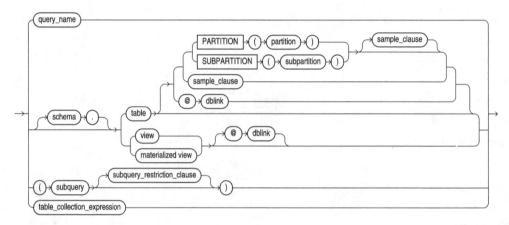

sample_clause::=

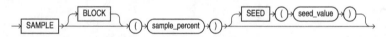

subquery_restriction_clause::=

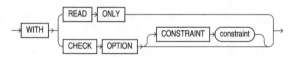

table_collection_expression::=

join_clause::=

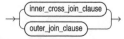

inner_cross_join_clause::=

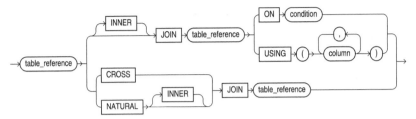

outer_join_clause::=

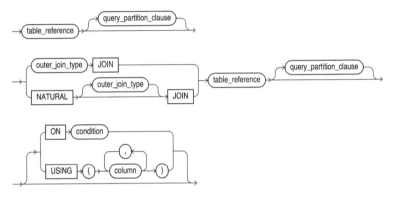

query_partition_clause::=

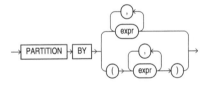

outer_join_type::=

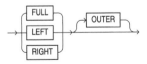

where_clause::=

hierarchical_query_clause::=

group_by_clause::=

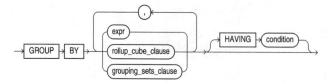

rollup_cube_clause::=

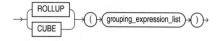

grouping_sets_clause::=

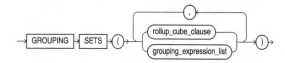

grouping_expression_list::=

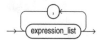

expression_list::=

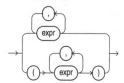

model_clause::=

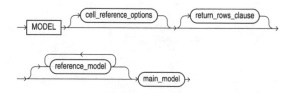

cell_reference_options::=

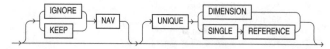

returns_rows_clause::=

reference_model::=

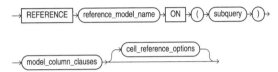

main_model::=

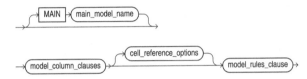

model_column_clauses::=

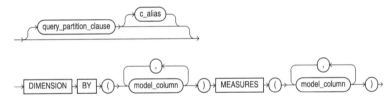

model_column::=

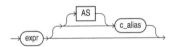

model_rules_clause::=

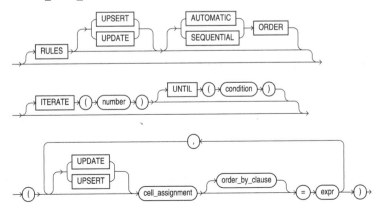

cell_assignment::=

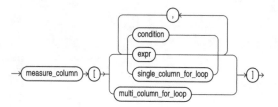

single_column_for_loop::=

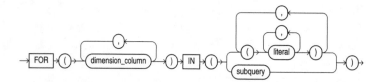

multi_column_for_loop::=

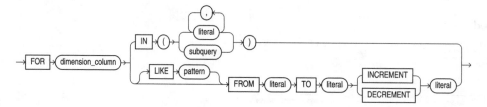

order_by_clause::=

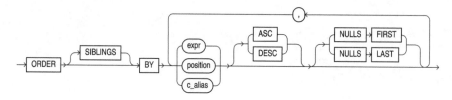

for_update_clause::=

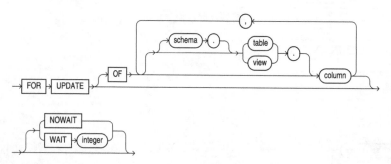

select ... into

Format:

```
SELECT expression [,expression]...
  INTO {variable [,variable]... | record}
  FROM [user.]table [,[user.]table]...
 [where...][group by... [having...]] [order by...];
```

set constraints

Format:

```
SET { CONSTRAINT | CONSTRAINTS }
{ constraint [, constraint]... | ALL }
{ IMMEDIATE | DEFERRED };
```

set role

Format:

```
SET ROLE
{ role [IDENTIFIED BY password] [, role [IDENTIFIED BY password]]...
| ALL [EXCEPT role [, role]...]
| NONE   };
```

set transaction

Format:

```
SET TRANSACTION
{ { READ { ONLY | WRITE }
  | ISOLATION LEVEL { SERIALIZABLE | READ COMMITTED }
  | USE ROLLBACK SEGMENT rollback_segment   }
  [NAME 'test']
| NAME 'test'  } ;
```

shutdown (SQL*Plus Command)

Format:

```
SHUTDOWN [ABORT|IMMEDIATE|NORMAL|TRANSACTIONAL [LOCAL]]
```

startup (SQL*Plus Command)

Format:

```
STARTUP options | upgrade_options
```

where *options* has the following syntax:

```
[FORCE][RESTRICT][PFILE=filename][QUIET][MOUNT[dbname]|
[OPEN [open_options][dbname]]|NOMOUNT]
```

where *open_options* has the following syntax:

```
READ {ONLY | WRITE [RECOVER]} | RECOVER
```

and *upgrade_options* has the following syntax:

```
[PFILE=filename]{UPGRADE|DOWNGRADE} [QUIET]
```

storage clause

Format:
storage_clause::=

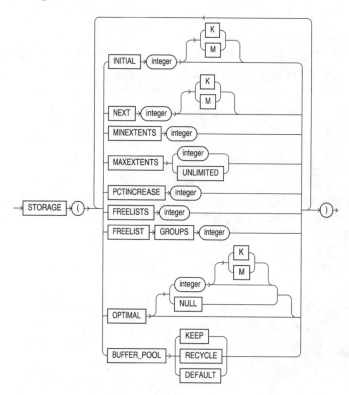

truncate

Format:

```
TRUNCATE
{ TABLE [schema .] table [{ PRESERVE | PURGE } MATERIALIZED VIEW LOG]
| CLUSTER [schema .] cluster }
[{ DROP | REUSE } STORAGE];
```

update

Format:

update::=

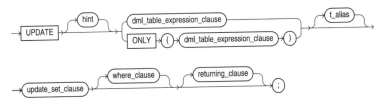

DML_table_expression_clause::=

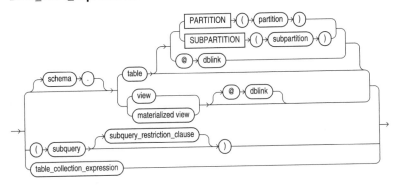

subquery_restriction_clause::=

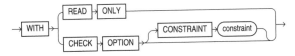

table_collection_expression::=

update_set_clause::=

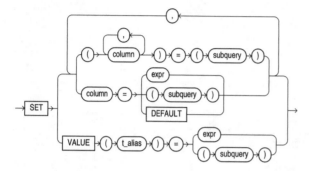

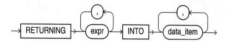

where_clause::=

→ WHERE → (condition) →

returning_clause::=

→ RETURNING → (expr) → INTO → (data_item) →

Index

G

H

I

P

Q

T

INTERNATIONAL CONTACT INFORMATION

AUSTRALIA
McGraw-Hill Book Company
Australia Pty. Ltd.
TEL +61-2-9900-1800
FAX +61-2-9878-8881
http://www.mcgraw-hill.com.au
books-it_sydney@mcgraw-hill.com

CANADA
McGraw-Hill Ryerson Ltd.
TEL +905-430-5000
FAX +905-430-5020
http://www.mcgraw-hill.ca

**GREECE, MIDDLE EAST, & AFRICA
(Excluding South Africa)**
McGraw-Hill Hellas
TEL +30-210-6560-990
TEL +30-210-6560-993
TEL +30-210-6560-994
FAX +30-210-6545-525

MEXICO (Also serving Latin America)
McGraw-Hill Interamericana Editores
S.A. de C.V.
TEL +525-1500-5108
FAX +525-117-1589
http://www.mcgraw-hill.com.mx
carlos_ruiz@mcgraw-hill.com

SINGAPORE (Serving Asia)
McGraw-Hill Book Company
TEL +65-6863-1580
FAX +65-6862-3354
http://www.mcgraw-hill.com.sg
mghasia@mcgraw-hill.com

SOUTH AFRICA
McGraw-Hill South Africa
TEL +27-11-622-7512
FAX +27-11-622-9045
robyn_swanepoel@mcgraw-hill.com

SPAIN
McGraw-Hill/
Interamericana de España, S.A.U.
TEL +34-91-180-3000
FAX +34-91-372-8513
http://www.mcgraw-hill.es
professional@mcgraw-hill.es

**UNITED KINGDOM, NORTHERN,
EASTERN, & CENTRAL EUROPE**
McGraw-Hill Education Europe
TEL +44-1-628-502500
FAX +44-1-628-770224
http://www.mcgraw-hill.co.uk
emea_queries@mcgraw-hill.com

ALL OTHER INQUIRIES Contact:
McGraw-Hill/Osborne
TEL +1-510-420-7700
FAX +1-510-420-7703
http://www.osborne.com
omg_international@mcgraw-hill.com

Sound Off!

Visit us at **www.osborne.com/bookregistration** and let us know what you thought of this book. While you're online you'll have the opportunity to register for newsletters and special offers from McGraw-Hill/Osborne.

We want to hear from you!

Sneak Peek

Visit us today at **www.betabooks.com** and see what's coming from McGraw-Hill/Osborne tomorrow!

Based on the successful software paradigm, Bet@Books™ allows computing professionals to view partial and sometimes complete text versions of selected titles online. Bet@Books™ viewing is free, invites comments and feedback, and allows you to "test drive" books in progress on the subjects that interest you the most.

GET YOUR FREE SUBSCRIPTION
TO ORACLE MAGAZINE

Oracle Magazine is essential gear for today's information technology professionals. Stay informed and increase your productivity with every issue of *Oracle Magazine*. Inside each free bimonthly issue you'll get:

- Up-to-date information on Oracle Database, Oracle Application Server, Web development, enterprise grid computing, database technology, and business trends
- Third-party vendor news and announcements
- Technical articles on Oracle and partner products, technologies, and operating environments
- Development and administration tips
- Real-world customer stories

IF THERE ARE OTHER ORACLE USERS AT YOUR LOCATION WHO WOULD LIKE TO RECEIVE THEIR OWN SUB-SCRIPTION TO ORACLE MAGAZINE, PLEASE PHOTOCOPY THIS FORM AND PASS IT ALONG.

ORACLE
MAGAZINE

Three easy ways to subscribe:

① Web
Visit our Web site at otn.oracle.com/oraclemagazine.
You'll find a subscription form there, plus much more!

② Fax
Complete the questionnaire on the back of this card
and fax the questionnaire side only to +1.847.763.9638.

③ Mail
Complete the questionnaire on the back of this card
and mail it to P.O. Box 1263, Skokie, IL 60076-8263

FREE SUBSCRIPTION

○ **Yes, please send me a FREE subscription to _Oracle Magazine_.**   ○ **NO**
To receive a free subscription to _Oracle Magazine_, you must fill out the entire card, sign it, and date it
(incomplete cards cannot be processed or acknowledged). You can also fax your application to +1.847.763.9638.
Or subscribe at our Web site at otn.oracle.com/oraclemagazine

○ From time to time, Oracle Publishing allows
our partners exclusive access to our e-mail
addresses for special promotions and
announcements. To be included in this program, please check this circle.

○ Oracle Publishing allows sharing of our
mailing list with selected third parties. If you
prefer your mailing address not to be
included in this program, please check here.
If at any time you would like to be removed
from this mailing list, please contact
Customer Service at +1.847.647.9630 or send
an e-mail to oracle@halldata.com.

signature (required)   date

X

name   title

company   e-mail address

street/p.o. box

city/state/zip or postal code   telephone

country   fax

YOU MUST ANSWER ALL TEN QUESTIONS BELOW.

① WHAT IS THE PRIMARY BUSINESS ACTIVITY OF YOUR FIRM AT THIS LOCATION? (check one only)
- ☐ 01 Aerospace and Defense Manufacturing
- ☐ 02 Application Service Provider
- ☐ 03 Automotive Manufacturing
- ☐ 04 Chemicals, Oil and Gas
- ☐ 05 Communications and Media
- ☐ 06 Construction/Engineering
- ☐ 07 Consumer Sector/Consumer Packaged Goods
- ☐ 08 Education
- ☐ 09 Financial Services/Insurance
- ☐ 10 Government (civil)
- ☐ 11 Government (military)
- ☐ 12 Healthcare
- ☐ 13 High Technology Manufacturing, OEM
- ☐ 14 Integrated Software Vendor
- ☐ 15 Life Sciences (Biotech, Pharmaceuticals)
- ☐ 16 Mining
- ☐ 17 Retail/Wholesale/Distribution
- ☐ 18 Systems Integrator, VAR/VAD
- ☐ 19 Telecommunications
- ☐ 20 Travel and Transportation
- ☐ 21 Utilities (electric, gas, sanitation, water)
- ☐ 98 Other Business and Services

② WHICH OF THE FOLLOWING BEST DESCRIBES YOUR PRIMARY JOB FUNCTION? (check one only)
Corporate Management/Staff
- ☐ 01 Executive Management (President, Chair, CEO, CFO, Owner, Partner, Principal)
- ☐ 02 Finance/Administrative Management (VP/Director/ Manager/Controller, Purchasing, Administration)
- ☐ 03 Sales/Marketing Management (VP/Director/Manager)
- ☐ 04 Computer Systems/Operations Management (CIO/VP/Director/ Manager MIS, Operations)
IS/IT Staff
- ☐ 05 Systems Development/ Programming Management
- ☐ 06 Systems Development/ Programming Staff
- ☐ 07 Consulting
- ☐ 08 DBA/Systems Administrator
- ☐ 09 Education/Training
- ☐ 10 Technical Support Director/Manager
- ☐ 11 Other Technical Management/Staff
- ☐ 98 Other

③ WHAT IS YOUR CURRENT PRIMARY OPERATING PLATFORM? (select all that apply)
- ☐ 01 Digital Equipment UNIX
- ☐ 02 Digital Equipment VAX VMS
- ☐ 03 HP UNIX
- ☐ 04 IBM AIX
- ☐ 05 IBM UNIX
- ☐ 06 Java
- ☐ 07 Linux
- ☐ 08 Macintosh
- ☐ 09 MS-DOS
- ☐ 10 MVS
- ☐ 11 NetWare
- ☐ 12 Network Computing
- ☐ 13 OpenVMS
- ☐ 14 SCO UNIX
- ☐ 15 Sequent DYNIX/ptx
- ☐ 16 Sun Solaris/SunOS
- ☐ 17 SVR4
- ☐ 18 UnixWare
- ☐ 19 Windows
- ☐ 20 Windows NT
- ☐ 21 Other UNIX
- ☐ 98 Other
- ☐ 99 None of the above

④ DO YOU EVALUATE, SPECIFY, RECOMMEND, OR AUTHORIZE THE PURCHASE OF ANY OF THE FOLLOWING? (check all that apply)
- ☐ 01 Hardware
- ☐ 02 Software
- ☐ 03 Application Development Tools
- ☐ 04 Database Products
- ☐ 05 Internet or Intranet Products
- ☐ 99 None of the above

⑤ IN YOUR JOB, DO YOU USE OR PLAN TO PURCHASE ANY OF THE FOLLOWING PRODUCTS? (check all that apply)
Software
- ☐ 01 Business Graphics
- ☐ 02 CAD/CAE/CAM
- ☐ 03 CASE
- ☐ 04 Communications
- ☐ 05 Database Management
- ☐ 06 File Management
- ☐ 07 Finance
- ☐ 08 Java
- ☐ 09 Materials Resource Planning
- ☐ 10 Multimedia Authoring
- ☐ 11 Networking
- ☐ 12 Office Automation
- ☐ 13 Order Entry/Inventory Control
- ☐ 14 Programming
- ☐ 15 Project Management
- ☐ 16 Scientific and Engineering
- ☐ 17 Spreadsheets
- ☐ 18 Systems Management
- ☐ 19 Workflow

Hardware
- ☐ 20 Macintosh
- ☐ 21 Mainframe
- ☐ 22 Massively Parallel Processing
- ☐ 23 Minicomputer
- ☐ 24 PC
- ☐ 25 Network Computer
- ☐ 26 Symmetric Multiprocessing
- ☐ 27 Workstation
Peripherals
- ☐ 28 Bridges/Routers/Hubs/Gateways
- ☐ 29 CD-ROM Drives
- ☐ 30 Disk Drives/Subsystems
- ☐ 31 Modems
- ☐ 32 Tape Drives/Subsystems
- ☐ 33 Video Boards/Multimedia
Services
- ☐ 34 Application Service Provider
- ☐ 35 Consulting
- ☐ 36 Education/Training
- ☐ 37 Maintenance
- ☐ 38 Online Database Services
- ☐ 39 Support
- ☐ 40 Technology-Based Training
- ☐ 98 Other
- ☐ 99 None of the above

⑥ WHAT ORACLE PRODUCTS ARE IN USE AT YOUR SITE? (check all that apply)
Oracle E-Business Suite
- ☐ 01 Oracle Marketing
- ☐ 02 Oracle Sales
- ☐ 03 Oracle Order Fulfillment
- ☐ 04 Oracle Supply Chain Management
- ☐ 05 Oracle Procurement
- ☐ 06 Oracle Manufacturing
- ☐ 07 Oracle Maintenance Management
- ☐ 08 Oracle Service
- ☐ 09 Oracle Contracts
- ☐ 10 Oracle Projects
- ☐ 11 Oracle Financials
- ☐ 12 Oracle Human Resources
- ☐ 13 Oracle Interaction Center
- ☐ 14 Oracle Communications/Utilities (modules)
- ☐ 15 Oracle Public Sector/University (modules)
- ☐ 16 Oracle Financial Services (modules)
Server/Software
- ☐ 17 Oracle9i
- ☐ 18 Oracle9i Lite
- ☐ 19 Oracle8i
- ☐ 20 Other Oracle database
- ☐ 21 Oracle9i Application Server
- ☐ 22 Oracle9i Application Server Wireless
- ☐ 23 Oracle Small Business Suite

Tools
- ☐ 24 Oracle Developer Suite
- ☐ 25 Oracle Discoverer
- ☐ 26 Oracle JDeveloper
- ☐ 27 Oracle Migration Workbench
- ☐ 28 Oracle9i AS Portal
- ☐ 29 Oracle Warehouse Builder
Oracle Services
- ☐ 30 Oracle Outsourcing
- ☐ 31 Oracle Consulting
- ☐ 32 Oracle Education
- ☐ 33 Oracle Support
- ☐ 98 Other
- ☐ 99 None of the above

⑦ WHAT OTHER DATABASE PRODUCTS ARE IN USE AT YOUR SITE? (check all that apply)
- ☐ 01 Access
- ☐ 02 Baan
- ☐ 03 dbase
- ☐ 04 Gupta
- ☐ 05 IBM DB2
- ☐ 06 Informix
- ☐ 07 Ingres
- ☐ 08 Microsoft Access
- ☐ 09 Microsoft SQL Server
- ☐ 10 PeopleSoft
- ☐ 11 Progress
- ☐ 12 SAP
- ☐ 13 Sybase
- ☐ 14 VSAM
- ☐ 98 Other
- ☐ 99 None of the above

⑧ WHAT OTHER APPLICATION SERVER PRODUCTS ARE IN USE AT YOUR SITE? (check all that apply)
- ☐ 01 BEA
- ☐ 02 IBM
- ☐ 03 Sybase
- ☐ 04 Sun
- ☐ 05 Other

⑨ DURING THE NEXT 12 MONTHS, HOW MUCH DO YOU ANTICIPATE YOUR ORGANIZATION WILL SPEND ON COMPUTER HARDWARE, SOFTWARE, PERIPHERALS, AND SERVICES FOR YOUR LOCATION? (check only one)
- ☐ 01 Less than $10,000
- ☐ 02 $10,000 to $49,999
- ☐ 03 $50,000 to $99,999
- ☐ 04 $100,000 to $499,999
- ☐ 05 $500,000 to $999,999
- ☐ 06 $1,000,000 and over

⑩ WHAT IS YOUR COMPANY'S YEARLY SALES REVENUE? (please choose one)
- ☐ 01 $500, 000, 000 and above
- ☐ 02 $100, 000, 000 to $500, 000, 000
- ☐ 03 $50, 000, 000 to $100, 000, 000
- ☐ 04 $5, 000, 000 to $50, 000, 000
- ☐ 05 $1, 000, 000 to $5, 000, 000

100103